THE MAN
WHO KNEW

ALSO BY SEBASTIAN MALLABY

More Money Than God
The World's Banker
After Apartheid

THE MAN WHO KNEW

The Life and Times of
ALAN GREENSPAN

SEBASTIAN MALLABY

A Council on Foreign Relations Book

B L O O M S B U R Y
LONDON · OXFORD · NEW YORK · NEW DELHI · SYDNEY

Bloomsbury Publishing
An imprint of Bloomsbury Publishing Plc

50 Bedford Square
London
WC1B 3DP
UK

1385 Broadway
New York
NY 10018
USA

www.bloomsbury.com

BLOOMSBURY and the Diana logo are trademarks of Bloomsbury Publishing Plc

First published in Great Britain 2016
Published by arrangement with The Penguin Press, an imprint
of Penguin Random House Group LLC

The Council on Foreign Relations (CFR) is an independent, nonpartisan membership organization,
think tank, and publisher dedicated to being a resource for its members, government officials, business
executives, journalists, educators and students, civic and religious leaders, and other interested citizens
in order to help them better understand the world and the foreign policy choices facing the United
States and other countries. Founded in 1921, CFR carries out its mission by maintaining a diverse
membership, with special programs to promote interest and develop expertise in the next generation
of foreign policy leaders; convening meetings at its headquarters in New York and in Washington,
D.C., and other cities where senior government officials, members of Congress, global leaders, and
prominent thinkers come together with CFR members to discuss and debate major international
issues; supporting a studies program that fosters independent research, enabling CFR scholars to
produce articles, reports, and books and hold roundtables that analyze foreign policy issues and make
concrete policy recommendations; publishing *Foreign Affairs*, the preeminent journal on international
affairs and U.S. foreign policy; sponsoring Independent Task Forces that produce reports with both
findings and policy prescriptions on the most important foreign policy topics; and providing up-to-date
information and analysis about world events and American foreign policy on its website, www.cfr.org.

The Council on Foreign Relations takes no institutional positions on policy issues and has no
affiliation with the U.S. government. All views expressed in its publications and on its
website are the sole responsibility of the author or authors.

British Library Cataloguing-in-Publication Data
A catalogue record for this book is available from the British Library.

ISBN: HB: 978-1-4088-5577-5
        TPB: 978-1-4088-5578-2
        ePub: 978-1-4088-5579-9

4 6 8 10 9 7 5 3

Designed by Amanda Dewey
Printed and bound in Great Britain by CPI Group (UK) Ltd, Croydon CR0 4YY

To find out more about our authors and books visit www.bloomsbury.com. Here you
will find extracts, author interviews, details of forthcoming events and
the option to sign up for our newsletters.

CONTENTS

BOOK III

THE CENTRAL BANKER

Preface

This book is based on almost unlimited access to Alan Greenspan, his papers, and his colleagues and friends, all of whom were generous in their collaboration. For a period of five years, starting in the autumn of 2010, I was a familiar visitor to Greenspan's offices in Washington, D.C., and saw him in other contexts, too: at home, hosting a dinner for a former British prime minister; at his suite in the Ritz on New York's Central Park South, where the staff welcomed him with a model of the Federal Reserve building made out of chocolate; on the Acela train between his two home cities, where he tipped the porters generously, proclaiming a belief in redistribution. At some point in this process, after we had logged more than seventy hours of recorded conversations, I stopped counting the time. The intriguing bits seemed to come at the least expected moments, and they were not always when the recorder was running. Once, after Greenspan had mentioned his love of automobiles, and particularly their ability to lift his mood from a dark patch, I sent a note over to his office, wondering how seriously he had meant this. Later that day, Greenspan replied:

Dear Sebastian,

In 1959 I bought a Buick convertible with tail fins and red leather seats. It did cheer me up driving on highways with J.S. Bach loudly pouring out of my car radio speakers. I do not recall being depressed prior to the purchase, however.

Best,

Alan

I looked around for a photo that matched Greenspan's description, and sent it over to him. Greenspan's assistant relayed his answer:

AG said this is his car! But his was red interior with black exterior (not white, as in the photo). He said he had air conditioning.

In the margins of conversations about money and power, the private man would surface unpredictably. Once, rather early in the process, I asked Greenspan about his romantic life. "I dated news anchors, senators, and beauty queens," he stated, a bit mischievously. I asked him what made him most happy. A sense of progress, a life trajectory angled upward at the steepest possible incline, he replied, with disarming honesty. I asked him why, despite having spent almost two decades as the world's most powerful economist, he still persisted in describing himself as a "sideman." The answers stretched back to the love and injury he had experienced as a child. His ambition, his shyness, the manner in which he navigated Washington—all had their roots in a 1930s boyhood on the northern tip of Manhattan.

Some of the best research discoveries came almost despite him. Several assiduous reporters had tried to lay hands on Greenspan's early writings, contained in his doctoral thesis; oddly, New York University, which awarded the degree, had lost it. But after several months of sitting at the round table in Greenspan's office, I noticed a pattern: when he referred to his youthful thinking, his eyes would drift up to a certain shelf; and, following his gaze, I spied a fat binder. One day, when Greenspan returned to the subject of his intellectual development, I looked up at that same shelf. I would love to read that early work, I said, staring purposefully at the binder. Despite the awkward nature of the content, he gave it to me.

I knew that in the 1960s, when Greenspan had been the de facto chief economist for the claque of libertarians clustered around the novelist Ayn Rand, he had delivered a series of lectures titled the Economics of a Free Society. I wondered if there were recordings, or possibly a text, affording an insight into Greenspan's worldview as he crested his late thirties. One day, as I tracked down Greenspan's friends and colleagues from those times, I found myself in a secluded cabin in the woods of Virginia, talking to Lowell Wiltbank, who had managed the computers and machines at Greenspan's small consulting firm. Learning that Wiltbank was himself a devotee of Rand's thinking, I asked whether he had kept memorabilia from her movement. His basement was stocked with it, he said. Before very long, I had three hundred pages of transcripts: the complete map of my subject's mind, at the height of his intellectual purism.

Inevitably, research of this kind involves drilling many dry boreholes. But the gushers repaid me: the personal files of the Republican provocateur Patrick Buchanan, which contained Greenspan's unapologetically conservative memos to Richard Nixon on the racial tensions and assassinations of 1968; the untold story of the Fed's record on derivatives and mortgages, teased out of interviews and documents released under the Freedom of Information Act; the sensitive memories of some of the women who loved him, foremost among them his wife, Andrea Mitchell. As I write in my acknowledgments, my own discoveries were augmented by an exceptional research team at the Council on Foreign Relations. Between us, we conducted hundreds of interviews and consulted thousands of pages of documentary sources in an attempt to reconstruct a life as vividly and accurately as possible.

I was moderately surprised when Greenspan agreed to cooperate with this project. I approached him after he expressed admiration for my history of hedge funds, which he cited in his own retrospective work on the 2008 financial crisis. But I imagined his attitude might be colored by an earlier book: my account of the World Bank under its tempestuous boss James Wolfensohn. Although my verdict on Wolfensohn had been broadly positive, it had not been received well: Wolfensohn sought to discredit me, and the World Bank bookshop decided not to display the stacks of copies it had ordered. During one of his tantrums, Wolfensohn's staff had arranged for a distinguished friend to call and calm him down. The friend was Alan Greenspan.

Despite this unpropitious background, Greenspan did agree to talk to me, even though he understood that he could claim no power over my account or my conclusions. On the advice of my literary agent, I tried to lock him in, asking that he sign an agreement promising cooperation with me and no other author. At this, Greenspan balked, observing that at some point I was likely to start doing things that he disliked; and since I was not offering to bind my hands, he was not about to bind his either. After that testy beginning, we proceeded on the basis of mutual autonomy—a fitting formula for the biography of a libertarian—and I would not in retrospect have wished anything different. The arrangement gave me full access to my subject combined with untrammeled independence. Married to one journalist, a courter of others over many years, Greenspan understood that he should not try to control me.

At the end of my writing, I hesitated to show my manuscript to Greenspan. Nothing in our relationship required me to do so, and I recognized the risks in putting my cards on the table. The mere extent of my research might come as a shock: in some cases, I had not told Greenspan about the documents I had unearthed because these often spoke for themselves and did not require his comment or elaboration. Besides, people generally do not find it easy to swallow an outsider's unvarnished account of their doings—like Wolfensohn before, Greenspan might react by firing back at me. Inevitably, the evidence had led me repeatedly to an understanding of my subject's actions and motives that was at variance with his own account—he was not going to like that. But after some deliberation, I did show Greenspan the pages. For one thing, openness seemed the more honorable course; he had been open with me, after all. For another, I wanted to submit my research to this final check. After five years of exhaustive efforts to get to the truth, it seemed right to test my results one last time against my subject's memory.

Three weeks after receiving my pages, Greenspan called me in London. We had two long conversations during which he vigorously disputed my interpretations in only a handful of places. The rest he accepted, noting with a chuckle that my history was perhaps more accurate than positive. I deferred to him on one detail about his relationship with his parents, and added a point about his motives in resisting derivatives reform in the late 1990s. In other instances, I weighed what he said but left my account substantially unaltered.

Positive or not, I hope this history is instructive. As the most influential economic statesman of his age, Greenspan spent a lifetime grappling with a momentous shift: the transformation of finance from the fixed and regulated system of the postwar era to the free-wheeling free-for-all of the past quarter century. No other individual was closer to the decisions that attended this change. The story of Alan Greenspan is also the story of the making of modern finance.

"Just prior to World War I emerged one of the historic disasters in American history, the creation of the Federal Reserve System."

—ALAN GREENSPAN, 1964

"The bottom line is that we really do not know how this system works."

—ALAN GREENSPAN ON THE FED'S OPERATION OF MONETARY POLICY, 1999

"Financial markets now view Chairman Greenspan's infallibility more or less as the Chinese once viewed Chairman Mao's."

—ALAN BLINDER AND RICARDO REIS, 2005

"Ages are no more infallible than individuals; every age having held many opinions which subsequent ages have deemed not only false but absurd."

—JOHN STUART MILL, 1859

Introduction:

"HE HAS SET A STANDARD"

On January 23, 1986, the members of the president's economic advisory board gathered in the Roosevelt Room in the West Wing of the White House. The group met in secret; to evade the irritating disclosure laws, the organizers had invited the CIA director and used his presence as an excuse to declare the meeting classified. Walter Wriston, the tall, slouched executive who had built Citicorp into the nation's top commercial lender, took his seat at the table; so did Milton Friedman, the diminutive libertarian iconoclast from the University of Chicago; and so did a dozen other luminaries from Wall Street and academia. After two hours of deliberation, a door opened. In walked Ronald Reagan.[1]

The president had one subject on his mind: inflation. With prices rising at around 4 percent per year, the country was far better off than it had been at the turn of the decade, when the rate had approached 15 percent. But 4 percent was still not low enough, at least not for Reagan. Inflation must be forced down to zero, "or we go right back to where we were."

One adviser suggested that the rate of acceptable inflation might have risen. But the president had no patience with appeasement.

"How the hell are we going to level it off?" he demanded.

"You are 100 percent right," Milton Friedman responded. "Only one goal is right and that is zero." If people grew complacent, Friedman reck-oned, inflation could be back up around 7 or 8 percent by the end of that year.

"Didn't Bastiat say that 'no civilization has survived fiat money'?" asked Reagan.

The president's appeal to a cultish nineteenth-century French econo-mist silenced most of his counselors. It seemed unwise to challenge Rea-gan on his core convictions—in this case, that a currency founded on nothing sturdier than the goodwill of bureaucrats would fail in its basic purpose, which was to act as a store of value. At the start of his presidency, Reagan had set up a commission to consider a return to the gold standard. At some deep level, the president believed that the remedy to the infla-tionary malaise of the 1970s was to go back to a simpler time, when money was a tangible substance.

Friedman waded in again. He sensed where Reagan was going and moved to redirect his thinking.

"Today fiat money is taken as standard," the professor insisted. The president was right to fear inflation; but rather than dream of a return to the gold standard, it would be better to avoid inflationary excess by limit-ing the bureaucrats' money-printing instincts. Central bank discretion should give way to a monetary autopilot: the law should lay down that the supply of money must increase by, say, 4 percent a year—not more and not less. "We have to tame fiat money by rules," Friedman said. "Don't think we can go back to a commodity money."

Friedman generally had the last word on such questions. Since the 1960s he had been the reigning academic commentator on monetary mat-ters, and his polemical skills were intimidating. "Everyone loves to argue with Milton, particularly when he isn't there," Reagan's secretary of state, George Shultz, wryly observed; a few contemptuous words from this gad-fly could reduce grandees to stutters.[2] But one man at the table was ready to stand up to Friedman.

"Why not a commodity standard?" a quiet voice demanded.

The quiet voice belonged to Alan Greenspan. He was in many ways a thoroughly unlikely figure. Neither a distinguished university professor nor a private-sector baron, he ran a low-profile New York consultancy. He had married briefly in his twenties; but now, at almost sixty years old, with an athletic frame, generous lips, and slick black hair, he played a curious dual role: introverted data guy and eligible society bachelor. Every Republican president since Richard Nixon had come to value his advice—he was the man who knew the arcana of the federal budget, next year's likely steel output, and the mysterious fragilities of finance. But he was also an accomplished dancer and a driver of ostentatious cars, and he courted beautiful women, not always sequentially.[3] The previous year, Greenspan had appeared on TV in a broad-shouldered power suit to pitch the latest Apple computer, fusing his own brand of nerdy sex appeal with Apple's insurgent image. After demonstrating how viewers could use the device to track their finances, dial into their bank accounts, and pay bills electronically, Greenspan signed off with evident pleasure. "If you have any money left over, congratulations," he closed, with a sardonic arching of his eyebrows. "You're doing better than the government is."

Reagan seemed to like Greenspan's remark about a gold standard. "I used to pay $50 for a suit," the president complained. "Now $50 will hardly get it cleaned." Vaulting from the mundane to the existential, he asked, "Is it possible for mere human beings to decide how much money should be put out?"

"The problem you have in the federal government is that it can print money," Greenspan observed sympathetically, in his trademark tone of soft authority. A gold standard might be the way to discipline the political classes: so long as there was a central bank that could create fiat money at will, politicians would always spend beyond their means, confident in the knowledge that their debts could be canceled by the printing presses. For precisely this reason, Greenspan had spent his twenties and thirties railing against the monetary status quo. Until Americans recognized that money-printing central banks were fundamentally deceitful—until they tied money to gold—inflation would remain a constant threat and the economy would rest on rickety foundations. Indeed, although few people remembered this, Greenspan had pushed this argument to its logical extreme. In what must surely rank as one of the twentieth century's great ironies, he had described the creation of the nation's central bank as "one of the historic disasters in American history."[4]

A year and a half after his exchange with Reagan, on August 11, 1987, Alan Greenspan was sworn in as Federal Reserve chairman. For the next eighteen and a half years, he embodied the idea that he had frequently denounced: that the discretionary judgments of a money-printing central bank could stabilize an economy.[5] Greenspan was so apparently successful in doing what he had deemed impossible that he became a global superstar, revered by economists, adored by investors, consulted by leaders from Beijing to Frankfurt. When he held forth at the regular gatherings of central bank chiefs in Basel, you could hear a pin drop; the distinguished figures at the table, titans in their own terrains, took notes with the eagerness of undergraduates. Through quiet force of intellect, Greenspan seemed to control the orchestra of the American economy with the finesse of a master conductor; he was the "Maestro," as an incautious biographer suggested. His oracular pronouncements became as familiar and comforting to ordinary Americans as Prozac and *The Simpsons,* the *New Yorker*'s John Cassidy wrote, slyly citing mood lifters that debuted the same year that Greenspan was appointed.

Greenspan's triumph was not merely remarkable in light of his own history as a critic of paper money. It was a refutation of powerful economic ideas—ideas that made it difficult even to conceive of a Fed chairman as a maestro. Since opening for business in 1914, the Fed had presided over inflation during two world wars, converted the recession of the 1930s into the Great Depression, and then, in the 1970s, proved feckless in the face of the most serious peacetime inflation in the nation's history. Surveying this procession of disasters, monetary theorists argued that central bankers would always be soft on inflation—they were subject to irresistible political pressure to juice up the economy.[6] Arthur Burns, who served as Fed chairman between 1970 and 1978, was ruthlessly bullied by Richard Nixon's henchmen; his successor, G. William Miller, was chosen by Jimmy Carter because he was politically loyal, then summarily removed after eighteen months in office. In 1979, Milton Friedman went so far as to write to Paul Volcker, Miller's replacement, confidently predicting his inevitable failure. "My condolences to you on your 'promotion,'" Friedman sneered, noting that the Fed faced double-digit inflation. "As you know, I do not believe that the System can rise to that challenge without major changes in its method of operation."[7]

Despite Friedman's contempt, Volcker proceeded to conquer inflation. But the idea that there were political limits to the Fed's inflation-fighting capacity still seemed true. Volcker had gotten away with toughness because double-digit price rises had created a national crisis; it would be hard to keep the pressure on once inflation had moderated. Indeed, toward the end of Volcker's tenure, Reagan appointees at the Fed staged a revolt against his tight-money policy, humiliating him so much that he considered resignation. The lesson seemed to be that a central banker such as Greenspan, who took office at a time when inflation was no longer enemy number one, was almost doomed to fail. Barring a return to the gold standard, only Friedman's monetary autopilot could be counted upon to ensure that the money in America's wallets would hold its value into the future.

Greenspan duly began his tenure amid modest expectations. Observers predicted that he would be "unable to dominate the Federal Reserve Board the way Volcker had . . . [and] unable to intimidate the politicians."[8] Sure enough, he was attacked repeatedly during his first years in office by the administration of George H. W. Bush; then, when a Democrat won the election of 1992, it was widely assumed that his days were numbered. And yet by the end of his tenure, Greenspan had achieved the exalted stature that Friedman had believed impossible. He received the Presidential Medal of Freedom, a British knighthood, and the French Legion of Honor, surviving in office for more than twice as long as Volcker, more than twice as long as Burns, and twelve times as long as the ill-fated Miller. Only William McChesney Martin, who led the Fed from 1951 to 1970, outlasted Greenspan by a hair. But in Martin's day, banking and credit mattered less and the Fed had little of its later stature.

Twenty-seven years after his caustic letter to Paul Volcker, Milton Friedman greeted the end of Greenspan's chairmanship by acknowledging a revolution. Greenspan had not only sustained Volcker's victory against inflation, he had also extended it. Prices had risen at an average annual rate of 5.2 percent in the Volcker era, and by 3 percent during his second four-year term. During the eighteen and a half years of Greenspan's tenure, they had risen at an average annual rate of just 2.4 percent.[9]

"Alan Greenspan's great achievement is to have demonstrated that it is possible to maintain stable prices," Friedman declared.

"He has set a standard."[10]

Milton Friedman died in November 2006, ten months after his tribute to Greenspan. He did not live to witness the financial crisis of 2008—or the dramatic reappraisal of his friend's reputation. In the years after Wall Street's meltdown, the reassuring maestro became a popular villain, blamed for inflating a monstrous bubble through heedless incompetence or wild laissez-faire ideology. From the vantage point of the postcrisis world, the fact that Greenspan had squeezed down consumer price inflation seemed almost beside the point. The crash had destroyed millions of jobs, wiped trillions of dollars off the value of household savings, and brought on the worst recession since the 1930s.

The financial crisis is indeed key to judging Greenspan's legacy. He cannot be blameless; the cost of the implosion was so great that more should have been done to avert or at least mitigate it. Yet although criticism is essential, it is worth stating something clearly at the start: much of the postcrisis commentary has reduced Greenspan to a caricature. He is accused, along with much of the economics profession, of believing blindly in models. He was in fact a leading skeptic of them. He is blamed for underestimating the propensity of financial systems to run wild. He had in fact spent fifty years warning of treacherous credit cycles. He is painted as an Ayn Rand–loving libertarian ideologue. Yet one of the many paradoxes of his rich life is that his bond with the uncompromising Rand coexisted with a malleable pragmatism. He was a Jew who advised the frequently anti-Semitic Richard Nixon. He was a conservative who could advocate tax hikes. He was a libertarian who repeatedly supported financial bailouts. He was an economist who often behaved more like a Washington tactician. A man who embraces the gold standard and then presides over the financial printing press is surely no simple ideologue.

Greenspan's roots as a gold bug render the crash of 2008 all the more perplexing.[11] He believed in gold as a disciplinary device—governments would not bail out Wall Street if they could not print the money with which to do so. And yet as Fed chairman, he delivered multiple rescues, cutting interest rates aggressively to cushion the shock of Wall Street's 1987 crash, the fallout from Russia's default in 1998, and the tech bust of 2000. The upshot of the older Greenspan's policies was precisely what the younger Greenspan feared: financiers were encouraged to take ever wilder risks, confident in the assumption that the Fed would protect them.[12] Why Greenspan was willing to cut interest rates and preside over a huge buildup in risk taking, and what might have happened if he had kept the cost of borrowing higher, are central questions in any judgment of his legacy. But if even this gold advocate shrank from sterner discipline, would another Fed chairman have acted differently? Was his use of monetary policy to backstop the financial system inevitable, given the political and institutional pressures he faced? Or did it reflect some weakness of character, some fear of confrontation, some lurking insecurity that had to be assuaged by power and popularity?

If Greenspan's stance on interest rates is puzzling, his regulatory stance is commonly seen as the unsurprising result of his libertarian ideology. In the view of most commentators, Greenspan resisted tougher regulation because he naïvely believed that markets were efficient. He trusted financiers too much, failing to imagine that their dazzling inventions could destabilize the economy. But the truth is more subtle and more complex than this account implies. Greenspan never was a simple efficient-market believer, and he sometimes voiced grave doubts about the risks in financial innovation.[13] If he nonetheless welcomed the advent of options, swaps, and newfangled securities, it was partly because he felt he had no choice. The inflation of the late 1960s had destroyed the comforting system of fixed exchange rates and regulated caps on bank interest rates; meanwhile, technological change and globalization made it impossible to resist the explosion of trading in derivatives. To cite just one telling illustration, between 1970 and 1990 the cost of the computer hardware needed to price a mortgage-backed security plummeted by more than 99 percent. No wonder securitization took off during this period.[14] So when Greenspan and his allies judged that certain regulations were obsolete, they were not the deluded victims of some libertarian fever. Rather, they were grappling with how best to manage the old system's inevitable demise. Policy makers could not have preserved the controlled financial system of the 1950s and 1960s even if they had wanted to.

Besides, it was by no means obvious that financial modernization should have been resisted, even if resistance had been feasible. The evident risks in the new financial methods had to be balanced against real benefits. Once currencies began to fluctuate, for example, exporters feared a dollar appreciation that would make their goods uncompetitive; importers feared a dollar decline that would push their costs up. Currency derivatives offered exporters and importers a way to meet in the futures market and cancel out each other's risks—far from rendering the world unstable, financial engineering promised to make it safer. In similar fashion, the securitization of mortgages allowed risks to be dispersed among thousands of investors; swaps and options, while dangerous if abused, had the same risk-spreading propensity. And when it came to managing the attendant perils, it seemed reasonable to bet that banks and investment houses would do better than regulators who operated at one or two removes. Contrary to caricature, Greenspan and his allies did not expect private actors to avoid manias and crashes, but they did hold the view that supervisors would do no better at averting them. They were not naïve efficient-market believers. They were government-can't-do-better realists.

Greenspan began his public and political career when he signed on with the Nixon campaign in the summer of 1967, at a time when modern finance had yet to be invented. Over the next four decades, he was involved in every significant financial debate: as chairman of President Ford's Council of Economic Advisers (CEA), as a Reagan administration confidant, as chairman of the Federal Reserve, and as a leading interpreter of capitalism. Along the way, the allies he collected came from both sides of the political divide. It was Jimmy Carter, a Democrat, who got rid of the last vestiges of interest-rate regulation for banks. It was Bill Clinton, another Democrat, who signed the banking reform of 1999 that ratified the breakdown of the Depression-era separation between banks, insurers, and securities houses. It was, for that matter, a global club of technocrats who, in setting rules for bank capital, deferred to banks' own risk models, effectively handing the teenagers the keys to the Mercedes. To paint financial deregulation as the product of some right-wing conspiracy is laughably off the mark. Intelligent people were grappling with deep forces driving financial evolution and making the best judgments they could. The sincerity of their purpose makes their errors all the more illuminating.

One of the virtues of biography is that it allows readers to understand decision making as it really is—imperfect, improvised, contingent upon incomplete information and flawed human nature. Greenspan and his contemporaries blundered: they were insufficiently wary of the distorted incentives within large financial institutions; they were too complacent about bubbles and leverage. But while one task for the historian is to judge past generations, a second is to show future generations how and why their capable predecessors strayed. After all, tomorrow's financial statesmen will grapple with the same limitations that Greenspan confronted. They will be expected to forecast crises but will lack the tools to do so. They will be called upon to eliminate financial risks when such risks are inescapable features of the human condition. The delusion that statesmen can perform the impossible—that they really can qualify for the title of "maestro"—breeds complacency among citizens and hubris among leaders. The story of Alan Greenspan may perhaps serve as an antidote.

Book I

THE IDEOLOGUE

One

THE FEELING OF
A CONQUEROR

rowing up in the 1930s, he fell in love with the railroads. The great locomotives, puffing and panting as they hauled their unimaginable loads, seemed less like machines than mythical creatures—"some species of mastodon," as a book of the time put it.[1] To watch the beam of light from the great monster's headlamps, to glimpse the hellish fire lighting the interior of the cab, to see the shadow of the fireman silhouetted against the glow—all this was to experience the thrill and terror of industry and progress, to see precisely what was meant by the American century. From around the age of eleven, the young Alan collected train timetables, memorized the routes and the towns along the way, and imagined himself traveling the continent: Duluth to Minneapolis, Minneapolis to Fargo, and then onward and westward to Helena, Spokane, and finally Seattle. It was a way of conjuring a world beyond Washington Heights, the neighborhood of immigrants he inhabited on the northern tongue of Manhattan; a way of escaping the squat redbrick apartment building with its ornate stucco moldings, of freeing his mind from the too-familiar streets filled with European accents—Yiddish, Irish, and German. Washington Heights had been developed just a few years earlier, after the New York subway stretched north to reach it in 1906. But although the subway had arrived, you could still see horses on the streets and men who cleaned up after them.[2] No wonder the railroads seemed romantic.[3]

Alan lived with his grandparents Nathan and Anna Goldsmith and with his doting mother, Rose. They shared a one-bedroom apartment at 600 West 163rd Street; Nathan and Anna had the bedroom, while Alan and Rose slept in what had been built as the dining room. It was a modest accommodation for four people, but it seemed a reasonable lot—better than the crowded tenements of the Lower East Side, where other immigrants lived, and not bad given that the country was in the grip of the Depression.[4] The Goldsmiths lived on the west side of Broadway, the dividing line that separated the salubrious part of the neighborhood from the rough-and-tumble east.[5] "The . . . gentility of the neighborhood . . . along with the style of the buildings, the parks nearby, and the cool breeze from the Hudson in the evening carried vague reminders of the bourgeois sections of German cities," a contemporary wrote.[6] German immigrants flocked to Washington Heights in such numbers that the area was sometimes known as Frankfurt on the Hudson.

To Nathan and Anna, born in Russia, driven to migrate to Hungary and then from Hungary to America, life in New York must have seemed a blessing almost divine—they had boarded their grandson's imaginary train, and after much adventure had arrived safely. As for Rose, born in Hungary though now as American as baseball, there was much to celebrate, too. She had a steady job as a salesperson at the Ludwig-Baumann furniture store in the Bronx, which paid enough to meet the rent of $48 each month, keep food on the table, and even spare Alan a quarter a week for pocket money.[7] Besides, she was happy to be living just half a block away from her sister, the well-to-do Mary. In summer Alan would stay with Mary at her vacation house close to Rockaway Beach, on the near end of Long Island. Alan and his cousin Wesley would spend hours walking the sands with their heads down, searching doggedly for lost coins. Then they would spend the fruits of their labor on candy.

Rose's greatest blessing was young Alan himself, born on March 6, 1926, the product of her brief marriage to Herbert Greenspan. The boy naturally expanded to fill the gaps in Rose's life—the husband who had left when their son was still small, the absence of other children. Each morning her young hero with his perfectly even features and broad smile would soldier off to the P.S. 169 elementary school on Audubon Avenue, and each afternoon he would return with extraordinary things. From very early on, he could add large numbers in his head, and seemed even to enjoy it. Rose trotted him out in front of aunts and uncles to perform. "Alan, what's thirty-five plus ninety-two?" she would ask. "A hundred and twenty-seven," came back the answer.[8]

A few years after he turned addition into a performance art, Alan developed a passion for baseball, and it was hard to say what thrilled him more: the excitement of listening to the radio commentary of the 1936 World Series or the discovery of a world that could be reduced to the statistics and symbols of a prodigious ten-year-old's devising. The statistics were straightforward, but pleasing all the same: a player who got a hit on three out of eleven appearances had a batting average of .273; one who succeeded five out of thirteen times had an average of .385; it was thanks to baseball that Alan memorized the conversion tables for fractions into decimals. But the symbols were where the creativity came in. Alan invented a notation that allowed him to track each play of the big games. If a player hit a ground ball, he would inscribe a careful x on his green scoring sheet. If the player hit a line drive, he would enter an ellipse; a circle with an x through it meant a high fly, and an α meant a deep hit into the outfield. Each fielder's position was assigned a number that could be combined with the symbols to create a precise record of the play: for example, an ellipse next to an 11 meant a line drive to right center field. Reflecting on his childhood some seventy-five years later, Alan remained convinced that his system was better than anything that even the newspaper writers had invented.[9] Rose, no doubt, had agreed with him.

Alan was too young to remember his father's departure, but the separation affected him deeply. To be a single child can be character forming. To be the single child of a single mother can be overwhelming. It has been said that Franklin Delano Roosevelt, the statesman who loomed over the America of Alan's youth, drew his confidence and ambition from his widowed mother's unrelenting attention: he was the work of her life, her monument.[10] Fortunately for Alan, his mother was far less controlling than the imposing Sara Roosevelt, who thought nothing of installing her married son in a town house adjoining hers, then cutting a door from her large bedroom through her daughter-in-law's much smaller one in order to gain access to Franklin's quarters. But though Rose was mild by comparison, her son was nonetheless the sole outlet for her love, and it seems likely that his sense of what he might achieve expanded correspondingly. "A man who has been the indisputable favorite of his mother keeps for life the feeling of a conqueror, that confidence of success that often induces real success," Sigmund Freud declared, possibly with more intuition than evidence.[11] At a minimum, Alan was prepared to believe that he could beat baseball writers at their own game, and that one day he might ride a train as far as the Pacific.

Yet if Alan felt confident in his intellectual abilities, he was less comfortable with people. He could master baseball through force of intellect; human chemistry was different. Part of his self-doubt may have come from his mother, for Rose was a hard act to follow. Pretty, vivacious, and gregarious, she could easily have made any child feel tongue-tied by comparison. At family gatherings, Alan's uncle Murray, who now went by the name of Mario and tried to pass as Italian, would play the piano with great flair; he had achieved success as a writer of musicals in Hollywood. But it was Rose who provided the accompaniment, a repertoire of period songs performed in the loose and haunting manner of a torch singer. Leaning over the baby grand piano in the living room of their apartment, flashing her infectious smile, Rose could make herself the center of the party.[12] Alan would be left feeling that he was somehow off toward the side—a "sideman," he would call himself.[13]

But the most obvious explanation for the young Alan's diffidence lay with his father. Herbert Greenspan had arrived in the United States as the four-year-old Haim Grunspann, a lowly "steerage alien" aboard a ship that docked in Ellis Island in August 1906.[14] Like Rose, he was good-looking, with the aquiline nose and fine cheekbones of the film star Gene Kelly. But while Rose was unfailingly sunny, Herbert could be awkward and withdrawn, and he may have passed down to Alan a tendency to live inside his own head. The fact of Herbert's absence reinforced that tendency greatly. After the divorce, Herbert moved back in with his family in Brooklyn, barely twenty miles away. But though he would promise to take Alan on outings, he often failed to keep his word.[15] "Alan hardly got to see him. But I do remember the ecstasy that Alan exhibited on those rare occasions when his father visited," his cousin Wesley remembered.[16] The experience of being let down by his father taught Alan that depending on the love of others could be a path to pain. It seemed safer to retreat into his own mind, to the controlled world of baseball statistics and railroad timetables.[17]

As a very young child, Alan expressed his longing for a father directly. His stern grandfather was no substitute—Nathan spoke in a forbidding Yiddish accent and was consumed by the world of his synagogue, which Alan found so alien that he later came close to refusing the bar mitzvah.[18] But Alan's uncle Irwin, the father of Wesley, was a more approachable figure.[19] Sometimes Irwin would set out for a walk holding Wesley with one hand and Wesley's younger sister with the other, with Alan tagging alongside. Pretty soon Alan would worm his way between uncle and cousin until his hand was being held, and Wesley was left to keep up independently.[20] But as Alan grew older, these transparent pleas for love were less frequent; he dealt with the gap left by his father by withdrawing into himself, and found that spending time alone made him feel comfortable and happy.[21] Even his school friends could see that he was unusually self-contained. Irwin Kantor, Alan's closest companion at the Edward W. Stitt Junior High School on 164th Street, spent hours at his apartment, absorbed in a game the two boys invented, a form of baseball with dice.[22] Years later, Irwin remembered Alan as a strange loner—no siblings, no father, a mother who was out at work, and grandparents who seemed stuck in an old world in which children spoke only when spoken to.[23]

"I think he really grew up with the radio, with his own thoughts," Greenspan's wife, Andrea Mitchell, would say later. "I don't know if it made him sad and lonely, but it certainly shaped the person he is. He's not easily accessible to people and he's very shy.

"*Very* shy," she added.[24]

If Alan's circumstances fed his natural introspection, they also nour-ished his ambition. A powerful voice inside him whispered that he was capable of greatness—his facility with numbers showed that this was so, and his mother's adoration removed all doubt of it.[25] Yet he also under-stood that the world would never recognize his greatness unless he demon-strated it beyond doubt, for he lacked the levity and carefree charm necessary to attain status without effort. If he was ever going to be some-one, he would have to work hard. By doing things, achieving things, the sideman would be noticed.

His father had a clear idea of how Alan's ambition might be directed. In 1935, Herbert published a tract called *Recovery Ahead!*, a paean to the New Deal that likened Roosevelt to a grand general leading the country to the "Delectable Mountains of prosperity." Herbert's motives for writing were commercial, not literary or scholarly; an ad for the book in the *New York Times* promised "a chart in which the writer predicts the month by month fluctuations of the stock market during 1935 and 1936."[26] Unem-barrassed by this startling claim of foresight, Herbert presented a copy of *Recovery* to his son, with an inscription hoping that the nine-year-old would take an interest in economics. "At your maturity you may look back and endeavor to interpret the reasoning behind these logical forecasts and begin a like work of your own," Herbert wrote. But although his son would ultimately follow his suggested path, the advice meant nothing at the time. Alan read a few pages of the book and then gave up. It was too much for a nine-year-old.[27]

Pushing the New Deal to one side, Alan focused his ambitions on baseball—as well as analyzing the game, he played it. As he entered his teens, he developed an athletic frame, and his agility and reflexes gave him what the sport demanded. He was a left-hander, which made him a natural first baseman; playing in a local park with older kids one day, he hit a curveball so confidently that an impressed high schooler declared he was headed for the major leagues. The compliment filled Alan with a powerful pride. He would go to Yankee Stadium and gaze down at his heroes: Lou Gehrig on first, Joe DiMaggio in the outfield, Lefty Gomez or Red Ruffing pitching—seventy years later, he could still recite the lineup from memory. And as he watched those champions playing, he sometimes imagined a fantastic reversal of his role.[28] One day, instead of looking down at that exquisite diamond, he might be down there himself. Instead of gazing, he would be gazed upon. He would take his position at the center of the universe.[29] He would be a major league first baseman.[30]

Alan completed junior high school in 1939, having skipped one year on the advice of his teachers. His next port of call was George Washington High School, a formidable structure with Italianate columns perched on a hilly promontory overlooking the Harlem River; the dramatic setting reinforced the building's mass and height, as if it were some temple lifted from antiquity. The school was among the best in the city: it boasted excellent teachers, and it served a neighborhood of ambitious immigrants determined to succeed in their new land by excelling in the classroom.[31] Alan continued to play baseball in high school, no doubt replaying that scene of himself at Yankee Stadium inside his head. But the truth was that his athletic progress began to taper off, and gradually he came to realize that his ambition needed a new outlet. This time he found it in music.

Alan's focus on music confirmed his mother's influence—and his father's lack of it. As well as presenting the boy with his book on economics, Herbert had taken him to visit an uncle, an accountant who lived in enviable splendor in an apartment on Central Park South; given Alan's aptitude for math, he might have decided in his teens to adopt this uncle as a role model. But nothing about the father appealed much to the son; he was far more drawn to his maternal family. Grandfather Nathan was a cantor in a synagogue in the Bronx; Uncle Mario could play the most complex piano pieces on sight; Cousin Claire was on her way to becoming a professional singer. And, of course, music was Rose's love. The sound of a Bach concerto or a music-hall ballad transported Alan to a happy place, where his mother was singing and the rhythm and melody bound the two of them together.[32]

At twelve, Alan had heard Claire play the clarinet. The rich sound captivated him, and he began to play, too; and as his baseball aspirations dimmed, he added the tenor saxophone to his repertoire. The big-band sound of the late 1930s, a fusion of 1920s dance music with blues and ragtime, swept him up in its wave. He practiced obsessively, sometimes sequestering himself in his room for as many as six hours in a day. He loved the music for its own sake, but something else was driving him as well. Music, like baseball, involved an element of performance. Here was another way for a loner to become a star, to earn the attention of the crowd without having to wade into it.

When Alan was fifteen, he made a musical pilgrimage to match his trips to Yankee Stadium. He took the subway downtown to the Hotel Pennsylvania, right by one of New York's main stations, to listen to Glenn Miller and his orchestra. The choice was no coincidence; Miller had created a variation on the big-band sound that revolved around the tenor sax and clarinet, Alan's two instruments. As he recalled in his memoir years later, Alan maneuvered himself right up to the bandstand, so that he was just ten feet away from Miller himself; and when the band started to play a dance variation on Tchaikovsky's Sixth Symphony, "The Story of a Starry Night," excitement triumphed over fifteen-year-old diffidence.

"That's the *Pathétique*!" Alan called out.

"That's terrific, kid," Miller responded.[33]

The thrill of being addressed by a jazz idol stuck in Alan's mind. Miller had uttered only three words, but that was more than DiMaggio or Gehrig had ever said to him.

Through Alan's adolescence, the tumultuous politics of the 1930s encroached periodically. Starting around the middle of the decade, Jews from Austria and Germany began flooding into Washington Heights, among them a teenager named Heinz Alfred Kissinger, who soon changed his name to Henry and enrolled in George Washington High, two years ahead of Alan. By the time Alan arrived there, the U.S. Navy had positioned a telescope in the soaring ecclesiastical bell tower that jutted improbably from the school's roof; its job was to survey the river down below lest it be penetrated by German U-boats. Two years later, some months after the trip downtown to hear Glenn Miller's orchestra, Alan switched on the radio in his bedroom during a break from clarinet practice. The newscaster was announcing Japan's attack on Pearl Harbor.

Alan ignored the march to war as much as possible. "I was more concerned about whether the Brooklyn Dodgers were winning than whether France was falling," he recalled, years later.[34] Rather than worrying about geopolitics, he joined an assortment of dance bands, playing a couple of jobs some weekends and earning $10 for his efforts. The music got the better of his grades; he continued to excel in math but failed to shine in other areas because he spent so much time with his instruments. When he completed twelfth grade, he received a special citation from the school's music department. His yearbook photo shows a young man with the strong features of his father: high cheekbones, aquiline nose, and chiseled jaw. The caption in the yearbook promises: "Smart as a whip and talented, too. He'll play the sax and clarinet for you."[35]

Emerging from high school in June 1943, Alan Greenspan had no interest in college. He secured a prestigious place at Juilliard, New York's elite musical conservatory, which aspired to rival the great classical training centers of Europe. But the school's formal approach was hardly the right fit for a Glenn Miller enthusiast, and Greenspan quit the following January. Meanwhile, he continued to play jazz. He took classes with a well-known teacher named Bill Sheiner, who held court at the Musical Mart on 174th Street in the Bronx. Sheiner directed Greenspan to sit next to a teenager named Stan Getz, who went on to become one of the greatest saxophonists in jazz history. The two students quickly became friends, and Greenspan later wrote that confronting such a talent made his own limitations obvious. But being less talented than Getz was more or less equivalent to being less intelligent than Einstein. In contrast to baseball, Greenspan knew that his musical ability promised a real chance of employment.

In the spring of 1944, Greenspan turned eighteen and was summoned by the draft board. It was a frightening time to be called up: American servicemen were dying by the tens of thousands. Greenspan rode the subway to the southern tip of Manhattan, where the draft board had set up an induction center at the Beaux-Arts customhouse on Battery Park, which had been built as a shrine to international commerce and now was party to its destruction. For a long while he waited in line with hundreds of young men. But when it was his turn to be processed, a medical check revealed a spot on his lung. "We can't tell if it's active," the sergeant said, ordering Greenspan to report to a tuberculosis specialist the next day. When the specialist could not determine whether the young man was sick, he was declared unfit for service.

Greenspan feared that his life might be over. And although that fear turned out to be unfounded, his life was surely changed: confronting deathly challenges with military comrades might have broken down Greenspan's mental walls and made him less of a loner; it might also have softened the disdain he came to feel in his thirties toward all things organized by government. In any event, aged eighteen and unbothered by such counterfactuals, Greenspan responded to his intimations of mortality by plunging deeper into music. His teacher, Bill Sheiner, told him of an opening in the Henry Jerome band, a traveling swing act that was looking to hire a clarinet and sax player.

Henry Jerome was not exactly Glenn Miller. He had a reputation for entertaining middle-aged couples in hotels and casinos; signing up with his outfit was like playing AAA ball rather than making it to the major leagues. But Greenspan showed up anyway at the audition at Nola's Studios in Midtown, a shy and loose-limbed youth with an ironic, self-measuring smile. Jerome liked what he heard and offered Greenspan the position at $62 a week—three times what his mother made at her department store.[36]

For the next sixteen months, Greenspan lived the life of a traveling performer, striking up conversations with neighbors in train compartments, finding that a southern accent could be hard to fathom, playing gigs as far afield as New Orleans, and enjoying himself immensely.[37] Along the way, moreover, he found that Henry Jerome was more exciting than his reputation had hinted. A little while before he signed Greenspan, Jerome's band had played at the Lookout House, a gambling joint on Dixie Highway in Covington, Kentucky. A rival orchestra that was drawing far bigger crowds at a nearby theater poached several of Jerome's musicians; "I had to start the whole thing over because the whole band was ripped out," Jerome remembered later.[38] Seeing opportunity in adversity, Jerome resolved to strike out in a fresh direction. A bold new style of jazz, forged in the heat of Manhattan's nightclubs by musicians like Charlie "Bird" Parker and Dizzy Gillespie, was beginning to eclipse the softer, sweeter big-band swing that had dominated the New York pop music scene since the late 1930s.[39] Jerome filled several of his open slots with musicians who had the improvisational skills needed to deliver the new "bebop" sound. "They were all musicians on the street, digging Dizzy and Bird," the bandleader recalled later.[40]

Jerome scouted around for a New York venue that would let him experiment with the new style, and found what he was looking for in the Childs' restaurant below the Paramount Theater. This cavernous cafeteria on Times Square was in some ways a strange setting, a far cry from the intimate jazz clubs that Parker and Gillespie played in. In the early part of the evening, it catered to everyone from midshipmen on shore leave to Westchester families visiting the city to see a show, serving pancakes and tuna salad sandwiches—there was nothing avant-garde about it.[41] But since the 1920s, Childs' had led something of a double life. Somewhere around midnight, the clientele would change, and the restaurant would feature "a dash of lavender," as a coy *Vanity Fair* writer put it. The modern magazine would have expressed that point a different way. In the small hours of the morning, Childs' became a gay hot spot.[42]

The Childs' gig gave Jerome's troupe exposure on national radio. The band often appeared in the eleven o'clock slot following prime-time dramas, its brassy trumpets and mellow sax riffs bursting forth as the news anchor finished delivering the latest war bulletins from Europe and the Pacific at the top of the hour. A suave hepcat of a host would introduce each number from the evening's lineup, improvising verbal riffs to match the licks rolling out of the horn section. "Well I don't care how far rigor mortis has set in," he began one night in the spring of 1945; "here's a tune that when you hear it—the Henry Jerome arrangement of it—you just gotta get up and dance, no matter what you're doing. Dig it."[43]

Greenspan was the junior figure in a fourteen-man ensemble. He was a good section musician, playing notes others had written. But unlike the great idols of jazz, he never made the jump to improviser or soloist. In Greenspan's recollection, he was happy with his role—when he had aspired to major league baseball, he had seen himself as a competent first baseman, not a pitching star; now that he played jazz, he was equally content to be a sideman. But his modesty had its limits. In the privacy of his mind, Greenspan knew he was special; he wanted to play the hero in the drama of his life, and he was determined to be recognized. Making $62 a week as a mere teenager was a wonderful first step. But if he wasn't going to do solos, he wasn't going to stick around indefinitely.[44]

In his time as a jazz player, Greenspan was a sideman in ways more than just musical. He took it upon himself to do the tax returns for fellow band members, thereby fingering himself as the intellectual in the group; he was "a better bookkeeper than musician," Jerome was heard to comment.[45] And his idea of downtime set him apart. World War II was the heyday of the union movement, and the band followed a routine prescribed by union rules: it would play for forty minutes, then take a twenty-minute break before beginning the next set. The other band members would sneak upstairs to the Walgreens drugstore during offstage interludes and smoke dope in the phone booths; Greenspan, for his part, would study books about finance. In the unlikely setting of the Childs' restaurant, Greenspan began his education about banking and markets. He learned about the life of John Pierpont Morgan, the financier who had shaped America's corporate behemoths before World War I. He devoured *Reminiscences of a Stock Operator,* the classic account of the speculator Jesse Livermore, who bet successfully against the market on the eve of the 1929 crash. And he resolved that once he tired of music, his next move would be to Wall Street.

In a strange kind of way, the hands of both Greenspan's parents lay behind his abrupt change of direction. If he was self-contained enough to stand apart from the band's culture, and self-confident enough to believe he could do better in a different world, he surely owed those strengths to the affirmation of his doting mother, whom he continued to live with when the band was not touring.[46] Yet if he gravitated toward finance, and if he possessed the mathematical aptitude to thrive at it, he owed a debt to his father, even if he seldom saw the man and was not inclined to thank him. It was almost as though he had had to exorcise his father before he could admit to sharing his interests. By joining a jazz band and taking after his mother, he had freed himself to discover finance and take after his father.[47]

In the summer of 1945, Greenspan quit the Henry Jerome band to prepare for an undergraduate degree at New York University.

Two

THE UN-KEYNESIAN

On August 14, 1945, half a million New Yorkers assembled in Times Square, right by the Childs' restaurant where Greenspan had performed with the Henry Jerome Orchestra. Their eyes were fixed on the moving electric sign on the New York Times Building, and at 7:03 p.m. they got the news flash they were waiting for: "Official— Truman announces Japanese surrender."

There was an immediate outpouring of joy. People in the streets tossed hats and flags into the air; office workers leaned precariously out of windows and showered confetti and streamers down on their heads; and the news radiated in all directions. In Harlem, couples jived in the streets and cars found it impossible to pass until sprinkler trucks dispersed pedestrians. In Italian American sections of Brooklyn, jubilant families set up tables outside and offered food, wine, and liquor to passersby. In the Garment District, brilliant patches of cloth, feathers, and hat trimmings mingled with the confetti that thickened the air. In the crooked streets of Chinatown, men, women, and children perched on fire escapes and waved American and Chinese flags and cheered the ritual dragons that danced their way along Mott Street and Doyers Street. Trucks laden with horn-blowing merrymakers pulled slowly through the dense ocean of humanity in Times Square. Men and women embraced. "There were no strangers in New York yesterday," the *New York Times* reported.[1]

Yet amid the scenes of jubilance, there was an undertone of apprehension. Appearing on the lawn in front of the White House with his wife, Bess, President Truman celebrated "the day we've all been looking for," but then added a warning: "We face the greatest task . . . and it is going to take the help of all of you to do it."[2] The nation had been pulled out of the Depression by war spending, fully half of which had been financed by debt; it had been "the largest public works project in the nation's history," in the words of the historian James Patterson.[3] But Japan's surrender signaled the end of the defense boom, and the nation now faced the challenge of demobilizing 12 million military personnel. Many feared that the returning servicemen would find nothing to do, and that queues of dejected, jobless youth would herald the return of the Depression.[4] Public opinion surveys reported that seven out of ten Americans expected to be worse off in the future, reversing the doubling of salaries they had enjoyed during the war. The writer Bernard DeVoto identified in the nation a "fear which seems altogether new. . . . It may well be the most truly terrifying phenomenon of the war. It is a fear of the coming of peace."[5]

The majority of Americans dealt with this fear by turning to their government. The experience of war had taught them how effective a federal super state could be; government planners had decided which factory should build what, and the result had been a triumph over fascism.[6] In 1944, Congress had responded to the mood of the nation by passing the GI Bill, offering generous stipends to returning servicemen who wanted to buy a home or enroll in a university. In the presidential campaign that fall, Roosevelt had upped the ante, promising more hospitals, more airports, and sixty million new jobs; he won the election in a landslide. By 1945, total federal spending had hit $95 billion, up from around $9 billion in 1939; expenditures during the war years were twice the total during the previous 150 years of U.S. history.[7] Roosevelt's sudden death from a cerebral hemorrhage in April 1945 did not shake the country's enthusiasm for his activist approach. In the wake of Japan's surrender, Truman promised to fight for a new law that would guarantee full employment.

Such was the intellectual climate when Alan Greenspan entered the School of Commerce, Accounts, and Finance at New York University. Statist faith was at its peak; laissez-faire ideas were in abeyance. "In 1945 no articulate, coordinated, self-consciously conservative intellectual force existed in the United States," declared George Nash, the great historian of the conservative movement. "There were, at most, scattered voices of protest."[8]

Arriving on the NYU campus as a shy nineteen-year-old, Greenspan could hardly fail to sense these intellectual currents. Since quitting the Henry Jerome band, he had spent the summer shuttling between the public library and his mother's apartment, diligently reading the text-books he would encounter in his first year of economics. He wanted to make the most of his studies, which he was paying for out of savings from his musical earnings, and he was determined to overcome the handicap of two years away from the classroom. When the university opened in September, he commuted back and forth from Washington Heights to the Greenwich Village campus, a cluster of faculty buildings around an incongruous marble arch on Washington Square, built in self-conscious imitation of the Arc de Triomphe in Paris. There the young Greenspan encountered a social climate dominated by the legions of returning ser-vicemen lounging around the ornate fountain in Washington Square Park. They were as sympathetic to government as any student cohort has ever been—the government was paying for their education.

Although New Deal progressivism dominated the country, Greenspan refused to be formed by it. He came of age in the era of Keynesian think-ing, but he emerged as an un-Keynesian. It is tempting to explain this par-adox in terms of the intellectual microclimate he inhabited, for the School of Commerce at NYU was at least partially at odds with the broader national zeitgeist. For one thing, the school had a strictly practical mission. Nicknamed the factory, its goal was to churn out accountants, insurance specialists, real estate managers, and such. The earnest young men who signed up for its classes went about the campus in formal shirts and ties, preemptively conforming to the dress code of the professions they aspired to.[9] Moreover, those professions were not always friendly toward the New Deal. In 1945, Ira Mosher, the leader of the National Association of Manufacturers, denounced the "unmitigated warfare that has been waged for a decade against the free competitive enterprise system."[10] Perhaps a little of that sentiment may have filtered into the School of Commerce, despite the generally pro-government outlook of Greenspan's generation.

Besides, university economics faculties were caught in a sort of time warp. By 1945, John Maynard Keynes's ideas had been embraced by New Dealers in Washington, but they did not yet dominate the undergraduate curriculum the way they did after 1948, the year in which Paul Samuelson, the self-described "brash whippersnapper go-getter" at the Massachusetts Institute of Technology, published his classic introductory textbook, *Economics*.[11] Samuelson's text cemented in the minds of undergraduates the case for a mixed economy, and if Greenspan had been exposed to it at the start of his studies, it is at least conceivable that he might have developed differently. "No longer is modern man able to believe 'that government governs best which governs least,'" Samuelson declared confidently in his textbook; and his writing's profound influence on students just a few years younger than Greenspan can be gauged from the vehemence with which conservatives denounced it.[12] In *God and Man at Yale*, published in 1951, William F. Buckley Jr. lamented that fully one third of the Yale class had been exposed to Samuelson's writings, and that "the net influence of Yale economics" was "thoroughly collectivistic."[13]

But when Greenspan began at NYU, Samuelson's textbook was as yet unpublished. Instead, Greenspan enrolled in courses taught by Walter Spahr, the head of the NYU economics faculty, whose view of the New Deal was ferociously critical. In a typical speech to the Economic Club of Detroit in 1949, Spahr decried "the March into the Death Valley of Socialism," exclaiming that "'Liberalism' means practically nothing but Socialism or Communism or being liberal with other people's money." Anticipating the objection that "the people" in question had voted for liberals, Spahr lectured his audience that "the last popular vote for Hitler was nearly 100% of the total vote cast."[14] Evidently, in those years when peace was new, the relics of the prewar economics lived on in the NYU faculty.

The question is how far any of this made a difference to the young Greenspan. Toward the end of his undergraduate career, he took Spahr's class on understanding business cycles. Ironically, Spahr's views on this subject anticipated the lectures and articles that Greenspan would produce in his thirties and early forties. In Spahr's opinion, Keynes and his disciples had business cycles backward: they favored budget deficits and money printing to battle recessions, but Spahr fervently believed that such activism would serve only to exacerbate swings in the economy. Yet if this was Spahr's opinion, he was ineffective at communicating it. His fierce off-campus speeches contrasted sharply with his quiet comportment at the university, and he smothered his ideological fire with a wet-blanket teaching style that made him the last person to win young minds over to conservatism. Standing before a packed classroom of fifty or so students, he would instruct his charges to open their textbooks at a certain page, then demand to know if anybody had a question about its content. The students were typically too bored or intimidated to venture a query, so Spahr would enjoin them to turn to the next page, whereupon he would repeat his question.

One day, as Spahr was torturing his students, a young naval veteran named Robert Kavesh looked over at his classmate Alan Greenspan, who was sitting next to him. Greenspan seemed to be hiding something from the professor, and when Kavesh looked closer, he saw what it was. Inside Spahr's textbook on business cycles, Greenspan had concealed a smaller volume about Keynes; and he was reading it with rapt excitement. The fact that Spahr was a staunch conservative was evidently of no interest to his pupil. Far from recruiting Greenspan to the conservative cause, Spahr had come close to driving him away from it.[15]

The truth is that the microclimate at the School of Commerce influenced Greenspan less than the young man's private reading.[16] The twin engines of his childhood—an introspective isolation on the one hand, a burning ambition on the other—were driving Greenspan to educate himself, with little influence from outsiders. He had friends at the university, and he was happy to play the clarinet in the college orchestra, sing in the glee club, and team up with Bob Kavesh, his neighbor in the business cycle class, to found a music appreciation club they called the Symphonic Society.[17] But just as he had won a coveted spot at Juilliard and then dropped out, and just as he had gotten his break in jazz and then turned to economics and finance, so as a student he cut his own path, curiously untouched by anything around him. If his later libertarianism had roots in his early life, these lay in his own nature, not in professorial nurture. The creed of individualism was bound to appeal to so pure an individualist.

Greenspan's course of private reading began with economic history. His boyhood fascination with the railroads returned in a new guise: he devoured books on the visionary entrepreneurs who had built the United States into an industrial powerhouse, all within the span of one man's lifetime. Historians might write about armies and navies and treaties, but the true making of the nation came down to the steam and steel that connected up a continent-sized country. Greenspan was especially enamored of James J. Hill, the impresario of the Great Northern line, whose ideas and ingenuity had turned the wilderness that was the great northwest into a thriving, productive economy.[18] In the mind of the young Greenspan, the industrialists of the late nineteenth century were not robber barons but pioneers and heroes. When the first doubleheader plowed across the Dakotas to the Pacific seaboard, the American empire was riding in that train of cars, and the plumes of smoke that streamed out from the engine signified as much as the burning powder over Gettysburg.[19]

Greenspan also imbibed Keynes, both indirectly and directly. He read the work of Alvin Hansen, an eminent Harvard economist who had embraced Keynes's writings during the 1930s. Hansen had seized upon Keynes's chief insight—the so-called paradox of thrift—and given it a new twist, influencing both policy makers and a younger generation of economists. Keynes's paradox described how a cyclical downturn could feed on itself: when the economy slowed, cautious consumers would seek to save, depriving businesses of customers and so exacerbating the slowdown. But Hansen believed that weak private demand and excess saving had become a structural malaise. The forces that had spurred spending in the nineteenth century had played themselves out; slowing population growth, the closing of the American frontier, and the maturation of the great capital-consuming industries such as railroads and steel signaled that spending would be weak indefinitely. Full employment and inflation were almost inconceivable under these conditions, Hansen believed; and this meant that the policy prescriptions that Keynes had advocated during the Depression were actually permanent imperatives. To counter what Hansen called secular stagnation, the government would have to discourage excess saving by redistributing money from the high-saving rich to the high-spending poor. It would have to boost public spending and tolerate large budget deficits.

Greenspan was not convinced by any of this. The contention that excess savings would pile up, with nobody willing to spend or invest them, seemed just too pessimistic. To a young man whose imagination had been captured by the virile railway magnates of the nineteenth century, it seemed obvious that there would always be new technologies on which to venture bets; the frontier was not purely geographical. It was all very well for Hansen, an economist already in his forties at the onset of the Depression, to have been shocked into a state of jaded gloom. But to Greenspan, the Depression was just the backdrop for his childhood; he failed to find it discouraging because he accepted it as normal.[20] What he recalled about the 1930s had nothing to do with excess savings or job lines; he remembered instead the thrill of visiting the World's Fair in New York in 1939, where he laid eyes for the first time on a magic box called television. Even as he commuted back and forth to New York University several years later, Greenspan could see the city changing under the impact of that box, as scrawny forests of antennas sprouted on rooftops. How could Hansen argue that progress was grinding to a halt? And how could anyone suppose that there was nothing left to spend money on?

As he read everything he found, Greenspan chanced upon a rebuttal of Hansen by George Terborgh, an obscure economist employed by the Machinery and Allied Products Institute. A more conventional student would not have given this author so much as a second glance—why read a nobody from a lobbying outfit when an eminent Harvard professor was arrayed against him? But with the quirky independence of an autodidact, Greenspan studied Terborgh's book *The Bogey of Economic Maturity* and agreed with what it said. Hansen's "stagnationist" position was excessively colored by "the dark valley of the thirties."[21]

As luck would have it, events soon vindicated Greenspan and Terborgh. The end of wartime rationing uncorked an exuberant surge of consumer spending as Americans bought washing machines, automobiles, electric ranges, cotton goods, girdles, nylons, cameras, film, sporting equipment, electric train sets—they had been denied all these during the war, and now they were happy to tap savings to spoil themselves.[22] Contrary to Hansen's pronouncements, consumer spending, economic growth, and inflation were not dead—indeed, consumer prices rose by 17.6 percent during Greenspan's second year in college. His skepticism of neo-Keynesian thought was thus confirmed. And so was his confidence in his magpie approach to his own intellectual development.

As he grappled with Keynes, Greenspan was changing. He had begun college as an unsure youth escaping from a dead-end job in a second-tier jazz band. Two years into his studies, he was emerging as a young man with a vocation. At the close of his junior year at NYU, he was the runner-up for the university's Beta Gamma Sigma Scholastic Award, a recognition of "scholarship, character, and seriousness of purpose."[23] His friend Bob Kavesh, who went on to a distinguished career as an economics professor, thought he had never seen anyone assemble bits of information so effectively from such eclectic sources. In discovering economics, Greenspan had discovered his calling.

It was an exciting time to enter the profession. Greenspan came to economics just as the United States came to dominate the field. Before the war, the London and Cambridge of John Maynard Keynes had shaped economic thinking. After the war, Boston, Chicago, and New York took over, with vicious academic fights among them.[24] What really captivated Greenspan was neither the missionary Keynesianism of the Bostonians nor the laissez-faire ideas of Chicago. It was the intense empiricism of the New York school, which shaped his approach throughout his career and explained what would be his greatest achievement.

The headquarters of the New York school were to be found some six miles north of NYU—at Columbia University and at the nearby National Bureau of Economic Research, which had been launched in 1920 by a Columbia professor named Wesley Clair Mitchell. The goal of the National Bureau was not to theorize about how the economy might function but rather to measure what it did; how much cotton or pig iron it produced; how many hours the average worker clocked up in a week; how much companies spent on new machines or buildings. Over the next quarter century, researchers at the National Bureau assembled the statistics necessary to document the business cycle and formulate the national accounts from which the gross domestic product is calculated. At the onset of the Depression, the Hoover and Roosevelt administrations had confronted a collapse in output without the benefit of knowing what that output was. By the time Greenspan graduated from NYU, armies of Wesley Mitchell acolytes were tracking every facet of Americans' productive existence.

In his junior year at NYU, Greenspan got a taste of this measurement project. He took statistics classes from Geoffrey Moore, a School of Commerce professor who doubled as a researcher at the National Bureau. Moore went on to become commissioner of labor statistics under Richard Nixon, and made a lasting mark on the profession by developing leading and lagging indicators of the business cycle. Moore recognized in the young Greenspan a like-minded data sleuth, and recommended him for a summer job at the prestigious banking house of Brown Brothers Harriman. Greenspan rode the subway down to the Brown Brothers building on Wall Street and soon found himself stepping into a sanctuary of thick carpets, gilded ceilings, and rolltop desks.[25] A young partner at the bank asked him to produce a weekly seasonal adjustment for the Federal Reserve's data on department store sales, and for the next two months Greenspan consulted technical articles on how seasonal adjustments are calculated, marshaling the data with the help of a slide rule.

As he labored over the numbers, Greenspan discovered something about himself. He found more satisfaction in this narrow task than in the grand but inconclusive debates about government versus markets that preoccupied some of his friends on campus. Something powerful inside him craved control over a confined domain. He wanted to be right, and to know that he was right; and he thrived on problems that he could solve alone, without seeking others' opinions. The critics of the New York school had lampooned the National Bureau for pursuing "measurement without theory." The shy young introvert was happy just to measure things.[26]

Greenspan graduated summa cum laude in 1948, having secured an unbroken string of A grades in all his classes after his first semester.[27] He accepted a scholarship to stay on at NYU and study for a master's degree in the evenings; his savings from his jazz days had run out and he needed to work during the daytime. An advertising agency made him a lucrative offer, but the ad business was not where his heart lay; instead, he took a more modestly paid position as a business researcher at the National Industrial Conference Board. At $45 a week, the job came with less money than his old gig in the Henry Jerome band, but it offered a chance to get established as a young economist.

The Conference Board had some two hundred member companies—a who's who of American business—and its approach to economics made it an extension of the empirical New York school. The board had developed the first version of the consumer price index, and had been the best source of data on unemployment during the Depression. At its big offices on Park Avenue, rows of researchers assembled numbers that its corporate members wanted: trends in mining, cotton harvesting, foreign trade, steel output, and so on. Greenspan made it his mission to master all the sources in the Conference Board's library, and he began to publish articles in the board's house journal. He produced learned analyses on small manufacturers' profits, housing starts, and consumer credit trends. The Conference Board's membership came to know his byline. The *New York Times* picked up one of his articles.

As he established himself at the Conference Board, Greenspan attracted a new kind of attention from his father. After deserting Rose soon after Alan's birth, Herbert had mostly disappeared from his son's life—especially after he remarried and began a second family. Now that Alan was succeeding professionally, Herbert reappeared, proposing that they go into business as partners; perhaps they could set up a consulting firm or even try their hands at trading. The proposals met with a stony reception. Alan had dealt with the lack of a father by retiring into his own world. He was not about to embrace a partnership with the man who had driven him into his shell in the first place.

Besides, there was something about Herbert that produced a visceral response from Alan. His father behaved awkwardly toward him, and this made him behave awkwardly in turn. It was bad enough to have inherited this social handicap from his father; it was worse to have him there to reinforce it. And Herbert, although intelligent, gave off a stifling odor of failure. He talked a good game about setting up a new enterprise—like many followers of the stock market in the 1940s, he was fascinated by price charts that told you when to buy stocks and when to get out of them. But Herbert lacked the character to deliver on his patter; he was still the same man who had promised to visit his young son in Washington Heights and then disappointed him, repeatedly. If Rose Goldsmith's unqualified devotion to Alan had fortified him with that feeling of a conqueror, Herbert Greenspan's aura of wasted potential provided a different sort of goad. The son was determined not to be like the father. He would prove that he was different by separating himself from him professionally.[28]

Greenspan was more open to substitute fathers.[29] In 1950, he completed his master's degree at NYU and enrolled in the PhD program at Columbia University. His adviser there was Arthur Burns, later the Fed chairman of the 1970s. Burns was an impressive figure, handsome and articulate; during his career in government, it was said that wherever he sat was the head of the table.[30] Milton Friedman, who studied under Burns at Rutgers University, wrote that his "greatest indebtedness," apart from that to his parents, was "unquestionably" to Burns, calling him "almost a surrogate father."[31] Greenspan reacted to Burns the same way; there was something about his old-world bearing, the thick hair parted in the center and the meditative tamping of his pipe, which commanded admiration and affection. "If only I could become somebody like him and then make $20,000 a year," Greenspan remembers thinking.[32] If Greenspan's own father provided something of an anti–role model, Burns personified the professional success that Greenspan aspired to.

Burns was the chief heir to Wesley Mitchell's empiricist tradition, and his influence restrained any enthusiasm that Greenspan might have felt for the new trends that had begun to stir in economics. After arriving at Columbia, Greenspan took a course in mathematical statistics, the field that would later be known as econometrics. The course showed how you could take the measurements generated by the empiricists and test the relationships among them, using the tools of regression analysis. In the absence of those tools, economists could make educated guesses about how one part of the economy related to another. For example, a surge in steel production logically signaled a burst of activity in steel-using indus- tries such as automobile manufacturing, which in turn provided grounds on which to forecast faster growth for the entire economy. But with the help of regression analysis, economists could do better than just guess. They could calculate the relationship between past accelerations in steel output and accelerations in growth, and so forecast the future with some- thing closer to scientific confidence.

Years later, Greenspan would deploy regression analysis to build a model of the economy, and would describe himself as "an empiricist mugged by econometrics."[33] But thanks to Burns's influence, he studied mathematical statistics at Columbia without fully embracing it. In his work at the Conference Board, he continued to sidestep the uncertain business of calculating relationships among economic variables, prefer- ring to stick with the empiricists' agenda of amassing data. Just measur- ing the economy was challenge enough: data series upon data series had to be cyclically adjusted, seasonally adjusted, and checked for consistency against other series—all without the assistance of computers. There was more value in this humble task than in fancy mathematics, Greenspan believed. Even the cleverest econometric calculation was limited because yesterday's statistical relationships might break down tomorrow; by contrast, finer measures of what the economy is actually doing are more than just estimates—they are facts. Even after he embraced econometrics, and even after he became chairman of the Fed, Greenspan never shed his conviction that the quality of an economist's data mattered more than the sophistication of his modeling.

In 2011, during one of our long conversations in his office in Washington, Greenspan plucked a faded green volume from a shelf. It was a copy of *Measuring Business Cycles,* Arthur Burns's classic study of the vicissitudes of the American economy, co-written with the father of empiricism, Wesley Mitchell. The text had been lovingly preserved since Greenspan's time at Columbia six decades earlier.

"Open it," Greenspan invited me.

I let the book fall open at random. The page was dominated by tables and charts: pig iron production, railroad stock prices, call money interest rates.

I looked up quizzically, and a wry gesture told me to try the exercise again. This time I flipped open a different page, and found myself gazing at a table that meticulously reported the peaks and troughs of bituminous coal production. Page after page heaved with minute inventories of America's industrial heyday. The Burns-Mitchell view of the economy had been built up from statistics on every raw material, every mine, every factory.

I understood why Greenspan was showing me his mentor's book. It was a window on the economic thinking of a different age, and he wanted me to see where his love of statistics had come from.

Three

THE REBIRTH
OF MONEY

O n June 25, 1950, ninety thousand camouflaged troops crossed
the border from North to South Korea. They punched through
the South's defenses with a cavalcade of Soviet tanks, overrun-
ning Seoul, the South Korean capital. Seven thousand miles away, in
Washington, D.C., the Truman administration suspected that the Krem-
lin lay behind the North's attack, and the president resolved to come to
the South's aid, even though he feared a global conflagration. Taking full
advantage of its air power, the United States rained bombs on the North
Korean columns; and General Douglas MacArthur, the camera-loving,
pipe-smoking, jut-jawed American commander in the region, executed an
audacious amphibious landing at the port city of Inchon, cutting off the
enemy's retreat and retaking the South Korean capital. But Truman's fears
of escalation proved all too justified. At the end of November, China sent
300,000 peasant infantrymen in warm padded jackets across the frozen
Yalu River that marked its border with Korea. The Chinese swarmed
American soldiers as they slept huddled on the frigid ground, stabbing
them to death through their sleeping bags.[1]

When the Chinese attacked, Greenspan was several weeks into his
PhD studies at Columbia University. Sometime in this period, he sat in a
classroom watching his mentor Arthur Burns demand of his students,

"What causes inflation?" Burns's answer was that "excess government spending causes inflation"—the modern notion that loose monetary policy might be at fault did not seem to occur to him. Burns was not alone in this belief. In the 1930s and 1940s, economists paid little heed to central banks; indeed, they dismissed finance as an insignificant sideshow next to the farms and mines and factories that formed the "real" economy. But the economists' indifference to monetary matters was about to be tested. In ways that neither the professor nor his student could anticipate, China's crossing of the Yalu River kick-started the rebirth of finance.

Until the time of the Chinese attack, Burns's view had been entirely reasonable. During World War II, the Fed had played a humble support role to the Treasury. The government spent whatever it took to win the war, and the Fed's job was to create enough money to make that spending possible. There was nothing coy about this arrangement. The Fed openly promised to buy however much government debt proved necessary to keep the Treasury's borrowing costs low: it guaranteed that the interest rate on long-term government bonds would never rise above 2.5 percent. Small wonder that Burns left the Fed and monetary policy out of his view of inflation. The purpose of monetary policy was not to stabilize prices. It was to finance the government budget and underwrite the war effort.

China's intervention in Korea scrambled this arrangement. The prospect of a protracted conflict forced the United States to redouble its military spending, and the Truman administration became more anxious than ever to have the Fed control its borrowing costs. In early December the president telephoned Thomas McCabe, the Federal Reserve Board chairman, at home, and insisted that interest rates on long-term bonds must on no account breach the 2.5 percent ceiling. "If that happens that is exactly what Mr. Stalin wants," the president lectured.[2] But the Chinese attacks also set in motion a parallel development: the prospect of a protracted conflict kindled fears of wartime rationing, and consumers rushed to load up on everything from cars to washing machines, triggering a surge of inflation. In November 1950, the consumer price index rose at an annual rate of 20 percent, and in the two months following China's invasion, it advanced even faster. The threat of radically unstable prices shocked the

Federal Reserve's leaders into doing what Burns and his contemporaries never imagined they would do. They resolved to control prices by forcing interest rates up, no matter how much Truman might invoke cold-war imperatives.

Given the prevailing assumptions of the time, the Fed was bold to pick this battle. Most postwar economists doubted that the Fed could control inflation even if it mustered the nerve to raise interest rates in defiance of the administration. Inflation, it was said, stemmed not from monetary choices but from bottlenecks in the economy. If companies had trouble getting the raw materials or workers they needed, they would bid their prices up and pass the costs on to consumers. The modern notion that it is the job of monetary policy to avoid such bottlenecks was understood but rejected. In theory, higher interest rates might deter consumers and companies from borrowing to spend; in theory, this might reduce demand for products, raw materials, and workers, avoiding bottlenecks and inflation. But most economists believed that other factors mattered more than interest rates: shifts in workers' negotiating power, gains in productivity by companies, new opportunities to sell abroad—any of these could have a more pronounced effect on prices.[3] "Today few economists regard Federal Reserve monetary policy as a panacea for controlling the business cycle," Paul Samuelson declared in the first edition of his famous textbook, published in 1948.[4] In the words of the monetary historian Robert Hetzel, "After World War II, monetary policy was an orphan."[5]

On the last day of January 1951, Truman impressed upon the Fed's leaders the gravity of the Korean crisis. He summoned the entire membership of the Fed's interest-rate-setting body, the Federal Open Market Committee (FOMC), over to the White House and did his best to frighten them. "The present emergency is the greatest this country has ever faced, including the two World Wars and all the preceding wars," he menaced. But the central bankers stood their ground. Chairman McCabe objected that military power depended on economic power, and that this required price stability. The administration then tried to beat the central bankers into submission: it issued a public statement claiming that the Fed had pledged to defend the 2.5 percent borrowing-cost ceiling. But the

Fed leaders countered by leaking their own account of the meeting, which pointedly excluded any such commitment. Faced with the reality that the Fed could unilaterally suspend purchases of Treasury bonds, the Truman administration backed down. Under the terms of a new "Fed-Treasury Accord," the long-term interest rate was finally allowed to rise.[6] Inflation came down abruptly, proving that monetary policy was not actually impotent.

The Truman administration was not quite done yet. It forced the resignation of Chairman McCabe and installed in his place a Treasury official, William McChesney Martin. But if Martin had been selected for his supposed loyalty to the White House, he soon proved his independence. Far from restoring the old interest-rate ceiling, he declared in his first speech that "unless inflation is controlled, it could prove to be an even more serious threat to the vitality of our country than the more spectacular aggressions of enemies outside our borders." It was a remarkable statement—the imperatives of price stability trumped the imperatives of war and geopolitics—and it signaled a profound change. The toothless central bank that Burns casually dismissed was now a force to be reckoned with.

Some years later, Fed chairman Martin encountered Truman on a street in New York. The former president paused, stared at him, and uttered one word.

"Traitor," he said, and then continued.[7]

G reenspan did not immediately grasp the significance of the Fed-Treasury Accord. He was too immersed in other work: his studies at Columbia and, increasingly, his research at the Conference Board. In the spring of 1952 he attracted attention with a two-part Conference Board article titled "The Economics of Air Power," which quantified the impact of the defense buildup that came with war in Korea. The research behind these articles was a triumph of detective work. Military procurement plans were classified in wartime, so Greenspan began by reading Pentagon officials' congressional testimony from the years before the war, when they had been happy to divulge how many aircraft were in a squadron, how many squadrons per wing, or the rate of noncombat losses. By combining that baseline with reports of the air force's operations in Korea, Greenspan estimated how many aircraft the force must be buying. He ferreted out the weights of particular aircraft from engineering manuals, estimating the proportions of copper, aluminum, and other materials in each case; finally he projected the impact of military demand on metal markets.[8] With defense spending accounting for about a seventh of the economy, the impact was considerable. The Conference Board's member companies devoured Greenspan's analysis, badgering him with requests for additional elaboration. An accelerating flow of freelance commissions began to come the young man's way, including a role as an economic consultant to *Fortune* magazine. After false starts in music and baseball, he had found a line of work he excelled in.

At the beginning of 1953, Greenspan got a call from an investment adviser named William Wallace Townsend. His firm, Townsend-Skinner, was a member of the Conference Board, and Townsend had phoned occasionally to discuss Greenspan's writings. But this time he had a different purpose. He invited Greenspan to lunch at the venerable Bankers Club, which occupied the top three floors of the towering neoclassical Equitable Building a few minutes from the stock exchange; during the 1920s the Equitable had been the world's largest office block. On the appointed day, Greenspan rode the subway downtown, walked into the Equitable Building's splendid marble entrance hall, and took the long elevator ride up into the sky over Manhattan. Stepping into the club's lobby, he looked every inch the corporate cosmonaut. His grandparents had come from the hardscrabble Yiddish settlements of Eastern Europe, but this well-built, slick-haired, bespectacled young man might have walked out of an IBM advertisement.

Greenspan asked somebody to point out his host. Townsend looked to be in his sixties, older than Greenspan had expected. But when the two men shook hands, it was Townsend who was most surprised. Knowing Greenspan only from his data-laden writings and earnest telephone manner, he had expected to meet a forty-year-old, not a man in his midtwenties.

Townsend lost no time in explaining the purpose of the meeting. His partner, Richard Dana Skinner, had died some years earlier, and his

son-in-law was leaving the firm to work elsewhere: he needed a new collaborator.[9] To Greenspan, the prospect was instantly attractive. He had
been at the Conference Board for more than four years, and he was growing restless. He was conscious, moreover, that even the most assimilated
of Jewish professionals had to be at least a little careful in choosing a
career path. His close cousin, Wesley Halpert, had been denied entry to
medical school, even though he had graduated from the prestigious City
College of New York; stymied by racial quotas, Wesley had become a dentist. Greenspan never complained about discrimination, nor did he even
discuss it much with Jewish friends; but he did understand that it might
make certain career choices difficult.[10] As recently as the war years, *Fortune* had insisted on discussing Jewish "klannishness," and you could
scour the lists of senior executives at many of the Conference Board companies in the early 1950s and not find a single Jewish name among them.[11]
Bill Townsend, for that matter, was not Jewish either. But he was offering
a partnership, undeterred by the discovery that Greenspan was thirty-
eight years his junior.

The new firm of Townsend-Greenspan opened for business in September 1953, operating out of a nondescript office on Broadway, not far
from the Bankers Club, where the two partners had first lunched together.
Quickly, executives who had followed Greenspan's writings at the Conference Board signed on as clients. The Wellington Fund, which later morphed into the Vanguard Group, came along first, followed by a string of
steel companies and a handful of other names, including two that would
later recruit Greenspan as a director—Mobil Oil and the aluminum giant
Alcoa. Operating as a consultant, Greenspan could bypass ethnic barriers
with no difficulty at all; he frequently made presentations in boardrooms
filled with avid listeners, knowing that he was the only Jew present.[12]
Besides, Greenspan was bypassing something else as well. He wanted
fame and fortune, but his personality was ill suited to climbing steep corporate ladders; he had no appetite for turf battles, no stomach for confrontation. As a business consultant he could succeed in his shy way, through
sheer mastery of numbers.

Greenspan's data sleuthing was perfectly matched to his new role at

Townsend-Greenspan. Building on work he had done at the Conference Board, he created a detailed map of the steel business, filling in gaps in the public data much as he had done with military procurement. For example, U. S. Steel's Fairless Works, a four-thousand-acre state-of-the-art complex, did not publish its production on a timely basis; Greenspan figured that if he knew how much iron ore was arriving at the mill, he could guess whether production was heading upward or downward. Unfortunately, statistics on iron ore deliveries were not published, but the sleuth knew that the ore came from Venezuela, and from the Mesabi Iron Range at the head of the Great Lakes, so he consulted reports on shipping tonnage and freight-car loadings, and he figured out the missing numbers. To convert his estimates of iron ore shipments into projections of steel output, he would consult engineering manuals on the quantity of iron ore needed to make various types of steel. Years later he would joke that he was the only Fed chairman to have studied a phone book–sized tome titled *The Making, Shaping and Treating of Steel.* Greenspan claimed to have read it in its entirety.[13]

Bit by bit, Greenspan expanded his grasp of the economy. Burlington Industries became a client, so Greenspan learned about the cotton industry. When Alcoa signed on, Greenspan replicated his steel map for aluminum. The analysis required minimal judgment, which suited Greenspan fine; the more he could rely on facts, the greater the confidence he felt in his projections. The facts could come from almost anywhere: engineering manuals, old congressional testimony, statistics on freight-car loadings; Greenspan's appetite for eclectic detail was unlimited. The more facts he assembled, the more his list of clients grew. The more clients he had, the more facts he assembled.

As Greenspan flourished in his new role, his partner emerged as another substitute father. The old man delighted in passing on what he had learned; the young man absorbed the teaching eagerly. "I wish I could be around to see what you will become," Townsend would say affectionately. This intimation of mortality proved all too justified: in 1958, Townsend died abruptly of a heart attack. Deprived of his mentor and still aged only thirty-two, Greenspan wondered whether he could keep the consultancy afloat. But he had built a powerful reputation, and his clients showed no inclination to abandon him.

Greenspan bought out Townsend's heirs so that he owned the whole company. But he kept Townsend's name on the front door in deference to the man who had opened a new world to him. "I wished he could have been alive to see what I achieved," Greenspan said later. "I credit a lot of what I did to him."[14]

Around the time he joined Townsend's firm, Greenspan paid his first visit to the Federal Reserve Board in Washington. Part of a research team from *Fortune,* he made his way through the Fed's formidable marble entrance and was shown to the office of Governor James K. Vardaman Jr. It was an unfortunate choice—Vardaman had been in the minority of Fed governors who refused to back Chairman McCabe in his fight with Truman, and he turned out to be as underwhelming as the Fed's building was impressive. The son of a prominent Mississippi segregationist, Vardaman had been installed at the Fed as a reward for his service as a naval aide. He had been sworn in wearing the uniform of a commodore, and he personified the shortcomings of the 1940s Fed, both in his excessive loyalty to the White House and in his intellectual limitations. "It was the most extraordinarily dispiriting experience I've ever had," Greenspan later recalled. "I mean, he literally knew nothing."[15]

Even though the encounter with Vardaman seemed to confirm Arthur Burns's dismissive view of the Fed, Greenspan's interest in money and credit was deepening. At Columbia University, he had picked out a PhD topic that hinted at his future path: he proposed to investigate the savings patterns of American households. Once he went into partnership with Bill Townsend, he shelved his academic ambitions—there were too many clients to visit, too many reports to write for them. But his interest in savings and the way they flowed through the economy did not go away. And in one of those small coincidences that can bend history's path, Bill Townsend's consulting firm turned out to be the perfect perch from which to ponder finance.

Before launching his consultancy, Townsend had made a fortune in the bond market. Then, together with his original partner, Richard Dana Skinner, he had devised a method for monitoring the lending markets in order to forecast equity prices. Years before such monetary analysis had become fashionable, Townsend saw that if banks pumped out a large volume of loans, investors would have more cash to throw around, and some of it would push up stock values. Through the 1930s and 1940s, when most economists ignored money and credit, Townsend held fast to this insight— when he recruited Greenspan in 1953, he was still putting out a newsletter on savings and loan institutions, a species of bank that lent only to home buyers, and he continued to track data on bank deposits and the bond market. Once Greenspan signed on, he, too, became involved in these projects, helping to marshal the statistics and contributing to the newsletters.[16]

As it turned out, finance was just then on the cusp of an awakening. During the Depression and its aftermath, the credit-creating machinery of Wall Street had been almost comatose. It was said that you could walk the famous canyons near the stock exchange and hear only the rattle of backgammon dice through open windows. But by the early 1950s, financiers were active once again. The GI Bill had promised mass home ownership, turning a generation of Americans into mortgage borrowers; and once they had acquired a taste for mortgage debt, other kinds of borrowing soon followed. By the time Greenspan joined Townsend, consumer loans were becoming so ubiquitous that the bill collector emerged as "the central figure of the good society," as one contemporary put it.[17] Meanwhile, a southerner named Charles Merrill shocked the Wall Street establishment by promoting stock market investment to ordinary Americans.[18] Thanks partly to Merrill's hard-hitting advertisements, the amount of money invested in mutual funds shot up fivefold between 1950 and 1960.

As more money coursed through the economy, its significance became more obvious. As Townsend had seen all along, surges in bank lending could multiply the purchasing power in the economy, driving up the price of stocks, and indeed all other prices. Contrary to what Burns had asserted, excess government spending was by no means the main cause of inflation— bursts of private lending could be equally destabilizing. This in turn meant that monetary policy mattered more than in the past. The friskier banks grew, the more it became vital that the Fed should restrain them.

After Townsend's death in 1958, Greenspan took over the firm's financial work, including the newsletter on the savings and loan industry. The new responsibility drove him to immerse himself in the financial and monetary debates that were swirling around him. Milton Friedman, the future father of monetarism, was in the process of transforming economists' thinking on central banking and finance. Through the 1940s, Friedman had accepted Burns's view of inflation as the product of excess government spending.[19] But by the late 1950s, he was approaching the point when he would declare that "inflation is always and everywhere a monetary phenomenon." As the financial system expanded, and with it the volume of borrowing and lending, the price of capital was coming to be recognized as *the* central price in a capitalist system. Far from being marginal to the real economy of oil and chemicals and steel, the central bankers and financiers who set that price drove just about everything.

As he read his way into these debates, Greenspan grew fascinated by John Gurley and Edward Shaw, whose contribution was to look beyond the banks to the financial system more generally.[20] Banks could create money by taking in a dollar of deposits and issuing several dollars of credits. But the same unnerving ability to manufacture spending power existed to various degrees in other parts of the financial system. The entire paraphernalia of the stock market, with its speculators and brokers and mutual funds, could be seen as creating money, too. Its function was to take illiquid ownership interests in companies and transform them into certificates that could be freely bought and sold, so that a stake in a mine or factory today could be cash in your pocket by tomorrow. The most fixed of fixed investments—a car assembly line or a steel plant—could be converted into spending power at the drop of a hat. And the more these ownership stakes circulated, the more their fluctuating prices affected the confidence of businesses and families—and hence the fortunes of the economy.

As he stretched his mind around Gurley and Shaw, Greenspan absorbed one further message. Some commentators emphasized the risks in this banking and finance, but Gurley and Shaw stressed the advantages.

A sophisticated financial sector offered citizens myriad ways to hold savings—an investor could commit money for the long term by owning a private company not quoted on the stock exchange, or he could avoid long-term commitment by holding a demand deposit. He could assume risk by buying a technology stock such as Xerox, or he could avoid risk by holding short-term government debt. By enabling people to construct portfolios that precisely suited them, sophisticated finance reduced the price at which citizens would commit savings. The result was a lower cost of capital, and therefore greater prosperity for all. Greenspan never shed this fundamentally optimistic conviction about finance, even when events repeatedly challenged him to do so.

One year after Townsend's death, Greenspan produced his own contribution to the understanding of finance. In a long paper delivered before the American Statistical Association in the last days of December 1959, he laid out the connections between the financial sector and the real economy, going further than almost any of his contemporaries in teasing out their interactions. Squarely confronting the notion that financial markets are merely a casino of meaningless side bets, he laid out an insight for which the Nobel laureate James Tobin would later capture the credit. Stock prices drive corporate investments in fixed assets, Greenspan observed. In turn, those investments drive many of the booms and busts in a capitalist economy.[21]

To put Greenspan's insight at its simplest, consider the construction industry. If the market value of an office block rises above the cost of building it, entrepreneurs will erect new office blocks to sell at a profit. As they procure steel and concrete and employ cranes and workers, the entrepreneurs' spending will set off a broader boom in the economy. But if the market value of office blocks falls below the cost of building new ones, the dynamic goes into reverse. Entrepreneurs will no longer have an incentive to put up new office blocks, because they will sell them at a loss. Their spending on raw materials, machinery, and workers will halt. The loss of this powerful source of demand may trigger a recession.

The same principle, Greenspan went on, applies equally to companies. If the market value of a company—that is, the value of its shares as determined by investors on the stock exchange—rises above the cost of the company's capital stock, entrepreneurs have an incentive to expand the company or create a new one. Just as the construction entrepreneur will erect an office block for $10 million if it can be sold for $15 million, so a manufacturing entrepreneur will build a new industrial enterprise for $100 million if he can expect to sell shares in it for $150 million. But if the company's market value falls below the cost of its distribution warehouses and production lines, entrepreneurs cease to have an incentive to invest in new capital assets. In the upswing, high share prices spur business investment, fueling a broader boom. In the downswing, low share prices destroy that incentive, triggering a slowdown.

Greenspan was assigning a greater significance to finance than nearly all of his contemporaries. Arthur Burns and other business cycle experts had viewed the stock market as a good forecaster of the economy; Greenspan countered in his article that stock prices were "not a forecast but rather a crucial determinant of economic activity."[22] The economics profession was starting to see that money, and not government spending or production bottlenecks, could be the cause of inflation; now Greenspan was adding that financial markets could be the cause of booms and recessions.[23] Greenspan sent copies of his paper to a number of eminent economists, and Milton Friedman himself was sufficiently impressed to write him an appreciative letter, even though the two men did not yet know each other.[24] Years later, Greenspan showed the paper to Lawrence Summers of Harvard, at a time when Summers was deputy Treasury secretary. "You had it right," Summers wrote in response. Alluding to Sweden's Nobel Prize committee, he went on, "I think the people in Stockholm should reallocate half of Tobin's money."[25]

Greenspan coupled his insight about the link between asset prices and investment with a related one about consumers. Just as a rising stock market triggers higher capital expenditures, so it will trigger additional spending by families. Finding that their stock portfolios have gone up, well-to-do

Americans will spend some of the windfall on one-off purchases: a car, a special holiday. If the portfolio gains persist, consumers will come to rely on them as a permanent source of additional income; they will allow their regular spending to go up commensurately. Though he did not use the term, Greenspan was describing the "wealth effect" that would later be well recognized. Again he was ahead of nearly all of his contemporaries.[26]

Having explained the effect of stock prices on investment and consumption, Greenspan delivered a policy lesson that makes for extraordinary reading in light of his Fed tenure. He insisted that central bankers must not ignore asset prices. As rising stock prices cause a surge in investment and consumption, Greenspan explained, there are two possible outcomes. If the stock market boom is allowed to run on, the spending surge will outpace the economy's ability to supply goods; bottlenecks will bring inflation. Alternatively, if the stock market boom turns suddenly to bust, entrepreneurs who had been eagerly erecting factories will freeze their projects; households with stock portfolios will cut back on spending; and the economy will collapse into recession. "The higher the stock market gets at its peak and hence the greater decline required to return to 'normal,' the deeper the decline in economic activity," Greenspan observed. If central bankers aspired to smooth out the peaks and troughs in the business cycle, they would have to control asset bubbles.

Greenspan drove home this point with a lesson from history. In the 1920s, the stock market had broken one record after another, yet the Fed had ducked its responsibility to choke off the bubble by raising interest rates. Instead, it had sided with commentators who rationalized the bubble, arguing that the abandonment of the rigid pre–World War I gold standard had inoculated the United States from boom-bust cycles, thereby neutralizing one of the main risks to investors and justifying a huge revaluation of the stock market.[27] As Greenspan put it:

> The belief, widespread at the time, that the business cycle had finally been controlled by the institution of a managed currency, induced a sharp drop in risk premiums, presumably to irrational levels. . . . The

sharp upward gyrations in stock prices—and other capital values—
made the subsequent stock market reversal inevitable.

New Dealers and Keynesians had advanced one explanation for the
Depression: as the economy had slowed, consumers and businesses had
cut spending, exacerbating the slowdown and setting off a vicious spiral.
If that was right, the remedy was extra government spending to make up
for weak private spending, plus a robust pep talk to buoy private-sector
confidence—"We have nothing to fear but fear itself," Franklin Roosevelt
had told the nation. But Greenspan was advancing an alternative theory:

[After the 1929 crash,] the resultant collapse in capital values took
huge chunks out of effective demand. It was not simply an issue of
people losing confidence—they were actually significantly poorer.
Their curtailment of expenditures were not so much fear induced, as
financially induced.[28]

Half a century after Greenspan wrote these paragraphs, the world succumbed to another violent stock market decline, and economists pronounced learnedly on "balance-sheet recessions"—ones that follow a
crippling destruction of wealth rather than a mere falloff in spending. The
pronouncements were frequently coupled with denunciations of the
Greenspan Fed: if only Greenspan had understood balance-sheet recessions and how painful they could be, he surely would have acted more
decisively as the bubble of the 2000s inflated. But the truth, as revealed in
Greenspan's 1959 paper, is that he had been thinking about balance-sheet
recessions for decades—in fact, he had been aware of them for longer
than many of his critics had been breathing. The fact that he nonetheless
allowed bubbles to inflate on his watch demands an explanation that goes
deeper than his purported ignorance.

Greenspan's attack on the 1920s Fed involved one further argument.
The Fed's mistake in the 1920s was not merely to rationalize the stock
market bubble by embracing the talk of a new era of stability, akin to the

"Great Moderation" that economists unwisely celebrated in the 1990s and 2000s. Rather, the Fed's key error was to underestimate its own contribution to the stock bubble. The rise in the market had set off a rise in investment and consumer spending, which in turn had boosted profits and stoked animal spirits, triggering a further rise in the stock market. The 1920s Fed had been the enabler of this feedback loop—in order for investment and consumer spending to take off, companies and consumers needed access to credit. Faced with a jump in the appetite to borrow, the Fed had decided to "meet the legitimate demands of business," as Greenspan put it. No doubt this had seemed safe: the resulting surge in lending was flowing to companies and households, not directly into asset markets. But money, once created, was bewilderingly difficult to trace. Like heat-seeking rockets, the newly minted dollars found their way into hot stocks, no matter which way they were fired initially.

Pursuing this logic in 1959, Greenspan adopted a radical position: the United States should return to the gold standard of the nineteenth century. By tying money and credit to a fixed supply of gold, the nation could prevent toxic surges in purchasing power, Greenspan asserted. If a rise in the stock market caused entrepreneurs to want to invest more, their rising demand for loans would meet a fixed supply of lendable funds, with the result that interest rates would jump, dampening the stock market before it generated a bubble. Thanks to gold's corrective discipline, the economy would be stabilized. "The pre–World War I gold standard prevented speculative 'flights from reality'—with their disastrous consequences," Greenspan insisted.[29]

For the rest of his career, Greenspan never quite recanted his belief that gold represented the ideal monetary anchor.[30] He became the steward of the world's preeminent paper money, yet he continued to argue that the Fed should conduct itself "as though there were a gold standard." His 1959 paper spells out what this ought to have entailed. Rather than allowing the money supply to expand to "meet the legitimate demands of business," as it did with disastrous consequences in the run-up to the 1929 crash, the Fed should have reacted to the danger posed by "speculative flights from reality." It should, in other words, have responded to the stock bubble by raising interest rates.

Greenspan's interest in finance was not purely abstract. He also tried his hand at commodity trading. He had been fascinated by speculators since his jazz days, when he read *Reminiscences of a Stock Market Operator;* and a few years later, his father had tried unsuccessfully to sell him on the idea of using charts to divine the markets' future. But around the time that he went into business with William Townsend, Greenspan came around to his father's ideas, though his door remained closed to any father-son collaboration. Plotting the movements of financial markets with pencil and paper, Greenspan began to seek out patterns that offered profitable clues about the future.[31]

One day, as he gazed at the shape of price movements in wheat futures, Greenspan spied an irresistible staircase formation. Wheat would trend upward, then lose half its gain; then it would head up again before giving back half of its progress. "This is easy!" the young seer exulted to himself. Right after wheat had completed one of its half retreats, Greenspan bought contracts for a thousand bushels. The futures rebounded, and he got out with a profit.

Greenspan soon came up with variations on this strategy. He noticed the asymmetry in commodity prices—the amount by which they can fall is limited because they cannot go below zero; but their potential to rise is unlimited. It followed that if you waited for low prices, usually reflecting a big harvest that caused a temporary glut, you could load up on wheat or corn or soybeans without troubling to find out about their prospects. If the price was already near zero, the potential loss was minimal; but if a transport strike or a natural disaster caused the market to tighten, the gain could be significant. Greenspan would accumulate stakes in several depressed commodities and then bide his time. The ones that did badly would decline by a couple of percent. The ones that did well would take off like rockets.[32]

In 1959, the year that he published his groundbreaking paper on finance, Greenspan took his trading to a new level. He had parlayed his expertise in steel and aluminum into a system that tracked inventories of metal products; if stockpiles of goods containing copper were abnormally low, for example, this was a signal that manufacturers would step up production—and that the boost to copper procurement would drive copper prices upward. Greenspan's inventory indicator was generating handsome trading profits, so he bought a seat on the New York Commodities Exchange (Comex), calculating that he would do even better if he stopped paying brokers' commissions and traded directly. The Comex was conveniently located just across the street from the Townsend-Greenspan office at 39 Broadway, and Greenspan would show up for ten or fifteen minutes at the morning opening, pop back again at lunch, and make a final appearance at the close of the trading session; he aimed to catch the most active periods in the market without stealing more than forty-five minutes from his consulting business. But after a few months of multitasking, Greenspan had to reckon with a rude surprise. Cutting out commission costs by trading directly had somehow failed to pay off. Unschooled traders in the metals pits were running circles around him.[33]

The experience shaped Greenspan's understanding of finance. As he watched the frenzied traders on the Comex floor, Greenspan learned that prices reflected economic fundamentals only imperfectly. They were driven, at least in the short term, by screams and hand signals and animal spirits.[34] The operators who thrived in this environment frequently knew nothing about the metals they traded or the news that might be driving the prices. Yet somehow they could sense turns in the market, so that they bought at the beginning of an upswing and got out before the market started down again.

In slow moments in the trading pit, Greenspan would sometimes ask a neighbor how he knew when to buy.

"I felt that the market was bottoming," the trader would respond gruffly, leaving Greenspan none the wiser.

"*What* did you do?" Greenspan would wonder to himself. "*Feel* the market? What, feel the wall? What does that statement mean?"

The meaning gradually revealed itself as Greenspan spent time on the trading floor. His rivals might not know inventories and fundamentals, but they understood two other terms: overbought and oversold. If the big traders in the pit went on a buying spree, sooner or later they would have bought all they could afford; in the absence of fresh buyers, the market's next move would have to be downward. Likewise, if the big men were dumping contracts, there would come a time when they would stop; with no more selling pressure, the next move would be upward. And if the pit was divided between big sellers and big buyers, then psychology kicked in. You had to read the body language of the adversaries: which side had more capital; which side had the balls to bet the biggest? Greed and fear and human ego trumped the dull particulars of inventories. Markets were not completely rational. They were simply too human.[35]

Some of this understanding found its way into the long paper that Greenspan presented to the American Statistical Association at the end of 1959. The writing was peppered with the language of traders—longs and shorts, bulls and bears, overbought and oversold—terms that did not appear in other academic papers of the period.[36] And although much of the argument focused on the consequences of bubbles, Greenspan also had some nuanced things to say about their causes. Investors were mainly rational—they responded to real events with real business consequences, whether these were technological breakthroughs from industrial laboratories or policy proposals from Congress. But investors filtered such news through their own moods and emotions; their judgments were too slippery and fragile to be called efficient. Anticipating the findings of behavioral economics in the 1970s and 1980s, Greenspan noted that lurches toward fear were generally more sudden and dramatic than lurches toward confidence. Markets could crash instantly, triggered by a modest shift in fundamentals. In contrast, bubbles inflated only gradually.[37]

If markets could be irrational, how could an observer know when they were overshooting? Years later as Fed chairman, Greenspan sometimes suggested that bubbles were impossible to recognize, but in 1959 he took the opposite position. In a market economy, he explained confidently, the future is by definition unknowable. New management tricks and technological advances are certain to scramble forecasters' projections; a war or natural disaster may come out of left field; the unexpected is to be expected. Because the future is necessarily uncertain, investors who bid risk premiums down to nothing have clearly taken leave of their senses. "When commitments are made on the assumption of certain cost-price stabilities existing for the next twenty years that is clearly irrational optimism," Greenspan proclaimed. At such moments of confidence, investors were forgetting the limits "of what *can* be known about future economic relationships."[38] Sooner or later, their hubris would be punished.

Four

AYN RAND'S
UNDERTAKER

In 1959, Alan Greenspan bought a brand-new Buick convertible, perhaps the most fabulous Buick ever to roll off the assembly line at any General Motors plant. It had a black finish on the outside and red leather seats on the inside; it was an exuberant, tail-finned, chrome-streaked status symbol, a garish motorized jukebox. Since the beginning of the 1950s, GM had produced an avalanche of impetuous confections—its quintessential ride was long, low-slung, and streamlined, like a cross between a jet aircraft and a killer shark—and the Buick Electra 225 confirmed this triumph of form over function. Even when standing still, the car exuded power and motion. Greenspan would take his seat behind the double hoop of the steering wheel, chrome on the smaller inner circle and a red finish on the wider outer one. In front, the angry snarl of the radiator grille preceded him; behind, his shoulders were seemingly enlarged by the broad sweep of the tail fins; above, on days when he could roll the roof back, there was just space and light and sky. Cruising along the brand-new interstate highways that spooled across the countryside like ribbons, with the wind in his dark hair and a terrific sense of well-being bubbling up inside him, the young consultant cranked the radio. He embodied the American Century and the Oil Century.[1] He was handsome, powerful, and upwardly mobile.

Soon after purchasing that Buick, Greenspan took the small team at his office to visit the Fairless steel works, an industrial wonder he had studied as he pieced together his map of the steel sector for his consulting clients. The young boss and three women—assistants who kept track of the data that Townsend-Greenspan analyzed—rolled out of Manhattan, through industrial stretches of New Jersey, eventually reaching Fairless on the eastern edge of Pennsylvania, one mile below Trenton. The roads seemed to be alive with people. In the first years after the war, cars had been so rare that buyers had paid dealers under the table to lay hands on one, but now three out of four families owned vehicles, and every passing masterpiece testified to the boisterous materialism of the 1950s. This was the decade when Americans were learning to enjoy electric carving knives, automatic shoe shiners, and motorized lawn mowers. In 1959, on the occasion of the centennial of the American Dental Association, they were introduced to a new gadget called the BROXO Electric Toothbrush.

Arriving at the steel complex, Greenspan and his entourage confronted another modern marvel, the crown jewel in the empire of the U. S. Steel Corporation. Big Steel, as the company was known, accounted for a third of the nation's steel output—the corporation president, Benjamin Fairless, dismissed critics as "Calamity Johns suffering from a midget complex"— and the eponymous Fairless Works announced its intimidating scale. Greenspan and his assistants watched how the ore was compressed in a vast sintering plant, melted in monstrous blast furnaces, turned into steel by open-hearth furnaces, then sent off to a battery of giant rollers and electric shears that flattened and shaped the material "as easily as a housewife might roll out a sheet of pie crust," as Fairless once bragged.[2] On any given shift, two thousand workers manned the operation, producing the indispensable ingredient of the modern economy: of the springs Americans slept on, the razors they used to shave themselves, the skyscrapers they worked in, not to mention the shark-like automobiles in which they crisscrossed the land.

Eight miles from this technological wonder, U. S. Steel had built a settlement called Fairless Hills. For a payment of just $100 down and $85 monthly, a worker could own a home in this company suburb; for an extra $10 a year, he had access to a bowling alley, a golf course, and a swimming pool. It was the American Dream, delivered courtesy of an imperial company; and if it meant living in a settlement named after the company's vainglorious president, this seemed scarcely less dignified than living in one of the Levittowns named after William J. Levitt, the emperor of suburban construction. There was a Levittown, in fact, just across the inland lake to the west of the Fairless steel works; but whichever suburb you visited, the cookie-cutter houses were planted at fixed distances from each other, "inhabited by people of the same class, the same income, the same age group," as the architectural critic Lewis Mumford complained.[3] Newcomers were invited to cookouts, potlucks, car wash drives, and family swim days. You joined or you were ostracized.

The consumerism on the roads, the intimidating scale of the steel works, the clipped-lawn residential settlements: all signaled the changes that surrounded Greenspan. The America of 1900—the America of railway barons and oil trusts that had thrilled the adolescent autodidact—had been divided between larger-than-life visionaries and rough-handed workers; the America of the 1950s was more technocratic and more bureaucratic, more homogeneous and suburban, and altogether more soft. In politics, the virile outdoorsman Theodore Roosevelt could hardly have been more different from the serene military bureaucrat Dwight Eisenhower. In business, the swashbuckling turn-of-the-century railway magnate James J. Hill was a world away from the quintessential 1950s industrialist Alfred P. Sloan of General Motors, who was happiest when contemplating financial controls and organization charts. In the mass ranks of the workforce, union men with picks and shovels were giving way to sales personnel, telephone operators, bank tellers, advertising copywriters, and civil servants; 1956 was the first year in which white-collar workers outnumbered blue-collar ones. American society at the start of the century had been shaped by the great migration that brought Greenspan's parents from Europe; it involved perilous ocean crossings, the wrenching loss of old-country culture, and inspiring tales of personal courage. By contrast, American society at midcentury was shaped by an utterly different migration, which shifted a quarter of the nation's population to the new suburbs, where frozen meals were consumed nightly in front of television sitcoms.

G reenspan seemed outwardly at peace with the changes around him. Having grown up with little, he was not against materialism; as soon as his work at the Conference Board had begun to bring in a steady income, he had moved out of Manhattan to a leafy neighborhood in Queens, not far from the beach in Rockaway where he had spent happy summers in his childhood. His new home was in a fresh redbrick duplex building close to a commuter train, and he shared it with his mother, who remained the fixed point in his life.[4] As a boy, he had dreamed vividly of going up in an aircraft, and had felt a confused mix of excitement at escaping the ground and anxiety at the realization that his mother was not with him. Now, as a man in his midtwenties, Greenspan had flown the congestion of Manhattan, and the sunny presence of his mother remained by his side.

Around the time that Greenspan moved out of Manhattan, a young Canadian painter arrived in the city. Thinking she might be lonely, a friend called her.

"I know an unusual man," the friend said. "I wonder if you might be interested in meeting him."

"Unusual how?"

"He's very, very intelligent," the friend said. "It's hard to find a girl for him."

A few days later the intelligent man called, and he did seem a bit unusual. At first, he seemed too diffident to ask her out. He kept her on the phone for half an hour, chatting about this and that, then finally offered her a choice of three activities. They could see a Broadway show, take in a ball game, or go to a concert at Carnegie Hall.

As luck would have it, the painter was a lover of classical music.

"Without a doubt, the concert at Carnegie Hall," she responded. "I've been dying to go there all my life."

And so Alan Greenspan made the acquaintance of Joan Mitchell. She was a striking beauty, with a slim figure, fine features, and blond hair; and her musical interests made her easy to talk to. On their first evening together, Greenspan walked into her apartment and found she had one of his favorite recordings on; his shyness fell away immediately. The couple went to Carnegie Hall, where they listened to Bach, and Alan told stories about the Henry Jerome band; and after the concert they went to the hotel where the band was performing. Joan met the band members, who told her that they had never expected Alan to stay with them. He had been too good at doing their taxes.[5]

Alan and Joan married in October 1952.[6] A rabbi presided over the small ceremony at the Pierre, a landmark hotel on Fifth Avenue. There had been some debate as to whether Herbert Greenspan would be invited; in the end he came, but left early. At a previous meeting, he had clumsily assured Joan that his son would not behave like him, and would not desert her at the first opportunity.[7] But family patterns could not be wished away. Even though the marriage took place amid the postwar baby boom, a time when the cultural power of the nuclear family was at its peak, Alan proved curiously immune to the norms surrounding him. He had married Joan, he later reflected, more with his head than with his heart. "This woman is very intelligent. Very beautiful. I'll never do better," he had reasoned.[8] But although Alan's musical bond with Joan was powerful, echoing his connection to his mother and anticipating his later marriage to Andrea Mitchell, the couple were ill matched in other ways. For one thing, Alan had little interest in his visual surroundings, a handicap in connecting with an artist.[9] For another, he was not prepared to compromise the way he lived. Since the early years of his life, he had spent time alone, pursuing interests that he chose, with little interference. His mother had given him her undivided love while imposing no constraints on him. She was unfailingly encouraging, yet also undemanding. She was a hard act to follow.

Alan and Joan ended their marriage after less than a year, with few recriminations. The couple agreed that they had different tastes. "Saturday mornings he loved to wake up and study numbers," Joan recalled. "He loved being in control of all these numbers."[10] While Joan wanted to have fun, Alan wanted to work; and when he was not working, he often disappeared to the golf course. Joan also wanted to move out of Forest Hills—the couple shared Alan's apartment, his mother having moved back into the city—but Alan resisted. Though he was too mild mannered to provoke a confrontation, Greenspan was not willing to bend in his choices. He wanted to control his time as he controlled those numbers—his habits of introverted independence allowed little room for the codependence of marriage. And no doubt his father had marked him. Having never seen his parents married, he was not really equipped to share his life with someone else.

If Greenspan's unyielding individualism left him ill-suited for marriage, he was bound to stand aloof from the mass culture of the 1950s, despite his eagerness to share in the prosperity it brought. He enjoyed golf and reveled in those splashy cars, but he was the last person to subsume himself in potlucks and cookouts, and his infatuation with the robber barons of the turn of the century put him at odds with his era. Companies such as U. S. Steel, the owner of the Fairless Works, had been forged by visionaries like J. P. Morgan and Andrew Carnegie; but now they were run by a new species of bureaucratic capitalist, reliable rather than risk seeking, controlled rather than passionate. Further down the hierarchy, corporate America was the dominion of Organization Man, as the title of a 1956 bestseller put it; and the distinguishing feature of Organization Man was orthodoxy, not creativity. "When white collar people get jobs, they sell not only their time and energy, but their personalities as well," the Columbia University sociologist C. Wright Mills lamented.[11] "What is the new loyalty?" the liberal historian Henry Steele Commager asked bitterly. "It is, above all, conformity. It is the uncritical and unquestioning acceptance of America as it is."[12]

A natural individualist like Greenspan inevitably rebelled against this absence of rebellion. He might almost have joined forces with Commager and his fellow liberals, who sneered loudly at the mass culture—"the bland leading the bland," as the historian Arthur Schlesinger Jr. jeered.[13] But right-wing versions of this disgruntlement suited Greenspan better, and these were growing louder and clearer by the 1950s. The forces of conservatism, demoralized and disorganized when the war ended, were gradually regrouping; by 1952, the Foundation for Economic Education, a libertarian outfit that distributed conservative tracts to its fan base, had a mailing list of nearly thirty thousand people. Three years later William F. Buckley Jr. launched the *National Review,* which quickly established itself as an influential platform for conservatives of various persuasions.[14] But although Greenspan would have made a natural recruit for Buckley's journal, or for some other recognized project of the new conservatism, he chose to keep his distance. Instead he fell in with a fringe group that was one part libertarian salon, two parts strange cult.

Toward the end of their marriage, Joan Mitchell had taken Greenspan to visit Ayn Rand, a Russian émigré and novelist known for her ferocious rejection of government intrusions.[15] They gathered at Rand's apartment on East Thirty-sixth Street in Manhattan, across from the Morgan Library, which housed the financier's rare books and art. The living room was decorated in the modern style: glass-topped tables, a black sofa, and a black lacquered dining table in the foyer that doubled as a workstation for typists who hammered out Rand's chapter drafts. A small study facing an airshaft provided a partial view of the Empire State Building. Cats had used the furniture as scratching posts, and the floor as a litterbox.[16]

Rand was short and square, all of five feet four inches tall, with dark hair cropped short and parted on the side in a slightly masculine fashion. She spoke with a pronounced Russian accent, and she glared at her guests out of dark, penetrating eyes. People differed wildly on whether she was offputtingly frumpy or vampishly sensuous. She "was quite plain to look at," Greenspan says in his memoir. She "was a very sensual woman. . . . Beautiful eyes, black hair, and very beautiful lips, prominent lips," recalled Jack Bungay, another disciple.[17] Rand went about in a short black cape that flowed impressively in the breeze, worn, as she admitted, in imitation of Supergirl. She smoked cigarettes from a tapered holder; and since the success of her 1943 epic, *The Fountainhead,* she had surrounded herself with male admirers who quoted from her novel the way Baptists quote from the Bible.[18] When her husband was out of sight, she liked to recline on her divan and invite an admirer to sit next to her, and if people suspected her of faithlessness, she did not seem to care in the slightest. Joan Mitchell had come to know Rand through a fellow Canadian, Barbara Branden, who was one of Rand's devoted acolytes—devoted despite Rand's ill-concealed designs on her husband, Nathaniel. Sometime after Greenspan's first visit to Rand's salon, the writer required her husband to vacate the apartment twice a week so she could sleep with Nathaniel, who was less than half her age.[19]

What interested Greenspan about Rand was her belief system; and, more particularly, the method by which she arrived at that belief system. Rand seemed completely certain in her judgments on everything from love to art to politics; by contrast, Greenspan was forever cautious. His love of data led him to distrust propositions that lacked empirical backing, and he had fallen under the sway of a philosophy called logical positivism, which taught that no truth should be accepted unless it could be directly verified. Some two decades later, A. J. Ayer, a leading logical positivist, remarked of this credo, "I suppose the most important [defect] . . . was that nearly all of it was false."[20] But in the mid-1950s, logical positivists were still certain that almost nothing could be certain. After a few evenings of listening to Rand at her apartment, Greenspan waded into the discussion, confident that his lack of confidence was justified.

"To be truly rational, you can't hold a conviction without significant empirical evidence," he insisted.

"How can that be?" Rand pounced on him. "Don't *you* exist?"

"I . . . can't be sure," Greenspan responded.

"Would you be willing to say you *don't* exist?"

"I might . . ."

"And by the way, who is making that statement?"[21]

Greenspan was astonished. He seldom encountered anybody who could outmaneuver him in argument, and now this fierce woman had sliced through his position like a butcher cleaving lamb. If a logical positivist could feel sure that everything was unsure, his feeling of conviction obviously negated his conviction; he was like the man who answers "yes" to the question "are you asleep?" To Greenspan, this revelation was shocking. If he, a social scientist, could not understand how to establish truth, how could he claim to understand anything? But the interchange with Rand was also liberating at the same time. She had shown Greenspan that he could rise out of his data and embrace moral or political positions. He would no longer feel the need to prove them in the way that he might prove that copper inventories were sub-average.[22]

It took a little while for the novelist and the consultant to admit that they were friends. Mocking his dark suit and lugubrious manner, Rand referred to Greenspan as "the Undertaker." "Well, has the Undertaker decided he exists yet?" she would ask her entourage—it was as though she meant to punish him for even trying to challenge her. Rand's soon-to-be lover, Nathaniel Branden, took it upon himself to save Greenspan from eternal darkness. Over a series of meetings in restaurants and at his apartment, he talked the Undertaker around, helping him out of his old logical-positivist clothing and into the philosophy that he and Rand would later call objectivism.

One day in 1954, Branden took a cab ride with Rand.

"Guess who exists?" he blurted out.

"Don't tell me," Rand said, "you've won over Alan Greenspan."

"Yes, I have," Branden announced. "And I think you're going to change your mind about him. I think he's a really interesting man with a very unusual brain."[23]

Greenspan began to show up regularly at the Saturday-night gatherings of Rand's entourage, which she called the Collective—her brand of irony was not subtle. The windows were usually clamped shut and the blinds were often drawn; one of Rand's cats had jumped to an untimely death, condemning visitors thereafter to endure the stuffy air in her apartment. But the force of Rand's intellect was enough to keep her guests awake. To a shy assimilator of industrial factoids, this small woman with her wildly vivid convictions was a tonic.

It was not just that Rand arrived at truth in a way that Greenspan found convincing. Her vision of the truth was deeply appealing. Raised in communist Russia in a family of Jewish anticommunists, Rand celebrated a brand of individualism so ferocious that it made Greenspan seem tame by comparison. As a child, Rand remembered, "I was so busy mentally with my own concerns that I did not develop any social instinct. . . . What I can't communicate is the unimportance that people in that social sense had for me."[24] If this sounded extreme, Rand's fictional heroes went further. Howard Roark, the architect-hero in *The Fountainhead,* is utterly oblivious to social pressure: "For him, the streets were empty. He could have walked there naked without concern." Contemptuous of society, Roark has a powerful sense of his own greatness, a characteristic with which the young Greenspan may also have identified. "I set my own standards," Roark announces in *The Fountainhead.* "I inherit nothing. I stand at the end of no tradition. I may, perhaps, stand at the beginning of one."

Worship of creative heroes and contempt for the masses suffused Rand's outlook. She had no patience with naturalism and its reverence for quotidian subjects. "At the age of seven, I could not understand why anyone should wish to paint or to admire pictures of dead fish, garbage cans or fat peasant women with triple chins," she said. "I refused to read . . . stories about the children of the folks next door. They bored me to death. I was not interested in such people in real life; I saw no reason to find them interesting in fiction." Naturalists might defend their focus on everyday subjects on the ground that they represented life as it really is; they derided Romantics as escapists. "An escape—from what?" Rand demanded. The proper subject for art was "greatness, intelligence, ability, virtue, heroism," and if portraying such qualities constituted an escape, "then medicine is an 'escape' from disease, agriculture is an 'escape' from hunger, knowledge is an 'escape' from ignorance, ambition is an 'escape' from sloth, and life is an 'escape' from death. . . . A hard-core realist is a vermin-eaten brute who sits motionless in a mud puddle, contemplates a pigsty, and whines that 'such is life.' If *that* is realism, then I am an escapist. So was Aristotle. So was Christopher Columbus."[25]

As a passionate Romantic, Rand favored the economic system that "demands and rewards the best in *every* man, great or average, and which is, obviously, laissez-faire capitalism." She had arrived in the United States as a near-penniless student, sailing into New York Harbor in 1926, the year of Greenspan's birth, and had been immediately enthralled by the skyline that greeted her. The Standard Oil Building, the Singer Tower, the Woolworth Building—these were the triumphant expressions of capitalism's creative power; they were "the will of man made visible." The industrialists who had commanded these structures into being were heroes in Rand's mind—she shared Greenspan's enthusiasm for the robber barons of yore, but she took it much further. James J. Hill, the railway magnate who had captured Greenspan's imagination, was her ideal, too; for he had not only interlinked the wilderness of the Pacific Northwest, he had done it, as Rand pointed out, while refusing land grants and other public assistance from the federal government. Capitalism was at its most perfect when it enabled such heroes, allowing them to pursue their visions without taxation, regulation, or other small-minded encumbrances. In *The Individualist Manifesto,* Rand's grandiose but unpublished attempt to do for capitalism what *The Communist Manifesto* had done for the left, the writer insisted that the capitalist system was superior not merely because it was efficient. It was to be preferred because it was natural, and therefore moral—it accepted man's selfish personality and did not try to change it. Liberated from socialism, religion, and other anti-individualist credos, free men would be driven by their natural egoism to build, invent, and prosper. "Selfishness is a magnificent force," Rand trumpeted.[26]

When Greenspan met Rand, she was already a decade into her most ambitious project: the novel *Atlas Shrugged,* which eventually weighed in at more than 1,100 pages. She approached her work with self-destructive mania, at one point writing for a thirty-three-day stretch without leaving her apartment, sustaining herself grimly with amphetamines and ambition. Sometimes, during special gatherings of the Collective, pages of the novel were passed around for comment, and on these occasions Greenspan felt as though his deepest private passions had been understood and vindicated. The heroine of the novel, an engineer named Dagny Taggart, could almost have been channeling Greenspan when she rhapsodized about the railroads, describing them as a metaphor for man's purpose—"a moral code cast in steel," she called them. Meanwhile, the hero was a steel magnate, allowing Greenspan to assist Rand by weighing in on the manuscript's descriptions of the industry that he knew intimately. Greenspan's enthusiasm for the novel, and his facility with metallurgical advice, expunged the stain of his logical-positivist protest. Rand now dropped the Undertaker moniker and dubbed him instead her Sleeping Giant, a quiet figure who would one day awake and achieve greatness.

In 1957, as the moment for the launch of *Atlas Shrugged* approached, the public reaction was awaited eagerly by members of the Collective. One young acolyte thought *Atlas Shrugged* would persuade Americans to turn back to the laissez-faire of the nineteenth century. Greenspan chimed in that the message of the novel was so "radiantly exact" as to compel agreement from every honest reader, and he presented the author with a miniature gold bar, a reference to the novel's paean to the gold standard.[27] Rand's publishers at Random House readied cigarettes emblazoned with gold dollar signs to support the launch, even though the editor had vainly entreated Rand to shorten her manuscript—"Would you cut the Bible?" Rand had retorted.[28] Barbara Branden loyally declared to her husband's lover, "Whether or not the world [deserves] to be saved will depend on how they respond to your book."[29]

As it turned out, the immediate public reception indicated that the world did not deserve to be saved. In the *New York Times,* the reviewer Granville Hicks complained that Rand's novel "howls in the reader's ear and beats him about the head in order to secure his attention, and then, when it has him subdued, harangues him for page upon page." Others agreed: "It would be hard to find such a display of grotesque eccentricity outside an asylum," the *Los Angeles Times* declared, while the *Chicago Tribune* managed to compare Rand to Hitler.[30] Perhaps most hurtful, Rand was also savaged by her presumed conservative allies. "I can recall no other book in which a tone of overriding arrogance was so implacably sustained," wrote Whittaker Chambers in the *National Review.* "Its shrillness is without reprieve. Its dogmatism is without appeal. . . . It supposes itself to be the bringer of final revelation. Therefore, resistance to the Message cannot be tolerated. . . . From almost any page of *Atlas Shrugged,* a voice can be heard, from painful necessity, commanding: 'To a gas chamber, go!'"[31]

The Collective quickly rallied to Rand's defense, and no defender was more ardent than Greenspan. The *New York Times* published his letter of protest on November 3, 1957:

> *Atlas Shrugged* is a celebration of life and happiness. Justice is unrelenting. Creative individuals and undeviating purpose and rationality achieve joy and fulfillment. Parasites who persistently avoid either purpose or reason perish as they should. Mr. Hicks suspiciously wonders "about a person who sustains such a mood through the writing of 1,168 pages and some fourteen years of work." This reader wonders about a person who finds unrelenting justice personally disturbing.

The letter marked a turning point for Greenspan. It was the first time he had taken a public stand on a question that went beyond data, and he had come out with both fists swinging. What was more, the next few months taught him to relish public fights, as Rand and her defenders got their revenge on the critics. *Atlas Shrugged* soon showed up on the *Times*'s bestseller list, alongside Jack Kerouac's *On the Road;* and within five years it had sold more than a million copies. Fan letters arrived by the thousands from readers whom one journalist described as "the largely abandoned class of thinking non-intellectuals."[32] Rand's opus was on its way to the extraordinary cult status it would attain later, vindicating her refusal to pare her manuscript to more manageable proportions. In 1991, in a poll sponsored by the Library of Congress, readers said that *Atlas Shrugged* had influenced their lives more than any other book except that other one no editor would cut—the Bible.[33]

The year before the publication of *Atlas Shrugged,* Robert Kavesh, Greenspan's classmate from his undergraduate days, moved back to New York after a spell at Harvard and Dartmouth. Now a business economist working at a bank, Kavesh looked up his old friend and was astonished by the change that had come over him. During his twenties, Greenspan had been a humble empiricist, ferreting out facts and seldom

venturing beyond them. But now, as he entered his thirties, both the humility and the empiricism were giving way. In business, he was transitioning
from being merely successful to being outright prosperous. In his thinking
and writing, he was increasingly opinionated. It was clear to Kavesh that
Ayn Rand had everything to do with the opinion part. Her relentless cross-
examinations had forced Greenspan to think through his positions and
come down clearly on questions that he might have sidestepped earlier—
especially the big issues of state activism versus laissez-faire. Greenspan's
debt to Rand was evident from the way he probed Kavesh about her. He
wanted to know whether Kavesh had heard of Rand, what he had read of
her writings, and how he had reacted to them. When Kavesh allowed that
he had read *The Fountainhead* some years before, Greenspan promised to
bring him a signed copy of *Atlas Shrugged* when it was published.

To a mainstream Keynesian like Kavesh, some of Greenspan's newfound clarity bordered on the wacky. As a student at NYU, Greenspan
had been an individualist by temperament, with a tendency to do much of
his learning on his own. But he had not been seized by individualism as a
philosophical creed, and though he had sat through Professor Walter
Spahr's classes, he had shown no great enthusiasm for a restoration of the
nineteenth-century gold standard.[34] Yet now he regarded gold as an indispensable bulwark against the government's manipulation of money, a
point that he would soon explain at length in his 1959 paper for the American Statistical Association. Kavesh decided that there was no point arguing with his friend—his views seemed implacably rigid. But he enjoyed
meeting Greenspan to play tennis on the waterfront downtown. Kavesh
was the better player, but Greenspan was fiercely competitive.[35]

Kavesh was right that Rand had changed his friend profoundly. Greenspan had been turned into a committed advocate of laissez-faire not by
some luminary within the economics profession but by a charismatic novelist. In some ways, this was merely typical of him. Since his days in the
Henry Jerome Orchestra, when he had read economic history while his
bandmates smoked pot, Greenspan had chosen his own path, and his
affinity with a cultish author was no more bizarre than his enthusiasm for
an obscure pamphleteer such as George Terborgh, the economist who

had debunked postwar predictions of secular stagnation. Besides, Rand's celebration of entrepreneurs and inventors seemed tailored to appeal to an individualistic consultant who was building his own business, and her romantic fascination with the industrial barons of the nineteenth century completed the connection. Indeed, as Greenspan grew more willing to assert his views, his affinity with the nineteenth century colored his approach to everything.

In September 1961, two years after presenting his groundbreaking article on finance, Greenspan followed up with an attack on government efforts to rein in monopolies with antitrust laws. This time the venue was a meeting of the National Association of Business Economists, but the tone was far less scholarly than the one he had adopted for the American Statistical Association. Indeed, it was combative:

> The world of anti-trust is reminiscent of Alice's Wonderland: everything seemingly is, yet apparently isn't, simultaneously. It is a world in which competition is lauded as the basic axiom and guiding principle, yet "too much" competition is condemned as "cutthroat." It is a world in which actions designed to limit competition are branded as criminal when taken by businessmen, yet praised as "enlightened" when initiated by the Government. It is a world in which the law is so vague that businessmen have no way of knowing whether specific actions will be declared illegal until they hear the judge's verdict—after the fact.

Greenspan proceeded to demand a complete rethink of America's attitude toward monopolies. In the early days of the republic, he recalled, Americans had feared the concentration of arbitrary power in the hands of government. They had felt differently about business, which has no power to compel obedience and relies instead on customers who freely choose whom to buy from. But these Enlightenment presumptions—for limited government on the one hand, for expansive commerce on the other—had been forgotten, Greenspan lamented. Franklin Roosevelt had attacked trusts—and then descended into a generalized attack on free enterprise.[36]

Greenspan's counterattack proceeded in three stages. First, critics of monopolies should remember that it was government meddling that created most of them, or so Greenspan asserted. For example, government subsidies and land grants to well-connected railway barons had created barriers to entry for unsubsidized competitors—James J. Hill being the heroic exception. If the principle of free enterprise had been properly adhered to, there would have been a level playing field in the first place, and hence no need for further government meddling in the form of antitrust law. "I am indebted to Ayn Rand's *Notes on the History of American Free Enterprise* for the identification of this principle," Greenspan acknowledged.[37]

Greenspan buttressed Rand's historical argument with a second, economic one. Monopolies were less pernicious than commonly suspected, he insisted. If they really did abuse consumers, their outsized profits would attract competitors—thus Standard Oil, which had controlled more than 80 percent of the nation's refining capacity at the turn of the century, soon faced a challenge from rivals such as Texaco and Gulf. In cases where no challenger emerged, this only went to show that the monopolist was not abusive—the exact opposite of what critics asserted. Citing the example of the aluminum giant that retained his consulting services, Greenspan argued that Alcoa faced no competition precisely because it behaved as though it did face competition. Alcoa was always seeking ways to cut prices and serve its customers better. Those who criticized its dominance were in effect attacking it for being "too successful, too efficient, and too good a competitor."

Greenspan concluded with a third argument, which fitted his emerging view of finance. In keeping with the Tobin-like analysis in his 1959 article, he pointed out that it was not just corporate managers who would want to challenge monopolists; the financial system itself would demand that they do so. If a monopoly extracted fat rents from its customers, its share price would soar; that would give entrepreneurs an incentive to create rivals to the monopoly, and it would give financiers an incentive to ply those rivals with abundant capital. The best guarantor of competition, Greenspan argued, was not the antitrust enforcement beloved by statists. It was the emergence of increasingly vibrant capital markets, which should be further encouraged with financial deregulation.

Greenspan's skepticism about antitrust enforcement was shared by many leading intellectuals of the era. But what distinguished Greenspan's contribution was its sweeping style—he had leaped the entire length of the continuum between intellectual caution and polemical audacity. In *The Constitution of Liberty,* published in 1960, the libertarian icon Friedrich Hayek had argued that government attacks on monopolies could do more harm than good; but he qualified his position by conceding that monopolies did cause abuses.[38] Two years later, in *Capitalism and Freedom,* Milton Friedman adopted a similarly nuanced position, conceding that antitrust legislation might be welcome.[39] Greenspan's Alice-in-Wonderland barrage was altogether cruder: "The entire structure of antitrust statutes in this country is a jumble of economic irrationality and ignorance," he stated flatly. Looking back on this outburst years later, Greenspan half apologized: "When you're young, there is a tendency for the world to be black and white in a way it never is thereafter," he offered.[40] But he was not really all that young. His polemic was republished in *Barron's* in February 1962, a month before his thirty-sixth birthday.[41]

Greenspan's refusal to concede anything to the critics of business was all the more remarkable given the dramatic shifts around him. It was one thing to defend the industrialists of the nineteenth century. But by the early 1960s businesses had grown larger and more politically connected: defending them without qualification required a determination to ignore reality.[42] In Greenspan's black-and-white moments, he imagined corporations run by bold proprietor-capitalists, like the robber barons he had idealized in his youth. But in the era of Organization Man, America's big corporations were run by technocratic empire builders who focused on controlling ever larger shares of their markets. When Greenspan drove his splendid Buick to the Fairless steel works, he experienced this imperial tendency firsthand. His destination proclaimed bigness: U. S. Steel controlled a third of the steel market. His means of transport proclaimed bigness: General Motors controlled half of the car market.[43] Companies this large were almost bound to distort Greenspan's ideal of free competition—their pay settlements set the standards for wages across the economy; their pricing decisions affected the rate of inflation; their bosses had easy access to the corridors of power—and if political decisions distorted legislation in their favor, only a naïf would have been startled. For Greenspan to assume perfect competition and no need for antitrust laws, he had to overlook the facts of the economy he inhabited.

Of course, a large part of him knew this. But Ayn Rand had set him on an intoxicating path that turned out to suit his temperament. Once he accepted that arguments could be valid without empirical proof, he launched himself into the construction of a broad worldview—a view that Rand's clique would embrace as the economic component of her philosophy of objectivism. While this worldview was under development, Greenspan was prepared to sweep details under the carpet; he wanted to get the big picture established and worry about messy real-world qualifications later. His loner's determination—that same determination that had found expression in baseball statistics, hours of solitary music drills, and dogged efforts to extract business insights from data—now found a new outlet in ideological inquiry; and the fact that Rand had dubbed him the Undertaker and the Sleeping Giant only reinforced his dedication. Ever since his childhood, Greenspan had known he was capable of greatness, but he also knew that he would have to earn it through hard work; he was too much the Undertaker—or too much the Sideman—to win the recognition that he craved without putting in a concentrated effort. In the early 1960s, the person whose recognition he desired most deeply was Ayn Rand. Contributing to objectivism became his priority.

In long discussions years later, Greenspan described this period of his life as a phase he had to go through.[44] He needed to complete the construction of his Randian philosophy before he felt ready to let reality intrude; only after that could he begin his shift from the libertarian fringe of the American debate to somewhere near its center. There is much truth to this self-appraisal. In contrast to foreign policy conservatives, who started out as moderate "realists" in the 1970s and grew progressively more radical in their belief that democracy could be spread by force of arms, Greenspan was radical early and moderate later. Invoking the famous quip that a conservative is a liberal who has been mugged by reality, Greenspan once mused, "I got mugged in the other direction."[45]

Five

AGAINST THE NEW FRONTIER

The sun shone brilliant and cold on John F. Kennedy's inauguration day. The young leader set off on foot, his top hat on his head and his radiant wife Jackie on his arm, down a path through the snow that blanketed the North Lawn of the White House. Citizens bundled in scarves and sleeping bags waited by the roadside to catch a glimpse of this almost regal procession; and when Kennedy approached the podium on the Capitol, his coat bravely cast aside, his optimism thrilled the nation. "Ask not what America will do for you, but what together we can do for the freedom of man," he declared. A tank mounted with a long-nosed ballistic missile trundled down Pennsylvania Avenue as part of the inaugural parade, a reminder that American idealism was backed by futuristic scientific weaponry. "There is a new generation in charge, with a new style and a new seriousness," the sage Walter Lippmann wrote. "People are beginning to feel that we can *do* things about problems after all—that everything is possible."[1]

No tribe was more optimistic than America's economists. After fifteen years of headlong postwar growth, the declinism of Alvin Hansen had been discredited. The predicted demographic bust had been buried by a happy rush of childbearing; and new technologies, from nuclear power to air flight, had more than made up for the closing of the American frontier.

By the time Kennedy promised to lead America to a New Frontier, advances in economic understanding seemed to promise growth that would be not only higher but more stable. Keynes had taught how to combat economic slowdowns by running a government budget deficit, and neo-Keynesians had grasped how slumps could be averted by the central bank as well: low interest rates, hitherto regarded principally as a means of helping the government to borrow, were now understood as a tool of economic management.[2] "The supply of money, its availability to investor borrowers, and the interest cost of such borrowings can have important effects on [GNP]," Paul Samuelson instructed in the 1961 edition of his bestselling textbook, revising the dismissal of monetary policy in his 1948 edition.[3] "The worst consequences of the business cycle . . . are probably a thing of the past," Samuelson wrote confidently, and conservative economists agreed.[4] At the end of 1959, Greenspan's mentor Arthur Burns proclaimed, "The business cycle is unlikely to be as disturbing or troublesome to our children as it was to us and our fathers."[5]

It was not just that economists understood how to prevent recessions. Thanks to new computer models, they believed they understood the relationships between growth, inflation, and employment so precisely that they could "fine-tune" the economy to deliver the ideal combination. In 1958, A. W. Phillips, a New Zealander at the London School of Economics, had documented the trade-off between unemployment and inflation, with the implication that technocrats could engineer permanently low unemployment if they were willing to accept modest inflation; and two years later Paul Samuelson and his MIT colleague Robert Solow, applying the Phillips curve to U.S. data, suggested that an enlightened administration might choose unemployment of 3 percent at the price of inflation of just 4.5 percent. Seizing on this happy verdict, the Kennedy administration promised "full employment," an objective that would benefit workers, salve racial tensions, and bolster America in its apocalyptic rivalry with the Soviet Union. In order to make good on this project, the administration proposed tax cuts and low interest rates. It was time "to get the country moving again," as Kennedy's campaign slogan had insisted.[6]

The Kennedy team proceeded to implement its experiment. Where it saw signs of price pressure, it treated them as the side effect of the econo-my's concentrated structure, not as evidence that all-out stimulus might stoke more inflation than intended. There was at least some truth to this claim. The giant corporations of the era had quasi-monopolistic pricing power, a fact that Greenspan swept under the carpet in his paper on anti-trust; and powerful labor unions had the muscle to extract extravagant wage hikes that set inflationary benchmarks for the economy. The admin-istration addressed this "cost-push" inflation with vigorous price and wage guidelines: the remedy for big business and big labor would be jaw-boning by big government. The steel industry in particular was recog-nized as a prime mover of cost-push inflation, so the Kennedy aides patted themselves on the back when they muscled the steel unions into agreeing to a wage increase of only 2.5 percent in 1962. When Big Steel later tried to welsh on its commitment, Kennedy was furious. "My father once told me that all steel men were sons of bitches," he reportedly said, "and I did not realize until now how right he was."[7] Kennedy threatened antitrust action against the steel companies, and FBI agents began telephoning steel executives in the middle of the night; finally the steel men relented. But this little unpleasantness was regarded as a minor glitch in an other-wise sound plan. Inflation averaged just over 1 percent during Kennedy's presidency, while growth barreled along at more than 6 percent per year. America was on a roll. The jawboning seemed to be working.

From his perch at his consulting firm, Greenspan was looking on in horror.

In the year of Kennedy's election, Greenspan moved his operation from the cramped offices at 39 Broadway to a more modern building on the east side of the stock exchange. The new Townsend-Greenspan premises at 80 Pine Street afforded double the space of the old one, and Greenspan installed himself in a large corner office with a spectacular view of the Brooklyn Bridge. Like one of Ayn Rand's heroes, he loved being high up in that building, gazing out over the cityscape that capitalism had made; his physical rise mirrored his financial one. "All of a sudden this poor kid was making a lot of money," Greenspan said later. "I could marvel at what I had done. . . . My self-esteem [improved] significantly."[8]

The new confidence was showing. Greenspan traded his Buick for an even more splendid blue Cadillac Eldorado convertible, and soon bought the license plate TG-1—both AG and TG were taken. Roaring back and forth to his new office, he regularly got speeding tickets on the East Side Highway; he could afford to pay them without noticing. To satisfy his musical tastes, he collected the highest of high-fidelity Harman Kardon equipment, which he installed at his apartment on Thirty-fifth Street, a block or so from Ayn Rand's building.[9] He played golf at the Quaker Ridge club, an emerald oasis where, according to club legend, George Washington himself had slept under a great oak and narrowly escaped detection by the British. As his range of business contacts expanded, Greenspan moved in ever grander circles. Sometimes, when Ayn Rand heard about a rarefied social gathering that Greenspan was attending, she would seem momentarily piqued. "Do you think Alan might basically be a social climber?" she once asked her lover, Nathaniel Branden.[10]

Townsend-Greenspan's business still revolved around heavy industry. But thanks to his financial writings, Greenspan was now drawing the attention of a new set, including at least one West Coast banker. In 1962, Louis J. Galen, the founder and CEO of a savings and loan named Trans-World Financial, offered Greenspan his first seat on the board of a public company. Ensconced in booming Southern California, Trans-World was a cash machine.[11] The population of the Golden State had more than doubled in the previous two decades, and home prices had shot up equivalently; blessed with such heady growth, mortgage lenders like Trans-World could scarcely fail to prosper.[12] Perhaps not surprisingly, the gusher of easy money was attracting promoters and hucksters. Some savings and loans in California hired pretty women to hand out gifts to new depositors, causing Greenspan's old collaborators at *Fortune* to tut-tut that such marketing gimmicks violated the "image of banker-like stability."[13] Bart Lytton, head of the eponymous Lytton Financial, was emblematic of the go-go atmosphere: during lawn parties at his Los Angeles home, he would parade about with a microphone hooked to his jacket so that guests who tired of lesser conversations could hang upon his words as they boomed out of surrounding speakers.[14] ("The only -ism for me is narcissism," Lytton once said cheerfully.)[15] The prospect of associating himself with this racy industry did not dismay the thirty-six-year-old Greenspan. He accepted Galen's offer.

Greenspan began to fly out to Los Angeles once a month for board meetings. He could see why so many people wanted to live there. In New York, there was nowhere to build but up. In Beverly Hills, where Trans-World was headquartered, mansions with exotic vegetation sprawled in the Mediterranean climate.[16] Greenspan took to staying at the Beverly Hilton and making time for golf. He shelled out several thousand dollars to join the legendary Hillcrest Country Club, known as "the leading Jewish country club in Southern California."[17] It was perhaps odd for a man who had almost refused to be bar mitzvahed to join a club that was described that way; but Greenspan did not seem to mind. The club was frequented by a who's who of Hollywood comedians who congregated at the so-called Round Table in a corner of the main dining room. Even Groucho Marx could be seen there, despite his famous quip that he wouldn't belong to any club that accepted him as a member.

At the end of 1961, Greenspan presented another paper at the annual meeting of the American Statistical Association, a sort of sequel to his groundbreaking 1959 article. Having dug deeper into the relationship between stock prices and business investment, he reported that the linkage was even tighter than suspected. High stock prices anticipated surges in investment not only for the economy as a whole, but also within industries; moreover, the time between stock price rises and jumps in capital expenditure was short, reflecting the power of the association that Greenspan had identified. If price signals from financial markets could drive shifts in the real economy so rapidly despite extensive regulation of finance, it followed that financial deregulation could make the transmission even slicker, so that capital would flow to the corners of the economy that would use it most productively.[18] After Greenspan completed his presentation, the research chief at the Wall Street brokerage Van Alstyne, Noel pronounced himself impressed. He asked Greenspan to stay in touch. Perhaps they could have lunch together?

What with Greenspan's travels, it took a little while for the two men to get together. But one day in late September 1962, Greenspan found himself seated at the top of the towering Equitable Building, in the same plush dining room in which Bill Townsend had offered him a partnership—naturally, the Bankers Club was another institution of which Greenspan was now a member. As the discussion wound on, Greenspan fielded questions about his view of the economy, and a few about his philosophical beliefs: Could a tree crashing in a forest be said to make a sound if there was no witness to hear it? The economist from Van Alstyne had brought along his research assistant, a slim, pretty brunette named Kathryn Eickhoff, who appeared baffled, understandably, by the talk of trees and forests. But Greenspan was more focused on other aspects of Eickhoff's appearance. When he got back to his office, he lost no time in calling her and inviting her to dinner that same evening.

Greenspan and Eickhoff went uptown to a small restaurant with curved booths along the edges and tables down the middle. He courted her respectfully, asking what she liked and what she believed in, and quickly discovered that this was his lucky evening. The young woman with the fine figure chose conversational territory that suited him perfectly. She proclaimed her faith in the moral correctness of free enterprise, the power of the individual to shape his world, and the responsibility of each person for his own choices.

Were these just her own ideas? Greenspan inquired pleasantly.

Eickhoff answered that she had been influenced by a Russian émigré—a novelist and philosopher named Ayn Rand. Just a few months earlier, Eickhoff had read *Atlas Shrugged* on a friend's recommendation. The experience, she confided, was an epiphany. It had changed her life.

Greenspan felt like a tennis player who sees a slow lob curling toward him, right in his sweet spot.

Would Eickhoff perhaps like to have coffee with Ayn Rand? he asked casually.[19]

The smash landed perfectly: Eickhoff was awestruck. A few days later, Alan took Kathy to hear Rand deliver a lecture, and afterward he introduced the young admirer to the charismatic grande dame. Alan and Kathy began dating, and Kathy soon discovered that Alan was an avid ballroom dancer. Sometimes they danced at Ayn Rand's apartment, where the Collective would roll back the carpets and put music on; once Alan took Kathy to a restaurant in Hartsdale, New York, and danced under the stars with her.[20] It was always ballroom dancing—Alan had no time for rock and roll or pop—and Eickhoff learned that he saw no reason to restrict himself to dancing with the girl he arrived with.[21] But if there was no music to dance to, and no meaty intellectual conversation to be had, Alan would just as easily retreat into his shell. Early in their relationship, Eickhoff had the misfortune of hosting a party at her apartment the same day that a new edition of the *Statistical Abstract of the United States* appeared. Greenspan commandeered the only comfy chair that Eickhoff had and read into the footnotes as the party continued around him.[22]

Kathy tried to get Alan to diversify beyond dinner, dancing, and conversations with Rand's circle. She quickly discovered that if he was going to do something, it had to have a score—and not necessarily a musical one. She took him to a place in Greenwich Village that had all-you-can-eat steaks and bowling; Eickhoff christened it Bo Ling because the *w* in the neon sign was broken. That adventure went down well, and was often repeated; but Kathy's attempts to get Alan to play bridge were less successful. One evening, at the home of Elayne Kalberman, Nathaniel Branden's sister, Greenspan got as far as sitting down at the table. But before the cards were dealt, he wanted everything explained. Why was an ace high to a king? Why were clubs worth less than spades? Why use all those bidding conventions, and were they really logical? Why, why, why, the questions continued, as if from a precocious toddler. After what felt like hours, Kathy and the Kalbermans gave up without playing even one hand. "He had a pathological objection to arbitrary conventions," Eickhoff observed later.[23]

Not long after they began dating, Kathy asked Alan for a job. A stock market bust in May 1962 had spoiled the atmosphere at Van Alstyne, and Kathy wanted to move on—though she assured Alan that she would stay at his firm only temporarily. Alan insisted on giving her a formal interview, and then agreed to hire her.

The firm that Eickhoff joined at the end of 1962 was in the midst of a transition. Thanks to the boss's broadening connections, Townsend-Greenspan was booming; but it had yet to make the leap from pencils and smudged ledgers to the new age of computing. When Eickhoff signed on, she was assigned to help with a product called the Major Economic Trends report. Each week, as the Treasury and the Federal Reserve came out with numbers on interest rates, the money supply, bank deposits, prices, consumption, and so on, Townsend-Greenspan assistants entered them into an imposing three-ring ledger with green, columned pages. Once all the data had been harvested, two researchers would sit next to each other at one of the desks under the large window in the main room of the suite. Guided by a fat instruction volume, they carried out the operations needed to transform the data into the report. To crunch the numbers, they used a rotary calculator—a bulky numeric typewriter that spat out its calculations on narrow spools of paper like the receipts from a grocery checkout. The machine could add or subtract fairly easily; but multiplication or division required iterative addition or subtraction. An innocent request—for example, that the calculator multiply two three-digit numbers—would set off a noisy grinding of the gears as the machine added and carried, added and carried, *ka-chunk, ka-chunk, ka-chunk.* The instructions went on for pages and pages, and the researchers plugged number after number into the rebarbative calculator and copied the outputs into their ledgers—it could take hours to calculate a handful of results. When they finally finished, the two colleagues would compare notes. If their numbers matched, the researchers sighed thankfully. If they conflicted, the *ka-chunk ka-chunking* started up again.

Eickhoff noticed that the instruction manual for the Major Economic Trends report repeated some operations pointlessly. When she alerted Greenspan, he was suspicious at first. The manual had been in service for years; how could there be a mistake in it? But Eickhoff was right, as Greenspan quickly recognized, and soon he was relying on his employee-cum-girlfriend for all manner of improvements around the office. A staffer who kept track of invoices for Townsend-Greenspan handed in her two-weeks notice, but Greenspan found her tedious so he failed to take in what she had said; when the two weeks were up and the bookkeeper said good-bye, Greenspan turned in desperation to Eickhoff, who, fortunately, had taken an accounting course in college.[24] Hiring clerical assistants was not Greenspan's strong suit, either, so Eickhoff soon took charge of interviewing processions of young women. When her romantic relationship with Greenspan petered out after a few years, she found that the boss dated many of the assistants she had recruited.[25] One young hire came to work with a skirt so short that when she reached down to open a low filing cabinet she practically undressed, which Greenspan thought was fine, Eickhoff remembered. "He never overlapped girlfriends for more than the day or two it took him to notify the other one that things had changed," Eickhoff added, noting that boss-secretary liaisons were routine in the sixties. "I don't think anyone that Alan ever dated would say that he harassed them. They might be upset only because he quit dating them."[26]

Upset or not, the staff at Townsend-Greenspan consisted entirely of women. When it came to the junior positions, this was typical of the times. In the years after World War II, women who had formed the backbone of the industrial workforce were pushed back into female-only jobs, especially in the rapidly growing service sector; as one historian put it, "Rosie the Riveter had become a file clerk."[27] But Greenspan was unusual in promoting women to positions of responsibility as well. In addition to Eickhoff, there were Bess Kaplan, an expert on government data, and Lucille Wu, who were steeped in the emerging science of economic modeling. Greenspan also recruited Judy Mackey, a former classmate from Columbia, who took over the task of compiling the firm's savings and loan report after being repeatedly passed over for promotion at her previous job with the Life Insurance Association.[28] Greenspan saw nothing problematic about advancing these women. He judged employees according to their abilities; and he could spot a bargain, too—because of widespread discrimination, talented women could be hired cheaply.[29] But Greenspan was too much of a loner—and too jealous of his sense of independence and control—ever to recruit a true peer to his firm, whether male or female.

Greenspan's headlong rise affected his connection to his parents. The more confident he felt about himself, the more his feelings hardened toward his father, Herbert. The man had abandoned his mother, disappointed him cruelly, failed to make anything of his own life, and yet still condescended to him infuriatingly. Alan permitted Herbert to visit him at the office once a year, on his father's birthday; and Herbert would spend part of these meetings inflating his own success and belittling Alan, doubting that his son would amount to much, even though he already had.[30] After an uncomfortable hour, the elder and lesser Greenspan would be shooed out of the building.

As to his mother, Rose, Alan felt a sense of filial duty, but his relationship with her was cooling. He supported Rose financially and set up a small board of directors for Townsend-Greenspan, consisting of Rose, himself, and Eickhoff. On the appointed day each month, Rose would show up at the offices on Pine Street, and the board meeting would consist of a fine lunch, usually at the nearby Fraunces Tavern.[31] But Alan seldom took part in these outings. He would greet Rose warmly, and then Kathy would lead her off, sometimes accompanied by the other senior women at the company. Rose grew popular at Townsend-Greenspan for her easygoing nature and spirited musical performances at the company Christmas parties. But Eickhoff recalls that, in the early 1960s, Alan grew impatient with his mother, however fond he felt of her.[32] "She would probably want to tell him what was going on with all the relatives . . . which would have been of no interest to Alan . . . here he is building a career, he's got a lot on his mind and . . . would much rather be doing other things."[33]

If Greenspan had a maternal figure in those years, it was that curious Russian novelist. Ayn Rand had grown depressed and difficult after the publication of *Atlas Shrugged,* but the two remained close—witness the extraordinary fervor of Greenspan's anti-antitrust article. Greenspan would see Rand frequently at the Italianate Roosevelt Hotel, which stood in the shadow of Grand Central Terminal, the largest railroad station in the United States and a symbol of the industrial might that they both romanticized. There, Rand and Greenspan, often accompanied by Eickhoff, would listen to one of the popular lectures on objectivism delivered by Nathaniel Branden, and afterward Rand and her inner circle would meet in the lobby and head off to one of the eateries in the basement. As they descended the grand staircase of the Roosevelt Hotel, Rand would link arms with Greenspan and Branden, one young escort on each side of her, and lead them down the steps. When Eickhoff watched this procession, she imagined a mother flanked by her two sons. To navigate the world he cared about, Greenspan seemed better off with Rand than with either of the two parents life had given him.[34]

A t the beginning of 1963, Greenspan sent two startling letters to his clients, reflecting his broad disaffection with Kennedy's economic policies.[35] His belief in the self-correcting magic of the gold standard—in boom times, a fixed supply of money guaranteed that rising interest rates would cool the economy, and vice versa—made Greenspan a natural enemy of fine-tuning. Walter Lippmann might exult that "we can *do* things about problems after all"; but if a laissez-faire system could rebalance itself, there was no need for such activism. The Kennedy team's faith in economic modeling struck Greenspan as folly, too. Around 1960, Mobil Oil had asked Townsend-Greenspan to prepare a general forecast of the economy, and in the course of delivering what his client wanted, Greenspan had concluded that such macroeconomic projections were more art than science. If state-of-the-art modeling could not pinpoint when the economy was headed for a slump, it followed that policy makers could not be expected to know when to order up a stimulus—fine-tuning seemed more likely to misfire than to hit its target.[36] But at the start of 1963, Greenspan focused his client letters on a narrower and more surprising claim. "The question of inflation has again arisen," he proclaimed, seemingly oblivious to the fact that in the two months just completed, inflation had come in at precisely zero.[37]

Greenspan proceeded to lay out a way of understanding price pressures that was diametrically opposed to that of the Kennedy administration. Rather than blaming inflation on cost-push pressures from big labor and big business, the letters linked it to the growth of money, which, as Greenspan noted, the Kennedy team was eager to encourage. History, Greenspan continued, proved that monetary expansions ultimately yielded inflation, even if the symptoms might be temporarily suppressed by wage and price controls or special circumstances. In the middle of the century, the monetary expansion during the Depression and the war had not resulted in immediate inflation; but as soon as the end of rationing had uncorked the economy, bubbling inflation had spilled forth—in 1946, the rate had hit 18 percent. Taking direct aim at the Kennedy team's view of inflation, Greenspan went out of his way to exonerate cost-push factors for that price surge. The postwar years were "not a period characterized by arbitrary periodic mark-ups of prices by industrial management, but rather reflected the upward financial pressures on prices resulting from the economic distortions initiated by the Government."

Greenspan's letters reflected the distance he had come since his days in Arthur Burns's classroom. Far from accepting that inflation reflected excess government spending, as Burns had lectured his students, he now embraced the monetarist view—that inflation reflected excess money. This was, at least conceptually, the logical corollary of the new thinking on central banking that Greenspan had absorbed in the late 1950s. If inflation occurred when the financial system created money too freely, then the trick was to monitor the rate of expansion. But this trick would not be easy to pull off. Different parts of the financial system created purchasing power in different ways. Measuring money would not be straightforward.[38]

In his first letter, sent in January, Greenspan concluded that monetary growth was not fast enough to be truly worrisome; the risks of inflation would remain small "unless and until the New Frontier economic policies take on something more of the chaotic financial juggling of the New Deal." But in his second letter, two months later, Greenspan sounded the alarm. The official monetary measures, he argued, had been rendered obsolete by changes in finance. Increasingly, banks were encouraging large customers to hold their money in time deposits, not demand deposits; and time deposits were excluded from the usual definition of the money supply. But starting in 1961, banks had issued "negotiable" time deposits that could be swapped for cash on short notice, turning them into money equivalents.[39] If you counted time deposits as money, the outlook became frightening, Greenspan wrote. Over the past year, this more inclusive definition of monetary growth had outstripped the growth of the economy by a wide margin. It followed that there were more dollars chasing each unit of output—and that, sooner or later, prices would advance destructively. Undaunted by the fact that there was no immediate sign of inflation, Greenspan's letter predicted that prices might rise at an average rate of 3.1 percent over the next five years, through the end of 1967. As it turned out, Greenspan's outlandish forecast proved more or less correct. Inflation hit 3.5 percent in 1966, then stayed at 3 percent or above for two decades.

Greenspan's monetarism, and his dissent from the economics of the New Frontier, owed something to Milton Friedman.[40] In *A Program for Monetary Stability,* published in 1960, Friedman had emphasized the destabilizing power of excess money creation, recommending that the central bank should target monetary growth that roughly matched output growth—in the absence of such a rule, discretionary policy would lead to inflation.[41] In 1963, the year Greenspan sent out his letters, Friedman and his coauthor, Anna Schwartz, followed up with an enduring statement in favor of laissez-faire, *A Monetary History of the United States*. A large section of this masterwork was devoted to arguing that the Fed had made the Depression worse than it need have been, allowing the money supply to collapse in the 1930s and so suffocating businesses. The implication was that discretionary monetary policy had failed disastrously, not once but twice—the Fed had helped to bring on the Depression by fueling the stock market bubble of 1929, as Greenspan had argued in his 1959 article; and it had also rendered the aftermath unnecessarily painful. It is likely that Greenspan's disapproving attitude toward central-banking ortho-doxy was fortified by Friedman's thesis. The year after the *Monetary History* appeared, he built on his client letters with an academic version of his critique, which appeared in the *Journal of Finance*.[42]

But by late 1963, Greenspan's mind was turning to a more ambitious project. He resolved to take his writings on asset prices, antitrust, and central banks and weave them into one grand statement of his economic philosophy.

In December 1963, an advertisement went out in the *Objectivist Newsletter*, a publication run by Nathaniel Branden to rally Ayn Rand's followers. The advertisement promised a series of ten lectures on the Economics of a Free Society, to be delivered by Alan Greenspan. A few days later, on a Saturday morning, Greenspan showed up at his office on Pine Street and dictated the text of his first lecture to a secretary, who duly typed it up, producing a transcript that ran to thirty pages.[43] On Monday and Tuesday, it fell to Kathryn Eickhoff to discipline the boss's prose. "It's not always apparent where grammar goes in Alan's sentences," she later said delicately.

For a period stretching into February 1964, Greenspan repeated this routine each week, testing the stamina of his assistants. Eickhoff would finish her edits by Tuesday evening, and the text of the lecture would be sent over to Rand and Branden for a further round of vetting. The two high priests of objectivism could be stern critics, always insisting that everything be made intelligible to a general audience. Over dinner on Wednesday evening with Greenspan, they would flag places where the complexity of his message clashed with the Randian imperative of lucidity; one time, Greenspan struggled to explain the futures markets in sufficiently clear terms, then eventually capitulated and cut futures out entirely. At other points in Greenspan's lectures, his explanations needed to be rescued from a narrowly technical framing. Rand demanded to know how everything connected to the broader issues of individualism and freedom. Greenspan was eager to comply, pushing his accumulated insights on economics to their logical and libertarian conclusions.

The morning after the dinner with Rand and Branden, Greenspan would return to his office armed with a newly polished statement of his philosophy. He would dictate the changes; the secretary would type; Eickhoff would take delivery of each page as it came off the typewriter. After Eickhoff had applied her last edits, the secretary would hammer out a final version; and with little time to spare, Greenspan would make his way uptown to the Roosevelt Hotel, ready to communicate the truth, an excited Eickhoff beside him. There, in one of the hotel's ornate meeting rooms, Greenspan would deliver his lecture—a handsome, rather 1940s figure with large heavy-framed glasses and dark slicked-back hair, older and graver in manner than his thirty-seven years justified. Greenspan read out the speeches carefully, following his prepared text. Rand and Branden frowned on extemporaneous departures from the version they had vetted.

Greenspan's purpose, he began, was to "show why a laissez-faire economy is the only moral and practical form of economic organization."[44] Attacks on the fairness of market prices should be understood for what they were: moral judgments that impugned the individuals whose free choices created those prices. It followed that the entrepreneur—or the "enterpriser," as Greenspan called him—was a hero; he was the essential figure who matched society's productive energy to ordinary citizens' desires, and did so in the most efficient manner possible. The United States had eclipsed its rivals by embracing this system, but the pragmatic, business-minded side of America was in conflict with a "moral and religious view, that material pursuits are evil and immoral," Greenspan lamented. "One has to be familiar with the destructiveness of this contradiction in American history to fully appreciate the contribution to America of *Atlas Shrugged*," Greenspan reminded his audience.

Presuming heroic patience from the objectivist faithful, Greenspan launched into a lengthy description of the most basic ideas in economics: why individuals specialize, why they engage in commercial exchanges, the difference between comparative and absolute advantage. He dwelled extensively on the purpose and origins of money, and especially on gold; he celebrated the era of "free banking," the time before the passing of the Federal Reserve Act in 1913, when banks issued private money backed by their gold reserves, with no interference from politicians. On a moral basis, Greenspan argued, this private money was superior to the government sort. "Private bank notes have value because the word of the banker is as good as gold," he explained; in contrast, government banknotes were backed not by honor but by coercive fiat—they were accepted because the law required them to be accepted. Echoing a famous passage on money in

Atlas Shrugged, Greenspan emphasized the violence implicit in such fiat currency systems: "The ultimate backing of paper currency is not the inviolate word of a private individual but the muzzle of a gun of a government bureaucrat."

Greenspan presented his preference for privately issued money as practical as well as moral. The advantage of private money, he contended, was that its quantity was limited. Lacking the government's ability to force the use of its banknotes, the "free" banks of the nineteenth century could only issue scrip that was credibly backed by their reserves of gold: they could not print endless amounts of it. Of course, this was in some ways a weakness, not an advantage: without the backstop of a central bank, private banks always invited the suspicion that their reserves were inadequate to support their promise to exchange scrip for gold; when these suspicions grew too strong, the banks were vulnerable to runs that forced them to cut off all lending, driving the economy into a recession. Indeed, it had been precisely such "money panics" that had spurred America's leaders to create a central bank "to furnish an elastic currency," in the words of the Federal Reserve Act. But Greenspan showered contempt on this logic, giving rise to what must surely be one of the most exquisite ironies of economic history.

The way Greenspan saw things, the money panics of the nineteenth century had actually been salutary.[45] They had inflicted brief contractions on the economy, to be sure. But they had also been a boon, for they had disrupted the inflation of asset bubbles. Thanks to the money panics, banks were regularly reminded not to let money creation run ahead of gold reserves, which meant that they would never pump out enough cash to fuel a truly dangerous bubble. It followed that the nation's leaders had derived exactly the wrong lesson from history. Noticing that the money panics came on when banks ran short of reserves, politicians thought that "the cure to these money panics . . . was to prevent the banking system from running out of reserves. It was as simple as that. The way to cure the patient, it was argued, was to lower his fever by putting the thermometer between two ice cubes. . . . Thus, just prior to World War I emerged one of the historic disasters in American history, the creation of the Federal Reserve System."

This "historic disaster"—the creation of the central bank that Greenspan would later lead—ushered in a brave new world of potentially unlimited reserves in the banking system.[46] Banks handed their gold over to the Fed. In return, they received title to deposits held at the Fed, and these deposits became the new reserves in the banking system. Unlike gold, these new reserves could be expanded elastically, by central bank fiat. The Fed might buy government bonds from the banks, and pay by decreeing an expansion in the banks' reserves—effectively creating money. Or it might "discount" other assets held by banks, taking in their business loans and crediting their reserve accounts with more invented money. Once such tricks became possible, banks were assured of access to funds; the economy had been inoculated from money panics. But, Greenspan continued, this clever new system had not turned out so well. "It did prevent shortages of reserves, but instead of perpetual prosperity, it created the greatest economic disaster the world has ever known—the depression of the 1930s."

Toward the end of his lectures, Greenspan resumed his attack on the economics of the New Frontier. With their commitment to full employment, the Kennedy and Johnson advisers were stoking inflation, pushing the Federal Reserve to pump up the economy by supplying bank reserves in ever increasing quantities. This was not simply a technocratic error; it was a failure to grasp the true driver of human progress. The New Frontier enthusiasts viewed the economy as a piece of machinery, to be fine-tuned as one might tweak the brakes on a car. But, Greenspan argued, "economic development is a function not of society, the economy, the system, etc., but of men. . . . To an extent which unfortunately we are too little aware, our society lives in the afterglow of their achievements." Lamenting that "the historical status of the great wealth producers of the past has declined with the growth of the welfare state," Greenspan invoked the heroes of his youthful readings: "The James Hills and the J. P. Morgans are an affront to a society dedicated to the worship of mediocrity," he insisted. Unless something drastic happened, creeping mediocrity would deaden every nerve in the nation. Borrowing a phrase from Ayn

Rand's repertoire, Greenspan gave warning that America was surrendering itself to "the primordial morality of altruism, with its consequences of slavery, brute force, stagnant terror, and sacrificial furnaces."

How could America halt its slide into this abyss? Greenspan's answer emphasized the role of elites—he preached a sort of libertarian Leninism. To recreate the free nation of the nineteenth century, there was no need to convert the masses to objectivism, he argued. Rather, "it is the intellectual leaders, who can doubtless be numbered in the hundreds, or at most thousands, who set the trend. They are the ones who have to be reached," he told his audience. "Communism started with a small dedicated few," the revolutionary instructed the band of eager brothers at the Roosevelt Hotel. And then he summoned them to arms. "Objectivism has a crucial advantage over communism and previous philosophical movements: the fact that it is right, consistent with reality, and consistent with life on this earth."

For Greenspan and his fellow objectivists, the struggle to save the nation coalesced around the self-consciously nineteenth-century figure of Barry Goldwater, senator from Arizona and, by the time Greenspan concluded his lectures, Republican presidential candidate. Four years earlier, Goldwater had published *The Conscience of a Conservative,* which invoked the "ancient and tested truths that guided our Republic through its early days," and pleaded for a very Randian vision: "that to regard man as part of an undifferentiated mass is to consign him to ultimate slavery."[47] Goldwater's book appealed powerfully to the college crowd that devoured Rand's novels; and the *Wall Street Journal* hailed it as proof that the nation's youth were moving "away from the state-welfarist political ideas that have dominated campus arguments since FDR first tilted his cigarette holder at a rakish angle."[48] Shortly after *Conscience* appeared on the bestseller lists, Goldwater sent a copy to Rand; "I have enjoyed very few books in my life as much as I have yours, *Atlas Shrugged,*" the accompanying note confided.[49] For her part, Rand celebrated the ascent of a Republican who resisted the welfare statism and "me-too-ism" of Dwight Eisenhower, for whom she had refused to vote.[50] Compromisers, Rand insisted, were worse than outright enemies. "There are two sides to every issue," she had proclaimed in *Atlas Shrugged*. "One side is right and the other is wrong, but the middle is always evil."[51]

Goldwater announced his presidential candidacy from his home in Phoenix in January 1964, promising Americans disaffected by the New Frontier "a choice, not an echo." The following month, Greenspan concluded his last lecture with an endorsement of the candidate. Goldwater might be an underdog, Greenspan conceded, but he or his equivalent might win in 1968; and if that happened, then an even purer candidate might emerge to his right, pushing the entire nation back toward the virtuous individualism of an earlier era. "Within one generation," Greenspan proclaimed eagerly, "we may see a United States presidential candidate fully committed to laissez-faire." A few days later, in the March edition of the *Objectivist Newsletter*, Rand herself expanded on Greenspan's commendation, acknowledging Goldwater's troubling Christianity but oddly forgiving it.[52] She was even willing to make peace with the wackier fringes of Goldwater's coalition, notably the secretive, borderline-racist, conspiracy-minded John Birch Society. As a committed atheist, Rand might have been expected to keep her distance from a society that required its members to believe in God; and as a committed individualist she might have been expected to bridle at the crushing of individual freedom involved in southern segregation. But when it came to the Arizona senator, the woman who painted compromise as evil turned out to be strangely open to it.[53]

After Rand's Goldwater endorsement, her New York acolytes mobilized. They launched a Goldwater political club and a Goldwater magazine, seeking both to support the candidate and to warn him off his religious inclinations. The Rand brand profited mightily from the excitement that the campaign generated. The Washington State Republican Party ordered copies of *Atlas Shrugged* to distribute to Goldwater followers. Subscriptions to the *Objectivist Newsletter* tripled. Goldwater's campaign staff featured several Rand devotees, notably Karl Hess, the speechwriter whom Goldwater called Shakespeare.[54] Kathryn Eickhoff was among the faithful who plunged into the Goldwater effort, encouraging objectivists to rally to his flag and venturing into public speaking for the first time since high school. When she delivered her first address, an attack on Lyndon Johnson's promise to create a Great Society by means of ever-growing spending plans, she felt thoroughly nervous. But Alan was there watching, and when the speech was over he asked what she would like to do to celebrate.

"You know, what I'd really like is to go tell my two heroes about it."

"And who would they be?" Alan asked her.

"Frank and Ayn," Kathy responded, referring to Rand and her husband, Frank O'Connor.

Alan and Kathy called Rand to see if it would be all right to come over. Then they made their way to Rand's apartment, and triumphantly presented her with a copy of Kathy's address.[55]

Buoyed by a diverse conservative groundswell, Goldwater captured the Republican presidential nomination. On the evening of July 16, 1964, a jubilant conservative movement watched its hero walk down the center aisle of the Cow Palace in San Francisco, arm in arm with his wife, to the strains of a brass band playing "The Battle Hymn of the Republic."[56] When he reached the stage, Goldwater clasped hands with Richard Nixon, the party's previous nominee, and the two men raised their arms in victory. Balloons fell from the ceiling. The crowd cheered and roared and cheered some more. Finally, Goldwater addressed the crowd in his deep, plainly accented speech. He praised limited government, private property, and freedom.

Two lines from Goldwater's address would be remembered for years afterward. "I would remind you that extremism in the defense of liberty is no vice," the senator declared. The crowd erupted; air horns blared. It was more than forty seconds before he could continue. "And let me remind you also that moderation in the pursuit of justice is no virtue!"

Watching on television, Greenspan wanted to applaud along with the delegates in San Francisco. The play on words was sheer genius. Extremism, in being allied to liberty, had become virtuous—what more could a revolutionary desire to hear from a presidential candidate?[57] In her postconvention analysis in the *Objectivist Newsletter,* Rand made the same point. "Now consider the term extremism," she wrote. "Its alleged meaning is: 'intolerance, hatred, racism, bigotry, crackpot theories, incitement to violence.' Its real meaning is: 'the advocacy of capitalism.'"[58]

But the enthusiasm of Rand's circle was not shared by everyone. Goldwater's words helped his opponents to paint him as a radical. The *Washington Post* concluded that if he were elected, "there would be nothing left for us to do but pray."[59] Governor Edmund Brown of California declared that "the stench of fascism is in the air."[60] Even members of Goldwater's own party were concerned. Moderate Republicans stormed out of the convention, and Eisenhower himself said he would not campaign for Goldwater.[61] The candidate attempted to tack toward the center for the general election, but that merely infuriated the libertarian faithful who had won him the nomination in the first place. Having set himself up as the anticompromise candidate, Goldwater destroyed himself by compromising.

As Election Day approached, Rand grew disenchanted. She declared that Goldwater should show more confidence in his conservative convictions, and she took it upon herself to write a speech for him to deliver at one of his final campaign appearances, at New York's Madison Square Garden. But although she sent the speech to the candidate, Goldwater ignored it; and when he faced the electorate a week or so later, his defeat was crushing. Outside the Deep South, where whites rallied to him thanks to his opposition to the Civil Rights Act, Goldwater won only his home state of Arizona, and then only just. It was the most lopsided popular vote since 1820.

Yet for Ayn Rand and Alan Greenspan, there was still much to look forward to. They blamed the setback not on conservatism but on the candidate: Goldwater had had "courage, frankness, integrity—and *nothing to say,*" Rand wrote afterward.[62] The candidate's lack of intellectual heft had been his main problem, she continued; Goldwater's speeches had reminded her of newspaper headlines running above empty columns.[63] It followed that the intellectual leaders of conservatism needed only to wait patiently. Soon a fresh election cycle would begin. As Greenspan had declared in his lectures, the day of laissez-faire was surely approaching.

Book II

THE POLITICIAN

Six

A LIBERTARIAN
FOR NIXON

On a Wednesday evening in July 1967, two white Newark police-men arrested a black cabdriver and beat him so badly that he could not walk. As they dragged him into the Fourth Police Pre-cinct on Seventeenth Avenue, they were spotted by residents across the street, and news of the brutality soon spread around the city. A few pro-testers hurled rocks at the Fourth Precinct that night; and the next eve-ning a larger crowd assembled, along with some expectant TV trucks. A woman with a crowbar stepped out of the crowd and began to smash the windows of the police station, and suddenly people were running down the streets, looting Almor Furniture, Morris's Dress Shop, and any other establishment that appeared to have a white owner. Molotov cocktails were hurled into the ransacked premises; fires soon spread over a dozen blocks; and the city fathers hit the panic button. New Jersey state troopers and the National Guard were summoned to restore order, and the result was a shooting spree far worse than the looting spree. A ten-year-old was killed by a stray bullet that hit him behind the ear. A mother leaning from her window was mistaken for a sniper and slain by a bullet to the neck. Finally, on Monday, July 17, the governor withdrew his men, after more than four days of battle.[1]

That same Monday, fifteen miles east of Newark in the very different setting of Manhattan, a baby-faced political operative named Pat Buchanan was hammering out a memo to his boss, Richard Nixon. He began by introducing an economist, Alan Greenspan, "a most level-headed and bright fellow." Then he explained that he had sought out Greenspan's counsel on "the Negro thing"—shorthand for the riots that had been breaking out sporadically since the summer of 1965, when the Los Angeles district of Watts had witnessed thirty-four deaths in six chaotic days. Buchanan had asked Greenspan how Nixon, already an undeclared contender for the Republican presidential nomination in 1968, could propose economic assistance that might assuage black rage while still sounding fiscally responsible. Greenspan had answered with bracing libertarian purity. "He said flatly that the Negro problem is not an economic problem and it is dangerous to think of its solution in financial terms," Buchanan reported.[2]

Three years after the excitement and disappointment of Barry Goldwater's campaign, Greenspan was wading into politics again—this time much more deeply. Around the time the Newark riots started, a Columbia University professor named Marty Anderson had suggested that he join the small group of advisers clustering around Nixon, and Greenspan had jumped at the opportunity. He had met Anderson, who was ten years his junior, when the younger man attended one of his objectivist lectures on the Economics of a Free Society; they had gone out for coffee afterward with Ayn Rand, and Anderson had observed how Rand deferred to Greenspan on all matters economic.[3] Over the next three years, Greenspan had found in Anderson a like-minded libertarian and, unusually for such a loner, a close friend; perhaps it helped that Anderson was an independent spirit, too, and that he shared Greenspan's experience of growing up with separated parents. By 1967, Anderson and Greenspan were starting to write a book together—a statement of libertarian economics based on Greenspan's lectures—and were hanging out on weekends with Anderson's girlfriend, Annelise, a hip, miniskirted doctoral student who wore her hair hanging loose to her waist. The trio would tool around in Greenspan's convertible Cadillac and listen to music in his latest trophy acquisition: an apartment in the brand-new, ostentatiously opulent United Nations

Plaza. The skyscraper had been constructed by Alcoa, a consulting client. In exchange for buying in early, Greenspan had secured a bargain.[4]

When Anderson landed a position as domestic policy adviser to Nixon in the summer of 1967, the book collaboration with Greenspan had to be shelved. But Anderson asked his friend to comment on his first policy paper, a recommendation to abolish the military draft.[5] As libertarians, Anderson and Greenspan had no trouble agreeing that conscription was an odious imposition on freedom, and after their successful partnership on that first paper, Anderson proposed that Greenspan meet the other members of the fledgling Nixon team to see if he could join the effort. By coincidence, Nixon's chief talent scout turned out to be Leonard Garment, a lawyer who had played jazz with Henry Jerome at the same time as Greenspan, more than two decades earlier. With both Garment and Anderson behind him, the stars seemed to be aligned; and soon Greenspan found himself sitting across an ill-lit restaurant table from Pat Buchanan, the young chief of staff, and explaining his views on the economy, the federal budget, and the "Negro thing." Buchanan was there with Ray Price, a Nixon speechwriter, who was struck by a line that Greenspan tossed out, suggesting that Nixon should move the nation "not left, not right, but forward."[6] The phrase seemed to reveal an appetite for trite political catch lines, suggesting that Greenspan aspired to be much more than a dry business economist. But dry he certainly could be. He held forth slowly and solemnly, not so much speaking as declaiming. During the course of that introductory dinner, he suffered his new acquaintances to endure a long lecture on the gold standard.[7]

Looking back on this period, Greenspan cast his involvement with Nixon as an unplanned adventure, a coincidental by-product of his friendship with Marty Anderson. "If it were not for Anderson, I may have made a lot of money being a private economist but that would have been it," he said, suggesting that he would not otherwise have ventured the career leap from New York to Washington.[8] Yet the tone of Greenspan's objectivist lectures indicates that he had been itching to turn his libertarian philosophy into a political program; and his bond with Anderson, a man who quixotically rang doorbells for Goldwater's campaign in the unpromising territory of the Upper West Side, further suggests that he was ready to do electoral battle if the right opportunity presented itself. His reputation as a private economist was still growing—he was the "kind of person who knew how many thousand flat-headed bolts were used in a 1964 Chevrolet and what it would do to the economy if you took out three of them," as a marveling acquaintance put it.[9] But having succeeded financially, and having completed the project of thinking through his Randian ideas, Greenspan was ready to add a new dimension to his life. Lacking the family responsibilities that anchor many adults as they pass their fortieth birthday, he needed the next challenge.

Besides, if Greenspan felt strongly about politics at the time of his Randian lectures, he felt even more strongly by 1967: in the intervening years, Lyndon Johnson had led the country on a course that made Kennedy look conservative. In the span of a single Congress, in 1965–66, Johnson had signed laws committing the government to provide health care for the poor and elderly as well as funding for education and the arts—all abominations to a libertarian. Johnson had also pushed Kennedy's economic policies to their logical extreme. In 1964 he had delivered a powerful fiscal stimulus by signing tax cuts into law, and he had proceeded to bully the Federal Reserve to keep interest rates as low as possible. When the Fed made a show of resistance, Johnson summoned William McChesney Martin, the Fed chairman, to his Texas ranch and physically shoved him around his living room, yelling in his face, "Boys are dying in Vietnam, and Bill Martin doesn't care!"[10]

If the tax cuts and low interest rates caused inflationary pressure, Johnson believed he could deal with it with more bullying and manipulation. When aluminum makers raised prices in 1965, Johnson ordered up sales from the government's strategic stockpile to push prices back down again. When copper companies raised prices, he fought back by restricting exports of the metal and scrapping tariffs so as to usher in more imports. The president battled uppity prices for household appliances, paper cartons, newsprint, men's underwear, women's hosiery, glass containers, cellulose, and air conditioners; when egg prices rose in 1966, he had the surgeon general issue a warning on the hazards of cholesterol in eggs.[11] It was just as libertarians had feared. The fine-tuners' ambition to achieve "full" employment while containing inflation was driving them to pile intervention upon intervention.

Meanwhile, the mood of the nation was shifting, reinforcing Greenspan's sense that politics was calling him. After the prosperous harmony of the 1950s and the heady optimism of Kennedy's New Frontier, American society seemed to be coming apart at the seams. The dignified pacifism of the early 1960s civil rights movement had given way to the Black Power rhetoric of Stokely Carmichael, who in 1966 stood up in Canton, Mississippi, and declared, "The only way we are going to stop them from whuppin' us is to take over. We've been saying freedom for six years and we ain't got nothin.'"[12] The women's rights movement was growing more radical, too: the early 1960s literary feminism of Helen Gurley Brown and Betty Friedan was making way for a more flamboyant variety which, by 1968, would involve the ritual dumping of girdles, bras, high-heeled shoes, false lashes, hair curlers, and other objects of female "enslavement" into a "freedom trash can."[13] Half a world away in Indochina, an American force that had numbered under a thousand in 1960 exploded to a half-million troops by the summer of 1967, pushing the cumulative death toll for American servicemen above ten thousand.[14] With draft notices going out to an average of a thousand college-aged men each day at the war's peak, university campuses became a hotbed for antiwar agitation that soon spilled out from the ivory towers and into the streets.[15] "Never have the young been so assertive or so articulate, so well educated or so worldly," *Time* marveled in declaring the under-25 crowd its "Man of the Year" in 1966.[16] The question was whether this rambunctious new force would shatter the establishment that had borne it.

To a libertarian business consultant now entering middle age, this cultural revolt was not appealing. Greenspan dressed himself each morning in a crisp white dress shirt and a neatly pressed dark suit, not tie-dyes or bell-bottoms. He kept his hair short and swept straight back from his forehead like the matinee idols of his youth, and his idea of a late-night jam session involved playing Bach and Beethoven on the clarinet to the accompaniment of a piano and violin.[17] "Turn on, tune in, and drop out" was not his thing; he hailed from a generation in which people smoked pipes—and put tobacco in them.[18] Besides, his mind was molded to an era far older than the one that he was born into. A man who revered the rugged individualism of the nineteenth century could not be in sync with the sixties.

Barely ten minutes' walk north from Greenspan's office, the cityscape itself screamed out that his ideals were in retreat, routed by a tide that was anathema to him. By the summer of 1967, the warren of social service agencies surrounding City Hall was doling out antipoverty funding "like a corner candy store," as even the city's welfare commissioner conceded.[19] The relentless growth of welfare spending was muscling out other parts of the budget, forcing the city to economize on police equipment and teacher salaries. Meanwhile, across City Hall Park, construction equipment chugged away on the early stages of a colossal $200 million Civic Center project financed by the Department of Housing and Urban Development, another Johnson creation.[20] Beneath the blades of the bulldozers patrolling the site lay the remains of handsome nineteenth-century Greek Revival and Victorian structures razed to make way for collectivist modernity.[21] For Greenspan or any other conservative who might have gazed upon the rubble, the metaphor would have been obvious.

Ten days after the end of the Newark riots, Greenspan followed up on his dinner with Nixon's advisers. "I should like to outline a policy position which I believe could be very effective for Mr. Nixon," he announced in a memo. Over the next two pages he rehearsed his libertarian creed, attacking the Johnson administration's policies for distorting the economy, stoking civil strife, and weakening America's international standing.[22] The root of the problem lay in the economics of the New Frontier, which Greenspan had criticized before: reckless budget deficits compelled fine-tuners to meddle with prices to keep the lid on inflation. But the habit of intervention had recently taken on a new dimension, Greenspan insisted. Welfare schemes were not only expanding, and thereby stoking deficits and inflation; they were breeding an entitlement mental-ity, a self-pitying expectation of government handouts, the opposite of the sturdy nineteenth-century self-sufficiency that Greenspan idolized. Each new government program reinforced the presumption that government should help, which in turn created more pressure to increase welfare spend-ing. "Once the principle of massive government assistance to any special group in the society is accepted, there is an open-ended expectation from all groups which can never be fulfilled," Greenspan lamented. Lyndon Johnson's inflation was not just a monetary problem; it was a state of mind, a crisis of too many social demands chasing too few possible providers of social services.

With the violence in Newark still fresh in his mind, Greenspan pitched the Nixon team on his theory of its causes. Material deprivation was not the source of the disturbances: "The average Negro family income in the United States would be considered modest affluence in virtually every other area of the world," Greenspan insisted. What ailed America's black population was not so much poverty as *anti*poverty efforts—"massive hand-out programs" which "have the ultimate effect of only degrading the Negroes as individuals and have led to the current upsurge in racism and class antagonism." And if the cause of the riots lay in inflated expectations of what government could deliver, the riots would intensify so long as lib-erals set the tone. "If the summer of 1967 is bad, the summer of 1968 is bound to be worse," Greenspan predicted.

Not everyone on Nixon's team shared Greenspan's perspective. Ray Price, who in his past career as a newspaperman had penned an editorial endorsing Johnson over Goldwater, recoiled at his opinions. "Frankly, I don't think this Greenspan memo adds up to a hell of a lot," he wrote to Buchanan in August. "He seems to posit the political debate as a simple choice between 'government handouts' and 'freedom of the individual,' with 'principle' of course equated with individual freedom. If every Fed-eral program for education, jobs, etc., is simply viewed as another hand-out, we might as well give up on this old land of ours. Freedom, yes; but freedom has many facets, and freedom from government is only one of 'em. Freedom from want and freedom from fear, freedom of movement, freedom to develop one's capacities, etc., all are among the freedoms we have to try to develop. . . . I think Greenspan's notion of 'principle' is too much one of dogmatic rigidity."[23]

Price's reservations did not deter Greenspan. He had an effective ally in the conservative Buchanan, who, at the tender age of twenty-eight, was already showing the pugnacious will that would make him a formidable populist presidential candidate and entertaining TV brawler. Buchanan took delivery of Greenspan's memo, underlined large portions of it, and where Greenspan urged Nixon to "convey an image of principle" rather than offering handouts, he wrote "good" in the margin. Then he forwarded the missive to Nixon with a cover note: "This fellow is an economist and a budgetary expert but more than that he is a sound thinker on a number of subjects." In early August, Buchanan followed up by sending Nixon two Townsend-Greenspan client letters, which fiercely denounced Johnson's budget policies as duplicitous and inflationary. On August 14 Nixon wrote to Buchanan, saying that "I think I should have a talk with Allen Greenspan."

A few days later, Greenspan walked into the lobby of 20 Broad Street, immediately adjacent to the New York Stock Exchange and just three blocks from his office. He made his way up to the twenty-fourth floor, to the offices of Nixon Mudge Rose Guthrie Alexander & Mitchell, the nearly century-old white-shoe law firm that had taken in the former vice president following his defeats in the 1960 presidential and 1962 California gubernatorial elections.[24] Nixon was ensconced in a lush corner office. Keys from major cities in Europe and Asia lined the walls; commemorative gavels rested on the walnut furniture; a gargantuan globe stood imposingly to one side, as if set there by an exhausted Atlas.[25] Behind Nixon's desk chair, a gallery of signed photographs from various heads of state filled an immense wooden cabinet, suggesting an old man stuck in past glories, not an ascendant candidate looking toward his next victory.[26]

Nixon greeted Greenspan and skipped past the introductory chitchat. He lobbed a series of probing questions on economic policy at his guest, the words flowing out of him in perfect sentences. In response, Greenspan launched into a long discourse on the federal budget, philosophizing about how statistics on taxes and spending could tell stories about the political styles of various presidents. As the conversation continued, each man grew increasingly impressed by the power of the other's intellect.[27] Nixon could see that Greenspan was a walking encyclopedia of statistical wisdom, the source of numbers and facts that would lend his candidacy authority. Greenspan could see that if he had ever harbored doubts about Nixon's potential, he should dismiss them straightaway—this was no washed-up politician grateful for the company. And yet there was something about Nixon that still left Greenspan with an odd feeling. The candidate's syntax was too exquisite; his attire was too impeccable; there was an impression of stiffness.[28] Eight years earlier, on a visit as vice president to Moscow, this same Nixon had had the panache to hold an impromptu "kitchen debate" against Soviet premier Nikita Khrushchev before an array of flashbulbs. But now, in the comfort of his own office, he seemed almost wooden. Sincerity, Greenspan would learn, did not come easily to Nixon.

Beyond the calm of the candidate's office, America was broiling. The Newark violence was only one of forty-six riots in that summer of 1967.[29] A total of eighty-one people died in the mayhem, and the destruction of property ran into the millions of dollars.[30] Polls suddenly found "crime and lawlessness" rocketing toward the top of citizens' concerns, displacing the cost of living and unemployment.[31]

Undeterred by the moderates on the campaign staff, Greenspan pressed his libertarian diagnosis more forcefully than ever. In a four-page memo to Nixon in late September, he blamed the urban riots squarely on the Great Society programs.[32] Government handouts represented a tacit admission of guilt by white Americans for the supposed exploitation of blacks, he charged; but no such exploitation was taking place—blacks who worked for white-owned companies or shopped in white-owned stores were freely choosing to do so.[33] By offering federal programs to make up for alleged exploitation, whites were guilty of claiming to be guilty when they were really innocent. They were providing black radicals with an excuse. "Any attempt in the present context on the part of the whites to improve the situation by handouts has been read as a sanction for violence," Greenspan contended.

Greenspan's communications with Nixon in these first few months would have made Ayn Rand proud of him. Like Rand herself in 1964, he was supporting a Republican presidential contender while also attempting to steer him in a libertarian direction. He was not always succeeding, to be sure. On September 26, the same day that Greenspan sent his riots memo, Nixon published his own reaction to the urban violence in *Reader's Digest*.[34] Echoing Greenspan, Nixon argued that the riots were not simply the result of poverty; they reflected a nationwide decline in respect for authority and the rule of law. But if Nixon's diagnosis resembled Greenspan's, his prescription veered in a different direction. Whereas Greenspan wanted to get government out of the inner cities and empower local businesses with tax cuts, Nixon called for the hiring of more and better police officers.[35]

Snubbed but undeterred, Greenspan made a bid to take his arguments public. At the start of November, he proposed to Nixon that he be allowed to draft an article on "What's Wrong with the Great Society" for publication in the *Harvard Business Review* "or some equivalent."[36] The article would convince readers that the Great Society was fundamentally "degenerative," that it was a cynical vote-buying scheme targeted at specific voting blocs, and that it would lead inevitably to budget deficits, inflation, regulatory controls, and "a divided, wretched social order." Again, Greenspan's proposal was ignored; Nixon was not about to embrace Greenspan's libertarian principles wholeheartedly. There was a reason why he balanced conservative advisers such as Buchanan and Marty Anderson with liberals such as Ray Price; the country had moved steadily to the left, and he was not going to win the presidency on a platform to restore the nineteenth century. Somehow, the Depression of the 1930s had increased Americans' appetite for government; and yet the opposite of the Depression in the booming 1950s and 1960s had further increased their appetite for government. Nixon could attack the Great Society at the margins, but a full-frontal assault would be electoral madness.

At the beginning of 1968, Buchanan asked Greenspan to write a statement for the campaign on farm policy. Federal subsidies to agriculture were among the more egregious special-interest handouts, and Greenspan cogently explained the laissez-faire case for ending them. The Nixon campaign followed its usual procedures, circulating the draft statement to its allies, and pretty soon Greenspan was on the phone with Buchanan.

"The Dakota wolves are after me," Buchanan remembers Greenspan saying. The lead wolf was Karl Mundt, a formidable South Dakota senator who reacted furiously to anything that threatened to reduce subsidies for his state's farmers.[37]

Buchanan briefed Nixon on the standoff. Greenspan had written a forthright anti-subsidy memo, and now farm-state senators were howling for his blood.

"They wouldn't be after Greenspan if he hadn't messed something up," Nixon responded.

Taking his cue from the candidate, Buchanan set out to repair the damage by writing a brand-new statement on the future of the nation's farms, this time praising subsidies effusively. Having composed something suitably emphatic about Nixon's unshakable commitment to agriculture, Buchanan made a trip to Washington to deliver his text to the Dakota wolf in person.

The senator called him in and sat him down. "Read it," he ordered.

Buchanan read the statement, which ended with a gushing quote from William Jennings Bryan's celebrated address to the Democratic National Convention in 1896. Bryan's oration is remembered as the Cross of Gold speech—the most famous attack in American history on Greenspan's beloved gold standard—but it was also a hymn to the heartland, to the men who break their backs to feed the soft people of the cities. Without the farmers of the heartland, the portly financiers of New York and Chicago would be forced to raise livestock in their living rooms. "Destroy our farms and the grass will grow in the streets of every city in the country," Bryan thundered.

"That's a wonderful speech," the wolf said, and dispatched Buchanan from his office.[38]

Humiliated by the Dakota senator, Greenspan might have given up on politics and returned to a life of lucrative business and Randian pamphleteering. But he did not. Money interested him only so much, and Rand's Collective was losing its allure; the cult was heading for a messy split, precipitated when Nathaniel Branden embarked on a romance with a young actress, causing the jilted high priestess to denounce him in a furious open letter. In any case, Greenspan had caught the political bug. The heroes of *Atlas Shrugged* might have retreated from an unjust society and left it to rot, but Greenspan was discovering that counseling the potential leader of the free world could be an addictive habit.

The presidential contest was just getting interesting. Nixon moved his campaign operation out of his law firm toward the end of 1967, and his people found quarters in Midtown; they were taking on new staff, preparing for the candidate's formal announcement. The new premises on Fifth Avenue were makeshift, with cardboard-quality walls; but the chaos and improvisation only added to the excitement.[39] Policy positions, draft speeches, advertising strategies, and logistical preparations flew about the office, and the buzz and throb of a major presidential bid echoed within every campaign aide who dreamed of working in the White House. One day the sympathetic *Time* journalist Nick Timmesch came by with the news that George Romney was running hard in New Hampshire, and Nixon risked falling behind if he did not jump in soon. On another occasion, Clare Luce—the writer, ambassador, seductress, and grandest of New York's grandes dames—paid a surprise visit to the campaign office, fizzing with wit and elegance.[40] The Nixon team threw a Christmas party at the Lombardy Hotel, and Greenspan showed up with a stunning woman on his arm. Her name has been swallowed by time, but she was enough to cause campaign colleagues to recalibrate their view of him.[41]

On January 31, 1968, just hours before the filing deadline, Nixon crossed the Rubicon. He plunged into the primary race, promising a crowd in New Hampshire the next day that he would address problems "beyond politics." His staff moved into more comfortable offices at 450 Park Avenue, with some overflow space across the street; and with this new phase of the battle, fresh opportunities opened. Marty Anderson headed out on the road with the candidate, leaving a vacuum at headquarters that Greenspan filled eagerly. With the exception of Fridays, when he was needed at the Townsend-Greenspan office to make sure the weekly mailings went out to the clients, Greenspan began to spend much of his time at Nixon's headquarters, preparing memos and updates for the traveling team on domestic and economic policy.[42] The campaign command center featured a teletype machine, a primitive fax machine, and a red phone reserved exclusively for calls from Nixon's field team. Whenever the candidate stopped for a few hours at a motel, Greenspan would hurry to get draft press releases and talking points across to Anderson before he headed off for the next rally.[43]

Some Nixon advisers drew salaries as high as $3,000 per month—more than $20,000 per month in 2015 dollars. Greenspan refused to be paid anything at all, a measure both of his substantial wealth and of his desire for independence.[44] But even without pay, he put his shoulder to the wheel, expanding his remit beyond economic and domestic policy and into the territory of opinion polling. Committing not only himself but his employees to this challenge, he set the Townsend-Greenspan team to work collecting the results of state and local polls; then he compared the latest readings with past trends and extrapolated likely numbers for states that had not been surveyed. It was a classic Greenspan data-sleuthing exercise, with the twist that his consulting firm had recently acquired its first computer. The futuristic IBM 1130 was the size of an office desk and boasted eight kilobytes of memory, a fraction of the capacity of a modern smartphone but positively thrilling to the pioneer geeks of the mid-1960s. An hourly employee at Townsend-Greenspan would transfer reams of raw polling data onto punch cards, then feed the cards into the majestic new machine, which strained and grunted for two hours before noisily spitting out an intricate matrix of columns and rows on sheets of perforated paper. The computer was used so extensively that the operator once logged ninety-six hours in a single week. He clocked up so much overtime pay that Kathryn Eickhoff, a salaried employee, grew irritated that he was earning more than she was.[45]

Greenspan's opinion-poll analysis boosted his standing in the campaign, inoculating him from the danger that his impractical libertarian views might marginalize him. Armed with his computer printouts, he became the man who knew; he could instruct Nixon's advisers on how they were faring in each state, which issues would sway voters most in which region, and what the likely outcome would be in terms of the popular vote and the balance in the electoral college. Starting in the 1950s, computerized forecasts had been used by news organizations to aid in reporting elections, and John Kennedy's advisers had used computer simulations to test how voters felt about the candidate's Catholicism.[46] But Greenspan pushed the art of polling analysis further; and when it came time for the Republican convention, in August 1968, his prediction that Nixon was the likeliest among Republicans to capture the White House may even have persuaded wavering delegates to throw their votes to him.

On the evening of Thursday, April 4, 1968, a shot snapped the truce in America's inner cities. As he stood on the second-floor balcony of a Memphis motel, Martin Luther King Jr. was struck by a sniper's bullet to the jaw, which shattered several vertebrae and severed his jugular vein. The death of a black civil rights leader at the hands of a white man reignited urban riots, culminating in the arrest of some twenty thousand people. To Nixon and his supporters, their calls for tougher law enforcement had been richly vindicated. But on the night of the assassination, a politician with a different perspective was emerging on the national stage. Having declared his candidacy for the Democratic presidential nomination, Robert F. Kennedy was on a plane, bound for Indianapolis.

Bobby Kennedy learned of King's shooting from a reporter on his aircraft. Once he landed, the Indianapolis police chief entreated him to stay out of black neighborhoods for fear of a riot, but Kennedy proceeded directly to a wind-blown lot surrounded by tenements, wearing his dead brother's old topcoat to protect him from the elements.[47] Standing before an audience of a thousand, he pulled out a few crumpled handwritten notes from his pocket and accepted the grave duty of informing the crowd of King's killing. As they gasped, Kennedy assured them he could feel their loss; after all, his own brother had been assassinated. Then he continued:

> What we need in the United States is not division; what we need in the United States is not hatred; what we need in the United States is not violence or lawlessness; but love and wisdom, and compassion toward one another, and a feeling of justice toward those who still suffer within our country, whether they be white or they be black. . . .

The speech left Kennedy's staff weeping. It succeeded with his audience, too; people later said that Indianapolis was spared destructive riots by Kennedy's inspired performance. The candidate, for his part, appeared grim but strong; few others in the nation had been forced to reckon with a political killing in the intimate way he had. After his speech in Indianapolis, Kennedy flew to Washington, D.C., where he toured a riot-torn section of the city, again defying advisers who warned him that his presence among looted and burning buildings might not be received kindly.[48] He attended King's funeral in Atlanta, viewing the body and marching in the procession. "Well, we still have Robert Kennedy," one of King's close supporters, John Lewis, later recalled telling himself.[49]

Watching the news from New York, Greenspan could barely contain himself. On April 8, the day before King's funeral, he sent a memo to "DC," a code name for Nixon that the campaign had adopted to preserve deniability if the documents fell into the hands of journalists. Greenspan accused Kennedy of "attempting to cash in on the tragic events of recent days by fostering guilt among the whites and accordingly presenting himself as a moral leader." Beneath his guise of righteousness, Kennedy was ducking his duty to come out and say clearly that violence was unacceptable. "He must be called on this," Greenspan insisted. "Does RFK consider violence in a free society morally justified or not? This is not an issue for vagueness or equivocation. It is important to tell the Black Power militants they are wrong. . . . It is not possible to be too strong on this issue." In Greenspan's eyes, the problem with Kennedy mirrored the problem with liberals in general—although they might pay lip service to nonviolence, they nevertheless accommodated violence by rushing to suggest that the rioters had fair cause to be angry. Cranking up his indignation to maximum volume, Greenspan went on: "[T]he Black Power militants are wrong. There is no conceivable moral justification for violence in a free society. This is not Nazi Germany or the Soviet Union."[50]

It was one of those moments when Greenspan's libertarian views got the better of his judgment. On questions of statistics, he was relentlessly empirical—ideology was subservient to data. But occasionally, when he strayed beyond the realm of numbers, he was less good at evaluating the evidence before his eyes: thus he had denounced all antitrust law, despite the concentrated nature of the economy in which he worked; and thus he was traducing Robert Kennedy. Far from equivocating on violence, Kennedy had actually spoken out the day after King's assassination, lamenting that Americans "seemingly tolerate a rising level of violence that ignores our common humanity."[51] And far from siding with the radical black leaders, Kennedy was in fact reviled by them. "The honky from honky Lyndon Johnson to honky Bobby Kennedy will not co-opt Dr. Martin Luther King," Stokely Carmichael told reporters the morning after King's assassination; "Bobby Kennedy pulled that trigger just as well as anybody else."[52] In assailing Kennedy, Greenspan was picking on the wrong target. If anyone was seeking to cash in politically on the shocking events of April, perhaps it was Alan Greenspan.

Nixon was too savvy to take Greenspan's advice; he never attacked Kennedy for his actions after King's killing. But he did adopt another Greenspan idea—a push for "black capitalism" in the inner cities. At campaign events, he lamented white America's attempts to assuage its guilt by buying off black Americans with an escalating array of social programs. "We have reached a point at which more of the same will only result in more of the same frustration, more of the same explosive violence, and more of the same fear," Nixon argued in one April speech, hewing closely to Greenspan's thesis that government aid and ghetto violence were caught in a vicious cycle.[53] Nixon would then lay out Greenspan's program of stimulating inner-city businesses with tax breaks—there would be credits to build housing, train low-skilled workers, and encourage businesses to locate in poor urban districts. This new program for black capitalism would replace the handout culture of government programs, fostering a sense of ownership and pride, and removing the frustrations that bred violence.

Nixon's embrace of Greenspan's ideas about black capitalism signaled that the fight with the Dakota wolves had been forgiven. Taking this cue, Greenspan's ally, Pat Buchanan, resumed his efforts to expand Green-span's influence. On May 18, 1968, Buchanan prepared a memo for Nixon, reporting on a mutiny at the campaign's Park Avenue headquarters. The cause of the trouble, Buchanan insisted, was Dr. Glenn Olds, a liberal academic best known for helping to create a domestic counterpart to the Peace Corps. As a favor to one of Nixon's business supporters, this Great Society professor had been given a role in the campaign, and he was developing all kinds of schemes that Buchanan found preposterous. The professor spoke of "doubling and tripling" the research staff to assist him in his head-hunting efforts, declaring that he meant to identify 2,500 people to man a future Nixon administration—"To Olds, his authority apparently is very great," Buchanan wrote tartly. Several members of the research team were threatening to quit if Olds was kept on, Buchanan asserted. "They speak of him as a 'totalitarian liberal'. . . . What they want is for Alan Greenspan—who will quit his job and go to work full-time— to be named Director of Research-Domestic Policy." Buchanan touted Greenspan as "a committed RN man, a hard worker, willing to give up his job. He has the confidence and support of everyone in research and they like the guy. . . . I do recommend that in any choice between the once-seen Olds and the often-seen Alan Greenspan, we come down on the side of Greenspan."

Nixon signed off on the promotion, and Greenspan was installed as the campaign's director of domestic policy research.

S ome two weeks later, on June 4, Robert Kennedy won California's Democratic primary. The results came in around midnight, and the candidate addressed his jubilant supporters in the ballroom of a Los Angeles hotel. Afterward the hotel manager led him off toward another room where the press awaited him. As Kennedy walked through the hotel's kitchen area, down a corridor narrowed by an ice machine, he stopped to shake hands with a busboy, and in that moment a Palestinian immigrant named Sirhan Sirhan stepped down from a low tray stacker and rushed forward and shot him. To many Americans, Kennedy's assassination marked the end of an era, burying the nation's postwar sense of possibility and progress. "Some men see things as they are and say why. I dream things that never were and say why not," Kennedy had declared during his campaign.[54] At his funeral in New York's St. Patrick's Cathedral, his younger brother Teddy quoted those words. The liberal cause had lost its leader.

Once the initial outpouring of grief faded, a cold fear possessed Americans. Assassinations had felled two national figures in two months, not to mention a president five years earlier. The nation was in the grip of shootouts between the police and the militants of the new Black Panther Party, firebombings by segregationist Ku Klux Klan vigilantes, strikes by labor unions, and protests by student radicals. Television viewers reacted by making ratings hits out of shows that stressed law and order, such as *Bonanza* and *Gunsmoke*. At Nixon headquarters on Park Avenue, the Secret Service determined that the candidate's office was insecure—he was a setup for a rifle bullet from the building across the street. The campaign moved Nixon into a room with less exposure, and the paneled office that had been prepared for him was assigned instead to the communications director. For the first few days, the communications man went uneasily about his work, glancing nervously out of the window.[55]

Nixon was well positioned for this climate of fear; he had been preaching authority over anarchy since the riots of the previous summer. But he faced a challenge from his right. George Wallace, the former Alabama governor now running as a segregationist independent, was haranguing the nation with a coarse version of Nixon's law-and-order policies, and working-class whites were flocking to him. "If I ever get to be President and any of these demonstrators lay down in front of my car, it'll be the last car they ever lay down in front of," Wallace growled, while lambasting welfare mothers for "breeding children as a cash crop."[56] Polls taken during the spring of 1968 showed Nixon losing several percentage points to Wallace nationwide, while in the states of the Deep South, Wallace was ahead of him. Riots in the ghettos following Kennedy's shooting only made Wallace stronger.

At the end of June, Greenspan's polling simulations convinced him that Nixon had to confront Wallace directly, though he was careful not to advise his boss to get down in the gutter. On July 4, he counseled Nixon to calibrate his statements so that they would "be loud enough for the George Wallace leaners to hear us, yet protect ourselves from charges of distortion."[57] "I suggest that rather than follow the George approach (which RN could never effectively emulate in any event) that we turn GW's simplisticness into 'Amateurism,'" Greenspan wrote in another memo, three days later. "While the local sheriff approach of 'knocking heads' may seem an emotionally satisfying solution to any particular riot, it will not bring tranquility to the streets of the nation. It will not allow the housewife to go shopping without looking over her shoulder."[58]

The following week Buchanan seized on Greenspan's polling results. In a memo dated July 13, 1968, he focused directly on Nixon's tactical dilemma: should he tack to the center, in an effort to steal votes from Democrats, or should he move right to siphon votes from Wallace? Nixon's moderate advisers favored the first route, not least because Nixon's support among Jewish and black voters languished in the single digits. But Buchanan gave the polling data a quite different spin. "All this endless talk we have been getting about RN losing unless he gets the Negro and Jewish vote is a pile of crap," he railed. "Since 1964 the Negroes are lost to the Republicans for a generation," he went on, referring to Goldwater's opposition to the Civil Rights Act; and "slobbering over the Israeli lobby is not going to get us anything." If blacks and Jews mattered, it was not because Nixon could win votes from them; it was merely that "the Negro loud-mouths are given access to the public communications media by a guilt-ridden establishment—and the Jews control that communications media. We don't want to antagonize these people—they can damage us. But they're not our voters; and if we go after them, we'll go down chasing a receding rainbow. The Irish, Italian, Polish Catholics of the big cities—these are our electoral majority—they, and the white Protestants of the South and Midwest and rural America." Capping off this outburst, Buchanan advised what he had often advised before: he pleaded with the candidate to listen more to Greenspan. It was vital, he insisted, "that Alan Greenspan be instructed to analyze the results of our polls." Evidently, Buchanan felt confident that Greenspan would support his ethnic strategy.

The morning after he fired off his memo, Buchanan set off with Greenspan for a meeting with the candidate.[59] Together with several other members of the Nixon staff, they assembled at New York's Marine Air Terminal, boarded a small chartered plane, and flew east over Long Island. Landing at East Hampton Airport, they switched to some waiting cars and drove on to Montauk, a small finger of land pointing out into the Atlantic. At the end of a winding dirt road, they reached a hilltop bungalow guarded by a pair of Secret Service men with walkie-talkies and sunglasses. More agents could be seen patrolling the scrub pine woods around the house. The visitors were shown into a glass-enclosed porch with a sparkling view out to the ocean.

Nixon entered, took a seat in an armchair, and propped his foot against a coffee table. He opened the meeting by laying down a rule: no discussion of running mates. Then he analyzed his campaign's prospects. In his failed presidential bid in 1960, he had sewn up 96 percent of the Republican vote, and he would need to do equally well this time. But since the King funeral three months earlier, the Wallace vote among Republicans had leaped from 2 percent to 8 percent. Nixon was losing twice as many

Republicans as he could afford; meanwhile, Wallace was stealing away independent voters whom Nixon also needed. In California in particular, Wallace supporters seemed likely to tip the state. If Nixon did nothing to check the insurgent, he faced electoral disaster.

Nixon went around the semicircle of advisers, a dozen or so men arranged on long couches. Each spoke for a few minutes, grappling with the question of how to attract the Wallace voter. As the Nixon speech-writer Richard Whalen later put it, intellectual voters wanted to know what the candidate thought about policy questions, but the lower-middle-class suburbanite wanted to know how the candidate *felt* about what he saw as *moral* issues. Yet if Nixon was going to show his feelings, he would have to shed his high-minded composure, and the establishment press would immediately denounce him. There was no easy solution to the candidate's predicament.

Feeling boxed in and frustrated, Nixon let loose a stream of invective. The blacks were against him. The Jews were against him. He cursed the whole world bitterly, and for a while his advisers paused to let him vent. To most of the men gathered around the candidate, there was nothing particularly shocking about this outburst. "Look, it was a very tense time; the idea that the guy blows up . . . So what?" Buchanan shrugged later.[60] But recalling this encounter years after the fact, Greenspan painted it as a turning point in his relationship with the candidate. "I saw a side of Nixon that absolutely devastated me," Greenspan said. "I had known him for months, worked with him for months and I had *never* heard a four-letter word come out of his mouth. He was always in a suit, a conservative lawyer from southern California, very smart. And then I saw this guy, who spewed out four-letter words that, having been in the music business, even *I* hadn't heard. And I said to myself, 'Oh my God, this is a Jekyll and Hyde.'"[61] The way Greenspan tells it, the meeting in Montauk decided him against taking a job in the administration after the election. "From that day forth I felt very uncomfortable and there wasn't even the slightest attraction to going in," he said.[62] "It so disturbed me that after the election, when I was invited to join the White House staff, I said, 'No, I much prefer to go back to my job.'"[63]

Nixon's performance that Sunday in Montauk was no doubt upsetting. Greenspan was a libertarian, an egalitarian, an instinctive opponent of social prejudice of all types; it cannot have been easy to stomach Nixon's vicious paranoia. But the idea that Greenspan made a principled decision to distance himself from Nixon is wrong. He had been perfectly happy to work closely with Buchanan, hardly a fount of racially inclusive views, and his polling analysis supported the theory that appeals to ethnic whites would be effective. Moreover, far from disengaging from the candidate in the weeks after Montauk, Greenspan redoubled his efforts to secure his election.

At the start of August 1968, Nixon descended on Miami Beach for the Republican convention. To television viewers, the setting at the Fontainebleau Hotel might have looked vaguely familiar—it was where James Bond had cheated death in the movie *Goldfinger*.[64] The Nixon operatives installed their candidate in a nearby Hilton, commandeering the top four floors and barricading the corridors with chicken wire fences covered in campaign posters. Thanks to some lobbying by Buchanan, Greenspan was squeezed into a room at the Hilton that he shared with another staffer. He wandered the corridors with his polling simulations to hand, eager to help wherever possible. At one point, Kathryn Eickhoff flew down from New York to bring him the latest printouts from the IBM 1130.

Having refused to discuss running mates at Montauk, the candidate announced his choice at the convention. Nixon was himself a robotic campaigner—a fellow Republican described him as "a walking box of circuits"—and he was far too insecure to elevate a man who might eclipse him. Even so, Nixon's selection made headlines for its blandness.

"I'm going to mention two words to you," a TV reporter told unsuspecting pedestrians after the running mate had been announced. "You tell me what they mean. The words are: Spiro Agnew."

"It's some kind of disease," said one man.

"It's some kind of egg," ventured another.

"He's a Greek who owns that shipbuilding firm," declared a third.

The running mate himself would not have batted an eye. "Spiro Agnew," admitted Spiro T. Agnew, "is not a household word."[65] The *Washington Post* dubbed Nixon's selection of Agnew "perhaps the most eccentric political appointment since the Roman Emperor Caligula named his horse a consul."[66]

Greenspan was among those who regretted Nixon's choice of running mate. He favored the hero of the right, California governor Ronald Reagan. But he was enjoying politics too much to be put off, and he was coming to understand that he must soft-pedal his conservatism. Ten days after the convention, on August 18, he became the subject of his first political newspaper profile, and it was not altogether welcome. The *Washington Post* columnist Hobart Rowen riffled through Greenspan's objectivist writings, quoting the lines that dramatized his distance from America's mainstream. "The entire structure of anti-trust statutes in this country is a jumble of economic irrationality and ignorance." "In the absence of the gold standard there is no way to protect savings from confiscation through inflation." "The welfare state is nothing more than a mechanism by which governments confiscate the wealth of the productive members of a society." Rowen strung the quotations together without comment, save for a final zinger: "It is strange to find a man somewhat to the right of McKinley as a key economic adviser to the new Nixon. Or is it?"[67]

A few days after the *Post* profile appeared, it was the Democrats' turn to stage a nominating convention. In anticipation of disturbances, seven-foot-tall barbed-wire fences surrounded the Chicago convention hall; bulletproof sheets of metal boarded up the gaps between pillars at the hall's entrance. But none of this was quite enough. For three days and three nights, rioters taunted the police, yelling "Fuck you, LBJ," "Sieg heil," and "Pig, pig, fascist pig." Thus provoked, the security men clubbed, Maced, and gassed the demonstrators, assaulting photographers and reporters for good measure.[68] Nixon's point man in Chicago, a young congressman by the name of Donald Rumsfeld, relayed the action unfolding below his hotel window. "They're breaking bones! Omigosh, look at that!" he told Nixon's political director by telephone.[69]

Nixon was delighted. To many working-class Democrats, the rioters were spoiled kids who had evaded the draft, loafed their way through college, and now traveled to Chicago to chant vulgarities at the very law enforcers who protected them. From the perspective of living rooms in small factory towns like Warren, Michigan—where one survey found only 4 percent of households thought the police had been "too rough"—such self-indulgence deserved a few good lumps; if this was what the Democratic Party had come to, they wanted nothing to do with it.[70] Opinion polls quickly registered the Chicago effect—a Townsend-Greenspan simulation showed Hubert Humphrey collecting only 11 electoral votes to Nixon's 461 in the wake of the convention.[71] Just one year earlier, when Greenspan had visited Nixon at the Rose law firm, pundits were barely admitting that Republicans had a shot at recapturing the White House. Now Greenspan found himself aboard a campaign that was heading for a landslide.

The day after the Democrats wrapped up their convention, Greenspan took stock of the political landscape. In another memo to DC—the Nixon code name—he thought his way onto the candidate's wavelength by invoking his previous presidential run in 1960. Then, Nixon's opponent, John F. Kennedy, had called for "a hopped-up America thrusting ahead to New Frontiers," Greenspan recalled. But now the national mood had turned. "The polls tell us that the country would like nothing better than to return to the quiescent, dull, 'boring,' environment of the 1950s." Given the mood of the nation, the bland and anonymous Spiro Agnew was an inspired choice for running mate, Greenspan maintained: "Charisma and pizzazz may be heavily discounted political assets." Nixon had positioned himself wisely as the man who could get the country back on track. "The remarkable performance of RN during the Republican Convention as a man of stability, coherence, and leadership has been quite effective," the memo insisted.[72]

Greenspan had come a great distance since his memos of the previous summer. Then he had fantasized about a "return to true liberalism." Now he was flattering the boss and parsing the polls for him. Whereas Ayn Rand had urged Barry Goldwater to stand up for libertarian principles in the fall of 1964, Greenspan now stressed that, to blunt the Democrats' attacks, Nixon should "not imply opposition to existing special interest welfare legislation."[73] Politics dominated Greenspan's thinking; much of his memo was devoted to positioning Nixon between Humphrey and Wallace, and to strategizing about how Nixon might carry off cosmetic shifts in his posture—shifts that would be "a matter of stress rather than content." In mid-September, Greenspan went so far as to warn Nixon of the political risks in specific proposals to cut government spending.[74] He was no longer the ideologue that Hobart Rowen imagined.

Greenspan still had one more lesson to learn, however. Not long before Election Day, a reporter quoted him as saying that Nixon "would be willing to take slightly more unemployment in the short run" for the sake of lower inflation. This doubtless reflected Greenspan's view—his critique of the New Frontier rested on the conviction that the Democrats were trying to push unemployment down too far, a folly that would ignite inflation and fail on its own terms. True to his new political persona, and betraying his old Randian one, Greenspan quickly disowned the quotation, insisting that his words had been taken out of context.[75] But the damage had been done. Humphrey seized the opening to excoriate Nixon for being willing to accept less than "full" employment. The Nixon men turned to Arthur Burns, Greenspan's professor from Columbia, to cast his student overboard. "I can say categorically," Burns told the *Washington Post*, "that this does not reflect Mr. Nixon's position. This world of ours won't accept anything but a full employment policy."[76]

Humphrey caught up with Nixon in the lead-up to Election Day. The race was too close to call after the polls closed, and the outcome remained uncertain throughout most of the evening. Around nine o'clock the next morning, Nixon climbed out of bed in his pajamas in the campaign's suite at the Waldorf Towers in Manhattan.[77] Turning on his television set, he found that the networks were calling the race in his favor; though the popular vote was remarkably close, he had won decisively in the electoral college. Having rallied resoundingly to Lyndon Johnson four years earlier, the American people had now repudiated him.

Nixon set up his transition headquarters at the Pierre in New York, the scene of Greenspan's wedding reception sixteen years earlier. Katharine Hepburn, Kirk Douglas, and the Greek royal couple were among the tenants at the Pierre, and Nixon moved into a kingly private suite with a fireplace and large French mirrors and an office with a fruitwood dining table.[78] Two banquet rooms with crystal chandeliers were converted into a briefing room and workstations for the press; and in a sign that budget cuts were not necessarily at the top of Nixon's agenda, the cost was passed along to federal taxpayers.[79] Meanwhile, Nixon's lieutenants busied themselves with the big question of the moment: which campaign adviser would land which job in the new administration.

In the days following victory, the campaign's chief of staff dispatched a special assistant to take the temperature of key advisers. After a week, the assistant reported back. Bill Safire, one of the campaign speechwriters, wanted a role on the president's staff: "He is quite willing and ready to sell his business to take such a position," the assistant reported. Marty Anderson, Greenspan's fellow libertarian, was willing to quit Columbia University: "Highly pleased with the prospect of a role in research at the White House," the assistant's memo noted. So it went on down the list—each campaign aide was as eager as the other. The only exception was the first name on the assistant's note. Alan Greenspan, the assistant reported, "is basically not interested in a government position except, as he put it, one or two that would be presumptuous for him to mention. By this, I take it he means Secretary of the Treasury or Director of the Bureau of the Budget."[80] The first guess was on the mark. Looking back on this period, Kathryn Eickhoff recalls that Greenspan secretly aspired to no less a role than that of Treasury secretary.

Whatever his misgivings about Nixon, Greenspan was ready to work for him. But he was not going to Washington for just any job; his life in New York was too lucrative and fulfilling. He had run his consultancy since the age of thirty-two. Now, aged forty-two, he was happy to adapt himself to the commando atmosphere of a campaign, but he was not prepared to be a cog in the bureaucracy of government—he would have to be a big shot. The Nixon men, for their part, were not convinced that

Greenspan was sufficiently reliable to be given one of the top jobs. He had offered loyal political counsel in the campaign's last stretch; but his early libertarianism was not forgotten, and his truthful gaffe about full employment hurt him. Though he had labored mightily to turn himself into a political animal, Greenspan had begun his conversion just a little late; and Nixon had never really grown to trust him. It was a lesson that Greenspan would later take to heart as he advanced in Washington.

Seven

DO-NOTHINGISM

On January 20, 1969, Richard Nixon took the oath of office in a pavilion at the east front of the Capitol. Although he was in many ways the anti-Kennedy—brooding and suspicious rather than confident and sunny—his economic message reprised the rhetoric of the New Frontier. Looking down upon the crowd beneath him, Nixon saluted America's extraordinary prosperity—"No people has ever been so close to the achievement of a just and abundant society," he exclaimed— and he affirmed his faith in fine-tuning, promising that America had "learned at last to manage a modern economy to assure its continued growth." With America's output expanding for the ninety-sixth consecutive month and unemployment at just 3.3 percent, the crowd had every reason to share the new president's optimism. Living standards were rising; the stock market index had more than doubled in a decade. What could possibly go wrong? The government was engineering the smooth growth of the economy. The dollar didn't fluctuate because it was pegged to gold. Interest rates moved within a narrow range and were restrained by regulation.

While Nixon was delivering his happy pitch, Greenspan's long-standing doubts about the New Frontier were nearing the point of vindication. In the spring of 1968, inflation had topped 4 percent for the first time since the Korean War, and by the time of the inaugural speech, both fiscal and monetary policy had been adjusted accordingly. Public spending had been curbed, with Lyndon Johnson's last budget actually yielding a surplus, and the Federal Reserve had started to raise interest rates.[1] This double-barreled tightening would have been disconcerting at the best of times, but there was a special reason to be fearful now. For the first time in Greenspan's adult life, companies and households had substantial borrowings: the total stock of private debt, which stood at 52 percent of GDP in 1945, had doubled to 107 percent by the time Nixon took office.[2] As interest rates rose, rising payments on the huge debt stock would hit Americans from one side. Lower revenues because of tight budgets and slow growth would hit them from the other.

Greenspan's consulting work catered increasingly to financial firms, which gave him a window onto the vulnerability of the economy. He would show up occasionally at New York lunches given by the first generation of hedge funds, many of which had borrowed money to load up on go-go stocks with "data" or "onics" in their names. When the stock market began to tumble soon after Nixon's inauguration, many of his lunch companions lost their shirts—go-go was gone, and the 1960s were over. On his trips out to the West Coast for the board meetings of Trans-World, Greenspan could see that the savings-and-loan industry faced a crisis, too. As interest rates rose, savings and loan associations (S&Ls) needed to compete with higher-yielding bonds in order to attract deposits. But they were prohibited from paying depositors more—like banks, which faced so-called Regulation Q caps on the amount of interest they could pay, S&Ls were hamstrung by the government.[3] As a result, the volume of deposits at the S&Ls began to tumble, landing lenders like Trans-World in an impossible bind.[4] They had extended long-term mortgages to home buyers, and could not recoup their money until the mortgages matured. But the depositors who funded those mortgages were heading for the exits.

Nixon's sunny endorsement of the New Frontier made it clear that he would ignore Greenspan's laissez-faire campaign advice. But the disaster brewing in the savings-and-loan industry showed something else: the president was wrong to do so. The New Frontier quest for full employment had caused inflation to rise, which had caused market interest rates to rise, which meant that S&Ls had to pay depositors a better rate or face a catastrophic loss of funding. But interest-rate caps prevented the S&Ls from adjusting: the government had first confronted the industry with the challenge of inflation, then prevented the industry from adapting to it. Even architects of the New Frontier were appalled by these distortions. In 1970 the future Nobel laureate James Tobin, a veteran of Kennedy's Council of Economic Advisers, published an attack on the costs of Regulation Q. He urged deregulation.[5]

By the end of Nixon's tenure, the cost of the president's decision to ignore Greenspan would be painfully clear. Greenspan, for his part, would perform a metamorphosis: from loyal Nixon campaign aide to unrelenting Nixon critic.

Whatever the uncertainties for the economy at the start of 1969, Greenspan was prospering impressively. *Barron's* had recently printed an inordinately long and deferential interview with him; it ran under the title "Worldly Philosopher" and extended over seven pages.[6] The philosopher had recently added a second board membership to his collection; he was a director of Standard Prudential United, a New York–based financing company. Meanwhile, Greenspan also retained his seat on the New York Commodity Exchange, and in 1969 became president of the National Association of Business Economists. He launched a joint venture with Standard & Poor's (S&P) that allowed Townsend-Greenspan to run forecasting programs on S&P's state-of-the-art computer; Kathryn Eickhoff worked a shift at S&P from midnight to four in the morning, sustained by doughnuts and coffee.[7] The joint venture helped to cement Kathy's post-Greenspan relationship with her future husband, a jazz bar owner named Jim Smith, who would close his premises at four a.m. and walk over to meet her for breakfast. It also led S&P's parent company to make an offer for 80 percent of Townsend-Greenspan's stock.[8] But Greenspan was not about to give up his autonomy, however rich it might make him.

Greenspan had told the Nixon team that he was eager to offer part-time assistance. He volunteered as the transition budget director before the inauguration; and another opportunity arrived soon after Nixon moved into the White House. Ignoring his defense chiefs, the new president set up a commission to consider an end to military conscription—he had no time for economic laissez-faire, but a libertarian position on the draft might be a vote winner. The management of the commission fell to Marty Anderson, who, with Greenspan's assistance, had composed the original campaign memo to Nixon on ending compulsory military service; Anderson now asked his old friend to serve on the commission. The invitation was rendered irresistible by another Anderson pick. The commission would also include Milton Friedman, the irreverent Chicago economist whose writings Greenspan followed closely.

Economics was just emerging as an imperial discipline, and the commission on the draft turned out to be a portent of the future. Conscription had frequently been debated in political terms: Would an all-volunteer force be overwhelmingly black? Would it be more likely to resist civilian oversight? Conscription had also been analyzed in military terms: Perhaps volunteers would fight more effectively than unwilling conscripts? Brandishing the ideas developed by Anderson and the commission's abolitionist staff, Friedman and Greenspan transported the whole argument onto economic territory. Having chosen the terrain on which to fight, they outmaneuvered the commission chairman, who openly favored conscription.[9]

The economists' assault featured two main arguments. First, conscription compelled a specific group of young, disproportionately low-income men to provide the government with labor at below-market wages. This was equivalent to a "hidden tax"—a forcible levy on conscripts that was not accounted for in the federal budget. Indeed, this stealthy tax on draftees was three times higher than the rate paid by equivalent civilians; servicemen were, in effect, bearing a heavy load so that everyone else could have an army on the cheap—it was a scandalously regressive income transfer. Building on this first argument, the economists asserted that because the true costs of military labor were obscured, military planners overused manpower and distorted the national labor market. A large supply of cheap draftees dulled the Pentagon's incentive to free up work-ers from low-skilled jobs that could be mechanized. The national econ-omy was paying a price because manpower was being wasted.

One day the army wheeled out General William Westmoreland, the famously hard-nosed former commander in Vietnam, to testify in the draft's favor. Seeking to silence the economists' jabber about hidden taxes and labor-market distortions, Westmoreland harrumphed that he did not want to command an army of mercenaries.

"General, would you rather command an army of slaves?" Milton Friedman shot back.

Westmoreland drew himself up and said, "I don't like to hear our patriotic draftees referred to as slaves."

"I don't like to hear our patriotic volunteers referred to as mercenaries," Friedman retorted. And then he went on: "If they are mercenaries, then I, sir, am a mercenary professor, and you, sir, are a mercenary general; we are served by mercenary physicians, we use a mercenary lawyer, and we get our meat from a mercenary butcher."[10]

"No enemy was ever as formidable to General Westmoreland as little old Milton Friedman," Greenspan later recalled with relish.

But however much Greenspan enjoyed Friedman's swordplay, he was not about to emulate it.[11] When one commissioner worried that the coun-try would never find enough volunteers to fill the places of conscripts, Greenspan's response was cautiously polite. "I'm sure the armed services could raise any reasonable number of personnel with improved compen-sation," he assured the man before changing the subject.[12] Recalling his work on the commission years later, Greenspan suggested that he could be mild because Friedman was so tough: "We all left it up to Milton because, if you have got a howitzer, why do you need a cop pistol?"[13] But the truth was that Greenspan had changed. He was less ideological than he had been in his years with Ayn Rand; he was more eager to get along with fellow power brokers. Besides, however strident he could be when committing arguments to paper, Greenspan retained some of the shyness of his youth. He did not like to confront people in person.

On the morning of February 21, 1970, the commissioners trooped over to the White House to present their final report to the president. Camera shutters whirred as the president sat at the middle of the Cabinet Room's large hexagonal conference table and talked casually with the commissioners.[14] Across the table from the president and to one side, Greenspan stood out from the group. In the era of loud jackets and exuberant lapels, he remained stuck in an earlier time: his suit was dark, his lapels obstinately narrow. But he was shaping the future anyway. Despite his diffidence on the committee, his side had won the argument; in less than three years, he had helped to shepherd the idea of an all-volunteer armed force from the typewritten pages of a campaign memo to the typeset pages of a bound report that now lay before the president. Some eighteen months later, Congress sent Nixon legislation based on the commission's findings, and Nixon signed it at an Oval Office ceremony.[15] The last draft call went out in December 1972. The burden carried by America's young men had finally been lifted.

While Greenspan was working on the military draft, the economy was flailing. By September 1969, inflation had risen to an annual rate of 5.7 percent, and the jobless rate had jumped to 4 percent, up from 3.3 percent in January. The *New York Times* reminded readers that the spike in unemployment represented "the sharpest rise since the presidential campaign of 1960." The significance of the comparison was not lost on Nixon, who believed that a weak economy had cost him the 1960 election.

Shortly before Labor Day in 1969, Greenspan and Milton Friedman attended a brainstorming session hosted by Paul McCracken, the chairman of Nixon's Council of Economic Advisers.[16] The subject of the meeting was rising inflation. Unstable prices, the participants agreed, strained the social fabric; they hurt some citizens more than others, leaving a "widespread view of unequal benefits in society." A fix was needed, clearly, but not a New Frontier–style regulatory clampdown on wages and prices that merely smothered the symptoms; the underlying causes of price pressure had to be dealt with. Excess demand was one side of the problem, which was why the Fed was raising interest rates and budget discipline was needed. But the other side of the inflation puzzle lay in supply—if government regulations were less onerous, producers would be freer to expand output, taking the pressure off prices. Greenspan and his colleagues singled out areas in which deregulation seemed most promising, among them the Regulation Q caps on deposit interest rates.

Unfortunately for the economists, the logic of their brainstorming session was not going to impress Nixon. True to the blithe rhetoric of his inaugural speech, the president wanted an economy that generated jobs—and never mind the inflationary consequences. Indeed, far from siding with the economists on the need for monetary discipline, Nixon was plotting ways to force the Fed into a looser policy. In October 1969 the president announced that the Fed chairman, William McChesney Martin, would leave office when his term expired the following January. He would be succeeded by Arthur Burns, Greenspan's old professor from Columbia.

It was not difficult to see why this switch appealed to Nixon. The president believed that Martin had denied him the presidency in 1960 by raising interest rates ahead of the election; if nothing was done to stop him now, Martin would repeat the trick by engineering slower growth ahead of Nixon's reelection bid in 1972. In contrast, Burns had managed to present himself to Nixon as a dependable ally. Although he was a conservative with a hawkish image on inflation, the professor had proved his loyalty to Nixon during the 1968 campaign, publicly rubbishing Greenspan's suggestion that higher unemployment might be necessary to bring down inflation.

To ensure that Burns understood what was expected of him, Nixon summoned him to the Oval Office.

"My relations with the Fed," Nixon began, "will be different than they were with Bill Martin there. He was always six months too late doing anything. I'm counting on you, Arthur, to keep us out of a recession."

"Yes, Mr. President," Burns said, lighting his pipe. "I don't like to be late."

Nixon continued: "The Fed and the money supply are more important than anything the Bureau of the Budget does."

Burns nodded professorially.

"Arthur, I want you to come on over and see me privately anytime," Nixon said, stroking Burns's considerable ego.

"Thank you, Mr. President," Burns responded.[17]

Having signaled that he wanted a soft line from the Fed, Nixon cast about for an alternative way of taming inflation. He had no interest in deregulation, and no stomach for monetary or budget discipline; like his New Frontier predecessors, he wanted to stabilize prices with some kind of magic fourth option. The most promising and least painful policy appeared to be some form of wage and price controls, and Nixon directed his team at the Council of Economic Advisers to consider how these might be implemented. He evidently wanted to out-Johnson Johnson in micro-managing the economy.

The CEA economists did their best to push back. True to the conclusions of the brainstorming session with Greenspan and Milton Friedman, they opposed a price control strategy that would merely treat the symptoms of inflation. Indeed, if inflation originated partly in excess regulation, as the brainstorming session had concluded, Nixon's plan to regulate wages and prices would only make things worse. At the start of 1970, the CEA published its annual *Economic Report of the President,* which emphasized the case for reducing regulatory "rigidities," presenting the relaxation of Regulation Q interest-rate ceilings as especially urgent. To advance that objective, the CEA announced the formation of a new presidential commission on the modernization of finance.

When the new commission's members were announced, they included Alan Greenspan.

On June 27, 1970, Nixon's commission on financial reform convened for its first meeting. The case for modernizing finance seemed more pressing than ever: a few days earlier, the Penn Central Transportation Company had collapsed, revealing the stresses that were building inside the old system. The railroad conglomerate was emblematic of the leveraging of the economy. It had borrowed wildly to go on an acquisition spree;

then, when the combination of rising interest rates and a slowing economy hit, its debts proved unsustainable. Fearful that the run on Penn Central might trigger the collapse of dozens of leveraged conglomerates, a panicked Federal Reserve promised to keep its discount window open to any bank that lent to a company in distress; and in order to help banks attract funds and channel them to wobbly industrial concerns, it suspended the Regulation Q interest-rate cap on very large deposits, freeing banks to compete harder to attract savings.[18] Inflation, and the Fed's response of higher interest rates, had created a fragility that only looser regulation could assuage. Contrary to the version of history that came to be accepted toward the end of Greenspan's career, financial deregulation was at least partly a response to instability. It was not simply the cause of it.

Greenspan shuttled back and forth to the meetings of the financial commission, but he was distracted. In the spring of 1970, Townsend-Greenspan had moved once more, this time to a brand-new glass and aluminum skyscraper that rose fifty stories above the southern tip of Manhattan. The premises at One New York Plaza gave Greenspan's consulting outfit twice the space that it had occupied before; and Greenspan's own office boasted floor-to-ceiling windows with views of Governor's Island, New York Harbor, and the Statue of Liberty. To get the most out of this executive crow's nest, Kathryn Eickhoff added an innovation designed specifically for the boss. At the old space on Pine Street, she had fretted that the corner office was unsuitable for greeting clients; Greenspan's mess of papers and statistical reports cluttered every surface. With the new setup at New York Plaza, Eickhoff kitted out a walk-in closet with desks lining the three interior walls. There, amid the litter of beloved data, Greenspan could immerse himself in study, his back turned to the world. But when clients came to visit, he would emerge from his hideaway like a butterfly from its chrysalis, alighting regally on a sofa. The view through the window behind him would be breathtaking; the coffee table in front of him would be pristine. Separated from his mess, he looked every bit the kind of man who advised the nation's president.

On the evening of Wednesday, August 5, Greenspan's team was hard at work on the thirty-third floor of One New York Plaza. Shortly after six o'clock some men from the telephone company knocked on the office door. Greenspan's computer handler, Lowell Wiltbank, answered and spoke briefly to the visitors; it seemed hot on the landing, but Wiltbank noticed nothing wrong and returned to his work. A few minutes later there was a more urgent knock. The same men from the telephone company were there, but this time a large plume of dark gray smoke accompanied them. In the office diagonally across from Townsend-Greenspan, a bad connection to a newly installed computer had burst into flames.[19]

Wiltbank rushed back to round up his colleagues, telling everyone to leave immediately. Greenspan was deeply absorbed in his work and did not want to budge; Wiltbank remembers seizing him and physically dragging him from his studies. The consultants crossed the hallway to one of the fire stairs and descended to the twenty-eighth floor; from there they took the elevator down to the safety of the sidewalk. By this time the fire had become a terrifying inferno, consuming four stories in a 2,000-degree blaze, buckling metal beams and blowing out windows.[20] Some tenants in the building had to be helicoptered off the roof. Two security guards boarded an elevator to go halfway up the tower, but the heat caused the system's electronic circuitry to misfire. The elevator hurtled directly to the thirty-third floor, where the security men died in the heart of the blaze.[21]

If the fire was not enough to distract Greenspan from the financial commission, Nixon's attitude hardly encouraged him to put his heart into it. In announcing the inquiry, Nixon had declared that the nation needed a revamped financial sector to channel savings to their most efficient purposes. There were suspicions, however, that the president's real objective was to placate Wall Street donors. After all, Nixon had never shown interest in rethinking the New Frontier; he was unlikely to embrace deregulatory advice from a commission. In January 1971, Nixon announced to a television news anchor, "I am now a Keynesian in economics"—a confession that the anchor compared to "a Christian crusader saying, 'All things considered, I think Mohammed was right.'"[22] But the truth was that Nixon had been a Keynesian from the moment he had taken office.[23]

The first test of Nixon's attitude to financial reform came on May 6, when Greenspan and his fellow commissioners packed into the White

House Cabinet Room to deliver a progress report to the president. The economy had by now deteriorated even further. Unemployment was approaching 6 percent, and the change of leadership at the Fed had frustrated Nixon. Once installed in office, Burns had proved too independent for the president's liking. His monetary policy was tough, and he had an infuriating habit of floating policy ideas that stole the administration's thunder. The more Burns seized the limelight, the more ineffectual Nixon looked. "Nixon fiddles while Burns roams," a Washington wit commented.[24]

The commissioners wanted to confront Nixon with tough news. The whole edifice of Regulation Q was creaking at the seams. They needed to make the president see the urgency of deregulation.

"Our financial system is just too vulnerable as it is now to shocks," warned Raymond Saulnier, a silver-haired commissioner who spoke in the soft seaside accent of his native Massachusetts.[25] Nixon trusted Saulnier as an "old hand" because of his service on the Council of Economic Advisers during the Eisenhower administration.

"We have a period of quiet now, but there's no real reason for believing it will last," Saulnier continued. "It really could come in quite suddenly."

Nixon seemed unconcerned by Saulnier's ominous prediction. He did not want to hear about deregulating finance; something else preoccupied him.

"I noticed in the material here you are not addressing yourself to . . ."

Nixon trailed off, but the commissioners could guess what the president was referring to.

"Not to the Federal—not to monetary policy, as such," one said awkwardly.

"Are you addressing yourself, for example, to the problem of the independence of the Fed?" Nixon asked. Now he was out in the open. He had placed a dagger on the table.

The commissioners informed Nixon that, no, they had not looked into the Fed's independence.

"Don't . . . don't . . ." Nixon stuttered. His tone veered from jovial to angry. "It's no sacred cow. I know the views; you've expressed some of them. But I think there's too much of a tendency among bankers and insurance people and government people and all the rest to say, 'Well, now, the Fed was set up back when Woodrow Wilson was president, and that was the creation and God created a perfect thing. . . .'"

"Mr. President, it was a commission that created that perfect thing," interrupted Saulnier.

Greenspan and the other commissioners laughed, but Nixon's mood darkened.

"The point that I made is don't doubt it if you think you want to discuss it," he said tersely. "Because I think any report by a group of this size which ducks that question—you have not addressed yourself to the total sector. . . . But you have to. You've got to go into it."

Nixon was becoming so insistent that he was repeating himself. He was daring the commissioners to pick up the dagger and plunge it into his enemy.

"Let's put it this way. You can't—those who examine the financial system at the present time cannot talk and reflect about it without talking about the Fed. The failure would be, it seems to me, that you were ducking one of the major institutions."

The commissioners hedged, knowing better than to argue. Nixon was right that they should examine the government side of the financial system, they told him, but they were concentrating on private finance just for the moment. Presently, Nixon seemed satisfied and backed off. His charm gradually resurfacing, he closed the meeting by presenting Greenspan and the other commissioners with cuff links and golf balls, emblazoned with the presidential seal.

"While this looks very expensive, it isn't," Nixon joked. "You don't have to report it."[26]

Six weeks later, on June 21, 1971, Greenspan found himself in Washington again, grappling with the financial instability that Nixon had declined to hear about. On the heels of Penn Central's failure the previous summer, the debt-burdened Lockheed Aircraft Company had turned to Washington for assistance. As the Defense Department's largest contractor, Lockheed commanded policy makers' attention; besides, it was a major employer in California, a swing state, and a generous contributor to political candidates. The Nixon administration duly proposed a rescue for Lockheed, but Congress put its own spin on the affair. Taking its cue from Arthur Burns, who had argued since Penn Central for a standing government authority to rescue systemically important companies, the Senate banking committee seized on Lockheed as a chance to give Burns what he wanted.

Testifying before the Senate, Greenspan refused to back his mentor. "I am in fundamental disagreement with this type of loan guarantee," he began. Government-directed lending "must inevitably lead to subsidization of the least efficient firms," damaging productivity and therefore living standards. Rather than channeling capital to the most deserving users, Burns and his Senate allies would allocate credit on political criteria, opening up "dangerous possibilities of waste and favoritism . . . even corruption." What the economy really needed was for weak companies to go bust, so that capital and workers would move to better-run establishments. The solution to the nation's problems was not to double down on New Frontier meddling. It was to reduce it.[27]

When lawmakers voted on Lockheed later that summer, Greenspan's message was ignored; Burns got his permanent bailout authority and Lockheed got its rescue. But Burns's success in expanding the Fed's remit did nothing to endear him to the White House, and soon he stuck his neck out even further. On July 16 he raised the Fed's discount rate, to Nixon's dismay. On July 23 he appeared before Congress and lamented the troubled state of the economy.

That evening Nixon invited three advisers to join him on the presidential yacht, *Sequoia,* for a Friday-night cruise on the Potomac.[28] The men kicked about ideas on how to deal with the wayward Fed chairman. Burns was behaving like a professorial Eeyore, talking down the economy with one gloomy comment after another, fueling the Democrats' attacks on

"Nixonomics." ("All the things that should go up—the stock market, corporate profits, real spending income, productivity—go down, and all the things that should go down—unemployment, prices, interest rates—go up," one Democrat had chortled recently.)[29] Building on a suggestion from John Connally, the Treasury secretary, Nixon and his henchmen settled on a plan. They would make Burns shut up by planting a negative story in the press about him.[30]

Burns had recently been urging the president to take a stand against inflationary wage increases. The Nixon men resolved to tell the press that Burns had simultaneously been lobbying behind the scenes for a personal pay raise. Coupling this charge of hypocrisy with crude intimidation, they would also inform reporters that Nixon was contemplating a reorganization of the Federal Reserve to curb the chairman's authority.

On July 27 the *Sequoia* smear surfaced in the form of a United Press International story. Burns, who drew a salary of $42,500, was said to be demanding a $20,000 raise. "Several advisers have urged President Nixon to double the size of the Federal Reserve Board," UPI added.[31] The next day Ron Ziegler, the president's press secretary, gave the story legs by refusing to deny it. With Burns now on the defensive, Nixon's men moved in for the kill. They would get a message to Burns demanding a positive speech on the economy.[32] If the Fed chairman wanted to avoid all-out war, he would have to cry uncle.

To complete their subjugation of the central bank, Nixon's operatives recruited Greenspan. They knew that he was close to Burns, and they viewed him as a loyal messenger.

Charles Colson, a member of the *Sequoia* trio who would later serve jail time for organizing Nixon's dirty tricks, tracked down Greenspan. He phoned him in New York and asked him to get Burns to change his tune on the economy.

Years later, Greenspan insisted that he refused to do Colson's bidding. But Colson's handwritten notes from the conversation suggest otherwise.[33] After taking Colson's phone call, Greenspan spoke at length to Burns. Then he reported back to the White House.

"What in the hell is going on?" Greenspan reported a "very disturbed" and "pissed off" Burns asking.[34]

Colson relayed Greenspan's efforts to H. R. Haldeman, the White House chief of staff, who gleefully shared the highlights with the president.

"The Arthur Burns ploy worked with a bang," Haldeman crowed to Nixon. "He talked to Alan Greenspan today and said, 'This is awful.' Then Greenspan said, 'Well I understand there's real concern in the administration by the political people about the great political harm that you're doing the President by running around making all these negative remarks.' And Arthur babbled on and on about how the last thing he'd ever do in the world is be political under the President, and he's not doing it for that, and what could he do?"

Nixon was eating this up. Haldeman continued.

"What he could do is make a damned positive constructive speech on the economy and what a great job the president is doing," the chief of staff said vehemently. He had already told Colson to get that message over to Greenspan, so Greenspan could take it to Burns. Greenspan had reported back that Burns first wanted "to see the President and straighten it out."

Nixon was not interested.

"No, no, no," he objected. "We've done this three different times, I've had these confidential talks . . . I'll be goddamned if I'm going to do it again. Why do I have to get him in here and have him molt again and say, 'I'm only doing what I believe is right. . . .' He's smart enough to know what the effect is."

"What Greenspan says is that . . ." Haldeman started.

"Greenspan is his friend."

"But Greenspan brokering this thing can do it effectively," Haldeman countered. "Greenspan says Arthur's ego is so great that honestly he thinks he is doing the right thing, and he doesn't think until now Arthur really realized he was doing political harm. But he thinks now he does, and he thinks this is a very effective way to do it and probably the only way. That you had to give him some shock treatment."

Greenspan's alleged endorsement of Nixon's dirty trick seemed to assuage the president.

"Greenspan thinks he's doing political harm, doesn't he?" the president asked.

"Yes," Haldeman answered.[35]

As soon as the meeting with Haldeman was over, Nixon called his Treasury secretary, John Connally, to break the good news.

"I thought you should know that your little tactic that you suggested got home to our friends across the street," Nixon said. His voice was loud and fuzzy and his breath hit the telephone in gusts as he leaned into the mouthpiece.

Connally let out a wheezy laugh. He knew right away that Nixon meant Burns, whose offices at the Fed were a few blocks west of the White House. Nixon, perhaps aware of the possibility that his Oval Office tape machine could one day be used against him, frequently identified people by their locations instead of their names.

"Well that's good, I'll tell you," Connally replied.

Nixon filled in Connally on the details of the smear, including the call between Burns and Greenspan, whom the president dubbed "our friend in New York."

"We got his attention," Nixon said. "Now all the rest of us . . . I'm not saying a word. . . . But I thought you should know. Just play it dumb as hell, too."

"Yeah, I will. In the morning, I'm having breakfast with him," Connally replied.

"But in the meantime, don't let up on him, understand? We've gotta have some way to get him to stay sweatin'."[36]

Within twenty-four hours, the Fed chairman had caved, and Nixon appeared at a press conference to disavow the shameful attacks on his good character. "Arthur Burns has taken a very unfair shot," the president said, explaining how Burns had in fact turned down a pay increase when the White House budget office had recommended one. A transcript of Nixon's remarks was forwarded to Burns, who soon was on the phone to express his gratitude.

"It warmed my heart," an elated Burns told Nixon's speechwriter, William Safire. "I haven't been so deeply moved in years. I may not have shown it, but I was pretty upset. This just proves what a decent and warm man the president is. We have to work more closely together now."[37]

Over the next months, the Fed shifted its focus from fighting inflation to fighting the election. Before the smear, Burns had raised interest rates to restrain monetary growth; after the smear, he desisted.[38] As a result, the economy accelerated to a giddy speed, growing at an annualized rate of 7.3 percent in the first quarter of 1972 and at a completely unsustainable 9.6 percent in the second one. The central bank had not been so clearly under the thumb of the White House since the Fed-Treasury accord of 1951. Politics had triumphed, and Greenspan had been party to its victory.

Two weeks after the smear, on Friday, August 13, 1971, William Safire had another brush with Nixon's brand of economic policy. He was told to pack his bag for a weekend retreat at Camp David, the president's country retreat, and not to tell anyone where he was going.[39] Arriving at the Old Executive Office Building at one p.m., Safire was joined by Herb Stein, a member of the Council of Economic Advisers, and shown to a White House limousine idling in a secluded entrance. The men piled into the backseat and took off for Anacostia Naval Air Station, where they boarded a helicopter.

Safire asked Stein if he knew what was going on.

"This could be the most important weekend in economic history since March 4, 1933," Stein replied, referring to the weekend in the depths of the Depression when FDR assumed office, declared a bank holiday, and launched the New Deal.

Two hours later Nixon greeted ten members of his staff in the wood-paneled living room of the Aspen Lodge, the largest of ten cabins that dotted the estate at Camp David. Eight advisers arranged their seats in a circle. Two sat against the wall, serving as note takers.

"No calls are to be made out of here except to get information," Nixon began.[40] Then he explained that he had convened the meeting to tackle the economy—multiple problems were coming to a head and it was time to take decisive action. Domestically, unemployment combined with entrenched inflation. Internationally, a collapse of confidence in the dollar threatened to undermine the international monetary system. Moreover, the two challenges were linked—the domestic and international troubles both reflected the steady buildup of debt in the economy. American business had leveraged itself to the point where it could not cope with the slower growth needed to fight inflation. Meanwhile, confidence in the dollar was falling because of Americans' debts to foreigners.

Besides the problem of its debts, the United States had to reckon with the fact that its two central economic objectives had proved incompatible. At the Bretton Woods conference in 1944, America had committed itself to a system of fixed exchange rates: the dollar was pegged to gold, and other major currencies were pegged to the dollar. The system had worked well for fifteen years, but then the New Frontier economists had embraced the goal of "full employment." To preserve the fixed exchange rate, the United States had to avoid inflation, which would undermine the value of its money. But to attain full employment, the United States had to do the opposite—it had to accept inflation in accordance with the implication of the Phillips curve, which indicated that rising prices could sustainably boost the number of jobs in the economy. As the goal of full employment trumped the fealty to Bretton Woods, rising inflation eroded confidence in the dollar.[41] Indeed, by the time Nixon's advisers gathered at Camp David, the dollar-gold link was close to breaking.

The floor was opened to debate. Nixon and his counselors confronted a choice between two options: They could take radical steps to rein in inflation and shore up confidence in the dollar. Or they could abandon the $35-per-ounce gold pledge, and with it the system of fixed exchange rates that had prevailed for a quarter of a century. The first option would involve austerity: a tighter budget, tighter monetary policy, and deregulation that would help suppliers to produce more. The second option would mean instability: with the gold anchor gone, the dollar would fluctuate unpredictably; and the money in Americans' pockets might be worth one thing today and quite another tomorrow.

There was little doubt about which way Nixon would jump. From the start of his administration, he had consistently made employment his top economic priority. He had no interest whatever in fighting inflation, as his bullying of Arthur Burns had demonstrated. After four hours of discussion that Friday afternoon and a postdinner bull session with a smaller group, the president resolved that the United States would leave the gold standard.

Herb Stein of the Council of Economic Advisers called Greenspan at home on Sunday to tell him that an announcement was coming. Greenspan duly settled himself in front of the television that evening to listen to the president. As Nixon was speaking, Greenspan reached down to pick something up and threw out his back. He was laid up in bed for weeks, and for the next few years he was forced to resort to special orthopedic chairs and to lie down periodically on the floor of his office.[42]

Greenspan would later joke that the shock of Nixon's announcement had injured him. The way he saw things, the abandonment of gold convertibility was not especially shameful—by 1971 the link had already lost so much credibility that Nixon's decision was hardly a surprise. Besides, it had proved to be an ineffectual discipline on inflation, making it hardly worth preserving.[43] What really bothered Greenspan was the policy that Nixon coupled with the abandonment of gold. Determined to fight inflation without enduring tighter budgets or higher interest rates, the president imposed wage and price controls on the economy. The interventionism of the New Frontier had reached its apotheosis.

During Greenspan's convalescence from his back injury, his mother, Rose, visited his apartment every day, stocking his refrigerator and trying to make him comfortable. For once in his life, Greenspan ceased to be as independent as Ayn Rand's cartoon heroes; his mother came to his aid, teaching him something profound about human beings' need for one another. After his recovery, Alan's old impatience with Rose was replaced by tenderness, and he began to call her faithfully each day. Their bond remained exceptionally strong until her death at ninety-two, twenty-four years later.[44]

Price controls were the last straw for Greenspan's relationship with Nixon. He had remained loyal to the president for longer than he later claimed—by August 1971, fully three years had passed since that campaign meeting at Montauk at which Nixon had revealed the dark recesses of his character. Over the intervening period, Greenspan had served as a no-holds-barred campaign adviser, as an interim budget director, as a consultant on everything from deregulation to the draft—and then finally as a go-between in the Fed's subjugation. But now, by announcing wage and price controls, Nixon had crossed a line. He had ignored Adam Smith's most basic insight about the preciousness of price signals: without them, producers cannot know what consumers want, and consumers cannot distinguish between scarcity and abundance.

Right up until the eve of the Camp David announcement, most administration economists had shared Greenspan's anti–price control convictions. "The imposition of the [wage and price] freeze was a jump off the diving board without any clear idea of what lay below," Herb Stein confessed later.[45] If Nixon's advisers had changed their position, it was not that they had been won over by some fresh analytical insight. It was simply that the drama of Camp David, with its secrecy and helicopters and sense of historical import, had gone to their heads—a policy that would have seemed plain foolish under any other circumstance felt intoxicating in the heat of the moment. "As my son said to me after the program was announced, 'Ideologically you should fall on your sword but existentially it's great,'" Stein recorded in his memoir.[46]

The hangover came fast, however. Writing the rules that would govern prices proved to be a daunting task, and the apparatchiks at the new Price Commission showed no sign of being equal to it. Donald Rumsfeld, the Nixon operative who had reported from the front lines of the Democratic convention in Chicago, set out to break the logjam, recruiting a young assistant named Dick Cheney to help him. A small team in Rumsfeld's outer office pulled an all-nighter, making seat-of-the-pants decisions on

hundreds of prices in a blaze of cigarettes and coffee. By the time the secretaries emptied the ashtrays the next morning, Rumsfeld's central planners had drawn distinctions between apples and applesauce; popped and
unpopped corn; raw cabbage and packaged slaw; fresh oranges and glazed
citrus peel.[47] A little while later, Cheney sent staffers to find out how shops
were implementing the resulting price controls, and the answer was not
encouraging. Each vendor was interpreting them differently, it turned out.
Merely ordering inflation to behave did not necessarily bring victory on
the economic battlefield.[48]

Despite his fury about price controls, Greenspan persisted with the
work of the financial reform commission. He conducted himself with
the same courteous diffidence he had shown on the commission to end
the draft, but the group converged on a platform that he found easy to
support anyway.[49] The commission called for the phasing out of Regulation Q, reflecting the almost universal agreement among experts that
banks and S&Ls must be allowed to cope with inflation by adjusting the
interest they paid to attract deposits. The commission also aimed to shatter the silos dividing different types of lenders. S&Ls would henceforth
be allowed to diversify out of mortgage lending and compete with banks,
while banks would be allowed to invade S&Ls' home turf, to underwrite
municipal bonds, and to sell mutual funds and insurance.

Since the crisis of 2008, this sort of silo-busting prescription has
acquired a bad name. By enabling the creation of too-big-to-fail financial
supermarkets, silo busting set the financial system up for a fall, with toxic
consequences for taxpayers. But in the early 1970s, sensible opinion took
the opposite line, and economists from both sides of the political divide
supported the commission's deregulatory prescriptions. For one thing, a
balkanized financial industry served customers poorly; by breaking the
silos and fostering competition, the commission aimed to cut costs that
penalized savers and borrowers. For another, narrowly focused lenders
threatened certain types of borrowers with episodes of credit drought.
When rising interest rates caused deposits to lurch out of S&Ls, for example, home buyers could not get mortgages elsewhere; rather than moderating in the face of rising interest rates, housing demand collapsed and the

building industry, which was prone to boom-bust cycles at the best of times, became even more volatile. Likewise, when savers withdrew money from regional banks, the small businesses that depended on them could no longer get loans, so business opportunities were wasted. In his attack on Regulation Q interest caps in 1970, James Tobin had emphasized their inefficiency but also their injustice. Wealthy Americans could find their way around regulatory constraints, whereas ordinary citizens were helpless.[50]

Besides, Nixon's financial reform commission favored deregulation because there was really no choice but to do so. Since 1970, Americans had been pouring savings into money-market funds, which mimicked the properties of bank accounts but which were not subject to Regulation Q.[51] If the government kept the regulatory screws on banks and S&Ls, capital would migrate to these money-market funds; and if the government responded by extending interest-rate caps to the funds, capital would migrate to Europe. Already, a booming trade in dollar-denominated bonds had sprung up in London, and if the government tried to regulate onshore credit markets more aggressively, Europe would gobble up more of the business. Nearly all the commissioners accepted financial deregulation as inevitable. The only question was whether Nixon would acknowledge this.

On a Wednesday morning three days before Christmas, Greenspan and his fellow commissioners arrived at the White House to see Nixon. The president seemed to be in good spirits. His rant about the Fed's independence apparently forgotten, he cracked jokes with the commissioners for the benefit of the cameras.

"Pick out three or four of the most controversial points," Nixon suggested to the commissioners, playing to the need of the journalists in the room for a lede.

"Well, we weren't afraid of controversy," one responded boldly. The commissioners began outlining what they thought were their headlines: more freedom for the S&Ls, an end to Regulation Q, and so on. Nixon listened politely.

When the presentation petered out, he said, "You don't go into the problem of the Fed."

"We do have some recommendations for reorganization of banking supervision," a commissioner ventured.

"Did you talk to him? Did you talk to Burns?" Nixon pressed.[52] His obsession had not changed after all. He had bullied the Fed into submission, and the economy's rate of growth was about to explode dangerously. But with the election looming, the president remained fixated on the Fed's supposed challenge to his authority over the economy.

When the meeting wrapped up, Nixon walked out of the Cabinet Room with Peter Flanigan, his point man on financial regulation.

"You know, Mr. President, the real politics of that proposal is that they treat savings banks—savings-and-loans—like regular banks," Flanigan told the president as they returned to the Oval Office. "Now, the big savings-and-loans . . . they're going to be able to compete when they can take checking accounts, but the little guys will be pushed pretty hard to the wall."

"Oh?"

"And that's why this thing wildly does inject competition into the financial world," Flanigan continued. The report had already circulated for comment, and Flanigan had endured a torrent of lobbying. Wheeling out a line that would prove potent in the years to come, one advocate for the smaller S&Ls had griped that the report was "anti-housing."[53]

"There's going to be a lot of crockery broken as we go along," Flanigan told Nixon.

"What's the upside? Are there a lot of other good things in it?"

"That's so much a key to it that what I think we ought to do is put it on the burner until after November," Flanigan said, referring to the election. "Do our own homework, but not get committed on it."[54]

Nixon agreed, and the fate of the commission was sealed in that moment. Greenspan had spent a year and a half on a report that was destined for some dusty shelf; he had been wise not to invest more energy in it. And yet this non-outcome proved more significant than it appeared, for it anticipated the story of financial reform during Greenspan's Fed tenure. Finance did change in the 1970s, but it was shaped not by the deliberate planning of an expert commission but by market pressures and crises.

The fact that Greenspan and his fellow commissioners proposed to phase out Regulation Q did not matter in the end; Regulation Q was neutered anyway as savings flooded into the new money-market funds, as unregulated dollar bonds multiplied in London, and as the Fed dealt with the panic following Penn Central by scrapping the Regulation Q cap on the interest that banks could pay to attract very large deposits. The pattern was the same in later years. Finance changed dramatically in the 1990s and early 2000s, but the change was not dictated by the deliberations of experts; earnest working committees pondered the meaning of the new swaps market or the rise of shadow banks, but Greenspan declined to throw his weight behind their ideas, and their findings failed to alter policy.

In this tentative approach to his regulatory responsibilities as Fed chairman, Greenspan was perhaps exhibiting a fatalism he had learned under Nixon. The evolution of finance could have huge consequences, to be sure, but efforts to shape it were liable to founder. Technological changes, the exigencies of crises, and money's mulish tendency to find its way around the rules—these forces decided things.

The week after Nixon brushed off the commission in the last days of 1971, Greenspan went to New Orleans for the annual meeting of the American Finance Association to deliver a speech on inflation.[55] Contrary to his expectations, Nixon's wage and price freeze was showing signs of succeeding. But far from making his peace with Nixon's policy, Greenspan chose to take a stand—he did not always punch his weight on Washington commissions, but when it came to statistical questions, he came out with both fists swinging. If inflation appeared to be moderating, Greenspan argued, it did not necessarily follow that Nixon's controls worked. Price pressures would return in the second half of 1972, he declared confidently.

Greenspan might easily have ducked this fight with the president. In denouncing Nixon's price controls, he was attacking the central plank of the administration's economic policy—and he had intimate knowledge of how the White House dealt with its critics. Moreover, some of his natural allies hesitated to take his side, especially when prices remained subdued into the next summer. As inflation fell to 2.7 percent in the year to June 1972, even Milton Friedman seemed willing to believe that Nixon's controls had notched up an unlikely victory. Perhaps the announcement of a wage and price freeze had introduced additional uncertainty into the economy, slowing business and dragging inflation down with it. Or perhaps the controls had succeeded in changing expectations of inflation—expectations that could be self-fulfilling.

"If there has been any impact it clearly has had to have been psychological (which I gather is your position)," Greenspan wrote to Friedman at the start of October 1972. "However I do find it rather difficult to believe that inflation psychology can be altered by Presidential edict."[56] The significance of official pronouncements for the economy should not be exaggerated, Greenspan maintained. His skepticism echoed his doubts about the power of FDR's pep talks during the Depression.

Friedman wrote back a week later, insisting that Nixon's program was working. As if to soften Greenspan's intellectual isolation, the letter ended on a personal note. "I am sorry, too, that you could not attend the wedding," Friedman wrote, referring to the recent marriage of his son. "I know you would have enjoyed it."[57]

Greenspan waged a lonely campaign against Nixon's policies for more than a year. Then, in the spring of 1973, inflation resumed its upward march, hitting 5.1 percent in the year to April. Just as Greenspan had predicted, the wage and price freeze had worked only temporarily; he could scarcely contain his sense of vindication. "That politicians advocate a legalized freeze on prices and think it will solve the problem, I find disturbing," he fulminated in the *Wall Street Journal* that April. "That the majority of economists, in a state of despair, acquiesce, I find inconceivable."[58] Harkening back to his correspondence with Milton Friedman, he rubbished the idea that Nixon's policies could succeed by altering expectations. "Inflation psychology is . . . a concept which removes the burdens of pursuing politically unpopular, truly disinflationary measures," he wrote contemptuously. "In a free society, controls cannot supersede the law of supply and demand. In a society in which they can, justice cannot prevail."

Price controls had worked just long enough to get Nixon reelected. But now their failure was spoiling his prize. Every new inflation number eroded Nixon's authority; meanwhile, the noose of Watergate was tightening around him. The more the president's fortunes deteriorated, the more Greenspan exulted. Writing in the *New York Times* in July 1973, with inflation now back up at 6 percent, he seized on the Watergate-fueled revulsion at the governing classes to put a political spin on his analysis. Inflation, he informed his readers, was fundamentally the consequence of politicians' compulsive meddling, which he traced back to John F. Kennedy—the early 1960s stimulus had delivered on Kennedy's campaign promise to "get the economy moving again," and its success had created an insatiable appetite among political leaders for a taste of the same glory. The cult of presidential activism, coupled with politicians' inability to pay a short-term price for a long-term benefit, condemned the economy to an endless frenzy of meddling. If only the nation's leaders could be a little lazier, Greenspan was saying. "Do-Nothingism" ran the title of his *Times* column.[59]

Three months later, in October 1973, the Arab states imposed an oil embargo on the Western economies. Greenspan had not needed this stroke of fortune to win the argument on inflation, but it ended all doubt about the viability of Nixon's policies. By the end of the year, the consumer price index was rising at an annual rate of almost 9 percent, and Greenspan celebrated his triumph with a final libertarian broadside. The controls were not merely failing; they were achieving precisely the opposite of what their authors intended: by destroying companies' incentives to invest, they were causing shortages of basic goods, and so forcing prices *upward*.[60] By screwing down the lid on inflation temporarily, Nixon had set himself up for bottlenecks and more inflation down the road. Two and a half years after that shocking decision at Camp David, the president was paying the price for his expediency.

In the decade since Greenspan had delivered his Randian lectures, America's political system had proved obstinately deaf to his message. The young seer had predicted the inflation that had come to pass. He had warned that each misguided intervention in the economy would create distortions that would lead to more intervention. He had been right twice over. In his campaign memos to Nixon, he had anticipated the resulting political fallout: entitlement programs would foster a sense that government must provide, creating pressure on politicians to deliver more than they were capable of. Disappointment would almost inevitably follow. Inflation, as Greenspan had suggested in his first memo to the Nixon team, was not just a monetary phenomenon, it was a state of mind. Rising expectations of government welfare created an impossible bind. The demand for government solutions outstripped the nation's capacity to supply them.[61]

Back in the fall of 1968, Greenspan had sounded like an anxious courtier, eager for a government position. By 1974 he was once again an angry man on the outside, contemptuous of politics. But if this change of tone was understandable, what happened next was a surprise. The Nixon loyalist of six years earlier stayed out of the White House. But the dissident of 1974 soon executed a dizzying U-turn—just as the Nixon presidency was imploding.

Eight

"A MINORITY OF ONE"

On the morning of August 8, 1974, Greenspan appeared before the Senate banking committee. It was six years to the day since he had watched Nixon accept the Republican nomination at the convention in Miami Beach, and he had matured well in the interim. Now past his forty-eighth birthday, he still boasted a full head of dark hair, a strong build, and a strong jaw; he still dressed in the same conservative suits he had worn since the fifties. His youthful belief that he would one day command the world's respect had been vindicated, amply. *Time* magazine had recently informed millions of readers that he was "erudite and witty"; and he was earning $300,000 per year—$1.4 million in 2015 money.[1] Yet traces of his boyhood shyness stuck to him, disguising his success behind a mask of modesty.

"Mr. Greenspan, that is quite a battery you have to introduce you," the committee chairman began.[2] Greenspan was flanked by a congressman on one side and a White House counselor on the other.

"Senator, I have rarely been in the middle of anything," Greenspan responded, in the self-deprecating manner of a sideman.

Eleven senators looked down at him. They had copies of his curriculum vitae, and they knew this statement to be nonsense. Oddly for a libertarian, Greenspan had emerged at the very center of the nexus between business and government: he now had a string of corporate directorships to his name, and he served as an adviser to the Federal Reserve, the White House budget office, the Treasury, and the Council of Economic Advisers. Far from being a sideman, Greenspan was appearing before the Senate committee as President Nixon's nominee to one of the three top economic jobs in Washington. He was to chair the White House Council of Economic Advisers, the committee of three eminent economists served by a powerful staff of experts on leave from academia.

Greenspan had hesitated before agreeing to serve a president whose economic policies he had reviled, but his misgivings had been calmed by several considerations. For one thing, Nixon had ended his disastrous experiment with wage and price controls in April, removing the clearest obstacle to Greenspan's joining the administration. For another, his long-standing hunger for high office remained with him, and the position of CEA chairman was several rungs more senior than anything Greenspan might have been offered at the start of Nixon's presidency. Finally, although others might have balked at the idea of joining an administration that was coming apart under the impact of the Watergate scandal, Greenspan saw the prospect differently. The nation was entering a dark moment, and Arthur Burns and several leading administration officials had entreated him to help.[3] "This government is paralyzed. But there's still an economy out there and we still have to make economic policy. You owe it to your country to serve," Burns had urged him.[4] A month or so later Greenspan told an interviewer, "What is at stake is so large that if anyone has the possibility of making a contribution, he should. It's one of the rare instances when the issue of patriotism comes up."[5]

So here was Greenspan on Capitol Hill, ready for what promised to be a gripping confirmation hearing. The news of his nomination had already generated a clutch of newspaper profiles, several of which portrayed him as the leader of a far-out sect. "To the congregation of conservative economists, Greenspan is high priest, and austerity is his faith," *BusinessWeek* declared, while *Newsweek* titled its profile "Fundamental Fountainhead." The *New York Times* spiced its coverage with quotes from Ayn Rand. "My impression is that Alan did not want to go to the Council in the first place, and I don't believe he would stay if he is asked to compromise on his principles," Rand told the *Times*. "Inconsistency is a moral crime," she added, a bit menacingly.[6]

After some introductory pleasantries, the chairman of the banking committee invited Senator William Proxmire to lead the questioning. A wiry ascetic, the author of a book on dieting and exercise, Proxmire was intelligent and strange: modest enough to refuse absolutely all campaign donations, vain enough to invest in hair transplants and a facelift. But Proxmire was, first and foremost, a Wisconsin progressive. He was not going to look kindly on Ayn Rand's chief economist.

"You said, 'What the economy badly needs is a strong dose of do-nothingism,'" Proxmire began, accusingly.

"That is correct, Senator."

"Is that still your view?"

Greenspan assured Proxmire that it was. Do-nothingism was "not a terribly philosophical term," the nominee apologized. But price controls had been a "shambles." Greenspan was apparently not going to soft-pedal his free-market views—whether for the senator's benefit or for the benefit of the president who had nominated him.[7]

Proxmire moved on. His staff had dredged up Greenspan's Randian claim that antitrust law was unnecessary. Calling Greenspan's attention to the fact that the Federal Trade Commission blamed price fixing for inflation, the senator suggested that a clampdown on monopolistic practices would take the pressure off prices.

"I would think that the effect on the price level has got to be negligible," Greenspan objected.

"Negligible?" Proxmire exclaimed. "I see." Like a lawyer confronting a witness who has just incriminated himself, he wanted to make sure he had understood Greenspan correctly.

"Antitrust action—the threat or the reality of it—coupled with jawboning, coupled with procurement policies, were among the ingredients that enabled Kennedy to roll back steel prices in 1962," Proxmire explained, presenting the standard case for the New Frontier approach to inflation. "Do you think that kind of action by a chief executive would be irrelevant?"

"Yes, sir; it is. It's treating the symptoms of the problem," Greenspan insisted.

But surely Greenspan would support a tough line on price fixers?

"No, sir," Greenspan answered.

"All right, why?"

Greenspan launched into his views on antitrust, restating his Randian paper unapologetically. With a very few exceptions, the entire edifice of antitrust law should be jettisoned. Monopoly power almost never harmed consumers.

"Let me ask you this one, Mr. Greenspan, and see if you can bat it back over the fence," Proxmire continued. "The steel industry has increased its prices by 30 percent this year, chemical industry by 30 percent. . . . A fantastic increase. Nothing ever like it. . . . Nonferrous metals increased their prices 48 percent. Oil by 82 percent. . . . This is why it seems to me that the concentration problem is so critical with respect to inflation."

Greenspan might have conceded the point. Proxmire's numbers were broadly correct, and the senator had the power to vote against his confirmation. But instead of giving in, Greenspan responded with an economics lesson.

"Let me see if I can distinguish between the general effect of inflation and the specific prices themselves," he began. The general price level reflected the amount of money in the economy relative to the supply of goods, but the specific price of certain commodities could shoot up independently, reflecting shortages or special circumstances. Those idiosyncratic price spikes would result in inflation only if more money was printed. In the absence of money printing, a price spike in some commodities would be offset by falling prices elsewhere. Therefore the rising cost of steel or chemicals should not be confused with inflation.

More senators weighed in, and the economics lesson continued. Senator Joe Biden of Delaware wanted to know whether Greenspan's past consulting ties would affect his policy judgments. The nominee had pledged to sever all connections with Townsend-Greenspan while in government service, and to give up his claim to its revenues so long as he remained in Washington; the CEA salary, at $42,500, represented a huge sacrifice.[8] But even if Greenspan cut his ties with his company, surely he would still be biased? Would he not favor the firms that would be his clients when he returned to the private sector?

"I don't think that my ideas change because of the particular job that I hold. I take ideas seriously," Greenspan responded. He had opposed quotas on foreign steel imports, even though these suited the steelmakers who paid him large retainers. "While I have nothing against making money, that is not what I am in business for," Greenspan said simply.

Biden had to admit that this had the ring of truth about it. Greenspan's ideas were far too extreme to reflect expediency. Even though he must surely understand that Randian libertarianism would harm his political prospects, Greenspan was not softening his opinions. To the contrary, he was calmly sticking to his positions. Intellectual honesty seemed to define him.

"I am glad that the president picked you," Biden declared. "If he picks a conservative, I want him to pick a straight one and a bright one."

Proxmire had been waiting for his moment to weigh in again. "I am not so sure that if you are going to pick an executioner that you want to pick one with the sharpest possible ax," he interjected.

"You want it clean," Biden responded. "If I go, I want a clean knife. Just, 'Bang.'"

Proxmire had his own knife out for Greenspan. "You have indicated at one time or another that you don't support the concept of a strongly progressive income tax."

"That is correct. I do not," Greenspan responded.

"You do not?" Proxmire exclaimed. The United States had taxed the incomes of the rich at a higher rate than those of the poor since the passage of the Sixteenth Amendment in 1913. Greenspan was saying, without so much as a hint of embarrassment, that he wanted to wind back the clock to the nineteenth century. The ease with which he confessed to this fantastical ambition was both disarming and horrifying. The man was a riddle. He was courteous, calm, and absolutely terrifying.

"The logic underlying the equity of the income tax per se, I find very elusive," Greenspan said evenly.

"Why isn't it simple?" Proxmire demanded. "The utility of a dollar is so much less for a man who earns $100,000 a year than a man who earns $10,000 a year."

Greenspan stood his ground, insisting that a progressive tax was "not consistent with a free society." But Proxmire came at him again.

"Would you, then, like to see a flat tax on all incomes?"

"That would be my ideal state, but I scarcely expect it to happen," Greenspan replied.

"But that is the direction you would want to have government policy move?"

"My view on this is perfectly clear," Greenspan answered. Then he added that nobody else in Washington agreed with him. "I am a minority of one," he said squarely.

The hearing had already lasted for three hours, and the senators understood that they confronted a puzzle. Greenspan had lectured Joe Biden on how seriously he took ideas; and if he tried to make the nation conform to his ideas, the results would be hair-raising. But if he truly accepted that he was a minority of one, his opening joke to the committee might turn out to be true. He might be so far off toward the fringe of the policy debate that he really would be a sideman. His practical impact on the government might be negligible.

Proxmire made one final attempt to bridge the gulf with Greenspan. The nominee's manner was so reasonable that it was hard to understand how his views could be so unreasonable.

"My problem with your nomination," Proxmire summed up, "is that it is very difficult, because you are honest, you are capable, and some of the things that you propose I enthusiastically applaud; but I have a great, great difficulty with the fact that you are a free enterprise man who does not believe in antitrust, does not believe in consumer protection, does not believe in progressive income tax.... The old-style laissez-faire capital system is dead," Proxmire continued; the challenge for intelligent policy makers in the late twentieth century was how to make the mixed economy work better. "With the greatest goodwill in the world, you are not going to go back to Adam Smith. You know that."

"I am aware of that," Greenspan conceded. But he was still not backing off. However popular the mixed economy, its existence was precisely the problem. The past decade had demonstrated how each encroachment by the state would fuel demand for the next one, driving the nation inexorably to price controls and stagflation. "My observations of the fundamental mechanisms by how this particular type of mixed economy works is one of the reasons why I am such a strong advocate of free enterprise capitalism," Greenspan insisted. "We have come to a point where the damage being done by our mixed economy policies is very patent."

Which part of Greenspan mattered? The reassuring style or the far-out ideas? The modesty or the Randian ambition? After questioning Greenspan closely, Proxmire concluded that the nominee's fringe libertarianism counted for more than the unassuming sideman pose—a CEA chairman who openly denounced the mixed economy was simply not acceptable.[9] But although he opposed Greenspan for his ideology, the senator befriended him for his character. After an overwhelming majority of his colleagues voted to confirm Greenspan, Proxmire developed an excellent relationship with him.

As it turned out, Greenspan never served in the Nixon administration. The day that he testified before the Senate, the president's press secretary announced that Nixon would appear on television and radio at nine o'clock that evening. A crowd of curious Americans collected around the White House, braving the August humidity and intermittent rain to watch the newsmen come and go, savoring the thrill of a dramatic moment in the nation's history. At 7:30 p.m., Nixon left the White House for the short walk to the Old Executive Office Building, and the crowd outside the gates waved U.S. flags and sang "America" as he walked slowly up the steps, his head bowed, alone.[10] Somebody put up a sign reading DING

DONG, THE WITCH IS DEAD. A little while later the president returned and delivered his promised address to the nation from his desk in the Oval Office.[11] Speaking in strong tones, his emotions firmly under control, Nixon announced his resignation, effective at noon the next day. The next morning Gerald Rudolph Ford Jr. was sworn in as the thirty-eighth president of the United States, famously declaring, "Our long national nightmare is over."

For the economy, it was not over. To the contrary, *Time* magazine complained of "feverish inflation, constriction of credit and throbbingly high interest rates." GDP had shrunk at an annualized rate of 3.9 percent in the previous quarter, the consumer price index was up 10.9 percent over the past year, and unemployment stood at 5.5 percent. "Middle-class people are being pushed into such demeaning economies as buying clothes at rummage sales and cutting contributions to their churches," *Time* lamented.[12] At his first press conference, President Ford was asked whether he would fight the war against inflation by reviving Nixon's tools—after all, every president since Kennedy had tried to intervene directly in the price-setting process. But Ford had already had his mind made up by his incoming chief economist, Alan Greenspan. "Wage and price controls are out, period," he responded bluntly.[13]

A month into the Ford presidency, on September 4, Greenspan was formally sworn in as the chairman of the Council of Economic Advisers. Greenspan's mother, Rose, put on a sleeveless dress for the White House ceremony, undaunted by the fact that she was past the age of seventy. When the president put his arm around her to pose for a photo, she barely came up to his shoulder. Ayn Rand came, too, bringing along her husband and some theatrical white gloves; she shed her combative atheism for long enough to allow Alan to place his hand on the Jewish holy book and swear the oath of office. Afterward, Rose and Ayn talked to the president, and Alan smiled a broad, untroubled smile that recalled his carefree youth as a ball-playing high school student. After a long journey, Greenspan had ascended to the apex of American life, and the two most important women in his life were at his side.[14]

Greenspan rented a two-bedroom apartment at the Watergate complex, the flowing, Italian-designed development overlooking the Potomac. Before Nixon's antics made the Watergate synonymous with scandal, it had been a magnet for the rich and notable; Greenspan had often visited Arthur Burns and his wife at their apartment there. But Greenspan appreciated the Watergate for other reasons, too. His considered view of the waterfront property, after weighing its curvilinear architecture and its cultural merits, was that it was a brisk eighteen-minute walk to his office; he also appreciated the fact that the Watergate leased out apartments on a thirty-day basis. True to Ayn Rand's fierce statements to the *New York Times,* he had warned people at the White House that he could not serve in a government that violated his principles. He wanted to preserve the feeling that he could quit Washington if he had to.[15]

It was not long before Greenspan's purity was tested, however. The morning after his swearing-in ceremony, he found himself sitting with President Ford in the gold-and-white East Room of the White House. Television camera crews bathed the whole scene in a blinding light.[16] "Inflation is our domestic enemy number one," the president declared to an audience of economists, and then he laid out how he proposed to tackle it. The administration would hold twelve minisummits to solicit opinions from around the country; then it would fashion the resulting input into a master plan for price stability. "The President cannot lick inflation," Ford lectured the meeting. "The Congress cannot lick inflation. Business, labor, agriculture, and other segments of America cannot lick inflation. Separately we can only make it worse, but together we can beat it to its knees."[17]

Greenspan was relieved that Ford had not fallen back on price controls. But a series of billowy civic meetings was not his preferred approach, either. Still, he played along loyally over the next weeks. In the middle of September he dutifully attended a gathering of supposed inflation experts from the health, education, and social services professions. Some way into the proceedings, a labor union chief complained that a policy of fighting inflation would favor rich bankers and harm ordinary workers. How could Greenspan defend that?

A warning light flashed dimly somewhere in Greenspan's brain, but he was already answering the question.[18] If the issue was who would see their incomes decline most, he was saying, why then the speaker was mistaken. If the government cooled inflation by clamping down on demand, Wall Street brokers would actually lose more because their incomes were more volatile. "If you want to get statistical," Greenspan said, "I mean let's look at what the facts are."[19]

A horrified booing filled the room. Somebody yelled out, "That's the whole trouble with this administration!"[20] Afterward, labor unions announced that Greenspan would be a candidate for their annual "dubious distinction" award, and Congresswoman Barbara Jordan of Texas suggested that Americans send Greenspan their grocery receipts.[21] Home builders in Oregon formed a group called Save Our Brokers. They mailed handkerchiefs to stockbrokers so that they would have something to sob into.[22]

The next day Ford saw Greenspan at the White House. "I understand you had fun yesterday," he said. "Welcome to Washington!"[23]

It was nice to have the president's support, but it did not make his inflation policy more credible. The minisummits produced a babble of contradictory ideas, mostly reflecting the lobbies that advanced them. Several prominent participants demanded a return to price controls, while others doubted that progress against inflation could justify the sacrifice that would be necessary. The chief economist from the IBM company presented a study showing that a painful $10 billion reduction in government spending would cut inflation by just one tenth of one percentage point, pushing up unemployment by far more. "Is it really worth it?" the man from IBM demanded.[24] Greenspan chaired a minisummit for economists at the Waldorf Astoria in New York, and the professionals considered a list of deregulatory initiatives that would take the pressure off prices—an approach much more to Greenspan's liking. But perhaps because he had advocated deregulation to no avail during the Nixon years, Greenspan responded warily. "These issues . . . have been raised many times before," he wrote in a memo. "There are solidly entrenched special interests working against such notions."[25]

On September 27, the minisummits culminated in a grand plenary. Two thousand clamorous participants crammed into the International Ballroom at the Washington Hilton, and the nation was treated to an Athenian experiment in economic policy. But at the end of two days of deliberation, the president was left clutching one single idea: the exercise in mass civic mobilization should be followed up by *more* mass civic mobilization. Ford now argued that given Washington's failure to rein in inflation, it was time for the American people to take the lead; they must be urged to relieve the pressure on prices by consuming less, recycling more, and boosting the national food supply by growing vegetables. On October 8, the White House unveiled its strategic contribution to this citizens' campaign. With the help of an ad agency, it had produced millions of red-and-white buttons that read WIN—"Whip Inflation Now" would be the slogan that inspired a national mobilization against price increases.

The economists in the administration were mortified.[26] Johnson's policy of cajoling captains of industry and union bosses had failed to restrain wages; the idea of cajoling the public at large was even more fanciful. It was one thing to ask people to plant Victory Gardens during World War II; it was another to expect them to dig vegetable plots now, with no goad from the Nazi threat and patriotism driven to an all-time low by the Watergate scandal. In an otherwise indifferent citizenry, the only flashes of enthusiasm for the WIN campaign came from discount retailers. A Denver grocery chain plastered its windows with WIN posters and proclaimed that its cheap products made it a champion inflation whipper.[27] An auto dealership in Pasadena offered a WIN button to anyone who would "test drive one of our inflation fighters."[28] A campaign to discourage consumption had been turned into a way of promoting it.

A few months later, in February 1975, Greenspan summed up the impact of the first major initiative of his public career. The WIN campaign "has not made a perceptible contribution to economic policy," he reported in a memo, "and I am unaware of any reason to expect it to do so in the future." It was time to acknowledge a failure. The WIN campaign should be allowed to make a "graceful exit."[29]

Yet Greenspan himself was not making for the exit. He had joined the administration promising to quit if its policies offended him, but association with the excruciating town-hall-and-vegetable-garden fiasco had failed to arouse his spirit of rebellion. On the contrary, he was emerging as a loyal team player—the part of him that had rallied to Nixon in the last months of 1968 trumped the part of him that stood on principle.[30] Greenspan seemed comfortable accepting that he was often in a minority, and that his views would not prevail. He was more of a sideman than Proxmire had anticipated.

It was not that Greenspan lacked intellectual backbone. He was clear on his own views and could stick up for them unflinchingly, as his Senate performance had demonstrated. But he did not feel compelled to force his positions on others—he had no need to dominate meetings, as his low-key performance on the draft commission had illustrated. At the start of the Ford administration, Greenspan insisted that unlike the previous CEA chairman, he would not serve as the public spokesman on economic policy; going on the record defending an initiative he disliked would have been anathema to him.[31] Once the spokesman's job had been passed off to the Treasury secretary, Greenspan was happy presenting confidential analysis to his political superiors and leaving them to decide what to do with it.

Recalling his time in the Ford administration years later, Greenspan told a story that summed up his approach to government service. At one point he had decided that Vice President Nelson Rockefeller was pushing a muddled energy policy; he had therefore done his duty by pointing out its flaws to the president. Ford had promised to block Rockefeller's initiative, but after a week he had called Greenspan into his office.

"Alan, you know, last week I promised you I was going to do this and frankly the politics were too tough," Ford said. "I want to apologize to you."

"Mr. President," Greenspan responded, "I am working for you and advising you. You don't have to apologize to me. I know what the problems are."[32]

Greenspan's sense of separation between his advice and the president's decisions came naturally to him. It was part of his loner psychology: he had relatively little need to feel that others approved of him, so he did not take offense if his advice was disregarded. It was also an extension of the habits he had learned as a consultant: he had spent two decades providing clients with analysis, and feeling blissfully indifferent as to what they did with it. But as well as coming naturally, Greenspan's sense of separation was convenient. It allowed him to remain true to his principles because the advice he gave was intellectually honest; but it also allowed him to flourish in his White House position, for it meant that he emerged as a popular team player. Senior officials from the president on down trusted his analysis because it seemed not to come burdened with any policy agenda. Precisely because he appeared not to want influence, Greenspan accumulated plenty of it.

In December 1974 Ford turned his attention to a new economic challenge: the economy was in recession. He was a bit exasperated by this turn of events—his economic advisers had allowed him to make speeches about inflation as enemy number one, while a far grislier enemy was sneaking up on him. The political price was already clear. The conservative commentator George Will had compared the halls of the Republican National Committee to "the set for a disaster flick, a political *Poseidon Adventure*."[33] A few days before Christmas, on December 21, Ford gathered his six top economic advisers plus Arthur Burns from the Fed and demanded to know what should be done.

Greenspan's preferred answer was, as usual, to do nothing—or at least to do as little as possible.[34] If companies were idling workers because their warehouses were full of unsold inventory, then the recession would end of its own accord once the excess had been sold off. For the government, the best policy would be no policy. Likewise, if the recession stemmed from a loss of business confidence, reflecting the spike in inflation, panicky government meddling might make things worse; for example, a budget stimulus might drive inflation up, damaging confidence further.[35] But because he felt more comfortable providing analysis than offering prescriptions,

Greenspan spent more time describing the troubles in the economy than laying out how the president should react; and the more he outlined the troubles, the less Ford was inclined to do nothing. At the end of the meeting, when the president checked off his decisions on an option paper prepared by his staff, he came down in favor of stimulating the economy by means of a tax cut.

Ford's decision confronted Greenspan with an uncomfortable dilemma. His own gloomy economic forecast had driven the president toward activism—Greenspan the analyst had inflicted a defeat on Greenspan the libertarian. But he was not about to sugarcoat his forecast in order to discourage economic tinkering; to the contrary, he had the consultant's self-protective habit of emphasizing bad potential outcomes.[36] And so rather than sweetening the data, Greenspan provided more data. Marshaling his team of staff economists at the Council of Economic Advisers, he came up with a statistical device to help limit the size of the tax cut: a weekly GNP estimate.

It was a classic Greenspan data-sleuthing exercise. The official GNP data came out once per quarter, but by cobbling together weekly numbers on retail sales, unemployment claims, and housing starts along with monthly numbers on machinery shipments, Greenspan's team could provide the president with real-time updates on national output.[37] If the libertarian in Greenspan was correct that the economy was going to stabilize itself, then the real-time updates would provide early proof that no stimulus was needed. If on the other hand the updates suggested that the economy was getting worse, then the empiricist in Greenspan would accept that stimulus was warranted.

Despite the fact that his economic principles were under fire, Greenspan was in his element. Shortly after deciding in favor of a tax cut, the president had left with his family for his traditional Christmas ski vacation in Vail, Colorado, where he stayed in a luxurious log cabin with a vaulted living room and crackling fires. Greenspan and other key advisers were billeted with various presidential friends dotted around the resort, mixing policy work with holiday socializing. Both obligations were fun. Greenspan enjoyed the company of the Ford team, even though it suffered from more than its fair share of difficult egos. There was the flagrantly ambitious Donald Rumsfeld, now serving as Ford's chief of staff. There was Dick Cheney, Rumsfeld's quietly effective young deputy with the lank comb-over, rounded shoulders, and squinted eyes, who brought along his daughters to enjoy the mountains. And there was the budget director, Roy Ash, who showed up at meetings with the president in a jazzy dark sweater with red-and-white stripes down the arms.[38] Ford himself retained the habits of a longtime congressman; he was used to working with a handful of advisers, and liked having the gang over for drinks at the end of the day. Greenspan became part of this inner circle, forging friendships that would last for years, and even permitting boisterous plaid to make an appearance in his wardrobe. A decade or so after disengaging from Ayn Rand's objectivist salon, although not from Rand herself, Greenspan found in the Ford team a compelling substitute.

By the start of 1975, Greenspan had carved out a special place for himself in Ford's cabinet meetings. The president's team understood that the proper size of the forthcoming tax cut would depend on just how weak the economy was, and thanks to his weekly GNP update, Greenspan was the man who knew—nobody else could shed light on this question. He had a way of expounding on the data that achieved two goals at once: he made it clear that everything was unclear, so that laymen could not possibly grasp what was going on; and then, having confused his audience into submission, he offered a rescuing hand in the form of his own forecast. If anybody else around the cabinet table tried to challenge his analysis, Greenspan swiftly cut him down. "He is extremely adept on his feet," a colleague noted in his diary on January 2. "No staffer knows the general subject of economics better than Greenspan—and he is quick to criticize anyone who misuses a phrase or term."[39] "He has the best bedside manner I've ever seen," another Ford administration colleague would recall, remarking on Greenspan's hypnotic effect on his superiors.[40] "*Extraordinary.* That was his favorite word. He'd go in to see Ford and say, 'Mr. President, this is an *extraordinarily* complex problem.' And Ford's eyes would get big and round and start to go around in circles."[41]

The more Greenspan parsed the mysteries of the economy, the more the president came to depend on him. The CEA chairman seemed to understand economic data like a horse whisperer understands a wild mare: he connected with them on a level that was invisible to most mortals. Yet because Greenspan drew a sharp line between analysis and prescription, his dominant alpha-male approach to economic forecasts combined with a mild diffidence as to policy questions. During the discussions of early 1975, Treasury Secretary William Simon argued forcefully that a tax cut was tantamount to going soft on inflation—a view that echoed that of Ford's likely challenger for the Republican nomination, California governor Ronald Reagan. By comparison, Greenspan seemed dovish, or possibly confused.[42] "Greenspan is on the fence—one day emphasizing inflation, the next day stressing the recession," his colleague noted in his diary.[43]

A few days before presenting his tax cut to the public, the president tried to force Greenspan off the fence. The administration was coalescing behind a plan for a $16 billion tax rebate, and Ford wanted to know whether that would hurt growth in the long run. Greenspan gave an honest answer, but it was also an answer that the boss wanted to hear. A one-time rebate would not affect the long-term budget or inflation much, one way or the other.

"As long as it's a one-shot deal and doesn't become permanent, it's not going to do much harm," Greenspan told Ford.

Ford seized on Greenspan's lack of objection and turned it into an endorsement. "If that's what you think should be done, then I'll propose it," he said, leaving Greenspan feeling startled but also gratified at the extent of his influence.

"The president of the United States is taking my advice," Greenspan later recalled thinking.[44]

On Sunday, January 13, 1975, Greenspan joined Rumsfeld, Cheney, and some other aides at the office. The president was to signal his intention to cut taxes that evening, using the format of an informal fireside chat, to be delivered from a White House library. Ford's speechwriter from his days in Congress had produced a draft of the address, but Rumsfeld was not impressed and wanted Greenspan's help in fixing it.[45]

After Ford had read out the speechwriter's draft on the teleprompter and watched a video playback, Rumsfeld seized the opportunity to suggest a few changes. Individual words were tweaked. Then phrases were improved. Then sentences went, and soon Rumsfeld and his allies were recasting whole paragraphs.[46] The more Greenspan got involved in this rewrite, the more he experienced a strange, contradictory sensation. He was conspiring in the overthrow of his own policy preferences: selling the case for a fine-tuning tax cut. But he was reveling in the feeling of being close to the action. Here he was on a weekend, crafting the president's message to the nation with a deadline approaching. In between the rehearsals and revisions, Ford invited Greenspan and the others to his residence on the second floor of the White House, where they watched snippets of the Super Bowl.

The next day the process was repeated all over again, with Rumsfeld, Greenspan, and colleagues scrambling to fill out the details of the president's State of the Union address, which would reiterate the call for a $16 billion tax rebate. The team worked steadily into the evening, piecing together the text and sustaining themselves with cookies, peanuts, and steak sandwiches. At one point, as Greenspan was pasting paragraphs of the speech into the right sequence, a colleague captured his sense of the moment, asking, "I wonder how I'm going to feel when I leave this place, looking from the outside in?"[47] There was nothing quite like the buzz of working in the White House.

Ford approved the final draft of the address at four a.m. the next morning.[48] Greenspan, for his part, faced his own moment of reckoning. Letters arrived from Ayn Rand's followers asking whether he had sold out; since when was a libertarian in favor of fine-tuning? Greenspan had preached repeatedly that budget discipline was key to controlling inflation; but now he had changed sides, going out of his way to marshal arguments that might mollify opponents of the rebate, such as Treasury Secretary William Simon. In a memo to Simon on the day of the State of the Union address, Greenspan explained that more government borrowing would not drive up prices so long as it happened soon, while private borrowing was in the ditch, along with the economy. "The problem will come in 1976 or after the economy has strengthened," Greenspan pleaded.[49] "We are all Keynesians now," he might as well have told him.

Greenspan reassured himself that he was making the world better. He had succeeded in improving the design of the rebate, insisting that it had to get to people before the economy recovered unassisted.[50] Besides, he and the president were steering a difficult course. If the $16 billion rebate seemed irresponsible to hawks such as Simon, it was still a triumph of restraint relative to the demands of liberal critics. The labor leader George Meany was among those demanding a far larger stimulus, and he had no doubt whom to blame for the administration's tightfistedness: "Alan Greenspan is there representing the philosophy of economic Darwinism—the survival of the richest," he growled bitterly.[51] Academics provided Meany with cover: "We're going to cut our own throats," said a professor at the University of Chicago, referring to the Ford team's reluctance to stimulate harder.[52] On January 23, 1975, Senator Hubert Humphrey, the Democratic presidential nominee of 1968, served warning that "unless the Administration gets with it, unless it begins to understand . . . we will go into a depression."[53]

The next day Greenspan appeared in Ford's office and sat himself down in an armchair directly across from the president's grand desk. His thick dark hair was swept back from his forehead, and although the colleague to his left was sporting a loud plaid jacket, Greenspan still wore his trademark dark suit—his sense of sartorial adventure was firmly suspended on days when he was in the office. To Greenspan's right sat a young speechwriter named Kaye Pullen. She was wearing a one-piece knit dress, short and tight. It was a very 1970s orange.

Pullen was looking a bit nervous, as though she feared spilling coffee on the presidential rug. She was thirty years old, she was the only woman in the meeting, and this was her first time in the Oval Office.

Greenspan introduced himself to Pullen and asked what she was working on. For a guy who had grown up in New York, Pullen later reflected, Greenspan had very nice southern manners. When Ford's meeting was over, Greenspan asked where Pullen's office was, and insisted on walking there with her.[54]

"My mother says, 'It seems to me that economic policy is about robbing Peter to pay Paul,'" Pullen ventured.

"It's pretty close," Greenspan indulged her. He mentioned something about Ayn Rand, and said that he would soon be off to a conference in a place called Davos. When he got back, he would be sure to be in touch with her.

Pullen got hold of Rand's novels but found them mostly impenetrable. The first was about an architect who blew up a building because it deviated from his original design; it was hard to relate to that when you worked in the Washington sausage factory. But when Greenspan called a few days later, Pullen happily accepted his invitation to dinner, and the two went to a place near Congress on Capitol Hill, the very citadel of sausage making. Pullen chattered excitedly, filling the space created by Greenspan's shyness with a stream of vivid stories. Her mother had sent her off to teenage parties in Nashville wearing long white gloves; she had been a reporter in Memphis covering civil rights; one time she and a news photographer had given chase to a local murderer known as the "cunning sex killer." Pullen was hitting her stride, impressing this big guy from the White House; and then, with one particularly vivacious wave of the hand, she knocked over a bottle of ketchup and spattered red gunk over the table.

Pullen felt an urgent longing to disappear into a dark hole. But slightly to her amazement, Greenspan didn't seem to think that the evening had been ruined. He just looked at the tablecloth and laughed an unfazed laugh. It was the beginning of a romance that would run and stop and start again.[55]

Toward the end of February 1975, Greenspan attained a new measure of fame—or perhaps infamy. A close-up of his face, with its heavy dark-rimmed glasses and soft eyes, filled the entire cover of *Newsweek*. Kaye Pullen's mother saw the photograph and was thrilled that her daughter was dating a celebrity, although she wished he were not Jewish.

The coverage inside *Newsweek* was less flattering than the photograph. A profile began by describing Greenspan as a "creeper"—"an unprepossessing presence who moves inchmeal through the roil of a Georgetown cocktail party leaving hardly a wake." People had begun to remark on Greenspan's curious combination of charm and awkwardness: he had a gift for getting along with powerful people, but his shyness flooded back when he navigated social gatherings. "He does not flow easily from one major conversational group of celebrities to another," the *Washington Post* reported, "but walks through various rooms looking as if he is going somewhere in particular—then you see him later heading back with the same purposeful expression."[56] Some people wondered why Greenspan bothered going to parties at all; he did not appear to be at ease in them. A few who remembered his Senate performance might have thought back to his opening remark—this man who professed never to be at the center of things seemed determined nonetheless to occupy a central place in Washington society. Some mysterious demon inside him must be driving him on. Perhaps, as the economic adviser to the leader of the free world, Greenspan felt compelled to claim the glamour that was due to him.

After labeling Greenspan a creeper, *Newsweek* allowed that he was likable, energetic, and possessed of the ear of the president. But it shared Senator Proxmire's suspicion that he was not to be trusted with it. "Greenspan's stern policy prescriptions have earned him a reputation as an insensitive Neanderthal," the magazine reported, adding that "many in Congress still doubt the wisdom of installing a CEA chairman who seems committed to the laissez-faire doctrines of a century ago."[57] A long essay accompanying the profile argued that Greenspan's supposed enthusiasm for austerity was especially risky in a time of recession. "Do Gerald Ford and his advisers know what they're doing?" *Newsweek* demanded. Unemployment had reached its highest point since 1941, but the inflation-obsessed hawks around the president were set against a real stimulus. The president, said one Democrat, was "getting the same kind of economic advice that Herbert Hoover was given," and the chief provider of that advice was the "ultraconservative" White House chief economist.[58] If austerity failed, Greenspan would surely be disgraced. "He'll be Alan Shortspan back in New York," *Newsweek*'s reporter quipped.[59]

Amid this storm of criticism, Ford's approval ratings hit the lowest point of his brief presidency.[60] Feeling the wind at their backs, the Democrats in Congress began to work up their own version of a stimulus, and in March both chambers passed a tax cut of $22.8 billion—a considerable expansion of Ford's original proposal. The president had to decide whether to veto the measure and take full responsibility for an unemployment rate that had passed the 8 percent mark, or bow to it.

Greenspan's position was now more uncomfortable than ever. After Ford had decided on a tax cut in December, Greenspan had responded by tracking the weekly GNP, and that gauge was now telling him that the worst of the recession was over.[61] Starting around mid-February 1975, he had "felt reasonably confident we were okay" and that "a marked recovery was a statistical necessity."[62] For Ford to sign a stimulus in late March would be to commit precisely the error that fine-tuners always made: by the time a recession captured Washington's attention and Congress drew up a bill, the stimulus was unneeded, wasteful, and potentially inflationary. But if Greenspan advised Ford to veto the tax cut, he would be exposing the president to political risk, potentially ruining his chances of election the following year. The weekly GNP gauge, however encouraging, could not provide proof of a recovery beyond all reasonable doubt. Given the uncertainty, could Greenspan really tell Ford to gamble on a do-nothing policy?

Ford demanded that his advisers state their recommendations to him in writing. Treasury Secretary Simon responded with a memo urging a veto. Arthur Burns supported him, maintaining that "if the tax bill becomes law, our national finances will be distorted for many years." Burns feared the bill's temporary provisions would become permanent: it was always easier to distribute candy to voters than to cut off their sugar supply later. "If you do not take a firm position on fiscal responsibility now, will you soon have another equally good chance to do so?" Burns demanded.[63]

With the Treasury secretary and the Fed chairman both opposed to the stimulus, Greenspan might have scuppered it if he had sided with them. But despite his frequent denunciations of deficits, Greenspan's nerve failed him.[64] On March 28 he advised Ford, "I recommend that the tax bill be signed but that you simultaneously come down very hard on expenditure increases."[65]

Ford quickly accepted Greenspan's advice.[66] He signed the tax reduction into law, then wielded the presidential veto over the next months in an effort to rein in spending. He did so with sufficient energy to upset the

Democrats: "This has been a government by veto," Senator John Pastore of Rhode Island huffed. "We've got the minority dragging the majority by the nose."[67] But Ford's veto campaign had barely any impact on the budget math: the federal deficit hit 3.4 percent of GDP in the year to June 1975, a larger shortfall than any that occurred under Lyndon Johnson. And unlike Johnson's big 1967–68 deficit, which was followed by the balanced budget enacted during his last year, Ford's 1974–75 deficit was followed by an even larger one. Just as Arthur Burns had predicted, Ford signed a measure extending the supposedly temporary tax rebate in December 1975, and the budget deficit for the year ending in June 1976 came to a shocking 4.2 percent of GDP, a postwar record.[68] Moreover, the stimulus hit the economy with the lousy timing that a critic of fine-tuning might have expected. It pumped up spending just as it was recovering anyway, with the result that annualized growth hit a blistering 9.3 percent in the first quarter of 1976 before crashing back to 3.1 percent in the following one.[69]

Greenspan had become the enabler for a policy that contradicted his principles. He had lambasted Lyndon Johnson's budget deficits; now he shared responsibility for permitting even larger ones. He had insisted that budget deficits were the cause of inflation; now he ignored his own lectures. He had required his staff at the Council of Economic Advisers to come up with a weekly GNP gauge whose express purpose was to signal whether a stimulus was needed; now, when that measure correctly indicated that no stimulus was justified, Greenspan had supported one anyway. Admittedly, he had supported the tax cut while simultaneously saying that spending should be restrained by means of vetoes. But this was a fig leaf. Given the nature of Congress, it was bound to be impossible to eliminate major programs; and Greenspan, who had long described inflation as a political problem, understood that better than anyone.[70] Only a few months earlier, Greenspan had promised Senator Biden that he would not change his ideas according to the job he held; and for a while he had kept his promise by drawing a bright line between his honest analysis and his bosses' policy compromises. But when it came to the tax question, Ford had asked him directly what ought to be done, and Greenspan had lacked the fortitude to join Burns and Simon in confronting the president with a tough message.

Greenspan's conduct was not shocking by the standards of Washington. There was a chance that the economy might fail to recover by itself, and he felt he should protect Ford against the possibility that his weekly GNP gauge was mistaken.[71] But the fact that Greenspan was following the ways of Washington was precisely the point. Half a year into his tenure, Greenspan had completed his journey from Ayn Rand's outsider salon to the inner circle of power; he might still condemn the status quo from time to time, but in truth he was now part of it. In voting against Greenspan's confirmation, Senator Proxmire had misjudged the man. Ideas were not what drove him after all; his courteous, clubbable, and nonconfrontational manner proved to be a better predictor of his conduct in office than his libertarian ideology. However disarmingly Greenspan might portray himself as a sideman, he was only human, after all. He wanted to be at the center.

Nine

BETWEEN THATCHER
AND KISSINGER

On a Monday evening in September 1975, an improbable, schoolmarm-like figure appeared upon the stage at the St. Regis-Sheraton in New York. Speaking with an accent, she lectured her audience that the pursuit of equality was a mirage—it was far more important to create wealth than to distribute it. The drive for so-called fairness was the product of ignoble sentiments: the envy of the underclass on the one hand, the guilt of the wealthy on the other. "Let our children grow tall," the lecturer declared, "and some taller than others if they have the ability to do so."[1]

The speaker might have been Ayn Rand, but the accent was British rather than Russian; and the bracing woman at the podium was the recently elevated leader of Britain's opposition Conservative Party, Mrs. Margaret Thatcher. New York was not sure what to make of this newcomer to the world stage, with her startling political philosophy and her baby blond hair. "The most operative word is lady—old-fashioned, proper, traditional lady," said a woman who heard Thatcher at a private luncheon, "she is a flower among the thorns." "She was prettier than I expected, softer, younger," agreed Barbara Walters, the rising queen of television news, who interviewed Thatcher on NBC's *Today* show. But the Conservative leader was not all soft. She carried a treatise by Hayek in her handbag. She was fond of tough quotes attributed to Abraham Lincoln: "You cannot strengthen the weak by weakening the strong."[2] And she bristled impatiently at unserious small talk. When Barbara Walters warned her, during a brief chat before their interview, that she might have to digress from political topics to the question of how it felt to be a woman in such a high post, Thatcher shook her head and sighed, "Isn't it too bad that there aren't more women around who feel as we do."[3]

After doing the rounds in New York, the Conservative leader flew to Washington to meet the president and his entourage.[4] Secretary of State Henry Kissinger had instructed Ford earlier that Thatcher was "a great gal," but "not experienced at all in foreign policy."[5] Ford and his national security aide, Brent Scowcroft, formed a similar impression. "She was very warm, very friendly, very composed," Scowcroft remembered. "We didn't see her as a heavyweight who was going to change the course of anything."[6] Katharine Graham, the publisher of the *Washington Post,* was not impressed by this grocer's daughter with intellectual pretensions: "I think she's just a vulgar fishwife," she confided (or so she thought) to the wife of a British newspaper owner.[7] But on her third evening in Washington, Thatcher appeared at a British embassy dinner in a black velvet evening suit and spoke from the heart about free markets and liberty. To a certain type of listener, she was more rousing by far than any British leader since Churchill.

One such listener was sitting right beside her. As the senior member of the Ford administration at the British embassy dinner, the chairman of the Council of Economic Advisers had been placed next to Thatcher, and she wasted no time in getting to the point with him.

"Tell me, Chairman Greenspan," she asked, "why is it that we in Britain cannot calculate M3?"[8]

It was an unusual dinner-party icebreaker. M3 was a broad measure of the money supply that counted deposits at S&Ls as well as bank deposits and cash; and quite apart from its arcane nature, the timing of this question was remarkable.[9] Central banks had only just begun to publish monetary measures, and the Fed would not commit itself firmly to a money-supply target for another four years; to know about M3 in the fall of 1975 was to belong to a rarefied club of hard-money believers.[10] But, however unlikely her question, Thatcher had unlocked her shy neighbor. For the rest of the evening, the two got along famously.

After the dinner, Greenspan made the short trip from Embassy Row on Massachusetts Avenue to his apartment at the Watergate. Kaye Pullen had let herself in and was waiting for him in the bare living room—Alan had done nothing to make the place feel like home, though by now this had less to do with the fiction that he might resign his job than with his serene indifference to interior decoration. Kaye was used to this routine by now, getting together with Alan after an evening spent separately; although they had been dating for eight months, they were not officially a couple in the eyes of Washington. But on this particular evening, she could tell that something out of the ordinary had happened. Alan was acting oddly, and for a moment she wondered whether the ambassador's butler had slipped him an extra gin and tonic. On further reflection, she realized that this theory was implausible: Alan's relationship with alcohol was as proper and controlled as his relationship with people. In all their months together, there had been just one occasion when Alan had ordered so much as a single drink at lunch—they had been eating at the White House mess, and Alan had broken with habit by asking for a beer to go with the Mexican food on that day's menu. But even this not terribly wild impulse had soon been squashed. Seeing Arthur Burns take a seat nearby, Alan had summoned the waiter back to his table and quietly told him that there would be no beer after all.[11]

Alan and Kaye talked—it was the usual evening debriefing—and it soon became clear why Alan was agitated. It was not what he had drunk; it was whom he had sat next to. Imagine, Margaret Thatcher had asked about M3! An obscure measure of the money supply embraced by followers of Milton Friedman! Which American leader would have heard of such a thing, let alone admit to an interest in the midst of a grand dinner party? After that get-to-know-you opener, Mrs. Thatcher had engaged Alan in a debate about market economics and the problems of the West: she talked like Ayn Rand, but she was likely to become the next prime minister of Britain.[12] Forced to choose between his libertarian principles and his urge to be at the center, Greenspan was capable of tempering his views, as his advice on Ford's tax rebate had demonstrated. But in his ideal world, Greenspan would be both a faithful libertarian and an influential power player—and sitting next to Thatcher had allowed him to dream that this combination might be possible.

Kaye had seldom seen Alan so excited.[13]

G reenspan's encounter with Margaret Thatcher came at a propitious moment. For free-market conservatives, 1975 was both dispiriting and hopeful: the West was reeling from unemployment and inflation, but there seemed to be an opening at last for libertarian remedies.[14] That spring, an essay by the eminent social scientist James Q. Wilson had circulated inside the White House; it argued that the nation's difficulties arose "not from government's having neglected the interests of its citizens, but from its having attempted to serve them."[15] The Harris polling organization reported that no more than 13 percent of the public felt confident in government, and most seemed to regard public assistance programs as false friends—the extra taxes they implied would outweigh their benefits.[16] Government regulation was losing favor, too. As an outside consultant, Greenspan had tried in vain to push the Nixon administration to embrace deregulation. But by 1975 some Democrats as well as Republicans were coming around to Greenspan's point of view; in the Senate, it was a Kennedy, of all people, who led hearings that year on airline deregulation. Margaret Thatcher's firm pronouncements demonstrated that Britain's economic troubles had generated a libertarian reaction. It seemed possible that the United States might follow.

Yet if Britain's Conservative leader illustrated what might be, there were also darker visions of the future. "You have an end-to-Western-capitalism syndrome," a business school dean worried; "businessmen see the big federal deficits, the capital shortage, world-wide inflation, the energy crisis . . . they see the continued encroachment of the bureaucrats."[17] *Time* magazine's cover asked flatly, "Can Capitalism Survive?" while in the pages of *Harper's*, the Democratic congressman Michael Harrington proclaimed, "National economic planning is an idea whose time has come."[18] In May 1975 the former vice president, Senator Hubert Humphrey, teamed up with Senator Jacob Javits to introduce a bill to establish an economic planning board; the board was to produce six-year plans every two years, as though this odd echo of the Senate's two-year/six-year electoral machinery might disguise the resemblance to the Soviet Union.[19] On June 3, 1975, Greenspan warned Ford that "a major philosophical issue which will emerge in the months ahead will be the role of government in economic planning."[20] Three weeks later he wrote again in the same vein, urging the president to place his trust in "the self-interest of the businessmen" rather than central planning. "One need only visit department stores in communist countries and compare them with those in the market oriented societies to get an immediate picture of where the consumer fares best," Greenspan lectured Ford, somewhat condescendingly.[21]

America seemed to be approaching a fork in the road. The Watergate scandal, the humiliation in Vietnam, and the stagflationary economy had buried the optimism of Kennedy's New Frontier. Some new kind of credo would have to take its place—either a Thatcherite philosophy of the conservative right or a doubling down on government controls of the sort advocated by Senators Humphrey and Javits. From his redoubt at the White House, Greenspan waded into this battle, denouncing the Humphrey-Javits bill as a plot by the intellectual elite, which "wishes to see its ideals more effectual than the market is likely to permit them to be." To his relief, the Humphrey-Javits legislation soon hit a wall in the Senate. But not all statist challenges would be seen off so easily—particularly not if they were mounted by a formidable bureaucratic brawler who operated from inside the Ford administration.

The brawler who concerned Greenspan was Henry Kissinger, Greenspan's fellow graduate from George Washington High School and the man who dismissed Thatcher as "a great gal" of no great consequence. Kissinger had descended from his perch at Harvard University in 1969, serving first as Nixon's national security adviser and then concurrently as national security adviser and secretary of state; he had no doubt of his ability to perform both jobs simultaneously. No other figure in Washington worked the system as deftly as he did—he was possessed of "an almost devilish psychological intuition, an instinct for grasping the hidden springs of character, of knowing what drives or dooms another person," a Harvard colleague said of him.[22] Whereas Greenspan was coy and ambivalent about acquiring power, Kissinger sought it out, treasured it, and lusted for it openly. His paranoid secrecy alarmed even Nixon, who was once driven to suggest that Kissinger might need psychiatric counseling.[23]

In May 1975, the same month that Senators Humphrey and Javits introduced their national planning bill, Kissinger directed his manipulative genius at the so-called commodity problem.[24] "The paramount necessity of our time is the preservation of peace," Kissinger told an audience in the first of three economic speeches that month, "but history has shown that international political stability requires international economic stability." In recent times, he continued, that stability had been threatened by "shortages and disputes over new issues such as energy, raw materials, and food." Grain, fertilizers, and petroleum had shot up in price, hitting the poorest nations that were net importers of all three; as a result, developing countries were demanding a "New World Order."[25] Such tensions, Kissinger warned, "must be overcome, or we face not only an end to the growth of the last thirty years but a shattering of the hopes of all mankind for a better future."[26]

Kissinger refused to contemplate such problems through a Thatcherite, free-market prism. The way he saw things, the miraculous growth of the postwar era was not the achievement of the invisible hand; rather, it was the result of the international architecture established at the end of World War II, with the United States at its center. "For thirty years, the modern economic system created at the Bretton Woods conference of 1944 has served us well," Kissinger declared; by creating a framework of stability, it had allowed commerce to flourish. It was hardly surprising that the collapse of the Bretton Woods system, marked by Nixon's abandonment of the gold peg, was now leading to trouble; it was the job of statesmen to come up with a fresh architecture to replace the old one. Kissinger duly proposed a series of price-stabilizing commodity agreements between producer and consumer nations. "Global interdependence is a reality," Kissinger averred. "There is no alternative to international collaboration."[27]

Even at the best of times, Greenspan never trusted Kissinger. He was too dark and too distant; strange secrets seemed to lurk inside the man that even he was not aware of.[28] But to Greenspan's way of thinking, what Kissinger was proposing was not merely untrustworthy. It crossed the border into being simply wrong—it amounted to price controls dressed up in diplomatic verbiage. Just as Nixon's disastrous price freeze had treated the symptoms of inflation only, so Kissinger's calls for "a Bretton Woods for the 1980s" missed the point: no international monetary architecture could succeed so long as inflation eroded the value of national currencies and forced periodic devaluations.[29] Kissinger's proposal to control commodity prices belonged to the same class of delusion—fixing the price of wheat or fuel was no more likely to succeed than fixing the price of the dollar. Even before Kissinger had gone public with his proposals for international price-stabilizing arrangements, an economist on the staff of the Council of Economic Advisers had sent a handwritten note to Greenspan, reporting on "an almost interminable series of meetings with the State Department that had been 'intellectually dishonest.'"[30] The secretary of state's speech was "filled with bombast and rhetoric," the economist complained after Kissinger laid out his vision.[31] When Kissinger created an interdepartmental working group to flesh out his program, attending its meetings "constituted one of the most frustrating experiences I have suffered through in my professional career," the CEA man reported.[32]

The frustration at the Council of Economic Advisers spread to the Treasury and the White House budget bureau, and pretty soon an anti-Kissinger backlash surfaced in the newspapers. A string of anonymously sourced articles portrayed the secretary of state as a clumsy interventionist; and on June 4 the *New York Times* reported complaints from well-placed government economists that Kissinger was making economic policy without going through the proper channels. "Speeches Irk Officials Who Prefer More Research," the headline said, pointedly.[33]

The day the *Times* article appeared, Kissinger called in one of his lieutenants.[34]

"I want to find out the source of all these newspaper articles," Kissinger instructed.

"I think it is basically coming out of the White House group," the lieutenant replied.

"Like who?"

"I know some of it came from Greenspan."

Kissinger did not register surprise at the suggestion that Greenspan might be knifing him. Perhaps he knew that Greenspan had been involved in faction fights before, showing up at the White House on a Sunday with Donald Rumsfeld and Dick Cheney to rewrite the president's fireside chat on the economy. "Speeches Irk Officials Who Prefer More Research"— the infuriating condescension of that *Times* headline sounded just like Greenspan.

"If people want to advertise their bureaucratic defeats, that is their problem," Kissinger growled menacingly.[35]

Kissinger was not about to retreat into his shell because of a few newspaper salvos. For some time now, he had been eyeing Iran, a key ally in the Middle East that was looking increasingly unstable. The surge in oil prices in 1973 and 1974 had flooded the country with cash, inflating a financial bubble.[36] Then the global recession had driven oil prices back down, cutting Iran's export revenues and threatening to burst the bubble. To make matters even trickier, the OPEC oil cartel was resisting the price fall by directing its members to pump less, which meant that Iran exported fewer barrels of oil as well as getting less for each of them.[37] The U.S. embassy in Tehran cabled Washington with reports of delayed construction projects, unpaid wages, and riots in major cities. The Iranian economy was in free fall. The regime itself might topple.

The prospect of upheaval in Iran was worrying enough for the Ford administration. The ruling shah was an American ally; besides, a revolution would disrupt oil production, driving up world prices yet again and suffocating the U.S. economic recovery. But however alarming instability might be, America's immediate problem was the shah himself; faced with riots against his regime, he was demanding a lifeline in the form of a 30 percent increase in the oil price set by OPEC. If Saudi Arabia, the cartel's dominant producer, cut back its own production sufficiently, the shah's 30 percent price jump could be made to stick. Iran would get the cash it needed to buy off protesters—and the United States would suffer a crippling blow to its economy.

In this cauldron of trouble, Kissinger spied opportunity. He was not going to take oil-price gyrations lying down; he believed that statesmen should shape destiny. And so he conceived a majestic triple play. The United States would offer the shah an alternative oil deal: it would buy up surplus Iranian crude in defiance of OPEC's quotas, requiring in exchange a discount on each barrel. The move would shore up America's ally, the shah. It would release more oil onto the global market, bringing down the price and providing a leg up for the U.S. economy. And it would weaken OPEC, avenging the humiliating oil embargo of two years earlier.

On June 12, eight days after the critical *Times* piece, Kissinger broached his plan with Ford at a meeting in the Oval Office, saying it would "maybe even crack OPEC." Ford immediately indicated that Alan Greenspan would have to sign off on it. He evidently did not want to make any significant economic decision without Greenspan's blessing, but he felt that if Greenspan was on board, the rest of the economic team would follow.

"Why don't you just talk to Alan alone?" the president suggested.[38]

Four days later, Kissinger summoned Greenspan to his office.

"The President wanted me to discuss something," Kissinger started. "This is only for you and is highly sensitive."

Greenspan listened politely to the outline of Kissinger's oil plan. He knew from the CEA staff memos that the State Department had a statist approach to commodity prices. But he said nothing of this to Kissinger.

"The idea properly packaged seems very attractive," Greenspan ventured. Then he added that it might take time to think through the details. "We may need a total strategy before we move," he cautioned.

Kissinger preferred to move first and strategize later. He had satisfied Ford's instruction to bring Greenspan in on the deal, and he had managed to elicit interest, if not quite approval.

"I think we should pick up what we can and develop a total strategy after Iran is signed up," Kissinger replied, wrapping up the meeting.[39]

Later that day, Greenspan had lunch with Charles Robinson, a dashing, bow tie–wearing entrepreneur who had participated in the D-Day landing and now served as Kissinger's undersecretary for economics. Greenspan reiterated to Robinson that the oil plan needed further thought. After all, Iran was willing to sell only 700,000 barrels a day of discounted oil, less than 3 percent of OPEC's daily output. As OPEC's swing producer, Saudi Arabia could easily shut off a few refineries to offset Iran's increased sales, leaving the world oil price exactly where it had been in the first place.[40]

Robinson reported to Kissinger that Greenspan was on the fence. He wanted another meeting.[41]

"Why do you and Greenspan have to see me again?" Kissinger asked, exasperated.

"He suggested it," Robinson answered. "He wants to explain this more fully."

"Come on, don't turn this small problem into a nightmare," Kissinger said. In two days, he had to deliver an address at a dinner of the Japan Society. It would be his first major speech on Asia since America's ignominious evacuation from Saigon two months earlier. He needed time to think about the global picture.

"I'll call him up and tell him I can't do it," Kissinger said.

"Hold his hand a little bit and that will solve his problem," Robinson counseled.

Kissinger called Greenspan the next day.[42] "I am working on my speech," Kissinger began, "so it is very important that—"

Greenspan cut him off. "Can I tell you briefly what I have been thinking about?" he began. He ran through some of the kinks in the deal, starting with the fact that the Saudis could simply offset extra Iranian sales by curbing their production. The plan had to anticipate this Saudi counterpunch, or it would fail. "You have to have pressure on Saudi Arabia," Greenspan concluded.

"But can't moving on this give us an option?" Kissinger urged.

"There are a number of technical problems about how we can do this," Greenspan answered. "They are solvable, but technical." In his usual way, Greenspan was asserting control with a calculated one-two punch: first, emphasize the complexity of the issue; second, offer himself up as the expert who could unscramble it. "It is not easy," Greenspan went on, "but I am trying to think of ways to do it and I think it can be done."

"It would give us an option," Kissinger repeated, trying to put the big picture back into focus. "It would give us protection against an embargo."

"That is certain," Greenspan said, humoring him.

"And a crack at the OPEC cartel," Kissinger added.

Again, Greenspan pretended to agree. The truth was that Saudi Arabia would have to cut production by just 10 percent to neutralize an Iranian side deal, a relatively small move given that the kingdom's output had already proved capable of swinging as much as 18 percent from month to month since the start of the year.[43] But Greenspan avoided telling Kissinger directly that his scheme was harebrained. His goal was just to slow him down by getting him to agree to a meeting.

"I haven't thought through how to play it and I would be more than anxious to get your views," Kissinger allowed. Greenspan evidently understood the technical details of oil markets in a way that he did not. He was coming around to the idea that Greenspan could be useful.

Greenspan sensed that Kissinger was lowering his guard. Pretty soon he would have him where he wanted.

"I am only concerned that before it is done you feel confident with the secondary effects," Greenspan said mildly.

"I am anxious to discuss it with you," Kissinger responded. "It may have to slip as late as Thursday."

"There is no rush," Greenspan assured him.[44]

The following week Kissinger invited Greenspan and the head of the Federal Energy Administration, Frank Zarb, to a lunch in his private dining room at the Department of State.[45] Zarb was a newcomer to the discussions over the Iranian oil deal, but Greenspan had worked on him enough to know that he would be an ally.

"Well, my first reaction was that it is an interesting idea," Zarb began. "A possible way to crack the oil cartel. But then I looked at the consequences and I have some questions." Ordinarily, it was private American oil companies that bought oil from Iran. If the U.S. government was going to act as the buyer, Congress would have to be on board, and the politics would get complicated. For example, the lawmakers would want a say in how large the Iranian discount would be, which would put them in a position of legislating the oil price. The scheme threatened to politicize a key sector of the American economy.

"We definitely do not want a government purchasing agency," Zarb said bluntly. "The notion of a government agency handling this sort of matter is inconceivable and inconsistent with our idea of a free enterprise system. The liberals have been pushing it in order to further their effort to nationalize the oil industry. So, success in this venture we are discussing would play into the liberals' hands."

Greenspan himself could not have put it better. This crazy oil deal was really about something much larger. If Kissinger was fond of grand strategic thoughts, he should spend a little time contemplating the state versus the market.[46]

Kissinger allowed that Zarb might have a point. "We might not want Congress to take too close a look," he conceded. But he evidently thought his plan was too brilliant to abandon.

"For us to work the deal would be a dramatic demonstration that our policy works," Kissinger urged. "And it would also shock the Saudis. There's no telling what they will do. But you can be sure they will want to do at least as well as the Shah. That might also give us a nice option."

"You mean they would want a similar deal?" Zarb asked.

"They will not let the Shah steal the march on them. What is least likely is they will cut production by 700,000 barrels a day," Kissinger insisted.

Greenspan could see why his staff at the Council of Economic

Advisers hated dealing with the State Department. Its arguments were back to front. For some reason Kissinger believed that a deal with Iran would spur the Saudis to make a similar sale to the United States. He did not seem to grasp that the Saudis played the role of swing producer within OPEC.[47]

"The Saudis . . . have the flexibility to absorb this and preserve the cartel," Greenspan said, mustering his reserves of patience.

"But it would affect price," Kissinger countered. He was still failing to see that Saudi Arabia could offset the Iranian sale, in which case the oil price would not actually be affected.

Perhaps sensing that he was losing the argument, Kissinger shifted onto what he thought was safer ground. A deal with the shah, he contended, "would highlight our leadership position."

Zarb shot back that the credibility of U.S. leadership might actually be harmed if the Saudis played the role of swing producer, as Greenspan predicted. The whole world would understand that the United States had tried and failed to break OPEC.

"I do not regard this as being a decisive break," Kissinger said, a little weakly. All the loose ends that Zarb and Greenspan were tugging on had him fighting to defend his plan. "It's really just a nibble, but it gives us flexibility with the others."

The back-and-forth continued until Kissinger played his final card. He reminded his guests that the clock was ticking. The shah's enemies were gaining strength and he needed the money quickly.

"It must be in the next six weeks, otherwise it's lost," Kissinger said urgently.

Greenspan was not going to fall for this car salesman's ploy. A limited-time-only bargain was easy to refuse if you did not want the vehicle.

"I'm concerned about the feasibility of bypassing Congress," Greenspan objected.

"Well, do you want to proceed or not?" Kissinger demanded.

Now, to Greenspan's chagrin, Zarb faltered. The ticking clock had rattled him, and he relented on the condition that the whole thing be kept away from Congress. "Yes, I think we should proceed," he conceded.

Greenspan jumped in, still hoping to stall Kissinger. "Is there any way . . . that we can be sure that that sort of legal operation is feasible?" he wondered. "Why don't we have some lawyers look at it?"

Kissinger seized on Zarb's assent and ignored Greenspan. The lunch ended with the understanding that Undersecretary Robinson would speak to the Iranians. For now, the secretary of state was winning.

One week later, on June 30, 1975, Robinson duly met the shah and his foreign minister.[48] The Iranians seemed keen to do a deal, but when Kissinger tried to make headway back in Washington, he found that Greenspan was counterattacking. The economic team had returned to the question of who or what would purchase the oil on behalf of the U.S. government. Without an answer to this practical question, Robinson's negotiations with the shah were not going to achieve anything.

"Couldn't Defense buy the oil?" Kissinger demanded at a meeting on July 14. Again, Greenspan, Zarb, and Robinson had joined him.[49]

"Defense buys all its oil on bids from companies," Greenspan said doggedly.

"As a historian, I say this country has had it," Kissinger sputtered. "I spend two-thirds of my time explaining to other countries why this country cannot do what is clearly in its own interest." The way Kissinger saw things, his Iran plan had implications that stretched far beyond one lousy deal. He and Robinson were simultaneously negotiating grain sales to the Soviets and a copper deal for Zaire; they were working on multiple commodity schemes designed to mold the global economy to U.S. interests. After all, the economic side of the U.S. government had let the entire Bretton Woods system go down in flames. Somebody needed to fix it.

"I want to break up the Group of 77," Kissinger went on, referring to the group of developing countries that had been protesting the deterioration in its terms of trade and demanding a New World Order. The Iran move was just one venture in a larger game. By buying off key third-world governments with commodity deals, Kissinger aimed to destroy their coalition.

"The Zairians told me that if they could get an agreement on cocoa and copper that they would drop the words 'new international economic order' from their vocabulary," Robinson offered, seeking to inject evidence that Kissinger's diplomacy might be succeeding.

"We must pick concrete issues and split them," Kissinger agreed eagerly.

"I call it the ice cream parlor approach. You put the ice cream on the table, you open the door, and the kids will come in by themselves," Robinson pontificated.

By now the economists' eyes were spinning.

"This is all too fast for me," Zarb interjected. "Your friends are your enemies and your friends." Invoking the defense secretary, Zarb continued, "I would rather work with Schlesinger. At least once you get him going, he goes in a relatively straight line."

"You think so?" Kissinger replied, a bit cryptically.

A fortnight later, at the beginning of August, Kissinger resolved that it was time to end-run Greenspan. He sent a memo to the president on August 6, pressing for "a decision to proceed with final steps" and promising "a crack in OPEC's price solidarity." "I am cutting through the fudge factory," he told Robinson the next day, instructing him to liaise with Greenspan and Zarb but not to give ground. "The guys will just have stupid nitpicks," he predicted.[50]

The next morning Kissinger saw Ford in the Oval Office. He told the president flat out that his economic advisers were petty obstructionists. "Zarb and Greenspan are dragging their feet," he said. "I have no doubt that they will approve it, but they want to prove their manhood." There was no more time to waste on their small-minded quibbles. It was vital to get a provisional answer to the Iranian foreign minister that day, Kissinger insisted.

"Go ahead," Ford responded.[51]

Having given the Iranians a provisional yes, Kissinger proceeded to the next stage. Eight days later, on August 15, his staff prepared another long memo for Ford, laying out what the State Department hoped would be the conclusive arguments for the Iranian oil purchase, including a way of keeping Congress out of it.[52]

"This will be a spectacular deal," Kissinger told Robinson. "The more we buy, the better."

"We need to clear it with Greenspan and Zarb," Robinson reminded him.

"There isn't a brain between the two of them," Kissinger answered. "I think I understand economics as well as they do."

"Greenspan apparently made some comment about we should make no more deals," Robinson cautioned.

"Look, just ignore Greenspan," Kissinger said firmly. "After this, they'll all come crawling." The case in favor of the deal was too powerful to resist, Kissinger believed. "Your arguments are conclusive," he told Robinson. "They ought to be—you got them from me."

But Greenspan was not to be ignored so easily. The president took delivery of Kissinger's long memo, initialed his approval, but added the proviso: "Would want Chuck Robinson to work with Frank Zarb & Alan Greenspan as he has in the past." Kissinger still lacked the green light he needed.

Seeking to build a coalition against Greenspan, Robinson visited Treasury Secretary Bill Simon in the Hamptons on August 17. Robinson felt that the discussion went well, with Simon nodding sympathetically as he made the case for the Iran deal. But victory proved elusive yet again. As Robinson got up to take his leave, the Treasury secretary made for the telephone; "Simon was attempting to reach Greenspan when I left," Robinson reported back to Kissinger.[53] Evidently, neither the president nor the Treasury secretary would take a firm position without Greenspan's say-so. Greenspan was the man who knew, and nobody would act without him.

At the end of August, the summer-long struggle over oil came to a close, and Greenspan emerged the victor. Irritated by the delays caused by unseen hands in Washington, the shah changed the terms of the deal: he announced that he must have a better price or he would sell oil just for a few months, not longer. Greenspan chose this moment to insist that only a long-term deal would be acceptable—he was open to the State Department's perspective, by all means, but only on conditions that made progress impossible.[54] On September 3, Kissinger's team cabled the Iranians one last time, outlining a final proposal. When the shah rejected it, the diplomats threw in the towel. "I conclude that there is no basis for agreement now," Robinson told Kissinger.[55]

One year earlier, confronted by an ideological adversary in the shape of Senator Proxmire, Greenspan had defended his libertarian philosophy forthrightly. Now, confronted by a scheming rival such as Henry Kissinger, Greenspan had proved equally adept at a shadier form of combat. By feigning cooperation, by never stating his opposition to the oil deal, he had achieved his purpose stealthily: "Revealing his thinking was not the outstanding attribute of Greenspan," Kissinger reflected, many years later.[56] But what was even more impressive was the aftermath of the victory. In postmortems of the aborted Iranian deal, both Kissinger and Undersecretary Robinson blamed the Treasury secretary for its failure; the CEA chairman somehow retained their respect and even friendship. Greenspan, unlike others, had never been "a bureaucratic factor," Kissinger averred.[57] The fact that Greenspan left few apparent bruises on his adversaries made his achievement all the more striking.[58]

On September 5, 1975, President Ford appeared in the Capitol Park in Sacramento, California, and a slight young woman in a nunlike red robe brandished a Colt .45 pistol at him before being clobbered by a Secret Service agent. Less than three weeks later, on September 22, Ford emerged from a San Francisco hotel and found himself at gunpoint once again; this time an older woman forty feet away got off one shot before being tackled by an ex-marine who was standing in the crowd with her. Greenspan was on the curb outside the hotel, and the shot sounded like a dull pop; an agent bundled him into the bottom of a limousine that sped off down a freeway. He lay there on the floor of the vehicle, pressed against a White House colleague. At some point a voice announced, "You can get up now."[59]

The second assassination scare took place three days after Greenspan's encounter with Margaret Thatcher, and it dramatized the scarier version of the nation's future. If Thatcher held out the prospect of a return to the individual responsibility of the nineteenth century, the attempts on the president signaled that America might descend into a poisonous despond in which citizens blamed government for their lot and, in extreme cases, felt free to vent their grievances by shooting at the president. "Violence is ever more condoned in this country especially if it has some pseudo con-nection with political positions and revolutionary ideas," Greenspan lamented in a memo soon after the second attack.[60] The increasingly left-wing atmosphere on college campuses deserved much of the blame, he continued. "Our university instructors are cynically disparaging the val-ues which made this country great." It was time for the president to defend American capitalism "in ethical and moral terms," Greenspan went on. Ford should give a major address on "the social-political-psychological roots of student nihilism, radicalism, and violence."

If the assassination scares were not enough, another alarming vision of America's future was playing out in New York City. Having borrowed too much, spent too much, and generally kowtowed to the unrealistic demands of its people, New York's municipal government had reached the brink of bankruptcy in May 1975 and come cap in hand to Washington. Most of the rest of the country seemed disinclined to help. New York had indulged its municipal employees shockingly: "You can't retire people after twenty years, at the age of thirty-eight or thirty-nine, at half their highest salary," one congressman complained, adding, for good measure, "You can have just so many porno movies."[61] Woody Allen captured the essence of this sentiment two years later in the movie *Annie Hall:* "Don't you see the rest of the country looks upon New York like we're left-wing, communist, Jew-ish, homosexual pornographers? I think of us that way sometimes and I live here."

At Greenspan's prompting, President Ford rebuffed New York's plea for a bailout. With much of the nation behind him, there seemed to be no reason to cave in to a city that exemplified the culture of the political left in all its gaudy irresponsibility. But almost immediately, New York hit back. Hugh Carey, the governor of New York State, accused Ford of "a level of arrogance and disregard for New York that rivals the worst days of Richard Nixon and his gang of cutthroats."[62] New York's mayor, Abraham Beame, invoked Nixon in a different fashion: "It's incredible to me that the President of the United States thinks more about the stockholders of Lockheed or Penn Central than the eight million people of our city."[63]

During the Lockheed hearings four years earlier, Greenspan had broken with his mentor Arthur Burns by opposing a rescue. Now he emerged at the helm of the hard-line faction once again, though this time he was doing so from within the government. To his way of thinking, Abraham Beame's invocation of Lockheed and Penn Central showed precisely why it was vital not to bail out New York. If America continued to slither down this slope, each bailout would furnish justification for the next, and pretty soon the government would backstop every debt in the nation. The essence of the Ford presidency, Greenspan argued at a White House meeting on September 25, should be to reverse this self-reinforcing pattern of softheaded decisions.[64]

Other Ford advisers agreed in principle with Greenspan, but they worried that New York's bankruptcy could trigger knock-on problems for the economy. Burns in particular predicted havoc. Banks were stuffed with New York bonds whose value would collapse, leaving banks too weak to lend; a credit crunch would follow. Even if the banks proved unexpectedly resilient, there were other possible channels of contagion. For one thing, a default in New York could destroy financial confidence in other American cities. Finding it hard to borrow, municipal governments would lay off police officers and teachers. As workers tightened their belts, business would fall off and the economy would spiral downward.[65]

It was not just Ford's advisers who feared the consequences of Greenspan's hard line. On October 3, 1975, German chancellor Helmut Schmidt lunched with the president at the White House.

"How's the Bundesbank? How's the mark?" Ford asked.

"Mr. President, never mind the Bundesbank or the mark," Schmidt answered. "If you let New York go broke, the dollar is worth *scheisse!*"[66] As Greenspan and other advisers listened, the German leader lectured

Ford that a New York default would have a domino effect on financial centers as far afield as Zurich and Frankfurt.

In the days after Schmidt's visit, Burns went public on the case for a rescue, and even the normally hard-line Treasury Secretary Simon sounded reluctantly open to the possibility.[67] Congressional leaders began to realize that punishing Sin City might mean punishing their own districts at the same time, and two bills offering New York billions in federal loan guarantees passed through the Senate banking committee. With an eye to the following year's election, Democratic presidential aspirants started to turn New York's plight into a cudgel. Senator Henry Jackson of Washington State quoted Abraham Lincoln shamelessly: "We are now engaged in a great civil war," Jackson announced, as though the financial troubles of New York plausibly could be compared to Antietam or Gettysburg.[68] Fearing that the political current would force its own solution on him, Ford scheduled a major speech about New York, to be delivered at the National Press Club in Washington.

Acting behind the scenes, Greenspan continued to resist the bailout. No matter that New York was his hometown; the diffidence that he had felt in pressing policy positions had by now clearly deserted him. He argued to Ford privately that a rescue would be unfair to the rest of the nation: Why lavish money on New York when the federal government was having to control spending in other areas? He insisted that a rescue would help New York only for a short time; pretty soon the city's addiction to deficit spending would swamp the additional money provided by a bailout. Finally, Greenspan maintained that the city's failure would be less risky for the national economy than most people supposed. The Joint Economic Committee in Congress had forecast that New York's bankruptcy would depress national growth by as much as 1 percentage point in 1976. But Greenspan's CEA team countered that the impact on other city budgets would be smaller than feared. Indeed, a New York City default would have welcome "demonstration effects which will contribute to the health of our fiscal system."[69]

The Greenspan team's optimism exceeded the supporting evidence.

Burns was right that default might trigger contagion; a Federal Reserve study released in November showed that 179 banks held state and city securities worth more than half their capital, so a sharp fall in their value would compel cuts in lending.[70] It was possible, moreover, that many institutional investors would be legally required to dump New York securities once the city defaulted, in which case fire sales would magnify the hit to the banking system. This prospect was disturbing enough to prompt the Council of Economic Advisers to undertake a state-by-state investigation of the rules governing defaulted bonds, but the resulting memo was not sent to Greenspan until twelve days after Ford's critical speech on the New York question, and even then it was vague in its conclusions.[71] But although Greenspan's no-bailout policy entailed risks that were as yet not analyzed, Ford trusted him anyway, relying on him for "arguments, logic, and articulation," as a colleague noted in his diary.[72] In the days leading up to the fateful speech at the National Press Club, White House advisers who favored aiding New York found themselves pushed to the wall. "I tried with minimal success to soften the harsh rhetoric of some of the best economic minds of the eighteenth century," Ford's chief speechwriter, Bob Hartmann, recalled bitterly.[73]

On October 29, Ford stood up at the National Press Club and declared bluntly, "I can tell you, and tell you now, that I am prepared to veto any bill that has as its purpose a Federal bailout." As well as citing the CEA's arguments against a rescue, the president drew the connection to the larger national challenges that had preoccupied Greenspan for years. "If we go on spending more than we have, providing more benefits and more services than we can pay for, then a day of reckoning will come to Washington and the whole country just as it has to New York City," Ford warned gravely. "When that day of reckoning comes, who will bail out the United States of America?"[74] Germany's chancellor, the Federal Reserve chairman, and a Lincoln-quoting senator had all clamored for a softer line, but Greenspan had succeeded in frustrating them.[75]

Greenspan's victory was not popular. By ten o'clock that evening, newsboys were hawking the early edition of the New York *Daily News*, its front page screaming with a 144-point type headline, "FORD TO CITY: DROP DEAD." From City Hall, Mayor Beame ripped Ford's speech as a "default of presidential leadership,"[76] while Governor Carey insinuated that Ford's "kick in the groin" reflected the political weakness of an unelected president.[77] A poll after the no-bailout speech found that a majority of Americans disagreed with the president's stand—and indeed that national support for a bailout had actually increased since he had spoken. Despite Americans' growing openness to antigovernment ideas, Greenspan's unvarnished message was too much for them.[78]

Two weeks after Ford's address, the New York Financial Writers' Association staged the Financial Follies, its annual send-up of current events set to old tunes with reworked lyrics.[79] An Arthur Burns impersonator appeared in one skit as the Loan Arranger, singing a pledge to prop up New York's banks while representations of the city's major financial houses polished his shoes gratefully. Then an actor dressed as Greenspan trotted out on stage and delivered an incomprehensible monologue on the economic outlook, and another figure representing a CEA member belted out a reworked version of an old Broadway number, "Buckle Down, Winsocki":

> *Keep it pure, our leader, keep it pure;*
> *Help the rich, our leader, not the lousy poor.*[80]

Even though Ford had ruled out a bailout as clearly as he could, the game was not yet over. Not only was public opinion running against Greenspan's tough line, but toughness itself was forcing new thinking—which in turn rendered toughness less defensible. In early November, New York's leaders prepared legislation to impose sacrifices on taxpayers and bondholders; by publicly tightening its belt, New York aimed to strengthen its appeal to would-be rescuers. Sure enough, the city's sympathizers in Congress stepped up the pressure for a bailout.

In mid-November, Ford attended an economic summit in France. Choosing his moment skillfully, Arthur Burns pointedly told Helmut

Schmidt and French president Valéry Giscard d'Estaing that a New York default was probable. The reaction was just as Burns foresaw. "The foreign leaders looked at Ford and said you have to be joking—it would be seen as the bankruptcy of America," a witness recalled later.[81] The president's resolve was cracking.

On November 26, Ford finally reversed course during a televised press conference at the White House. He called upon Congress to grant a $2.3 billion temporary line of credit to New York, explaining that "Americans have always believed in helping those who help themselves."[82] New York had indeed made strides toward addressing its problems. It had embraced spending cuts, imposed a $200 million tax hike, reduced interest payments to bondholders, cut retirement benefits for municipal workers, and arranged to borrow $2.5 billion from the city's pension fund. Even so, Ford's call for a bailout constituted a climbdown. Previously, Greenspan had argued that New York could fix its problems by itself. Now Ford was insisting that Washington should help, even though there was no way to be sure that New York would implement all the reforms it promised. Sure enough, New York needed a second package of federal loan guarantees in 1978, and the city continued to draw on federal support for more than a decade.

Greenspan had seen New York as an opportunity to break the expectation of federal bailouts created by Penn Central and Lockheed. Ford had tried to follow his advice, but in the end it proved politically untenable. Perhaps this should not have come as a surprise. Just as bailouts created a self-reinforcing momentum, with each rescue strengthening the case for the next one, so the refusal of a bailout generated a sort of self-canceling momentum, with Ford's denial of assistance causing New York to make itself more deserving of assistance. Partly because of these dynamics, Americans have almost never been able to resist bailouts—not in the mixed-economy 1970s, not in the Reaganite 1980s, and not in later decades, either. Even when the intellectual tide turned in favor of conservatives on questions of tax and regulation, Americans continued to look to the government for rescues whenever crises struck. A dozen years after New York's rescue, Greenspan himself would join the bandwagon.[83]

A round the time that Ford caved on New York, Greenspan's relationship with Kaye Pullen reached an inflection point. The couple had
been happy together for the best part of a year. Because they were both
working long hours—in Greenspan's case, six days a week—it was nice to
unwind with someone who shared and understood the intensity of the
White House experience. Friday night was date night, and they would go
out to dinner: Alan would listen to all kinds of stories about Kaye's family,
but he never mentioned his own; he was at once generously supportive
and eerily private. No doubt the pain inflicted by an absent father was not
something he cared to revisit. No doubt his mother was too close to be the
subject of date-night gossip.

On October 1, 1975, when Kaye turned thirty-one, Alan took her to
the Jockey Club at the Fairfax. He ordered the smallest bottle of champagne on the menu, knowing that he would drink only one glass of it. But
soon after that birthday dinner, Alan asked Kaye gently whether she
wanted more out of this relationship than he could give. He was married
to his job, he said, and until he got to the top of the mountain, he would
never have much time for anything outside it. It was a slightly unpersuasive
protest: plenty of men of Greenspan's generation married without shoul-
dering much responsibility for home or children. But Kaye accepted Alan's
reasoning sadly. He had always been considerate and honest with her, and
she never resented the way she was treated; "I was nuts about him," she
confessed simply. After that conversation, the two stopped dating.[84]

Fresh from that well-managed soft landing, Greenspan appeared at a
tea dance at the Admiral's House off Embassy Row, Vice President Rockefeller's official residence. Rockefeller had a habit of inviting movie stars,
media magnates, and other American royalty to his parties; and on that
day at the end of November, Greenspan spied Barbara Walters, the television news celebrity who had interviewed Margaret Thatcher. Walters was
a sleek brunette in her midforties; she combined a steely journalistic core
with a sweet feminine manner, leading the Russian poet Yevgeny Yev-
tushenko to dub her "a hyena in syrup." To many of her viewers, she was

the very definition of alluring. Asked whether she felt that television exploited her as a sex object, Walters replied: "I should hope so."[85]

Greenspan boldly approached Walters and introduced himself, announcing that he was the chairman of the Council of Economic Advisers. The title "sounded important if rather dull to me," Walters recalled later.[86] But Walters responded warmly anyway, finding Greenspan pleasant, unassuming, and a "very nice dancer." Greenspan pressed his advantage, telling Walters that he actually lived in New York on the weekends and that he would like to call her. Walters offered her phone number, and Greenspan followed up the very next weekend. "I welcomed this call, the first of many, from the tall, quiet stranger," Walters recorded in her memoir.[87]

Alan and Barbara embarked on a romance, though it was not without its complications. Barbara was already involved with a different financial Alan: Alan "Ace" Greenberg, the husky, bald trader who was not yet quite the chief executive of Bear Stearns, and not yet quite divorced from his first wife. Having two Alans pursuing her became a source of confusion for Barbara's assistants, especially because Greenspan and Greenberg had the habit of leaving only their first names when they telephoned. "Even if they asked either gentleman to please leave his last name, it was not much help," Walters wrote later. "Greenberg. Greenspan. They sounded so much alike that both [assistants] were in despair." Barbara's solution was to ask her assistants about the caller's tone of voice. If the man on the other end of the line "almost whispered," Walters knew it must be Alan number two, the one with hair who worked in Washington.

Confusions aside, dating Barbara Walters had clear compensations. It certainly caught people's attention, and for a man with a lingering lack of social confidence, that mattered. When Ford read the news that Greenspan was dating Walters, he clipped the article and sent it to his chief of staff with a message: "Dick Cheney, note p.2. I don't believe it."[88] When Barbara visited Alan at the office, she made a similar impact. "There'd be rumors, Barbara Walters is going to come this afternoon," a very distinguished CEA colleague recalled. "There was a flutter of anticipation and let's just make sure that our doors are open and that we get a chance to see

her in the corridors."[89] One time Greenspan attended a Brookings conference on the economy, and he seemed his usual serious self—"some would
say dull," a fellow participant remembers. But when the technical debates
were over and his fellow economists headed for the bar, Greenspan was
swept off in a limousine with his famous girlfriend. "Gosh, how can a guy
like that lead a life like this?" his colleagues wondered.[90] Greenspan would
not have been upset to know that they were thinking that.

Alan persuaded Barbara to read *Atlas Shrugged,* just as he had Kaye
Pullen before her. The book failed to impress Barbara, though she briefly
regretted that her parents had not named her Dagny, like the novel's heroine.[91] Barbara was not impressed by Alan's social skills, either. He struck
her as "frugal"; he "wore the same navy blue raincoat until it practically
fell apart," and "rarely remembered to pick up a check or buy a Christmas
or birthday gift."[92] At dinner parties, Greenspan would not mingle before
sitting down to eat, and if he was seated next to a woman he didn't know,
he could be awkwardly difficult to draw out. "He was not the sort of man
you would notice when he walked into the room," Walters added, piling
one complaint onto the other, "and often I would have to introduce him to
friends more than once because they wouldn't remember him."[93] But Barbara's attitude to Alan's vulnerabilities was to do her best to protect him—
after all, she had social poise to spare; she would make up for his lack of it.
Once, at a dinner party given by Diane von Furstenberg, creator of the
iconic wrap dress, California governor Jerry Brown ripped into overrated
presidential advisers, belatedly noticing Greenspan's presence and allowing that maybe, just maybe, he might profit from Greenspan's counsel. Barbara leaned forward, raised her eyebrows, and said, "Maybe you would!"[94]
With this charismatic woman by his side, Alan could feel serenely confident in any social setting.

In his own quiet way, Alan repaid Barbara's assistance. He made her
feel calm and secure; he was neither judgmental nor domineering.[95] In the
spring of 1976, Barbara was invited to jump from NBC's early morning
Today show to ABC's flagship evening news program—she was offered an
annual salary of $1 million to become the first female evening news
anchor, making her more than three times as valuable as ABC's incumbent

evening host, Harry Reasoner. Barbara agonized about whether to take up the offer, and Alan served as her sounding board night after night, at one point analyzing ABC's accounts to verify that it could deliver on its extravagant pay promise. Alan gave the thumbs-up on the network's financial soundness, and Barbara eventually resolved to take the job, a decision she never regretted.[96]

Alan turned fifty in March 1976, and Barbara arranged a dinner party for him. Frank Zarb, Ford's energy czar, recalls taking a call from the news queen—she knew he was swamped with government business but hoped that he could find the time to come; Zarb assured her sincerely that he would not miss the dinner for anything.[97] Henry and Nancy Kissinger were there, and Oscar and Annette de la Renta were there; and there were Joe and Estée Lauder and Punch and Carol Sulzberger.[98] Some of Alan's friends thought a great moment had arrived—perhaps, after so many years of bachelor life, Alan might finally remarry. Kathryn Eickhoff reckoned that this relationship with Barbara was different from the rest; this time Alan was matched with someone three years his junior, not more—and someone who was at least his equal in professional status.[99] Alan and Barbara were close enough that Barbara got to know Alan's mother, Rose; she admired her strong bond with her son, and invited Rose to her apartment to play the piano. In July 1976, Alan took Barbara to a state dinner at the White House for Queen Elizabeth II. It was the quintessentially glamorous occasion for a glamorous celebrity couple.

Yet sometime between that dinner and the Republican convention the next month, the relationship shifted down a gear or two. There was no acrimonious blowup; Alan did not do acrimony. But Barbara could not bond with Alan in an area that mattered intensely—she had no deep relationship with music—and contrary to the speculation of his friends, Alan was not ready for marriage.[100] The couple agreed to a new kind of understanding. It was something more than a friendship, and something less than a committed romance. It suited Alan perfectly.[101]

After that second soft landing, Alan continued to see Barbara; but he also picked up again quietly with Kaye Pullen. On the last night of Ford's presidency, January 19, 1977, Alan took Barbara to an inaugural party that flowed with Iranian caviar; a line of celebrity-spotting students outside the reception called out to Barbara as she arrived there.[102] But when that party was finished, Alan switched personas and girlfriends. He met Kaye for a late dinner at a restaurant in Georgetown, where they ate steak and french fries together.[103]

G reenspan's last year in the Ford administration underlined how hard it was to resist the forces of statism. In December 1975 he fought a rearguard action against a congressional plan to control energy prices, which, as he wrote in a memo, "would extend government direction of the economy and discourage those who would rely on the free market."[104] Ford shrugged off Greenspan's advice and signed the energy bill anyway. That same month, Greenspan recommended a veto of the Home Mortgage Disclosure Act, a bill that aimed to fight discrimination in lending by requiring banks to disclose details of their customers. The lending disclosures implied that "an efficient capital market is undesirable and that allocation of credit by political group pressures is superior," Greenspan complained; but Ford ignored him again and signed the legislation.[105] The following April, Greenspan endorsed changes to the bankruptcy code that would make it easier for cities to secure protection from creditors— the idea was that this option would make New York–style bailouts less necessary.[106] This time the president sided with him, but the victory was hollow. Neither investors nor political leaders trusted the reform's untested provisions, so cities continued to get bailouts by arguing that the alternative would be chaos.[107] The government's role was expanding.

The spring of 1976 also marked a strange comeback for Hubert Humphrey, the senator and former vice president who had cosponsored the central-planning bill a year earlier. Humphrey teamed up with Representative Augustus Hawkins, a California Democrat, to promote a law that would mandate full employment, ambitiously defined as an adult unemployment rate of just 3 percent; the federal government was to act as "employer of last resort," hiring anyone who could not find a job at "prevailing wages."[108] Early drafts of the legislation quixotically allowed unemployed workers to sue the federal government for failure to provide jobs; and it called for a permanent antirecession program that would ramp up public works whenever unemployment crept above 4.5 percent.[109] In March, Greenspan appeared before the Joint Economic Committee of Congress to point out the pitfalls in the Humphrey-Hawkins bill: experts disagreed on what constituted "full employment," so it was dangerous to enshrine one number in the law; it would be folly to commit to an employment goal that would detract from the fight against inflation.[110] The following month Greenspan weighed in again, insisting that the bill's emphasis on government planning implied a dangerously exaggerated faith in economists' ability to forecast the economy.[111] But however cogent Greenspan's arguments, Congress was evidently a long way from his worldview. The Humphrey-Hawkins legislation passed in a diluted form two years later, becoming the basis on which Fed chairmen would be summoned to testify before Congress at six-month intervals.

Greenspan's warnings about the limits to economic forecasting were timelier than he realized. His last months in office were marked by an error that first haunted him—and then saved his career prospects. Since the beginning of 1976, there had been pressure to boost Ford's election chances by ramping up government spending—the stimulus would come on top of the previous year's tax rebate. Greenspan might have backed this spending boost—after all, he had a strong interest in the election outcome because it was widely assumed that he would become Treasury secretary in a second Ford term. But the economy was growing at an annualized rate of 9.3 percent in the first quarter of 1976, and Greenspan resisted calls for further pump priming.[112] On April 16 he counseled Ford that a ramp-up in government spending would not be necessary to keep the economy humming.[113]

As it turned out, Greenspan was mistaken. The rebound of early 1976 was caused by a sugar high from Ford's 1975 tax rebates. Consequently, it did not last; in the second quarter of the year, growth collapsed to an annualized rate of 3.1 percent. Greenspan confidently insisted that the third quarter would bring better news, as government departments rushed to spend remaining cash before the close of the fiscal year caused them to forfeit it.[114] But government spending remained weak into the fall, and the economy slowed further to an annualized growth rate of 2.1 percent. Greenspan's misguided optimism arguably cost Ford the election.[115] Henry Kissinger taunted Greenspan for his bad call years after they left office.[116]

Ford's narrow loss frustrated Greenspan's long-standing ambition to become Treasury secretary. But it was a blessing in disguise. By the time of Ford's electoral defeat, the inflationary pressures in the American economy were building dangerously—inflation as measured by the consumer price index would top 14 percent in 1980. "By 1977, 1980 was already baked into the cake," Greenspan reflected as he looked back on those years. Whoever presided over economic policy in the late 1970s was therefore doomed to suffer huge reputational damage. If Ford had been elected, Greenspan mused, "I may well have ended up as Secretary of the Treasury but I would never have become Fed chairman."[117]

Ten

THE FIRST HOUSING CONUNDRUM

O n the day of Jimmy Carter's inauguration, January 20, 1977, Greenspan took the noon shuttle back to New York and pro- ceeded to his office.[1] Townsend-Greenspan was still located at One New York Plaza, scene of the dramatic fire in 1970; and the business was still prospering, despite the boss's two-and-a-half-year absence. Kath- ryn Eickhoff and the three other women vice presidents had kept the data flowing and the clients contented, churning out austere analyses on manu- facturing profits, steel output, and so on. But although Greenspan was happy to be reunited with his ersatz family, he allowed himself one mod- est grumble. Eickhoff had been telling clients that a hot housing market was driving consumer spending: people were taking out second mortgages on their homes and using the proceeds to remodel their kitchens or pur- chase new cars, turbocharging the economy. Eickhoff's observation had a sting in its tail. If the housing market turned cold, consumer spending could nose-dive. The economy could turn out to be more fragile than any- body realized.

"Where are your data on this?" Greenspan demanded once he had settled back into his job.

"Well, we don't have any data exactly," Eickhoff answered. "But every meeting that we go to, we can find somebody at the table to explain how you do this mortgage extraction in that particular community."

Greenspan did not like this answer. He was not impressed with anecdotal evidence. The Townsend-Greenspan brand was based on dealing strictly with facts.

"Why didn't you get the data then and find out whether you were right?" he pressed Eickhoff.

Eickhoff pleaded lack of time. Everybody at the firm had been paddling hard to stay afloat with Greenspan not there.

"Well, if you're right, it's in the data," Greenspan insisted.

"Fine," Eickhoff retorted. "I'm right; we're right; you go find it."

Over the next weeks, Greenspan spent hours sequestered in the library.

"Kathryn, you were wrong," he announced eventually. "You had absolutely no idea of the size of this phenomenon."[2]

It was not the most gracious way to concede that Eickhoff had been onto something. But over the next year Greenspan made the most of her insight about mortgages and consumption. It was the sort of idea that appealed to him deeply, not least because it harkened back to his magisterial 1959 paper. Eickhoff's point was an example of how a change in the value of an asset—in this case, housing—could have powerful effects on spending by individuals. Likewise, Greenspan's 1959 paper had emphasized that a change in the value of a different type of asset, corporate stock, could determine spending by companies on new plant and machinery. Moreover, Eickhoff's insight appealed to Greenspan because it was overlooked by his rivals. Most economic forecasters focused on the national accounts, the data set that presents output by companies, households, and the government, which adds up to the gross domestic product (GDP). But capital gains are nowhere to be found in these accounts. If the value of a home increased by $100,000, and the homeowner took out a second mortgage for 80 percent of that amount, that extra $80,000 of spending power did not show up in the national accounts—not in the personal disposable income number, not anywhere.[3] The impact of changing asset prices was occurring under the radar.

Greenspan set his team to work quantifying the home-price effect in detail. He wanted to know how much mortgage lending was being channeled to families who already owned homes—and who were therefore likely to spend the proceeds on things other than housing. No data existed on this "home-equity extraction," as it later came to be known. But Greenspan estimated how much new mortgage debt might have been created as a result of the construction of new homes, and he calculated how much debt existing mortgage holders would normally repay in any given period. By taking his estimate for new mortgages and subtracting repayments on old mortgages, Greenspan arrived at the expected change in the total amount of mortgage debt in the economy. Now he was just one step away from the statistic he wanted. If the expected increase in mortgage debt was smaller than the actual change, the difference must represent additional mortgage lending to existing homeowners—home-equity extraction. Thirty years after his undergraduate vacation job at Brown Brothers Harriman, Greenspan had lost none of his taste for statistical sleuthing.[4]

By August 1977, Greenspan was ready to lay out his results in detail to his clients. When home values had gone up in the early 1970s, he reported, less than a third of the increase had been extracted to support spending. By contrast, during the second quarter of 1977, virtually the entire increase in the market value of existing homes had been monetized. This was a remarkable finding. Thanks to the financial industry's eagerness to hand out new mortgages, consumer purchasing power had expanded by almost 5 percent during the quarter; and although Greenspan did not drive home this point, total spending in the economy (counting in spending by government and companies as well as consumers) might have been boosted by almost 3 percent.[5] The implication was that GDP growth in the second quarter, which had come in at an annualized rate of 8.1 percent, might have come in nearer to 5 percent without the miraculous boost from housing. The flip side was that if the housing boom came to an end, the economy would slow. There was a "danger that the rise in home prices could take on a speculative hue," Greenspan observed. "The assumption of ever rising prices for new homes is not valid."[6]

The clients on the receiving end of these data did not always know what to make of them. They paid Greenspan as much as $30,000 annually to receive his economic letters and hear from him in person once every quarter—the retainer matched the entire salary of the average in-house analyst who listened to his presentations.[7] In return for this princely compensation, Greenspan would show up at his clients' offices with the outsized leather briefcase full of data that he carried with him at all times, like the presidential football; some clients suspected he had one arm longer than the other. His manner of speaking was both impressive and mysterious: "It suggested he was stewing a vast amount of data in his head, and letting out only a little of the steam for his public to sniff at," a client recalled years later.[8] Most of his audiences were money managers at mutual-fund houses, pension funds, or banks, and they were in the business of making yes/no, buy/sell decisions on specific stocks and bonds. But Greenspan floated above this dull binary game, forcing his listeners to consider multiple scenarios. If the dollar fell a little, three knock-on trends might develop; if it rose, there could be two consequences. Meanwhile, if inflation ticked up, there were four possible versions of the future. Greenspan would speak on and on, his expression seldom altering, his heavy-lidded eyes hidden behind thick glasses. The clients paid top dollar for his ruminations because there was no doubt about his mastery of data. But after he departed they would huddle together anxiously at post-Greenspan meetings. What had he really said? What did it mean for their portfolios?[9]

Greenspan traveled relentlessly, visiting clients across the country. His staff joked that he could only keep up with his schedule because he had learned to live out of a suitcase as an itinerant jazz player.[10] But as he crisscrossed the country, Greenspan was deepening his grasp of economics, too. His experience at the Council of Economic Advisers had expanded his intellectual ambitions: for the first time, he had been surrounded by colleagues who were more formally qualified than he was. When he returned to his firm, he resolved to ramp up the sophistication of its macroeconomic forecasting, and to this end he retained the consulting services of a young ex-CEA economist named John Taylor, later to become a renowned Stanford professor and insistent Greenspan critic.

Although he was now past the age of fifty, Greenspan himself returned to New York University to take courses in econometrics.[11] Twenty-seven years after enrolling in the graduate program at Columbia, he completed his doctorate.

Greenspan's PhD thesis, submitted in late 1977, was not a conventional dissertation. It was a strange mixture of articles written over many years, including the 1959 paper on asset prices; it ranged from math-heavy technical submissions to a layman-friendly article published in the *Economist.* But although the style was eclectic, the thesis served to capture the central strands in Greenspan's thought, distinguishing him sharply from the dominant camps in late 1970s economics. Unlike Milton Friedman and his fellow monetarists, Greenspan never put stock in stripped-down models that forecast the future path of the economy by tracking a favored measure of the money supply; he was far too interested in the workings of industry and government budgets to zone out all those details.[12] Unlike both monetarists and Keynesians, Greenspan emphasized the key role of financial markets in driving the economy, and he was leery of the intellectual hubris that underpinned Keynesian fine-tuning. Finally, unlike many conservative economists in the late 1970s, Greenspan never fell in love with "rational expectations." In its earliest versions, the rational expectations school argued that both fiscal and monetary policy could be powerless to affect growth and jobs, because citizens offset it. For example, if the government ran a budget deficit in the hopes of stimulating growth, rational individuals would expect the government to have to increase taxes later to pay the interest on the debt—and they would prepare for the higher taxes by saving more in the present, thus negating the intended stimulus. Greenspan agreed that fine-tuning was counterproductive, but he did not agree that it was impotent. Indeed, he had doubted the power of the expectations channel in his correspondence with Friedman about Nixon's price controls, and in his ridiculing of Franklin Roosevelt's conceit that fear alone caused the Depression.

Greenspan opened his PhD submission with an argument that drew directly from his 1959 paper. By ignoring the impact of asset prices on spending, Greenspan contended, the reigning forecasting models were "abstracting from reality in a somewhat unrealistic manner." The mistake was understandable: capital gains and losses were not part of the national income accounts, and their absence had "tended to bias model builders away from data which are not readily available." But still, Greenspan continued, economists ought to do better; and he cited the impact of home-equity extraction, which was "largely missed in the standard models."[13] Moreover, Greenspan insisted, it was not just that rising home prices could boost spending; the effect also worked the other way around, with higher spending tending to boost home prices. Because of such feedback loops between finance and the "real" economy, unsustainable trends could appear sustainable for a long time, as higher asset prices boosted spending, which boosted asset prices, which boosted spending. Eventually, the feedback loops would drive prices to completely unsustainable levels, and the bubble would burst, landing the economy in serious trouble. Although he was writing in the heyday of efficient-market faith, Greenspan did not believe that markets were always rational and stable any more than he had done as a commodity trader in the 1950s.[14]

With the unfair benefit of hindsight, Greenspan's position was both impressive and ironic. Years before his critics charged that the Fed during his tenure had been blind to wealth effects and bubbles, Greenspan was at the cutting edge of thinking on these questions. And he was ahead of his time in another sense, too. Both in the 1970s and later, most forecasting models essentially left finance out. They assumed that the channeling of capital from savers to spenders was a utility-like function that would not alter growth; they did not reckon with the fact that shifts in the financial sector, such as a greater willingness to facilitate home-equity extraction, could change the path of the economy.[15] In the wake of the 2008 crisis, this underestimation of finance was held up as one of the economics profession's cardinal errors. But Greenspan was never guilty of this mistake. Ever since his study of John Gurley and Edward Shaw in the 1950s, he had emphasized the significance of shifts within finance, and by the 1970s he was all the more convinced that economic forecasters had to factor finance into their thinking. "Our financial institutions are more flexible and complex than we had supposed a couple of decades ago," he observed in his thesis. "Certain elements of the financial system are sometimes dominant; sometimes quiescent." Such shifts from dominance to quiescence—from bullish risk taking to a bearish desperation for safety— could change spending and output dramatically; and Greenspan strove to build this observation into the forecasting model at his firm, tracking bond issuance and money-market funds as well as plain-vanilla banking. The approach harkened back to Greenspan's mentor and partner, Bill Townsend. But it was also "ahead of the game," as John Taylor remembered years later, in 2011.

Greenspan was awarded his PhD in late 1977, and Barbara Walters held a small dinner in his honor. Arthur Burns and his wife Helen attended, as did Greenspan's old NYU undergraduate friend, Bob Kavesh, and a very proud Rose Greenspan. At the end of the evening, Barbara passed out cigars that she had brought back from Cuba after interviewing Fidel Castro.[16]

Even as he lived an ambitious private life, Greenspan remained engaged in public policy. He joined *Time* magazine's board of economists and the Brookings Panel on Economic Activity. He taught the receptionists at his firm to pay special attention to phone calls from the press—they were to inquire about the reporter's deadline and make sure that Greenspan responded fast enough to have his quotes included in the article. Journalists, for their part, repaid Greenspan's attention with flattering profiles. Soon after his return to his consulting firm, a prominent *New York Times* commentator reflected that Greenspan had forged "probably the most intimate and influential relationship an economist has ever enjoyed with a president."[17] Somehow Greenspan managed to convince journalists that he was virtuously indifferent to power and status, even as his courtship of journalists suggested otherwise. "If power interests you, you would miss the change," Greenspan mused to the *Times,* reflecting on his shift from the White House back to private life. "I wouldn't say I was unaware of power—or didn't even like it—but my professional work interests me more."[18]

Greenspan's media appearances delighted his mother. Whenever he was due to appear on TV, one of his assistants would call Rose and tell her the time and channel.[19] But Greenspan's hunger for the spotlight was less welcome to some of his colleagues. Kathryn Eickhoff accused him of suffering from "Potomac fever": halfway through a discussion about some delicate statistical question, the boss would break off abruptly because a journalist or congressman was on the telephone. "There were times when I could have killed him, because we were in the middle of something important for the firm," Eickhoff recalled; and his public shtick about how his "professional work" mattered more to him than fame only added insult to injury.[20] Even so, Eickhoff could never be cross with Greenspan for long. "It's really difficult not to get along with Alan," she reflected years later. "He doesn't give off enough emotional content for you to be offended."

Greenspan's place in the spotlight obliged him to comment on the new economic ideas stirring in the Republican Party. These contrasted sharply with his own public opposition to budget deficits.[21] In June 1978, the voters of California passed a referendum known as Proposition 13, which imposed an immediate cut in property taxes. When the leader of the Prop 13 movement was accused of dangerously expanding California's budget deficit, he retorted that his tax cut would compel legislators to hack "the barrels of lard out of the government budget." The idea that preemptive cuts in revenue would somehow elicit responsible spending cuts seemed wishful, and research later showed it to be wrong.[22] But recognizing the political attraction of tax cuts, Greenspan gave Proposition 13 a qualified endorsement: "Such brutal sledge-hammer techniques turn out to be necessary to prevent government from continuing to increase its share of overall economic activity," he ventured.[23] Greenspan had recently told *Fortune* that "it would be a mistake to enact a general tax cut," and that "economists ought to recommend what they think is right and let the politicians make the political judgments."[24] Now he was violating his own injunction.

A fortnight later, on July 14, 1978, Greenspan testified before a Senate subcommittee. The hearing had been called to study a tax bill introduced by a Republican duo—Representative Jack Kemp of New York and Sena-tor William Roth of Delaware. The Kemp-Roth bill relied on a new type of tax logic, more radical even than the approach embraced in California. Lower tax rates would stimulate growth and therefore extra tax revenue, the bill's proponents claimed; tax cuts would pay for themselves. Some three months earlier, the Congressional Budget Office had debunked this so-called supply-side theory—the 1964 tax cut, a favorite precedent for supply-siders, had generated enough growth to offset only a quarter to a third of the lost income.[25] But Kemp and Roth were undeterred—either by research or by ridicule. "Sound the trumpets and hear the heralds," Walter Heller, the former Kennedy CEA chairman, sneered in the *Wall Street Journal*.[26] "Lunch is not only free, we get a bonus for eating it. P.T. Barnum, move over."

As the Senate hearing convened, Senator Roth began by presenting a birthday cake to his counterpart, Representative Kemp, in honor of the one-year anniversary of the introduction of their bill. "I might say that this is one of the few times that the American people may not only have their cake, but eat it too," he said, parrying ridicule with self-parody. Roth then proceeded to congratulate himself and his Republican col-leagues on their budget conservatism even as he peddled his tax cut—to his way of thinking, there was no contradiction. Back in the 1960s, the Democrats had been the ones to champion tax cuts, justifying their policy with the mistaken idea that inflationary budget deficits could lastingly boost employment. Now the Republicans had seized upon the equally mis-guided fallacy that tax cuts were self-financing.

Rather than denouncing the fallacy of Kemp-Roth, Greenspan tiptoed around it. He ventured that the economy was in such dire need of sharper incentives that tax cuts, particularly on corporations, were imperative—even if they involved a larger deficit. Without improved incentives, what Greenspan termed "the British disease" of industrial stagnation beck-oned. "Since the cost of stagnation politically, socially, and economically is so large, we have to lean over backward to avoid it."

Naturally, Roth was delighted. "I think you set forth the facts for sub-stantial, across-the-board tax cuts as well as I have heard them set out," he said, enthusiastically. But then he demanded to hear more. One of the most quoted economists in the nation was sitting there in front of him. The senator was determined to nail down his support as explicitly as possible.

"Mr. Greenspan, looking at the *Wall Street Journal* article that appeared on July 12, 1978, titled 'The Kemp-Roth Free Lunch,' I'm sure you've seen the article?"

Roth was referring to Walter Heller's P. T. Barnum taunt. Greenspan signaled that he had indeed read it.

"I wonder if you agree with the thrust of it?" Roth asked. He was fishing for the Republican former CEA chairman to neutralize the Democratic former CEA chairman.

"My good friend, Professor Heller, is fighting a strawman," Greenspan obliged. "The problem he raises is not the issue." Contrary to Heller's article, tax cuts would not widen the budget gap, Greenspan maintained. The reason was that they would be followed by spending cuts.

Greenspan was not about to endorse the supply-side fantasy of self-financing tax cuts in its entirety. But he was willing to give Republican leaders what they wanted anyway by embracing the Prop 13 faith that tax cuts would create pressure for spending cuts. For more than a decade, Greenspan had insisted that there was a ratchet effect in government spending, with each new program whetting the public's appetite for the next one. Now he was happy to imply that cutting Leviathan would be simple.[27]

Three months after his tax testimony, in October 1978, Greenspan extended his arguments on housing finance in the unlikely setting of Utah State University.[28] He had been invited to this remote outpost, perched on a flat bank in a mountainside eighty miles north of Salt Lake City, to deliver a speech, and he used the occasion to address the question implicit in his writings on home-equity extraction. Something had changed in the financial sector, triggering a deluge of new mortgage loans. What was it?

Greenspan began by noting a collapse in the relationship between interest rates and the housing market. Until the start of the 1970s, rising interest rates had caused mortgage finance to dry up: housing demand fell and so did house prices. But by the mid-1970s, Greenspan noted, rising interest rates were no longer having that effect. At the time of Greenspan's speech in Utah, the Fed had just increased the short-term interest rate to 9 percent, but mortgages were still easy to come by and house prices were booming.[29]

The reason, Greenspan told his audience, was that the rules of the game had been changed by the government. The construction industry, furious at periodic real estate busts imposed by high interest rates, had lobbied Washington for relief. Washington had duly responded; but, Greenspan said sourly, "as is typical with any political endeavor in this country, we inevitably overdid it." In 1970, Fannie Mae, a government-sponsored enterprise (GSE) set up during the Depression, had been allowed for the first time to buy private mortgages, and in the same year Congress created a second GSE called Freddie Mac to compete with Fannie. Goading each other on, Fannie and Freddie stood ready to buy mortgages from banks and S&Ls, with the result that these lenders gained a huge new source of funds—there were "massive expansions of mortgage credit availability." One decade earlier, new mortgage creation had seldom exceeded $15 billion per year. Now six times that quantity was normal.

This revolution, Greenspan went on, had consequences beyond housing. "The mortgage market has basically exploded into a major new financial vehicle that dwarfs the federal deficit, dwarfs corporate borrowing, and dwarfs state and local borrowing," Greenspan declared. "It has become the most dominant element in the whole financial system." The government-sponsored enterprises had driven up house prices, boosting the wealth of families and so boosting consumption; a politically conceived change in the financial plumbing was effectively driving spending on vacations, education, large automobiles—everything. The upshot was that the mortgage explosion had not merely delinked the housing sector from interest rates; it had delinked the whole economy from interest rates, at least temporarily. Thanks to Fannie and Freddie, lending was cheap and plentiful even though the Fed had raised the short-term interest rate to its highest level in almost four years. Monetary policy was apparently tight, but financial conditions were in practice loose.[30] The economy was growing at a heady rate, and the trend was not sustainable.[31]

Greenspan was describing a version of what he would later call the conundrum.[32] In testimony before Congress in February 2005, he famously noted that the Fed's efforts to raise interest rates were not having their usual effect, possibly because a flood of foreign purchases was pushing down interest rates on long-term bonds, so higher short-term interest rates did not translate into higher long-term interest rates. The implication, which Greenspan emphasized repeatedly after the crisis of 2008, was that the Fed had been nearly powerless to defuse the housing bubble—rates for long-term mortgages were barely responding to the short rates that the Fed guided. But this breakdown in the relationship between long rates and short rates was in fact less novel than Greenspan implied. As he had written in his PhD thesis, shifts within finance were constantly altering the economy's behavior. Foreign bond purchases in the 2000s provided one example of this truth. The advent of Fannie and Freddie in the 1970s provided another.

Having shown how economic growth had been temporarily delinked from interest rates, Greenspan gave warning that trouble was looming. Years later it would be argued that the opening up of a new credit hose— huge lending from foreign countries, especially China—caused asset-price inflation. In 1978, Greenspan explained that the opening up of the mortgage hose was causing consumer price inflation. Fannie and Freddie were creating spending power that had already pushed CPI inflation back above 8 percent a year, and the effect was all the more powerful because the Federal Reserve was too weak willed to counter it. With a clarity that is ironic in hindsight, Greenspan described how the Fed was falling down on the job. Rather than pushing back against the stimulus from financial innovation by raising short-term interest rates more, the Fed was letting the financial system have its way, with the result that there was "a huge excess of credit in the system."[33] When the Fed finally got tough, the party would stop. But the longer it delayed, the more the bursting of the housing bubble would be painful.

"A recession is almost surely going to occur," Greenspan concluded in his Utah speech of October 1978. "Any attempt to find a way to somehow push under the rug the imbalances that have been created, especially in the financial markets of recent years, is likely to fail." Precisely the same warning might have been addressed to Greenspan himself in January 2006, on the day of his retirement as Federal Reserve chairman.

Whatever the prospects for America's economy, Townsend-Greenspan was thriving. In 1979, the firm hired David Rowe, the first PhD economist to sign on for a full-time staff position. Rowe had been trained by Professor Lawrence Klein of Wharton, the father of Keynesian macroeconometric modeling who would win the Nobel Prize the following year, and by Klein's colleague Albert Ando, who would eventually help to create the Fed's macromodel. Studying under these two masters, Rowe had come to see the difference in their styles: Ando was a perfectionist, spending months crafting each equation that went into his model; Klein was an ambitious visionary, at one point launching an effort to combine disparate national forecasts into an econometric model of the entire world economy. When Rowe moved into his new office at One New York Plaza, he wondered which pattern Greenspan would follow—Ando-style craftsman or Klein-type visionary. He quickly discovered that the answer was neither.

Rowe eventually labeled Greenspan the "street-smart economist." Unlike Albert Ando, he was not about to spend months tweaking a single equation, for he doubted that real-world relationships remained stable long enough to justify such effort. In Greenspan's opinion, each part of the economy reflected multiple influences that were constantly in flux: for example, household spending might be driven by house prices or job prospects or fears of inflation or any number of factors, and the drivers that most mattered would vary from one period to another. Likewise, unlike Lawrence Klein, Greenspan mistrusted grand hypotheses about how the economy functioned. He was not interested in what ought to happen according to some elegant theory; he was interested only in what would happen as a result of messy reality. Consequently, he set about building his forecast on discreet insights. Greenspan knew that rising metal prices often signaled an industrial revival; that rising inventories might portend a slowdown; that planned growth in government spending usually signaled good times for the defense industry. Even if none of these relationships was fixed or certain, each contained a useful hint. If you collected enough canaries, you got a sense of what might happen in the coal mine.

Greenspan would not have been upset by Rowe's description of him. He was after all a business economist, with roots among the empiricists at Columbia University and the National Bureau for Economic Research. He remained more interested in measurement than in theory; he was not so much a modeler as an empiricist with a big computer. Exposure to more orthodox economists at the Brookings Institution or the Council of Economic Advisers did nothing to shake his confidence in his eclectic approach. And because he was not dazzled by theory, he felt free to focus on data—on ferreting out information that others did not have rather than obsessing about the mathematical assumptions that linked the data points together. If Greenspan discovered a correlation that seemed to have a good record of predicting the future, he would embrace it happily—and never mind the fact that it might seem orthogonal to a more conventional economist. "Which single indicator do you find most useful?" people would frequently ask. "Scrap steel prices," he would say, relishing the bemused looks that greeted him.

Rowe came to appreciate his street-smart boss, both intellectually and personally. He knew that introverted intellectuals could be hell on wheels to work for—they refused to take the time to explain what they wanted, then blamed you for not doing it. Greenspan was not like that at all: he was happy to have Rowe into his office to discuss statistical issues, provided that no journalist or congressman was demanding his attention. He had a sense of humor, too. One day Rowe remarked to Greenspan that whenever their discussions went on for longer than a few minutes, Rowe would end up seated while Greenspan paced about the office, often in his socks.

"I guess that's because my brains are in my feet," Greenspan said. "Yours must be someplace else," he added.

Around this time, Greenspan got a call from the storied brokerage firm Merrill Lynch: Don Regan, the profane ex–marine colonel who ran Merrill, was asking to meet him. Greenspan went over to Regan's office at Merrill's hulking steel-fronted headquarters and was confronted with an offer that he was not supposed to refuse: Merrill would buy Townsend-Greenspan and Greenspan would become Merrill's chief economist. Regan had a number on a piece of paper, and Greenspan took a look. "That's a big bundle of cash!" he told himself. Keeping his composure, he told Regan he needed time to think. It was a Friday, and Regan asked him to respond by Monday morning.

Greenspan went home and thought to himself, "You know, if this were a shoe factory this would be one hell of a price-earnings ratio. Of course I would sell it." The next day, Saturday, Regan's unbelievable offer kept crowding his mind, paralyzing him with indecision. When he awoke on Sunday morning, he was still heavy with anxiety. But then, in the shower, the weight suddenly lifted.

"I said to myself 'Oh my God, now I know what was bothering me,'" Greenspan recalled. "'It's my independence.'" His head knew that the offer was compelling; his heart rebelled against the prospect of being folded into someone else's organization chart. After that epiphany, Greenspan turned down Don Regan—an act that came back to haunt him when Regan became Ronald Reagan's Treasury secretary.

If Greenspan's choice of freedom over money revealed something of his character, the way he arrived at his decision was even more illuminating. Faced with a life-altering choice, he had been uncharacteristically rattled; but over the course of thirty-six hours, he had consulted precisely nobody. He was still seeing Barbara Walters, who had leaned on him heavily as she had pondered her own career move from breakfast to evening TV, but he had not felt inclined to ask Barbara to reciprocate. "There was nothing to consult anyone about," he said, years later. "There was no factual information I didn't have. . . . A fact is a fact. Once you know it is a fact, there is nothing more to be discussed."[34]

Perhaps Greenspan's solitary decision making said something about his relationship with Walters; after all, he was also seeing other people. Around this period, Greenspan was invited to spend the weekend at a home in New Jersey, where he would play tennis with Brendan Byrne, the governor of the state, and Peter Benchley, the author of *Jaws*. Greenspan accepted the invitation and asked if he could bring a date, a woman from his office. But Greenspan's solitary decision making also spoke volumes about him. His most vivid experiences played out within the confines of his head. The solitary boy lived on inside the famous adult.

G reenspan's pessimistic Utah speech soon proved to be prescient. As he predicted, the delinking of interest rates from mortgage lending was not absolute; in the end, the Fed hiked interest rates enough to make an impact on the housing market. The tipping point came soon after he spoke. At the start of 1979, with the Fed's short-term policy rate now up at 10 percent, mortgage lending started to fall, silencing the engine that had propelled consumption. In the first three months of the year, annualized growth came in at 0.8 percent, down from 5.5 percent in the previous quarter.

Greenspan's warnings about New Frontier economics were coming true also. As growth slowed, inflation paradoxically sped up: price controls and other regulatory meddling had succeeded in suppressing investment and productivity gains, dampening growth; meanwhile, they also created bottlenecks, fueling inflation. The resulting stagflation left policy makers wondering whether to stimulate the economy or apply brakes to it. Money-supply data were not much help in resolving this dispute; financial innovation rendered the numbers hard to interpret. Spending power concealed itself in places that the familiar monetary measures missed: in money-market funds; in instant credit provided by department stores; or in a truly futuristic innovation known as the automated teller machine, which facilitated shopping sprees at all times of the night or weekend. In the face of these uncertainties, Greenspan sided with the hawks who prioritized fighting inflation. "A recession is unavoidable. The sooner we have it, the better off the economy will be," Greenspan told *Time* in April 1979. The overhang from the long mortgage binge had to be purged out of the system.[35]

Greenspan gave the Carter administration credit for its conservative stance on the budget and deregulation. "I find remarkably little difference anymore between the liberal left and the conservative right on general economic issues," he told the *New York Times*. "Now everybody's looking to restrain inflation, improve production, and increase investment."[36] In keeping with this bipartisan pronouncement, Greenspan offered some informal help to Senator Edward Kennedy as he readied his presidential bid, and he did the same for Jerry Brown, the California governor whom he had met with Barbara Walters and Diane von Furstenberg. But even as Greenspan the intellectual shifted toward the middle ground, the travails of the economy caused a collapse in Jimmy Carter's popularity ratings, encouraging Greenspan the politician to position himself for a top job in a future Republican administration.[37] In August 1979, 84 percent of Americans told Gallup that they thought the country was on the wrong track. Many appeared to sympathize with the writer Tom Wolfe, who had called Carter an "unknown down-home matronly-voiced Sunday-school soft-shelled watery-eyed sponge-backed Millennial lulu."[38]

Since leaving the White House, Greenspan had remained in touch with Gerald Ford, who was mulling a political comeback. On his trips out to California, Greenspan would visit Ford in Palm Springs, where the former president had installed himself in a ranch house overlooking a golf course; the two would play a round and Greenspan would keep his old boss up to date with the latest goings-on in the economy. But if Ford chose not to plunge back into politics, Greenspan had a backup plan. Marty Anderson, his old Randian friend who had brought him into the Nixon campaign, was now hard at work for California's former governor.

In the first days of May 1979, Anderson visited Greenspan to ask whether he would help Ronald Reagan, even if his allegiance to Ford might make things awkward. "I'm not asking for your political support,"

Anderson told his friend. "I just want to know if you can advise him on what he should do *if* he is elected."[39]

Greenspan accepted readily. He would be happy to begin advising Reagan straightaway, provided it was understood that this was not an exclusive commitment.[40]

Anderson duly arranged for Greenspan to meet Reagan at Stanford University, where Anderson and other influential Republican thinkers congregated. The encounter went well, and afterward Reagan instructed Anderson to involve Greenspan in the campaign as much as possible.[41] At the start of September, Greenspan duly flew out to Marina del Rey, an affluent corner of Los Angeles wedged between the bohemia of Venice Beach and the brutish utilitarianism of the city's international airport. A handful of other Reagan advisers were there, too: George Shultz, Nixon's former Treasury secretary; Caspar Weinberger, the future defense secretary; and Edwin Meese, who would serve as a top White House counselor and later as attorney general. At 9:30 a.m., after a quick breakfast of coffee, juice, and rolls at the Marina City Club, the men settled into a discussion of the themes that might animate Reagan's candidacy.[42]

Greenspan kicked off the proceedings with a forecast for 1980. He had settled into his familiar role, commanding the attention of colleagues because he had more facts than they did.

"Next year will be an unmitigated disaster," Shultz said, summing up Greenspan's somewhat technical remarks for the group's noneconomists. "Continuing high inflation, economic instability, demands for wage and price controls. It will be a chance to shift the debate in a conservative direction."

The discussion continued until lunch, dwelling in detail on the arcana of the federal budget. After the break, the group reconvened, and this time Reagan himself joined the proceedings. Greenspan was struck by his manner: the candidate projected ease and warmth; there was an attractive roundness to his voice, perhaps learned long ago from acting.[43] But Reagan could also disengage, like a daydreaming child. As they settled in for the afternoon session, the actor became the audience.

The discussion moved on to the case for deeper deregulation and the need to move spending programs out of Washington to state and local government. At one point Reagan intervened to clarify the proper pronunciation for the name of that apparatus he aimed to control: Was it "gov-ERN-ment" or "GUV-mint?" Otherwise, he was silent.

Marty Anderson emphasized that Reagan's cabinet must be forceful enough to get Reagan's economic priorities accomplished.

"On those priorities," Shultz said. "I recommend you read Alan Greenspan's paper." The former Treasury secretary evidently viewed the aspiring Treasury secretary as something of a guru.

"New issue," came a voice that had been silent for a while. "Money. No nation can survive under fiat money."

It could have been Greenspan, circa 1964, delivering his Randian lectures on the economics of freedom. But the speaker was Ronald Reagan.

"Could we reestablish a monetary standard or discipline?" the candidate asked in his mellow voice. "For instance, could we coin $200 gold pieces from the Fort Knox reserves?" Reagan evidently associated Nixon's break with the gold standard with ruinous inflation. He wanted to go back to the old verities.

"You are reversing cause and effect," Greenspan told the candidate, displaying a greater bluntness than he sometimes did with politicians. "We went off the gold standard because the printing of money increased and inflation developed." Inflation had forced the country off the gold standard, not the other way around. And that led Greenspan to a surprising conclusion.

"We must resolve the fiscal and inflation problems," Greenspan said. "If we can do that, there is no need to return to the gold standard."

The small group around Reagan cannot have guessed the full significance of Greenspan's statement. But he had summarized a fundamental change in his worldview—one that would set the stage for the two decades of his Fed tenure. For more than a generation, conservative economists had believed in monetary rules, just as conservative social-policy experts emphasized the rule of law. The monetary rules came in assorted guises: one camp favored a gold standard to preserve domestic price stability, often combined with fixed exchange rates to preserve the dollar's international value; a second camp favored Milton Friedman's proposed autopilot, whereby the rate of money expansion would be fixed according to a rule so that politicians could not tinker with it. Whichever camp conservatives favored, they preferred rules to discretion. Rules would prevent inflation, avoid exchange-rate fluctuations, and forestall bubbles. But now Greenspan was breaking with this intellectual tradition. He still feared inflation and asset bubbles as keenly as ever—witness his writings on home-equity extraction—but he no longer viewed rules as the right antidote. He would still be willing to humor Reagan by paying occasional lip service to the virtues of the gold standard. But he no longer believed this message.

In one sense, Greenspan's new stance was only logical. It would clearly be futile to go back onto the gold standard so long as inflation raged, because inflation would undermine the credibility of the gold peg and the Nixon shock would be repeated. Equally clearly, if raging inflation could in fact be contained, then going back to gold would have been proved unnecessary. Yet in another, deeper way, Greenspan's new stance reflected a changed understanding of democracy. Modern pluralistic systems, Greenspan was saying, were messy and willful; after witnessing government up close, he knew this conclusively. It was idle to expect such systems to submit to rules—political pressures would destroy them. Technocrats who hoped for enlightened economic policy would have to roll their sleeves up and wage political battles.

Eleven

REPUBLICAN DREAMERS

On the evening of September 30, 1979, the world's financial states-men gathered in Belgrade, Yugoslavia. The annual meetings of the IMF and World Bank were to open the following day with a speech from Josip Tito, the Yugoslav strongman, who would harangue his audience about inequality and then rapidly absent himself, lest shoulder rubbing with financiers diminish his revolutionary aura. But tonight the assembled dignitaries were to hear from one of their own. Arthur Burns, the former chairman of the Federal Reserve, was to deliver an address on "The Anguish of Central Banking." Given the surge of inflation across the Western world, it seemed an appropriate topic.

"One of the time-honored functions of a central bank is to protect the integrity of its nation's currency," Burns began. "And yet, despite their antipathy to inflation and the powerful weapons they could wield against it, central bankers have failed so utterly in this mission." The roots of this paradox lay in "philosophic and political trends" that had begun during the Great Depression, Burns continued; he looked as though he were puffing on his pipe, even when he wasn't. Rehearsing the thumbnail history repeated so often by his student, Alan Greenspan, Burns noted that the 1930s had turned a nation of hardworking individualists into a people who looked to the government to battle unemployment; the postwar era had brought an extension of this attitude, so that by the 1960s Lyndon Johnson's Great Society programs had committed the expanding state to placating multiple political constituencies. It was hardly surprising, Burns pleaded, that the central bank had been caught up in this profound change. As he put it,

> Viewed in the abstract, the Federal Reserve System had the power to abort the inflation at its incipient stage fifteen years ago or at any later point, and it has the power to end it today. At any time within that period, it could have restricted the money supply and created sufficient strains in financial and industrial markets to terminate inflation with little delay. It did not do so because the Federal Reserve was itself caught up in the philosophic and political currents that were transforming American life and culture.

Burns's pronouncement was doubly remarkable. For one thing, he was not arguing that the Fed lacked the tools to vanquish inflation: he was rejecting the widespread view that monetary policy was impotent. As recently as 1978, he had suggested that budget policy, not monetary policy, was the key driver of prices; and even when he was not blaming the budget deficit, he resisted the idea that the Fed was responsible, instead pointing the finger at cost-push factors: commodity-price shocks, over-mighty labor unions, rent-seeking monopolists, regulations that created bottlenecks and scarcities.[1] On occasions when he acknowledged the power of interest rates, he nonetheless took refuge behind a version of Greenspan's conundrum. In congressional testimony in July 1975, he noted that it was long-term interest rates that really influenced the economy, and that "all of us recognize that the influence the Federal Reserve has on long-term rates is negligible."[2] In declaring unambiguously that the Fed did have the power to control inflation, Burns was announcing the arrival of a new consensus.

But Burns's speech in Belgrade was also striking for another reason. In blaming the political culture for the Fed's lack of determination, he was invoking a truth that modern commentators forget: despite the aura of independence that has grown up around central banks, they do not exist in a vacuum. To the contrary, their mandates come from lawmakers; their legitimacy derives from the climate of expert opinion; and they ultimately depend on the sympathy of voters. If Burns had tried to extinguish inflation under Nixon, he would have suffered even more punishment from the president's henchmen; and even under Ford and Carter, there were limits to his freedom. At a minimum, a Fed leader wanting to defy his political overlords would need the legitimizing support of the economics profession; but in the 1970s many economists argued that the cost of fighting inflation would exceed the benefit.[3] Because there was neither a political nor an intellectual consensus in favor of higher interest rates, Burns had felt unable to act. Thanks to the constraints imposed by the zeitgeist, the Fed was omnipotent in principle but still impotent in practice.[4]

Sometime after Burns had begun speaking, a huge, rumpled, egg-headed figure entered the auditorium. Not seeing a convenient chair free, he slouched down against the back wall like an overgrown schoolboy and crossed his legs in front of him. The strange impression he created—powerfully gigantic in stature, meekly childlike in posture—mirrored Burns's message; for the six-foot, seven-inch latecomer was none other than Paul Volcker, the newly appointed Federal Reserve chairman. In principle, Volcker was the world's most powerful economic policy maker, with the weaponry to eliminate inflation at will. But he was doing his best to impersonate a 240-pound kindergartner.

Burns continued. Not only did central bankers face political constraints; their task was intrinsically treacherous because the economy and the financial system were forever changing. Central bankers understood that an expanding money supply could herald inflationary pressure; but given the protean nature of finance, they were unsure whether time deposits, money-market funds, and such should be counted as money. They recognized that changes in monetary policy took effect gradually; but the duration of the lags was unpredictable. They knew that higher interest rates would restrain prices, but they had no clear sense of how large the effect might be. Because of these manifold uncertainties, monetary experts could not be expected to speak with one voice. Mustering the intellectual consensus necessary to defy political pressures was therefore all but impossible.[5]

As Burns spoke, Paul Volcker listened at the other end of the huge hall.[6] Anyone with a window into his thoughts would have been startled. Whatever the impression created by his schoolboyish posture, this giant was not mild. He was rebellious, possibly dangerous. Burns's long lament came down to the claim that the political and intellectual assumptions of the age constrained the Fed's actions. It was precisely the argument that Volcker rejected.[7]

Burns was coming to the end of his lecture. "Fairly drastic therapy will be needed to turn inflationary psychology around," he announced, stressing that the therapy could not be administered only or even mainly by constrained central bankers. In addition to tougher monetary policy, governments would have to play their part by disciplining their budgets, and they would have to unleash supply by deregulating industry and lowering business taxes. "I wish I could close this long address by expressing confidence that a . . . forceful program for dealing with inflation will be undertaken in the near future," the professor concluded. "That I cannot do today. I am not even sure that many of the central bankers of the world, having by now become accustomed to gradualism, would be willing to risk the painful economic adjustments that I fear are ultimately unavoidable."

The day after the speech, Volcker suddenly left Belgrade. He did not care that the IMF/World Bank meetings had barely begun. He was heading back to Washington with a mission: to refute Arthur Burns's message.

Paul Volcker is often held up as the model Federal Reserve chairman—the standard against which others must be judged, including Alan Greenspan. Everything about him seemed to radiate frugality and discipline; with his wearily stooped shoulders, lumpy features, and bald head, he looked like an Old Testament prophet. He was raised by a fiercely ethical town manager in a small New Jersey suburb: "Do not suffer your good nature . . . to say yes when you ought to say no," ran a quotation from

George Washington on the wall of his father's office.[8] As a student at Princeton, he imbibed the writings of the austere Austrian Friedrich Hayek, who taught him that inflation could reduce unemployment only by disguising real wage cuts. "Hayek's words forever linked inflation and deception deep inside my head," Volcker told his biographer William L. Silber. "And that connection, which undermines trust in government, is the greatest evil of inflation."[9]

Volcker's legendary stature is built on what he did after listening to Burns in Belgrade. Arriving back in Washington, he convened a secret weekend meeting of the Federal Open Market Committee, which usually gathers every six weeks to decide the Fed's monetary policy. Emerging from that confabulation on October 6, 1979, Volcker drew himself up to his full height and unleashed his Saturday Night Special, a sharp break in the way the Fed would conduct business. Rather than targeting a particular short-term interest rate, Volcker decreed that the Fed would henceforth target the supply of money in the banking system—he would switch from manipulating the price of credit to policing the quantity of it. Under the old system, the Fed might raise the official short-term borrowing rate by what felt like a hefty amount, but the economy might continue to surge if home-equity extraction or some other market change made long-term credit cheap and plentiful. Under the new system, by contrast, the Fed would impose a straitjacket on the quantity of money and credit. If that meant that interest rates went through the roof, so be it.

Volcker could have halted inflation simply by raising interest rates aggressively. If he had pulled that lever hard enough, the appetite for loans would have collapsed and the money supply would have been brought under control without being directly targeted. But Volcker understood that a fierce-sounding new policy would get the public's attention: it would signal that the Fed really meant business. The more the giant could shock people, the likelier they were to stop expecting inflation. If workers pulled back from demanding pay raises and companies thought twice before hiking prices, inflation might subside without requiring drastic treatment.

The Saturday-night shock was the most impressive moment in the Fed's history since the Fed-Treasury Accord of February 1951, when

Chairman Thomas McCabe had defied President Truman by refusing to hold down the government's borrowing costs. At the time of Volcker's announcement, in October 1979, consumer price inflation was running at 12.1 percent; three years later, when Volcker ended his experiment with monetary targets, the rate had plummeted to 5.9 percent. To force inflation down, round upon round of tightening proved necessary; and in the summer of 1981 short-term interest rates breached the extraordinary height of 20 percent, prompting Representative Henry González, a Democrat from Texas, to denounce Volcker for "legalized usury beyond any kind of conscionable limit."[10] The economy endured a double-dip recession, and unemployment hit double digits, too. But the payoff was clear. Inflation not only halved during Volcker's three-year monetarist experiment, it kept falling into 1983. By dint of iron-willed persistence, Volcker turned the inflationary 1970s into the disinflationary 1980s.[11]

Nobody, least of all Alan Greenspan, likes to question this achievement. At the time of Volcker's elevation to the top job at the Fed, Milton Friedman himself had predicted he would fail—like Burns, he believed that the political constraints on central banks were insuperable.[12] But Volcker trampled those constraints under his large feet, and even the most hostile reactions could not stop him. Bankrupt home builders protested by mailing two-by-fours to his office; struggling carmakers sent him the keys of unsold vehicles; furious farmers drove their tractors to Washington and encircled the Fed's headquarters.[13] But unlike Ayn Rand's Atlas, Volcker refused to shrug off his responsibility, patiently carrying the world on his shoulders even when lawmakers threatened to impeach him. Month after month, the giant sat stoically through furious congressional hearings in his cheap suits, blowing clouds of cigar smoke as if to hide himself from his critics, occasionally shaking his domed head as if to say that he pitied the simpletons who abused him. "I've always considered him the most important Chairman ever," Greenspan said flatly, years later.[14]

And yet despite his courage and achievement, the legend of Paul Volcker requires qualification, for if he is allowed to stand too tall, others will be left to shrink unfairly. The first thing to be noted is that Volcker's victory against inflation owed much to timing. He assumed the Fed chairmanship in August 1979, at a moment when Americans craved bold leadership. Confidence in the dollar was evaporating fast: the moment favored a big man with a big sense of his own destiny. As one pollster put it, "For the public today, inflation has the kind of dominance that no other issue has had since World War II. . . . It would be necessary to go back to the 1930s and the Great Depression to find a peacetime issue that has had the country so concerned and so distraught."[15] If ordinary people wanted Volcker to act forcefully, Wall Street was even more desperate for a firm hand. Around this time, Merrill Lynch dispatched a team to hyperinflationary Brazil to learn how to navigate a world in which prices might do anything.[16]

Even though circumstances cried out for decisive monetary tightening, Volcker proceeded cautiously during his first weeks, contrary to the legend that has grown up around him. The first two meetings of the Federal Open Market Committee held under his guidance, in August and September 1979, raised interest rates only modestly. As a result, the inflationary fear in the markets continued to build, and investors fled the dollar in favor of gold. On Monday, October 1, perhaps reacting to Burns's speech the previous evening, gold rose by fully 4 percent. The next day it spiked a further 6 percent—investors' determination to dump dollars implied an expectation of hyperinflation. Now, with both the public and the markets clamoring for a dramatic move, the political constraints that Burns emphasized magically loosened: with the nation behind it, the Fed could clamp down on inflation and ride out any recriminations from the White House. Yet even with this strong wind behind him, Volcker coaxed the timid members of his Open Market Committee as gently as he could. He pleaded that the switch to monetary targets might bring down inflation expectations painlessly, sparing the economy a prolonged recession. He reassured his colleagues that they could always turn back. "If we adopt a new approach," he said, "we are not locked into it indefinitely."[17]

Volcker did not so much lead his committee into battle as deliberately wait for the panic in the markets to do the leading for him. In this sense, he did not quite refute Burns's Belgrade speech. In ordinary times, the Fed would indeed be hard-pressed to defy political currents, just as Burns argued; it was only when the times were out of the ordinary that the Fed acquired the latitude that Volcker was now exploiting. In 1951, the Fed had stood firm against President Truman because inflation had hit the terrifying rate of 20 percent. In 1979, the combination of 12 percent inflation and a crashing dollar gave Volcker the chance to show his greatness. Fed chairmen who preside over calmer periods, like American presidents who govern in peacetime, face an altogether different set of challenges and opportunities.

Greenspan anticipated the Volcker shock, or at least something like it. A short while before the Saturday Night Special, he told *Fortune* that inflation was destined to come down, basing his forecast on opinion polls. Prices would stabilize "not because politicians become wise and courageous, or because some economist invents an easy and painless way to slow inflation," he explained, but "because Americans generally, especially the middle class, are getting so fed up with inflation that the federal government will be compelled to adopt effective inflation-slowing policies."[18] Commenting on the Saturday Night Special later in October, Greenspan had nothing but respect for Volcker, whom he praised as "a tough guy." But he regretted that the fight against inflation had not been pressed further. If the goal was to discipline wild money creation, the government needed to clamp down on federal subsidies for mortgages.[19]

Among the politicians channeling the public's inflation rage was Greenspan's new acquaintance, Ronald Reagan. In November 1979, a month after the Volcker shock, Reagan formally launched his campaign for the presidency. He spoke in swelling tones of America as "a shining city on a hill," paraphrasing John Winthrop, the Puritan father of the Massachusetts Bay Colony. *Time* characterized Reagan as a "romantic conservative," while others dismissed him as naïve.[20] "Reagan steps out of the pages of *Reader's Digest*," sniffed the *New Republic*. "He is as direct as Daffy Duck."[21] But whatever one's view of the candidate, his position on inflation was clear. He excoriated rising prices not just for disrupting the economy but also for threatening "family life itself." Inflation was the demon that compelled women to forsake their homes and join the workforce.

Back in September, at the meeting in Marina del Rey, Reagan had invited Greenspan to endorse his favorite cure for inflation: the gold standard. Gold appealed both to the romantic within him and to Daffy Duck; it evoked the heroic individualism of the nineteenth century—rugged pioneers paying for homesteads with leather pouches of metallic coin—and it was seductively simple. Two months after declaring, he returned to the same idea again, this time with Milton Friedman.

On Monday, January 21, 1980, coincidentally the day on which the gold price hit its all-time high, Reagan huddled in earnest discussion with Friedman at the candidate's nondescript Los Angeles headquarters, at 9841 Airport Boulevard; rather than a marina and a sea of fancy yachts, the view from Reagan's office featured aircraft hangars. Inflation was the first topic on the agenda. Consumer prices had actually accelerated since the Volcker shock in October.

"What if we announce a plan to mint and sell gold?" Reagan suggested. If Americans had gold coins in their pockets, they would feel confident that the government would not expropriate their wealth by engineering inflation.

"Gold is an unstable basis for a monetary system," Friedman answered. The gold price, which had leaped from $559 per ounce at the start of January to around $850 by the time of this meeting, was proof that gold was a fickle store of value. "The gold bandwagon is a false path. . . . The key to fighting inflation is to hold down monetary growth and control the budget."[22]

Reagan had struck out a second time. He had tried his gold infatuation on the top Republican economic consultant, and now on the top Republican economics professor. Not finding satisfaction, he resolved to bide his time. Perhaps some future adviser would prove more sympathetic.

If Reagan's gold nostalgia reflected the broad public horror at double-digit inflation, his stance on the budget was equally reflective of the moment. The Kemp-Roth tax-cutting proposals, which Greenspan had expediently endorsed in 1978, still enthused congressional Republicans, and Reagan was happy to embrace them. In January 1980, around the same time as the meeting with Friedman, the candidate spent a few days with Representative Jack Kemp, the more fiery partner in the Kemp-Roth alliance, and with two of Kemp's tax-cutting allies, Arthur Laffer and Jude Wanniski. Both Kemp and his sidekicks were given to messianic eccentricity. Laffer in particular believed that there was no need whatever to offset tax cuts with cuts in spending, and he had nothing but contempt for anyone who disagreed with him. "In the latest gyrations of highly-situated government officials in this country, we hear the litany of personal sacrifice ad nauseam," Laffer wrote in his newsletter at the time of his encounter with Reagan. "Federal Reserve Chairman Paul A. Volcker states that the American standard of living will just have to be lower, if we're ever to come to grips with inflation. Treasury Secretary G. William Miller assures us that slow growth is good"—Laffer underlined the key names like an obsessive recluse plotting the destruction of his enemies. Then he spelled out his message to these puritanical killjoys. "More often than not, acts which are pleasurable are also good for you," he preached. "Cutting tax rates is the primary example"—tax cuts would pay for themselves.[23] Reagan, who liked sunny messages, was quickly won over. Emerging from those January meetings, Kemp announced triumphantly that the Republican front-runner was "ninety percent with us."[24]

Greenspan had no sympathy for the Kemp-Laffer tax dogma, just as he could not honestly endorse Reagan's nostalgia for the gold standard. He had planted one foot in the Reagan camp with the help of Martin Anderson, but by January 1980, Reagan's emerging stance on economics was a bad caricature of Greenspan's. Greenspan had long favored tough monetary policy, but Reagan's belief in gold was simpleminded, as Greenspan had tried to tell him. Greenspan had long favored tax cuts, but Reagan embraced these naïvely—without any of the spending cuts that would make them affordable. From Greenspan's perspective, Reagan was congenial in his small-government instincts, but alarming when it came to policy detail; and on social issues he was anathema. In the words of David Stockman, a brilliant young congressman and Greenspan protégé, Reagan stood for "the anti–gun control nuts, the Bible-thumping creationists, the anti-Communist witch-hunters, and the small-minded Hollywood millionaires to whom 'supply side' meant one more Mercedes."[25]

Greenspan showed his mixed feelings about Reagan by keeping a safe distance. The Reagan camp was "reaching around for solutions and considering some innovative ideas," Greenspan told the *Wall Street Journal* in November; "I didn't say they were all necessarily *good* ideas."[26] Meanwhile, he carried on his social life, attending the premiere of *Superman* at the Kennedy Center with Barbara Walters and escorting her to the White House for a state dinner in honor of the Middle East peace accord. Barbara disloyally enjoyed Henry Kissinger's response to *Superman*—"I want to thank Warner Brothers," Kissinger had said in his Germanic baritone, "for making a movie about my life"—but Greenspan did not let this bother him; the fact that Israel and Egypt had buried the hatchet under a different secretary of state served to contain Kissinger's ego, at least marginally.[27] In between the glittering parties, Greenspan maintained an impressive intellectual flow. In late 1979, he collaborated with *Fortune* on a long-run economic forecast, correctly predicting that falling inflation, lower corporate taxes, and deregulation would boost the incentives for business investment, turning the 1980s into a boom era.[28] In March 1980, he published an essay in *Challenge* that was equally prescient, but in an eerie way. Reflecting on the fragilities in finance, Greenspan showed how deeply he understood the demons that would haunt him as Fed chairman.[29]

Greenspan's *Challenge* essay was prompted by the fiftieth anniversary of the 1929 crash, which had heralded the Depression of the 1930s. If the nation was vulnerable to a repeat, Greenspan began, it would come not from the equity market but from housing. After all, home prices had nearly tripled during the 1970s, and because that bubble had been built on debt, a reversal would impose a long period of weak growth on the economy. Moreover, the risks from the housing bubble were magnified by the "extraordinarily complex development of international finance." Bankers' creativity outstripped public understanding of the risks entailed: "There are very likely to be structural inadequacies in these new financial innovations which the standard bailout procedures of the central banks do not fully address," Greenspan wrote soberly. Banks and quasi banks were increasingly interconnected by daisy chains of lending, so that the failure of one could bring down others, and capital-asset ratios had been allowed to shrink alarmingly. Any bank that got into trouble "would have to be bailed out by its central bank or international agencies, or be absorbed by institutions not yet in difficulty," Greenspan predicted.

Despite his own record of opposing bailouts, Greenspan reassured his readers that a repeat of 1929 was highly unlikely—because bailouts were a certainty. At the first sign of a banking failure, central banks would ride to the rescue, even if they damaged long-run growth in the process. "The overriding mandate of the world's monetary authorities to prevent a credit deflation almost assures policy overkill," he wrote. "Deflation would be quickly aborted—to be followed shortly by . . . economic stagnation. . . . Thus, in today's political and institutional environment, a replay of the Great Depression is the Great Malaise," Greenspan concluded.

On March 10, 1980, Greenspan moved to distance himself from the economic naïfs in his own party. Appearing before the Senate banking committee, flanked by five other former CEA chiefs, he joined with his cowitnesses in rejecting the fantasy of self-financing tax cuts.

"There remains the desperate yearning that somehow we can resolve our very difficult inflationary problems without taking the harsh measures," he lamented. But harsh medicine was inevitable, because the budget deficit was actually far larger than it appeared to be. If you counted in loan guarantees, the true measure of government spending exceeded what was captured in the conventional budget. Whatever the wishful thinkers around Reagan might say, it was time to rein in Leviathan.

Senator William Proxmire, the senior Democrat who had opposed Greenspan's appointment to the CEA six years earlier, was delighted with this testimony.

"There are four times as much in dollars outside of the budget as within the budget," he marveled. "My question is this: Do you see that as a real loophole?"

"I would most certainly say so, Mr. Chairman," Greenspan responded.

"That is a very welcome warning," Proxmire said, appreciatively. He noted that federal loan guarantees had recently been used to bail out the car company Chrysler; meanwhile, loan guarantees continued to mount up for New York City. Given all this government-backed money creation, it was no wonder that inflation was accelerating.

Proxmire turned next to Walter Heller, the architect of the Kennedy-Johnson tax cut. Noting that some Democrats had lately grown eager to balance the budget, Proxmire demanded whether Heller would endorse his party's shift to deficit cutting.

"You are quite right . . . the world has changed," Heller acknowledged. He added that he welcomed deficit reduction so long as Congress avoided rigid limits on spending.

"I'm not talking about inflexible limits," Proxmire responded testily. "What concerns me very much is what Mr. Greenspan has brought out I think brilliantly here," the senator continued, alluding to the growth of off-budget loan guarantees. Surely it was time to take an ax to the excesses of the 1970s.

Heller pleaded that several types of government spending had already been reined in considerably.

"Does that take into account the enormous increase in the off-budget credit?" Proxmire demanded.

"That does not."

"Shouldn't that be included?" Proxmire pressed him.

Heller dodged and weaved until the two men reached a stalemate. But a strange reversal had transpired. Proxmire was siding with the libertarian, Alan Greenspan, and assailing Walter Heller, the Democrat. The world really was changing, as Heller had said; and the effect on a conservative economist such as Greenspan could be disorienting. When he surveyed the policy landscape, Greenspan could see a Democratic Fed chairman, Paul Volcker, who embodied his own hard-money ideals; he could see a Democratic Senate banking chairman, William Proxmire, who embodied his budget conservatism. Meanwhile, portions of Greenspan's own party were headed off to wishful la-la land. They were not so much do-nothing as know-nothing.

Yet if Greenspan aspired to hold high office, he could not afford to dwell on this reshuffling.

O ne way Greenspan's problems with the Reaganite wing of his party could be resolved was with a successful Gerald Ford candidacy. Since the summer of 1979, polls had indicated that Ford was more likely than anybody else to beat Reagan in the Republican primaries, and the president's former lieutenants were urging a fresh bid for the White House.[30] The *Washington Post* noted that almost all the Ford old-timers were holding off on joining other campaigns, although some, like Green-span, were no doubt playing footsy with Reagan on a "nonexclusive" basis. Ford, for his part, was in no hurry to commit. "We seem to be doing bet-ter not being a candidate," he told the *Post* in September 1979, using the majestic plural.[31] For the rest of the year and into 1980, Ford waffled back and forth. He insisted that he was not planning a campaign. He insisted that he knew better than to say "never" in politics.

By the time of Greenspan's testimony to Proxmire, the moment of truth was approaching. The early primary states had already voted; if Ford wanted to capture enough delegates for the nomination, he would have to plunge in quickly. On March 5, 1980, with time dwindling, Ford allowed himself to be interviewed by Barbara Walters, and declared that his likeli-hood of running was around fifty-fifty. He then delivered a series of attacks on Carter's record and picked up the endorsement of Henry Kissinger, not to mention much feverish newspaper attention. On March 12, two days after Greenspan's Senate appearance, Ford met several former advisers in Washington to discuss his chances of winning. A journalist asked Greenspan what he would counsel Ford to do. "There are certain types of decisions nobody should give advice on," Greenspan answered coyly. "You know—'Should I marry Jane?'"[32]

A couple of days later, Greenspan flew out to Ford's home in Rancho

Mirage, California. A kitchen cabinet had formed around the ex-president: there was Thomas Reed, a former air force secretary who had launched a draft Ford committee; John Marsh, a former White House assistant; and three political consultants. Greenspan was the only senior policy figure in the group—a testament both to his proximity to Ford and to his chameleon-like ability to double as a political operative. For two hours on March 15, Ford's advisers debated his prospects. But their conclusion was grim. At this late stage, Ford's chances of overtaking Reagan seemed negligible.[33]

Emerging from that consultation, Ford marched off to face the reporters camped outside his ranch house. At last, the equivocation was gone: "I am not a candidate. I will not become a candidate," he declared firmly. Afterward, he shed his suit and tie and stormed off to the golf course with three loyalists in tow, Alan Greenspan among them. That day, Ford played some of the worst golf of his life, spraying erratic shots alarmingly, clobbering palm trees, missing easy chips, and finally finishing after darkness had descended. His aides told friends to keep their distance. "Stay the hell away from him," one told a caller who sought to console the ex-president, "and make sure anybody you care about does the same."[34]

With Ford out of the race, Greenspan pedaled back to Reagan. His close relationship with the ex-president gave him an advantage, because Reagan advisers were intrigued by the prospect of Ford as a running mate. It was an outlandish idea: there had never been a case in history of a president later becoming vice president. But polls continued to show that Ford was popular, and having him on the ticket would boost Reagan's chances against Carter. In June, Reagan planned a courtesy visit to Ford in Rancho Mirage; and as the day of the visit approached, Reagan's campaign manager, Bill Casey, briefed him carefully on what Ford might want from him.[35] Ford would recommend bringing Henry Kissinger into the campaign, Casey reported, suggesting that Reagan could accept that. But Ford also had ideas on economic policy, Casey continued, and the campaign manager offered a preview of the details based on a long talk with Alan Greenspan. "Greenspan told me that Ford will express concern and skepticism about your going all out on Kemp-Roth," Casey warned Reagan. "He's concerned about the budget-inflationary impact."

Two years earlier, Greenspan had given a green light to the Kemp-Roth tax plan. But privately, Casey reported, Greenspan was arguing that voters would be skeptical of a free budget lunch—and Casey himself seemed ready to agree with him. "Greenspan has constructive ideas on how to handle this," Casey told Reagan. "To make our tax position credible we must emphasize a corresponding commitment to reduce the size and scope of government."

Casey then rounded off his memo with a note on the dress code for the upcoming meeting. "Ford intends to wear a dark blazer and open gold shirt," he confided.

Reagan duly visited Ford, and the two discussed the running-mate idea without reaching any conclusions. But one month later, on July 7, Greenspan reaped the reward for his long conversation with Casey: he was named chairman of Reagan's Budget Advisory Group.[36] Ford's one-time budget director and his deputy would join the advisory group, too. Greenspan and his fellow old-timers were making their bid to shape Candidate Reagan. A battle with the wishful fringe was looming.

A few days after Greenspan signed up with Reagan, old-timers and insurgents alike descended upon Detroit, host of the Republican nominating convention. The Reagan campaign installed itself on the sixty-ninth floor of the soaring Detroit Plaza Hotel; and on July 13, the day before the formal proceedings got under way, Ford gave another interview to Barbara Walters. Asked about his vice presidential ambitions, Ford gamely played them down. But he was tanned, fit, and on TV. He was evidently not tired of the limelight.

After the interview, Ford said to Walters, "If you see Alan Greenspan tell him I'd like to speak to him." Walters duly passed the message on, but thought nothing of it until later.[37]

The next day, Monday, July 14, was Ford's sixty-seventh birthday. Escorted by his wife, Betty, he went over to Reagan's hotel suite, and Ronald and Nancy toasted him with champagne and presented him with an antique Crow Indian pipe.[38] When the conversation turned to the vice presidency, Ford declared that he and Betty wanted a quiet retirement. But that evening Ford appeared before the convention crowd at Detroit's Joe Louis Arena and delivered a rousing oration.[39] "This country means too much to me to comfortably park on the bench," he declared, before thrilling the assembled faithful with a thundering crescendo. *"Count me in!"* he roared. The question was, in what capacity?

Encouraged by Ford's mixed signals, the Reagan team resolved to press him. Bill Casey, the campaign manager, and Dick Wirthlin, the pollster, visited Kissinger on Tuesday, informing him that Reagan would not defeat Carter without Ford on the ticket—in view of the electoral arithmetic, Ford had an obligation to his party to serve as running mate. Kissinger promised to relay this message to Ford, whom he would see that evening.[40]

When Kissinger told Ford about the Reagan team's approach, Ford sought out Alan Greenspan. His favorite economist was not hard to find. Together with some large fraction of the Republican high command, he was attending a party on a yacht belonging to a party money raiser. The overture from Reagan sounded like the real deal, Ford said; it was not just some media rumor. The former president was visibly excited. "For the first time, I thought it was possible," Greenspan told the *Wall Street Journal* later.[41]

Ford and Greenspan left the yacht for Ford's suite on the seventieth floor of the Plaza, one floor above Reagan's. They were joined there by Kissinger and several other advisers. Starting around midnight, the group hashed out the possibility of a Reagan-Ford alliance, each speaker building upon the last until the whole room believed in the "Dream Ticket."[42] The old battles over the Iranian oil deal now apparently forgotten, Ford instructed Kissinger and Greenspan to hash out the terms of the engagement.

On the third day of the convention, Wednesday, July 16, negotiations over the Dream Ticket opened in the morning. Kissinger and Greenspan proposed that Ford should be made into a sort of executive vice president. He would assume responsibility for foreign policy, the budget, and various other functions. In fact, he would not be a vice president so much as a copresident.

If this was a lot to expect from the Reagan camp, there was still a risk that it was not enough to get Ford to do it. Characteristically indecisive, Ford still had cold feet. Betty hated the idea of a return to Washington. The excitement of the previous night was fading.

Partway through the morning, Greenspan took a break from the negotiations to urge Ford not to back out. He understood that the former president and Betty were enjoying retirement. But echoing the pitch that Arthur Burns had made to him during the dying days of Nixon's presidency, Greenspan told Ford he had a duty to his country.

"Look, for God's sake, if I'm going to do this, would you be willing to come in and help me out on the economic side?" Ford demanded.

"If I'm sitting here and strongly suggesting that the vice presidency isn't a bad idea, I have no choice but to say yes," Greenspan responded.[43]

At five that afternoon, Ford returned to Reagan's hotel suite, flanked by his Secret Service detail. He announced that he would like to bring Alan Greenspan and Henry Kissinger into the administration with him. Reagan listened pleasantly, raising no objections. After half an hour or so, Ford left, stopping on the landing to greet Reagan's national security adviser, Richard Allen, who was on his way in to see the candidate.

When Allen entered Reagan's suite, a handful of advisers sat hushed on a large U-shaped couch. It was as though they had fallen under the collective spell of an unseen hypnotist.

Allen asked if Reagan needed anything.[44]

"Oh, no," the candidate replied, "but thanks."

As Allen turned to leave, Reagan asked, "What do you think of the Ford deal?"

"What deal?" Allen responded.

"Ford wants Kissinger as secretary of state and Greenspan at Treasury." It seemed that Greenspan was about to get the job that he coveted, in the most roundabout way possible.

"That is the craziest deal I have ever heard of," Allen retorted. Quite apart from the fact that the glassy-eyed figures on the U-shaped couch might be shut out of some plum jobs, Reagan was supposed to be the standard-bearer of the party's new guard. His campaign promises directly contradicted what Ford and the old-timers stood for.

Crazy or not, Allen realized nervously that the Dream Ticket might be unstoppable. In just a few hours, Reagan would announce his selection for vice president. Little had been done to prepare the ground for a running mate other than Ford.

An hour or so later, Barbara Walters was reporting live from the floor of the Joe Louis Arena. Standing in front of an American flag, blond hair falling in waves to her shoulders, she held the microphone straight up in front of her and cited "highly informed sources" who knew that "top advisers" had been "wrestling with the problem of how to make Jerry Ford say yes." "One Ford intimate told me, 'The decision the former president must now make is to weigh the national interest against his personal feelings,'" she confided. "The odds are still against Ford saying yes, but the answer is not yet a formal and definite no."[45]

At 7:30 p.m., Ford himself appeared on CBS with Walter Cronkite. With the television cameras trained on him, his political appetite was whetted. He declared that he would seriously consider running for vice president if he received assurances of a "meaningful role," adding that he and Betty had already joked about taking up residence in the vice presidential mansion.[46] Determined to keep up with her rivals, Barbara Walters rushed over to the CBS booth to seize Ford on his way out; and when she had her turn to grill the ex-president on air, he explained that the Dream Ticket would entail "a far different role than any of the vice president–president relationships I have known in the past thirty years in Washington."[47]

In his suite at the Plaza, Reagan had emerged from a catnap and parked himself in front of three muted television sets. When he saw Ford appear on one of the screens, he asked that the volume be turned up. Richard Allen, who was watching Reagan closely and taking notes through the evening, thought that the candidate looked appalled by Ford's talk of power sharing.

Seeing an opening, Allen suggested that Reagan issue a statement ruling out a copresidency.

"I can't," Reagan said weakly. Then, after a pause, he asked, "Who else is there?"

"There's Bush," Allen suggested.

Reagan demurred. George Bush represented the establishment wing of the Republican Party, and he lacked Ford's poll ratings. Besides, Bush had likened Reagan's advocacy of self-financing tax cuts to "voodoo economic policy."[48]

Reagan continued to sit before the televisions, snacking on his favorite jelly beans. One floor up from where he was sitting, negotiations over a Dream Ticket carried on. Just after eight p.m., according to Allen's notes, the candidate asked whether Ford didn't "realize there is no way in the world I can accept? What kind of presidential candidate would I be in the eyes of the world if I were to give in to such demands?"

About half an hour later, Reagan got word that Ford wanted to speak with him. He went into his bedroom to dial Ford, and emerged after a few minutes. The talks had moved, he told his aides. Kissinger had taken himself out of the running for secretary of state. As far as Allen could tell, Greenspan had not taken himself out of anything.[49]

At the convention center below, the news anchors buzzed with Dream Ticket speculation. Determined to trump the competition, Barbara Walters let viewers in on the story of Ford's using her to pass a message to Greenspan. Having thus established her insider authority, she predicted that Ford's ultimate decision would hinge on the advice he got from Greenspan and Kissinger.

As the television stars were talking, the convention delegates went through the ritual of reporting their votes for the prospective nominees, and at 11:13 p.m. the Montana delegation clinched Reagan's victory, making his nomination official. There were cheers on the convention floor, and a few in the candidate's hotel suite, too. But the Dream Ticket negotiations were still grinding on. If they were not concluded soon, it would be too late to nail down an alternative vice presidential candidate.

When the conclusion did come, it was as abrupt as the negotiations had been extensive. At 11:30 p.m. Ford appeared in Reagan's hotel suite. "Look, this isn't going to work," he said.[50] He had evidently gotten cold feet about the whole idea. He was gone after five minutes.

When Ford had left, the Reagan team was silent.

"Well, what do we do now?" Reagan demanded.

"We call Bush," Allen ventured.

Reagan looked at his other advisers. Nobody was proposing anybody else. Nobody was objecting.

"Well, let's get Bush on the phone," Reagan ordered.[51]

Within a few minutes, Reagan offered Bush a place on the Republican ticket, which Bush accepted giddily; and just after midnight, Reagan announced his vice presidential choice to a surprised public. Greenspan had come close to landing the big job, but it had slipped through his fingers in the end. His adversaries within the Republican Party might be dismissed as economic dreamers. But the Dream Ticket itself had been a dream. There was no way that an ex-president would agree to serve on terms that a new president would find acceptable.[52]

G reenspan's failure to emerge as Treasury secretary in waiting did not mean that he stopped wanting the position. He had negotiated persistently on Ford's behalf, risking the resentment of the Reaganites. Now, to preserve his political prospects, he needed to soften the memory of his side's demands—notably the demand that he himself should take a prime position in the cabinet.

The next day, Thursday, July 17, Greenspan began to massage history. He had an ally in Barbara Walters, who appeared on the evening news shortly after 6:30 p.m., blond hair spilling over a pink-and-white jacket. Right before her appearance, an ABC reporter had reprised the Greenspan-for-Treasury saga, explaining that the combined Greenspan-Kissinger demand had poisoned the deal for Reagan. But when Walters put her spin on the story, she focused on the Kissinger angle, and she set Ford up as the fall guy. "What brought down the Dream Ticket was indeed Henry Kissinger, and it wasn't his fault," she announced. "Gerald

Ford himself, without Kissinger's asking, said he wanted within his administration people with whom he could work; people like Henry Kissinger and economist Alan Greenspan. The Reagan negotiators took this to mean that Ford wanted Kissinger as secretary of state and this is where the negotiations broke down," Walters contended. "Henry Kissinger was the stumbling block, and nothing was the same once his name came up."[53]

A few minutes later, Walters appeared on air again, this time in a khaki suit and a wide-collared maroon blouse. Her colleague Ted Koppel gave her a drumroll. "It is such an incredible story that it is undoubtedly going to be chewed over both by politicians and those of us in the media for some time to come," he said of the Dream Ticket. "Let's start chewing with someone who knows what's going on." The action moved to Walters sitting high above the convention floor, accompanied by none other than Alan Greenspan.

Greenspan reached for a preinterview sip of water, the bright-white cuffs of his dress shirt extending far beyond his pin-striped sleeves. He wore his trademark heavy spectacles, and his hair looked as though it had been slicked back with Brylcreem.

Walters leaned in for her first question. "Dr. Greenspan," she began, as though meeting him for the first time—she evidently did not believe that she needed to disclose their relationship. "Some of the Republicans are saying that Ford never had any intention of accepting this position, and why did he do it, and create all this controversy? Just to get even with Ronald Reagan?"

"Well that's just not true," Greenspan responded, leaping to the defense of his patron. "I've known Gerald Ford for quite a long time and there are no occasions which even remotely suggest to me he could do such a thing."

"He would have accepted it if it had been worked out, that's what you're saying?" Walters leaned farther forward and pointed her pen gently in Greenspan's direction as she attempted to put words into his mouth. If she could get him to say that Ford had been ready to take the vice presidential slot, then she could force him to come clean about other possible reasons for the Dream Ticket's failure.

Greenspan sensed where the conversation was going. "Well, not necessarily," he parried.

Walters switched tack. "Let me ask you," she said, requesting permission for something she would certainly do anyway, "what the plan was, what did Ford want, what was it going to be?"

"Well basically, Governor Reagan was interested in what Ford—in what I would call an enhanced vice presidency."

"Well let me be specific," said Walters, reaching for her notes. "What we understand is that Ronald Reagan was going to be chairman and chief executive officer and Ford would be the chief operations officer, and the budget committee, and foreign policy, and so forth." Walters allowed her hand to fall up and down as she emphasized all Ford's responsibilities. "Reagan would make the broad decisions but Ford would implement them." At "implement," her hand formed a fist and came down as if to emphasize the finality of implementation. "Is that true?"

"Well, essentially that," Greenspan said, a bit uncertainly.

"Ford would run it—the day-by-day operations," Walters coaxed him.

"In effect," Greenspan answered warily. He was fencing on a stage that Barbara commanded. If his goal was to soften memories of Ford's Constitution-stretching demands, the interview was going badly.

"Now, we have heard," Walters continued, "the Reagan people couldn't swallow Kissinger and that's what broke everything off. Why didn't Ford then back down?"

"The actual negotiations went well beyond any discussion as I gather of personalities even though I wasn't there at that time," Greenspan said vaguely.

Walters was not going to let him get away with that. "Get back to this business about Kissinger," she snapped. "My understanding—"

Walters stopped suddenly, and unexpectedly switched tone; had Greenspan grimaced at her off camera? "I don't mean to be that, that, that abrupt about it," she stammered, reaching over to her guest apologetically. It was a moment of softness, and then gone. "My understanding was— and we all seem to have heard the same story—that the Reagan people could not seem to accept Dr. Kissinger. Is that false?"

"Well, that may or may not be true," Greenspan waffled.

"Then what was the final breakdown?" Walters demanded.

This was the crux. Either Greenspan had to confess that the Dream Ticket had been scuppered by personnel demands, or he would have to blame Ford's maddening indecisiveness.

"The final breakdown was Gerald Ford never quite was able to get himself to say yes," Greenspan answered. "He was moving toward it. I personally thought he would say yes, but he never quite made it."

The confession elicited another momentary respite. The camera panned out, showing Barbara still leaning in toward Alan, her right hand gently draped over the edge of the armrest. "Is it workable? Is it workable," Walters resumed, her voice rising again, "to have . . . a vice president who is really in charge of foreign policy, budget—by the way was there a chief of staff?"

"No there would not be in the usual sense."

"So Ford would be."

"Yes. But wait a second," Greenspan countered. Time was rushing, and he had one last chance to place a favorable construction on the past forty-eight hours. "The president's burdens are just much too large and it strikes me that an enhanced vice presidency is almost an inevitable new element within the federal system," he ventured.

Moments after that, the interview ended. Greenspan had done his best to soothe the ruffled feathers of his adversaries. The Dream Ticket had not been just a vulgar power play. It had reflected a farsighted vision of America's constitutional future.[54]

Having played the political broker in Detroit, Greenspan switched back to his more familiar role as data master and economist. He hung on to his position as Reagan's chief budget adviser, and waged open war on the conceit that the Kemp-Roth tax cuts would pay for themselves. In August he worked up estimates of how much extra growth and government revenues the tax cuts would really generate, sensibly concluding that every $100 in cuts would generate only $17 in new revenues, meaning that they would expand the budget deficit by $83. If Jack Kemp had put the voodoo into Reagan's economic policy, Greenspan aimed to be the exorcist.[55] It followed that Reagan's tax plan would be affordable only if it was phased in slowly, with deep spending reductions in the meantime.[56] But Reagan was trapped. He had already promised tax cuts, a balanced budget, and a defense buildup besides. His rivals scoffed that his economic plan depended on smoke and mirrors.

Eager to counter the critics, the Reagan team announced that the candidate would soon give a major address on the budget. The project was known internally as the "mirrors speech," but agreement on the name did not extend to the contents. Greenspan's old friend Martin Anderson believed that balancing the budget was the easiest to sacrifice of Reagan's three priorities. The defense buildup was sacrosanct, and the tax cuts were the only thing distinguishing Reagan from Carter's generally conservative economic program. But a few hours before Reagan was due to appear in Chicago to lay out his fiscal vision, Anderson was forced to think again. James Baker, a canny Texan political operative who had parachuted into the campaign with Bush's selection as running mate, insisted that the goal of a balanced budget could not be tossed aside so easily.

Baker combined the polish of a Princeton education with the earthiness of his southwestern roots; he could pose convincingly in tailored suits while chewing a wad of Red Man tobacco. More important to Anderson, he was the savviest campaign tactician in the Republican Party. If he said the budget plan was a mistake, everyone would take him seriously.

"We just can't go with these $50 billion deficits," Baker protested, alluding to the shortfall that Anderson had proposed to tolerate. Reagan would be eviscerated for advocating so much red ink. "There must be something you can do," Baker insisted.[57]

Anderson had installed himself at the Palmer House Hilton in downtown Chicago. Greenspan and a defense expert named William Van Cleave were there with him, and that evening the three of them were due to brief the national press on the mirrors speech. Now Baker had thrown their script for a loop. If the $50 billion deficits were unacceptable, the Palmer House trio had to come up with a way of reducing them—quickly.

Anderson proposed an escape strategy. The Senate Budget Committee had recently produced a rosy growth forecast that made Reagan's plans seem more affordable. Over the span of five years, it would give Anderson an additional $224 billion to work with. But before he could embrace the Senate's numbers, Anderson needed buy-in from Greenspan. "A happy Greenspan, fully confident about the program, was crucial to a successful press briefing that night," Anderson recalled later.[58] The press knew Greenspan as the man who knew. His endorsement was crucial.

Unfortunately for Anderson, Greenspan was uncomfortable with the Senate's forecast. It assumed nominal growth of around 12 percent per year; because the trend rate of real growth was about 3 percent, this implied annual inflation of about 9 percent. In other words, the Senate forecast would prove responsible only if the broader response to inflation was irresponsible.

Greenspan told Anderson to dial back the Senate's projected windfall by a fifth. But even with that revision, he seemed anxious. The doubtful Senate forecast would be the icing on the hopeful numbers that Anderson had already baked into the plan. The combination would be indigestible.[59]

Greenspan suggested that the fact sheets for reporters simply omit all numbers rather than containing false ones.

Anderson was alarmed. Reagan was under attack as the smoke-and-mirrors candidate. He had to lay out specifics.

Greenspan asked for the sheet of paper with the campaign's budget projections. He commandeered the one big soft chair in the room and withdrew into a private reverie. Anderson could feel the clock ticking. The press briefing was just an hour away; if there were going to be numbers in the fact sheet, the budget table had to be typed, photocopied, and stapled to the other materials.[60]

Greenspan continued to stare silently. Eventually, Anderson asked him one more time whether they could go with the dialed-back version of the Senate numbers.

Greenspan looked up quizzically at his old friend. After sixteen years of steady comradeship, after their shared migration from Ayn Rand's salon to the Republican front line, he was not going to resist him. The numbers were not pretty, but they were good enough.[61]

Anderson snatched up the budget table before Greenspan could get cold feet again. He headed downstairs to the press room, sat down at an old Royal typewriter, and bashed out a table that contained the essence of Reagan's economic program.

When the press conference got under way, Greenspan delivered the performance that Anderson wanted. Exuding technocratic seriousness, and using the supply-side wing of the Republican Party as a convenient foil, he presented Reagan's budget as a model of sobriety, gravely cautioning reporters that it was "a risky proposition" to justify tax cuts on the assumption that they would be self-financing. The effect on the assembled journalists was exactly as planned. "The names Kemp and Roth don't appear in Reagan's speech," Elizabeth Drew marveled in the *New Yorker,* capturing the essence of the candidate's pivot. "Reagan has entered the orthodox conservative mainstream. He has been pushed into a new policy by his new advisers."[62]

Reagan had attained policy respectability, with an assist from Greenspan—he was on his way to the White House. But neither Reagan nor Greenspan could anticipate what was to come, courtesy of a lumpy giant with a bald head who had been watching from the sidelines.

Twelve

"DO WE REALLY NEED
THE FED?"

E lected in a landslide as a candidate of clear convictions, Ronald
Reagan could be paradoxically elusive. He exhorted his country-
men to reach for greatness, to "believe in ourselves and to believe
in our capacity to perform great deeds. . . . Why shouldn't we believe that?
We are Americans." But the content of this greatness was sometimes hazy,
for Reagan managed to entertain radical notions while simultaneously
fuzzing them. He supported deep tax reductions, cuts in welfare spending, and (privately) a return to the gold standard, but he always took care
to soften his convictions with self-deprecating humor. When the joke
went around that Reagan's right hand didn't know what his far-right hand
was up to, some thought that Reagan himself had originated it. He made
light of his reputation for doziness. "I am concerned about what is happening in government—and it's caused me many a sleepless afternoon,"
he told reporters. "It's true hard work never killed anyone but I figure,
why take the chance?"[1]

Like a majority of voters, Alan Greenspan was willing to bet on this
inchoate figure, even though the political shifts of the late 1970s had
landed him closer to Democrats such as Senator Proxmire than to the
Republicans of Jack Kemp's circle. After conferring respectability upon
Reagan's budget plan in Chicago, Greenspan continued to build his

standing with the candidate. His friend Martin Anderson arranged for him to brief Reagan thoroughly on domestic issues over the course of a long, transcontinental flight; Greenspan used the opportunity to charm Reagan, largely by listening to his amusing stories and ignoring the tedious briefing book that Anderson had prepared for the session.[2] Greenspan was also invited to the Virginia estate of Senator John Warner and his wife, the actress Elizabeth Taylor, where he helped to prep Reagan for the first presidential debate; Reagan thanked him afterward, writing that he was "comforted in the knowledge that you were there and participating."[3] Inevitably, as his relationship with Reagan deepened, Greenspan's long-standing ambition for high office bubbled up again. In mid-November 1980, a week and a half after the election, he flew out to Los Angeles to take part in a forum with the president-elect and his brain trust. Sharing a cab from the conference center to the hotel with some fellow economists, he made one of those quips that is more revealing than funny: "The future Treasury Secretary is in this taxi," he blurted out, paying the cabdriver before anybody else got out his wallet.[4]

Greenspan's hopes for the Treasury job were disappointed. The Reagan team opted for Donald Regan, the garrulous Merrill Lynch chief with a strong peak of gray hair who had tried to buy Greenspan's consultancy. But Greenspan was too dogged to allow himself to be discouraged. Praising his rival as "an extremely intelligent and tough person," he quickly found an alternative role for himself as the quiet counselor to Reagan's budget chief. Taxes and spending would be the first testing ground for the promised Reagan revolution. Greenspan would be in the thick of it.

The new budget chief was David Stockman, the bumptious thirty-four-year-old who had sneered at Reagan's base of gun nuts and crass millionaires. A colleague once described Stockman as "flashing like a meteor across the sky," and Stockman himself confessed roguishly that he might be "the most conniving character in history."[5] But whatever Stockman's brains and energy, he faced a monumental task. A lousy economic outlook was forcing a rethink of Reagan's campaign pledges: it would be harder than ever to cut taxes and boost defense spending while simultaneously avoiding a huge budget shortfall. Encouraged by Greenspan, Stockman was ready to ax social spending to make the numbers balance. But his job was going to be complicated by Jack Kemp and the supply-siders, who denied the need for austerity. The tax cuts, Kemp's people insisted flatly, would pay for themselves.

On December 18, 1980, Greenspan dined with Stockman and several senior Republicans at the Century Club in Manhattan. Stockman had spent the day trying to sell Reaganomics to Wall Street, and had met with a skeptical reception. Spooked by the supply-siders, investors anticipated big deficits; to compensate for the consequent inflation, they were driving up interest rates on bonds. Stockman promised the bond vigilantes that Reagan's tax reduction would be offset by commensurate reductions in spending. "The tax cut has to be earned through the sweat of the politicians," he promised.[6]

The reaction from the other diners at the Century Club showed what Stockman was up against.

"The Street's delirious!" snarled Jude Wanniski, one of Jack Kemp's tax-cutting allies. "Stockman spent the whole day selling root canal and threatening to heave widows and orphans into the snow.

"If the administration wastes its political capital on budget cutting and imposing a lot of societal pain and sacrifice, the battle for marginal tax rate reduction, the gold dollar, and supply-side prosperity will be lost," Wanniski insisted. "We'll end up with Republican austerity as usual."[7]

The outburst presented Greenspan with a dilemma. He had assured the media in Chicago that Reagan's budget numbers added up; if Wanniski and his cohorts hijacked the process, Greenspan would deserve some blame for the debacle. But beating down supply-siders was like a frantic game of Whack-A-Mole. As Reagan's campaign budget adviser, Greenspan had smacked them hard. Now they were burrowing up again.

Some ten days later, soon after the Christmas break, Greenspan attended a bull session on the budget in David Stockman's office. Despite Stockman's assurances to Wall Street, the group that he assembled was not committed to balancing the budget. Jack Kemp's supply-siders were there in force, but so, too, was a doctrinaire contingent from the monetarist camp—followers of Milton Friedman who believed that inflation could be painlessly tamed by means of monetary targets. Greenspan's presence represented a faint hope that both flanks could be quieted.

The group launched into a debate about the economic forecast that would underpin Reagan's first budget. The supply-siders insisted that thanks to the tonic of tax cuts, growth would accelerate. The monetarists were adamant that thanks to the magic of monetary targeting, inflation would fall rapidly, bringing down interest rates. The dueling perspectives would turn out to be incompatible. High growth implied strong demand for capital and therefore high interest rates—if the supply-siders were right, the monetarists were unlikely to be. Victory over inflation implied a recession—if the monetarists were right, the supply-siders would probably not get the growth that they predicted. But nobody around Stockman was insisting that this contradiction be resolved, and so the group was coalescing around a nonsensical compromise. Growth would be high, but interest rates would be low. Greenspan was conspicuously silent.

Toward the end of the meeting, Stockman turned to Gail Fosler, a Republican staff economist on the Senate Budget Committee. She had rushed over on short notice, dressed as she usually dressed over the holiday period: in jeans and a turtleneck.

"So Gail, what do you think?"

Unintimidated by the radicals around her, Fosler responded honestly. "The only thing you have in this town is your integrity," she said. "If you present this as the president's forecast, you will lose your integrity."

The session soon broke up. Fosler and Greenspan chatted on the way out and headed off together to a cafeteria.

Fosler was wondering why she had even been summoned to Stockman's office in the first place. She was known in Washington as a critic of the ideologues—they surely would not have wanted to include her. But some powerful somebody had clearly decided that she should be present. Washington invitations did not go out by accident.

To test her theory of who might have invited her, Fosler looked at Greenspan and asked, "I bet you are not very happy that you had me come to that meeting?"

Greenspan gave her a sidelong smile. "You did what I expected you to do," he said.[8]

Fosler eyed Greenspan again. He was more Machiavellian than he appeared. Since his days in the Ford administration, he had learned to fight bureaucratic battles while preserving his own capital. If he was going to offer unpopular good sense, he would do so through proxies.

S oon after Reagan's inauguration on January 20, 1981, Greenspan vis-ited St. Louis, Missouri. He was there on business, but he took the opportunity to meet privately with Murray Weidenbaum, a rumpled eco-nomics professor who would soon become chairman of the Council of Economic Advisers. Weidenbaum and Greenspan both served on Stock-man's economic forecasting committee, and Weidenbaum was furious with the rosy growth assumptions of the supply-siders.

Greenspan knew perfectly well that Weidenbaum was right. But he nonetheless urged Weidenbaum to let the matter slide. The forecasts were the product of hours of fractious haggling between supply-siders and monetarists. If the incoming CEA chairman insisted on reopening the debate, budget policy might end up worse rather than better.[9]

When Weidenbaum arrived at the White House, he ignored Green-span's counsel. He was not going to stand behind a forecast that absurdly combined rising growth with falling interest rates; he was not going to tip-toe around Washington, hiding behind crafty proxies and picking battles timidly. If the forecasting mess was not cleared up, Weidenbaum informed Stockman, he would escalate the fight all the way to the Oval Office.

Stockman conceded that the contradiction should be straightened out. But he urged Weidenbaum not to alienate the supply-siders by rubbishing their high-growth forecast—they were too powerful in Congress. Instead, the forecast could be cleansed of contradiction by ignoring the monetar-ists and projecting continued inflation. Backing the supply-siders over the monetarists would also have the effect of easing Stockman's budget arithmetic.

Weidenbaum accepted Stockman's direction. After all, the monetarists were asserting that inflation would soon collapse to 2 percent; the idea that Paul Volcker would reduce inflation by that much seemed like a crazy fantasy. "Nobody," Weidenbaum roared, "is going to predict 2 percent inflation on my watch. We'll be the laughing stock of the world."[10]

Stockman told Weidenbaum to plug in whatever inflation number he could live with. He just wanted the estimate for growth to be as high as possible because high growth would make the future deficits look manageable. The CEA chairman duly projected growth of 12.9 percent in 1982: 7.7 percent inflation plus real growth of 5.2 percent.

When Weidenbaum presented his forecast, neither the monetarists nor the supply-siders were happy. As Stockman later recounted in his memoir, somebody taunted the professor:

"What model did this come out of, Murray?"

"It came right out of here," Weidenbaum responded, slapping his belly with both hands. "My visceral computer."[11]

Weidenbaum had shown more courage than Greenspan, but not necessarily more wisdom. He had insisted on a forecast that was internally consistent, but he had picked the wrong side in the battle. As it turned out, the monetarists who thought inflation could be vanquished were not far from being right: the Fed succeeded in bringing inflation down to 3.8 percent by 1982, much lower than the 7.7 percent that Weidenbaum anticipated. Meanwhile, the supply-siders who predicted a growth bonanza were disastrously wrong: the economy shrank by 1.4 percent in 1982, an abysmal performance relative to the real growth of 5.2 percent that the visceral computer had projected. Weidenbaum's high-inflation, high-growth forecast had allowed Stockman to balance the budget on paper; but when the forecast proved wrong, the low-inflation, negative-growth reality depressed tax receipts, delivering what was by contemporary standards a budgetary calamity. The deficit hit $128 billion in the year to September 1982, and $208 billion the year after. It was the worst budget performance in the postwar era.[12]

Greenspan's political antennae had served him well. By hiding behind proxies and picking his fights, he had avoided association with a fiscal humiliation. But even as he dodged this danger, Greenspan was learning a new lesson, too. For Reagan's top economic officials, and even for the Treasury secretary whose job Greenspan coveted, there was not much glory in presiding over the budget. For an economist with limitless ambition, the real prize lay elsewhere.

The current holder of that prize was lurking in a marble edifice, a long-legged twelve-minute stroll from the White House. While Stockman and Weidenbaum concocted their forecast, Paul Volcker was driving the policy that would frustrate it.

More even than the announcement of the Saturday Night Special, Volcker's actions after Reagan's election qualified him for the history books. During the summer of 1980, the Fed's monetary straitjacket had caused a recession; by the election, unemployment stood at 7.5 percent. The compensating payoff was still nowhere to be seen: inflation had come down only moderately.[13] The climate was ripe for an attack on the central bank; and in mid-November, at the Los Angeles gathering of Reagan's brain trust, the president-elect's advisers issued a menacing statement. Warning that the Fed's independence "should not mean lack of accountability," they demanded clearer monetary targets from the central bank and encouraged Congress in its efforts to "monitor the Fed's performance."[14]

Two days later, on Wednesday, November 19, Arthur Burns visited Paul Volcker in Washington. He installed himself in a wing chair in front of the fireplace and lit his pipe. Volcker spread his long frame out on a couch and enjoyed one of his cheap stogies.[15]

Burns was evidently agitated. He had just come from Los Angeles, where Friedman and others had lambasted Volcker. "Milton wants to abolish the Fed," he began. "He wants to replace you with a computer."

Volcker remained calm. "It's a metaphor, Arthur."

"I understand, Paul, but it's more than that." Burns went on to describe how the Los Angeles proceedings had been dominated by Friedman's obsession with a monetary rule. The whole tone of the discussion had portended trouble for the central bank. Burns seemed so frantic that Volcker grew worried. "I thought he was going to have a heart attack," he recalled later.[16]

Volcker hardly needed to be told that politicians might attack him; already the Carter administration had come after him. But Burns insisted that the assault on the Fed had grown more dangerous than before: the political constraints that he had emphasized in his lecture in Belgrade were about to assert themselves with a vengeance. Milton Friedman was at the head of a powerful coalition: monetarists who agreed with him that the Fed could be supplanted with a simple rule, and supply-siders who resented the Fed for tough anti-inflation policies that made tax cuts unaffordable.[17]

Two months later, with Reagan newly installed in the White House, his staff let it be known that he would visit the Federal Reserve building. Remembering Burns's warning, Volcker bristled at the thought: the symbolism of the commander in chief marching into his office had to be avoided.[18] To prevent the image of a presidential invasion, Volcker demanded that the meeting be shifted to a safer venue. He would lunch with Reagan at the Treasury.

As if to draw attention to the occasion, Reagan refused to be driven to the Treasury building. It had been a long time since a president had walked the streets of Washington, but Reagan strode out of the front door of the White House, a handsome, rangy figure surrounded on all sides by aides and Secret Service men, followed by a delighted press corps.[19] On the steps up to the Treasury, the president stopped to kiss seven-year-old Sandy Kotz of Detroit, the winner of the Tiny Miss North America beauty pageant, who wore a sash that read, "Young Republicans."[20] Once inside the building, Reagan took his seat at the head of the table in a wood-paneled conference room.[21]

"You know," he began, "I was very pleased to read a prediction that the price of gold will nosedive below three hundred dollars an ounce. If that's true, it would mean we've made great strides against inflation."

"I could not agree with you more, Mr. President," Volcker answered, delighted that the conversation was beginning with a softball.

"Well, I expect we'll make even more progress going forward," Reagan said genially.

The clutch of reporters and photographers who had been allowed in for the start of the meeting now left the room.

"But I do have a question that I'd like you to help me with," Reagan continued.

"If I can," Volcker replied warily.

"I've had several letters from people who raise the question of why we need the Federal Reserve," the president announced. "What do you suggest I say to them?"

It was a stunning question. The Fed had been around since 1914. Reagan appeared to be suggesting a return to the nineteenth century.

Thanks to Arthur Burns's warning, Volcker was prepared for something like this. "Mr. President, there have been concerns along those lines, but I think you can make a strong case that we've operated quite well. Unfortunately, we are the only game in town right now fighting inflation. . . . Once the budget gets under control we'll have a better shot at taking the pressure off prices."

The answer did the trick. It addressed Reagan's question, and switched the focus to budget policy. At the mention of the deficit, Don Regan, the Treasury secretary, weighed in, agreeing that the budget must be moved back toward balance. After some talk about taxes and spending, Volcker got Reagan onto the subject of fishing.[22] The more he could avoid monetary issues, the more he would preserve his independence.

When the lunch was over, Volcker returned to his marble-fronted redoubt. Budget policy might be chaotic, with dueling camps of ideologues forcing mainstream economists to the sidelines, but nobody had told the Fed chairman to change course. The era of central-bank supremacy was dawning.

Despite his doubts about Reagan's budget math, Greenspan made a public show of cheering along loyally. In one weeklong stretch in the middle of February 1981, when the president unveiled his economic plan, Greenspan made five separate trips to Washington, attended countless

White House meetings, and appeared on seven television shows, never defending the radicals in his party but always telegraphing respect for the official policy. The *New York Times* profiled him as a sort of minister without portfolio, a shape-shifter who could both advise on the inside and operate on the outside as an authoritative commentator. His professional versatility seemed to mirror his curious double persona. He appeared absentminded, soft-spoken, and indifferent to social convention: he bought his suits in batches. Yet he was powerful, connected, and impressively well paid. His annual income came to more than half a million dollars, the equivalent of close to $1.5 million in 2015.[23]

In his media appearances over the next months, Greenspan emphasized the importance of one part of Reagan's plan—the spending cuts. Safeguarding his reputation by distancing himself from the supply-siders, he insisted that balancing the budget was now more crucial than ever; and he pressed his point by invoking a new argument. In the past, Greenspan had denounced deficits because the Fed would print money to buy the resulting government bonds, therefore fueling inflation. Now, thanks to Paul Volcker, the Fed had retired from the money-printing business, so deficits would be financed by government's borrowing from private lenders; the borrowing would drive interest rates up, and the result would be a higher cost of capital for banks, businesses, and households. In the years before Volcker's Saturday Night Special, in other words, deficits had meant inflation that penalized savers; after Volcker's policy revolution, deficits meant high interest rates that penalized borrowers. And that shift was troubling for a reason that Greenspan was supremely qualified to diagnose: high borrowing costs threatened to destabilize finance. Savings and loans were being forced to pay more for deposits, raising their cost of funding above the fixed income they received on their mortgage portfolios. As Greenspan put it to the *New York Times* in March, "The most important thing at the moment is to get interest rates down and avoid what I think is a potentially very dangerous financial problem in the thrift institutions."[24]

While Greenspan urged deficit reduction to bring down interest rates, the supply-siders advanced a different remedy. Like druids brandishing a magic talisman, they echoed the president's faith in the gold standard. The way the supply-siders saw things, Volcker's monetary medicine was failing to convince the markets that inflation was coming down, with the result that interest rates remained elevated. In contrast, a return to the gold standard would instantly signal that inflation was over; it would have a transformative effect on expectations. Thanks to this psychological revolution, interest rates would plummet painlessly; there would be no need for the "root canal" spending cuts that Greenspan and the old guard advocated. Of course, embracing the gold standard meant depriving the Fed of its power over the nation's money. Just when Volcker was emerging as a superman, the supply-siders wanted to neuter him.

To long-standing believers in a gold anchor, the supply-siders were perverting a venerable idea. In the 1950s and 1960s, Greenspan had favored the gold standard as a way of disciplining the government: unable to finance deficits by printing dollars, politicians would be forced to balance income and expenditure. But now the supply-siders were embracing gold not as a guarantor of budgetary restraint, but rather as a cover for budgetary recklessness: the way they saw things, tax cuts would have no adverse consequences—for inflation or for interest rates—if only the nation returned to the gold standard. Greenspan, always a skeptic of the government's power to shape expectations, was not about to buy this view. The government's credibility as an inflation fighter would have to be earned over time. It could not be conjured instantly, whether by Nixon's price controls or by the supply-siders' gold standard.

Whatever Greenspan's misgivings, the gold camp was advancing. In May 1981, it scored a tactical victory when Arthur Burns was named ambassador to West Germany, removing the doyen of the anti-supply-side old guard from the debate in Washington. The *Wall Street Journal* speculated drily about a follow-on appointment: Greenspan might be dispatched as ambassador to Tokyo.[25] The following month, the supply-siders pressed their advantage, forcing the administration to announce the formation of a gold commission, tasked with considering gold's role in the monetary system.[26] But what was really worrying was the posture of the president himself. His long-standing hankering for gold remained. And the higher unemployment went, the more he was encouraged in his fantasies by his business friends, who were desperate for an alternative to the Fed's stern discipline.

In July, Gordon Luce, the boss of a California savings bank, wrote to the president to complain about Volcker. Reagan soon wrote back: "I've passed your essay on to our economic types to see if they have an answer to whether the Fed is really necessary," he assured him.[27]

Sure enough, Luce's complaints made their way to Murray Weidenbaum at the Council of Economic Advisers, complete with a note scrawled in the presidential hand. "Do we really need the Fed?" Reagan demanded.[28]

Hoping to calm Reagan, Weidenbaum crafted an artful one-page rejoinder. He began by admiring the "well-written and thoughtful piece" that the president had forwarded to him, and he conceded that the Fed lacked credibility as a bulwark against inflation. But rather than concluding that the central bank should be replaced with a revived gold standard, Weidenbaum invoked the model of the 1950s Fed—the one that had stood firm in the face of Truman's inflationary demands, and that had contained inflation successfully until the late 1960s. The problem was not with central banks per se, Weidenbaum argued, but rather with a central bank that failed to deliver stable monetary growth—"usually," Weidenbaum lamented, "because previous Administrations gave them conflicting signals." The solution lay in making those signals consistent. Rather than attacking the central bank, Reagan should emphasize his support for it.[29]

On August 13, 1981, Reagan appeared before reporters at his beloved California ranch, decked out in cowboy boots and a tough-guy denim jacket. Seated at a rustic table and grinning for the cameras, he signed into law the budget-busting tax cuts that the supply-siders wanted. The next day he turned his mind back to gold, and the influence of the supply-siders was never more apparent. Writing to Gordon Luce again, the president assured him that the "economic types" agreed wholeheartedly with the critique of the central bank—they had no quarrel with the verdict that it lacked credibility. Then he leaped to a prescription that turned Weidenbaum's memo on its head.

"Our system of government and our Constitution are based on the proposition that 'Rule of Law' is superior to 'Rule of Man,'" Reagan declared. "Yet, in monetary policy there really are no rules governing how money is created by the Fed. It is my hope that we can put restraints on the creation of money. Perhaps the Gold Commission will be coming up with recommendations along these lines," he wrote expectantly.[30]

A s the supply-siders advanced, the mainstream economists at the White House began to panic. Four years earlier, Jack Kemp's maverick followers had been ridiculed as P. T. Barnum wannabes; now they had Reagan behind them. The president evidently regarded powerful central-bank technocrats as an offense against his antigovernment instincts. "Hold your hats, friends, because the gold bugs are coming," the *Washington Post* columnist Hobart Rowen proclaimed; "and they have an ally in the White House named Ronald Reagan."[31]

It fell to Greenspan's ally Martin Anderson to come up with a way of derailing the gold bandwagon. Now on the staff at the White House, Anderson still regarded Greenspan as his favorite collaborator on such issues. In the spring of 1981, when the members of the gold commission had been appointed, Anderson had tried to have Greenspan included so that he could subvert the process from the inside; that ploy had failed, but Anderson continued to confer with Greenspan on ways of countering the gold camp.[32] The two comrades had experienced the same intellectual journey on monetary matters. Both had embraced the gold anchor in their Randian years. Both now regarded it as impractical.

At the end of August, two weeks after Reagan's second letter to Luce, Anderson and Greenspan discussed a ruse that might frustrate the gold lobby. Greenspan would publicly call for a "gold bond"—the Treasury would issue five-year debt whose interest and principal would be repaid in gold rather than dollars. Greenspan would present this gambit as a win for the gold camp; after all, it would require the government to curtail its habit of repaying debts with funny money. But the proposal's real purpose would be to play for time. The precise specifications of the gold bond would involve plenty of arcane detail, creating an excuse for the administration to extend the gold commission's deadline. The risk of the commission's throwing its weight behind a full return to the gold standard would thus be forestalled. A problem delayed might be a problem averted.[33]

On Labor Day, September 1, the president let loose another reminder of his impatience with conventional monetary policy. "The Fed is independent, but they're hurting us," he told an audience of supporters.[34] But that same day, Greenspan launched his counterattack, laying out his gold-bond proposal on the op-ed page of the *Wall Street Journal*. As he had planned with Anderson, Greenspan cloaked his thinking in respect for the gold camp: "The restoration of a gold standard has become an issue that is clearly rising on the economic policy agenda," he began, conceding that the discipline of gold had powerful attractions. But then he introduced a wrinkle: even if the gold standard represented the ideal monetary policy, there were daunting obstacles to getting there. To begin with, the U.S. government would have to decide the price at which to reestablish convertibility. If it set the price of gold too low, it would be flooded with purchase orders and its gold stocks would be depleted, forcing it off the gold standard permanently. If it set the price too high, owners of gold would rush to sell to Uncle Sam, and the dollars they received would inflate the money supply and cause inflation. Because of these risks, Greenspan suggested, monetary and fiscal discipline should be restored before a return to gold was attempted, allowing enough time for the dollar price of gold to stabilize around some market-determined value. "Concrete actions to install a gold standard are premature," Greenspan concluded.

Having explained why even the most ardent gold advocate might wish to bide his time, Greenspan presented his gold bonds as a reasonable idea that believers could support in the interim. The more the Treasury issued these obligations, the more it would acquire a vested interest in lower inflation, because the cost of repaying creditors in gold would rise in dollar terms as the greenback lost value. Meantime, the new instrument would create a means of judging whether the country was ready for a full return to the gold standard. If the yields on dollar bonds fell to the same level as the yields on gold bonds, the convergence would signal that investors had as much confidence in dollars as in gold. At that point the dollar could be repegged to gold, with less fear of a repeat of Nixon's humiliating devaluation.

Greenspan's proposal had real attractions. Indeed, he would continue to push for inflation-proof bonds until 1997, when the Clinton administration obliged by creating Treasury Inflation-Protected Securities (TIPS). Yet if Greenspan's advocacy of gold bonds was sincere, his verbiage about the gold standard was not: it was merely a way of humoring the gold camp and perhaps of tipping his hat to his own youthful convictions. After all, Greenspan was the man who had celebrated the publication of *Atlas Shrugged* by presenting Ayn Rand with a miniature gold bar. He still dined periodically with Rand at the University Club in New York and had no wish to offend her.

Greenspan's mature conviction, however, was the one he had explained to candidate Reagan two years earlier: the case for the gold standard could be refuted by a paradox. "A necessary condition of returning to a gold standard is the financial environment which the gold standard itself is presumed to create," Greenspan noted in his *Journal* essay. "But, if we restore financial stability, what purpose is then served by a return to a gold standard?"

Two weeks after the publication of Greenspan's *Journal* article, on September 16, 1981, Paul Volcker testified before the Senate Budget Committee. If there was going to be a moment when Volcker lost his inflation-fighting nerve, this surely would be it—although Greenspan and the White House were trying to protect his flank, the Fed's enemies in the gold camp were bearing down upon him. But Volcker firmly stood his ground, directing the blame for high interest rates away from the Fed and toward the budget deficit. Congress had just enacted the supply-siders' tax cut, Volcker observed. If Congress wanted to bring borrowing costs down, it should now rein in spending.

Senator Lawton Chiles, a Florida Democrat, did not take kindly to Volcker's lecture. It was all very well for the Fed chairman to urge spending restraint, but politics would not permit it—not with the economy already reeling from the Fed's tight monetary policy. If Volcker pressed his case too ardently, he was asking for trouble.

"We are going to have an explosion," Chiles menaced. If Congress didn't do something to help people battered by recession, there would be pressure "to knock out the Federal Reserve Board altogether. . . . You have given us a good lecture about how much we should cut spending. I just do not think, however, that . . . is in the realm of possibility."

Chiles was honoring a venerable tradition. Politicians bullied the Fed; the opposite was not supposed to happen.

"You are the political expert," Volcker responded, gruffly. "What I am saying . . . is that the challenge before the Congress and the Administration now is to do what cutting they can do. . . . Shooting the messenger or the head of the Federal Reserve is not going to do anybody any good."

"But it is going to be a lot easier to cut the head off the Federal Reserve System than to make these huge cuts," Chiles retorted. "That is what I am afraid is going to happen."

"Let's just clarify the point," Volcker growled. "It may be easier to cut the head off the Federal Reserve, but even when the Federal Reserve is running around headless you will still have exactly the same problem you started with."[35]

Two days later, on September 18, the gold commission gathered for its next meeting. Volcker's defiance in the Senate had shown how isolated he was—it was not just Kemp's supply-siders and Reagan's business friends who were losing patience with him. Even if he and Greenspan were right that high long-term interest rates reflected the ballooning budget deficit, their argument was as popular as broccoli, particularly when compared with the gold camp's sweet confections.[36] The supply-siders even argued that as well as curing inflation and high interest rates, gold would miraculously fix the budget. Lower interest rates, courtesy of gold, would save the government money on debt-service payments; presto, no more deficit.[37] With such beguiling arguments as these, gold's momentum seemed unstoppable.

Then, suddenly, it did stop. Addressing the commission members in the Treasury's ornate Cash Room, where citizens had exchanged gold and silver in the years after the Civil War, Treasury Secretary Don Regan lamented that the gold standard was dauntingly complex—the technical issues involved in restoring it were widely disputed. There was no chance of coming up with a "fast or simple" answer, the Treasury secretary continued, repeating the argument that Greenspan had made in the *Wall Street Journal*. To allow time to think through the issue in all its permutations, the commission's planned October deadline would have to be extended—maybe for six more months, or maybe even for longer.

With that, the Treasury secretary killed the sense of urgency permeating the gold commission: it was now an open-ended talking shop. It did not take the supply-siders long to guess the source of their setback. On September 25, Jude Wanniski fired off a letter to Greenspan, inviting him to a "Gold Lunch" and challenging him to debate the propositions in his *Wall Street Journal* essay. "Because you have such enormous influence on administration policy, I think it would benefit the President and the nation if you were at least aware of our viewpoint," Wanniski protested angrily.[38] But the truth was that Greenspan and his White House allies understood Wanniski's viewpoint all too well, and Greenspan's deliberate delay tactics were about to succeed exactly as intended. By dragging out the gold debate for a further six months, the administration allowed time for inflation to fall, so that the screams for an alternative to the Fed lost much of their saliency. When the gold commission eventually came out in favor of the status quo in February 1982, the best that the supply-siders could claim was that their issue had been debated.[39]

In 1971, the Nixon White House had recruited Greenspan to help rein in the central bank. One decade later, the Reagan White House had recruited Greenspan to do precisely the opposite. And Greenspan had played his assigned role deftly. Just as he had stymied Henry Kissinger on the Iranian oil deal, Greenspan had feigned empathy with his adversaries and played skillfully for time, morphing from ardent advocate of gold into its most devious opponent.[40] The Fed's power had been preserved. The prestige of the Fed chairmanship, already growing, expanded even further.

At the end of 1981, the Reagan administration sought out Greenspan's help again, this time on the question of the government's pension promises. The revered Social Security system, which mailed regular checks to thirty-six million beneficiaries, was running short of cash; if nothing was done before the spring of 1983, there would be insufficient revenues to keep the checks flowing.[41] To fend off that political disaster, the Reagan team needed a survey of possible fixes; and on December 16 the president signed Executive Order 12335, creating the National Commission on Social Security Reform, with Greenspan as its chairman. A bevy of aides arrayed themselves in a semicircle around Reagan as he sat at the Oval Office desk. A flash went off, and the group was captured for posterity: nine sober-suited men, with Greenspan looking grimly grave, the most sober of all of them.

Given Greenspan's libertarian roots, reforming Social Security seemed like the ideal challenge for him. By the time Reagan created the commission, Milton Friedman had fathered a minor cottage industry devoted to privatizing government pensions; now Greenspan was in charge of a group that could presumably act on these proposals.[42] Seven months earlier, in May 1981, Greenspan's ally David Stockman had proposed fixing the Social Security deficit with deep benefit cuts, and Greenspan had cheered along, declaring that it was time to "restore some sanity to the system."[43] The president himself could be counted upon to support bold reform. In his earlier run for the presidency, in 1976, Reagan had demanded a sweeping overhaul. "People like me shouldn't get Social Security," the president would say. "My friends at Burning Tree"—the president was referring to an exclusive golf club in the Washington suburbs—"they don't need Social Security."[44]

Despite the president's instincts, Greenspan's mission as chairman of the Social Security commission was anything but Friedman-like. Stockman's proposed benefit cuts had generated a costly political backlash: Representative Claude Pepper, the octogenarian Florida Democrat who had become the popular face of the program, had raised a clenched fist in

mission had accomplished almost nothing. It had failed even in the narrow task that the White House had set for it. The Democrats exploited Social Security ruthlessly during the campaign; the existence of the bipartisan Social Security commission did not inhibit them in the slightest. Claude Pepper himself stumped tirelessly in two dozen states, demonstrating that some eighty-two-year-olds with hearing aids are fully capable of work. Thanks partly to Pepper's efforts, the Democrats picked up a net gain of twenty-six seats in the House. The only good news was that the election was over.

Greenspan resolved to hold the next commission meeting somewhere outside Washington. Away from the atmosphere of Capitol Hill, the members might be less distracted from the task; and with the campaigning behind them, they might even be less partisan. A week after the election, the commissioners duly assembled at a nondescript Ramada Inn in Alexandria, Virginia. Outside, a group of seniors calling themselves the Gray Panthers picketed the meeting. "No ifs, ands or buts, no Social Security cuts!" they chanted.[60]

Partway through the deliberations, Senator Dole stood up and left, accompanied by a Democratic commissioner. This was actually a good sign. Disclosure laws required that the meetings be open to the public, so naturally the real bargaining took place in private huddles, safely away from the TV cameras. A little while later, several more commissioners exited through a side door; presently Dole marched back into the hearing, a look of purpose in his eyes, and bent down to talk to Greenspan. Even though Greenspan was chairing the meeting, he quit the room, too, leaving a member of the commission staff to filibuster for the cameras.[61]

Greenspan followed Dole until they found the cabal of absentee commissioners clustered in a back room. After months of fruitless stalemate, Dole had apparently discovered a faint glimmer of hope. The Democrats were ready to accept tweaks in the Social Security benefit formula that amounted to cuts.

Greenspan knew that the Democratic move might herald a breakthrough. But he also understood that this was not for him to determine. Despite the myth that later grew up around the commission—that

Greenspan led an exercise in technocratic compromise by removing Social Security from the political realm—the truth was that the real negotiating power lay with the White House. Greenspan duly got on the phone to James Baker.

Baker dearly wanted to resolve the Social Security question. But he needed more than token cuts, because the president favored radical ones. "I'm gonna go on the radio; I'm gonna go above the heads of the Congress; I'm going to tell the American public," Reagan would threaten periodically. "There's got to be a better way, and you're just going around there, you're not coming in with something good."[62]

After listening to Greenspan's description of the Democratic concessions, Baker dismissed them as inadequate. It was not Greenspan's fault. Baker had chosen Greenspan for the commission because he needed a political ally who could double as a dry economist, and Greenspan was playing the role perfectly. But despite Greenspan's best efforts, his commission seemed destined to fail. It held a final meeting in December, which broke up after a few minutes.[63]

Despairing of talking to his colleagues on the commission, Greenspan addressed the public. On January 3, 1983, with the commission's deadline just a fortnight away, he used his regular slot as a commentator on public television to make a final plea. Failure to repair Social Security's finances would reinforce Wall Street's expectation that the government would never fix the budget deficit, he said; it would confirm that policy was paralyzed. So long as Wall Street thought that Washington was dysfunctional, interest rates would remain excruciatingly high. The economic recovery would be delayed indefinitely.

The day that Greenspan made his plea, Senator Bob Dole published an op-ed in the *New York Times*—he, too, had decided to negotiate via the media. Dole noted that Republicans and Democrats were not that far apart; a handful of technocratic tweaks would be enough to salvage Social Security. Daniel Patrick Moynihan read the op-ed at his desk on the Senate floor and walked across the aisle to compliment his colleague.

"Are we going to let this commission die without giving it one more try?" Moynihan asked.[64]

Dole and Moynihan agreed to a final rescue effort. But they needed a new negotiating format. The full commission was too big, and obstreperous members on either flank made real bargaining impossible. The senators rounded up Greenspan and two other moderate commissioners, and then they made contact with James Baker at the White House. A Dole-Moynihan cabal had now supplanted the Greenspan commission.

Two days later, on January 5, the cabal gathered at James Baker's home on Foxhall Road in Washington. Because the ultimate deal would need the president's support, Baker and his staff did much of the talking for the Republican side, but they turned to Greenspan to make sure the numbers worked—it was he who had mastered the technical details, and no plan would fly without his blessing. Over the next week the negotiators continued in secret, sometimes convening in Baker's basement and sometimes at the presidential guest quarters at Blair House, across Pennsylvania Avenue from the White House. On Saturday, January 8, there was a break to watch the Washington Redskins defeat the Detroit Lions in the National Football League play-offs; and then the bargaining began again, ranging over a potential cost-of-living-adjustment freeze and whether Social Security benefits should be taxable. One year earlier, the Greenspan commission had been asked to come up with a fix to present to the White House. But now the White House was shaping the deal directly.[65]

On the morning of Saturday, January 15, 1983, the Dole-Moynihan cabal met at Blair House for its last session. It agreed on a series of pragmatic fiddles that would extend Social Security's solvency at least into the 1990s. Cost-of-living increases would be delayed; scheduled payroll tax increases would be brought forward; affluent retirees would pay taxes on their benefits: together, these measures would contain the system's deficit.[66] The meeting broke up around noon, in time for the participants to watch the Redskins take another step toward that year's Super Bowl victory.

Once the negotiators had a deal, the next step was to sell it politically. James Baker was ready to deliver the endorsement of the president, but he wanted some cover; he proposed that Tip O'Neill, Democratic Speaker of the House, join Reagan in blessing the compromise. But when O'Neill heard what the White House was asking, he let out a torrent of unprintable abuse. There would be no joint endorsement.

Baker disappeared into the White House to consult the president. If O'Neill refused to endorse the package, they needed some other political insurance: Reagan could not be out there alone, taking all the heat for cutting benefits. At around seven o'clock that evening, Baker returned to Blair House with the verdict. The president would back the deal, but only if it had the support of the full Greenspan commission.

Greenspan walked out of Blair House, an owlishly bespectacled figure with slicked-back dark hair, braced against the sharp chill of the evening. Exiting the presidential guesthouse, he turned toward the elegant north front of the White House, then rounded the corner into Lafayette Square, where the rump commissioners were waiting in a nearby office. After months of aimless proceedings, this was his moment. He needed to deliver the commissioners' support, even though the majority had been cut out of the deal that they would now put their names to.

Facing his fellow commissioners, Greenspan explained the Blair House agreement and called for a vote. To his surprise, Claude Pepper wanted a word with him.

Speaking in his rich southern brogue, Pepper asked, "Alan, you've been following these hearings very closely, and you know where I stand in general on all this. Now do you think that I, given my general point of view, can sign this document?"

Greenspan looked at the congressman with his rumpled face and bulbous nose. A few months later, a presidential aide would tell *Time* magazine that Pepper was almost alone among Democrats in his ability to frighten Ronald Reagan. But now Pepper was turning to Greenspan for advice. Greenspan was the man who knew. Pepper would vote however Greenspan told him.

"I can assure you that you have *no* concerns about signing this final document," Greenspan informed him.[67]

When the vote was taken, twelve out of fifteen commissioners fell into line—including the doughty white-haired populist. It was just about enough, and Greenspan ran upstairs to phone the president to say that he had an agreement. When he came downstairs afterward, he found Claude Pepper holding forth to a scrum of reporters, flashbulbs popping all around. Despite Pepper's propensity to say whatever came into his head, the moment passed without trouble.[68]

Around midnight, the group broke up. The members of the Greenspan commission had come together on a compromise that would later be remembered as a model—while the Fed was emerging as the dominant force in economic policy, outbreaks of pragmatic statesmanship from other parts of the government would be treasured for their rarity. But now it was time for the commissioners to go their separate ways, and they walked out into Lafayette Park and gazed over at the White House. The cold evening had brought snow. The usual mud of politics was covered in a soft white blanket.

Thirteen

A REPUBLICAN VOLCKER

On Friday, August 13, 1982, while Greenspan was still treading water with the Social Security commission, a Yale-educated Mexican technocrat arrived at the Federal Reserve building in Washington. He had made this journey many times before and had learned to expect the lemon-meringue pie that was served unfailingly in the Fed's executive dining room.[1] But this visit was unlike the others of the past few months. Rather than briefing the Fed chairman on looming risks, Mexico's finance minister, Jesús Silva Herzog Flores, had come to announce that those risks were no longer hypothetical—they had materialized. Having borrowed prodigiously from American bankers, Mexico could not repay. Its stash of foreign currency was dwindling by the hour. It would default when the markets opened on Monday.

Paul Volcker had been braced for Silva Herzog's news since the beginning of the week, when a heads-up from his staff had caused him to cut short a fishing trip to Wyoming.[2] He knew that Mexico's bankruptcy was America's problem—and his own problem, personally. Before rising to the position of chairman of the Federal Reserve Board in Washington, Volcker had headed the New York Federal Reserve, the most important of the twelve regional banks that, together with the board, make up the Federal Reserve System. During his four years as the New York Fed's president, between 1975 and 1979, Volcker had shouldered the responsibility for regulating most of the so-called money center banks. The buildup of Latin American loans had occurred on his watch, and he had failed to prevent it. Upon taking the helm at the Federal Reserve Board in Washington, moreover, Volcker had assumed even greater responsibility. The Washington Fed employed an army of sophisticated bank supervisors, yet Volcker had failed to marshal these troops to stem the flood of Latin American lending.[3] As a result, America's top banks had lent Mexico so much that the country's default now threatened their own viability.[4] The nation's financial system was on the brink, and Volcker deserved a large slice of the blame.

If this failure tarnished Volcker's reputation as a disciplinarian, his response to Silva Herzog's news confirmed that he was not tough all the time—despite his reputation as an unbending Old Testament scourge, he was capable of printing money in a crisis. Indeed, even before Silva Herzog's visit in mid-August, Volcker had discreetly provided Mexico with a series of unannounced Fed loans: $600 million in April, $200 million in June, another $700 million at the start of August.[5] Now that these attempted rescues had proved too small to do the job, Volcker resolved to prop Mexico up with a blockbuster bailout. Joining forces with Donald Regan at the Treasury, he put together a monumental $3.5 billion war chest—it was 50 percent larger than the federal bailout for New York that Greenspan had resisted seven years earlier.[6] Thanks to Volcker's lifeline, Mexico would have the resources to keep paying back the bankers after all. Having secured this promise of support, Silva Herzog went home a hero.

Volcker was inevitably attacked for allowing American lenders to expose themselves so much that such a bailout had become necessary. William McChesney Martin, who had chaired the Fed through the 1950s and 1960s, declared that Volcker was "very good" at conducting monetary policy but a "complete flop on bank supervision."[7] Volcker's regulatory failure was especially disappointing because his own monetary policy should have alerted him to the financial risks. As Greenspan had argued in the spring of 1981, the battle against inflation had upended the relationship between borrowers and lenders, rendering some kind of debt crisis almost inevitable.[8] Before Volcker's policy revolution, borrowers had taken on debt carelessly, believing that inflation would erode its real value; after the Volcker revolution, inflation was falling, forcing borrowers to repay more than they had bargained for.[9] The Fed chairman's tough monetary policy ensured that his lax regulatory policy was dangerous.

When Volcker was cross-examined in the Senate about Mexico's failure, his answers anticipated his successors' self-defense in the wake of future crises. "None of us enjoys perfect foresight," he pleaded, adding that regulators could not be expected to second-guess the decisions of Wall Street's experts. "It remains central to our financial and economic system that the individual lenders reach their own credit judgments," he maintained; and although he conceded the case for stricter bank regulation, he emphasized the risk in clamping down on Wall Street. "The danger of overreaction—of encouraging inadvertently an abrupt retreat from lending—is equally real," he lectured the Senate. Regulation was needed, certainly; but it had "to be balanced against letting the system work."

The redoubtable Senator Proxmire was incensed. "Danger signals were apparent to all but the willfully obtuse," he rumbled; "Mr. Chairman, as we go through these hearings, I think we must get the answer to a very simple question: Where were our regulators?" The way Proxmire saw things, the Fed's army of bank supervisors "advised, they monitored, they cajoled, they encouraged—in fact, they did everything except what they are paid to do, and that is to regulate." The banks' indifference to the Fed's polite coaxing recalled Henry Higgins's remark about women in *My Fair Lady,* Proxmire continued. "She will ask you for advice, your reply will be concise, and then she will do precisely what she wants," he fulminated.

Fixing Volcker with his fiercest stare, Proxmire asked him directly, "Were the regulators forceful enough?"

"I suppose, in retrospect, probably not," the giant conceded meekly.[10]

As if humiliation on the regulatory front were not enough, it was followed by the abandonment of Volcker's monetary revolution. The $3.5 billion rescue for Mexico had staved off an immediate banking collapse, but it had not eliminated the risk of some future meltdown, especially because a sharp recession at home was driving thousands of borrowers into bankruptcy, adding to the banks' losses. "We are in a very sensitive period," Volcker told his Federal Open Market Committee colleagues on August 24, pointing to "concern—and I'm afraid to some degree justified concern—about the stability of the banking system."[11] At the FOMC's next meeting, on October 5, Volcker reiterated his fears, comparing the potential for banking failure to 1929 and declaring it was time for the Fed to execute a pivot. The moment had come for the Fed to switch focus from stabilizing prices to stabilizing finance. By a vote of 9 to 3, the committee resolved to cut interest rates rather than targeting a steady rate of money growth. It was the end of the experiment with monetarism.

Volcker announced this turning point with as little fanfare as possible. He said nothing whatever for a full five days; then he used the occasion of a meeting in Hot Springs, Arkansas, to slip the news out. "I thought I had a good idea a week or so ago," he began coyly; "I had a little sense that maybe we wouldn't put our usual emphasis on M1 as an operating target." The shift from monetary targeting to the direct manipulation of interest rates was just a "little technical matter," he went on; it was reversible, quite possibly temporary, and certainly not worth front-page headlines. A quarter of a century later, central bankers would come to regard clear communication as a central part of their tool kit. But in 1982, Volcker deliberately muddied his message. Torn between the fight against inflation and the fear of a financial meltdown, he set off in two directions all at once. His interest-rate policy was going one way, his communications policy the other.[12]

To those who understood that the monetarist chapter was over, Volcker appeared to have unbuckled his protective armor. During his three years in office, the Fed chairman had endured plenty of personal attacks—"This guy is killing us," the White House chief of staff, James Baker, had protested, as recently as the summer.[13] But Volcker had been able to defend himself by hiding behind the claim that he was targeting stable monetary growth, and therefore the punishing level of interest rates was not really his responsibility. Now, having abandoned monetary targets, Volcker could no longer take refuge in this way. Henceforth he would directly decide interest rates, so he could hardly pretend that high rates were not his doing. He had abandoned the rule guiding his policy, replacing it with nothing more concrete than his personal judgment.

In April 1983, the full extent of Volcker's vulnerability became apparent. At a meeting of the President's Economic Policy Advisory Board, Milton Friedman pointed a finger at the central-bank chief and turned to address Reagan. "Because of the policies of the Fed under that man, we've had an inflationary surge in the money supply which is going to have to be corrected," Friedman insisted.[14] Unable to hide behind a framework that might legitimize his decisions, Volcker endured the assault in silence. It was his judgment against Friedman's. Nobody defended him.

On April 18, 1983, the conservative *Washington Times* reported that Reagan would not reappoint Volcker.[15] His four-year term as Fed chairman would expire in August, and Treasury Secretary Donald Regan had convinced the president that he did not deserve another one. The White House denied the story, but the truth was that the political team around Reagan wanted a Republican at the Fed—somebody who would set interest rates with at least half an eye to the following year's election. The mere fact that the president had not yet reappointed Volcker seemed to confirm the *Washington Times* piece—if Volcker was going to be the man, why turn him into a lame duck by keeping quiet about it? The chairmanship of the Fed was evidently up for grabs. And by popular consent, the front-runner was Alan Greenspan.

Quite how Greenspan emerged as the top choice was a subject of some fascination.[16] It was evidently not because he stood for policies that differed from Volcker's—"Greenspan is a Republican Volcker without the cigar," *Newsweek* commented.[17] On monetary issues, certainly, the two men were indistinguishable: Greenspan had emphasized the need to subdue inflation for at least as long as Volcker had; he had protected Volcker against attacks from the gold camp; his belief in policy discretion rather than rules made him a fan of Volcker's break with monetary targeting. On regulatory issues, admittedly, Greenspan was more laissez-faire. But the difference was obscured in the wake of Mexico's collapse, because Greenspan refused to position himself as a critic of Volcker, however much the media invited him to do so.

Appearing on *Meet the Press* on January 2, 1983, Greenspan had been given an opportunity to disparage Volcker's regulatory record. In light of their reckless lending to Mexico, surely banks should be kept on a tighter leash? an interviewer had asked him.

Greenspan was not taking the bait. "Do I think regulation would help?" he asked. "I doubt it."

The interviewer tried again. At the very least, he suggested, banks should have been prohibited from lending too much to one country?

Again Greenspan resisted. He was happy to concede that the banks had been reckless—bankers, like financial markets generally, were not always efficient. But he doubted that regulatory restraints would make the world safer. "It's very difficult to impose those arbitrarily because somebody's got to make that judgment," he explained, referring to the question of how much lending to one country might cross the line into excess. "The trouble is that the person who is probably most able to make that judgment is an international banker," he went on. "I don't know of anybody in the government bureaucracy who is better able to make that judgment."

If Greenspan had not emerged as the Fed's chairman-in-waiting by promising a fresh policy approach, how had he done it? The answer came down to personal connections. Despite his low-key style, Greenspan had relationships in Congress and powerful allies in the White House; he had followers on Main Street and Wall Street; he had friends at the newspapers and political talk shows; and Barbara Walters, the queen of television news, had recently escorted him to Henry Kissinger's sixtieth birthday party. The success of the Social Security commission had only burnished Greenspan's allure; he had emerged as the pragmatic technocrat whom everyone could get along with. Liberal economists fell over one another to sing his praises. "Alan has managed to avoid all the way-out positions," Otto Eckstein said approvingly. "He's not a simple-minded supply sider, he's not a simple-minded monetarist, he's an all-around conservative economist."[18] "I had an image of him as the worst, flaming, right-wing bastard in the world," Arthur Okun chimed in. "I still disagree with him but I enjoy arguing with him and I like him."[19]

With the passage of the decades, Greenspan's youthful diffidence had matured into a subtle strength: with just a few exceptions that were remarkably rare, his demeanor ensured that he did not alienate people. "He talks very quietly, and his manner does defuse people who might disagree," mused Robert M. Ball, a Democrat who had served on the Social Security commission. "I don't think he has such a thing as a personal enemy," Barbara Walters reflected. This same relentless equanimity could make Greenspan a bland friend—"Sometimes you just want to say, 'Damn it, Alan, tell me a dirty joke. Or at least listen to one,'" his undergraduate comrade Robert Kavesh said teasingly.[20] But even if Greenspan's personality lacked the rough patches to which soul mates might adhere, there was no doubt that his composure paid professional dividends. By forming acquaintances with anyone who was anyone—by proving incapable of anger and not giving offense—Greenspan had built a vast network. He had risen to prominence as the man who knew. Now that the Fed chairmanship appeared to be open, the key to his stature was that everybody knew him.

Paul Volcker, for his part, was of two minds about his future. When he had assumed the Fed chairmanship, his wife, Barbara, had remained in New York; her health was not strong, and after four years on the job, it was time for Volcker to return to her. But the chairman was reluctant to move on. He had force-marched the nation through two punishing recessions, and the rewards were only just materializing now: in the first quarter of 1983, inflation had come in at less than 4 percent. It was a remarkable victory, but it was still fragile. Volcker could not stand to leave his post until his legacy had been consolidated.

On Memorial Day weekend, Paul sat with Barbara in the lime-colored office of their East Side apartment.

"I'm asking for a meeting with the president next week," he told her.

Barbara's spirits seemed to lift. "Are you going to submit your resignation? You know that is what they would like. Everything I read says they still don't trust a Democrat."

"Not exactly . . ."

Barbara began to cry. "We have no money and I have no life," she pleaded. "I have never stood in your way and I am proud of what you have accomplished. But now that you've beaten inflation your job is done."

"For now."

· "What is that supposed to mean?"

"It's just the end of the beginning—"

She cut him off: "You really think you're America's Churchill?"

It was a reproach more fitting than she knew. Less than four years earlier, Arthur Burns had lectured the world in Belgrade about how central banks were impotent. But her husband had turned the chairmanship of the Fed into a job of Churchillian proportions.

Volcker proposed a compromise. "I will tell the president that if he chooses to reappoint me I will leave midway through—after two years."[21]

In the late afternoon of June 6, 1983, Volcker sat in the West Sitting Room of the White House, waiting to meet the president.[22] Despite the *Washington Times* article, he knew he was still in the running to succeed himself. The Treasury secretary might want him gone, but plenty of Reaganites had come to respect his triumph over inflation. Besides, the Treasury secretary had no great love for Volcker's putative rival, Alan Greenspan. In a rare exception to the rule that Greenspan made no enemies, his refusal to sell his consultancy to Regan back in 1979 had left a residue of ill will, exacerbated by the rumors in 1982 that Greenspan might be recruited as an economic czar at the White House. Moreover, Regan was the kind of man—gregarious but shallow, with the empty bravado of a salesman—that Greenspan found hardest to deal with; and the supply-siders on Regan's Treasury staff resented Greenspan for his reservations about tax cuts. "I would rather kiss Paul Volcker on the mouth, cigar and all, than have Alan Greenspan as Fed chairman," a leading Treasury official told *Newsweek*.[23]

Presently, Nancy Reagan entered the West Sitting Room in a red evening dress. She was known for spending lavishly on clothes. Her wardrobe for her husband's inaugural events—"a bacchanalia of the haves," some critics griped—was said to have cost $25,000.[24]

"Madam First Lady, you look quite beautiful," the inflation killer offered.

The president hove into view. "Congratulations on your good taste, Mr. Chairman."

The first lady soon left, and Volcker made his pitch to Reagan. "Mr. President, we are in a sensitive period, both domestically and internationally, and you do not need a lame duck as Fed chairman right now," Volcker began. It was a way of needling the president into making a choice. Endless public speculation about the future of the Fed was not helping anyone.

"But there is something I should tell you before you announce a decision, whatever it is," Volcker went on. "I think I've been here long enough so if you choose to reappoint me, I would expect to stay for only the next eighteen months or two years. I thought you should know this before you decide."

"Paul, I will be in touch shortly," Reagan responded.[25] That evening he wrote in his diary, "I met with Paul Volcker—? do I reappoint him as Chmn. of the Fed Aug.1 or change. The financial mkt. seems set on having him. I don't want to shake their confidence in recovery."[26]

It was not that the financial markets lacked confidence in Greenspan. Two days after Volcker's visit to the White House, a poll of investment managers showed that if Volcker was not reappointed, 37 percent wanted Greenspan to get the job, with the second most popular option, Milton Friedman, garnering a mere 11 percent.[27] But the same poll confirmed Reagan's intuition that change would involve risk: fully 77 percent regarded a Volcker renomination as the first best outcome. Ironically, the same factors that had made Volcker vulnerable the previous autumn made him hard to budge now. Mexico's debt crisis had been contained, but it was by no means over; it seemed risky to entrust its management to a new Fed chairman. And because Volcker had replaced the monetary rule with personal discretion, he had captured the credit for the economy's revival.[28] "For their finest accomplishment, reduced inflation, [Republicans] are deeply indebted to a Democrat appointed by Jimmy Carter," wrote the conservative commentator George Will. "The Democrat—Paul Volcker—may be more important than Ronald Reagan this summer when the recovery hangs by a thread."[29] It was a remarkable tribute to Volcker's Churchillian stature. The central-bank chief mattered more than the president.

"I think we'll re-appoint Paul Volcker for about a year & a half. He doesn't want a full term," Reagan confided to his diary.[30]

A few days later, on June 18, 1983, the president announced his choice of Volcker in his weekly radio address to the nation. Greenspan proved that he could lose with grace. "The President's indecision was unfortunate," he wrote to Volcker in July. "But in the end—as he seems usually to do—he came out on the right side."[31] Milton Friedman sent Greenspan a commiserating letter. "I continue to believe that President Reagan made a serious mistake in reappointing Paul Volcker instead of appointing you as Chairman of the Fed," he averred. "Delighted to have kept a friend, but sorry to have lost a Chairman."[32]

There was no doubt that Greenspan had craved the job. "It's in the very nature of the human species to seek to achieve personal fulfillment and to somehow create a sense of self-esteem," he told a television interviewer in August; despite the distance he had come, the sideman was still burning to make his mark, to the maximum extent of his abilities.[33] But life outside the government had its attractions, too. The business of being Alan Greenspan had grown more lucrative than ever: at the time of the contest for the Fed chairmanship, he was delivering some eighty paid speeches per year and pocketing almost $1 million from them.[34] Besides, Greenspan did not object to earning more. For a man of his stature, there were many ways to do so.

At the start of 1984, Greenspan moved his consultancy into an art deco building at 120 Wall Street. The tower had once been occupied by coffee merchants, and a few still hung on; every so often the smell of roasting coffee beans would waft through the air-conditioning system. But by now Townsend-Greenspan was a diminishing part of Greenspan's professional empire, for rather than growing his firm, Greenspan himself had grown beyond it. As well as milking the speaking circuit, he served as the pitchman for Apple's TV ads, sporting his Woody Allen glasses and a broad-shouldered black business suit. He accompanied Henry Kissinger on visits to Kissinger's consulting clients, providing an economic view that complemented the geopolitical one—evidently, by now, their shared commercial interests trumped old policy rivalries.[35] Meanwhile, Greenspan held directorships on an A-list of corporate boards, among them Mobil, General Foods, the aluminum giant Alcoa, and J.P. Morgan. He experimented with joint ventures, too. A few years earlier, Greenspan had teamed up with a computer-services company called ADP, which had been built by the New Jersey senator Frank Lautenberg. Together they provided a souped-up version of the Townsend-Greenspan offering, bundling consulting, computing, and data processing into one product.

In September 1984, Greenspan allowed his fame to be affixed to an investment company. It was the brainchild of Marvin Josephson, a celebrated Hollywood talent agent. Coming from the movie business, where big money followed big names, Josephson created a fund-management outfit around two bankable stars, recruiting Greenspan as the romantic lead and a financial rainmaker named C. Roderick "Rory" O'Neil to play opposite him. Greenspan-O'Neil Associates acquired suitably lavish premises in Midtown Manhattan, and Greenspan would show up once a month to give his view on the economy. The firm's investment thesis was not exactly cutting-edge. Its stock pickers would listen to Greenspan's assessment of the business cycle and buy stocks that would do well if he was right: if Greenspan foresaw accelerating growth, banks might be poised for a good run; if he foresaw a downswing, utilities offered some protection. The resulting investment returns were barely respectable—after all, Greenspan was offering little more than the advice he gave to the roster of more sophisticated investment teams that retained him as a consultant. But the firm's clearest failure had to do with marketing. Greenspan had been recruited on the theory that he would attract business from corporate pension funds, but he refused to use his Rolodex to land clients; indeed, he even discouraged the marketing staff from approaching companies he knew intimately. It was an example of how, in certain contexts, Greenspan's scruples could dominate his behavior: he had been willing to lend his name to Josephson's venture, but he was not willing to risk his reputation by urging friends to entrust money to it. Greenspan-O'Neil folded after about two years, costing the movie man $2 million.[36]

If this failure demonstrated that Greenspan could wander into projects in a half-committed way, it was not the only example. His multiple board memberships required little more than listening; the corporate culture of the time did not encourage activist directors.[37] Even the prestigious J.P. Morgan appointment fitted this model.[38] Greenspan was thrilled to be a Morgan director: the board featured a who's who of corporate titans, and ever since Greenspan had conceived a youthful fascination with the nineteenth-century robber barons, J. Pierpont Morgan had occupied a special place in his imagination. Years later, Greenspan would recall the awe he felt at entering Morgan's theatrical headquarters at 23 Wall Street, passing through the unmarked corner entrance, proceeding underneath the opulent Louis XV chandelier with its 1,900 crystal pieces, and taking his place in the boardroom beneath the portrait of the glaring, walrus-mustached patriarch, with his bulbous nose and starched wing collar. To the kid from Washington Heights, it was almost as though he had realized his boyhood fantasy of playing baseball in the major leagues.[39] But now that he had entered the sanctuary, Greenspan was not expected to do much. To the contrary, Morgan board meetings would feature a large lunch, capped off by an elaborate pastry; no liquor was served, but some of the directors had taken care of that deficiency before arriving. After lunch there would be a collective lighting of cigars, and the directors would process downstairs to the boardroom and sit back in comfortable chairs as a fog of distinguished somnolence descended upon the gathering. The entire ritual, a Morgan insider remembers, "was consistent with the way firms generally viewed their outside directors. You sort of took care of them, you made them comfortable, and kept them interested but you didn't necessarily feel that they were running the show, as opposed to you running the show with them as adjuncts."[40] Morgan's chairman, Lewis Preston, had no desire whatever to foster vigorous debate. By mustering a handful of probing questions, Greenspan performed above expectations.[41]

A round the time he launched his ill-fated investment firm, Greenspan was approached by Arthur Liman, a prominent attorney in New York's financial circles. Liman needed some help for his client Charles H. Keating Jr., a lanky former Olympic swimmer with a wide smile and whiter-than-snow teeth, known for his fervent campaigns against pornography. Horrified by any hint of sexual license, Keating would lecture schoolgirls on proper behavior, telling one group in his hometown of Cincinnati that "men get lewd, sinful thoughts when they see a woman wearing shorts," and specifying that "Bermuda shorts, too, can be an occasion of sin."[42] To recruit supporters for his antipornography campaign, Keating mailed out membership cards with a message denouncing "the pit demons of pornography." "Just take this card in your hand. Hold it. Feel the bond with me, and with the hundreds of thousands of decent, God-fearing people across the country who stand in unbending line against the forces of absolute evil."[43]

When Keating's life intersected with Greenspan's, he had recently purchased a mortgage bank called Lincoln Savings and Loan, based in Irvine, California. Though keen to eradicate pornography, Keating was a financial libertine; he wanted Lincoln to break out of its regulatory silo— to diversify out of mortgage lending by taking direct ownership stakes in corporate stock and real estate. Keating needed a well-placed ally to persuade the regulators to approve his plan, which was why his lawyer, Arthur Liman, had chosen to approach Greenspan.

Greenspan signed on as Keating's consultant, and in November 1984 he submitted a brief to the Federal Home Loan Bank Board, which regulated Lincoln. This was not a heavy lift: the brief simply restated Greenspan's long-standing support for financial deregulation.[44] It stated that rules limiting thrifts' investments "are unsound in principle and will prove harmful in practice." It rejected the notion that direct investments in corporate stock or real estate were riskier than mortgage lending, suggesting to the contrary that they "should lower the industry's overall level of risk and place it on a sounder footing." "The industry as a whole *requires* the broad ability to make direct investments in order to restore and ensure its economic stability," Greenspan asserted.[45]

Unfortunately for Greenspan, the regulators were not won over by his letter. Concerned that allowing thrifts to make riskier investments would heighten the threat of their failure, they vowed to come up with a rule that would restrict direct real estate bets.[46] The regulators' obstinacy drove Keating to step up his campaign, dragging his consultant in much deeper. On December 17, 1984, Greenspan consented to join Keating on a visit to Capitol Hill, where they explained their position to Senator Alan Cranston of California. Their methods of persuasion were not purely intellectual: Senator Cranston brought his campaign finance director to the meeting, and Keating and his associates would ultimately donate $850,000 to political organizations connected to the senator.[47] Then, in February 1985, Greenspan applied his signature to another letter for Keating. This time he argued that if regulators insisted upon direct-investment restrictions for S&Ls, Lincoln deserved a special exemption from them.

Greenspan may have regarded his second letter as an innocent extension of his established deregulatory views; if he opposed investment restrictions for S&Ls in general, why shouldn't he argue that a particular S&L should be excused from them? But his testimony now crossed the line from broad policy advocacy into the riskier territory of vouching specifically for Keating and his people. Greenspan assured regulators that Lincoln's management was "seasoned and expert in selecting and making direct investments"; that it had "a long and continuous track record of outstanding success in making sound and profitable direct investments"; and indeed that Lincoln's investments were "highly promising" and "widely diversified." To deny Lincoln's request for an exemption, Greenspan concluded, would be "a serious and unfair hardship on an association that has, through its skill and expertise, transformed itself into a financially strong institution."[48]

These statements were, to say the least, incautious. To begin with, Greenspan had sounded the alarm repeatedly about the fragility of S&Ls. The entire industry was "basically running on virtually no tangible capital," he complained in a television interview in March 1985; why did he suppose that Lincoln was more stable than the rest of the industry?[49] Indeed, a little digging in the public record would have suggested that Lincoln might well be less solid than its peers. A few years earlier, the Securities and Exchange Commission had charged Keating with abusing funds at one of his other companies. Keating had ultimately signed a consent decree without admitting guilt, but the run-in had cost him a coveted appointment as Reagan's ambassador to the Bahamas.[50] Greenspan might also have wondered about Lincoln's headlong growth; from his time as a director of Trans-World, Greenspan surely knew that the flashiest and most ambitious thrifts were often the ones that fell hardest.[51] Years later, Greenspan would write that he had vouched for Lincoln before Keating "was exposed as a scoundrel."[52] This was fair—but only barely. The truth was that in the rush of a full life, Greenspan had ignored the red flags that were there to be discovered.

After Greenspan moved to the Fed, Keating's true character was revealed in its entirety. He wiretapped supervisors who were examining Lincoln's books.[53] He flew into a rage with them, screaming to his secretary, "Get Alan Greenspan on the phone for me"—though by this time Greenspan had wisely instructed his office to direct Keating's calls to the Fed's general counsel.[54] Finally, in 1989, Lincoln collapsed, and the federal government was forced to pick up the pieces, selling Keating's "highly promising" direct investments for whatever anyone would pay for them. There was a preposterous hotel project, complete with a swimming pool lined with mother-of-pearl tile; there was a half-built residential community near Phoenix, where Keating meant to ban pornography.[55] The S&L's failure ended up costing taxpayers an astonishing $3.4 billion—more than any other thrift of the era.[56]

"I was wrong about Lincoln," Greenspan said later.[57] It was an understatement.

If Greenspan's failure to secure the Fed job freed him to dabble in some dubious business ventures, Paul Volcker faced his own set of challenges. As the economic recovery continued into 1984, he began to push up interest rates, reversing the loosening that had followed Mexico's near meltdown. The tightening was undoubtedly needed—inflation was creeping up again.[58] But Reagan's political counselors did not see things that way: they had no patience with interest-rate hikes in an election year, especially not from a Democratic Fed chairman. "If the Fed continues on their tight path now, it will have an effect on November and December," Treasury Secretary Regan complained publicly on May 9, 1984. "Is that politics and does that have us worried? You bet your life it has us worried."[59]

Political attacks were the least of Volcker's problems, however. The same day that the Treasury secretary came after him, financial markets panicked about Continental Illinois National Bank and Trust Co., the eighth-largest bank in the nation. Continental had traditionally financed America's auto and steel business from its stately bastion on South LaSalle Street in Chicago, but in the late 1970s it had expanded hastily, buying up loans that had been originated by others. Then Continental discovered, as many were to rediscover in 2007 and 2008, that banks that make loans with a view to selling them are sometimes tempted to lend carelessly. As Continental's loans proved uncollectible, traders from Asia to Europe began to fear that it might fail; and the day that Regan harrumphed about Volcker, the jitters turned into a full-blown panic. Banks cut credit lines to Continental as quickly as they could; and the clearinghouse of the Chicago Board of Trade, Continental's neighbor and one of its largest customers, withdrew a $50 million deposit. History's first electronic bank run had begun. There were no mobs of frenzied customers outside Continental's doors. There were just numbers flashing on computer screens, heralding disaster.[60]

On Friday, May 11, the Federal Reserve Bank of Chicago hastily propped up Continental with a loan of $3.6 billion—more even than it had taken to stabilize Mexico. But despite that infusion, Continental was still teetering. It had taken in an astronomical $40 billion in deposits, mostly in the form of bulky chunks of capital from other financial institutions, many of them foreign. Once this hot money began to run, the exodus of cash could quickly overwhelm the Fed's emergency loan. In desperation, Continental sought help from its competitors.

Hoping for a line of credit that would be large enough to change the game, David Taylor, Continental's lean, aristocratic chairman, turned to the one bank that all the industry revered—J.P. Morgan. There was a rich echo in this turn of events. The most famous moment in Morgan history had occurred during the market panic of 1907, when J. Pierpont Morgan himself had led Wall Street's elite in rescuing the financial system, at one point locking his fellow bank chiefs in his library until they pledged to support his bailout program. Now, seventy-seven years later, Pierpont's successors rounded up the nation's banking chiefs to back Continental, urgently pleading that its failure would hurt all of them. This time there was no locked library, no majestic wall tapestries or illuminated manuscripts—there were simply frantic calls to credit officers, one of whom was contacted while windsurfing.[61] By Sunday evening, the House of Morgan had persuaded the nation's top lenders to step up. It pulled together a private credit line of $4.5 billion to backstop the Fed's backstop.

Even that was not enough, however. Together, the Fed loan and the Morgan syndicate represented less than a quarter of Continental's deposits; amazingly, Continental was larger than the combined size of all the banks that had failed during the Depression.[62] When the markets opened on Monday, Standard & Poor's fueled the panic by lowering its rating of Continental's debt; and on Tuesday morning the front page of the *New York Times* proclaimed that Continental's collapse could trigger "a wave of failures worldwide."[63] Western banks had already been battered by the Latin American shock, and now Continental's woes threatened to push them over the edge. In the American Midwest, some fifty banks were said to have deposits at Continental that exceeded their total capital.[64]

At ten o'clock that Tuesday morning, a worried Paul Volcker convened a meeting with his fellow bank regulators, the comptroller of the currency, and the head of the Federal Deposit Insurance Corporation. The Reagan Treasury was enthusiastic about the idea of the Morgan-led "private solution," but the markets were screaming that something bigger was needed. The scale of the challenge dwarfed 1907, when Pierpont Morgan had succeeded in ending the panic with a war chest of around $300 million—about $3.3 billion in 1984 dollars.[65] Now, with a single institution requiring a bailout many times larger, a private solution would not work. The Fed, which had been founded after 1907 precisely to end the unnerving reliance on private bailouts, had created the stability that had allowed finance to expand. As a result, when crises did occur, they happened on a scale that demanded Fed action.

Volcker suggested to his fellow regulators that they should meet the leaders of the Morgan syndicate. He asked J.P. Morgan to gather Wall Street's elite at its headquarters the following morning.

The next day, Wednesday, May 16, 1984, Volcker slipped into New York and entered the Morgan offices through the service garage. The last thing he wanted was for financial traders to know of his visit; the news would only intensify the panic. He also did not want to be late for his next engagement. He was due to attend that afternoon's commencement exercises at Columbia University, where he would be awarded an honorary degree. His absence would be conspicuous.[66]

Volcker made his way from the garage up to the Morgan boardroom. The imposing portrait of Pierpont glared down on him from the wall, and when the meeting got under way, some of those present invoked the patriarch's past glories. A few of the bank chiefs suggested grandly that they could save the system once again, without the taxpayers' involvement. But it was just talk. They were not about to risk their money on the scale that would be necessary.

William Isaac, the young chairman of the Federal Deposit Insurance Corporation (FDIC), explained that he was readying a rescue package of $2 billion for Continental. Prompted by Don Regan at the Treasury, he wanted the assembled bankers to cover a quarter of that sum. But several of the bankers resisted even this modest request, doubting whether a further $2 billion could possibly make much difference. So long as Continental's creditors entertained any doubt whatever about the bank's survival, they would race each other for the exit.

The meeting broke up, and Volcker prepared to leave for the commencement ceremony at Columbia. But before he departed, the FDIC chairman pressed an idea on him. At present, only deposits up to $100,000 were covered by FDIC insurance, and these represented just a tenth of total deposits at Continental. If the government pledged to protect other creditors—larger depositors as well as investors who owned Continental bonds or short-term paper—the panic could be calmed. The FDIC's $2 billion rescue loan would then be enough to end the run on Continental.

Volcker was not keen on guaranteeing uninsured creditors. "That would set a bad precedent," he cautioned. "Frankly, I think that between your capital infusion and our loans at the discount window we should be able to stabilize Continental."

"That's easy for you to say," the FDIC man responded. "All your exposure is collateralized." He was pointing out that the Fed's emergency loans were provided against the security of Treasury bonds or other assets. If Continental went down, the Fed would take possession of its collateral. But the FDIC was more exposed. "We're on the hook for $2 billion if Continental is forced into bankruptcy," he continued. "I can't afford to let that happen."

"Well, I've got to go and get that damn honorary degree or people will start thinking we've really got a problem," Volcker harrumphed. "Just try to keep the wording as vague as possible."

The following day, the government and Wall Street jointly unveiled the largest bank bailout in U.S. history. The FDIC duly provided the $2 billion loan, having arm-twisted the bank chiefs into underwriting part of it. The Morgan syndicate's private credit line was expanded to $5.3 billion, and the Fed promised to keep its discount window open until the crisis abated. But the most lasting consequence of the disaster was the one against which Volcker had warned. The government issued a statement declaring that no Continental creditor, large or small, would be permitted to lose money.

Back in 1970, Arthur Burns had initially resisted pressure to bail out

Penn Central; then he had reversed himself completely. In 1975, Gerald Ford had resisted calls to bail out New York City; then he had caved under pressure. Now even the Churchillian Paul Volker had followed the same path. On Mexico and again on Continental Illinois, he had thrown public money at defaulters and allowed private creditors to escape unscathed. The doctrine of "too big to fail" had been established.

Greenspan himself had mellowed on bailouts. The month after Continental's rescue, he devoted two of his regular public television commentaries to the affair, conceding that the Fed's actions "may well have been necessary given the potential dangers of a major run." But he still focused on the dark side. Creditors to large banks could now expect to be rescued, whereas creditors to small banks presumably could not; armed with the advantage of implicit government insurance, big banks would now grow bigger than ever. At the same time, moreover, big banks would grow more reckless, too. Hitherto, large, uninsured creditors had supposedly restrained bank managers from taking too much risk; if they saw signs of unsound lending, they would quickly yank their money out. But now that large creditors were de facto insured, that restraining discipline was gone; risks would build up, and more large banks would fail in the future. The government would be on the hook for almost limitless bailouts, requiring "taxpayer money and probably a good deal of Federal Reserve printing press money as well," Greenspan predicted.[67] The warnings contained in his *Challenge* essay, written to mark the fiftieth anniversary of the 1929 crash, were coming true. The larger the financial system grew, the scarier the prospect that it might crack. Any bank that got into trouble "would have to be bailed out by its central bank," Greenspan had observed in his essay.

If the Continental rescue had been both necessary and appalling, what was the solution? The answer, Greenspan insisted at a discussion convened by the *New York Times* in August 1984, was that banks should protect both taxpayers and themselves by maintaining thicker capital cushions. For a moment, it sounded as though Greenspan were demanding regulatory action; for the previous few years, the Fed had tried halfheartedly to impose capital standards on U.S. banks, never summoning the nerve to force large lenders to comply with them. But having seemingly laid out a policy prescription, Greenspan quickly undermined it.

"Mr. Greenspan, do you have a figure in mind for what the appropriate capital-asset ratio should be at this time?" a journalist inquired, reasonably.

"Yes, I do, but that's irrelevant because it depends on the individual bank," Greenspan replied. "It depends on the type of liabilities it has. For example, a bank which has nothing but certificates of deposit that mature in ten years can do with a lot less capital than one which has borrowed overnight money."

Greenspan's logic was correct: if Continental had locked up funding for ten years, it could have brushed off rumors about its health without overnight depositors running. Indeed, Greenspan's logic could be extended to the other side of a bank's balance sheet, too. A bank that lent to dicey start-up businesses needed more capital to buffer losses than a bank that only lent to the U.S. government—the appropriate amount of capital depended on the individual bank, exactly as Greenspan suggested. But if Greenspan was arguing that the right capital-asset ratio could not be described by a rule—just as the right monetary policy could not be described by a rule, and just as the right amount of lending to a Latin American country could not be described by a rule—then he was offering a counsel of despair. He was insisting that banks should hold more capital; and yet he was also arguing that regulators could not force them to do so, because they had no way to decide how much capital was needed.

One of the *Times*'s journalists forced Greenspan to confront the implication of his thinking. Banks were risky, yet Greenspan had no advice on how to rein them in. Should the banking system therefore "be structured as a noncompetitive utility?"

"I think we're getting to the really crucial issue," Greenspan responded. "Look, there are extraordinary advantages to the American standard of living in having the type of banking system that we have had. In other words, we keep looking at the problems but remember that the financial

institutions that we've developed in this country have been a very important factor in why we have this pre-eminent standard of living. . . ."

Banks were hazardous, Greenspan was conceding; and no capital rule
could tame them. But reducing banks to tame wards of the state was not
the right answer, because prosperity depended on sophisticated finance.
The experts who decided how money flowed through the economy were
providing a vital service. Even though they made mistakes, there was no
way to do without them.

Greenspan's bottom line marked a shift in his outlook. Since the 1950s
and 1960s, he had argued that bankers must be trusted to manage their
affairs; far from wanting to turn finance into a "noncompetitive utility," he
had favored deregulation. But this part of his thinking had rested on the
presumption that financiers would pay for their errors—they should be
free to manage their own risks, but they must also be *incentivized* to manage them. Precisely because he was adamant that financiers should bear
the cost of their mistakes, Greenspan had denounced the creation of a
lender of last resort—the founding of the Fed had been "one of the historic disasters in American history." By the same token, Greenspan had
consistently opposed financial rescues during the 1970s, opposing assistance for Penn Central, Lockheed Martin, and New York City. But sometime in the mid-1980s, this two-part logic was allowed to blur. Greenspan
continued to favor the deregulation of finance; but it grew obvious that
government safety nets were there to stay—financiers would *not* pay for
their errors. An affluent democracy was simply not willing to let its financiers go bust. Yet Greenspan continued to support deregulation anyway.

Greenspan was perfectly aware that his worldview was fraying. He
could see, for example, that the progressive expansion of deposit insurance had dulled banks' incentive to hold the extra capital buffers that he
thought necessary.[68] In the laissez-faire nineteenth century, banks had
needed ample capital to attract deposits; in the paternalistic late twentieth
century, depositors knew that the government insured them, so capital
was passé. But even though market discipline was atrophying, Greenspan
retained more faith in financiers than in regulators who faced no market
discipline at all. A bank's judgment about how much capital to hold might

be distorted by the government backstop; but a regulator's judgment would be worse than distorted—it would fail to reckon with such elementary matters as the duration of a bank's borrowings or the riskiness of its lending. Neither banks nor markets were perfectly efficient, Greenspan understood. But however inefficient banks might be, regulators might well be even less efficient.

Greenspan's willingness to give bankers the benefit of the doubt owed something to his Randian roots. Ever since his anti-antitrust article of 1961, he had underestimated the destructive power of skewed incentives within companies.[69] Greenspan's experience on the board of J.P. Morgan may have colored his view, too.[70] More than any other major institution on Wall Street, Morgan embodied his ideal of what a bank should be—financially self-sufficient, intellectually independent, culturally moored to the ethos of the nineteenth century. But whatever the roots of Greenspan's deference to bankers, it would have huge consequences for the evolution of finance. Greenspan had lived through the Mexico crisis and the Continental Illinois crisis—he had seen that financiers were capable of grievous errors. And yet he still believed that bankers were better placed than others to allocate credit. There would be blowups, to be sure. But there was no better prescription.

"Life is risky," Greenspan concluded at the *New York Times* forum in the summer of 1984.[71] Despite the many financial disasters that ensued, this passive bottom line remained the best that he could offer.

Fourteen

WITHOUT THE CIGAR

On December 28, 1984, Greenspan sat alone in his favorite restaurant in New York, a plush Midtown establishment called Le Périgord. He was waiting for his date, who arrived somewhat belatedly, disheveled but beautiful, cold from the snow that was carpeting the city. From the moment she sat down, the conversation flowed, ranging from childhood to baseball to music. She had grown up with a piano-playing mother; she had been a passionate teenage violinist; she connected with music in the visceral manner that mattered so deeply to Alan.[1] Adding to these points of connection, the date, Andrea Mitchell, was NBC's White House correspondent, and she shared Alan's fascination with politics and Washington. Over plates of lavish French cooking, the two talked about elections and diplomacy and even the vexing question of monopolies, and Alan seized the opportunity to invite Andrea back to his apartment to show her his 1961 denunciation of antitrust law. "What, you didn't have any etchings?" Andrea would tease later. But in Greenspan's recollection, they did go to his apartment, and she did read the anti-antitrust essay, and they did discuss it together. Andrea thought that Alan was testing her seriousness, but the truth was simpler. As he put it later, "I was doing everything I could think of to keep her around."[2]

With that dinner in December, Alan acquired an additional reason to be in Washington. Andrea was less confident in her looks than Barbara Walters, but she combined a TV star's poise with a no-nonsense reporter's direct manner.[3] She had, by her own admission, an insatiable appetite for political gossip; and in the initial phases of their courtship, Alan would sometimes play the insider card with her—after all, Andrea had first shown interest in him when she had telephoned his office seeking a well-informed economist who would help with a news piece. Now, on business trips to the capital, Alan would make a point of visiting Kathryn Eick-hoff, who had just taken a post at the White House budget office, and after catching up a bit, he would slyly ask to use her telephone. Then, with the old girlfriend looking on, he would place a call to the new one. Dialing Andrea from a White House extension had an effect more powerful than roses.[4]

Greenspan usually managed to keep his private life private. Officially, he had remained connected to Barbara Walters, escorting her to the White House Correspondents' Dinner as recently as April 1984. Unofficially, he had chanced his luck with multiple others; he was never shy in this department. But the relationship with Andrea began to go public within two months of that first date. Alan had come down to Washington to see Andrea on the day she had interviewed his idol Margaret Thatcher, and he had had dinner at her home with a handful of journalists and politicos, including his old colleague David Stockman. Stockman was so exhausted that evening that he leaned back in his chair and passed out. The chair fell backward, and his head smacked into the wall, denting the plaster in the Mitchell dining room. An ambulance arrived to collect Stockman, and Andrea and her guests followed anxiously by car. But when word got out that Reagan's budget director was in the emergency room, a reporter showed up at the hospital. The Greenspan-Mitchell liaison was no longer quite the secret the two might have preferred.[5]

The liaison was not yet a commitment; Alan maintained a second girlfriend in New York.[6] But Andrea nonetheless found in Alan an ideal companion, warmly witty and diverting in a way that belied his public image as a dry prognosticator. Besides, he offered her a special mixture. As a prominent professional woman, Andrea wanted a man she could feel proud of, and Alan certainly was that. But she also wanted a man who would not control her; and Alan, with his sideman's self-containment, was the least controlling power figure a woman could hope for.[7] During her gutsy rise through the television news business, Andrea had battled her fair share of male condescension, confronting city politicians who would bat away her questions by calling her a "little girl." At NBC, a boss had refused to send her to cover the nuclear disaster at Three Mile Island, explaining that a woman of childbearing age should not be exposed to radiation. Mitchell shot back that men's testicles were as vulnerable to radiation as women's ovaries. She was on the plane to Three Mile Island the next day.[8]

Alan was not going to talk down to Andrea like that, but he would not be weak, either. He was outwardly shy but inwardly possessed of a rock-solid belief in himself—the mirror image of Andrea, who was outwardly confident but inwardly gripped by doubts. It was a case of opposites attracting. Where Alan could be tongue-tied and averse to confrontation, Andrea's mother wondered how her daughter had developed "such a fresh mouth." But for somebody so successful, Andrea could be surprisingly fragile, bursting into tears in the face of professional setbacks. When she was passed over for the job of chief White House correspondent a few years later, she was inconsolable. A friend coaxed her out to dinner, and people in the restaurant came to her table to ask for her autograph. But Andrea kept dissolving.[9] She needed a strong prop, and Alan provided that.

If Alan helped Andrea, the reverse was also true in a way that neither could have predicted. In February 1985, around the time that Stockman collapsed in Mitchell's dining room, Don Regan traded positions with James Baker, leaving the top job at the Treasury to become chief of staff at the White House. Regan's new position was even more powerful than his previous one, and he treated it as such: he liked the sound of "chief" more than the sound of "staff," Nancy Reagan said knowingly.[10] From Greenspan's perspective, Regan's elevation was unwelcome, for now the man with the office right next to the president's harbored a deep grudge against him. There was no way that Regan would back Greenspan to become Fed chairman. Indeed, Regan privately promised the Fed chairmanship to

Beryl Sprinkel, a dyed-in-the-wool monetarist with a notorious foghorn of a voice, who became chairman of the Council of Economic Advisers that April.[11]

Don Regan had his weaknesses, however: the sort of weaknesses that could be helpfully exposed by none other than Andrea Mitchell. A few months into his new assignment, Regan asserted to a journalist that women didn't care about the nuclear arms race. "They're not . . . going to understand throw weights," he maintained, referring to the amount of lift needed to propel a missile and its warhead. A little while later, Regan unwisely consented to a live interview with Mitchell on NBC's *Today* show. With the cameras running, Mitchell leaned over and asked, "Mr. Regan, what is throw weight?"

There was an interminable silence as Regan sat speechlessly, like a child frozen with stage fright. Eventually he attempted to fill the silence: "Well, uh," he said, "from the point of view it's—it's the amount of actual warheads that come from the, uh, curve of the missile from the time it leaves to the time it actually lands, and how much do you actually drop."[12]

A little more than a year later, Mitchell humiliated Regan all over again. In November 1986, as the Iran-Contra scandal began to curdle the White House, the chief of staff admitted to reporters that the administration had condoned Israel's arms shipments to Iran, even though it ostensibly supported a weapons embargo on the Iranians. Shortly thereafter, the president held a rare press conference, hoping to tamp down the Iran-Contra fires with a convincing explanation of his policies. But it soon became apparent that the president was ignorant of what his chief of staff had already confessed. Facing off against the White House press corps, Reagan denied that his administration had blessed Israel's weapons sales.

Mitchell stood up in the press room, an intense, petite figure with a strikingly wide smile. Reciting what the president's chief of staff had already admitted to, she invited Reagan to comment further on the administration's stance toward Iranian arms purchases.

"I never heard Mr. Regan say that, and I'll ask him about that, because we believe in the embargo," the president replied testily.

When the press conference ended, Mitchell went off to her White

House cubicle to write her story for the next morning. Fifteen minutes later, a voice came through the press room loudspeaker, announcing that the president would clarify something he had just said. When the statement came, it was a complete about-face: it alluded to Israel's role in piercing the embargo, reversing the president's earlier position. Mitchell could not think of a time when a president had performed so dramatic a U-turn. She sprinted out to NBC's camera position on the White House lawn, handing the statement of correction to a colleague who was broadcasting live.

When Mitchell returned to her cubicle, the phone was ringing. It was an apoplectic Don Regan, yelling and cursing and threatening to have her fired. How dare she embarrass him with the president in front of the entire world? He would make it his personal mission to end her career in Washington.

Mitchell felt intimidated, but it was not her job that was at risk—Regan's was. The chief of staff had been caught briefing the press behind the president's back, and not even bothering to tell him. Because of this and many other acts of arrogance, Regan's reputation went into a free fall. Three months later, at the end of February 1987, he was ejected from the White House.

A few days after Regan was forced out, Treasury Secretary James Baker moved to install Alan Greenspan as Federal Reserve chairman. Baker had wanted to drop Volcker in 1983, favoring Greenspan as the replacement. The way he saw things, there was no reason for a Republican president to stick with a Democrat at the Fed; there was every reason to turn to an economist who had been a Baker ally since the days of the Ford administration. Greenspan had exorcised the voodoo in Candidate Reagan's economic policy. Greenspan had helped torpedo the supply-side extremists on gold. Greenspan had done loyal service on the Social Security commission. Greenspan had even helped to prepare Baker for his Senate confirmation hearings in 1985, before he became Treasury secretary. In a bit more than a year, Baker would be running Vice President

George Bush's bid for the White House. Now was the time to ensure that the Fed chairman was dependable.

On Monday, March 18, Baker raised the issue of Volcker's replacement during a meeting with the president. It was time to dispense with Jimmy Carter's appointee. Once in his eight years as president, Ronald Reagan surely had the right to pick his own central-bank chief.[13]

That night, Reagan wrote in his diary, "We're going to see if Alan Greenspan will take the job if Paul will step down gracefully."[14]

After securing a green light from the president, Baker contacted his candidate. Could Greenspan come to Washington for a meeting at his house—the scene of the secret basement negotiations on Social Security? Greenspan thought that this was odd; why meet at Baker's home rather than his office? He agreed anyway.

The next morning, Greenspan reported to Baker's nice old Georgian colonial on Foxhall Road in Washington. There he found not only the Treasury secretary but the White House chief of staff—not the old one who resented him, but a friendlier new one. Donald Regan's replacement was Howard Baker, the respected former Senate majority leader, who was as easygoing as his predecessor had been gratingly imperious.

Eyeing the two Bakers, Greenspan knew something was up. The president's chief of staff was not in the habit of absenting himself from the office without a compelling reason.

Howard Baker soon explained the reason. "Paul Volcker may be leaving this summer when his term runs out," he said. "We're not in a position to offer you the job, but we'd like to know—if it were to be offered, would you accept?"

Greenspan did not hesitate. Nineteen years earlier, a Nixon transition operative had noted his ambition: Greenspan, the Nixon man reported, "is basically not interested in a government position except, as he put it, one or two that would be presumptuous for him to mention." Now the most presumptuous of all presumptions was on the point of being realized; Greenspan was in line for the position that, as many commentators said, might rival even the president's in importance. Alan Greenspan, the shy sideman, would step into the shoes of his mentor Arthur Burns.

And he would do so at a time when central-bank bosses were the new Churchills.

Greenspan told the Bakers that if the job was offered, he would accept. After a few pleasantries, the meeting concluded.

It was not entirely clear that Volcker really was leaving. Having assured Reagan that he would stick around for only half his second term, he had sailed past that marker with no hint of deceleration. In February 1986, some two and a half years in, he had suffered the rare indignity of losing a vote on monetary policy at the Fed's board—by then, four of the seven Fed governors had been appointed by Reagan, and they ganged up to force a cut in interest rates ahead of the midterm elections.[15] Inflation was in fact falling—over the next year, consumer prices would rise by less than 2 percent—so the Reaganite revolt turned out to be justified. But Volcker stormed out of the room, slamming the door as he left, and proceeded to his office, where he drafted a resignation letter.[16] Then, just as quickly, he calmed down. By the time of Greenspan's conversation with the Bakers, he seemed committed to his job. His wife wanted him to leave, but that had not decided the issue the last time.

And yet relative to 1983, the tide had shifted against Volcker. On the big question of inflation, the giant had emerged strong, but on the regulatory front, he was at odds with both the banking industry and the Reagan administration. In December 1984, around the time that Alan and Andrea met for their first date, J.P. Morgan had launched a fateful deregulatory push against the Depression-era Glass-Steagall Act, which restricted banks from underwriting and dealing in securities. From Morgan's perspective, breaking out of this silo was a matter of survival. With the computerization of Wall Street, tradable debt securities had powerful advantages over old-fashioned commercial loans. Trading allowed creditors to sell out of an exposure whenever they pleased, and this privilege induced them to provide capital at lower interest rates, reducing the cost of borrowing to companies and households. Trading also delivered the debt into the hands of those investors who could absorb the risk most easily, reducing the cost of capital still further. And trading magically adjusted interest rates on a continual basis, ensuring that the rate on IBM's thirty-day paper or Mobil's five-year bond reflected the up-to-the-minute judgments of thousands of experts, not just the outdated opinion of one bank's credit department. Wall Street was increasingly packaging everything from consumer loans to mortgages as tradable securities. J.P. Morgan had to move with the times or be overtaken by them.[17]

Morgan set out its case for entering the securities business in a paper titled "Rethinking Glass-Steagall."[18] Its key contention was that the goal of the 1933 Banking Act, of which Glass-Steagall was part, had been to strengthen the nation's banks, and that this goal would paradoxically be served by repealing Glass-Steagall. At the time of the act's passage, it had been thought that the casino culture of the securities business had rendered commercial banks unsound; therefore, the solution was to separate securities dealing from federally insured deposit taking. Morgan countered by presenting evidence that banks with securities affiliates had been no more likely to fail in the Depression than banks that confined themselves to simple loans.[19] Besides, Morgan continued, whatever might have happened in the 1930s, there was surely no way that securities underwriting would impair bank safety now. To the contrary, plain-vanilla lending had been proved disastrously risky by the shocks from Mexico and Continental Illinois, whereas securities houses—not least the Morgan spin-off, Morgan Stanley—had spent the first half of the 1980s reporting glorious earnings. By way of a punch line, Morgan also noted that the United States was out of step with the rest of the advanced world. Universal banks were the norm in Japan and Europe; indeed J.P. Morgan's European operations were busily issuing and dealing in corporate securities. "We may be in the ironic position of becoming a global securities firm without being able to underwrite in our own market," Morgan's chairman, Lewis Preston, said pointedly.[20]

As a J.P. Morgan director, Greenspan enthusiastically supported the "Rethinking Glass-Steagall" paper. "Greenspan was very instrumental in getting that document out," an insider told Ron Chernow, the masterful chronicler of Morgan's history.[21] But when Preston hand-delivered a copy of the report to Paul Volcker, he got a different response.[22] Perhaps because he regretted his softness on the bankers as they had rushed into

Mexico, Volcker was determined to stop them from rushing into securities. Morgan's outside counsel, Bruce Nichols of Davis Polk, likened Volcker's reaction to that of a small-town cop who obsessed about outsiders speeding through his territory.[23]

Lewis Preston was not backing off, however. He marched into battle with Volcker, marshaling whatever arguments he could find to get the securities ban lifted. His lawyers discovered a chink in the statute: the letter of Glass-Steagall stated that banks should not be affiliated with firms engaged *principally* in the securities business.[24] Presumably, this meant that some amount of securities activity must be permitted? Emboldened by this theory, Morgan joined with Citicorp and Bankers Trust in formally petitioning the Fed for permission to set up securities affiliates, pledging that the new business would account for no more than 5 percent of revenues.

Volcker stalled manfully, delaying Morgan's petition for two years. But by the spring of 1987, he was the only one of the five sitting Fed board members who had not been appointed by Reagan, and there was no doubt about the president's support for Morgan's argument. Indeed, James Baker's Treasury was readying a comprehensive push to deregulate banking, seeking not only to break down the Glass-Steagall barrier but also to relax rules restricting mergers between banks from different states, and even to allow nonbank companies to invest in the banking industry.[25] The way the Treasury saw things, the problem of too big to fail in banking was eclipsed by the reverse danger: American banks were too small to compete, and their lack of competitiveness drove them to gamble on riskier loans, heightening the threat of future crises. Back in the 1950s, the United States had boasted fifteen of the world's top twenty-five banks, but now only two U.S. lenders ranked among the biggest twenty-five; meanwhile, thanks to the regulatory barriers to consolidation, fourteen thousand commercial banks dotted the country. Deprived of economies of scale, even the bigger American lenders were only half as profitable as the giants in Japan and Europe.[26] "When we wake up and realize that financing is being controlled by a cartel of foreign banks, the American people are going to be very unhappy," one banking executive growled angrily.[27]

Paul Volcker continued to believe that the alleged advantages of financial modernization paled next to the risks of financial hubris. But his enemies were armed with lawyers, backing from the Treasury, and—it had to be admitted—some reasonable points. It was true that the securities business had been more stable than the lending business, at least in recent years. And it was true that other countries were spawning global banks that made American competitors seem puny.[28] Volcker's sense of encirclement came to a head on April 30, 1987, when the Federal Reserve Board finally put Morgan's petition to a vote. The chairman made a last-ditch attempt to persuade his colleagues to keep Morgan in its box, arguing that if the banks wanted the law changed, they ought to petition Congress.[29] But a majority of the Board of Governors were deaf to this appeal. The giant was losing his authority.[30]

From the Reagan administration's perspective, Volcker's foot-dragging on the banks was one more reason to replace him.[31] The favored alternative, Alan Greenspan, had fretted publicly about the problem of too-big-to-fail banks, but unlike Volcker, Greenspan was willing to take both sides of this issue. As a director of J.P. Morgan, he was identified with the push against Glass-Steagall, and he assured the Treasury privately that he also supported broader bank deregulation.[32] Big banks that were subsidized by the ever expanding public safety net were a threat to society, Greenspan believed. But if big banks grew bigger as a result of deregulation, this market-driven expansion was to be celebrated.[33]

Four years earlier, Greenspan and Volcker had seemed almost indistinguishable in policy terms. But now a gap had opened up. If Greenspan was Volcker without the cigar, the cigar stood for support for Glass-Steagall.[34]

James Baker called Greenspan from time to time. "It's still under discussion," he would report; or "Volcker is thinking about whether he wants to stay." Baker had conferred with leading Republican senators, and they all wanted Volcker to depart; apart from anything else, getting rid of Glass-Steagall would deprive Democrats of campaign contributions from investment banks, which were lobbying to keep commercial banks out of their business. But however much Baker wanted to be rid of Volcker, he was leery of a public fight. The giant had come to embody the government's commitment to fighting inflation. Muscling him out would be risky.

On May 19, 1987, the Fed's board held another vote on banking regulation. For a second time within three weeks, Volcker found himself in the minority. Against his wishes, four more banks gained limited powers to enter the securities business.[35]

The following week, on May 26, 1987, the giant finally crumbled. There was no point sticking around to lose vote after vote; there was no good reason anymore not to give his wife what she wanted. Volcker met Howard Baker, the White House chief of staff. He told him that he did not want a third term in office.

Baker protested, a bit mildly. Then he asked, "If you don't stay, who would you suggest?"

Volcker said he could think of only two people: John Whitehead, the former chairman of Goldman Sachs who had become deputy secretary of state; or Alan Greenspan.[36]

Chief of Staff Baker relayed the news to Treasury Secretary Baker. At last, things were moving. They had secured Volcker's departure, and Volcker even regarded their chosen successor as a worthy steward of the economy. If Volcker was disposed to be cooperative, some of his inflation-fighting credibility might be transferred to the new man. Greenspan was perfect for the job. He was a Republican long marcher and loyal administration ally. On top of all that, the outgoing Democratic chairman of the Fed was willing to endorse him.

James Baker phoned Greenspan with the news. "You'll be getting a call from the president," he promised.

On Monday, June 1, 1987, Greenspan was at his orthopedist in New York. His back pain dated from the day on which Nixon had imposed price controls—his moment of maximum alienation from any Republican White House. Sixteen years later, his back still troubled him. But his alienation was a distant memory.

A nurse appeared to say that the White House was calling. The receptionist had assumed that the call was a prank, but it seemed to be for real. Would Greenspan take it?[37]

Greenspan went into his doctor's private office, picked up the telephone, and heard the relaxed, friendly voice of Ronald Reagan. "Alan, I want you to be my chairman of the Federal Reserve Board."

Greenspan told the president he would be honored. Reagan chatted a bit and the call ended.

Greenspan stepped back into the hall, and the nurse peered at him anxiously. "Are you all right?" she asked. "You look like you've gotten bad news."[38]

Later that day, Greenspan went to Washington, where he was due to attend a birthday dinner that Andrea was giving for the *Washington Post*'s White House correspondent, Lou Cannon. Most of the guests were reporters, with the exception of Margaret Tutwiler, James Baker's spokeswoman at the Treasury. Andrea sat Margaret next to Alan at the foot of the table, and noticed that the two of them were especially jolly, laughing and talking with great animation. It was only after everyone else had left that Andrea discovered why.

"Today, the president called and asked if I wanted to be chairman of the Federal Reserve," Alan told her simply.

Andrea wanted to know how this would change their lives. Their commuting relationship had given each of them a way out of a full emotional commitment. Now Alan would live in Washington; what would that mean for them? Besides, Andrea would now be dating a senior government figure. There might be conflicts of interest.

The next morning the White House press corps was informed that the president would appear at ten o'clock for an announcement. The reporters knew this meant a senior personnel shuffle—maybe a new FBI director? Andrea's NBC colleague Chris Wallace wondered aloud who it could be. Perhaps a replacement for Paul Volcker?

At this, Andrea was uncharacteristically quiet. Wallace looked at her suspiciously and said, "Oh, my God, it's Alan, isn't it?"

Andrea could not lie to her colleague. But she could plead: if Wallace tipped off the news editors at NBC, he would land her in deep trouble. "If you tell them, Alan's credibility is in tatters with Jim Baker. He'll never trust him, or me, for that matter."

Wallace agreed to tell the editors only that they should carry the briefing live. He would not tell them more than that.

At ten o'clock precisely, Reagan appeared in the White House briefing room, flanked by Alan Greenspan and Paul Volcker. The image instantly conveyed the news: the lumpy Old Testament scourge would be replaced by the slick candidate of the Fortune 500. There was a flurry as the White House reporters processed this transfer: in a few minutes they would have to become instant experts on the Fed—what the heck was the inflation rate? Andrea, for her part, did not know whether to react like a reporter or to beam with pride at her man. As she would write later in her engaging memoir, she was not sure whether to rejoice or slump in her seat to avoid notice.[39]

Among the millions who learned of Greenspan's elevation courtesy of the television news were the employees of Townsend-Greenspan.[40] There had been no opportunity to warn the team at 120 Wall Street in advance. But once the White House ceremony was done, Greenspan showed up at his offices and convened a staff meeting.

Two dozen or so employees crammed into an interior conference room with no windows; it was like a meeting of a large extended family. At one time or another, most of the people there had donned Economets T-shirts—Economets being the name of the Townsend-Greenspan baseball team—and everybody had known Alan for years, as a son-in-law might know a patriarch. The analysts at Townsend-Greenspan knew the boss was happy pondering data in the closetlike enclosure that Kathryn Eickhoff had conceived. They knew he liked to help himself to Coco Pops in the little kitchen in the office. Now he was standing before them at sixty-one years old. His hair was thinning on his forehead and a large patch on his crown was bald. But his star had risen magically. He was at once familiar and impossibly distant.

Looking around at this band of loyalists, Greenspan announced that after thirty-four years with the firm—in fact, after nearly as many years of *being* the firm—he would finally be leaving. It was the end of an era, and for some of the folks there, almost the end of a lifetime. Bess Kaplan had arrived at Townsend-Greenspan in the early 1950s as an expert on government data; Lucille Wu had joined just a little after that to work on the early versions of the Townsend-Greenspan forecasting models. Neither had married; Alan and the firm truly were their family. One of the younger researchers, a man named Ben Melvin, who had once twitted Greenspan by wandering into his office dressed in a gorilla mask, came over to a colleague and kissed her forehead. Then he walked out of the meeting.[41]

Greenspan's employees pondered whether they could keep the business going. But the firm had no future without its famous chief—he alone brought clients in and made the enterprise viable. People began reluctantly to look for work elsewhere, and the grim task began of clearing out the office. In the last days of Townsend-Greenspan's existence, there was no dinner or company event to mark the burial. There were three decades of statistical reports lying in heaps in the conference room, ready for the trash collectors.[42]

Soon after the White House announcement, Greenspan got a call from Arthur Burns's wife, Helen. His old mentor was fading fast; he would be dead before the month was finished. But Helen wanted Alan to know that she had told Arthur of Alan's appointment. Arthur had pronounced himself delighted.

"That meant something to me," Greenspan said, years later.[43]

On July 21, 1987, Greenspan appeared before Senator William Proxmire and his fellow members of the Senate banking committee. Thirteen years had passed since the testy hearing that preceded Greenspan's elevation to the Council of Economic Advisers, when Proxmire had excoriated him for his free-market views, including his frank opposition to progressive taxes. Greenspan and Proxmire had since bonded. Both men were intelligent loners, ensconced in the nation's power structure and yet somehow aloof; both men were fearsomely driven—"I get the feeling he's a Martian, he's so disciplined," a Senate aide once said, perhaps reflecting on Proxmire's daily ten-mile runs and his compulsive scolding of an employee who ate chocolate doughnuts.[44] Proxmire and Greenspan had often been allies on budgetary issues, too. The senator took pride in exposing frivolous government spending, handing out Golden Fleece Awards to projects such as a National Science Foundation study of why people fall in love; he appreciated Greenspan's frequent calls for budget discipline. But now that Greenspan had been nominated as Fed chairman, Proxmire was not going to be a pushover. He was never soft on anyone.

Greenspan was introduced by Senator Daniel Patrick Moynihan, his comrade on the Social Security commission. They made an odd couple: Moynihan in his trademark polka-dot bow tie and floppy professorial gray hair, Greenspan in a conservative dark suit with flashy banker's cuff links.[45] Affecting a mock-serious manner, Moynihan declared that the man seeking confirmation as Fed chairman that morning was doubtless "the most distinguished saxophone player ever to come before the committee."

"I always thought it was the clarinet," Proxmire interrupted. With his sharp cheekbones and strong jaw, Proxmire looked a good deal younger than his seventy-one years. The hair transplants and facelifts had achieved something.

Moynihan leaned over and exchanged whispers with Greenspan. "It's both, Mr. Chairman," he reported.

Proxmire wanted to move on to serious business. Last time around, he had opposed Greenspan's appointment to the CEA, fearing that he would force his inflexible Randian ideas on the Ford administration. This time Proxmire had the opposite concern. He feared Greenspan might be too compromising.

"For almost all of the past thirty-six years the Federal Reserve Board has been headed by three remarkable chairmen—William McChesney Martin, Arthur Burns, and Paul Volcker," the senator declared. "If there is one distinguishing hallmark of their service as chairmen of the Fed, it was their consistent independence."

Proxmire knew this had not actually been true of Arthur Burns, but he did not want to speak ill of someone so recently dead. Still, his meaning was clear: his real fear was that the less-than-independent Burns might be the model that Greenspan would follow.[46] After all, there was going to be huge pressure to cut interest rates ahead of the 1988 election, the more so because all sitting members of the Federal Reserve Board had been appointed by Reagan. "This isn't patty-cake; the presidency of the United States is at stake," Proxmire lectured; "are you the man who can say no to the administration?" At the Council of Economic Advisers, Greenspan had been "a get along, go along, comfortable and increasingly popular chairman," Proxmire recalled. "Now you may have to reverse that congenial, cooperative spirit."

Having warned Greenspan not to go soft on inflation, Proxmire moved on to the challenge of too-big-to-fail banks. He demanded to know whether Greenspan would match Volcker's determination to resist financial mergers, pointedly noting that Greenspan's business connections might bias him on the subject. After all, Greenspan had been a director of J.P. Morgan and, as Proxmire put it, "a paid advocate" of Sears, Roebuck, the retailing giant that sat atop a fast-growing consumer-finance operation. Given all his business ties, could Greenspan be counted upon to oppose "excessive financial concentration"?

Senator Phil Gramm, a Texas Republican with a penchant for irreverence, mocked Proxmire for harping on about the Fed's independence. "I'm sure as Dr. Greenspan listened to you," he drawled, "he made a little note that when you call him next month to give him advice, he will hang up."

Everyone burst out laughing. The senators on the committee respected Proxmire's intelligence, but they found his grandstanding irksome. He was more clever than they were, and more pure. Gramm was welcome to tease him.

"I won't call him," Proxmire protested, indignantly. "If I did, it would be the first time in thirty years that I've ever called a Fed chairman to give advice on anything."

Proxmire was wearing a light jacket with a dashing check and heavy designer glasses. He looked like a peacock. Gramm looked like a gray turtle.

"Well, I have called our current Fed chair on many occasions, Dr. Greenspan," the turtle revealed, evidently reveling in his own impertinence. "He's always taken my call and I want to make it clear I don't think there's anything wrong with the head of the Federal Reserve Board talking to Congress, listening to them. Every once in a while, a few of them are right."

Proxmire left the hearing for the Senate chamber in order to vote. Not missing a roll-call vote—not once, in more than two decades—was another facet of his righteousness.

While the committee chairman was gone, a sympathetic senator hoped that Greenspan would "have the iron will to resist pressure from anybody in any form that you think is wrong." With the exception of Senator Gramm, the politicians were urging Greenspan to stand up to the politicians. The case for central-bank independence, which came to be accepted internationally over the next decade, had clearly penetrated the Senate.

The hearing wound on, and Greenspan gave a comprehensive tour of his views on credit and money. He believed that monetary growth would determine the inflation rate in the long term, but that it was no guide to price stability in the short term. He understood that information technology would bring an explosion in tradable securities, and that traditional banking was bound to be a dying business. He was open to mergers among banks; and if these combinations created conflicts of interest, internal Chinese walls could deal with them.

Soon Proxmire returned from voting and started in again. "I am going to be the skunk at the picnic, at this love feast we are having here this morning and give you some questions in the 'nobody's perfect' department," he declared. Then he made a stink that would be recalled years later.

"I have here a study by the Joint Economic Committee," said the chairman, brandishing a report that compared the forecasts of the Greenspan CEA with the economy's subsequent growth. "[For] the three years 1976, 1977, 1978 the forecasts of the agency which you headed were wrong by the biggest margin of any in the eleven years 1976 to 1986."[47] When it came to forecasting inflation, Proxmire added, Greenspan's CEA had broken all records for inaccuracy—his prediction for 1978 had been less than half the actual amount. "How do you answer to the facts that your forecasts were so far off?" the senator demanded.

After the great financial crisis of 2008, Greenspan's critics would remember Proxmire's question as a sort of gotcha occasion—the moment when the maestro mask was torn away, revealing the sallow face of a mundane careerist.[48] The senator was attacking the witness at his very core: Greenspan was the man who did not know, Proxmire was insinuating. Faced with this effrontery, Greenspan could have pushed back directly: Proxmire was misrepresenting the Joint Economic Committee study, which in fact indicated that forecasts by the Greenspan CEA had been more accurate than the first two forecasts issued under Jimmy Carter.[49] But instead, Greenspan calmly deflected the attack. His wide lips curled into an impish smile. He was going to win by charm rather than logic.

"There is a very substantial difference, Senator, between forecasting in the administration and forecasting outside," Greenspan began in his grave voice. He was appealing deftly to the politicians' self-hatred. His excuse was that the political pressure constraining a White House official had overwhelmed his technocratic objectivity.

The senators laughed appreciatively.

"And I will explain to you, as best I can, with imminent sense of the failure of my mission," Greenspan went on, affecting a theatrical modesty as the laughter continued. The forecasts that Proxmire cited were not really forecasts at all, he explained. "Those are projections that the president's economic policy, if implemented, is supposed to create," Greenspan said sardonically. "The difficulty is that it is almost never implemented."

"But let me just interrupt to point out that every other chairman of the Council of Economic Advisers had the same problem, and they didn't miss by as much as you did, not nearly as much," Proxmire countered, inaccurately. But the more Proxmire insisted, the less persuasive he became. He was not carrying the crowd with him.

"I feel sorry for me and happy for them," Greenspan replied, to more chuckles from the committee.

"Well, then you had an opportunity to be a forecaster with Greenspan-O'Neil," Proxmire pressed, referring to Greenspan's failed asset-management venture.

"All I can say is I acknowledge that that did not work very well, and I take my share of the responsibility."

"Well, I hope . . . when you get to the Federal Reserve Board everything will come up roses. You can't always be wrong," Proxmire harrumphed. His ammunition was exhausted.

"All I can suggest to you, Senator, is that the rest of my career has been somewhat more successful," Greenspan replied, drawing more laughter from the committee. The shy man with the bald patch had seen off the showman with the transplants; he was more appealing, more self-deprecating, and somehow more human. Besides, by this stage in his lifetime, Greenspan was well known to his inquisitors: he had testified before them countless times; he socialized with them; he advised them. And when it came to allegations about whose forecast was off by how many percentage points, the senators understood that they were treading on quicksand. It was easier to chuckle at Greenspan's sly jokes than to arrive at a firm view about the accuracy of his projections.

As the hearing drew to a close, Proxmire got the last words in.

"I would like to conclude, Dr. Greenspan, by saying, this is an extraordinary kind of a situation. . . . Your forecasting record, as I have pointed out, has not been good. It's been bad. You are opposed to the antitrust laws of this country, but you will carry out the laws, although you oppose them. . . . Your position on banking and commerce, again, is that you would obey the law, as I understand it, but you think, if you erected Chinese walls, you can still merge banking and commerce. . . . And you will move in with a board of clones—not clowns, clones. . . . They have all been appointed by President Reagan.

"Nevertheless, you are a very good man. We are going to act on your confirmation swiftly."

True to Proxmire's promise, the full Senate voted less than two weeks later, and Greenspan was confirmed as the chairman of the Federal Reserve Board by a vote of 91 to 2. When it came down to the crunch, even the redoubtable senator from Wisconsin examined his conscience—and supported him.

Book III

THE CENTRAL BANKER

Fifteen

"GREENSPAN'S IRRELEVANT"

O n August 11, 1987, Alan Greenspan arrived at his new office. It was quite unlike his former habitat—the soaring towers of lower Manhattan, symbols of the audacity of capitalism. The Fed's fortress in Washington was a mere four stories high; its clean white marble evoked solidity and power—or "dignity and permanence," in the words of its architects. A statue of an American eagle perched over monumental bronze doors, gazing out at the classical pillars of the Lincoln Memorial; the ceiling of the lobby was decorated with a plaster relief of the goddess Cybele, symbol of abundance and stability.[1] The fact that the Fed building had been erected in the 1930s, soon after its leaders had exacerbated instability by rendering money insufficiently abundant, was by now mostly forgotten.

"The elevator will be here momentarily, Mr. Chairman," an attendant promised.

"Please, call me Alan," the sideman responded.

"We don't do that here," the attendant answered.[2]

Greenspan reflected on the distance he had traveled. As a boy in Washington Heights, he had dreamed of playing major-league baseball—but even then he had identified with George Selkirk, the Yankees' workmanlike right fielder. Now he was presiding over the Federal Reserve System, consisting of the Federal Reserve Board in Washington and the twelve regional Federal Reserve banks. He was Babe Ruth or Joe DiMaggio.[3]

Greenspan's new empire employed a total of 23,000 staff, with Washington accounting for 1,500 of these.[4] Fortunately, he was not expected to manage the system as a chief executive might manage a conglomerate; he had no experience of marshaling a large organization, and less interest in learning how to do so. Instead, the presidents of the twelve regional Feds ran their own operations, answering to boards of directors that were dominated by businessmen and bankers from their districts; and Greenspan was not really expected to run the Federal Reserve Board in Washington, either. By tradition, the chairman delegated managerial tasks to his fellow governors, who would lead oversight committees named Reserve Bank Affairs, Consumer and Community Affairs, Payments System Policy, and so on. Greenspan took a particular liking to the competent governor Edward W. "Mike" Kelley Jr., a lanky Texan executive who understood how to meet a payroll and make a big organization function. Kelley was happy to take a backseat on monetary matters, which commended him all the more to Greenspan.

While others kept the trains running on time, Greenspan's job was to provide intellectual leadership. He would be the public face of the Fed, testifying before Congress on the economy, delivering speeches that would be minutely parsed for clues as to the future path of interest rates. He would chair the weekly meetings of the Federal Reserve Board, at which the governors voted on issues of financial regulation and the level of the discount rate—the interest rate at which the regional Fed banks stood ready to lend to private banks on the rare occasions they were strapped for short-term money.[5] By convention, the chairman of the Federal Reserve Board was also the chairman of the Federal Open Market Committee, which set targets for traders at the New York Fed, who in turn manipulated the overnight money market—either "loosening" borrowing conditions by injecting newly created dollars into the banks or "tightening" by withdrawing them.

Through his command of the bully pulpit and his chairmanship of the discussed their views; he did more schmoozing in those days than his aloof predecessor had managed in a typical six-month period. The Fed's most sacred duty, Greenspan urged, was to safeguard its victory over inflation, and there was no room for complacency. In the year to December 1986, the consumer price index had risen by a mere 1.1 percent; by August 1987, the rate had almost quadrupled, to 4.3 percent. If things carried on this way, the sacrifices of the Volcker era would be for nothing.

When the Federal Reserve Board met on September 4, Greenspan got what he wanted. Despite the staff economists' forecast, and despite the fact that Greenspan had been in the building for less than a month, the board signaled its vigilance on inflation by raising the discount rate by half a percentage point.

It was the Fed's first discount-rate hike in more than three years. A message for Greenspan came in from Paul Volcker. "Congratulations," it read. "You are now a central banker."

Greenspan's dispute with Prell revealed a paradox about his early tenure. On his arrival at the Fed, the financial regulators on the staff had trembled at the prospect of a libertarian boss, while the economists had looked forward to welcoming a kindred spirit. But Greenspan swiftly upset expectations in both camps. In regulatory discussions, he struck an unexpectedly mild tone; he seemed happy to follow the advice of the lawyers and supervisors who had served Volcker.[13] But when it came to economics, Greenspan broke sharply with his predecessor's style. Volcker had been a technophobe, recoiling at data presented in the form of a printout—"I don't want any computer output!" he once admonished an adviser.[14] Greenspan veered to the opposite extreme, reveling in columns of dot-matrix numbers, the more detailed the better. And he was not simply going to swallow the senior staff's advice. Indeed, his instincts would often lead him to reject it.

If Greenspan's differences with Mike Prell's forecast reflected his long-standing preoccupation with finance, they also stemmed from his early formation as an empiricist in the 1950s. Even though he had moved with the times, attempting to build a model of the economy at Townsend-Greenspan, he had never been entirely won over by the approach that came to dominate the profession. Mike Prell's forecasting process was built around a model that consisted, like any model, of a series of hypotheses about what affected growth: if the government ran a deficit, it would inject more spending into the economy and so boost output; if the dollar fell, domestic manufacturers would sell more; and so on. By deciding what factors mattered, the Fed also decided what factors to leave out—either because they were too small to be significant, or because they duplicated something else that the model was already tracking. But just as he had done as a consultant, Greenspan approached the puzzle of the economy in his own idiosyncratic way. Because he did not believe that economic relationships were static, he was reluctant to accept that certain data should be overlooked—at any given time, there was no telling which statistical series might provide the crucial clue to everything. The more closely Greenspan studied the data, the better shot he had at some revelatory insight, so he was constantly slicing and dicing the numbers, pummeling them for clues about the future. If there had ever been a tribunal for the torture of data, Prell said, Greenspan would have been the first defendant.[15]

Just as Greenspan thought Prell underestimated how economic relationships could shift, Prell thought Greenspan underestimated the limits to statistics. After all, no data series is perfectly accurate; in manipulating the numbers to extract a more precise insight, Greenspan was like a man who squeezes a lemon long after the juice is gone from it. For example, the Fed tracked manufacturing inventories, knowing that a buildup might foreshadow lower output as retailers sold goods they had on hand rather than ordering more from the factories. But to Greenspan this was not enough. He wanted to know what share of inventories was imported—after all, a decline in orders for imports would not affect domestic production. He also wanted the value of the inventories to be recalculated by subtracting retailers' markups—otherwise, they would overstate the potential hit to manufacturing output, Greenspan insisted.[16] To be sure, both Greenspan adjustments were sensible in theory. But Prell doubted how much either would be worth in practice. If the inventory data were only approximate in the first place, it was unscientific to suppose that Greenspan's clever adjustments could make them more accurate. Moreover, if the distortions that bothered Greenspan were present more or less continuously, they could be safely ignored because forecasters cared about *changes* in inventories. "Sometimes one could mistake arithmetic for analysis," Prell commented.[17]

At his second FOMC meeting, on September 22, Greenspan's differences with the staff came to the fore again. Following his interchange with Prell five weeks before, the staff had raised its growth forecast sharply.[18] But the chairman was still prodding. This time he seized upon the disparity between gross national product data, which supported the staff's projection of moderate growth and inflation, and the industrial production index, which pointed to a risk of inflationary overheating. Greenspan was inclined to think that the industrial production data were more accurate.

Prell was not impressed. "At this point, we don't see a big disparity," he objected. He acknowledged that industrial production was growing more rapidly than GNP, but the gap appeared to be within the normal range and he doubted that the discrepancy was significant.

As it turned out, Greenspan was right. Over the next three months, the economy grew much faster than the Fed staff projected. Although Greenspan's successful call was quickly forgotten—he was overtaken by events, as we shall see presently—his insights anticipated the data deconstruction that would mark his tenure, and his debate with the staff said much about the state of economics. Eight years earlier, Volcker's elevation had coincided with the rise of monetarism—the audacious idea that a single economic relationship linking money and prices was so totally dependable that central bankers could ignore all other variables. But by the late 1980s, monetarism had been discredited, and no alternative theory had replaced it. "There is greater not less confusion at the business end of macroeconomics, in understanding the actual causes of macroeconomic fluctuations, and in applying macroeconomics to policy-making," the prominent MIT professor Stanley Fischer observed in 1988, confessing to the limitations of the models that he had helped to develop.[19] Across academia such pessimism became standard. "Today, macroeconomists are much less sure of their answers," N. Gregory Mankiw of Harvard declared in the *Journal of Money, Credit and Banking*.[20]

By a happy coincidence, Greenspan's empiricist training suited him ideally to this uncertain moment. The models were misfiring because Greenspan was right: economic relationships are not static. In normal conditions, industrial production would track the broader measures of national output; but sometimes that relationship might break, and the essence of the forecaster's job was to divine what had disrupted it. Mike Prell's staff economists understood this well; they did their best to modify the results from their model by adding in factors that it was not designed to anticipate. But Greenspan's feel for the kinks in the data was difficult to match. He could sense when a model's competent extrapolation was worth less than human judgment.

Mankiw compared the state of economics in the late 1980s to the astronomy of an earlier era, when the old Ptolemaic system had been discarded, but the new Copernican ideas were not yet much use to navigators. During that confusing interregnum, there had been no dependable rule book; ships had been steered by improvising pragmatists. In economics, likewise, the rules in the best forecasting models had been exposed as unreliable. It was a time for improvising pragmatists, and Greenspan was the pragmatist par excellence.

To Andrea Mitchell, Greenspan's elevation to the Fed was a mixed blessing. On the night that he told her about his nomination, she had asked what this would mean—now that they would be living in the same city, would they really be a couple? The answer, it turned out, was not entirely clear. When Alan moved from New York to Washington, he did not move into Andrea's home, tucked away on a steeply winding, wooded street; instead, he set up on his own, renting a functional apartment at the Watergate complex, just as he had done during the Ford presidency. He brought almost no belongings from his old life with him, save for a handful of cherished technical books. Andrea's mother came to Washington to order some furniture for the apartment. Even after she was done, the place still felt anonymous.[21]

To the extent that his fierce work schedule allowed it, Alan spent time with Andrea. But he occasionally spent time with other women, too: at the small private lunch on his first day at the Fed, he invited a journalist named Susan Mills, a producer for the *MacNeil-Lehrer NewsHour,* to join him and his cousin Wesley Halpert.[22] One magazine writer described Andrea dropping Alan off at work one morning when he was waiting to be confirmed. What was their relationship? the writer asked. "Everyone wondered," Andrea recalled. "At times, so did we."[23]

Life wasn't made easier by Andrea's profession. A knight from the House of Government was romancing a daughter of the House of Journalism—it was a forbidden liaison, a case of Montagues and Capulets. Andrea recused herself from covering the economy to avoid a conflict of interest, but Alan struggled to come up with a similarly clean fix. Before his elevation, he had courted the media; the economics reporters on the *Wall Street Journal* kept a list of experts who would return calls fast, and Greenspan's name appeared at the top of it. After his elevation, Greenspan continued to welcome journalists to his office, and went out of his way to flatter them. Whereas Volcker would set the tone of a press interview by pretending not to notice a visiting journalist for the first minute or so, Greenspan made reporters feel that he actually valued their opinions. Greenspan even played tennis occasionally with Nathaniel Nash of the *New York Times.* One time on the White House tennis court, Nash drove a powerful forehand at him when he was playing at the net. The ball smashed into Greenspan's chest, and he crumpled to the floor. "He's killed the chairman!" Nash's partner thought. But to everyone's relief, Greenspan was soon on his feet again.[24]

At the start of October 1987, Greenspan appeared on ABC's Sunday morning show *This Week with David Brinkley.* He had promised Brinkley an appearance before he had been nominated to the Fed; and although the fact of his elevation provided ample excuse to walk away, Greenspan would not do so. The man who had gone out of his way to avoid being a public spokesman during the Ford years now found it impossible to resist a prime-time interview.

The program began with an introduction that captured Greenspan's central challenge—to establish credibility. The Fed chairman, an ABC reporter explained, was "in some ways the most powerful man in the country . . . everything from the price of bread to the cost of home mortgages is in the hands of this man who regulates the money supply and sets interest rates." But nobody felt confident that Greenspan would use his power well, especially with an election year approaching. "Can Alan Greenspan, with his Republican ties, withstand pressure for easy money that would also risk inflation?" the reporter demanded.

A few minutes later, the camera cut to Greenspan, sitting with David Brinkley and two other inquisitors: the conservative commentator George Will and Sam Donaldson, ABC's bearlike White House correspondent. Greenspan's large-lens glasses framed the length of his face from the bridge of his nose to its tip. He was wearing a navy blue suit and light-blue tie, as if someone had advised that blue looked good against the gray panels in Brinkley's studio.

"Mr. Chairman, thank you for coming in," Brinkley began.

"Thank you. I'm glad to be here," Greenspan answered softly. He had appeared on these Sunday morning television shows many times before. Nothing in his manner betrayed the fact that he had become the most powerful economist on the planet.

"Are you enjoying your new job?" Brinkley asked.

"So far," said Greenspan, a smile crossing his face and his eyebrows arching coyly.

"All right," said Brinkley, dispensing with the pleasantries. He had lured the Fed chairman into his lair, and his job was to establish whether the public skepticism was right: Did Greenspan have the fortitude to live up to the Volcker legacy?

Brinkley, Will, and Donaldson proceeded to take turns pummeling the Fed chairman. They attacked him for his complicity in Reagan's budget deficits. They asked him to make monetary policy on air. They demanded that he predict the next recession. At one point, George Will leaned forward earnestly, hands clasped on his crossed legs, and declared that no indebted democracy could resist lightening its load with a burst of inflation. "So," Will taunted, "Greenspan's irrelevant." A quarter of a century later, research on the importance of clear signaling by central banks drove Greenspan's successor, Ben Bernanke, to hold regular press conferences, with all manner of questions answered live under the glare of the cameras. But if Greenspan's central mission was to establish credibility, the interview was not advancing his prospects.

As it wound to a close, Greenspan wondered what else they might throw at him.

"Are you worried about speculation in the stock market?" Donaldson demanded. "Do you think it's getting out of hand?"

"I don't think so, not yet," said Greenspan, rubbing his lower lip contemplatively. "I'm always worried about the stock market, but—"

"Every day, every hour?" Brinkley asked.

"Yeah." Greenspan nodded.[25]

Sixteen

LIGHT BLACK MONDAY

A few weeks after his arrival at the Fed, Greenspan called Ken Duberstein, the deputy chief of staff at the White House. Duberstein was a wise counselor who would later become Reagan's chief of staff. He was also a friend, and Greenspan needed a favor.

"Help!" Greenspan began. The president and Mrs. Reagan had invited him to a state dinner at the White House. But Mrs. Reagan did not approve of unmarried couples at formal events. Andrea had not been invited.

"Do you mind interceding with Mrs. Reagan and asking her if I can bring Andrea?" Greenspan pleaded. He explained that this would mean a lot. It would be the first time that he had attended a big public event with Andrea.

Duberstein knew Andrea well because she covered the White House. But he was not convinced that the first lady's sense of etiquette was his problem. "Alan, you are a big boy, you ask her," he retorted.

"No way," Greenspan protested. He did not sound like a big boy; he was doing his best to come over as a small boy—charmingly shy and awkward. "I am not calling Mrs. Reagan on the phone about this," Greenspan went on. "Please, do me this favor."

"Alan, you are a big boy," Duberstein insisted. Greenspan was the most powerful economist in the world. Surely he could place a call to Mrs. Reagan.

Greenspan protested some more, and eventually Duberstein said he would think about it.

A few moments after putting down the phone, Duberstein received another call. This one was from Andrea.

"Please!" she implored. "Do me this favor. This would mean so much to us. Will you please call Mrs. Reagan?"

"Alan could do it," Duberstein objected.

"Oh please, Ken, it would mean so much to me."

A little while later, Duberstein found himself in conversation with the first lady. He mentioned Greenspan's request.

"What should I say?" Nancy Reagan inquired of him.

"I think you should authorize me to tell Alan, if he calls you, you'll consider it."

Duberstein called Greenspan with the news. The door had been opened, but Alan still had to do his part. It was up to him to push on it.

"Oh my God, I don't want to call Nancy!" Greenspan protested. "You do it! I don't want to do it!"[1]

In the end, Alan overcame his inhibitions; and on October 14, 1987, he escorted Andrea to her first White House state dinner. After covering many such occasions as a reporter, Andrea was thrilled to be on the inside; and she did her best to live up to the occasion by wearing an Oscar de la Renta gown that, as she wrote later, "almost broke the bank."[2] There were cabinet secretaries and celebrities and sports stars; there were ostentatious jewels and a buzz of beehive hairdos. After the dinner, the jazz vibraphonist Lionel Hampton played for the assembled throng. Acknowledging the guest of honor, José Napoleón Duarte of El Salvador, the jazzman dedicated a piece to "one of the great presidents from down there in that foreign country."[3]

The day after the state dinner, Treasury Secretary James Baker met Greenspan for breakfast and gave a press briefing at the White House.[4]

Nancy Reagan's glittering party had revived the glamour of the Gilded Age, but the financial markets threatened to upset the mood of celebration. Greenspan's appearance on the Brinkley show had certainly not helped: his remarks had been received as a signal that the Fed meant to tighten interest rates, and both stocks and bonds were sliding.[5] Interest-rate hikes in other countries were adding to the pressure by encouraging investors to shift money out of dollars. Baker meant to use his press conference to calm Wall Street's jitters. To address the problem of dollars fleeing the country, he lectured Germany's Bundesbank for raising rates.

"We will not sit back in this country and watch surplus countries jack up interest rates and squeeze growth worldwide on the expectation that the United States somehow will follow by raising its interest rates," Baker said, showing scant regard for the Fed's independence.[6]

Greenspan did not give Baker's pronouncements too much thought. He went about his normal business for the rest of the day: a background interview with a newsmagazine at three o'clock; a meeting with Congressman Chuck Schumer at four o'clock; a tennis match with a colleague, Fed governor Wayne Angell, at six; a reception at the White House followed by a dinner with Andrea. But investors on Wall Street had parsed Baker's statements carefully—far from being reassured, they found the prospect of a currency war alarming. The following day, Friday, October 16, the Dow Jones index dropped almost 5 percent, capping off its worst week since 1940. "It's the end of the world!" one trader bleated.[7]

Baker realized that his remarks had backfired. Early on Friday afternoon, he returned to the White House, this time to a meeting with the president, Alan Greenspan, and Beryl Sprinkel, the head of the Council of Economic Advisers who had aspired to be Fed chairman.

Nobody knew what to do, and Sprinkel was concerned that the worst was not over. The German move would oblige Greenspan to raise interest rates to defend the dollar; but higher rates would spell disaster for the stock market.[8]

Reagan confided later to his diary that he agreed with Sprinkel—the Fed might be too tight for the stock market's health. But he noted that

Greenspan disagreed. The Fed chairman regarded the market's fall as "an overdue correction."[9]

A complete account of Greenspan's view would have been more complicated. In the weeks after his nomination as Fed chairman, Greenspan had spoken at length with E. Gerald Corrigan, the president of the New York Fed, who had given him an earful about the dangers of financial instability.[10] Lumbering, chain-smoking, brilliant, and profane, Corrigan had spent the past several years handling crises from Mexico to Continental Illinois, and he saw no reason to suppose that the world was about to become calmer. Greenspan needed little persuading on this score; in his half decade or so before arriving at the Fed, he had noted repeatedly that an extraordinary buildup of debt was making the economy more vulnerable.[11] American households were devoting three times more of their income to interest payments than they had at the end of the Korean War. Nonfinancial corporations had allocated 10 percent of earnings to interest payments in the mid-1950s; now that share had leaped to 60 percent. This leveraging of America had lifted the economy to new heights, facilitating a burst of investment and spending. But it had also created vertigo. Because families and firms were on the hook to pay back debts, they were constantly at risk of toppling into bankruptcy.[12]

By the time Greenspan moved into his new office in Washington, he was thoroughly aware of Corrigan's preoccupations.[13] Financial fragility would be a central challenge of his tenure, possibly rivaling inflation. Worse, the twin challenges might come into conflict. In his comments on the struggling thrift industry in the early 1980s, Greenspan had noted that Volcker's tough monetary policy might destabilize lenders—most of the financial sector depended on short-term funding, so interest-rate hikes quickly fed through into rising costs that threatened viability. There might be times when the Fed had to choose between raising interest rates to ensure price stability and cutting interest rates to ensure financial stability—and given the extraordinary cost of financial failures in a leveraged economy, the Fed might feel obliged to prioritize financial sta-bility.[14] The implication was profoundly unsettling for Greenspan. Just when Paul Volcker had established the Fed's inflation-fighting credibility, leveraged finance might force his successor to abandon it.

Soon after his arrival in Washington, Greenspan asked to see the Fed economist who was in charge of tracking the stock market. Pretty soon, half a dozen PhDs reported to his office.

"I wasn't expecting quite so many," Greenspan said, in a tone of shy levity. He would have to get used to the fact that if he asked to see one specialist, that person's boss, and probably that boss's boss, would want to be in on the meeting.[15] But Greenspan wasn't about to object. With this much intellectual firepower at his beck and call, he felt like a kid in a toy store.

Greenspan announced that he thought the stock market was too high; he hoped it would subside gently rather than crashing. In the back of his mind, he remembered the precedent of the 1920s Fed, which he had exco-riated for passivity in the face of a stock bubble. Now, looking around at his lieutenants, Greenspan asked what he could do to improve the odds of a calm outcome.

The staff offered him two options. He could raise interest rates, which might crimp corporate profits and raise the cost of leveraged buyouts, thereby letting some air out of the stock market. Or he could try giving a speech: if the Fed chairman declared that stocks were too high, investors might take notice. The catch was that neither of these options was certain to succeed—they might have no effect on stock prices or, alternatively, too much effect, triggering the crash that Greenspan was afraid of. No other weapon looked better. One popular remedy for equity bubbles was to raise margin requirements—the rules restricting loans to investors who wanted to buy stocks. But the staff had researched that option and dis-carded it. Equity investors who wanted to borrow would always find a way of doing so.[16]

Because there was no sure way of defusing the bubble, Greenspan commissioned some contingency planning. If the market did crash, what would the Fed do about it? The staff set about producing a pink-jacketed manual that considered contingencies ranging from a dollar collapse to a stock market crisis. But the result was not exactly comforting. According to the Pink Book, the Fed could not legally support a crashing market by purchasing stocks, so it would have to use indirect methods. It could browbeat securities firms into buying stocks on its behalf, but this would represent a troubling infringement on free enterprise. It could close the stock exchange, but suspending investors' ability to sell would only exacerbate the panic. It could step up its "open-market operations," buying short-term government securities with newly created money, and hope that the financial system would funnel that money into stock purchases. This last option seemed most promising, but it was a worryingly roundabout remedy.[17]

The stock market, in short, posed a serious problem. But as Greenspan had observed frequently, serious problems in finance do not always come with obvious solutions. Hence his apparent optimism in that encounter with Ronald Reagan, Beryl Sprinkel, and Jim Baker on Friday, October 16, 1987. He appeared hopeful about the stock market because hope was all he had. If the market's fall of almost 5 percent that day turned out to be the harbinger of something worse, the guardians of finance would have few good options.

The following trading day, October 19, 1987, went down in history as Black Monday. Stocks fell sharply in Tokyo and London, and when trading opened in New York and Chicago, the pattern was repeated. Around midmorning, Greenspan convened a conference call of the Federal Open Market Committee. The market had fallen by almost a tenth in the first hour and a half. This was twice as bad as Friday.

Greenspan was due to fly to Dallas after lunch to address a meeting of the American Bankers Association. Manley Johnson, the Fed vice chairman, used the conference call to urge Greenspan not to go—his planned speech on banking regulation would sound out of touch if the market continued its free fall.[18] But Greenspan still thought the best policy was to stay calm and project confidence. Eighty years earlier, J. Pierpont Morgan had learned of the 1907 Wall Street crisis while attending a conference of Episcopalians in Virginia; he had refused to rush back to New York, reasoning that a hasty return would telegraph panic. As a former Morgan director, Greenspan was steeped in the stories of the patriarch's composure.[19] He resolved to stick to his schedule and fly down to Dallas.

The FOMC conference call ended. Johnson himself was due to make a speech that day at the annual meeting of the American Stock Exchange, which was taking place in Washington. Following Greenspan's business-as-usual example, Johnson made his way over to the Mayflower Hotel on Connecticut Avenue.

When he entered the hotel conference room, he confronted a mob scene. Every financial journalist in the city had arrived to hunt for interviews. Every prospective interviewee seemed to be running for the telephones.

Johnson found one of his hosts and asked what was happening. The previous speaker, he soon learned, had been David Ruder, the chairman of the Securities and Exchange Commission. Ruder had apparently told reporters that if the equity sell-off continued, it would be time to consider closing the markets temporarily.[20] Sure enough, just as the Fed's Pink Book had predicted, Ruder's suggestion had triggered pandemonium. If the market was at risk of closing, it might become impossible to sell. Therefore investors wanted to sell now, immediately.

Johnson stood up and improvised a short speech, announcing that the Fed was monitoring the situation. Then he beat a retreat as quickly as possible. He knew he was not supposed to telegraph panic, but the market was panicking anyway.

When he got back to the Fed, Johnson found that Greenspan had already left for Dallas. He called together a small group of senior officials and established a crisis center in the mahogany-paneled Special Library, a den lined with leather-bound volumes on the Fed's history, across the hall from his office. Sitting at a small round table, the group began to consider its options, ticking off the contingencies outlined in the Pink Book. Pretty quickly, a plan started to emerge. The Fed's job was not to stop the market from falling—the market would have to find its own level. Rather, it was to contain the collateral damage from the crash. Just as with a run on a large bank, the task was to prevent contagion.

It was difficult to say what that contagion would look like. When Continental Illinois had been hit by a run, a few conversations with its managers had established which other banks were exposed to it. But a stock market crisis was different. Thousands of brokers and investors held stock portfolios. Somewhere, some of them would be in deep trouble. With the value of their holdings down, they would no longer look creditworthy to their bankers; and if they lost access to borrowing, they might be forced to dump stocks in a hurry, driving the market down further. But although Johnson and his colleagues could be certain that the financial system was cracking, it was impossible to foresee where the fissures would emerge earliest.[21]

Facing an invisible enemy, Johnson's impromptu crisis committee needed some fresh tactics. During the Continental Illinois crisis, the Fed had lent directly to the troubled bank. This time, following the least-bad option outlined in the Pink Book, the strategy would be to pump money into the short-term borrowing markets. Abundant liquidity would help investors and brokers get access to credit, hopefully tiding them through the shock from the stock market.

Thirteen hundred miles away, Greenspan's plane landed in Dallas. He was greeted at the airport by a representative of the Federal Reserve Bank of Dallas.

"How did the stock market finally go?" Greenspan asked immediately.

"It was down five oh eight," said the man.

"Great," Greenspan said. If the market had lost only 5.08 points, his decision to stick to his schedule had been vindicated. "What a terrific rally."[22]

The man from the Dallas Fed looked pained, and Greenspan realized what had really happened. The Dow Jones Industrial Average had dropped 508 points, nearly a quarter of its value and the largest single-day loss in history.

Greenspan reached the Adolphus Hotel in Dallas and checked in as fast as possible. Once in his room, he got hold of Manley Johnson, who was manning the crisis response team at the Fed's headquarters. By now it was around eight p.m. on the East Coast, and some of the regional Fed presidents had alerted Johnson to pockets of trouble—sure enough, the fissures were emerging. In New York the market's plunge had overwhelmed the "specialists" at the stock exchange, who made markets in particular stocks by standing ready to buy or sell at any moment. With the market falling like a stone, the specialists were understandably refusing to buy—with the result that, for everybody else, selling had become impossible. Unable to convert shares into cash, everyone on Wall Street suddenly valued cash above all else. Lenders called in credit lines. Those who had cash sat on it.

Johnson had asked the Fed's general counsel, Michael Bradfield, to ready a public statement assuring investors that the Fed would supply ample money to the markets. Bradfield wanted to be careful to delineate what the Fed could and could not do, and he and Johnson had gone through a dozen possible wordings.[23] Now, with Greenspan back in touch, the crisis group at headquarters convened a series of phone calls, looping in some of the regional Fed chiefs as well as the White House and the Treasury.

Gerald Corrigan, the president of the New York Fed, was not impressed by Bradfield's statement. He was impatient with lawyers at the best of times, and a crisis was not the right moment to get hung up on legal niceties. "It was this long-winded, highly technical discussion about section X, part B, subpart A of the Federal Reserve Act," Corrigan recalled later. "I said wait a minute, I said that's the last damn thing we need. What we need is a statement that has about ten words in it."[24] The Fed just needed to announce that it would flood the system with money. Anything else was superfluous.

Not everyone agreed. "Maybe we're overreacting," somebody cautioned. "Why not wait a few days and see what happens?"[25]

"We don't need to wait to see what happens," Greenspan snapped. "We *know* what's going to happen." He had not taken the lead in determining what sort of statement the Fed should make—he could always see the flaws in any proposed action. But when it came to diagnosis rather than prescription, he was absolutely clear. The market drop had wiped out paper wealth equivalent to the GNP of France, or California plus Florida. No financial system could sustain such a blow without suffering huge stresses.

"You know what people say about getting shot?" Greenspan recalls telling people on one of the conference calls. "You feel like you've been punched, but the trauma is such that you don't feel the pain right away? In twenty-four or forty-eight hours, we're going to be feeling a lot of pain."[26]

As recently as breakfast time that morning, Greenspan had doubted that the Fed had the tools for dealing with a crash. But when a collapse of historic magnitude arrived, the Fed had no choice but to respond—even if its tools had to be improvised.

While the central bankers debated their options, another crisis was brewing. Nine hundred feet above the streets of his city, Leo Melamed, a wiry, hot-tempered Polish immigrant who ran the Chicago Mercantile Exchange, left a dinner in the Sears Tower and descended sixty-six stories to ground level.[27] It had been a day of vertiginous descents: the equity futures contracts traded on the Merc had led the New York stock market downward. In the months before the crash, anxious investors had bought a newfangled product called "portfolio insurance." Their brokers had placed contingent orders to sell stock-index futures on the Merc, and these orders triggered automatically when the New York market began falling. But this insurance strategy accelerated the avalanche on Black Monday. Automatic sell orders in Chicago caused stock futures to collapse, driving down the underlying share prices in New York, which in turn triggered more selling in Chicago.

Melamed did not yet know whether his exchange would survive the carnage. After a normal day of futures trading, Merc members who had lost money were supposed to settle up with the clearinghouse that served the exchange, and the clearinghouse would distribute the proceeds to the day's winners. But today's after-hours clearing would take place on an unusual scale. Losers were on the hook to produce an astonishing $2.5 billion, about twenty times more cash than they typically delivered.

When Melamed got back to his office, his secretary handed him a list of phone calls: Alan Greenspan, Beryl Sprinkel, Senator Don Riegle, and so on. Melamed had no regard for senators: once, when he had received a visit from the senator-astronaut John Glenn, he had rebuked his secretary so loudly for showing the man in that Glenn had overheard the yelling.[28] But Melamed felt differently about Greenspan, whom he had tried to recruit to the Merc's board. Now that the Merc's fate hung in the balance, Melamed was glad that Greenspan was at the Fed.[29] It was good to have a central banker who had once been a futures trader.

Melamed returned Greenspan's call and got through to his room at the Adolphus.

"Will you open tomorrow morning?" Greenspan asked. He wanted to know whether the market's payment system was working. If the losing speculators defaulted, the winners would not get their dues. They would lose faith in the market, and no further trading would be possible.

"Mr. Chairman," Melamed responded bravely, "I don't think we have a problem, but to tell you the truth, it's too early to tell."

Greenspan assured Melamed that the Fed was going to help. Fedwire, the Fed's system for moving money from bank to bank across the nation, would remain open overnight. If Chicago futures dealers were trying to get their hands on cash in order to settle trading debts, they would have all night to wire in cash from other cities.

Before putting the phone down, Greenspan told Melamed that he should call again at any time he needed. Strictly speaking, Melamed's exchange and the brokerages that formed its membership lay outside the Fed's safety net. But the failure of a clearinghouse would spook the whole system. If the Merc had a problem, Greenspan wanted to know about it.

Greenspan stayed up until around midnight. He had never been in the eye of such a storm before; and although his mind stayed crystal clear, he sometimes sounded to his colleagues like a fascinated onlooker, calm almost to the point of detachment. He was still determined to deliver his planned speech in Dallas the next day, however much Manley Johnson and Gerald Corrigan recommended that he cancel it.[30]

Shortly before he turned in that evening, Corrigan reminded Greenspan that he was not just a bystander. He was the leader of the free world's financial system. "Alan, you're it. Goddamn it, it's up to you," Corrigan urged. "The whole thing is on your shoulders."[31]

Greenspan turned in for the night. Despite Corrigan's admonition, he slept perfectly soundly. Meanwhile, in the North, the Merc was fighting for survival.[32]

Just as Melamed had feared, collecting $2.5 billion overnight was proving difficult. On ordinary evenings in Chicago, the Merc's losing speculators drew on lines of credit from the city's big banks and delivered the cash to the Merc's clearinghouse. But now the day's losses far exceeded the size of the credit lines—Morgan Stanley alone was down $1 billion. The banks, moreover, were not inclined to lend more than they had to. For all they knew, Morgan Stanley might go bust within the week. Why would any banker lend to it?

Around three a.m., Melamed could see he was in trouble. He thought of taking Greenspan at his word and waking him. But what could Greenspan do? Melamed decided instead to ask a colleague to call Morgan Stanley's top executive and beg him to pay up. He warned the New York Fed that it might be impossible to clear all trades before the next day's opening.

Just before seven a.m., with half an hour before the Merc was scheduled to open, Melamed called Continental Illinois. Having survived the crisis of 1984, Continental was one of the four Chicago banks that serviced the Merc's members. Morgan Stanley was among its customers.

Wilma Smelcer, the Continental executive who managed the Merc's clearing account, reported that most of the losing speculators had paid up. But the exchange was short $400 million.

"You mean we're down to $400 million on $2.5 billion? That's pretty good."

"Yes, but it's not good enough," Smelcer told him. Until the Merc collected all the money to clear all its trades, it would be in default to yesterday's winners. It would have to close before it racked up any further unpayable obligations.

Melamed was not going to swallow that. A few years earlier, he had suffered a gallbladder attack and refused to be taken from his hospital bed for X-rays until the Merc trading session was over. His secretary, summoned to his bedside, had found him with one tube attached to his arm, another in his nose, a cigarette in his mouth, and a telephone to his ear.[33] He was not going to permit a middling bank official to decide the Merc's destiny.

"I'm certain your customer is good for it," Melamed assured Smelcer. Continental should credit the Merc's clearing account on Morgan Stanley's behalf and recoup the money later. "You're not going to let a stinking couple of hundred million dollars cause the Merc to go down the tubes, are you?"

"Leo, my hands are tied," Smelcer pleaded.

Now Melamed brought out the big gun. "Please listen, Wilma; you have to take it upon yourself to guarantee the balance because if you don't, I've got to call Alan Greenspan, and we're going to cause the next depression."

There was a long silence at the other end of the phone. Finally Smelcer got back on the line: the chairman of Continental had just walked into her office. Then there was more silence.

Melamed could feel the time slipping away. In just a few minutes, the Merc was due to open.

Finally Smelcer delivered the verdict. "Leo, we're okay," she said. "You've got your money."[34]

Greenspan rose early that Tuesday to review the public statement that the Fed planned to release before the markets opened. The hotel operator interrupted him with a call from the White House. It was Howard Baker, the president's chief of staff.

"Good morning," Greenspan said, with an air of playful nonchalance. "What can I do for you?"

"Help!" Baker responded. Greenspan seemed admirably calm in the face of the crisis, but there were times when a man could be *too* calm. "Where are you?"

"In Dallas," Greenspan answered. "Is something bothering you?"[35]

There was. As the market had crashed on Monday, Treasury Secretary James Baker had arrived in Sweden at the invitation of King Carl Gustaf to go elk hunting. Having learned the news at the airport, he had reboarded his Concorde without seeing the king or any elk; but he was not yet back from his junket.[36] Howard Baker and the White House did not relish the responsibility of managing the worst financial crisis of the Reagan years with both its top economic officials out of town.

"You've got to get back here!" Howard Baker told Greenspan. "I looked around and there's nobody in town but me, and I don't know what the hell I'm doing."

Greenspan said he couldn't get a flight until after his speech.

"Alan," Baker replied, "we've still got airplanes and I'm going to get you back up here."[37]

Greenspan could see that it was time to stop trying to be Pierpont Morgan. The world had accelerated since the patriarch's era, and there was no point playacting business as usual when the market was collapsing. Besides, Greenspan had tried to edit his Dallas speech to make it appear relevant, but it was like taking the *Congressional Record* and rewriting it into a suspense novel. The best thing he could do was to forget Dallas. He would reassure the markets most if he returned to his command post.

Before Greenspan boarded the plane, he needed to approve the Fed's public statement. From his office in Washington, Manley Johnson convened another conference call. Michael Bradfield, the general counsel, was still working with a draft that ran to about three paragraphs.

Greenspan indicated he was content to go with Bradfield's version.[38] The way he saw things, there was a fine line between a forceful promise to create liquidity and an excessive gesture that might backfire, stoking fears of inflation and damaging investor confidence. It was one of those moments when the Fed's warring objectives were pulling in opposite directions: financial stability argued for a bold statement; price stability argued for caution.[39] There was no sure of way of judging the balance, but Bradfield's proposal seemed as good as any.

Gerald Corrigan thought differently. He weighed in forcefully, urging that the statement should be shorn of legalistic hedges. The Fed just needed to make clear that it would lend money freely, through whatever channels it saw fit. It should be an open-ended commitment—a declaration of "whatever it takes," in the phrase that central bankers came to love after the 2008 crisis.

In the end, brevity won out: "The Federal Reserve, consistent with its responsibilities as the Nation's central bank, affirmed today its readiness to serve as a source of liquidity to support the economic and financial system," the statement read. Greenspan later thought it was as perfectly concise as the Gettysburg Address.[40]

Having won the battle of the statement, Corrigan pressed his next prescription. He was the man with the plan—though still only forty-six years old, he had more crisis experience than the rest of the Fed's leaders. As soon as the FOMC conference call was over, he followed up with Greenspan personally.

"Alan, we're going to have to back this up," Corrigan insisted in his rumbling voice. Promising to pump money into the markets was a good start, but ever since this idea had appeared in the Pink Book, it had been seen as an indirect solution. The money would reach distressed institutions only if banks played their part. As president of the New York Fed, Corrigan declared he would call the city's major banks and tell them to keep lending—whether to firms like Morgan Stanley, with losses in Chicago, or specialists on the floor of the stock exchange, who lacked the capital to make markets. "I just want you to know that I'm going to start to make calls," Corrigan told Greenspan.

Greenspan was taken aback. He had spent most of his career arguing that the government should not tell bankers whom to lend to. He asked Corrigan how he would convey his message.

Corrigan told Greenspan that he would strike the right balance. The formula for these phone calls was not written down in any central banker's manual, but Corrigan had been through this before—he knew how to do it. He would call up a bank chief and stipulate that all business and credit decisions should be the bank's alone; the Fed would not second-guess them. But then he would deliver his punch line: "There is a bigger picture out there. You've got to be sensitive to the well-being of the system as a whole. If the system becomes unglued, you won't be insulated." Corrigan would infuse this lecture with his trademark mix of charisma and menace. The bank chiefs would get the message.[41]

Greenspan signaled his assent. He had little choice: the Fed had to lead the nation through this crisis. Then he boarded a military jet and headed back to Washington.

In the first hour of trading that Tuesday, stocks recouped two fifths of Monday's losses. The Fed's statement seemed to be having the desired effect, and Corrigan was on the phone, urging the banks to keep lending. But around 10:30 that morning, the rally petered out. Seeing the market turn against them, the New York specialists, still nursing losses from the previous day, all but halted the purchasing of shares, and the fall became a cliff dive. Years later, commentators would blame computerized "high-frequency traders" for market gyrations.[42] But 1987 proved that human traders were just as capable of exacerbating crises.

Now everyone began to panic. In Chicago, the Mercantile Exchange suspended trading in stock-index futures and the Options Exchange suspended trading in stock options. John Phelan, the head of the New York Stock Exchange, called Howard Baker at the White House to announce that he, too, intended to suspend trading. By late morning the market had given up its early gains and was falling like a stone. The system was disintegrating.

With Greenspan still out of touch, Howard Baker called Corrigan to ask how he should respond to Phelan's plan to suspend trading.

Corrigan declared that closing the stock exchange would be a cata-strophic error.

Why did he feel so strongly? Baker prodded him.

"Because if you close the goddamn thing, you're gonna have to figure out how the hell to open it."

There was a moment of silence.

"I always believed you have to trust the guy who's on the front line," Baker said presently. He would take Corrigan's advice; but if the advice proved to be wrong, the New York Fed chief would be history.[43]

Corrigan was sure of his message, and he was equally sure that the system would freeze up if the banks did not maintain their lending. Bank credit was essential to the smooth functioning of the clearinghouses in Chicago; it was essential to the securities firms that were members of the clearinghouses; it was essential to the investors who were the customers of the securities firms. If any link in this chain failed for lack of ready cash, the rest of the chain could follow. Already firms such as Goldman Sachs and Kidder Peabody had extended loans to customers who had lost money on Monday. Because the banks had pulled back, those customers had not been able to repay their brokers—by noon on Tuesday, Goldman and Kidder combined were owed about $1.5 billion.[44] To make it through this cash crunch, the brokers turned to their bankers. If the banks refused to help, the brokers would be in trouble.

Corrigan could not be certain how the banks would respond to these distress signals. He had done his best to browbeat them, and the Fed was pumping liquidity into the money market, buying short-term Treasury securities for cash. But the banks that got the cash seemed to be playing it safe and scrambling to buy back Treasuries rather than lending the money to other banks or brokers. As a result, the interest rate on Treasury bills fell way below the rate for private borrowers. This so-called TED spread, a standard gauge of market fear, hit a record that stood unbroken until the depths of the 2008 crisis.[45] Low rates on Treasuries were all very well, but they were not going to help the brokers and traders who were gasping for liquidity.

With Greenspan still airborne, Corrigan was getting desperate. If yesterday's fall had almost sunk the Merc, another meltdown could sink the whole system. With no good options left, Corrigan contemplated an extreme response. If the banks refused to keep the money flowing, the Fed might have to shoulder some of the risk itself—it might have to find a way to use its discount window to lend to the brokers.[46] The central bank's safety net, supposedly for banks, would thus be extended. In the heat of a crisis, the Fed would backstop almost anything.

L anding at Andrews Air Force Base just outside Washington, Greenspan boarded an official car and placed a call to Manley Johnson.[47] The news was grim: there were trading interruptions in Chicago; the New York specialists had stopped making markets; sell orders were swamping the stock exchange's ability to process them. Paper chits were piling up; order-processing machines were breaking down; the men who depended on the machines were close to breaking also.[48] At one point in the mayhem, four specialists trying to make a market in a major blue-chip stock found themselves besieged by furious sellers; "Finally I yelled 'shut up' and shoved the biggest one of them back into the crowd," one of the specialists recounted later.[49] Now at his wit's end, John Phelan felt the exchange needed a time-out before it could recover.

After hearing from Manley Johnson, Greenspan took a call from Howard Baker. The chief of staff wanted to know what he should do about Phelan's plan to suspend trading. Greenspan insisted that the market must remain open. He agreed with Corrigan.

The trouble was that the White House could not require the market to keep trading. The law gave the government the power to close the exchange in an emergency; it did not provide it with the authority to force it to keep open. Viewing markets with suspicion, Congress had been careful to ensure that trading could be stopped; it had failed to imagine that the best antidote to chaotic trading might be, paradoxically, more trading. Yet that was plainly the case now. If stock prices were overshooting because some market makers were on strike, the worst thing to do would be to close down the exchange and take all market makers out of action.

Baker asked the White House lawyers how he could put Phelan in a box. The lawyers suggested that the president declare that he expected the market to stay open—if Phelan did not know the law, he might hesitate to defy Reagan.[50] There was no guarantee that this would work, but it was the best the lawyers could come up with.

Much like the Fed, the administration was finding itself short of crisis-fighting options. Also like the Fed, it now abandoned its free-market principles. Howard Baker and the Reagan team began calling contacts on Wall Street, doing everything they could to persuade people to support the market. "It is really important for the country that you start buying," they implored—the subtext being that we might remember if you don't, and also that we're calling everyone we know, so you stand to profit handsomely if you buy this rally early.[51] Dozens of corporations chose this moment to buy back their own stock, responding, as one report said, to "a none-too-gentle nudge from Washington."[52] But the market kept on falling.[53]

A few minutes past noon, Stanley Shopkorn, the cigar-chomping head trader at Salomon Brothers, took a call from Dick Grasso, a senior official at the New York Stock Exchange. Shopkorn had been on the receiving end of calls from the administration, too, but the message from Grasso was altogether more pointed. The specialists were overwhelmed, Grasso declared. Unless something happened fast, there would be no market to trade on.

Shopkorn responded by conferring with Bob Mnuchin, his counterpart at Goldman Sachs, and together they agreed to flood the market with buy orders.[54] Shopkorn agreed to buy up to $500 million worth of shares that the specialists could not absorb, and Mnuchin did the same; and the show of confidence from two respected players on the Street was enough to turn the market. From around 12:30 p.m. onward, stocks headed up. The Reagan team breathed easier, and the stock exchange did not close after all.

Now back in Washington, Greenspan went over to the Treasury and spent an hour with Jim Baker, newly returned from his aborted elk hunt. Greenspan reported that the Fed was flooding the markets with liquidity;

Baker and the Treasury team were duly impressed by the unique power of the central bank during a panic.[55] Together, Greenspan and Baker conceived another measure that might give the market life, and they went over to the White House to sell it to Ronald Reagan. The president should announce his willingness to work with congressional Democrats to cut the budget deficit, they urged. Reagan did what he was asked; and although budget politics remained firmly gridlocked over the next weeks, Greenspan felt sure that the promise of sound fiscal policy had boosted market confidence.[56]

In the last two hours of trading on Tuesday, stocks recovered their losses and ended in positive territory. By the end of the week, the panic was over. America's financial system had survived its worst moment in the postwar era.

Greenspan's conduct during the crash boosted confidence in his leadership. Both Howard Baker at the White House and James Baker at the Treasury would later describe Greenspan as a pillar of strength—he had arrived back in Washington around lunchtime on Tuesday, and the market had recovered.[57] The Fed's one-sentence press release that morning was remembered as a stroke of genius, more powerful than any act of Congress; and James Baker doubted that Volcker would have acted so decisively to pump money into the financial system.[58] A month after Black Monday, the *Wall Street Journal* published Greenspan's picture on its front page. "Fed's New Chairman Wins a Lot of Praise on Handling the Crash," proclaimed the long headline. "Alan Greenspan Was Aided by His Ability to Foresee Problems and by Planning."[59]

How far Greenspan deserved this praise was a different matter. The miraculous Fed press release had not been mainly his idea; the White House calls to Wall Street were not his initiative; he had been tempted to resist Corrigan's browbeating of the bankers.[60] Postmortems of the crisis found that Corrigan's phone calls to the bank chiefs had been especially potent—perhaps more so than even Corrigan himself suspected. During the week of the crisis, the ten largest New York banks almost doubled their normal lending to securities firms, enabling brokers to meet cash calls from the Chicago clearinghouses and stave off a disastrous spiral of fire sales.[61] Corrigan's effect on John S. Reed, the chairman of Citicorp, was particularly spectacular. On Tuesday alone, Citi's lending to brokers skyrocketed to $1.4 billion, up from the usual $200 million to $400 million per day. Corrigan must have bitten off Reed's ear.[62]

It was no accident that Greenspan got the credit for saving the markets, whether or not he deserved it. He was not necessarily the best crisis manager at the Fed, but he was undoubtedly its best politician. He had spent years cultivating allies in the White House, the Treasury, and the media, fighting through his natural shyness to attend society functions and state dinners. Now that investment had come good. Greenspan was the man whom everybody knew, and if the Fed got something right, people were inclined to see his lucid mind behind it—after all, he was the chairman. In his brief time at the Fed, moreover, Greenspan had already done a masterful job of winning over his potential foes. He flattered Wayne Angell, a particularly volatile governor, by complimenting him on his television performances and inviting him to play tennis; he invited other senior colleagues and their wives over to Andrea's for dinner.[63] As a private consultant, Greenspan had clashed with the Fed's general counsel, Michael Bradfield, even trading heated personal insults after disagreeing about the regulation of the S&Ls on a public panel. But now Greenspan made amends, treating Bradfield and his wife to a concert at the Kennedy Center. When the *Journal*'s crack reporters called around their sources for comments on the new chairman, they encountered nothing but warm praise. Greenspan had covered all his bases.

If Black Monday boosted Greenspan's reputation, the same could not be said for laissez-faire capitalism.[64] The presumption of market efficiency, which had dominated academic finance since the late 1960s, now demanded a rethink. Statisticians pointed out that extreme falls in prices occurred far more commonly than was assumed in the efficient marketers' equations. Behavioral economists invoked psychological experiments that showed the limits to investors' rationality.[65] For Greenspan, who had never bought into the efficient markets hypothesis, none of this revisionism upset his settled views; but there were other lessons from the crash that did challenge his thinking.[66] Black Monday forced him even further from his youthful conviction that central banks ought to allow private financiers to go bust; and it drove him to reconsider his belief that a steep fall in the market would drag down the real economy. Combined, these two lessons amounted to a fateful change in Greenspan's approach to central banking.

The first rethink led Greenspan to repudiate his Randian lectures. In 1963 and 1964, he had celebrated "money panics" as salutary enforcers of economic discipline. By the time of Continental Illinois' rescue, Greenspan had begun to soften his stance—modern democracies were not prepared to take the pain of big financial failures, so a lender of last resort would have to dampen money panics. But after Black Monday, Greenspan completed his conversion. Testifying before William Proxmire and the Senate banking committee in February 1988, he argued that central-bank rescues were not merely inevitable given democratic pressures. They were desirable.[67]

This was music to the old peacock's ears. "Thank you very, very much, Dr. Greenspan. You've done an excellent job," Proxmire gushed. "We're in your debt and you rise in esteem every time you appear before us."

The key to Greenspan's new thinking lay in a distinction that had been curiously absent from his youthful writings. Financial crises, the mature Greenspan now recognized, involved both rational and irrational components. To the extent that investors and creditors were waking up to real risks, a sharp market correction could be salutary. But in the heat of a crisis, panic was likely to feed upon itself, so that corrections overshot dramatically. The Fed's strategy during Black Monday had been "aimed at shrinking irrational reactions in the financial system to an irreducible minimum," Greenspan told the Senate banking committee: he was laying out a rationale for repeated interventions later. Moreover, the case for fighting crises had been compounded by the growth of finance itself. In 1964, when the younger Greenspan had contemplated the money panics of the previous seventy years, he could just about construct an argument for letting financial institutions fail; finance was still sufficiently small to make this a believable (but still radical) prescription. But by the late 1970s, as Greenspan had noted in his *Challenge* essay, finance had grown scarily complex; and by the time of his arrival at the Fed, the sheer size of the financial sector made a contagious failure unthinkably costly. In the twenty-three years since Greenspan's Randian lectures, the sector's debt as a share of the economy had more than quintupled, rising from 7 percent to 37 percent. Banks and other depository institutions had expanded their assets almost a hundredfold, from $46 billion to $4.1 trillion, or from 66 percent of GDP to 84 percent. The outstanding stock of corporate bonds had gone from 15 percent of GDP to 23 percent.[68] The leveraging of America, which Greenspan had discussed with Corrigan during the summer, had been accompanied by the emergence of a financial system that simply had to be propped up—it was not just individual banks that were too big to fail; the whole nexus of exchanges and brokers and clearinghouses collectively fitted that description. If Greenspan was retreating from the Randian principles of his youth, it was because his eyes were open.

If the Fed had to fight market irrationality during a crash, Greenspan also recognized its role during the aftermath. Rejecting the do-nothingism of his past—he had claimed in his Randian lectures that activist monetary policy "opened a Pandora's box of business instability"—Greenspan cut interest rates after Wall Street's dive, believing that the market shock would otherwise slow the economy. The logic of his magisterial 1959 article was very much on his mind. Having experienced a bout of terrifying volatility, businesses would no longer feel confident in their stock prices; uncertain how the market might value their assets, they would be reluctant to invest in building more of them. The resulting decline in capital investment would be compounded by weaker consumption. Expecting a pernicious drag on growth after Black Monday, Greenspan guided the federal funds rate down from over 7½ percent just before October 19 to around 6¾ percent in the middle of November.

Yet within a few months, Greenspan's fear of slower growth turned out to be self-canceling. The economy grew at a blistering 6.8 percent in the fourth quarter of 1987; far from rising after Black Monday, unemployment actually came down a bit.[69] The market crash proved to be less toxic than Greenspan had feared, and the antidote of lower interest rates proved more powerful than anticipated. At his appearance before Proxmire's committee in February 1988, Greenspan expounded on why this had been so. Stock market panics in the pre-Fed era had dragged down the economy because they had triggered a reinforcing jump in interest rates; during the panics of 1893 and 1907, brokers had been forced to endure borrowing costs as high as 74 percent.[70] But now that the nation had an active central bank, no such spike in interest rates needed to happen—an activist Fed could clean up the mess left by a bursting bubble. It followed that Greenspan was free to worry about bubbles a little less obsessively than he had done in the past; he could focus his efforts instead on targeting lower inflation. In sum, the crash of 1987 led paradoxically to less fear of a crash. It had been Light Black Monday.[71]

After the Great Crash of 2008, Greenspan's reaction to 1987 would come to seem complacent.[72] Yet he was not alone in his conclusions. Far from the pressures of public office, in the quiet of Princeton, a shaggy-bearded rising star in academia was struck by a similar logic. The crash, he argued in the *Review of Financial Studies* in 1990, had revealed terrifying weaknesses in the nation's financial system. The Chicago clearing-houses in particular had been shown to be fragile, and there was little they could do to reduce their vulnerability. In theory, a clearinghouse could protect itself during a crisis by suspending payments to winning traders—that was effectively the course that Wilma Smelcer had proposed to Leo Melamed. In practice, nonpayment by one clearinghouse would trigger panic among the members of others—it would cap one institution's losses by compounding losses elsewhere in the financial system. Yet although the financial system appeared scarily fragile, it had one potent saving grace: if you factored in the presence of an active central bank, the vulnerability of the clearinghouses magically evaporated. "When the financial system is conceived broadly to include the government as the 'insurer of last resort,' the current institutional setup seems satisfactorily robust," the professor concluded.[73] There was no need to worry about financial stability—so long as the Fed stood ready to act in the next crisis.

If that was the verdict from Princeton, it was perhaps not surprising that the Fed chairman should share it. But the Princeton perspective was memorable for another reason, too. The shaggy young professor was Ben S. Bernanke, Greenspan's successor as Fed chairman.

Seventeen

THE GUN-SHY CHAIRMAN

S haped like a claw grasping at the Atlantic, Walker's Point is a narrow spit of land that juts southward from the Maine coastline. Cold
ocean currents from Nova Scotia slosh past the point's rocky eastern
shore, and the quiet cove to the west teems with striped bass and lobster.
A single road connects Walker's Point to the mainland, leaving the penin-
sula in the state of isolation that first attracted its namesake—Bert Walker,
a Missouri banker who bought the land in 1902, shortly before a small
Hungarian girl named Rose Goldsmith arrived at Ellis Island. No doubt
Walker would have been gratified to know that his grandson, George
Herbert Walker Bush, would one day seek solace at his oceanfront com-
pound, midway through his bid for the U.S. presidency.[1]

On Memorial Day weekend in 1988, when George H. W. Bush made
the pilgrimage to Walker's Point, he needed to recharge his batteries. His
campaign was not going according to plan. Having inherited money, connections, and manners, he was used to doing well: "He had always seemed
a little like Scott Fitzgerald made him up," a friend once remarked of him.[2]
As Reagan's sitting vice president, Bush enjoyed the advantage of incum-
bency as well; he basked in the reflected glory of an economy that was
notching up its twenty-third consecutive quarter of expansion, the longest
peacetime boom in American history. Yet despite Bush's advantages, he

trailed Massachusetts governor Michael Dukakis, the top Democratic contender, by as much as 10 percentage points; and to make matters worse, the long boom was threatening to stall out on him. After cutting interest rates in the wake of Black Monday, the Federal Reserve was beginning to tighten. Contemplating his prospects in the coming November, Bush could see the central bank hovering like a storm cloud above him.

On Monday, May 30, 1988, Bush ventured out from his compound to watch the Memorial Day parade in the nearby village of Kennebunkport. The skies opened and rain poured down upon him. The next day, as the vice president sat through a marathon of campaign strategy sessions, his advisers kept coming back to the economy. Their counsel was dampening, and screamingly dull—the candidate was bored by economics. "This fellow, George Herbert Walker Bush, with an honors degree from Yale in economics, knew no economics," recalled Paul MacAvoy, the indignant dean of the Yale School of Management, who went out to advise Bush at Walker's Point in 1980, during the candidate's first presidential run. "He was not a Hayekian; he was not a Keynesian, he was nothing, he knew nothing!" MacAvoy had long experience with politicians, but his time with Bush still left him agog. "He sat facing the ocean," the professor marveled, "and we [advisers] would sit with our backs to the water and we would start in on shoe imports or the classical paradigm and he would look over our shoulders and say, 'Oh my god, MacAvoy, they're going out in the pencil boat. They're going to see the seals! Oh, damn it.'"[3]

After suffering through the briefing sessions, Bush stepped out to see the press, dressed in a baseball cap and a crisp windbreaker. Even when he was not wearing a suit, he still managed to look dapper.

"There was some expression of concern," Bush said, recounting for reporters what he had heard from his campaign team. His advisers had assured him that "we were rocking along pretty well on inflation, and making great progress in terms of growth"—he had "a lot of confidence" in Greenspan and the Fed, he stipulated. Then he pulled the trigger.

"As a word of caution, I wouldn't want to see them step over some [line] that would ratchet down, tighten down on the economic growth,"

Bush informed the scrum. "So I think there is more room for the economy to grow without unacceptable increases in inflation."[4] "Watching for signs of inflation is fine," he conceded. But the Fed "is at the lower end in terms of growth of the money supply."[5]

It was a warning, an omen: the Walker's Point declaration of May 1988 set the tone for Alan Greenspan's next four years in office. The Bush family retreat in New England might radiate gentility and charm, but when it came to the Fed and interest rates, George H. W. Bush was primed to do ungentle battle.

A few months into his life as Fed chairman, Greenspan was settling into a smooth rhythm. He would wake each morning at five-thirty or six, conscious that the first hours of the day would be his most intellectually productive. He would lie in bed for several minutes, thinking through the knottiest questions on his plate; and after this period of prone pondering, he would commit his epiphanies to paper before the tide of the day's business swamped them. Next, he would crack open the old-fashioned leather briefcase with the curled top that he brought home from the office. Not pausing for breakfast—eating would divert his body's energies from his brain to his stomach, he believed—he would start reviewing draft speeches and poring over technical papers produced by the Fed's economists. If his back was troubling him, Greenspan would go through the papers while soaking in a hot bath. His staff got used to deciphering steam-smudged marginal notes, the product of the chairman's morning cogitations.

A bit after seven o'clock in the morning, a driver and a security guard would interrupt Greenspan's studies. The Fed chairman had been assigned a security detail after Paul Volcker had received threats; but the minders constituted an informal crew, and Greenspan often felt he was being accompanied rather than protected. With his posse downstairs waiting for him, Greenspan would pack up his papers and walk out into the curving corridor of the Watergate building; then he would ride the elevator down to the lobby and board the waiting black limousine. The journey from apartment door to car door constituted almost half of his commute: the drive to the Fed building took less than five minutes.

Arriving at the office, Greenspan would permit himself breakfast, often with a guest: the Treasury secretary, an FOMC colleague, a senior staff economist, a journalist, a politician. Then he would launch into a series of meetings. On days when he was due to chair a board session, Bill Wiles, the secretary of the Board of Governors, would stop by to deliver a pro forma briefing, and Greenspan would proceed into the boardroom to preside over the day's business. There would be matters regarding financial oversight; decisions about whether a proposed bank merger should be allowed; debates on whether a lender that violated the Fed's rules should be punished or just cautioned. Greenspan would run the meetings evenhandedly, much as he had done with the Social Security commission; he avoided weighing in too hard on regulatory dilemmas, preferring to preserve his capital for arguments about interest rates, which were conducted mainly in the separate forum of the Federal Open Market Committee. On days when there were no board meetings, Greenspan would hold court to a steady stream of visitors, including figures from his rich past—Kathryn Eickhoff, Marty Anderson, assorted friends from Wall Street.[6] The discussions were not confined to economics, not by any means—his guests were often startled to discover that Greenspan could handicap a close-fought Senate primary election or tell you which congressman was likely to cast the swing vote on which House committee. A bit after six o'clock in the evening, the chairman would be on his way out of the door: to a drink or a dinner at the old-line Metropolitan Club; to a private soirée arranged by a powerful hostess; or to an embassy reception. Having made a point of showing up at parties since his days in the Ford White House, Greenspan had now acquired an additional reason to get out: Andrea reveled in it.[7]

While he was still new to the job, Greenspan's social appetite flagged just occasionally. Four months into his tenure, Laurence Tisch, the billionaire boss of the CBS television network, invited Alan and Andrea to the

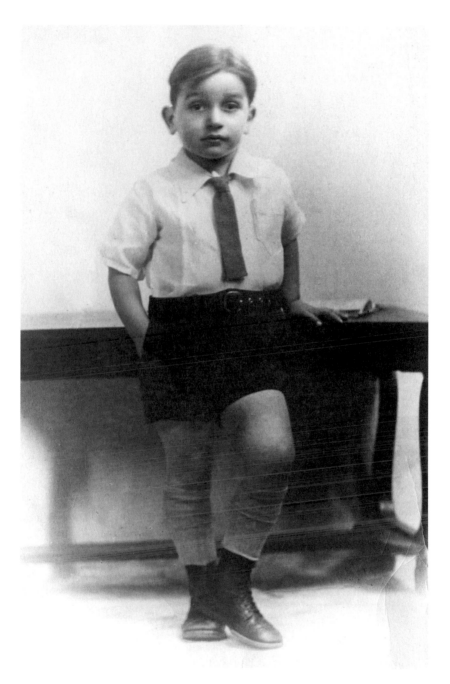

Greenspan grew up in the immigrant community of Washington Heights, on the northern tip of Manhattan. As a young boy, he entertained his relatives with feats of mental addition.

The single child of a single mother, Greenspan's isolation was relieved by his cousins. Greenspan is on the left, about nine years of age.

At sixteen, Greenspan's interests had progressed from baseball to jazz. Pictured here on vacation at Lake Hiawatha, New Jersey.

GREENIDGE, GERTRUDE
Up and coming

GRIFFITH, LLOYD
Lloyd is liked by everyone,
He's swell and really full of fun

HABER, MARILYN   Steno Office,
Spanish Office, Steno Auxilium
A pretty girl who's also smart,
A treat to give the boys a start

GREENSPAN, ALAN   Band, Orchestra and Dance Band, Lunch Squad
(4), President Class 8-1
Smart as a whip and talented, too,
He'll play the sax and clarinet for
you

GUGGENHEIM, LENORE
She's the kind we like to meet—
Personality from head to feet

HALLE, RITA
The old country's contribution to
the new

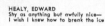

HAMERSCHLAG, HARRY   French
Auxilium, French Club, Ushers' Corps
He'll answer every question in history—
All of which to us is a mystery

HANDLEMAN, EVELYN
Pretty as a picture set,
She reminds us of Etta Kett

HEALY, EDWARD
Shy as anything but awfully nice—
I wish I knew how to break the ice

HERVEY, ELIZABETH
One in a million

HAMMERMAN, ROY   Service Squad,
Career Club, Lunch Squad, G.O. Office, Tennis Team, Swimming Squad
There is nothing that our Roy can't
do—
Without him the girls would all be
blue.

HAUSMAN, IRVING   Chem. Office,
Tumbling Team, Pin Committee
In the chem lab you'll find him on
the floor,
Cause he's been puttering around
with H_2SO_4

HEIT, JOSEPH   French Club, Spanish Club, French Auxilium, Portuguese Club
Finer fellow you cannot find,
Really sincere and refined

HERZFELD, MARILYN   Social Arts
Club, Mrs. O'Rourke's Office
Mickey's quiet and neat—
She's hard to beat

HIGGINS, MARGARET
Behind this mask of quiet bliss
There lives a charming, quiet miss

HIRSCH, HERBERT   Band, Intramural Basketball, Swimming Club,
Class President, Senior Messenger
(Official), Jazz Band
A sense of humor—it can't be beat
He's a guy you really ought to meet

HOFFMAN, ANITA   P. T. Office
Swim Office, A and P, Social Arts
Club
O my goodness! it must be a lie—
The Paramount bows when she goes
by.

HOLELA, NATHANIEL
Swimming Team, Prom Committee,
Swimming Monitor, Intramural Basketball Team, Lunch Squad
Swimming team member, to us he's
Big Nat
A swell guy to know, they'll all tell
you that

HIGH, VIVIAN   President of 5-7,
Swimming Office, Latin Auxilium,
Treasurer 8-1, Treasurer Senior Class
Always neat, always sweet—
A girl like Vivian is "alreet!"

HIRSCHFIELD, MURIEL   Spanish Office, Cherry Tree Rep., Grade Advisers' Office
Lovely to look at,
Delightful to know

HOLDER, HILDA   Basketball Club,
Leaders' Club, Swimming Club,
Dancing Club, Swimming Office
Stay as sweet as you are

HOROWITZ, DOROTHY
Dotty is quiet and rather shy—
Above all, she's a regular guy

Greenspan attended George Washington High School, two years behind Henry Kissinger.
He excelled in math but failed to shine in other areas because of his intense focus on music.
He appears here in his yearbook, second in the top row. The caption proclaims,
"Smart as a whip and talented, too. He'll play the sax and clarinet for you."

After high school, Greenspan toured the country with Henry Jerome and His Orchestra, playing saxophone and clarinet. Seated at far left, he never showed the confidence necessary to make it as a jazz soloist—an experience that reinforced his sense of himself as a shy "sideman."

THE Economic Society of the School of Commerce, Accounts and Finance, New York University, was founded in 1933.

The purposes of the Society is to further the study of economics among the student body. The organization has gone about accomplishing its objective by having open discussion among its members, research projects, and addresses by authorities both from within and outside the University. The faculty adviser to whom a great deal of appreciation is due is Mr. Joseph S. Keiper.

Both Professor Spahr and Dr. Backman have spoken before the Economic Society. This year the following economists have been scheduled as speakers: Rufus Tucker, General Motors Corporation; Edwin B. George, Dun & Bradstreet; Glenn Saxon, Yale University; Solomon Fabricant, National Bureau of Economic Research; A. D. Kaplan, Brookings Institution; Bradford B. Smith, United States Steel Corporation; and Martin R. Gainsbrough, National Industrial Conference Board.

ECONOMIC SOCIETY

President	Alan Greenspan
Vice-President	Martin Stoller
Treasurer	Barney Seligman
Secretary	Shirley Block

Greenspan enrolled at New York University at a time when Keynesian faith in government was at its peak, yet he nonetheless emerged as an anti-Keynesian. He served as the president of NYU's undergraduate Economic Society, seated at center.

Greenspan's strong relationship with his doting mother persisted into adulthood, giving him what Freud called "the feeling of a conqueror." President Ford joked that Greenspan would never commit to another woman until she died.

By his mid twenties, Greenspan was earning enough as an economic statistician to live the 1950s dream and move out to the suburbs. Although this was the heyday of the nuclear family and the baby boom, Greenspan's brief marriage broke down. He remained unmarried between the ages of 27 and 71.

From his late twenties, Greenspan forged an intense bond with the cult libertarian novelist Ayn Rand, who became a sort of second mother. He advised her on the economic passages in her monumental novel *Atlas Shrugged*, and shared her radical laissez-faire faith in untrammeled capitalism and the gold standard.

After the failure of his brief marriage, Greenspan embarked on
a long series of romances. Here pictured with Kathryn Eickhoff,
who was both a senior employee at his consultancy and his girlfriend.

Greenspan joined the Nixon campaign in 1967, offering libertarian policy advice and doubling as Nixon's polling analyst. Amid the riots that followed the assassination of Martin Luther King Jr., Greenspan persuaded Nixon that government spending in inner cities should be replaced by a push for "black capitalism."

Greenspan, right, served on President Nixon's financial reform commission, which argued that the dismantling of postwar regulation was inevitable and desirable. It took until the 1990s for the commission's recommendations to be adopted more or less fully.

In 1974, at the height of the Watergate scandal, Greenspan accepted Nixon's offer to serve in the White House. However, Nixon resigned before Greenspan was confirmed to the position.

Greenspan invited his mother, left, and Ayn Rand and her husband, right, to meet President Ford when he was sworn in as the chairman of the Council of Economic Advisers.

Greenspan forged a close relationship with Ford, becoming more influential than the Treasury secretary. His bonds with other Ford advisers, notably future vice president Dick Cheney, lasted for four decades. Pictured here with Ford on vacation in Vail, Colorado.

Greenspan battled back trouble for much of his life, still managing
to play tennis into his eighties. Pictured here on the floor
of the chief of staff's office at the White House.

In January 1975, Greenspan met Kaye Pullen, seated to his right,
at a meeting in the Oval Office. They soon began an on-off courtship
that lasted through the end of the Ford administration.

Greenspan began
dating the TV news
star Barbara Walters
after meeting her in
November 1975 at
a tea dance given by
the vice president.
Pictured here with
Henry Kissinger.

An Anglophile, Greenspan was close to several British
leaders. Pictured here with Queen Elizabeth, Prince Philip,
and Betty Ford, with Barbara Walters behind him.

While serving President Ford, Greenspan entrusted his consulting firm to a troika
of female vice presidents. The staff of Townsend-Greenspan is pictured here
on a visit to the White House. Kathryn Eickhoff is to Ford's immediate right.

Martin Anderson, pictured right, befriended Greenspan after meeting him with Ayn Rand during the 1960s. Anderson brought Greenspan into Nixon's campaign. Twelve years later, he did the same with the Reagan campaign, hoping that Greenspan could help the candidate absorb some understanding of economics.

At the Republican convention in 1980, Greenspan and Henry Kissinger tried to get Reagan to pick former president Ford as his running mate. For a few hours, this audacious project seemed likely to succeed, allowing Greenspan to realize his ambition of becoming Treasury secretary.

In August 1987, President Reagan nominated Greenspan to succeed Paul Volcker as Fed chairman. The choice owed much to Greenspan's strong bond with Treasury Secretary James Baker, pictured right. Critics suggested that Greenspan might be a political stooge with no stomach for inflation fighting.

Greenspan cemented the independence of the Fed by resisting pressure to cut interest rates during the George H. W. Bush administration. Despite the standoff, Bush nominated Greenspan for a second term, fearful that firing him would damage market confidence.

Bill Clinton's youth and political leanings set him apart from Greenspan.
But the two men bonded intellectually, making Greenspan
the most influential Fed chairman in its history.

Greenspan was invited to sit next to First Lady Hillary Clinton
at her husband's State of the Union address to signal his
support for Clinton's plan to cut the deficit.

Greenspan kept up an active tennis and golf schedule during his years
as Fed chairman. Pictured here with Treasury Secretary Lloyd Bentsen.

Greenspan began dating Andrea Mitchell of NBC in 1984. Pictured here in 1996, after Mitchell completed the New York Marathon.

Greenspan married Mitchell at a picturesque inn in Virginia. General Colin Powell, hero of the Gulf War, accused him of "sensual exuberance."

TIME

The Clintons: Their Future

Who Wrote Shakespeare?

THE COMMITTEE TO SAVE THE WORLD

The inside story of how the Three Marketeers have prevented a global economic meltdown so far

Rubin, Greenspan and Summers at the U.S. Treasury last Wednesday

www.time.com

After the successful management of the Asian financial crisis of 1997, and despite Russia's default in 1998, *Time* lauded Greenspan, Treasury Secretary Bob Rubin, and Deputy Secretary Lawrence Summers as "The Committee to Save the World." Even though Greenspan had actually questioned the bailouts, he dominated *Time*'s cover.

In January 2000, when Greenspan was nominated to his fourth term
as Fed chairman by President Clinton, his star was higher than ever.
At his confirmation hearing that month, Senator Phil Gramm
called Greenspan "the best central banker we have ever had."

Elected in 2000, George W. Bush quickly buried his father's
resentment of Greenspan, seeking to burnish his economic
credentials by embracing the Fed chairman.

Greenspan was sworn in to office for the fifth and final time by Vice President Dick Cheney, an old ally from the Ford administration. The ceremony took place at Ford's home in Colorado.

Greenspan shared a happy moment with the actor Andy Griffith as they attended a White House ceremony. To Greenspan's right is singer Aretha Franklin.

Greenspan's post-retirement memoir broke publishing records. Even Fidel Castro liked it.

As he prepared to leave office, Greenspan was showered with accolades, including the highest civilian award in the United States, the Presidential Medal of Freedom. The praise rendered the comedown after the 2008 crash all the more painful.

Kennedy Center Honors, a grand occasion at which the actress Bette Davis was to be among those feted. Andrea bought a special dress; this would be her biggest evening out since the White House state dinner for the Salvadoran president. But on the morning of the Honors, a Sunday, Alan got cold feet. He had a packed agenda the next day: a Fed board meeting in the morning, a lunch at the conservative American Enterprise Institute, meetings in the afternoon with Treasury Secretary Baker, with the number two at the German central bank, and with no less a figure than President Reagan. He had been up late for a dinner party at Andrea's on Saturday evening. Now he wanted to stay home and study.

"You what?" Andrea demanded, when Alan explained what he had decided. Quite apart from her own disappointment, Andrea shuddered to think what CBS's boss would make of his substitute social partner. Alan had passed his tickets for the Kennedy Honors on to Wayne Angell, the peppery Fed governor from Kansas with whom he played tennis. It was an act of social sacrilege, like failing to show up at your friend's wedding and deputizing a colleague.

"It's done," Alan answered. "I need to work. I cannot stay up late."[8]

These lulls in sociability were brief, however. That week following the Honors, after getting through his meeting with Reagan, Greenspan was in the swing again, dining with Barbara Walters at Washington's Madison Hotel on Tuesday and breakfasting with Henry Kissinger the next morning. Most weekends he would go to Manhattan, where he made amends with Laurence Tisch, golfing with him at the Century Club, an exclusive enclave some twenty miles north of the city. Tisch was a billionaire at a time when there were just a handful of billionaires in the entire nation, but he could spend an eternity lining up a twenty-five-cent putt. He had clearly worked hard for every penny he had earned, Greenspan liked to tease him.[9]

When he was not golfing in the suburbs, Greenspan would eat brunch with Felix Rohatyn, the boss of the investment bank Lazard Frères, and stay in touch with his cousin Wesley Halpert, who had led him on coin hunts on the beaches of Queens during boyhood vacations. Denied the opportunity to become a doctor by anti-Jewish quotas, Wesley had become a dentist, and Alan had become a conscientious patient. On several occasions each year, Greenspan would visit Wesley's town house at the very end of Fifty-third Street, on the eastern edge of Manhattan—sometimes he would go to the clinic on the lower level to get his teeth cleaned; sometimes he would go to Wesley's residence on the upper level to eat dinner. It was a case of Say's law, Greenspan later quipped. Supply creates its own demand, Jean-Baptiste Say had observed, a century before: by selling his wares and earning an income, a supplier becomes a consumer, thus boosting demand—including demand for his own output. In similar fashion, Wesley supplied the food that sullied his cousin's teeth, thereby ensuring Alan's continuing demand for his dental services.[10]

For his first year or two at the Fed, Greenspan maintained his apartment in the United Nations Plaza, which he had owned since he had first grown rich in the mid-1960s. He would stay there for a night or two, using it as a base for his golf games and his social rounds, but never failing to make time for visits to his mother. Now in her mideighties, Rose was a sad shadow of her former self: her mind remained clear, but she suffered from depression. Alan would make his way to her modest apartment on the West Side of Manhattan and sit with her in the living room that she seldom ventured from, struggling to fill the silences. He was still her brilliant son, the grown version of the handsome prodigy of half a century before—the boy with the even features and dark hair who solved math problems in his head to entertain the relatives. But now nothing made her eyes light up, not even her perfect progeny; as she confessed regretfully to him one day, his greatest successes had arrived when she could not take any pleasure in them. Alan would stay with Rose for an hour or so, doing his best to reverse the pattern he had always known. For the first sixty years of his life, she had been the one to illuminate the room with gaiety and chatter; now it was his turn to provide the sunshine, and it did not come easily. Presently he would rise and take his leave. But he expressed his love for her on every morning of her final years, faithfully telephoning her by nine o'clock, even if it meant setting an alarm when he was in a different time zone.[11]

As he entered his late eighties in his own turn, Greenspan recalled his mother's fading strength with a rare flicker of emotion. His mother's incapacity to enjoy his grand success was "pretty awful," he said, his voice thickening just slightly.[12]

D espite Candidate Bush's outburst at Walker's Point, Greenspan was in fact a monetary dove during his first year or so in office. He had arrived at the Fed determined to protect Volcker's inflation-fighting legacy, but the near-death experience of Black Monday altered his priorities.[13] Price stability now seemed to matter less than financial stability, at least for the time being, and Greenspan repeatedly resisted hawkish colleagues at the Fed who wanted to raise interest rates. "If we were to indicate that we were tightening, the shock to the markets I think would break the stock market," he worried to the Federal Open Market Committee in February 1988, explaining why the lowest jobless rate in nine years was not reason enough to raise borrowing costs. Three months later, the specter of financial fragility was still holding him back. "There is a stock market out there that I think could get pretty shabby," he fretted at the FOMC meeting in May—even though it had been more than half a year since the trauma of Black Monday.

Because of this preoccupation with financial stability, Greenspan committed the opposite error to the one that Bush accused him of. Far from squeezing the economy too much, he was allowing core inflation to accelerate, risking Volcker's legacy. Thanks to this monetary looseness, real estate prices started to take off—and by an irony apparently lost on Bush, the property mania raged especially fiercely in picturesque New England.[14] Describing the vice president at Walker's Point on that Memorial Day weekend, the *Washington Post* noted that the quaint little homes around the art galleries and seafood restaurants were fetching astronomical prices.[15] The Fed's loose monetary policy, aimed at managing the risks from fragile equities, was perversely encouraging New England's mortgage lenders to foment a new source of fragility.

With inflation showing up in consumer prices and housing, Greenspan came under pressure from his Fed colleagues. At the FOMC meeting following Memorial Day, Boston Fed president Frank Morris warned him bluntly about a "kind of euphoria in commercial building" in New England; and many of the other regional Fed presidents, who were less closely allied to the Reagan administration than the Fed governors in Washington, shared Morris's frustration with Greenspan's loose policy. After all, the economy had grown at a sizzling rate of 5.4 percent in the second quarter of 1988, and unemployment was now at its lowest level since the Nixon era. Another few months of rapid growth seemed certain to stoke even higher inflation. What was Greenspan waiting for?[16] A month later, at the start of August 1988, the discontent with Greenspan burst out into the open. The *New York Times* quoted a chorus of private economists who accused Greenspan of outright cowardice. "I think he's gun-shy," one critic said bluntly.[17]

Greenspan had won plaudits for his handling of the crash. But now, a year into his Fed chairmanship, his credibility was at stake. If the gun-shy label stuck, it could take years to unstick it.

Two days after the *Times*'s broadside, on Friday, August 5, 1988, Manley Johnson attended a parade at one of the capital's oldest landmarks, the Marine Barracks in southeast Washington. The ceremony honored James Baker, a former marine officer, who was resigning from the helm of the Treasury to take over Bush's campaign for election. Johnson made his way through the security check, past the young, white-gloved marines, and readied himself to watch the eerie, floating, ceremonial stride that these young warriors performed so earnestly.[18]

Johnson spotted one of Baker's deputies at the parade and approached him. He had a message to deliver. In the past forty-eight hours, the mood at the Fed had shifted. The chairman had held off on tightening for a surprisingly long time, but now Wall Street economists were accusing him of being chicken. That very morning, the critics had been fortified: strong data on employment had appeared, confirming that the economy was overheating.[19] The pressure for a rate hike was building, Johnson warned Baker's aide. The Treasury should brace itself.

The message should not have come as a surprise; by any objective measure, it was indeed time to tighten. But in keeping with the spirit of the Walker's Point declaration, the man from the Treasury pronounced himself aghast.[20] A rate hike now, three months ahead of the election, was exactly what the Bush camp was most dreading.

Two days later, on Sunday morning, Baker appeared on NBC's *Meet the Press*. The Treasury secretary wanted to discuss Bush's run for the White House, but the interviewer kept bringing up the Fed. How would the Bush campaign fare if Alan Greenspan chose this moment to tighten monetary policy?

"I think the Federal Reserve has done an extraordinarily good job of maintaining the balance between preserving growth on the one hand and being vigilant against inflation on the other," Baker hedged.

"But if they nudge interest rates upward because they feel it's necessary to control inflation—"

"You're asking me to talk with you about a hypothetical," interrupted Baker. "They have not said that they're going to do that."

Two days later, on Tuesday, August 9, the hypothetical became actual. The Fed marked the end of its post–Black Monday monetary looseness by hiking the publicly announced discount rate by half a percentage point. Greenspan had responded to his critics: he was not shy of his gun. But he had confirmed the Bush team's darkest fears. The Republican National Convention was a week away, and Bush was still trailing Michael Dukakis.

After the board meeting Greenspan went over to Baker's office at the Treasury.[21] If he was going to manage the political fallout from the rate hike, he had to warn Baker face to face, before the news of the Fed's move hit the newswires.

"I'm sure you're not going to be happy about this," Greenspan began after the two men sat down in Baker's office. "But after a long discussion of all the factors," he continued, "we arrived at a decision to raise the discount rate."[22]

"You just hit me right here," the Treasury secretary said, gesturing at his stomach.

"I'm sorry, Jim," Greenspan answered simply.

Baker began to roar and shout, but the Fed chairman stood his ground stoically.[23] There was a paradox about his personality: polite, soft-spoken, Greenspan hated to confront others; but when he found himself on the receiving end, he reacted perfectly serenely. His confidence in his own powers of judgment allowed him to shrug off abuse—to dismiss it as a pitiful symptom of his assailant's vulnerability. Perhaps, Greenspan reflected in this case, Baker was screaming so as to cover his own back; he needed to be in a position to assure Bush that he had protested the Fed's move with maximum ferocity. After more than a decade in and out of Washington, Baker had emerged as the ultimate pro. He never lost control, except in a controlled fashion.[24]

The following Sunday, Greenspan's guess was vindicated. Baker made another appearance on one of the morning TV shows, purring with professional composure. A higher discount rate was not so bad, he now maintained.[25] However much he might pressure the Fed behind the scenes, Baker evidently understood the case for cooling the economy.

Greenspan's interest-rate hike in the summer of 1988 ended up helping the vice president. The tightening was too mild to dampen the economy—after a slight deceleration in the third quarter of the year, growth roared back in the fourth one.[26] But the tightening did contribute to a turn in New England. The housing market cooled off at last: for the first time in five years, New England home prices lagged the national average. Happily for Bush, his opponent, Michael Dukakis, was the governor of Massachusetts; and Dukakis had made the prosperity of his home state a central theme of his campaign, so that the end of the New England boom ripped the core out of his message. Bush seized the opportunity to deride the vaunted "Massachusetts Miracle" as the "Massachusetts Mirage." By the middle of October, polls put the vice president comfortably ahead. Bush won the election in a landslide, aided by a Fed move that he had vehemently resisted.

It did not necessarily follow that Bush or his team would stop attacking Greenspan. Jim Baker understood enough to keep criticism private, but he was heading off to serve as secretary of state, where he would have nothing to do with monetary policy. His successor as Treasury secretary, Nicholas Brady, was a Wall Street executive with far less experience of Washington; he was high on courtesy and low on analytical rigor, and he had an Irish temper, like Greenspan's old antagonist Don Regan. A few days after the election, on November 18, Brady appeared on NBC's *Today* show, brimming with unsolicited monetary advice. "I don't see anything in the figures right now that would indicate that interest rates are going to rise," he said, brazenly ignoring the clear signs that growth was too high to be sustainable.[27]

Brady was not the only Bush adviser who promised trouble for Greenspan. The Fed chairman was also worried about his old supply-side adversary, Representative Jack Kemp, now frequently described as a future Republican president. Handsome, ebullient, and famous since his days as a young football pro, Kemp was seen as a youthful version of Reagan—another sunny crowd-pleaser from the entertainment industry. Kemp had no patience whatever with austerity of any kind, whether it arrived courtesy of higher taxes or higher interest rates. Awkwardly for Greenspan, he seemed set to take a job in the Bush cabinet.

On Thursday, December 1, 1988, Greenspan walked into Manley Johnson's office. He was looking a bit flustered.

"There must be some mistake," Greenspan began. That evening, Kemp's retirement from the House of Representatives was to be marked by a grand reception at the Omni Shoreham Hotel in northwest Washington. A thousand guests would be on hand, including President Ronald Reagan and President-elect George Bush. Greenspan had not received an invitation.

Johnson had a good relationship with Kemp, and Greenspan wanted his assistance. "Can you do me a favor and call up Jack and just make sure, you know, I know where my table is?" Greenspan asked Johnson.

Johnson did not see why Greenspan was so keen to go. Rubber-chicken dinners in cavernous ballrooms were nothing much to lust after. In fact, Johnson himself had been invited to the event but was thinking of skipping it.

"Why do you want to go?" Johnson asked. He suggested to Greenspan that he could show up in his place—there would be a free seat at his table.

Greenspan was not going to be left out of a power gathering like this one. He insisted to Johnson that he must have been invited in his own right. The address on the card must have been wrong; there had to be some error somewhere. But it was now already the midafternoon. He needed Johnson to call his buddy and straighten out the confusion.

Johnson tracked down Kemp in a suite at the hotel, where the honoree was getting ready.

"Jack, Alan thinks that there's been some kind of administrative screwup, you know, about his table, about his invitation to your event tonight and everything like that."

"There's no screwup; I didn't invite him," Kemp answered.

Johnson tried to humor his old friend. It was a mistake to exclude Greenspan.

Kemp pushed back. He didn't like Greenspan's economic views. The man was an enemy of supply-side tax cuts.

"That's petty, Jack," Johnson protested. "You know he wants to be at your event, and everybody in the administration is going to be there. He's the chairman of the Fed. You cannot not include him."

Kemp went around in circles a bit more, then eventually relented. "All right, tell him he can come."

"I'm not going to tell him that he can come. He's the chairman of the Fed. You tell him."

Kemp agreed, and that night Greenspan took his place among the throng at the Omni Shoreham.[28] The event raised big dollars for two conservative think tanks—tickets had sold at $1,000 a pop—and Kemp amused the crowd by passing a football to Reagan: the rising standard-bearer of tax-cut conservatism was linking up with the older one. The veteran conservative intellectual William F. Buckley Jr. stood up and compared Kemp's departure from Congress to "the retirement of Niagara Falls from Niagara."[29] Speaker after speaker paid tribute to Kemp's supply-side views. Jim Baker hailed Kemp as "the idea man behind the Reagan Revolution."

Surrounded by members of his own political party with whom he had little in common, Greenspan must have reflected on the challenges ahead. Thanks to Manley Johnson, he was physically inside the room. But he was intellectually estranged from it.

T wo weeks later, on December 13 and 14, Greenspan chaired an FOMC meeting. The news was not good—it was too good. The staff's Green-book, the briefing prepared ahead of each meeting, stressed that the economy was growing rapidly; inflation, already up to 4.2 percent, was set to continue rising. Greenspan's rate hike in August had evidently not been enough. Contrary to what Treasury Secretary Brady seemed to believe, interest rates might have to rise as much as two full percentage points to keep the lid on prices.[30]

Earlier that year, Greenspan had resisted rate hikes because of his fear for financial stability. Now the same dilemma raised its head again—although by now financial stability was about more than just the stock market.

"There is a whole set of risks that everybody around this table is familiar with—mostly in the financial area, thrifts, LDCs, LBOs, etc., etc.," observed Ed Boehne, the president of the Philadelphia Fed. He was referring to the bogeymen who had spooked the monetary establishment for some years: LDCs (or less developed countries) had yet to crawl out from under their collapsing debts, while LBOs (or leveraged buyouts) were still propping up the stock market. Raising interest rates might be the right policy to combat inflation, but American corporations and consumers had piled up mountains of debt.[31] If the Fed tightened abruptly, there would be an epidemic of bankruptcies.

John LaWare, the Fed governor who took the lead on financial regulation, echoed Boehne's anxieties. "I've got a metallic taste in my mouth when I start trying to quantify—and this is the difficult part—the implications on these fragile elements in our financial system of a 200 basis point rise in interest rates," he said. "More recently, we've had the question of real estate overhang. A higher set of interest rates is obviously going to at least prolong the resolution of that overhang." If New England mortgage lenders had behaved recklessly during the boom, a higher cost of funds was the last thing they needed.

Greenspan listened to his colleagues' concerns—and more or less ignored them. It was a striking turnaround: financial fragility now mattered less to him than controlling inflation. More than a year had passed since Black Monday, and the sustained tranquility of the stock market had taught him a lesson: if the imperatives of financial stability and price stability were pulling him in different ways, he could prioritize stable prices, knowing that if markets crashed he had the power to contain the damage. Moreover, the warning of the previous August stuck in his mind: if Wall Street came to believe that he was gun-shy, inflation expectations would rise, and it would take enormous effort to force them back down again. The future central-bank consensus—that price stability trumped other objectives—was not yet entrenched. But it was taking shape beneath the surface.

After some back-and-forth around the table, Greenspan prevailed upon his FOMC colleagues to set their financial-stability concerns aside and raise the federal funds rate.[32] A month later, on January 24, 1989, the chairman defended his move in testimony before the House of Representatives, and his tone made it clear that more tightening was coming.[33] But the day after that testimony, Greenspan reaped the inevitable whirlwind. No less a figure than the newly inaugurated president went out of his way to slap him: "I haven't talked to Alan lately, but I don't want to see us move so strongly against fear of inflation that we impede growth," Bush told the *New York Times*. "We have to keep expanding opportunities for the working men and women of this country."[34]

It was the Walker's Point declaration, all over again. No matter how low unemployment went, it could never fall enough in Bush's eyes. If Greenspan was going to emulate the Churchillian Volcker, the new president would retaliate by emulating Nixon's Fed bashing.

On Sunday, February 5, 1989, Greenspan made his way over to the White House for an evening meeting. The president's economic advisers were waiting for him in the Roosevelt Room to discuss a secret contingency plan. Their boss was getting ready to unveil a savings-and-loan rescue the next day—the stresses at the S&Ls had finally triggered federal action. At a cost of $90 billion, the S&L bailout would be the largest financial rescue in American history, and there was a risk it could go wrong: the announcement might ignite panic, alerting customers to the weakness of the thrifts, and trigger a run on deposits. The president's advisers wanted Greenspan's assurance that if the worst happened, the Fed would prop up the S&Ls with emergency loans, even though the thrifts were technically outside the Fed's safety net.[35] They also wanted Greenspan to sit behind Bush when he announced the plan. He would not have to speak, but they needed him in the camera shot.[36]

Greenspan assented on both counts. He was willing to backstop the S&Ls, and he was willing to be photographed. His libertarian rejection of bailouts was long gone; what he wanted above all was the space to fight inflation. If the Fed chairman could help the administration deal with the thrifts, perhaps it would cut him slack on monetary policy.

The day after the bailout was announced, the FOMC convened for its next meeting. The tension between the Fed's inflation-fighting objective and its financial-stability objective was even more acute than usual. One governor noted that raising interest rates would have the effect of "taking some of the modestly solvent and profitable thrifts and throwing them over on the other pile."[37] A regional Fed president chimed in that an increase in borrowing costs of just half a percent would saddle S&Ls with additional losses of about $1 billion—losses that taxpayers would be forced to swallow.[38] Moreover, if tighter monetary policy led to a recession, newly unemployed homeowners would default on their mortgages, compounding the S&Ls' problems.[39] Black Monday had been scary because it had happened so fast, but the remedy had proved relatively simple. By contrast, the slow-burning S&L mess could be far more expensive to taxpayers.

If the S&L crisis presented one obstacle to higher interest rates, the Fed was also hamstrung by its own internal confusion. Paul Volcker's early tenure had coincided with the ascendancy of monetarism, which simplified and clarified the FOMC's mission—to deliver stable growth of money. Now, in the Greenspan era, the Fed found itself in a doctrinal no-man's-land.[40] Officially, the Fed still operated in a monetarist fashion: it steered the economy by tinkering with the supply of credit. Unofficially, the Fed's attention was shifting from the quantity of credit to its price—from the money supply to the interest rate. Legally, the Fed was supposed to target full employment as well as stable prices. Practically, it had decided that its priority should be to bring down inflation—but nobody was sure how far or how quickly. The committee was also uncertain about its stance on exchange rates. In the late 1980s, some major central banks used monetary policy to manage their currencies rather than domestic economic conditions. The Fed, for the most part, was not in the currency-targeting camp, but Greenspan and his colleagues sometimes felt they should react to the level of the dollar.

Midway through the February 1989 meeting, Lee Hoskins, the president of the Cleveland Fed, hinted at a way out of this fog. The Fed should be clearer about its intentions—both to itself and to the public. Monetary policy, to be successful, needed an anchor—for a long time the Fed had been guided by its promise to maintain the dollar-gold link; later, following a disastrous period of confusion that had opened the door to stagflation, the Fed had been guided by its promise to maintain stable growth of money. Now, if it was not returning to the earlier anchors, the Fed needed a new one. It should announce an explicit inflation target.

Hoskins was airing an idea that would come to be embraced by central banks the world over. Only a few months later, at the end of 1989, New Zealand became the first convert, enshrining an inflation target in law and granting the central bank the independence from political interference that would make the target achievable.[41] Given the pressure on the Fed from the Bush administration, the attractions of a New Zealand–style bargain were obvious: if the Fed formally committed to an inflation target, it would have a potent excuse to ignore White House demands for lower interest rates. But when Hoskins raised the idea of an inflation target in February 1989, he did not win the argument.

Don Kohn, the head of the Fed's Division of Monetary Affairs, pushed back. Speaking with the implicit backing of Greenspan, he cautioned, "It's what we do more than what we say—read our actions rather than our lips." Besides, there was a risk in announcing a formal inflation target, Kohn pointed out. The Fed might miss the target through no fault of its own—a drought or a war could push inflation up, even if monetary policy was perfect. If the Fed committed to a target and then missed, it would squander credibility.[42]

With confusion as to its monetary tools, no clarity about its inflation target, and with the competing objectives of financial stability and exchange-rate management threatening to encroach, the Fed seemed to be adrift, laying itself open to a humiliating repeat of the inflationary 1970s. As Arthur Burns had argued in Belgrade in 1979, intellectual uncertainty among monetary experts made it harder for a central bank to stand up to pressure from the politicians. But precisely when the Fed appeared most vulnerable, Greenspan proved himself most resolute. In the two weeks after the February 1989 meeting, he raised the federal funds target no fewer than three times, delivering a cumulative jolt of three quarters of a percentage point. On February 24, the Fed hiked the publicly disclosed discount rate for good measure, and instructed bank examiners to discourage certain types of loans—a measure that would restrict real estate lending, exacerbating the crash in New England. Ignoring the warning contained in the Walker's Point declaration, and discounting his colleagues' anxiety about precarious S&Ls, Greenspan leaped from low-key, incremental tightening to an aggressive show of force. Unlike his mentor Arthur Burns, he was not going to be intimidated.

The paradox of February 1989 went unremarked by contemporaries.

The Greenspan Fed had rejected a proposal to impose clarity on its doctrinal confusion—to replace gold targeting and money targeting with inflation targeting. But even as it rejected inflation targeting in theory, it was inching toward it in practice. At a time of maximum danger for the S&Ls, Greenspan was ready to raise interest rates. Price stability trumped financial stability.

George Bush swallowed the shock of three successive interest-rate hikes as calmly as he could, masking his annoyance behind jocular teasing. On March 6, 1989, when Greenspan celebrated his sixty-third birthday, he received a card embossed with the presidential seal. "Dear Alan, Happy Birthday!" it began. "May you have many happy returns and may all your days ahead be full of low inflation and yes low interest rates—long and short term."[43] Pressure applied jokingly could be jokingly shrugged off; and Greenspan kept the card appreciatively, filing it with various letters from Presidents Ford and Reagan. But if the Fed's February tightening had its intended effect, the economy would cool and more S&Ls would fail. The message from the White House was likely to get sharper.

Two days after his birthday, on March 8, Alan flew with Andrea to London. They checked into one of the Marriott hotels—Alan's commitment to upholding the integrity of the dollar extended to buying American. On Thursday and Friday, the couple fitted in a little time together between meetings, but the highlight came on Saturday. Alan was to see Margaret Thatcher, the bracing free-market icon he had met during the Ford years. When his audience with the prime minister was over, Alan and Andrea were to stay at the country home of Robin Leigh-Pemberton, the governor of the Bank of England.

A limousine arrived to fetch Greenspan and Leigh-Pemberton on Saturday morning. It headed northwest out of London, into the exurban countryside, arriving at the prime minister's sixteenth-century country residence in time for lunch. Then entering her final eighteen months in office, Mrs. Thatcher was in the mature stage of her public life; and whereas Greenspan remained modest in his manner and increasingly moderate in his opinions, power had only magnified the prime minister's Napoleonic demeanor. Over lunch and afterward, Mrs. Thatcher congratulated Greenspan for the Fed's record on inflation, repeatedly turning to her own central bank chief to demand why he had failed to perform as competently. The hectoring continued well into the afternoon, and somewhere in the English countryside, Andrea sat imprisoned in a Bank of England car, circling aimlessly. Her driver was under instructions not to deliver Ms. Mitchell to the Leigh-Pemberton estate until the governor was in a position to receive her; and as the afternoon progressed, her hapless host evidently remained stuck in the prime minister's clutches. Eventually, word came that Ms. Mitchell would be received by Mrs. Leigh-Pemberton alone, and Andrea was given tea and shown to her room—a room exclusively for her, as her nonhusband would sleep elsewhere. It was early evening by the time Greenspan and Leigh-Pemberton arrived. The Englishman headed straight to the drinks cabinet and poured himself a neat whiskey.[44]

In the second quarter of 1989, the Fed's February tightening began to have its intended effect on the economy. Growth began at last to slow—in some places, abruptly. New England's bubbly economy was hit hardest: with real estate prices no longer rising, construction workers could not find jobs, and debt-laden firms began to miss their payments. The *Boston Globe* detailed a dramatic rise in New England's bankruptcy filings, and a go-go mortgage lender named Eliot Savings Bank, which had boasted during the boom years that it did "deals the other banks thought were crazy," collapsed ignominiously.[45] New Hampshire's bankruptcy court was so overwhelmed that torrents of paperwork piled up in cardboard boxes stacked around the floors of the courthouse.

At first the blowback appeared limited. In early May, following the news that unemployment had risen, the CEA chairman, Michael Boskin, wrote to the president: "We need to be prepared to (quietly) nudge the Fed to ease if this slowdown is other than temporary."[46] The administration refrained from public attacks on the Fed; and thanks to the resolute February rate hikes, Wall Street commentators who had deplored the gun-shy chairman now sounded respectful. "I think Alan Greenspan is the best Federal Reserve chairman we have had in the postwar period, bar none," one gushed. "If he gets us through this [period] with a soft landing—that is, with a slowdown in growth without a recession—I'll underscore my comment."[47] Hoping to achieve such a soft landing, Greenspan cut the federal funds rate slightly in June and again in July. He had squeezed the economy enough to slow it down. Now he felt ready to resume easing.

On Friday, August 11, Greenspan headed off for a long weekend on Nantucket, where he stayed at the home of Senator John Heinz, ketchup heir and moderate Republican. Turning on the television to watch the Sunday morning talk shows, Greenspan saw Dick Darman, Bush's budget director, on NBC's *Meet the Press*. Darman had been James Baker's deputy at the Reagan White House and later at Treasury; he was one of the smartest operatives in Washington, but not one of the most modest. By force of personality and intellect, he frequently eclipsed the amiable Treasury secretary, Nicholas Brady, whom one commentator dismissed as "the nice man serving as Treasury secretary until Dick Darman takes over."[48] Darman's fans—foremost among them, Darman himself—agreed that he was shrewd, charming, and extremely funny. He was also lethal to be on the wrong side of.[49]

On this particular morning, Darman was gunning for Greenspan. The Fed, he suggested, "may have been a little bit too tight." Then he added a warning. "If we do have a recession, I think it will be because they erred on the side of caution."[50]

Greenspan was shocked. "What!?" he protested at the television screen.[51] Raising the bogeyman of a recession seemed gratuitous; despite the slowdown in New England and the trouble at the S&Ls, nationwide growth was still running at a healthy rate of 3 percent or so. Nor did Greenspan need a lecture about high interest rates; he had already begun cutting them. Perversely, Darman was going to achieve the opposite of what he claimed to want. By agitating for a cut in interest rates, he would make it impossible for Greenspan to deliver without compromising the Fed's independence.

Jack Kemp, by now installed as Bush's secretary for Housing and Urban Development, scribbled a felt-tipped message to Darman. "D.D. You are the 1st ever to take them on! You're right & I (we) thank you— J.K."[52] Then, realizing he had missed an opportunity for a football metaphor, Kemp fired off another note. "Dick—You're the Q.B. who can lead us to victory! Don't give up—Your 'right tackle' Jack."[53]

Fearing that Darman's example might encourage copycat attacks, Greenspan opened a correspondence with him, flattering the budget director by appearing to take his monetary ideas seriously. If Darman felt he had a private line to the Fed chief, he might be less likely to go public with his criticisms. But the challenge posed by Darman was not so easily contained. Greenspan soon found himself confronted by a fresh round of attacks—this time from inside his committee.

Nine days after Darman's outburst, on August 22, Boston Fed president Richard Syron confronted his colleagues with more trouble from New England.[54] The losses at the S&Ls were now spreading to the larger banks, setting off a vicious cycle. As New England's lenders faltered, they extended fewer loans; fewer loans meant lower growth; lower growth meant yet more bankruptcies, which weakened the lenders further. The region was suffering the full force of a real estate hangover.[55]

"I may be stretching a point, but I think there may be a little lesson from the region," Syron suggested in his strong Boston accent.[56] Once New England's bubble had burst, it had set off a chain reaction that no policy could halt. If this sequence repeated itself across the country, Greenspan's hopes for a national soft landing could look quaint in hind sight. Cleaning up after an equity bubble was one thing. Cleaning up after a housing bubble might be quite another.

Two months after Syron sounded the alarm about housing, the Fed confronted another shock from the financial system. With the growth slowdown that summer, investors had begun to worry about junk bonds, the high-yielding debt used to finance corporate takeovers. On Friday, October 13, 1989, the jitters came to a head with the collapse of one of the largest leveraged deals of the decade, the $6.75 billion buyout of United Airlines. The collapse screamed out that the buyout boom was over. The Dow Jones Industrial Average ended the day down nearly 7 percent—a far bigger drop than it had registered on the Friday before Black Monday.

Wall Street's warriors went home for the weekend, asking themselves what the next Monday would be like. The answer arrived sooner than expected. On Sunday morning the *Washington Post* and the *New York Times* quoted an anonymous "senior Fed official" who pledged, "Markets will be able to count on us to make sure the financial system stays liquid." The Fed had apparently decided to rerun its old playbook from 1987. The markets would not be permitted to freeze up. There was no reason to panic.

Greenspan had no difficulty guessing the source of the news stories. On Saturday, Manley Johnson had suggested a liquidity pledge, arguing that the Fed should get out ahead of stock market instability rather than waiting for a meltdown, as it had in 1987. Greenspan had rejected Johnson's pitch, objecting that there was no need to promise a safety net preemptively. Staging a rescue when all other options had been exhausted was one thing; conditioning investors to expect support at the first sign of trouble was quite another. Johnson had evidently ignored Greenspan and taken his case to the newspapers.[57]

Gerald Corrigan read the Sunday newspapers and called Greenspan from New York. As a veteran Fed official, Corrigan pronounced himself outraged; the leak shattered the Fed's tradition of vigorous internal debate and limited external communication. Of course, the anonymous senior official was correct: if Monday brought a full-blown crash, the New York Fed stood ready to supply the markets with liquidity. But Corrigan did not like having his hand forced by news stories.

Greenspan overcame his normal aversion to confrontation, and let Johnson know that he was angry. He never heated up enough to raise his voice; he turned cold and icy. The Fed's firepower was limited, he told Johnson; it was not to be wasted on panicky leaks to the newspapers. Besides, no central bank should train markets to assume there was a floor under equity prices; if speculators thought that the Fed had their backs, their bets would only grow wilder.[58] By the end of his tenure, Greenspan would come to be remembered as the creator of the "Greenspan put"—a reference to the put options that traders buy to limit their potential losses. But in 1989, Greenspan was furious with Johnson for announcing such a put in public.

On the Monday following the minicrash, tourists and camera crews clustered outside the stock exchange like rubbernecking witnesses at some motorway disaster. "I feel like I'm watching a car accident," said a twenty-four-year-old New Yorker waiting to get into the visitors gallery.[59] Tan-coated sentries guarded the entrances to the stock exchange. Across the street, anarchist squatters from a nearby park carried placards that read: SELL TODAY, JUMP TOMORROW.

Greenspan watched the clock tick down to the market's 9:30 a.m. opening. On the phone with him were the rest of the FOMC members, whom he had convened by conference call.

"One gets the impression of looking at a Cape Canaveral blastoff," Greenspan joked. Then he turned serious.

"Those articles in the *Washington Post* and the *New York Times* yesterday were not authorized releases," he said pointedly. "They were not done by myself nor anyone I'm aware of."

Corrigan weighed in. The leaks were "undermining discipline in the marketplace." They were "amateurish." They "cut right at the very heart of the Federal Reserve," he said menacingly.

Manley Johnson kept quiet, grateful that nobody was calling him out by name. Greenspan might have little stomach for confrontation, he reflected grimly to himself, but the pit bull from New York took care of that department for him. Still, Johnson could at least console himself that his policy would prevail. By speaking to the newspapers, he had created a fait accompli—thanks to the expectations he had stoked, the Fed felt compelled to supply more money to the markets.[60] When the stock market opened, Fed intervention duly calmed investors' nerves. Buoyed by the Manley Johnson put, Wall Street recovered.

Later that day, Greenspan went over to the *Washington Post* building, where he was met in the lobby by the newspaper's Fed reporter, John Berry. Greenspan knew Berry well: of all the journalists covering the Fed, Greenspan gave the uncomplicated Berry most access, finding in him a useful means to get his message out to Congress and the markets. The two men rode the elevator to the executive dining room, where they were greeted by the *Post*'s proprietor, Katharine Graham. The grande dame of Washington society had befriended Greenspan, introducing him to Meg Greenfield, the *Post*'s editorial page editor, and to Warren Buffett, the famed investor and *Post* shareholder. Greenspan would sometimes go over to Greenfield's house on the northern edge of Georgetown for parties; and every year after the Gridiron Club dinner—an elite Washington ritual that brought together media barons and public figures—he would team up with Warren Buffett to present his views on the economy to a select group of *Post* guests and advertisers. For a man who deplored his colleague's leaks to reporters, Greenspan was remarkably cozy with the media.[61]

Sitting in the *Post*'s executive reception room, Greenspan assured Berry and his colleagues that the minicrash was behind them. But over the next months, the challenge of financial fragility persisted. Investors' withdrawal from junk bonds exacerbated a larger problem: creditors of all kinds were scared of lending. Regional Fed presidents swapped stories of small businesses stymied by tightfisted banks; home builders were scrambling for funding; in February 1990, Drexel Burnham Lambert, the investment house that had pioneered junk bonds, collapsed, with the Fed resisting entreaties to save it. Amid this drying-up of credit, growth slipped to under 1 percent. The recession predicted by Darman began to seem all too possible.

By the spring of 1990, Greenspan's record at the Fed was the mirror of his reputation later. After a brief period as the gun-shy chairman in the wake of Black Monday, he had emerged as the hard man who stood up to the White House and to the doves within his own monetary policy committee who wanted to cut interest rates. Greenspan had shown he could be hard on Wall Street, too, opposing the Manley Johnson put and allowing Drexel to go down without assistance. Critics who later scolded Greenspan for a monetary policy that enabled bubbles, and for a regulatory stance that permitted Wall Street to run wild, seldom reckoned with this early part of his tenure. Given the pressure from the Bush administration, the intellectual confusions about monetary policy, and the scary fragility of finance, Greenspan might have been expected to go soft— especially because the public had lost its appetite for the fight against inflation.[62] But instead of buckling, Greenspan hung tough. He raised the discount rate on the eve of the Republican convention in the summer of 1988. He brushed off warnings from a popular new president by hiking the federal funds rate after Bush's inauguration in 1989. And the following August, when the formidable White House budget director came after him on television, Greenspan adamantly declined to budge, even as New England's bubble imploded and S&Ls failed across the nation.[63]

Seven years earlier, when Paul Volcker had been in the thick of the inflation fight, the Reagan administration had repaid him with whispers that he would not be reappointed. In March 1990, the Bush White House dealt with Greenspan the same way: an anonymous White House source confided to the *Los Angeles Times* that the Fed chairman would be gone when his term expired the next summer. Greenspan's offense, the anonymous source specified, was his obstinate failure to cut rates—a failure that cruelly undermined a president who deserved better. The way the White House saw things, Bush had made the tough decision to clean up the S&Ls, a mess that he had not created. He did not deserve a monetary policy that drove more S&Ls under and raised the cost of the bailout, thereby expanding the budget deficit and forcing Bush to contemplate a tax hike that would undo the central pledge of his campaign—"Read my lips, no new taxes," the candidate had promised famously. The *LA Times* quoted a "longtime" Bush adviser who confided that the president was "mad as hell" with the chairman. "I can't believe he will reappoint him and I don't know a soul in the White House who thinks he will," the adviser declared bluntly.[64]

During the weeks after the press leak, Greenspan stood his ground firmly. Because he refused to bend on monetary policy, the cost of the S&L cleanup increased, and the budget deficit ballooned alarmingly. At the end of June 1990, the president invited congressional leaders to a breakfast in the White House family dining room; and after some intensive horse-trading, the outline of a deficit-reduction strategy emerged—some of the gap would be closed by cutting government spending, but there was no way around the need to raise more revenues from citizens. An aide scratched out a summary of the agreement on a yellow legal pad; soon the president's three-word campaign centerpiece of "no new taxes" had fallen victim to 130 words posted on a bulletin board outside the White House press room.[65] The president had been forced into a U-turn. He was ready to raise taxes after all.

The backlash was not long in coming. The Republican faithful who had worked for Bush's election felt betrayed: "Read my lips: Bush blew it," seethed a prominent conservative in the *Washington Post*. "This essentially guarantees a conservative challenge to Bush in 1992," he added, anticipating a bruising contest in the upcoming Republican primaries.[66] But Bush's policy climbdown was momentous for another reason, too. Since the time of the Walker's Point declaration, he had made a public show of taking on the Fed; yet now he was retreating ignominiously. Arthur Burns's Belgrade lecture had been turned upon its head. Rather than the president's forcing compliance from the central bank, the central bank had stood its ground, obliging the president to abandon his campaign promise.

Eighteen

"YOU'RE THE BIG GURU"

The first signs of war came from a helium-filled surveillance balloon gliding high above the Mutla Ridge outside Kuwait City.[1] As the balloon hurled radar waves at the dark desert floor, the blips on the screen of its American operator coalesced into a picture of menace: 80,000 troops from Iraqi leader Saddam Hussein's Republican Guard were pouring into Kuwait under the cover of the night, streaming south toward the emirate's capital. Within minutes, alerts went out to Washington that an invasion was under way. By that afternoon, Kuwait City had fallen and Iraqi forces were streaming toward Kuwait's oil fields.

Two weeks later, on August 17, 1990, Andrea Mitchell headed off to the Gulf as part of the Pentagon press pool. She was of two minds about leaving Alan, even for a short trip.[2] Five years after their first date at Le Périgord, he had finally moved into her house on a quiet, wooded street, bringing not much more than the collection of technical books that had come with him from New York; and she was thoroughly enjoying life as the more talkative half of Washington's leading power couple. But she also wanted, or needed, to be covering the big story; and soon she was trailing Defense Secretary Dick Cheney as he bounced between Saudi Arabia and the smaller Gulf sheikhdoms. At one point, in a break between sessions in elaborate royal palaces, Cheney visited U.S. troops at an airfield, and his entourage followed in a fleet of limousines and buses. Emerging from the air-conditioned vehicles into the blazing desert was like walking into an oven. A crowd of airmen standing in front of their barracks shouted, "Tell them to send pillows."[3]

While Andrea was covering Cheney, Alan also enjoyed access to him. Greenspan had known the defense secretary as the quietly effective chief of staff in Ford's White House, and had befriended him over indulgent feasts at Le Steak, a Washington institution mainly known for its enormous plates of salty french fries.[4] The two had stayed in touch via get-togethers with ex-President Ford, including policy symposia in the Colorado mountains; and Alan and Andrea would sometimes go out for dinner with the defense chief and his wife, Lynne, a prolific conservative author.[5] Greenspan and Cheney had watched each other climb life's ladder separately but in parallel, and each recognized within the other the ingredients of his own ascent. Cheney, like Greenspan, had risen by dint of intelligence, diligence, and attention to detail; his position at the pinnacle of American life served to validate Greenspan's, for it showed that talent and hard work were properly rewarded. Beyond this special bond connecting like-minded success stories, Greenspan and Cheney were drawn to each other by a mutual interest. Each man recognized the other as a man who knew. An exchange of ideas would profit both of them.

Now, with a military crisis looming over the economy, Greenspan wanted Cheney's insights on the likelihood of further conflict. Already oil prices had spiked nearly 12 percent on the day of the invasion and climbed a further 30 percent over the ensuing two weeks; to any economic forecaster with open eyes, the prospect of a full-blown war against Iraq was the elephant in the room.[6] Greenspan could remember how production had surged and slowed in response to the wars in Korea and Vietnam; regular conversations with Cheney now would keep him abreast of the key unknown in the economy. But a private line to Cheney served another function, too, providing Greenspan with an invaluable weapon in his long-running struggle with his own colleagues.

Three years into his tenure, Greenspan had mostly prevailed in these struggles, just as he had seen off the pressure from the White House. He had shown himself capable of challenging the Fed staff's economic forecasts, matching the technicians in his command of statistics. He had captured the credit for the Black Monday rescue, whether or not he entirely deserved it. He had lived down the accusation that he was a gun-shy chairman, and gone toe to toe with an elected president. But by the time of Kuwait's invasion, he was on the back foot. The FOMC faction that favored lower interest rates, partly for fear of the impact of a recession on the nation's fragile banks, was growing more insistent as the economy softened—the National Bureau of Economic Research would later determine that a recession had begun in July 1990, on the eve of the Kuwait invasion. With the White House and the Treasury likewise clamoring for lower interest rates, an uprising against Greenspan could not be ruled out. Volcker had been outvoted by his fellow governors at the Fed. Greenspan could not take dominance for granted.

A few days after Andrea set off with Cheney, on August 21, Greenspan presided over the next FOMC meeting. The case for cutting interest rates was in one sense stronger than ever: if the U.S. economy had been flailing under the impact of the credit crunch before Kuwait's invasion, the outlook now was surely worsening. Rising oil prices would claim a growing share of Americans' spending, leaving less demand for U.S. products; and geopolitical uncertainty would hurt bonds and stocks, raising the cost of capital to companies. Already a falling bond market had raised long-term borrowing costs by more than 50 basis points: Saddam Hussein had effectively tightened U.S. monetary policy without the Fed's doing anything.[7] But rather than supporting the economy and countering the Saddam effect by cutting short-term interest rates, Greenspan wanted to be tough. Inflation was accelerating, and might accelerate still further with oil prices heading up.[8] For a Fed chairman who wanted more than anything to remain credible as an inflation foe, the challenge was how to keep monetary policy tight without losing colleagues' backing.

When the FOMC debate got under way, several members sounded the alarm about the weakening economy. "People are poorer; they have less money to spend; their wealth is reduced," one governor remarked, before expounding on the difficulty of borrowing—"The junk bond market is gone; the banks are not forthcoming."[9]

As to the Kuwait invasion, the committee seemed not to know quite what to make of it. Mike Prell encouraged people to consider the budgetary angle. War might expand the federal deficit.

"The increment is less than a couple of Texas S&Ls, presumably?" one of the governors asked, dismissively.

"That's true," Prell conceded.

When it was his turn to speak, Greenspan transformed the tone of the discussion. He did not want to dwell on how weak the economy might be, because he did not want to cut interest rates. Instead, he delivered a lecture on the situation in the Gulf, which his colleagues had passed over so airily.

"The crucial issue confronting us right at the moment is that the odds of an actual war in the Middle East are 50-50," Greenspan announced, his voice laden with the confidence of someone who has special information. "If you look at the form of the buildup that we're engaged in there, it's fairly apparent that this is not a military establishment that is going to sit there for a very long period," he said, displaying a feel for the difficulty of keeping large numbers of men in the blistering heat. "We are bringing in fairly significant tactical offensive weapons. The chances of this all positioning itself and doing nothing and Saddam backing down easily have to be on the low side."

If Saddam Hussein seemed unlikely to back down, the same was true for the United States, Greenspan explained to the committee. Saudi Arabia's oil refineries were clustered in an area not far from Kuwait, rendering them vulnerable to attacks launched from Iraq's new bases; some Iraqi pilots had already volunteered for kamikaze raids, Greenspan confided to his colleagues. Saddam Hussein's ability to threaten Saudi Arabia, coupled with his control over Kuwait's oil, would pose unacceptable risks to U.S. energy security. "If Saddam is perceived to be increasing his power and his clout and his control over the West, he is going to be able to name OPEC's level of output. He has terrorist groups out there and he can control Indonesia and every far-flung oil producer in the world." In Greenspan's opinion, Saddam had to be confronted.[10]

Having cowed his colleagues with his military insights, Greenspan advanced his monetary prescription: do nothing. It was a surprising bottom line: the prospect of war presumably increased the odds of a recession. But Greenspan spun an elaborate story about how a do-nothing policy would send a reassuring signal to the world. "It is crucial that there be some stable anchor in the economic system," he declared, equating stability with inactivity. "It's clearly not going to be on the budget side," he said, alluding to the inconclusive negotiations between the Bush White House and Congress about the implementation of the president's tax U-turn. "It has to be the central bank. It's got to be we!"

Greenspan's appeal for Zen-like stillness, not to mention his grammatical flourish, impressed Richard Syron, the normally hardheaded president of the Boston Fed. "I think of the whole situation in a sort of 'BS,' Before Saddam, and 'AS,' After Saddam, way," he mused gravely. Before the invasion of Kuwait, Syron had favored lower interest rates. But after listening to Greenspan, he saw the case for yogic immobility. "I must confess to being somewhat dismayed by your odds," he continued, referring to Greenspan's assessment of the prospects of a war against Saddam. But then he added hastily, "I'm not disagreeing with them because I'm sure you know more than we do."

Some members of the FOMC were less entranced than Syron. "Doing nothing so as to do no harm is one side of the coin," one conceded. "The other side of that coin is paralysis."[11] Greenspan's claim that inactivity would promote stability seemed puzzling, to be polite; clearly there could be times when stability demanded action. But although several FOMC members seemed bemused by Greenspan's do-nothing prescription, they lacked the confidence to second-guess him. When it came to the military outlook, Greenspan clearly had the upper hand. He had staked out a preference for leaving interest rates unchanged, and nobody felt sure enough to challenge him.

Pressing his geopolitical advantage one final time, Greenspan appealed to the FOMC members for unity. "I don't think I have asked specifically for support in a large number of meetings, going back a number of years," he told his colleagues; "I'm not saying that people should violate what they think are their principles." But on this particular occasion he demanded deference. "This is the type of meeting in which it would be helpful if we had a very substantial consensus," he instructed, as though the prospect of war demanded monetary unity—for reasons that experienced statesmen would apparently find obvious.

When the secretary called the roll, Greenspan won unanimously. Interest rates would not be cut, despite the fact that the economy was in recession. So long as inflation posed a threat, Greenspan was not going to risk a looser policy.

The day after the FOMC meeting, Greenspan called Dick Darman at the White House. If he did not give the formidable budget director a chance to berate him privately, Darman was likely to go after the Fed in public. The previous summer, with growth running at 3 percent, Greenspan had shrugged off Darman's televised attack. Now, with the economy weaker, that might not be so easy.

Greenspan explained that he had not cut interest rates this time, but that he was "in the mode to." "The CPI set us back," he told Darman, referring to the latest signs of inflation from the consumer price index. There had also been "concern about the dollar," whose recent decline would be accelerated if the Fed cut interest rates. But Greenspan assured Darman that he was "still looking for an opportunity to ease." The fact that any central banker anywhere could describe himself in these terms was not something Greenspan emphasized.[12]

Darman seethed on the other end of the phone line.[13] He was sometimes described as the most ruthless Washington infighter since Kissinger, but like Kissinger before him, he was finding Greenspan to be a worthy adversary. The Fed chairman seemed so modest and friendly, but he was as obstinately obsessed with inflation as the Old Testament Paul

Volcker. As Jim Baker's deputy Treasury secretary, Darman had been part of the team that pushed Volcker out. He expected more gratitude from Greenspan.[14]

Like the doves on the Federal Open Market Committee, Darman was particularly nervous about the bleak state of the banking system. Some two hundred banks had failed during 1989, the largest number in any year since the Depression.[15] With the economy flailing, 1990 seemed certain to be worse. Already the Fed had spent the first half of the year propping up the sprawling Bank of New England with loans from its discount window, and the Federal Deposit Insurance Corporation had created a special war chest in the expectation that New England's property bust had doomed the bank to failure.[16] A few more big bankruptcies on that scale would wipe out the deposit-insurance fund, forcing taxpayers to recapitalize it and compounding the Bush administration's budget headaches.[17] And quite apart from the direct impact on the budget, Darman worried about the effect on the economy. Weak banks would be in no position to extend credit and fuel growth. Surely the Fed ought to step in with lower interest rates.

One month later, toward the end of September 1990, Greenspan was invited to dinner at the palatial home of Prince Bandar bin Sultan, Saudi Arabia's legendary ambassador in Washington. Andrea was invited, too—there was no question anymore as to their status as a couple. The other guests were to include Greenspan's old friend Ken Duberstein and his wife, as well as the defense secretary, Dick Cheney.

For a Fed chairman eager to maintain his geopolitical advantage over his FOMC colleagues, this was not a dinner to be missed. But the invitation coincided with the start of Yom Kippur. Jewish families were supposed to be fasting that evening, not feasting at the table of the Saudi ambassador.

Ken Duberstein conferred with Andrea by phone. "What are you going to do about the Bandar dinner?" he asked her.

"Of course we're going," Andrea replied. Neither she nor Alan had really focused on the calendar.

Duberstein felt more inhibited, but allowed that he would probably go, too.

"God will understand!" Andrea said firmly.[18]

The meal was predictably sumptuous: a Western dinner in the French style followed by several courses of traditional Arabic food. Afterward, the women were led off by Bandar's wife, Princess Haifa, and were soon trying on veils. The men remained with Bandar for cigars, brandy, and wide-ranging conversation.[19] Greenspan already sensed that the odds of war were growing—earlier that same day, he had paid a visit to Brent Scowcroft, the White House national security adviser.[20] He left the dinner with his impressions confirmed. It would be hard to avoid a Gulf conflict.[21]

Two days after the Saudi dinner, on Sunday, September 30, 1990, President Bush appeared alongside congressional leaders in the sun-drenched White House Rose Garden. Following weeks of bitterly partisan negotiations since the president's climbdown on taxes, a weekend marathon of talks had yielded a more detailed deficit-reduction blueprint.[22] Coming on top of the distress in the banking sector and a likely war in the Gulf, the promised fiscal tightening seemed sure to knock the wind out of the economy. Now more than ever, Darman and the Bush team would look to the Fed for lower interest rates.

The following Tuesday, October 2, the FOMC convened for its next meeting, and this time Greenspan pivoted. He had shown fortitude in standing up to the White House, but he was nothing if not pragmatic. The promised deficit reduction would surely neutralize the threat from inflation; and besides, a small cut in interest rates would send the right signal to the warring factions in Congress—if they cut the deficit, the Fed would reciprocate. Addressing his FOMC colleagues, Greenspan suggested that the committee should authorize two modest rate cuts of 25 basis points each. If Congress went ahead and passed the budget deal, Greenspan would follow up by announcing either one or both of the cuts, depending on the latest data from the economy.

The backlash was swift. Two months earlier, Greenspan had bull-dozed the committee with his military talk. But now he was trying to link monetary policy to congressional politics, a subject on which his col-leagues had their own opinions. Besides, the linkage appeared to involve the Fed in horse-trading with lawmakers. Surely central bankers should avoid political entanglement?

"Wouldn't it be wiser to link it more to those economic considerations so we don't have this precedent of having acted because fiscal policy has acted?" one FOMC member demanded.[23]

"Make it economic, not political," agreed another.[24]

"There's a lot more fiscal restraint promised down the road, and I'd hate to see us get into a linkage where we sort of condition people to think that there is always going to be a monetary policy offset," chimed in a third.[25]

"I think there is a danger of our losing sight of what the fundamental job of a central bank is, which, of course, is to bring down inflation," lec-tured a fourth.[26]

"The more I think about that, the more I think it would be embarrass-ing," a fifth member fretted.[27]

Greenspan listened—and ignored the critics. As with military matters, so with the budget: the truth was that the chairman knew more than his colleagues. The Fed could not afford the luxury of ignoring politics—after all, Congress ruled over the budget and the budget impacted the economy. Even the proudly independent Paul Volcker had responded to budgetary developments, publicly supporting deficit cuts even though Congress had not always thanked him for it.

"We're voting on the directive now," Greenspan announced, silencing a particularly uppity critic.

When the roll was taken, Greenspan won—but barely. Four dissent-ing votes were cast against his proposal, with only seven in favor; the Fed-eral Open Market Committee was now more divided than at any time since Greenspan's arrival. "The tradition of all-powerful chairmen such as

Paul Volcker and Arthur Burns is now a memory," the *Wall Street Journal* announced on its front page when it got wind of the vote tally.[28]

The day after the uprising, Greenspan showed what he was made of. He doubled down on his support for Bush's budget plan, testifying before a House committee that it was "credible" and "enforceable."[29] As soon as the budget package made it through Congress, Greenspan reached down from his high pedestal and gave the politicians their reward, cutting the federal funds rate by a quarter of a percentage point. He was not deterred by the dissenters on his board, just as he was not intimidated by administration critics. When it came to setting interest rates, he was anything but a sideman.

G reenspan's quarter-point cut offended his critics on the FOMC, but to the administration it appeared inadequate. July's depressing job losses had been followed by more layoffs each month, and by the end of October the ranks of active workers had shrunk by almost half a million. The signs of a recession had grown unmistakable. And it was not a normal recession.

For most of the postwar era, the economy had contracted when the Fed had raised interest rates to choke off inflation. As higher interest rates fed through into lower borrowing and spending, businesses got stuck with warehouses of unsold goods; they cut production and waited for inventories to run down, and the consequent layoffs rippled through the economy. But in the fall of 1990, the problem was not high interest rates but rather high debt. The economy was slowing not simply because the Fed was disciplining credit but because overextended banks and customers were disciplining themselves.[30] Darman and the doves on the Federal Open Market Committee were turning out to be right. The United States was experiencing what economists would later call a balance-sheet recession.[31]

In mid-December, with the economy still weak, Treasury Secretary Nicholas Brady seized a chance to push Greenspan to ease faster. Manley

Johnson, the Fed's young vice chairman, had announced his intention to step down; and Brady sent a memo to the White House, weighing in on Johnson's replacement. The priority, Brady insisted, was "someone who will support economic growth." He recommended the elevation of his own former adviser, a Harvard professor named David Mullins Jr., who had been installed as a Fed governor six months earlier. "Mullins has already proved his commitment to growth," Brady declared confidently.

Dick Darman, eager to put his own stamp on the Fed appointment, summoned Mullins to his office at the budget bureau.

"One of the problems we have at the Fed," Darman instructed, "is that Manley Johnson thinks right in terms of his economics, but he's too nice a guy."

"And you're suggesting I would never have that problem," Mullins responded.

Darman smiled knowingly.[32]

Having given Mullins his instructions, Darman turned his attention to the governorship that Mullins would vacate. To fill this seat in the Fed's boardroom, Darman favored Lawrence Lindsey, a combative economist at the White House. Lindsey was a born bureaucratic bomb thrower, sharp-witted and feisty; Darman had once dreamed of Lindsey's storming down the corridors of the Old Executive Office Building, lobbing a grenade through every open door he passed by.[33] Sending Lindsey over to the Fed would be a double victory, Darman thought. The White House would rid itself of a troublemaker, and it would sic a troublemaker on Greenspan.

On January 14, 1991, President Bush duly nominated Lindsey to the vacant Fed slot, and the heat mounted on the Fed chairman. The White House invited eight prominent economists from industry and academia to lunch; and when the group assembled, each guest was asked whether the Fed should cut interest rates more deeply. Put on the spot in front of the president, all eight economists supported the administration's easy-money bias. "Alan, in my travels you stand alone in your view," Brady wrote to Greenspan after the White House lunch. There was a "lack of forceful leadership by the Fed," he complained bitterly.[34]

Facing pressure from the White House and his FOMC colleagues, Greenspan could usually rely on his standing with the press and in Congress. If newspapers praised him and senators hung upon his words, there was a limit to what his enemies could do to him. With Andrea's assistance, Greenspan had taken to staging elaborate Fourth of July parties on the grand balcony of one of the Fed's buildings; the couple paid personally for a splendid spread of food, and senators mingled with Supreme Court justices and leading members of the press, accompanied by a gaggle of excited children. Meanwhile, Greenspan's rock-star status was affirmed on a regular basis when he testified in Congress. His Capitol Hill lectures were a good deal less provocative than the lectures he had once delivered for Ayn Rand, but they were punctuated by tumultuous clatterings at the press table, as reporters bolted to relay the great man's thoughts to an expectant global audience. Once, after an especially vigorous commotion, Senator Don Riegle joked that his banking committee had a line in its budget to cover broken chairs. It was a cost of taking testimony from the Fed chairman.[35]

Now, however, with the recession dragging into its sixth month, Greenspan's defenses showed signs of failing. On January 23, 1991, he appeared before Senator Riegle's committee alongside Nicholas Brady and his old adversary, Jack Kemp. This time the reception was less deferential.

Alfonse D'Amato, the scrappy Italian-American senator from New York, fixed his gaze upon Greenspan. "What I'm going to say, maybe it's not polite," he warned him.

"If you're still so worried about inflation, you're a year late. . . . I'm sick and tired of hearing that nonsense. We've got a real recession!"

Greenspan slumped forward slightly in his chair, his face lugubrious and impassive. Brady sat unnaturally still, like a man trying to stay out of a bar brawl. Only Kemp was bubbling with delight, and not trying to conceal it.

D'Amato kept going. "You're the big guru," he snarled. "We all sit here and then you say, 'Oh, I see some light. Oh, things may be getting better.'

"Where the hell do you live that you see things getting better?"

Greenspan's eyes narrowed. He buried his chin in his hand as if to stop himself from lashing out. Kemp's hand was cupped over his mouth, but his grin was so broad that it was showing at the edges.

"People are going to starve out there and you're going to be worried about inflation," D'Amato ranted, as Kemp leaned back gleefully and draped his arm over the seat next to him.[36]

With unemployment rising, inflation at 6 percent, and banks on the brink of failing, Washington seemed ready to turn on the Fed chairman.

Three days later, on January 29, 1991, President Bush appeared on the podium of the House of Representatives to deliver his State of the Union address. His focus was inevitably on the bombardment of Iraq: "What is at stake is more than one small country," he announced; "it is a big idea: a new world order." Then he marshaled his prestige as a wartime leader to bombard the central bank as well. As the network television coverage cut to a close-up of Brady, the president declared, "Sound banks should be making sound loans—now. And interest rates should be lower—now." The chamber applauded heartily.

If this assault on the Fed's tight policies was brutally direct, an even greater challenge lay concealed in the president's passing reference to bank lending. The Treasury was getting ready to unveil an ambitious reform of banking rules—"the most sweeping banking package put forward in half a century," the *Washington Post* called it.[37] Greenspan agreed with much of the Treasury's thinking: that banks should be allowed to spread across state borders; that they should no longer be barred from underwriting securities, selling mutual funds, or offering insurance; and that, in return for their new freedoms, they should be required to finance their lending with less debt and more capital. But Greenspan could not afford to celebrate, for the Treasury was also readying a coup. It aimed to seize the Fed's authority to supervise the banking system.[38]

The Treasury's plot was especially chilling because it was so reasonable.

It made no sense for banks to be regulated by four separate overseers, the administration pointed out; it would be better to consolidate power at the Treasury, which answered directly to the taxpayers who were on the hook to pay for bank bailouts. To achieve the desired consolidation, the administration proposed to roll the Office of the Comptroller of the Currency, the Office of Thrift Supervision, and the supervisory part of the Federal Deposit Insurance Corporation into a new Treasury unit called the Federal Banking Agency; and this superagency would also gobble up the Fed's supervisory authority. No longer would banks be free to shop around for an indulgent regulator: they would face one consistent set of rules. No longer would the Fed call the shots on tighter or lighter capital requirements, which in turn influenced how much banks could lend to support growth. The Treasury would.

Confronted with the Treasury's turf grab, Greenspan had no choice but to fight it. With his libertarian roots, he had limited enthusiasm for bank supervision; but the Fed's regulatory clout was essential to his authority. Stripped of their mission to supervise one thousand or so of the nation's lenders, the regional Federal Reserve banks would become shadows of their former selves, and the stature of the twelve Fed presidents would shrivel accordingly. To retain the Fed presidents' loyalty, Greenspan had to defend them—and he needed that loyalty not just because he wanted to prevail in monetary debates at the FOMC, but also because he wanted their support in Congress. Each of the twelve regional reserve banks had its own board of directors, packed with local captains of industry and finance; each captain knew senators and congressmen, and no doubt contributed to their campaigns for reelection. The Fed's sprawling network provided Greenspan with powerful allies. If the Treasury was out to gut his power base, Greenspan would counterattack.

Fortunately for Greenspan, his shaky standing with Senator D'Amato was nothing as compared to the precarious stature of his chief rival, the Treasury secretary. By the start of 1991, Nicholas Brady had become a figure of ridicule in press profiles: he was a "profoundly unexciting man," "a guaranteed ratings loser on interview shows" who "raised diffidence to an art form."[39] Two days after the president's State of the Union, a front-page article in the *Wall Street Journal* quoted a battery of Brady bashers: the Treasury secretary was unable "to defend his positions under scrutiny," one sneered contemptuously. The headline on the *Journal* article summed up the message: "Is Brady's Treasury Up to Doing Its Job? Many People Doubt It."[40]

The day this devastating hit job appeared, Brady made one of his joint appearances with Greenspan before the House Banking Committee. Representative Cliff Stearns, a Republican from Florida, demanded to know why the S&L cleanup was dragging on expensively.

Brady was caught off guard. "I thought you were asking a technical question," he said uncertainly.[41]

Stearns tried again. The thrifts' bad loans had been transferred to a government-run Resolution Trust Corporation. But the RTC still held billions of them on the taxpayers' behalf. The deeper the recession grew, the less the toxic loans were worth—and the higher the eventual hit to the federal budget. "Everything in the RTC inventory has gone down, and it could have been sold off six months ago," Stearns said accusingly.

"And could what?" Brady asked again. He was clearly bewildered.

"It could have been sold six months ago."

"Well, believe me, anything we could have sold six months ago, we would have sold and are attempting to sell," Brady insisted. Then he tried to pin the problem on the Fed. "The level of interest rates unquestionably affects the value of real estate," he stressed. "There isn't any question in my mind: if the interest rate comes down, the value of real estate will go up."

"Mr. Greenspan, with that in mind, are interest rates coming down?" Stearns pivoted.

Greenspan perked up in his chair, chuckling as he tugged a microphone toward him. He evidently knew about Brady's humiliation in the *Journal* that morning; indeed, he might well have known about it before it appeared, given his courtship of journalists. Either way, squaring off against Brady on this particular day was like dueling with a man whose trigger finger had been amputated.

"I think the secretary is referring to, essentially, the value of mortgage interest rates, which to a large extent reflect a wide variety of forces, none of which I intend to forecast at the moment," he responded. The defensive body language from the D'Amato hearing had vanished completely. The Fed chairman was in his element.

Brady sat tensely with a smirk frozen on his face. Stearns pressed Greenspan again: Would he agree that the economy was in a recession?

"Yes, I would," Greenspan answered.

"If we are in a recession, it would seem to me that the interest rates should come down," Stearns said. "And I think Mr. Brady is saying to you that, if the interest rates would come down, we could alleviate the S&L problem quite a bit."

"I'm not *sure* he's saying that," Greenspan replied artfully, not missing a beat. The sly reference to the confused figure in the morning newspaper hit home. The room broke out in laughter.

Over the course of the following weekend, Brady concluded that a full-frontal attack on the Fed was more than he could muster. Already one regional Fed president had denounced the Treasury's reform plan in the *Los Angeles Times,* and the *Times* had taken the Fed's side, reporting that lenders supervised by the central bank had a lower failure rate than rivals overseen by other regulatory agencies.[42] The attack in the *Wall Street Journal* had proved that Brady's enemies were circling; and Greenspan's deft testimony had shown that he could land a killer punch. The press had painted Brady as a confused weakling. Greenspan only had to hint as much to get the better of him.

On Tuesday, February 6, when Brady officially unveiled his reform plan, Greenspan emerged with a half victory. The administration now proposed a scaled-down version of its turf grab—it no longer aspired to kidnap the entire banking system.[43] Instead, the Fed would surrender its authority over the large bank-holding companies that increasingly dominated lending, and would be partially compensated with an increase in the number of state banks that it supervised.[44] The United States would be left with two bank regulators, the Treasury and the Fed, though the Fed would clearly be the junior partner.

Greenspan had not finished yet. He wanted more than half a victory.

In the last days of February 1991, the Bush administration's hand was strengthened. Before sunrise on February 24, U.S.-led forces launched a ground invasion of Iraq, advancing rapidly behind a deafening artillery barrage, kicking up enormous clouds of dust, capturing thousands of Iraqi troops, and encountering almost no resistance.[45] Only one hundred hours later, the Gulf War was over—it was the swiftest American victory since the Spanish-American War, the *Washington Post* suggested.[46] Relief swept through the neighborhoods surrounding the nation's military bases; ecstatic citizens waved miniature U.S. flags in front of the White House; Mayor David Dinkins of New York promised the "greatest ticker-tape parade" in history.[47] Lifted on this wave of patriotism, Whitney Houston's rendition of "The Star-Spangled Banner" became the fastest-selling single in her record label's history.[48] The president's approval rating hit 91 percent. The country was behind him.

Over the next days, the administration struggled to convert military success into momentum for its flagship bank reforms. It met with subtle resistance—resistance that appeared to come from none other than the Fed chairman. In public, Greenspan was cautiously neutral: he was not going to take on a hugely popular president with an argument that boiled down to the Fed's bureaucratic self-interest. But whenever Greenspan met privately with a senator or congressman or journalist, he would earnestly confide his doubts about the Treasury's proposal. The formulation of monetary policy depended on insights that came from banking supervision, Greenspan would say; even the watered-down Treasury blueprint would jeopardize the Fed's management of the economy. Moreover, the Fed stood ready to rescue the banking system as the lender of last resort—it needed to supervise the large players it was backstopping.[49] "Ultimately, the Fed is responsible for the nation's financial system," an unnamed senior Fed official told the *New York Times*. "We can't have that responsibility without the input that comes from direct contact with the biggest banks."[50]

While Greenspan waged a low-key battle with the Treasury, others attacked the reform plan more directly. The powerful association of community banks—powerful because its members did business in nearly every congressional district—had everything to lose from Brady's proposals: the liberalization of interstate branching would free large, efficient lenders to invade the community bankers' home ground; meanwhile, proposed cuts in federal deposit insurance would drive savings out of fragile community banks and into larger rivals that could expect a rescue from the government. The post-2008 concern—that too-big-to-fail banks would use their implicit government safety net to grow bigger still—was already in the air. "The most free-market people in the history of mankind never had the nerve to fail a major bank," the chief community-bank lobbyist complained. Thanks to this unofficial government backstop, the nation's big banks were always getting bigger.[51]

Even though the Treasury's enemies might have been his natural friends, Greenspan did not support the community bankers' argument. The way to stop banks from burdening the taxpayer was not to fight bigness, he maintained. To the contrary, large financial companies would make the system safer by diversifying risks; they would smooth the economy's path by shifting capital deftly to the users who most needed it. If financial behemoths were exploiting an implicit government backstop, the answer was not to shrink them; it was to eliminate their subsidy by insisting that they self-insure—they should fund their operations with more capital. There was nothing remotely insuperable about banking fragility, Greenspan assured the House Banking Committee on April 30. Banks "didn't fail for decades," he observed; "the problems are of fairly recent origin and they are very readily capable of being dispensed with." "None of us like this too-big-to-fail doctrine and we all look forward to its demise," he concluded breezily.

Greenspan's new optimism about taming the too-big-to-fail problem was not altogether honest. He had spent much of his career lamenting that banks would act prudently only in a parallel world, one with no government bailouts, no central bank to act as a lender of last resort, and no deposit insurance. Something like this libertarian utopia might have confronted the nineteenth-century industrialists whom Greenspan had idolized in his youth, but in the late twentieth century, the too-big-to-fail problem was far less tractable than Greenspan now pretended. As he addressed Congress at the height of the bank-reform battle, Greenspan skipped over this inconvenient truth. By assuring his audience that the too-big-to-fail problem was soluble, he brushed aside the community bankers' reasonable objection that deregulation would allow big banks to grow bigger.

Even as he welcomed the advent of the megabanks, Greenspan fought the administration's reform at every opportunity. The Fed's indefatigable congressional lobbyist would tell him whom he had to see, and Greenspan would head off to Capitol Hill, sometimes meeting several senators and representatives in a single outing. The central bank's mission was nothing less than to safeguard the stability of the nation, Greenspan would say; without the authority to keep tabs on the big banks, it would be mission impossible.[52] Somehow he imbued this message with an electric mix of flattery and menace: lawmakers would emerge invigorated but worried, thrilled to have been let in on the mysteries of finance but burdened with a fresh insight into how precarious the world was. Even the most hostile congressional barons were magically subdued; they might not be precisely sure what Greenspan did, but they still shuddered to think what could transpire if he were ever to stop doing it. For a while, Representative Henry González, the combative chairman of the House Banking Committee, was determined to curtail the Fed's ability to act as a lender of last resort, arguing that doomed attempts to keep banks afloat only increased the eventual cost of closing them.[53] But a discreet visit from the Fed chairman caused González to back off. Greenspan had "expressed a serious concern," the congressman explained vaguely.[54]

By the middle of May, the Treasury's reform plan had been shredded.

The ambitious supervisory restructuring was dead; the Fed's emergency lending powers were protected. Despite the hit to his authority from the recession, Greenspan had now waged war with the Bush administration on two fronts. He had defended the Fed's monetary independence, and he had protected its regulatory authority.

On May 16, 1991, Alan escorted Andrea to the British embassy for a black-tie dinner. The occasion marked the visit of Queen Elizabeth II, and Andrea was wearing a white gown and a pair of white kid gloves that reached above the elbow. With America's president beside her, the queen greeted each guest one by one; and as Alan and Andrea moved up the receiving line, Bush attempted a chivalrous gesture. Taking Andrea by the arm, he announced, "Your Majesty, this is one of our premier American journalists"; then, turning to Andrea, he said, "Hello, Barbara." The gaffe over Alan's TV girlfriends only rendered the president more solicitous. The next day he sent a White House keychain and a personal note to Andrea at home. "It was the 'excitement' of the Queen's evening; it was my 'heart'; it was the 'medicine'; it was that I'm 'almost 67'; it was that you 'looked great'; alas it was that I screwed up. A thousand sorries. Here's a peace offering! Am I forgiven? Con Afecto, George Bush."[55]

Despite his eagerness to appease Andrea, the president's relations with Greenspan were fraying. He had conceded defeat over the banks, but the struggle over interest rates continued. By the time of the queen's party in May 1991, the Fed had cut the federal funds rate to 5.75 percent, down from 8 percent the previous October. The way Greenspan saw things, this was quite enough—even though the economy had shed jobs in April, he believed a turnaround was imminent. The president's advisers, however, disagreed fiercely. "We have ample room to lower interest rates," Nicholas Brady declared on television.

By tradition, the Treasury secretary met with the Fed chairman for weekly breakfasts to share views on the economy. Brady regarded these encounters as an opportunity for combat. He would gird himself for battle by having his staff work up some charts, whose message was inevitably that interest rates were far too high—never mind the fact that no chart the Treasury assembled was likely to surprise the Fed chairman.[56] Greenspan, for his part, would attempt unsuccessfully to humor Brady; but this was a rare case in which his charm failed to work its magic. Brady was not fond of Greenspan's dry humor, having felt its brunt. He was cold to Greenspan's dazzling mastery of policy detail, because he preferred to leave details to subordinates.

The standoff between the Fed and Treasury was taking its toll on the economy. Greenspan's first term in office would expire in less than three months, and the administration's failure to announce his reappointment was unsettling financial markets.[57] A poll of money managers found that fully 75 percent favored Greenspan for a second term; the closest runner-up was Paul Volcker, and only 9 percent backed him.[58] The Bush team, like the markets, had no clear alternative in mind. Manley Johnson's name had been bandied about in the press, but his relationship with Brady was not much cozier than Greenspan's. Gerald Corrigan's perch in New York made him an obvious candidate, but he had fallen out with Darman. The administration briefly considered naming David Mullins, Manley Johnson's successor as vice chairman, or the Harvard professor Martin Feldstein, who had served as CEA chairman under Reagan.[59] But any replacement for Greenspan would have to win backing in the Senate. Given its defeat on banking reform, the administration was eager to avoid another test of wills in Congress.[60]

Bush met several times with Brady, Darman, and his CEA chief, Michael Boskin. If they were not going to replace Greenspan, they should at least use the whip of his reappointment to tame him.[61] Darman urged that Greenspan be asked to endorse the administration's goal of 2.75 percent growth. The Fed chairman seemed to have some kind of inflation target in his head. Darman thought he ought to have a growth target.

"Goddamn it," Darman exclaimed at one of these sessions. "Look at this money supply. It's right down at 2.5 percent. This guy is going to take us into the tank!"

Brady looked up in surprise and asked, "That's what we wanted, isn't it?"

Darman and Boskin explained that the administration's 2.75 percent target was for growth, not money.

"Now wait a minute," replied Brady. "What's the difference between the real growth rate and the growth of the money supply?"[62]

After a month of fractious paralysis, the Bush team finally came up with a scheme for handling Greenspan. It devised a series of questions that would flush the chairman out, forcing him to clarify his intentions for the economy. Darman by now regarded Brady as a dolt, and would soon say as much to a reporter.[63] But protocol laid down that the Treasury secretary was the administration's official point of contact with the Fed chairman, so Brady got the job of posing the questions.

Brady sat down for one of his frustrating conversations with Greenspan. He started working through the Bush team's question list, but there was only one that really mattered. Would the Fed chairman run the central bank in such a manner as to achieve the president's growth objective?

"Yes, I believe in the man," Greenspan answered.[64]

Brady thought that was enough: Greenspan would do whatever it took to support the president's program, managing the economy in such a way as to give him a decent shot at reelection. The Treasury secretary duly relayed the good news to Bush. "I think we should stick with who we've got," he reported. But then he added a kicker—"unless you want me to take the job."

"Mr. President," Brady went on, "I'm happy where I am. Unless you tell me to take it, I'm not volunteering."[65]

Bush let Brady's trial balloon float by without incident. Years later, the president's former advisers remained unsure whether Brady had meant his offer seriously. In any event, Bush's nonresponse to Brady's half suggestion cleared Greenspan's path, and on the late afternoon of Wednesday, July 10, 1991, the Fed chairman appeared at the president's side in the briefing room of the White House. At last the uncertainty was at an end. Greenspan could look forward to another four years as the world's most powerful economist.

"What are you going to do differently in your next term?" a reporter demanded, as Brady and Darman looked on expectantly.

"I haven't a clue," Greenspan responded.[66]

G reenspan's self-deprecating quip soon turned out to be prophetic. In the weeks leading up to his reappointment, he had expected a brisk recovery, driven by a classic inventory-restocking cycle. During the recession, scared businesses had cut back production and run down their stocks, but now inventories were so low that production seemed certain to bounce back: "The end of inventory liquidation," Greenspan observed to his FOMC colleagues in May 1991, "has been the classic element to turn around the economy in every pickup after recession that we've seen in the post World War II period—and I'm sure earlier." But in the weeks after his reappointment, no strong recovery materialized; instead, unemployment rose, hitting 7 percent in October. Addressing a business audience that month, Greenspan confessed that the economy was advancing into "a fifty-mile-an-hour headwind." The insufferable Richard Darman had been right. Banks and their borrowers were in worse shape than Greenspan had understood. Balance-sheet problems were smothering the inventory cycle, inhibiting growth for longer than the Fed chairman had expected.[67]

Greenspan's underestimation of the banking mess was supremely ironic. Ever since the publication of his magisterial 1959 paper for the American Statistical Association, he had been quick to see the links between banking, asset prices, and the real economy. In 1977, when he had returned to his consultancy after his stint at the White House, he had led the pack in pointing out how strong household balance sheets, buoyed by rising house prices, had unleashed a deluge of home-equity extraction that was driving the business cycle. Greenspan's sensitivity to the power of finance was sufficiently developed that even the best critiques of his policy during 1990–91 do not explain where he went wrong. Looking back on the balance-sheet recession a year later, Ben S. Bernanke, the

Princeton professor who had commented so thoughtfully on Black Monday, proposed a rethink of how money affected the economy: it was not just the price of credit that mattered; the health of banks and borrowers determined how much lending took place, and hence also the amount of spending and growth in the economy. But although Bernanke's emphasis on the "credit channel" was more scholarly than Greenspan's, he was essentially restating what the Fed chairman knew anyway. It was revealing that Bernanke acknowledged a minority tradition in macroeconomics that anticipated his own approach. Among the pioneers whom he cited were John Gurley and Edward Shaw, the authors who had influenced Greenspan in the 1950s.[68]

If Greenspan was intellectually equipped to anticipate the balance-sheet recession, why did he nonetheless miss it? In another painful irony, the empiricist who prided himself on his command of data turned out to be short of information. Toward the end of 1991, Greenspan hosted a meeting in the Fed's boardroom with outside real estate experts from academia, industry, and Wall Street; and he was shocked to discover that they knew more than he did. The real estate research team at Salomon Brothers had assembled proprietary data on office blocks and other commercial structures; these showed that an enormous glut of buildings was under construction, and hence that builders were in trouble.[69] It followed that the banks' problems were significantly worse than Greenspan had understood. The Fed's supervisors had known for months that banks were struggling with uncollectable bad loans; what they did not know was that yet more loans would soon be turning bad as the oversupply of commercial buildings imposed losses on developers and hence their creditors.[70] Back in 1977, Greenspan had been the private economist who pointed out the interplay between housing, finance, and the economic cycle. Now, in 1991, other private analysts were setting him straight. It was not the last occasion on which Wall Street's endeavors in real estate finance would run ahead of him.

By the end of 1991, Greenspan's miscalculation had grown obvious. In November the economy shed 57,000 jobs, its worst performance in six months, and consumer price inflation was down at 3 percent, confirming there was room for looser policy. In a form of confession, Greenspan cut the federal funds rate not once but twice in December, for a cumulative easing of 75 basis points. Yet although this activism might have appeased the administration if it had come earlier, it was no longer enough. With the 1992 election approaching, the White House advisers feared that the clock was running out on them.

The final year of the Bush presidency brought a tawdry rerun of the themes that had played out since its beginning. The spirit of the Walker's Point declaration came back with a vengeance, but now it grew altogether nastier. When Greenspan refused further cuts in interest rates during the first months of 1992, Richard Darman put it about that there was something creepy about the Fed chairman, this unmarried sixty-five-year-old who telephoned his mother every day—perhaps he was a bit like Norman Bates, the mother-fixated figure in Alfred Hitchcock's *Psycho*? At the very least, Darman whispered, Greenspan resembled Woody Allen—intelligent but neurotic and unstable.[71] Nicholas Brady, for his part, resorted to his own brand of psychological warfare. He suspended all contact with Greenspan—not just the regular working breakfasts but also the invitations to play golf at Augusta National. Alan and Andrea would no longer be welcomed at Brady's Washington parties, either—"Whoosh! Boom! Stop!" Brady sputtered.[72] If Greenspan could not be persuaded by means of charts and data, perhaps he could be ostracized into obedience.

Early in Greenspan's tenure, commentators had painted Greenspan as a Republican stooge, unlikely to defend the Fed's autonomy. But he had long since proved tougher than anyone had dreamed, and 1992 confirmed his obduracy.[73] The Fed conceded a quarter-point rate cut in April, then sat on its hands—even though the faltering economy afforded ample scope to justify more easing. In June the administration tried to ratchet up the pressure on the Fed: the president himself declared to the *New York Times* that rates should be reduced as much as possible.[74] But at the next FOMC meeting a week later, the committee shrugged off Bush's remarks, barely even stooping to acknowledge them. It was quite a change in the culture. At the start of the 1970s, the Nixon team's attack on Arthur Burns had succeeded in altering his policy; and during the 1980s, the Reagan Treasury's pressure on Volcker accomplished its goal of getting him outvoted by his own committee. But now even Fed governors transplanted from the administration felt obliged to insist upon their right to differ with the president—the grenade-throwing Lawrence Lindsey, installed at the Fed explicitly to make trouble for Greenspan, mused that the Fed should react to Bush by *raising* rates to punish him.[75] In fact, if not in law, the Fed was establishing its independence.

Although they would not bend to Bush, Greenspan and his colleagues were flummoxed by the economy. By June 1992 unemployment stood at 7.8 percent, up from 6.8 percent fifteen months earlier, when the recession had theoretically ended. Having earlier based his expectation of an inventory-driven recovery on the pattern of postwar business cycles, Greenspan now held forth about the money panics of 1873, 1893, and 1907, lecturing his FOMC colleagues about "a phenomenon we have seen many times in the past . . . it's the classic balance sheet/market value crunch." The federal funds target had already been hacked down to 3.75 percent, the lowest overnight borrowing rate in fully two decades. But evidently more monetary medicine was needed.[76] By the time of the November election, Greenspan had cut the federal funds rate to 3 percent, an extraordinarily low level.

From George H. W. Bush's perspective, it was too little, too late. He was forced to face the voters with unemployment still above 7 percent, and naturally he was defeated. "I think that if interest rates had been lowered more dramatically that I would have been reelected president," Bush declared later. "I reappointed him, and he disappointed me."[77]

Greenspan took no pleasure in the defeat of his own party. But the 1992 election brought a troubled period to a close. By running a gun-shy policy after the 1987 stock market crash, Greenspan had allowed the economy to overheat, setting the stage for the 1990–91 recession. He had then switched to playing the hard man, but he had stuck with that approach too long, underestimating the drag on the recovery from the real estate bust. Along the way, he had been challenged by the White

House and the Treasury; by his own FOMC colleagues; and by hostile critics in Congress. If Greenspan had left office at this moment, five and a half years into his tenure, he would have been remembered as a stout defender of the Fed's monetary and regulatory prerogatives—but not more than that.

Nineteen

MAESTRO

He liked to jog, but the jogs ended at McDonald's. He frequented barbecue and Tex-Mex joints, hamburger dives and southern meat-and-threes; at Doe's Eat Place in his hometown, he would devour a cheeseburger with jalapeño, lettuce, tomato, mayonnaise, pickles, and onions—all for under four dollars.[1] If George H. W. Bush was at ease amid the bobbing lobster pots at Walker's Point, William Jefferson Clinton was Big Mac man, a garrulous, flirtatious natural force that sprang out of Arkansas' louche swamp, powered by an uncanny flair for politics and people. At a crucial moment in his campaign for the presidency, Clinton met an elderly woman who cried as she recounted her struggles to pay for both medicine and food. The candidate reached down, held her in a hug, and sobbed, "I'm so sorry."[2]

Soon after his victory at the ballot box, President-elect Clinton invited Greenspan down to his transition headquarters in Little Rock, the Arkansas state capital. Paul Volcker had bargained intensively over the circumstances under which he would meet the new President Reagan, but Greenspan was willing to make the five-hour trip to this southern backwater, gritting his teeth only a bit over the tiresome layover and flight change. He would often say that he disliked politicians, especially after his experience during the Bush years. "This is a town full of evil people," he had

confided recently to a New York friend who was considering an administration job. "If you can't deal with every day having people trying to destroy
you, you shouldn't even think of coming down here."[3] But the truth was
that Greenspan courted politicians assiduously. After all, the Fed did not
exist in a vacuum. To pilot the economy successfully, it needed to remain
on cordial terms with Congress and the White House.

Arriving in Little Rock, Greenspan emerged from the aircraft walking wearily, a little stooped; if he had resembled an undertaker in his
youth, the impression had only grown stronger. Dodging the news cameras at the airport, including the one posted by Andrea's team from NBC,
he climbed into a car and rode over to the big redbrick Governor's Mansion with its white pillars and broad expanse of flat lawn. Inside, he was
ushered through a stately foyer with cream-colored walls and an antique
French chandelier. Then he was made to bide his time. Clinton's tardiness
was legendary.

After twenty minutes, his host finally appeared, bounding into the
room, a blur of meaty energy. "Mr. Chairman," Clinton said, striding
toward Greenspan and smiling, reaching out to shake hands. Slightly to
his surprise, Greenspan felt genuinely welcome.[4]

The president-elect knew what he wanted from the Fed chairman. His
campaign had featured promises to match his gargantuan appetite: he
wanted to halve the federal budget deficit, cut taxes on the middle class,
boost spending on education, and provide for more training—even as he
renewed the nation's infrastructure. Now that he had been elected, Clinton had to choose which promises to keep. It would be a lot easier to go
for deficit reduction if Greenspan offset the drag on the economy by lowering interest rates.

"We need to set our economic priorities," Clinton told Greenspan.
"I'm interested in your outlook on the economy."[5] It was good that he was
muddying his real question.[6] He respected the central bank's independence enough not to pitch for lower interest rates explicitly.

Greenspan felt immediately comfortable. Presidents and presidential
aspirants had been asking him about economic priorities for twenty-five
years, since before Clinton had graduated from college. And with one

slightly shaming exception—his time inside the Ford White House—
Greenspan had argued consistently for budgetary restraint.[7] The national
debt had ballooned to the point where interest payments had become the
third-largest federal expense after Social Security and defense, he now
told Clinton. It was time for the government to live within its means, not
burden future generations.

Greenspan made a further point, answering Clinton's unasked question. Whatever the new president chose to do about the deficit, the federal
funds rate was now down at 3 percent, which meant that the cost of short-
term borrowing was roughly zero after accounting for inflation; the Fed
could not be expected to cut interest rates any further. However, the thirty-
year bond rate was up above 7 percent, and this was where Clinton's deficit
reduction could make a difference. High long-term rates reflected the
market's expectation of inflation, Greenspan explained; and that expectation in turn reflected the deficit. Bond traders remembered that the budget gaps of the late 1960s and 1970s had brought double-digit inflation;
they feared that history would repeat itself. A show of fiscal discipline from
Clinton would douse inflation expectations, bringing long rates down to
the level that Americans had enjoyed under John F. Kennedy.

For a young leader who styled himself on Kennedy, that prospect was
beguiling. If Clinton could reassure the bond market, a virtuous circle
would ensue. Lower interest rates would spur purchases of homes, cars,
dishwashers, and even vacations—these days, everything was bought on
credit. Lower interest rates would simultaneously help businesses to borrow funds to ramp up production. Meanwhile, lower yields on bonds
would drive investors into equities; the stock market would take off, creating yet another boost to consumption and investment. The old Keynesian
idea that budget deficits boosted the economy would be turned on its
head: because of the effect of deficit reduction on interest rates, austerity
could be expansionary. "The latter part of the 1990s could look awfully
good," Greenspan mused, dangling a shiny orange carrot in front of Clinton's nose. "I was not oblivious of the fact that 1996 would be a presidential election year," he recalled later.[8]

Greenspan's pitch was flimsier than he admitted. It involved two assertions that were at least open to doubt: first, that cutting the budget deficit would bring down inflation expectations; second, that lower inflation expectations would bring down the long-term bond rate. The truth, as Volcker had demonstrated, was that the link between deficits and inflation expectations could be broken; thanks to a determined central bank, inflation expectations had fallen in the Reagan years, even as the deficit had *expanded* to a postwar record. Equally, it was by no means clear that inflation expectations were the main driver of the long-term bond rate. Of course, other things being equal, investors who anticipated inflation would charge more for long-term loans. But high long-term interest rates might also reflect other factors: a recovering economy and hence a healthy appetite for loans; a paucity of savings, whether from Americans or foreigners; and so on. The Fed staff gently pointed out to Greenspan that if deficit reduction brought down long-term interest rates, it might not be for the reason that he claimed. Rather than bringing down inflation expectations, a smaller deficit might bring down the long-term interest rate simply because it meant less government borrowing. Reduced government demand for loans would mean that loans were cheaper.[9]

Even though Greenspan's choice of argument appeared eccentric to the economists on the Fed's staff, he had a way with politicians. His meeting with Clinton ran on for two and a half hours, with the president-elect soliciting advice on all manner of questions, including the quality of foreign leaders with whom Clinton would be working. Whenever Greenspan thought he might have talked enough, Clinton's body language urged him on; Greenspan had not expected to remain for lunch, but lunch arrived anyway. They made an odd pairing, this kibitzing couple: the indulgent, ebullient baby-boomer Democrat, his hands always reaching out to gesture and to touch; the shy, austere Republican with thick lenses and a fashion sense that had frozen in the 1950s. But somehow the two men bonded anyway. Each had grown up without a father; each had played the saxophone; each delighted in the other's intellect, which bridged party division. Besides, the Fed chairman and the future president each had a powerful reason to want to get along. Greenspan was eager to forestall a repeat of the Fed bashing of the Bush era. Clinton had campaigned on the economy—he wanted Greenspan's cooperation.

After the meeting, Clinton delivered his verdict on the Fed chairman. "We can do business," he confided to his running mate.

Greenspan, for his part, arrived at a similar conclusion. "I don't know that I'd have changed my vote, but I'm reassured," he told a friend in Washington.[10]

Three weeks later, Alan and Andrea celebrated Christmas in their usual way: at the home of Al Hunt and Judy Woodruff. Al was the *Wall Street Journal*'s Washington bureau chief, and Judy an accomplished television journalist; the couple had three children, including a three-year-old who was Andrea's goddaughter. Alan and Andrea had become part of the family, joining in for Christmas breakfast and an excited opening of stockings, then following the kids into the living room to unwrap what Al called "more presents than was really good for us." The gift supply was so abundant, Al chuckled, that Alan emerged from every Christmas with a firm intention to raise interest rates; the children tore through glossy paper until it carpeted the floor, and Al unveiled his masterstroke, a special gift for the Fed chairman. There was nothing material that Alan wanted, so Al came up with a series of inventive gags: a life-sized cutout of Paul Volcker, an autographed photo of the hostile supply-side columnist Bob Novak, and so on.

For Christmas 1992, Al's gift was especially successful. A few days earlier, the president-elect had sat for an interview with Hunt and his *Wall Street Journal* colleagues, and over the course of their discussion, Clinton had spoken warmly of the Fed chairman. "I had a very good meeting with Greenspan," Clinton had told Hunt; "I liked him," he had added. Al gift-wrapped the transcript of the interview and presented it to Alan, who responded like a boy engrossed in his first Lego set. Zoning out the children, Alan pored over the text; in one revealing passage, the president-elect drew a connection between the unstable complexity of modern finance and the case for reassuring continuity in the person of the Fed chairman.[11] Greenspan could not have put it better himself. Clinton sounded as though he might be the first president ever to internalize the truth that Fed independence was in his own interest.

Moreover, Clinton was increasingly inclined to follow Greenspan's preferred route on the budget. Even before the encounter in Little Rock at the start of December, his advisers had pressed their own argument for attacking the deficit: by getting its finances in order, the government would demonstrate America's ability to solve its problems, and the boost to business confidence would invigorate the economy.[12] As the first Democratic president since Jimmy Carter, Clinton had to show investors that he was not going to bring back stagflation; if only he could prove that he was different, long-term interest rates would fall significantly. But although Clinton understood the argument, he was not quite ready to bet his political capital on it. He was reluctant to give up his spending plans. And the idea that Keynesian theory could be turned upon its head sounded a little suspicious.[13]

On January 7, 1993, Clinton's economic team convened at the Governor's Mansion in Little Rock. Alan Blinder, a distinguished Princeton professor who would join Clinton's Council of Economic Advisers, addressed the group; "I've been asked to do the pedantic stuff," he confessed disarmingly. Then he did his best to settle Clinton's budget doubts. In the long run, he said reassuringly, there was no question that a smaller deficit would increase growth: capital would be freed for private use, boosting investment and productivity. But in the short and even medium run, austerity entailed a risk. The drag from a tighter budget would probably prove stronger than the boost from cheaper borrowing. The balance would depend, Blinder concluded, on how fast the Fed or the markets delivered lower interest rates.

Clinton was turning an alarming red. "You mean to tell me that the success of the program and my reelection hinges on the Federal Reserve and a bunch of fucking bond traders?" he demanded.[14]

Blinder reiterated that growth would depend on how interest rates responded to a tighter budget. Perhaps Clinton should seek a quid pro quo from the Fed before cutting the deficit? "You need some pre-assurance from Greenspan," he suggested to Clinton.[15]

The following day, Friday, January 8, Greenspan got a report on the proceedings. Lloyd Bentsen, the courtly, silver-haired Texan senator who would become Clinton's Treasury secretary, arrived in Greenspan's dining room for lunch. He was accompanied by Bob Rubin, the Goldman Sachs chief who would head Clinton's National Economic Council, a new White House unit designed to be less academic and detached than the Council of Economic Advisers.[16] Fortunately for Greenspan, neither visitor bought Blinder's "pre-assurance" talk: both understood that the Fed chairman could not be expected to make promises on interest rates. It helped, no doubt, that Bentsen was a friend and tennis partner of Greenspan's; he had watched the outgoing Bush administration's attempts to constrain the Fed, which had backfired humiliatingly. Rubin, for his part, barely knew Greenspan, and suspected that a partisan Republican might lurk under the chairman's technocratic demeanor; but Rubin had spent his career in the markets and understood that the more independent and credible the central bank, the milder would be the pain of squeezing down inflation. Bentsen and Rubin sat down with Greenspan, laid out their framework for deficit reduction—and then left. They did not solicit the Fed chairman's endorsement. They did not even ask for his opinion.

Greenspan was getting the best of both worlds. He had pushed Clinton toward deficit cuts. But nobody was pushing him on interest rates.

As the Bush administration exited and the Clintonites arrived, Greenspan managed the transition expertly. He took care to bid respectful good-byes, attending a dinner for the departing defense secretary, his old friend Dick Cheney, and making time for a midafternoon ceremony held in Cheney's honor at Fort Meyer, near the National Cemetery in Arlington. He was equally assiduous about how he said hello, building on his good start with the president-elect and Bentsen. He asked David Mullins, the Fed vice chairman, to use his Arkansas connections to set up a breakfast with Thomas F. "Mack" McLarty, Clinton's childhood friend and incoming chief of staff; and he invited McLarty to address the directors of the regional Fed banks when they visited Washington—for McLarty and the Clinton team, Greenspan's offer constituted a valuable opening to a wealthy group of private-sector leaders. Learning that the first lady, Hillary Clinton, planned to take up health-care reform, Greenspan told McLarty that he would be delighted to discuss the issue with her: the fact that Clinton was proposing to extend government control over a vast swath of the economy did not keep Ayn Rand's protégé from offering his assistance.[17] Meanwhile, Laura Tyson, the upbeat Berkeley economist who was to head Clinton's Council of Economic Advisers, received some practical advice: Greenspan had studied her television performances and offered her a tip—to tone down her body language. Too many hand gestures and facial expressions could undermine her credibility, Greenspan counseled. The CEA chairwoman should simply present facts, with as little visual commentary as possible.[18]

Even with Washington in transition frenzy, Greenspan continued to visit New York frequently. His mother was now ninety, lucid but unhappy, and he took every opportunity to relieve her loneliness. There were social, professional, and medical reasons to be in New York, too. The day after the visit from Bentsen and Rubin, Greenspan took the shuttle from National Airport to LaGuardia and checked into the Stanhope Hotel on Fifth Avenue—by now he had sold his apartment in the United Nations Plaza. Once installed at the Stanhope, he donned an evening jacket and black tie for a party given by Barbara Walters; the next day he ate brunch amid the old-world elegance of the Harmonie Club on East Sixtieth Street, returning to Washington by shuttle in time for afternoon tennis. A few days later, on January 21, Greenspan doubled back to Manhattan for a lunch at the New York Fed, and five days after that he boarded the shuttle once again, this time for a battery of tests at the New York Hospital–Cornell Medical Center. There were two hours of biochemical blood profiling and heart monitoring by echocardiogram and electrocardiogram: though he enjoyed remarkably good health, Greenspan believed in meticulous monitoring. The marathon of testing was capped off with checkups by two different doctors. After a brief respite at the Waldorf Astoria, Greenspan flew back to Washington. He had another tennis match that evening.[19]

The morning after his bout with the doctors, Greenspan had breakfast with Lloyd Bentsen, newly installed as Treasury secretary. Despite Alan Blinder's talk of "pre-assurance" from the Fed, Bentsen still showed no sign of pressuring the chairman to cut interest rates. To the contrary, he wanted to enlist Greenspan's help in pressuring the president. The Treasury secretary and his colleagues were coalescing around a plan to cut the deficit by $145 billion, but Clinton was still sitting on the fence, fearful of a slower economy. Just as Greenspan's old friend Marty Anderson had turned to him to instruct Candidate Reagan on the economy, so Bentsen now asked Greenspan to explain the budget stakes to Clinton.

At 9:30 a.m. on Thursday, January 28, Greenspan arrived at the White House for a meeting with Bentsen and the newly inaugurated president. The responsibilities of office had not diminished Clinton's appetite for discussion, and he listened earnestly as Greenspan emphasized that, if nothing was done about the deficit, it would grow to unmanageable proportions. "You cannot procrastinate indefinitely on this issue," the Fed chairman said bluntly.[20] The tutorial extended for an hour. The president gave it his full attention.[21]

It was not just the administration that wanted Greenspan's opinion. Later that same day, Greenspan testified before the Senate budget committee. Kent Conrad, a Stanford-educated North Dakota Democrat, had digested the message that a responsible budget could have wonderful effects. But he wanted Greenspan to elaborate.

Seated before the microphone, looking up at the dais of legislators as he had done so many times before, Greenspan assured Conrad that a credible budget would bring down bond rates. The effect could be substantial because long-term interest rates were weirdly high—far above the levels that had been normal before the inflation surge of 1979, and "clearly well in excess of what they should be in a noninflationary environment," Greenspan lectured.

"Could you put a number on that?" Conrad inquired. "Two points higher?" The senator was tempting Greenspan to be dangerously specific. To assert that deficit reduction would reduce interest rates was already quite bold. To quantify the reduction would be to stray far beyond the evidence.

Normally Greenspan was a master of evasion. Confronted with an invitation to get himself into trouble, he would meander around the subject, piling clause upon subclause, leaving his audience to suppose that they might have understood if only they had listened harder. The Nobel laureate Robert Solow once compared him to a bespectacled sea squid: sensing danger, Greenspan would flood his surroundings with black ink and then move away, silently.[22] But now, confronted by Kent Conrad, Greenspan's instincts failed. The senator was demanding to know how big the inflation premium in long-term interest rates might be. Having stressed the premium's significance so many times, Greenspan could hardly refuse to answer.

"I would say two, maybe more," Greenspan obliged. If the markets perceived a credible shift in fiscal discipline, the inflation premium would disappear, reducing long-term interest rates. "I mean, we've had them much lower. We're now somewhat over 7 percent, and they have been well under 5."[23]

It was an extraordinary assertion—far bolder than Conrad seemed to realize. Long-term interest rates had not actually been below 5 percent since 1967, a time when the global economy had been utterly different.[24] Back in 1967, Regulation Q had held down interest rates artificially, and barriers to cross-border capital flows had bottled up Americans' copious savings inside the country, further restraining borrowing costs. It was by no means obvious that the long-term interest rate of 1967 offered any sort of guide as to how far interest rates could fall in the 1990s.[25]

Having secured one answer from Greenspan, Conrad demanded another. "How much deficit reduction do we need over a four-year period or a five-year period to be credible, to get the interest rate reduction we all agree would be stimulative?" he asked him. The senator evidently thought Greenspan should be able to assign a numerical value to anything.

"I don't think it is the actual dollar amount as much as the specific means by which it is done," the guru hedged cautiously.

Conrad was not satisfied. "I have tried my best to get an answer, but I have not achieved one," he declared accusingly.

Greenspan flinched. He was supposed to be the man who knew. He hated to disappoint people.

"Are you looking for a number, Senator?" he asked obligingly.

Conrad nodded. Precisely how much deficit reduction would it take to bring down inflation expectations?

"Let me just say to you that I don't find the number that President Clinton has given to you to be off-base," Greenspan offered.

"Which number?" Conrad demanded. He wanted Greenspan to go on the record as clearly as possible.

"The $145 billion, as I remember it."

"I think you just made news!" Conrad exclaimed triumphantly.

"Splendid," Greenspan deadpanned, to giggles from the senators.

Sure enough, the following day's *New York Times* reported Greenspan's "ringing endorsement" of the emerging Clinton program.[26] The Fed chairman seemed so invested in the case for deficit cuts that if the economy weakened as a consequence, he could be expected to lower interest rates, the *Times* speculated. Thanks to Greenspan's testimony, a new policy consensus was taking shape. In the place of the loose budget policy and tight monetary policy of the Reagan-Volcker years, there would be tight budget policy and loose monetary policy.

For the Fed and Alan Greenspan, the new consensus was almost too good to be true. For years, politicians had spent wildly and forced the Fed to play bad cop. Now politicians promised to provide the discipline, allowing Greenspan to play the openhanded uncle. By leading the nation in its grueling war against inflation, Paul Volcker had built the Fed chairmanship into a heroic role. One decade later, Greenspan would be able to control prices just as surely as Volcker—but without the blood and sacrifice. If Volcker's stout performance had turned him into a latter-day Churchill, the stage was set for Greenspan to emerge as a likable wizard: a maestro.

G reenspan's Senate testimony had a profound impact on budget poli- tics. The Clinton adviser Dick Morris later summed up economic policy in this period: "You figure out what Greenspan wants, and then you get it to him."[27] Even allowing for exaggeration, there was truth in Morris's sound bite—now that Greenspan had laid out his views, he had set the terms of the debate for both the administration and Congress. A week after the Senate testimony, on February 5, Clinton's economic team set out its budget options in a lengthy memo to the president, pointedly noting that "Greenspan believes that a major deficit reduction (above $130 billion) will lead to interest rate changes *more than offsetting*" the contraction caused by less government spending. Some Clintonites quib- bled with the $130 billion target, but not with the impeccable authority of its source. Lloyd Bentsen objected that Greenspan's preferred target was actually higher—$140 billion.[28]

After weeks of uncertainty, Clinton finally resolved to throw his lot in with the budget hawks. On February 17, he announced his commitment to deficit reduction in his State of the Union speech, and Greenspan was wheeled out to perform his familiar role as validator in chief—the White House arranged for him to listen to the address from a perch between the first lady, Hillary Clinton, and the second lady, Tipper Gore. When the president reached the part of his speech dealing with his budget plan, the TV cameras zoomed in on the red-suited first lady and the dark- suited Fed chairman, each applauding enthusiastically. Critics were quick to grumble that Greenspan was sullying the Fed with politics: "To my knowledge, this was the first time that the head of the supposedly inde- pendent Federal Reserve had shown his support for a president at such a highly charged public event," former Treasury secretary Brady har- rumphed, apparently forgetting how the Bush administration had wanted Greenspan in the camera shot for the announcement of the S&L bailout.[29] David Mullins, whom Brady had installed as Fed vice chairman, was equally livid. But Greenspan was doing more or less what Volcker had done when he had lobbied for deficit reduction in the Reagan years. The chief difference was that Greenspan was succeeding.

Two days later, Greenspan appeared again before the Senate, describing the Clinton plan as "serious" and "credible." He evidently had two audiences in mind: Congress, which would ultimately vote on the president's budget; and investors, who had the power to reward the budgeteers with lower interest rates.

Phil Gramm, the Texas senator who had teased William Proxmire at Greenspan's confirmation hearing, now turned his wit on the Fed chairman.

"Alan, I saw you in all of your splendor in the photograph in the paper between the first lady and the second lady," Gramm drawled. "People asked me who that handsome guy was and I said, it's Alan Greenspan, who controls the money supply of the United States. And had I been the president, I would have had you in exactly the same spot."

The committee broke into laughter.[30]

Gramm was soon proved right. Greenspan's deliberately visible support for Clinton's budget plan impressed investors, and long-term interest rates began to fall, just as the Fed chairman had promised. The fiscal hawks on Clinton's economic team were overjoyed: they had done the responsible thing on the budget; here was a rare case in politics of virtue being rewarded. No less a figure than the president himself announced enthusiastically to the nation that the yield on the thirty-year bond had dipped below 7 percent, its lowest level in sixteen years; and for the next several weeks, the mood in the White House bounced up and down with interest rates. "I used to think if there was reincarnation, I wanted to come back as the president or the pope or a .400 baseball hitter," quipped James Carville, Clinton's ebullient campaign strategist. "But now I want to come back as the bond market. You can intimidate everybody."

Over the spring and summer, the good news persisted. At the end of May 1993, an amended version of Clinton's deficit-reduction plan made it through the House of Representatives, and long-term bond yields fell; in August, the plan was triumphantly signed into law, and yields fell even further.[31] The interest rate on thirty-year bonds fell by a total of 1.4

percentage points between the start of January and the middle of October, from 7.4 percent to about 6 percent: it was not quite the 2 percentage point reduction that Greenspan had touted to Senator Conrad, but it was nonetheless remarkable. And yet even as Greenspan appeared triumphant, something odd was going on: the mechanism that supposedly controlled long-term rates was not behaving as predicted. In his Little Rock conversation with Clinton, the Fed chairman had described how deficit reduction would bring down inflation expectations, and how lower inflation expectations would feed through into lower long-term interest rates.[32] But much as the Fed staff had warned him, inflation expectations hardly budged—the University of Michigan's surveys showed that they were defiantly stable.[33] Greenspan was like the math student who gets his calculations wrong but somehow comes up with the right answer.

Discussing this puzzle privately with his FOMC colleagues, Greenspan admitted to some misgivings. "This bond rate decline is running faster than I think it probably should," he confessed in March 1993; in the absence of falling inflation expectations, it was hard for him to see why long-term interest rates should be collapsing. Indeed, given unchanged inflation expectations, falling bond yields and the corresponding rise in bond prices might be regarded as an irrational bubble. "Frankly, if I were in the private sector at this stage, I would be having fits on the bonds in my portfolio," Greenspan remarked to the committee.

Governor Lawrence Lindsey tried to push Greenspan to follow the logic of his own analysis. "We have overextended financial markets," he agreed. "You said so yourself; you said you would be quitting the bond market." The right response to a bubbly bond market was to raise interest rates, Lindsey continued. Better to squeeze some air out of the bubble now than to let it inflate further.[34]

At the next FOMC meeting, in May 1993, Richard Syron of the Boston Fed restated Lindsey's warning. Unsophisticated savers were pouring money into bond funds. The moment the rally stopped, the dumb money would stampede for the exit.

Given his long preoccupation with finance, Greenspan might have been expected to heed these signals. In his magisterial 1959 article, he had complained that the Fed ignored asset bubbles at its peril; indeed, his support for the gold standard was grounded in the fear that central banks would accommodate "speculative flights from reality" in markets.[35] But at the FOMC meetings in March and May, the mature Greenspan behaved precisely as the young Greenspan had feared: he refused to listen to the hawks, preferring to keep the federal funds rate ultralow, fueling the dramatic rally in bonds that he himself viewed as excessive.[36] The mature Greenspan was driven to these choices by the inherent uncertainties of finance. Even though Greenspan, the former Wall Streeter, had far more confidence in his view of the markets than any previous Fed chairman, he could only guess as to their right level. No Fed chairman—indeed, no market seer or investor—can ever be completely sure that a bubble is inflating. To raise interest rates in the face of a bubble is always to pay a certain price to head off an uncertain threat—and to incur the wrath of politicians and the public, who love nothing better than a soaring market.[37]

Perhaps unsurprisingly, Greenspan was careful not to advertise the tension between his youthful writing and his mature behavior. He seldom spoke about his 1959 paper; and when a *Wall Street Journal* reporter tried repeatedly to obtain a copy of his PhD dissertation, of which the 1959 article was a central part, the library at New York University replied that the dissertation had gone missing.

By the fall of 1993, even the cautious economists on the Fed's staff were concerned about the bond market. They did not presume to know what the "right" level of the market was, but they were increasingly unnerved by it. Long-term interest rates were continuing to tumble in the absence of a fall in inflation expectations, and it was unclear whether the government's reduced borrowing needs were enough to justify the repricing. And yet the dominant view of the bond market—championed by the irrepressible baby boomer in the White House, aided and abetted by the lugubrious child of the Depression at the Fed—survived unquestioned and unchanged. Ever lower interest rates were only good. They had been down at 5 percent under Lyndon Johnson; why shouldn't they be down that low under Bill Clinton?

Mike Prell, the head of the Fed's research and forecasting division, set his staff to work on the drivers of the bond market. What was really pushing rates so low? If inflation expectations were stuck, what were the decisive factors?

On September 21, 1993, Prell presented the fruits of his staff's work to the Federal Open Market Committee. The message was startling—although Prell was far too courteous to say so, the research suggested that Greenspan's pitch to the president-elect in Little Rock had been fundamentally misguided. Long-term interest rates were not primarily driven by inflation expectations, Prell's findings suggested, and even the effect of less government borrowing on the demand for capital might not be the key driver. Rather, the main factor explaining long rates was the recent level of short rates. "The persistence of low short rates will gradually lower investors' perceptions of what is normal and sustainable," Prell explained. After all, the long-term interest rate was composed of a sequence of short-term rates. If investors learned to take rock-bottom short rates for granted, they would bid down the long rate.

Prell presented his evidence in a dry, just-the-facts way: Greenspan's strictures on body language were clearly unnecessary in his case. But his message was provocative enough. Rather than falling because of Clinton's deficit reduction, long-term interest rates were falling because of Greenspan's own monetary policy. The Fed had slashed the federal funds rate to 3 percent back in September 1992; one year on, investors were coming to behave as though cheap money were the new normal. Moreover, the longer Greenspan kept short-term credit ultracheap, the further long-term bond yields would come down: Prell suggested they could end up even lower than Greenspan's 5 percent target. And contrary to what Greenspan had argued publicly, ever lower long rates would not be a good thing. Because they were not supported by a fundamental shift in inflation expectations or the supply and demand for capital, they could not be sustained. When the Fed eventually raised short rates, long rates would shoot up—or to put the point another way, the bond bubble would implode precipitately.

Greenspan had clashed with Prell before, and this time he hit back with a thought experiment. If the FOMC took the staff advice literally, it could cut the federal funds rate to zero and look forward to ever lower long-term interest rates. Surely Prell was not suggesting that such a strategy would work? The Fed's superloose stance would ignite inflation fears, driving the long-term interest rate *upward*.

Prell was not impressed. Greenspan's reductio ad absurdum shed little light on the Fed's immediate policy choices. Of course, if the federal funds rate was pushed to an extreme, it could be decoupled from long-term rates. But in the real world—as opposed to the world of thought experiments—short rates drove long ones. Prell's staff had tested the correlations going back four decades, and the results were quite clear. Even during the 1980s, when inflation and inflation expectations had been on everybody's minds, their influence on long-term interest rates had been marginal.

Vice Chairman David Mullins, who would soon leave the Fed for the efficient-market-minded hedge fund Long-Term Capital Management, could scarcely contain himself. Prell's model was "transparently nonsensical and violates enormous evidence which has been accumulated on the way markets work, including market efficiency," he insisted. A core assumption of academic finance was that investors were forward-looking—what mattered was not their experience of short rates in the past, but rather their expectation of short rates in the future. Wouldn't Prell's model be better if he included "some measure of inflation and inflation expectations?"

"It is possible that such a model as you hypothesize might be serviceable," Prell retorted condescendingly. "But I suspect that we have experimented enough that this formulation has proven more robust. I think saying that this model is nonsensical and totally at odds with reality runs up against the point that . . . it has worked," he added tartly.

Mullins hit back. "The reason I say it's nonsensical is because it doesn't make logical sense," he insisted.

The two slugged away at each other for a while. Mullins was confident in his own brilliance; the Fed staff was confident that he was irritating. Presently, Mullins threatened to explain "another theory that I don't know if we want to get into."

"We don't," Greenspan said curtly. He had heard enough efficient-market dogma from Mullins. But he was not going to take his cues from Prell, either. He would not be railroaded into doing battle with a potential bubble—raising interest rates in order to bring the bond market down was a fool's errand. Perhaps the lesson of 1987 was in the back of his mind: if a bubble did burst, the Fed could handle the consequences. But there was another factor, too. In the climate of Washington, it felt altogether safer to focus the Fed's efforts single-mindedly on containing inflation. This was the heroic undertaking that Volcker had established for the central bank; this was the mission that the White House at long last seemed willing to respect; and whereas financial bubbles could not be identified with certainty, the signs of incipient consumer price inflation seemed easier to monitor. The case for focusing on asset prices—the case Greenspan had himself advanced in 1959—was swept under the carpet.

Three months later, Greenspan endured a final assault on his position. In an argument that anticipated the debates of coming years, Governor Lawrence Lindsey explained to the FOMC why low inflation might offer a false signal for monetary policy. The consumer price index appeared stable because imports were getting cheaper: low-cost emerging nations were joining the world economy; globalization restrained prices for everything that could be traded. In this environment, the Fed could supply a surprising amount of easy money without being punished by inflation. But it did not necessarily follow that easy money was desirable. As Lindsey reminded his colleagues, rock-bottom interest rates prevented savers from earning a return on the cash in their bank accounts; it induced wealthy Americans to shovel savings into equities, commodity futures, holiday homes in Wyoming—and into the bond market. Meanwhile, ordinary Americans were being tempted into borrowing imprudently.[38] The resulting fragilities—asset bubbles on the one hand, precarious towers of household debt on the other—could upset the smooth path of the economy just as surely as inflation.

Greenspan's monetary policy during 1993 has never attracted much criticism. He was presiding over a period of deficit reduction and falling inflation; having peaked at 6.3 percent on the eve of the Gulf War, consumer price inflation dropped to 2.7 percent by the time of Lindsey's attack on him. With inflation so nearly defeated, what was not to like? Yet the seeds of Greenspan's controversial later choices were planted at this time—and Lindsey diagnosed the pitfalls in his chosen path with admirable foresight. By refusing to respond to the evidence of a bubble, Greenspan was neglecting a potential danger to the economy's progress. By defining the Fed's mission narrowly in terms of price stability, he risked fighting the last war—the war of the 1970s.[39]

Two months later, on January 21, 1994, Greenspan headed over to the White House to deliver a warning to the president. He had finally decided that the time had come: the Fed would have to raise interest rates. Regardless of what he felt about the bond market, seventeen months of zero real interest rates were enough: inflation, remarkably, was still subdued, but the economy had grown by 5.4 percent in the final quarter of the previous year—a rate that promised bottlenecks and higher prices in the not-too-distant future. Back in 1988, Greenspan had been slow to rein in the expansion because he had worried about the fragile equity market. This time he wanted to raise interest rates before inflation reared its head. If he was going to make price stability his primary objective, he wanted to be sure that he delivered it.

Addressing Clinton and his entourage, Greenspan explained the Fed's dilemma. It could raise interest rates modestly if it acted against inflation early, or it could wait and be forced to tighten more aggressively later. Either way, Greenspan emphasized, the administration should resist the urge to criticize the central bank. The Fed would be deaf to the attacks, but the markets would hear them. If investors began to worry that the Fed would be prevented from acting firmly, inflation expectations would rise, forcing the Fed to respond with even higher interest rates.

Fifteen months after their first meeting in Little Rock, this was the first test of the odd couple's relationship. Greenspan could see that Clinton was annoyed—why raise interest rates before inflation had materialized? His irritation underlined the political problem with Lawrence Lindsey's advice. There was no telling what Clinton would have said if the Fed had jacked up rates to pop an alleged bond bubble.

After a moment, Clinton's composure returned. "I understand what you may have to do," he conceded.[40]

Greenspan felt relieved. The Little Rock camaraderie had survived its test: Clinton was not like his predecessor, George H. W. Bush; he was not going to come after him, not even in private. Whatever Clinton's reputation for baby-boomer indulgence, he was the most disciplined president in memory when it came to Fed independence.

Two weeks later, on February 3, 1994, the FOMC convened for its next meeting. The members of the committee knew that it was time to tighten—indeed, most had wanted to do so at the previous meeting. Greenspan proposed that they should mark the change in monetary direction with a change in procedure: they should announce their action in a press release. This innovation would be in keeping with the push for open government that was sweeping through Washington; recently the Fed had been browbeaten into publishing the transcripts of past FOMC meetings. More to the point, an FOMC press release would magnify the impact of a move in the federal funds rate. In the new world of deep and global capital markets, the Fed did not so much control borrowing costs as aspire to influence them. a hike in the federal funds rate would have a significant effect only if traders reacted by bidding up market interest rates. If the Fed wanted to play the influence game, it would have to speak clearly and publicly.[41]

"What I'm saying is that the first time we move the funds rate after this extended period, we are hitting a 'gong,'" Greenspan said. "And I think we ought to stand up and hit it." A few years later, his percussion metaphor would give way to a vast scholarly literature on the significance of central bank communication.

Greenspan promised that his press release would be a one-off: it would not establish a precedent. Nobody objected. But when the Fed chairman proposed a tightening of a quarter of a percentage point, he confronted a revolt. A majority on the committee wanted to hike the rate by twice as much as he suggested.

Greenspan had never yet lost an argument on monetary policy. Sometimes he won by wielding obscure facts: he had understood troop positioning in the Persian Gulf because of his direct line to Dick Cheney. Sometimes he rallied colleagues by appealing to duty, commonly claiming that the FOMC was meeting at an uncommonly momentous time, requiring unity on monetary policy. On still other occasions, Greenspan exploited disagreements within the committee to steer it into a stalemate—whereupon it would postpone its decision, issuing an "asymmetric directive" that left the chairman with the power to move the federal funds rate between meetings. In February 1994, faced with the most serious FOMC revolt of his tenure, Greenspan combined a head feint with a dash of intimidation.

Seeing that his committee wanted to tighten by more than he proposed, Greenspan began by hinting that smaller might paradoxically be bigger. Acknowledging a suggestion from a colleague, he reflected that a hike of 25 basis points might be seen as the start of several moves; it might therefore pack a bigger punch than a hike of 50 basis points, which would be dismissed as a one-off adjustment. Because of the expectation of successive rate rises, the quarter-point rate rise would "subdue speculation in the stock market," Greenspan mused; "[by] having a sword of Damocles over the market we can prevent it from running away," he added. Apparently, the chairman was happy for monetary policy to target asset prices if this helped him to win over his critics.

Having humored his colleague, Greenspan switched course: smaller would be smaller, he now firmly insisted. Indeed, a quarter-point rate rise would be preferable to a larger one precisely because it would be judiciously gentle, and so would avoid scaring the equity market. "The stock market is at an elevated level at this stage by any measure we know of," he reflected sagely. "I've been in the economic forecasting business since 1948, and I've been on Wall Street since 1948, and I am telling you I have a pain in the pit of my stomach." If the rest of the committee wanted to trigger a repeat of Black Monday, they could go ahead and vote for a 50 basis point increase, Greenspan's implication went. If the economy blew up, they would be responsible for the disaster.

Rounding off his appeal, Greenspan played on his colleagues' sense of loyalty. "I also would be concerned if this Committee were not in concert because at this stage we as a Committee are going to have to do things which the rest of the world is not going to like," he admonished. "We have to do them because that's our job. If we are perceived to be split on an issue as significant as this, I think we're risking some very serious problems for this organization."

Their heads spinning a little, the rest of the committee paused at this. They did not want to push their chairman into a corner, particularly not on the first rate hike in fully half a decade—and the first ever to be announced in a press release. Perhaps, one member suggested, they could move a quarter point now, but hold open the possibility of a further hike before the next meeting?

"That's perfectly fine with me," Greenspan responded. The FOMC was about to do what it so often did: agree to an asymmetric directive that left the power to decide policy between meetings in the hands of the chairman.

But this time Greenspan was denied victory. Lawrence Lindsey—the governor who had already upbraided Greenspan for neglecting asset prices, the governor whom the Bush White House had rightly regarded as trouble—declared that he could support an intermeeting hike only if Greenspan committed to consult the FOMC by conference call beforehand. Moreover, Lindsey wanted to tie the chairman's hands on the timing. He demanded that the conference call be held within two days of Greenspan's upcoming congressional testimony.

At this, Greenspan grew testy. "I've been Chairman of this Committee now for over six years," he retorted. "I hope I have enough credibility to know when a telephone call is appropriate."

"But there will be a phone call?" Lindsey pressed.

"Yes," Greenspan conceded.

With that, the committee rallied round and Greenspan won the vote, sidestepping the humiliation that Volcker had suffered when he had lost a vote on monetary policy and come close to resigning. But the FOMC meeting of February 1994 nonetheless marked a turning point in three ways. First, there was that press release; despite Greenspan's promise that it would set no precedent, the Fed never returned to its old practice of changing short-term interest rates without announcing anything. Second, Lindsey's intervention put an end to interest-rate moves between meetings on the chairman's discretion; after the troublemaker drew a line, Greenspan abandoned this method of bypassing his committee.[42] Third, after half a decade in which the Fed had not raised interest rates, the February 1994 meeting delivered a rate hike.[43] Nobody could be sure how markets would react. The next weeks might be bracing.

The day after the FOMC meeting was a Saturday. The newspapers reported that Senator Paul Sarbanes, Democrat of Maryland, had compared the central bank to "a bomber coming along and striking a farmhouse"—evidently, the Bush administration's penchant for Fed bashing was alive and well in some quarters.[44] But Greenspan went about his weekend business as usual. He rode his limousine across town to the Senate tennis court, where he was due to play with Lloyd Bentsen; and the next day he went to the French ambassador's residence for brunch before playing tennis yet again—this time with Wayne Angell, who had just stepped down as a Fed governor. Angell footfaulted sneakily, which offended Greenspan's deep desire to win.[45] But if the Fed chairman aimed to get on the tennis court four times per week, he needed people to play against, and Angell was better than a ball machine.

On Monday the markets reopened for business. Equities seemed mercifully calm; bonds were selling off a bit. All things considered, it was a reassuring mix: Greenspan had feared another stock market crash; but given that the rate hike had signaled the Fed's vigilance on inflation, he felt confident that bonds would rally. But by the last days of February, Greenspan was proved dramatically wrong. The thirty-year bond rate, which had been climbing anyway thanks to the economy's hot growth, now jumped from 6.3 percent at the start of the month to around 6.7 percent at the end of it. It was the outcome that Mike Prell's research had anticipated, and that Greenspan had brushed aside: higher short-term interest rates would lead to higher long-term ones. Moreover, Prell was being vindicated in an oddly powerful way. Somewhere in the belly of the bond market, something strange was stirring.

The personification of that something was seated at a bow-shaped trading desk in Midtown Manhattan, a portly figure with a bristling mustache and a bald pate, blinking at a phalanx of computer screens. His name was Michael Steinhardt, and he was in the vanguard of a new phenomenon: bond-trading hedge funds. After the recession of 1990, Steinhardt had seized the opportunity presented by the Fed's loose policy: he took out short-term loans from his brokers, paying the rock-bottom short-term interest rate, then lent money to the government by buying longer-term Treasury bonds, collecting the higher long-term rate. Thanks to the easy profits in this "carry trade," Steinhardt and his fellow hedge funders had expanded at a monstrous pace. Until around 1990, the very biggest hedge fund had less than $1 billion in assets. By the start of 1994, Steinhardt was managing $4.5 billion, and the number of hedge funds had leaped from a bit over one thousand in 1992 to perhaps three thousand a year later.[46] In at least one Treasury bond auction, in 1991, Steinhardt and another hedge funder contrived to buy 100 percent of the bonds offered—they owned the entire market.[47] In this brave new incarnation of Wall Street, the determinants of long-term borrowing costs were not merely inflation expectations, the pattern of short-term interest rates, or similar abstractions in economists' models. They included the emergence of an unfamiliar breed of superman speculator.

The rise of bond-trading hedge funds, along with hedge-fund-like operators inside Wall Street houses such as Goldman Sachs, was partly helpful to Fed policy. Reacting to a cut in the short-term rate by gobbling up bonds and driving down the long-term rate, traders amplified the Fed's decision to loosen—precisely what the Fed wanted when it was trying to stimulate the economy. In the wake of the S&L bust and the crippling losses at other traditional lenders, hedge funds were especially useful: by borrowing short and lending long, they were standing in for wounded banks—partially compensating for what Ben Bernanke, the Princeton professor, had termed the broken credit channel. But the hedge funds' amplification of monetary policy could be alarming, too—particularly because the power of the amplifier was variable and unpredictable. The hedge funds built their bond portfolios by piling debt upon debt: they lent money to the government by buying bonds, then pledged the bonds to their brokers as collateral so that they could borrow more, then used the proceeds of that borrowing to buy more bonds from the government. For every $100 million of U.S. Treasury bonds in Michael Steinhardt's portfolio, he had borrowed an astonishing $99 million, financing only $1 million of the purchase with capital belonging to himself or his investors. The result of this audacious leverage was that markets were primed to react fast. A fall in the bond market of just 1 percent would wipe out Steinhardt's entire equity stake, so he had no choice but to bail out at the first sign of trouble.

This was what explained the sharp jump in long-term interest rates that confronted the Fed in the last days of February. Hedge funders like Michael Steinhardt were rushing to sell bonds, and once the rush began, it cascaded unpredictably. Brokers who had happily lent hedge funds $99 million for each $100 million of collateral were now forced to reassess. With the bond market falling, the hedge funders' collateral was worth less, so the brokers changed their terms: henceforth, Steinhardt and his friends would be allowed to borrow $19 million, not $99 million, for every $1 million of real money. This abrupt withdrawal of credit put Wall Street into shock. Hedge funds were now forced to dump four fifths of their bond portfolios.

At the Fed's early February meeting, Greenspan had fought his colleagues to avoid an interest-rate hike of half a percentage point. By March 1, the rates on five- and ten-year Treasuries were up by half a percentage point anyway. Huge losses at the hedge funds were mirrored by losses on the bond-trading desks of the big banks; and rumors about their viability ricocheted around the Street, causing a temporary suspension of trading in shares of J.P. Morgan and Bankers Trust on the New York Stock Exchange. The insurance industry lost as much money on its bond holdings as it had paid out for damages following the recent Hurricane Andrew; "I'm starting to call this Hurricane Greenspan," quipped one insurance analyst. Anticipating the 2008 crisis, a hedge fund that traded exotic mortgage-backed securities blew up in particularly fine style, triggering a panic among its lenders and forcing yet more fire sales.[48] By the end of March, the five- and ten-year interest rates had jumped a further half a percentage point. Lawrence Lindsey's warning—that the bond bubble would pop—was beginning to prove prescient.

The market disruptions did not amuse the president. Thanks at least partly to prodding by Greenspan, Clinton had risked his political capital on deficit reduction, betting that the bond market would reward him. But the five-year bond rate was now *higher* than it had been at the time of his election, and the ten-year rate was at almost the same level.[49] In a further proof of his self-discipline, Clinton did not lash out against the Fed. But on March 31, 1994, he interrupted a vacation in California to phone Robert Rubin, the ex–Goldman Sachs chief who served as the top economic adviser in the White House.

For about half an hour, Rubin did his best to soothe the president. Long-term interest rates were only loosely tied to inflation expectations, despite what Greenspan might have said; besides, finance had evolved and the bond market was behaving unexpectedly. The new world of leveraged traders was a world of unpredictable connections: everyone was borrowing from everybody else, and any interruption to this chain could send interest rates off course, regardless of fundamental economic logic. Meanwhile, the market for debt securities had expanded dizzyingly over the past dozen years, and Wall Street firms were hiring physicists and equipping them with supercomputers as they designed ever more fanciful products. Complexity and leverage were weakening governments' ability to anticipate the market's moves, let alone control them.

The president finished his telephone conversation and walked out to face a small scrum of reporters. "No one believes that there's a serious problem with the underlying American economy," he declared bravely. "Some of these corrective things will happen from time to time, but there's no reason for people to overreact."[50]

For the Fed chairman, however, some soul-searching was in order. On an FOMC conference call on the last day of February 1994, Greenspan recognized the truth he had resisted earlier: the bond rally of 1993 had indeed been a bubble. "Looking back at our action, it strikes me that we had a far greater impact than we anticipated," he admitted. "I think we partially broke the back of an emerging speculation in equities. . . . In retrospect, we may well have done the same thing inadvertently in the bond market. . . . We pricked that bubble as well," he concluded. Later in his Fed tenure, Greenspan would strenuously resist the notion that a small shift in the federal funds rate could deflate a bubble—his denial was part of the case he developed for neglecting asset prices. But now he conceded that a modest act of tightening had forced speculators to retrench. Monetary policy could be a powerful tool—if the Fed chose to use it.

Greenspan offered up another confession for good measure. Every so often, he mused to his Fed colleagues, it paid to catch Wall Street unawares: shocks were the best antidote to complacency. "We also have created a degree of uncertainty," he reflected; "if we were looking at the emergence of speculative forces . . . then I think we had a desirable effect." Again, this observation contradicted Greenspan's subsequent stance: later in his tenure, he would be known for *not* surprising the markets. For much of the 2000s, he moved interest rates steadily and predictably, telegraphing his intentions via speeches, congressional hearings, and the FOMC's post-meeting statements; and the impact of his transparency was exactly as he had anticipated in 1994—traders were emboldened to leverage their portfolios, confident that the cost of borrowing would not move against them unexpectedly. If the Greenspan of 2004 had acted on the Greenspan observation of 1994, the bubble of 2006 might have been less disastrous.[51]

As the bond market continued its fall, Greenspan went further. Not only did the Fed have the ability to prick bubbles, it should be acutely conscious of its power, because bursting them could send the economy into a tailspin. The chief danger to stability, he told his FOMC colleagues on March 22, was not necessarily inflation; rather, "the only real danger to this economic outlook, as I see it right now, is the financial structure." A central bank that sought to dampen costly swings in the economy should not be blind to finance, Greenspan seemed to be saying: "If the financial system were to be ruptured, it would not be terribly difficult to bring the economy down very quickly." Lest his colleagues doubt his warning, he invoked the crash of 1929. "Go back and read the business annals," he implored. "They show economic conditions looking absolutely terrific three weeks before the roof caves in." A little later in the discussion, Greenspan invoked the 1920s again. Just as in the 1990s, inflation had been absent and growth had appeared strong. The implication was that getting employment and inflation right might not prevent a central bank from being humbled by finance.

During the so-called Great Moderation of the coming years, neglecting the fragility of finance would prove to be a costly error. Seen with the benefit of hindsight, therefore, the cycle of 1993–94 was a dry run for the future. Yet the more immediate lesson of this episode could be read the opposite way: finance was indeed fragile, but it might not affect the real economy. When the dust settled after Hurricane Greenspan, it was evident that Lawrence Lindsey had been right to diagnose a bubble, and right that its implosion could produce a nasty shock. But the shock was nasty—and then gone; the economy had been growing so strongly that it shrugged off the turmoil in the markets. Like the equity crash of 1987, the bond crash of 1994 barely mattered for Main Street. Having ignored Lindsey's warnings and then escaped unscathed, Greenspan was encouraged to take risks with financial stability later.

Twenty

ALAN VERSUS ALAN

Raised on the mid-Atlantic seaboard, educated at Princeton, his face framed by thick glasses and a domed pate, Alan Blinder could almost be taken for a young version of Paul Volcker. He had played basketball as a teenager; and though, unlike the towering Volcker, he never made the Princeton team, no other player at Syosset High School could equal his record for consecutive free throws.[1] Following the Volcker template, Blinder was instinctively a Democrat; he had a stern sense of social justice and a suspicion of Wall Street. And while he had chosen a career in academia—chairing the Princeton economics department—Blinder had a Volckerite hankering for public service. Dismayed by the supply-side coup during the early Reagan period, when, as he put it, "nonsense was worshipped as gospel," he firmly believed that economists had a duty to engage in public debates—otherwise, "the quacks would continue to dominate the pond."[2] Earnest, idealistic, humanized by a self-deprecating wit, Blinder was out to make the world a better place by writing about it, teaching about it, or perhaps even by running it.

At the beginning of 1994, Blinder was serving as one of the three principals on the Council of Economic Advisers in the Clinton White House. He was also moonlighting occasionally as a math tutor for the president's daughter, Chelsea: bonding with the first family was a perk of proximity.[3] Then, at the start of February, the Fed's number two slot opened, and Blinder quickly emerged as the front-runner to fill it. As an eminent monetary economist, and now as a solid member of the Clinton team, Blinder was an obvious pick. His selection would make him the first Democratic appointee to the Fed board since the 1970s. The *Washington Post* quickly described him as the natural successor to the chairmanship.[4]

If this speculation was unhelpful to Greenspan, it was only the half of it. Upon hearing of Blinder's likely arrival, Greenspan asked David Mullins, the outgoing vice chairman, to check into Blinder's writings. Mullins quickly discovered that in one crucial respect, Blinder was actually the anti-Volcker. In a book published seven years earlier, Blinder had trumpeted an unorthodox complaint: American policy makers erred "by exaggerating the perils of inflation."[5] Rising prices were "more like a bad cold than a cancer on society," Blinder maintained; and whereas the Fed under Volcker and Greenspan had elevated the fight against inflation above concerns for employment, Blinder argued for parity.[6] "Unemployment represents a waste of resources so colossal that no one truly interested in efficiency can be complacent about it," he lectured; it caused revenue losses that ran into the trillions.[7] Moreover, one argument commonly advanced for prioritizing inflation—that it was extraordinarily costly to reverse—did not impress Blinder in the least. "The myth that the inflationary demon, unless exorcized, will inevitably grow is exactly that a myth," he asserted; there was neither theoretical nor statistical support for it. To the contrary, it was the ravages of joblessness that were impossible to reverse. Once output was lost because of unemployment, the hit to prosperity could *never* be undone. Labor unutilized in one year was not available to boost output in the next year. It was gone forever.

"Don't worry," Mullins told Greenspan, "it's not like he's a Communist or anything. It's just in his early publications he's noticeably soft on inflation."

"I would have preferred he were a Communist," Greenspan said.[8]

The timing of Blinder's arrival at the Fed made things all the more awkward. Greenspan was partway through a tightening cycle that was likely to strain his relationship with the White House; Blinder would provide the Clinton team with a dovish ally within the FOMC. Everybody remembered how the Reagan team had used Manley Johnson to undermine Volcker. Moreover, the Fed's old confusions over monetary doctrine were starting to creep back, and the arrival of an outspoken freethinker like Blinder could only exacerbate them. During the first year of Clinton's presidency, Greenspan had united the Federal Open Market Committee around a focus on inflation, refusing to target asset prices. He had been helped in this endeavor by the changes around him: the challenge of financial stability had receded as Black Monday and the S&L bust had slipped to the back of people's minds; the case for focusing on inflation had been reinforced by the alleged payoff from lower long-term interest rates. But by the time the White House nominated Blinder to the Fed vice chairmanship, in April 1994, the bond-market blowup had disrupted this consensus. Financial stability had again emerged as a concern, and Greenspan's promise that focusing on inflation would bring down long-term interest rates had collided with the fact that long-term interest rates were now rising.

Blinder did his best to discourage reporters who sought to portray him as the Fed chairman-in-waiting. Nobody had ever jumped from the vice chairmanship to the top job at the Fed, he pointed out to them. Nevertheless, Greenspan's position suddenly looked precarious. His second term in office would expire in 1996, the year that he turned seventy. His new deputy was respected, Democratic, and twenty years younger. As if to add to Greenspan's troubles, the Clinton administration was simultaneously filling another vacant Fed governorship with an outspoken dove—an economist from Berkeley by the name of Janet Yellen. "A new coalition will form around Blinder," the chief economist at a large Wall Street firm predicted. "I think this is the beginning of the end for Greenspan."[9]

Although his seventieth birthday approached, Greenspan remained a vigorous figure. His regimen of exercise and doctors, combined with a fortunate genetic heritage, fended off the ravages of time; the back trouble that had been especially debilitating during his forties was now in abeyance. He sometimes walked with a slight shuffling stoop, but he could still produce a skilled golf swing, controlling the twist in his torso as the club went up, enjoying the momentum of body and grooved iron that lofted the ball into the distance. It was not quite the same feeling as driving a convertible Buick Electra on a brand-new interstate highway at the height of the American century, but it was not totally different: that same sense of power and motion, that same taste of affluence and well-being. In golf as in all things, Greenspan exhibited a will to win. He never conceded a short "gimme" putt. If he forced his opponent to play the shot, there was a chance he might miss it.

Not so infrequently, especially with summer approaching, Greenspan would leave his downtown office early to ride out to the old-world Chevy Chase Club in Washington's suburbs, the capital's answer to the New York sanctuaries to which he had belonged earlier. On balmy weekday evenings, he would set forth from a clubhouse that recalled antebellum Savannah, then play a round with John LaWare, the Fed governor responsible for bank oversight; or with Arthur Levitt, the chairman of the Securities and Exchange Commission; or with Kathy Kemper, a former tennis pro who was a fixture at Washington's power parties. Greenspan would often rent a cart to lug his clubs around, and as he whirred around the emerald landscape he might venture a quiet joke. But on other occasions he was too distracted to speak much. According to one regular partner, Greenspan could be so absorbed in his own thinking that he would take off in the buggy while the other player was still maneuvering himself into his seat. He sometimes came close to spinning his victim out of the side of the cart, leaving a mess of tasseled cleats and polo shirt heaped upon the fairway.

In the spring of 1994, confronted with the challenge from Blinder, Greenspan's competitive instincts kicked in with a vengeance. He had dealt with troublesome Fed governors before, putting them in charge of committees that would force them to expend energy on secondary issues, and managing the choreography of FOMC meetings so as to blunt their influence. Lawrence Lindsey, sent over by the Bush White House with the express purpose of needling Greenspan, was assigned to the committee on consumer and community affairs, which dealt with allegations of racial discrimination in bank lending; he soon found himself addressing booing crowds of hecklers in church halls. When it came to the challenge of Vice Chairman Blinder, Greenspan's methods would be different. But he was determined to contain him.

His efforts began with a new attempt to fix the Fed's doctrinal confusion. In the heat of the bond-market meltdown, in late February and March, Greenspan had sounded half open to the idea that the Fed might react to bubbles. Now, feeling threatened, he reverted to safe ground, defining the Fed's role narrowly in terms of stable prices. And because the hope that low inflation would mean low borrowing costs had been complicated by the plunge in the bond market, Greenspan sought out a new rationale for price stability.

Greenspan's chief prospect lay in an old hunch that low inflation boosted productivity. In the absence of inflation, firms would be unable to raise prices to consumers, he reasoned; they would therefore try harder to squeeze efficiency out of their operations.[10] It was not an entirely convincing hypothesis: firms have an incentive to cut operating costs regardless of the level of inflation. But Greenspan set Glenn Rudebusch, a Fed staff economist, to work on the links between inflation and productivity, testing all manner of permutations in the data. Every few weeks, Rudebusch would serve up some freshly crunched numbers, and Greenspan would devour them; one time Greenspan called Rudebusch from his car phone, eager to hear about his latest progress.[11] If only the inflation-productivity linkage could be proved, Greenspan would have the argument he needed to maintain the focus on inflation.

In May 1994, facing questions as to why the Fed was raising interest rates to head off inflation that had not yet materialized, Greenspan went public with his theory. Testifying before Congress, he proclaimed, "The lower the inflation, the higher the productivity growth rate." Conceding that the Fed's number crunching was still in progress, he pointed to "the extraordinary gains that seem to be occurring in the underlying growth rate of this economy, which I suspect—but I grant cannot conclusively demonstrate—is the result of low inflation." The implication for the fight against inflation was clear: the Fed should on no account "dissipate the gains that have been made because I suspect they are quite formidable."[12] Driving home his message to the senators, Greenspan concluded that "not only is it important to bring the inflation rate down from 10 percent to 5 percent, which everyone agrees to, but it's increasingly becoming evident that the lower we get under 5 percent, the more stable and growing the economy."

The truth was that Greenspan was gambling with his credibility. As it turned out, the productivity justification for squeezing inflation proved even less robust than the promise of reliably lower long-term interest rates. Although Rudebusch's data experiments found that productivity gains and stable prices might be correlated, it was impossible to establish causation; and when the Fed staff redid the calculations with revised GDP data, even the correlation crumbled.[13] Barry P. Bosworth, an economist at the Brookings Institution, observed to the *New York Times* that earlier academic research had failed to find an inflation-productivity connection, at least in economies with inflation below 20 percent; and he suggested, rather obviously, that Greenspan might simply be looking to head off political attacks on the Fed as it raised interest rates. "I think it's a bit of throwing everything at the fan and seeing what sticks," Bosworth said contemptuously.[14]

A way from the public eye, the case for focusing on inflation ran into new trouble—and Greenspan's challenge in facing down Blinder and the monetary doves grew even more daunting. At the July 1994 FOMC meeting, assuming himself to be on entirely safe ground, Greenspan remarked that a spurt of inflation could not durably boost job creation. The idea advanced in 1958 by the New Zealander A. W. Phillips, that higher inflation meant more employment, had long since been discredited; stagflation had shown the trade-off to be illusory except in the short term—"I think it doesn't exist," Greenspan said bluntly. Even if he was struggling to prove the benefits of low inflation, whether in the form of low long-term interest rates or higher productivity, the opposite claim that inflation might actually be desirable had surely been discredited.

A minute or two later, Lawrence Lindsey homed in on a section of the Fed staff forecast that suggested quite the contrary. Buried among the materials the staff had prepared for the meeting, Lindsey had found a set of charts that implied that inflation could be wonderful. By allowing faster price increases, the charts indicated, the Fed could create millions of jobs—and never pay a price for doing so. Inviting his colleagues to study the last chart in particular, Lindsey said incredulously, "It means, as I understand it, that simply by printing money we can increase the long-run aggregate amount of output in the economy."

Don Kohn, the director of the Division of Monetary Affairs, responded with his trademark calmness. He was easily the smoothest of the Fed's senior barons. Mike Prell, the head of the research division, could scarcely conceal his disdain for his supposed superiors on the FOMC; Ted Truman, the head of the international division, could fly off the handle with the governors and yell at them furiously. But nothing seemed to ruffle Kohn, even when he was confronted with the most extraordinary of facts. The Fed staff's model appeared to assume that inflation would be a boon for American workers. The Phillips curve was creaking back to life, like a self-regenerating zombie.

"If you believe that there are some costs to inflation, those are not embodied here," Kohn conceded to Lindsey. "The model itself doesn't have, I don't believe, losses in output from higher inflation rates," he reiterated a bit later.

"Ever?" Lindsey demanded. The implication of zero losses from inflation was surely crazy. Lindsey was determined to embarrass the staff by exposing its absurd conclusions.

"I don't believe so," Kohn said amiably.

Mike Prell tried to back up Kohn, but Lindsey was not to be placated.

"If I heard you right, we *never* have a net loss in output resulting from a choice to go for inflation?" he pressed disbelievingly. When he got into this sort of argument, he looked like he might blow his top. Richard Darman's vision of his tossing grenades through office doors became disconcertingly plausible.

Greenspan weighed in, eager to dispatch the troublemaker. "The argument as to why we get a net loss is 'the Federal Reserve will react—do something,'" he suggested. But for an avowed foe of inflation, this was incredibly thin stuff. Greenspan was conceding that inflation itself might not be damaging. It was the remedy—high interest rates—that was painful.

Anticipating the obvious rejoinder, Greenspan added: "The question is, we are the Federal Reserve and why should we react if that's true?" This was indeed a reasonable question. Greenspan did not volunteer an answer.

"We should let inflation go up. It's as simple as that," Lindsey concluded sarcastically. Such was the logic of the staff economists' model. Politicians who accused the Fed of a groundless inflation obsession might be closer to the mark than they realized.

"Is there anyone around the table who thinks that by printing money, the present value of output of this economy will go up?" Lindsey continued. "If there is, I will join them in voting to cut the discount rate to zero."

"Oh, no, you don't mean that statement as you said it!" Greenspan protested.

"Why not?" Lindsey shot back mercilessly.

As luck would have it, this was Alan Blinder's first FOMC meeting. He appeared understandably bemused: the most august group of monetary policy makers in the world seemed somewhat at sea about the basics of its mission. Responding to Lindsey's last retort, Blinder blurted out that the Fed had a legal duty to protect stable prices. The Federal Reserve Act required it to do so.

Greenspan could not resist the opportunity to bait the newcomer. Was he not supposed to be a dove? Would Blinder wish to follow the letter of the Federal Reserve Act if 11 percent inflation were actually better for the economy than 10 percent?

"If 11 percent is better than 10 percent . . ." Blinder repeated uncertainly. He had evidently been thrown off guard. "If there's no cost to inflation—I am a little bit surprised at the tenor of this conversation around here!"

Teasing aside, the argument had illustrated an alarming fact: nobody could really say why inflation mattered.[15] Neither Greenspan's intuition nor the number crunchers on his staff could show why Blinder's past writings were wrong—perhaps inflation really did resemble a mere head cold? The awkward truth was that, reacting to the 1970s, the Fed had developed a loathing for inflation that exaggerated its real toll. Surveying the evidence three years later, the future Nobel laureate Paul Krugman would observe, "One of the dirty little secrets of economic analysis is that even though inflation is universally regarded as a terrible scourge, efforts to measure its costs come up with embarrassingly small numbers."[16]

The month after that disconcerting FOMC meeting, the Federal Reserve's leaders convened in Jackson Hole, Wyoming. Since the start of the 1980s, when Paul Volcker's love of fly-fishing had led him to accept an invitation to a symposium in Jackson, the long, flat-roofed Jackson Lake Lodge had been transformed for a few days each August into a sort of central bankers' summer camp. FOMC members, distinguished professors, and foreign monetary chieftains gathered in the shadows of the spectacular mountains, mixing sessions on economics with whitewater rafting and moose spotting. Greenspan attended faithfully, escaping the swampy Washington summer, often staying at a guesthouse on the splendid estate owned by James Wolfensohn, the networking Wall Street charmer who in 1995 became president of the World Bank. There would be dinner in the Wolfensohns' exquisite designer cabin, with its sprucewood pillars soaring thirty feet up to the cathedral roof; Andrea would often come, accompanying Wolfensohn's wife, Elaine, on hikes and horse rides. Alan, for his part, was less interested in scenery. He preferred pastimes that allowed you to keep score—ones where you could tell if you were winning.

Greenspan's driver arrived early on a Thursday morning to take him to Dulles Airport. Later in his tenure, Greenspan would sometimes accept a ride in Wolfensohn's private jet. But this year, like most years, he made his way to Jackson just like any normal member of the global elite, flying out to Colorado and then changing planes for the onward hop northwestward. To the north of Jackson lay the National Elk Refuge and the Grand Teton National Park, and beyond that a traveler would reach Yellowstone, home to geysers and grizzlies. It was the sort of heroic wilderness in which Ayn Rand's Atlases might have sought refuge from a collectivist world. A car drove Greenspan along the flat bed of the stunning valley and wound its way up to the Jackson Lake Lodge, where the monetary establishment was waiting for him.

The topic for the Jackson Hole symposium in 1994 was "Reducing Unemployment"—testimony to the fact that objectives other than inflation remained on central banks' agendas. Standing before the hundred or so people lucky enough to be allowed into this economic sanctum, Greenspan opened the proceedings, a familiar figure with large black-rimmed spectacles and large ears, beloved by the world's newspaper cartoonists. Politely, Greenspan stipulated that jobs were a matter of concern. "We are keenly interested in what we can do to maximize sustainable employment growth and to reduce unemployment," he intoned earnestly. Then he introduced his caveat. There were limits to the power of monetary policy to conjure up jobs, he insisted—he was not about to mention the contrary assumptions embedded in the Fed staff's model. Referring obliquely to the arguments over inflation's costs, Greenspan repeated his unproved productivity hunch. Such costs would probably exceed what economists had so far measured, he suggested.[17]

For the next two days, a brisk debate ensued: between inflation fighters and doves; between economists who wanted monetary policy to focus on prices only and those who believed in also targeting employment. The high priest of the inflation-only faction was Donald Brash, the governor of the Reserve Bank of New Zealand—the first central bank to adopt an explicit inflation-only target. Brash was thin, bespectacled, and mild of manner, but his message was not mild in the least: contrary to the teaching of his countryman A. W. Phillips, he insisted that central banks had no business trying to create jobs, because they had no power to do so. "There is a growing body of evidence suggesting that inflation hinders growth," Brash continued, not pausing to mention what that evidence might be. Focusing exclusively on inflation was "the best contribution monetary policy can make to growth and employment prospects."

For the counterpoint to Brash, the conference organizers had turned to Alan Blinder. Given his outlook, Blinder was the obvious leader of the dovish faction. After all, he had written that "inflation, like every teenager, is greatly misunderstood—and that this gross misunderstanding blows the political importance of inflation out of all proportion to its economic importance."[18] He had once even mocked Greenspan's patron Gerald Ford, who had declared that inflation would "destroy our country, our homes, our liberties"—"Destroy our homes?" Blinder had quipped. "Gee, I thought inflation destroyed my mortgage."[19] But in assigning Blinder a prominent slot on their agenda, the symposium organizers were also recognizing his official status. Blinder would be speaking not just as a leading academic dove but as vice chairman of the Fed—and according to the rumor mill, as a future Fed chairman.[20]

Blinder took the stage, looking faintly nervous. He had a slight tic in his right eye, and he exuded a tense air, even when what he had to say was authoritative and humorous. "While I am not young by any reasonable criterion, I am very young as a central banker," he began, perhaps drawing a contrast with Greenspan; then he recalled that he had attended the Jackson Hole symposium "several times before, but always as an academic speaker, where my role was clearly to say something and maybe even to say something interesting." Now, Blinder deadpanned, "in my new job, my new role is to say nothing and certainly not to say anything interesting."

Blinder proceeded to the substance of his remarks, staking out territory that stood between the Phillips curve faith of the 1960s and the inflation-targeting creed of Don Brash and his disciples. "Where employment is concerned, in the short run macroeconomics is everything and in the long run macroeconomics is nothing," he postulated, capturing the consensus in the economics profession. Contrary to what A. W. Phillips had claimed, central banks had no power to change the unemployment rate in the long run; instead, long-term unemployment reflected *microeconomic* factors such as the flexibility of the workforce, just as Brash and the inflation targeters argued.[21] But in the short run, Blinder insisted, macroeconomics—meaning, the level of demand—certainly did matter. If the total amount of spending in the economy fell below the economy's ability to supply things, unemployment would move above its "natural" rate—the rate at which wage increases would be steady and inflation would be stable. In these circumstances, a demand-boosting stimulus could get people back to work.

What followed became known as *l'affaire Blinder.* Eager to extract some drama from the symposium, the *New York Times* proclaimed that Blinder, "a leading candidate" to accede to the Fed chairmanship, "publicly broke ranks with most of his colleagues"—even though the Fed's short-run ability to boost jobs was acknowledged by everyone, Greenspan included.[22] The next day the *Times* ran a second pot-stirring story, painting Blinder as a dissident, out of the mainstream; and the day after that it followed with an editorial. Soon the *Economist* and the *Financial Times* weighed in, and the normally fair-minded *Newsweek* columnist Robert Samuelson declared that Blinder lacked the "moral or intellectual qualities needed to lead the Fed."[23] It was an astonishing accusation, and Blinder was left wondering how this feeding frenzy had begun—and more to the point, why Greenspan had failed to stop it. Surely the Fed chairman could have protected Blinder from the second and third waves of attack? He knew the Fed reporters well, and a few calming words from him would have caused them to back off. After all, the differences between the two Alans had been mischievously exaggerated. Nothing in Blinder's remarks warranted the media assault that now descended on him.

Blinder could only guess at Greenspan's role in the affair—which was perhaps the best proof of Greenspan's deftness. Conceivably, the Fed chairman was entirely innocent: maybe he had neglected to stick up for Blinder because his mind was on other things; or maybe, as Greenspan himself said later, he thought it was a mistake to dignify press attacks by reacting to them.[24] Equally conceivable, however, was that Greenspan might be capable of dirty tricks: on this theory, he had stayed mum because he was happy to see his putative successor stabbed by the media. As the blood pooled around his ankles, Blinder could not know for sure. The Fed chairman's fingerprints were not on the dagger.

Greenspan left Jackson the day after Blinder's speech and flew to San Francisco with Andrea. They were to take their annual weeklong vacation in Carmel Valley, at a tennis camp created by John Gardiner, a pioneer of the luxury sports industry whose stylish retreats were favored by film stars and political rainmakers. Lloyd Bentsen, Treasury secretary and tennis friend, had suggested to Alan and Andrea that they would enjoy Gardiner's place: it was beautiful, comfortable, and just wild enough to feel a little funky. Alan and Andrea stayed in an adobe house on a hilltop, and the camp organizers lent them a beat-up VW Beetle to tootle up and down the slope. There were drills and games all morning, and Alan would flash his surprisingly strong forearms, which were sadly wasted on a man who lived in suits; and Rick Manning, the Yale-educated head pro, would tease Alan good-naturedly, much to Andrea's amusement. Then they would stop for a delicious lunch; and Alan would nap and read or play a bit more tennis. The gardens were exotic, and stars lit up the night sky. It was, Andrea recalled, "perfectly romantic."[25]

Feeling rested and fit, the couple flew back to Washington. On Sunday they took part in one of the capital's A-list rituals: they trooped off to watch the Washington Redskins open the new football season at RFK Stadium. The main event was not really the football; it was the experience of riding the owner's private elevator up into the sky and stepping into the pregame party in the Vince Lombardi Room. There the Redskins' vinegary octogenarian proprietor, Jack Kent Cooke, played host to presidential aspirants and ambassadors and power journalists, not to mention a large contingent of ladies in "Chanel, silk, French twists and lorgnettes," as one visitor recorded.[26] When the game started, the guests proceeded over a catwalk to the owner's box, a cluster of Naugahyde seats with hovering waitresses and too much wine; and Cooke presided powerfully as if this were the Oval Office East, an important telephone by his side and important sycophants around him. It barely mattered that the team played miserably, losing by an embarrassing margin. Watching the Redskins from the owner's box was "a ruling-class ritual on an emotional, if not esthetic, par with Wimbledon and Ascot for the British," as one student of power put it.[27]

Monday was Labor Day, and Alan and Andrea played more tennis at the Chevy Chase Club. Andrea, who had taken up the sport comparatively recently, enjoyed playing with Alan so long as he did not resort too frequently to his sneaky left-handed slice, a shot that later caused Christopher Meyer, the British ambassador, to dub the Fed chairman Greenspin.[28] After the Chevy Chase Club, the couple attended a potluck barbecue arranged by Alan's tennis-and-golf friend Kathy Kemper. Greenspan's official diary records that Andrea was to contribute a pasta salad to Kemper's casual buffet, and that the dress code called for "T-shirts and flipflops." History does not relate how the Fed chairman interpreted this directive toward ease. But at least for a moment, the fights about the central bank's mandate retreated to the periphery of his vision.

The fall of 1994 was a low point for the Clinton presidency. The economy was growing respectably and unemployment dipped below 6 percent for the first time in four years, but Democrats sustained a crushing blow in the midterm congressional elections. The rising force in politics was now another ebullient baby boomer from the South: Newt Gingrich, the incoming House Speaker.

Gingrich was a conservative Republican, but he was not the sort of politician who naturally appealed to the Fed chairman. Greenspan had enjoyed a close relationship with Tom Foley, the Democrat whom Gingrich had ejected from the speakership; like Bill Webster, the CIA chief who had served Reagan and Bush, Foley shared a birthday with Greenspan, and the three power brokers met for lunch on March 6 each year to celebrate, united by establishment ties and unbothered by party differences.[29] Gingrich, by contrast, was a populist scourge of the establishment. He was not inclined to lunch with people from the opposite side of the aisle; indeed, it was hard to imagine him extending any sort of courtesy to anyone. His views on economics combined a patina of brilliance with the fantasies of Jack Kemp. The United States should aspire to growth of 5 percent per year, he insisted. This was fully twice the sustainable, noninflationary rate, according to the Fed's estimate.[30]

As he picked himself up from the midterm elections, Clinton also bridled at the Fed's restrictive view of the economy. He doubted the need to raise interest rates preemptively, before inflation had arrived; and he rejected the assumption that the natural, or noninflationary, rate of unemployment was stuck at its historic level of around 6 percent. Confiding to the authorized chronicler of his administration in late 1994, Clinton argued that global competition deterred companies from raising prices, and that the decline of labor unions had reduced workers' ability to agitate for extra pay. For both these reasons, inflation was a distant threat; unemployment could be allowed to fall lower without igniting price increases. Sometimes, when Greenspan was due to come over to the White House, the president would entertain his advisers with an imitation of the Fed chairman: a cheerless old man droning on about inflation. The bloom from that first meeting in Little Rock seemed to be fading. The president respected Greenspan; it was not clear that he liked him.

A few days after the congressional elections, facing potential hostility from the new House Speaker and the wounded president, Greenspan bravely risked his popularity: he confronted his FOMC colleagues with a proposal to raise the federal funds rate by a hefty 75 basis points. It would be the steepest hike of his tenure, and it would take the cumulative tightening in 1994 to fully 2.5 percentage points; it was as though Greenspan had listened to Gingrich and Clinton wax lyrical about the economy's potential and had resolved to pick a fight with both of them. The chairman's proposal was especially provocative because it was based on little more than a personal judgment that the economy needed it. The consumer price index was rising at a relatively subdued 2.6 percent per year. Why throttle the economy?

When the FOMC debate got under way, Alan Blinder was adamant that a 75 basis point hike would be excessive. The case for a sharp tightening was based on the assumption that there would be no corresponding jump in long-term interest rates; where did this assumption come from? Greenspan was going on the theory that the Fed's earlier rate hikes would not be adequate to keep inflation in check; perhaps he was fiddling too nervously with the monetary thermostat? Blinder had gone to the lengths of getting the Fed staff to run different scenarios through its forecasting model, and the results had confirmed his suspicion that 75 basis points would be too much. "Nobody has to believe these numbers," he conceded, referring to the simulations by the staff, "but I don't know where else to get numbers other than trying to put this policy through an econometric model." Blinder's implication was obvious: Greenspan was going with his gut, ignoring scientific method.

Greenspan stood his ground calmly. Blinder was welcome to his models: he was an academic. But the mechanism linking the Fed's interest-rate lever to the real economy was a prime example of a phenomenon that could *not* be modeled: it changed character so fast that a statistical study of its past told you little about its future. The bond-market convulsion of February served as a reminder of this truth: no model knew about Michael Steinhardt, so no model had been accurate. Further back in Greenspan's memory, the rise of home-equity extraction in the mid-1970s had demonstrated the same point: thanks to new players in mortgage finance, hikes in short rates did little to restrain the economy. And so rather than relying on the Fed's staff model to assess the effect of tightening, Greenspan had taken to gaming through the market's probable reactions in his head. If monetary policy operated through the psychology of traders, then he, too, would think like a trader, summoning up the lessons he had learned in the commodity-futures pit.

Greenspan's attempts to imagine his way into the mind of the market produced some bewildering pronouncements. "What bothers me about doing only 50 basis points," he told his FOMC colleagues at the November 1994 meeting, "is that even though the markets are saying that that is what we probably are going to do, I think we have to distinguish between what they are forecasting we are going to do based on our past behavior and what they think we ought to do." To critics such as Blinder, this circuitous psychologizing was blather—"Nobody really knows about market psychology," Blinder said bluntly. Moreover, Greenspan's effort to think his way into the mind of the market was not appropriate, either: a central bank representing the broad interests of Americans should not be obsessing about mood changes on Wall Street. "It sends a signal that I find very unfortunate: that we can be led around by the markets," Blinder objected. The Fed was rightly savoring its newfound independence from politicians. It would be perverse to discard that independence by capitulating to the whims of baby-faced traders in yellow suspenders.

Once Blinder had finished, Greenspan had his turn. "Okay, I propose that we move 75," he announced briskly. The committee rallied behind him without a murmur. For all Blinder's eloquence, nobody was listening to him.

Greenspan's ambitious rate hike of November 1994 met with skepticism from both wings of the economics profession. On the right, Greenspan's old friend Milton Friedman chided him for overreach. "The desire to fine-tune the economy is almost irrepressible," he told the *Washington Post*. "If we knew enough, it could be useful, but because we don't, it is almost misguided." On the left, critics focused on the unpredictable vagaries of markets, which made the effect of Fed moves correspondingly uncertain. "There is a great hubris in the belief that by changing the cost of financing, the Fed can control the pace of economic activity," observed Hyman Minsky, an economist who would later be celebrated for his prescient analysis of bubbles. Yet despite the plausible pushback from Blinder, and despite this barrage of attacks, Greenspan was ultimately vindicated. After the record rate hike of November 1994, long-term interest rates did not spike up, as Blinder had feared; instead they stabilized, just as Greenspan had expected. By means of this tightening and a further one the following February, the Fed engineered a soft landing, slowing the economy down without triggering a recession.[31] Inflation was kept firmly under control throughout 1994 and 1995; unemployment stayed below the "natural rate" of 6 percent and gradually drifted downward.[32] Neither too hot nor too cold, this miracle soon came to be known as the Goldilocks economy.[33]

The soft landing of 1994 defused the Jackson Hole argument. There was no point debating whether to prioritize inflation or employment: the economy was performing brilliantly on both measures. There was no point speculating about the end of the Greenspan era; as Blinder himself later concluded, "Never disagree with Greenspan on tactics: He will be better."[34] The Fed chairman's emergence as a maestro advanced by two impressive bounds. If the first step had come in 1993, when the politicians relieved the pressure on the Fed to act as a bad cop by committing to a tighter fiscal policy, the next steps followed in 1994–95, when Greenspan steered the economy away from the inflationary rocks without beaching it on the shoals of a recession. In the process of his first triumph, in 1993, Greenspan had shrugged off the challenge from Larry Lindsey; as he accomplished his second one, in 1994, he had outmaneuvered a formidable vice chairman and academic star who had been touted as his natural successor.[35] Frustrated and defeated, Blinder soldiered on through 1995 and then resigned in January 1996. Thereafter, Fed governors seldom posed a challenge to Greenspan. The era of the imperial Fed chairmanship was beginning.[36]

And yet there were two doubts about the maestro's progress. More than anybody cared to notice, his success reflected luck: if consumer price inflation stood at an impressively low 2.7 percent at the end of 1994, down from 6.3 percent on the eve of the Gulf War, this success had materialized despite significant errors. The Fed had underestimated the credit crunch of 1991–92, and so had run tighter policy than it had intended. It had misread the economy in 1993, wrongly attributing declining long-term interest rates to falling inflation expectations.[37] And yet regardless of the Fed's errors, deeper forces were conspiring to bring down inflation: global competition, advancing technology, declining labor-union membership. In this unfamiliar new economy, periods of monetary looseness were more likely to result in bubbles than in consumer price spikes. But nobody bothered with such obscure quibbles. Greenspan was presiding over low inflation and strong growth. His reputation prospered marvelously.

The other doubt about the maestro's emergence was more immediate. Almost inevitably, the big interest-rate hikes of 1994 were going to cause a blowup.

Twenty-one

THE ZIPSWITCH
CHAIRMAN

O range County, California, is the home of Disneyland—and therefore of the Sleeping Beauty Castle. In late 1994 it became notorious for a fantasy castle of the financial variety. The county treasurer, Robert Citron, contrived to lose an astonishing $1.6 billion of taxpayers' money, and what was more alarming was the manner of his humiliation. The treasurer and his advisers had conjured up a make-believe portfolio, muttering a series of mysterious spells: ratio swap, periodic floor, spread lock, Treasury-linked swap, knockout call option, wedding band. On December 6, these shadowy spells broke—a month after the Fed's 75 basis point rate hike, Orange County filed the largest municipal bankruptcy in U.S. history. Nor was Orange County the only victim of the new dark arts. Around the same time, companies such as Procter & Gamble and Gibson Greeting Cards succumbed to similar enchantments, losing tens of millions of dollars.

In the seven years since Greenspan's arrival at the Fed, a profound change had taken place in the heart of the financial system. Financial derivatives, which had proliferated in the 1970s in response to the new volatility of interest rates and exchange rates, took on a bewildering complexity. Before, banks had traded relatively simple products: futures and options on stocks, interest rates, and currencies. Now Wall Street was hiring armies of young men with physics PhDs to dream up esoteric instruments. The quants delighted in slicing ordinary bonds into strange "strips"; the flows of money they generated were separated into interest-only payments and principal-only repayments, creating new securities known as IOs and POs; there were inverse IOs, inverse POs, and even a mind-boggling creature called the forward inverse IO. Firms such as Morgan Stanley assembled teams of scientists to apply ideas like chaos theory to markets, and hedge funds such as Long-Term Capital Management began to bet not on the direction of a market's move but rather on *how far* it would move in either direction. The sheer speed with which derivatives proliferated was remarkable. As of the end of 1987, the face value of privately negotiated derivatives—mostly interest-rate swaps—amounted to under $1 trillion. Seven years later, the number had soared more than tenfold, reaching $11 trillion.[1]

In the wake of the disasters at Orange County, Procter & Gamble, and Gibson Greeting Cards, *Fortune*'s Carol Loomis did her best to understand what was happening. Loomis was the doyenne of financial journalists, the writer who had exposed the workings of the first ever "hedged fund"—she was not easily bamboozled. Cornering the boss of Bankers Trust, the bank that had sold fancy derivatives to P&G and Gibson, she demanded to know how these instruments functioned: "What is a wedding band?" she asked him. The boss, Charles S. Sanford Jr., who was himself a former trader, turned out to be hazy: the sorcerers in his kitchen had brewed up their mysterious spells, but he had little idea how they functioned. Sanford suggested that Loomis direct her question to one of his derivatives experts, and the next day a Bankers Trust official called to explain that a wedding band "was a swap containing a series of barrier options." This lurch into barrier options caused Loomis to feel as though her mind were shutting down, as she reported to her readers.[2] In the sheer opacity of its jargon, Bankers Trust anticipated the notorious CDOs-squared that came to light in the 2008 crisis.

Sanford's fuzzy grasp of his own bank's products raised a question for Greenspan. The Fed chairman had always believed that private risk management would be superior to oversight by regulators. A decade earlier, after Mexico's default and the Continental Illinois failure, he had made this point explicitly: bankers were evidently guilty of taking on bad risks, but it was their job to evaluate borrowers, and it was their companies' capital that was on the line—however fallible they were, they would be less fallible than civil servants. But the losses that bubbled up from the derivatives markets in 1994 might reasonably have prompted a reconsideration of this creed. Finance had grown so complex that private risk takers no longer understood their own portfolios. And Charles Sanford's confusion was only the start. The really woeful ignorance was to be found among his firm's clients.

Those wedding-band swaps illustrated the problem nicely. They promised a profit so long as interest rates remained within a narrow range, inflicting losses the moment that rates moved above the band or below it. This sort of arrangement had no obvious risk-management purpose; it was a gamble, pure and simple. It was a gamble, moreover, that the clients were almost bound to lose, precisely because of the derivatives' complexity. The sorcerers at Bankers had deliberately dreamed up products that their clients could not understand; they were preying on the innocent. In taped conversations that later came to light, Bankers employees referred routinely to the "ROF-factor"—short for "rip-off factor"—in their deals. Celebrating the befuddlement of his clients, one trader looked forward to "a massive, huge fucking gravy train"; "this is a wet dream," he added. Another Bankers Trust employee mused thoughtfully about the experience of selling complex derivatives. "Funny business, you know?" he said to a friend. "Lure people into that calm and then just totally fuck 'em."[3]

The Fed, to its credit, dealt with Bankers Trust sternly. The examiners at the New York Fed favored the traditional response of a private rebuke; a public humiliation could undermine a bank's credibility, perhaps triggering a run and knock-on instabilities. But the Washington Fed favored a tougher approach, and was willing to take the risk of reprimanding Bankers publicly. The dispute resulted in a standoff between the Fed's two most powerful branches, with the Washingtonians grumbling that the New Yorkers were too soft; eventually the matter was brought before Greenspan and the Fed's Board of Governors. Generally, Greenspan did not like to clobber the private sector, and he knew Charles Sanford personally. But he did not shrink from a tough line, especially when John LaWare, the governor in charge of regulation, with whom he played golf, came out in favor of a public shaming.[4] An enforcement action was duly brought, requiring Sanford's firm to hire outside counsel to investigate past abuses.[5] People were impressed. "No matter how you slice it, Bankers Trust has agreed to change its conduct," one analyst observed. "There is no question that these were bad boys."[6]

It was one thing to get tough with a bank, another to grapple with the broader challenge posed by newfangled financial instruments. Bankers Trust was not the only abuser of the new products; Orange County had got its fix of poison courtesy of Merrill Lynch, suggesting that the whole business of designer swaps might be a cauldron of trouble. Derivatives, said the former FOMC member Richard Syron, were now "the eleven-letter four-letter word"; and Senator Byron Dorgan, Democrat of North Dakota, promised a bill barring banks from trading in derivatives for their own accounts—a measure that anticipated the spirit of the "Volcker Rule," passed after the 2008 crisis.[7] The stage was set for regulatory action, if only the Fed would go along with it.

The day after Orange County's bankruptcy, at the height of the derivatives panic, Greenspan appeared before the Joint Economic Committee of Congress. Senator Ron Wyden, Democrat of Oregon, gave voice to the nation's misgivings. The government, he charged, had "not acted as an adequate watchdog over the derivatives market and some of these pretty exotic instruments."

Greenspan was being invited to lay out a response to the new finance. Instead, he laid out the case for doing nothing. Derivatives, he explained firmly, were a zero-sum game. Unlike leverage, they did not magnify risk; they merely redistributed it. Of course, some zero-sum gamblers would be zeroed out. But in a healthy market system, risk takers should be ready to lose their shirts; "I don't consider it to be something which gives me great concern," Greenspan lectured. Meanwhile, the risk-shifting properties of derivatives would move financial exposure to the investors who could absorb it best. "I must say we think that's very helpful," Greenspan concluded.[8]

Greenspan's description of derivatives was only half accurate. In theory, if they were managed properly, the new products would have the benign effects that he outlined, shifting risks to institutions that could manage them most safely. But the benign potential of derivatives came bundled with two significant downsides. The complexity of the most exotic contracts made it easy to rip off clients: this lesson emerged from the abusive selling of toxic mortgage securities before the 2008 crash, but the same lesson could have been learned more than a decade earlier, courtesy of the Bankers Trust scandal. Equally, complexity made it possible for crazy risks to build up inside financial enterprises, unbeknownst to their own managers. This was the lesson taught in 2008 by AIG insurance, a venerable enterprise laid low by derivative sorcerers. But the same lesson might have been absorbed in 1994. Charles Sanford's fuzziness about his own company's wedding-band swaps was a portent of the future.

Greenspan ignored these early clues about the dangers lurking within finance. In part, he ignored them because regulatory questions failed to engage him intellectually. When it came to the federal funds rate, he would fight his committee doggedly over a difference of 25 basis points; on regulatory issues, he followed the majority. This reflected his sense of his own strengths. Monetary policy hinged on canny economic forecasting, his strong suit. Regulatory policy hinged on a fine understanding of precedent and rule books, and such legalisms bored him. But the main reason why Greenspan glossed over the derivatives danger lay elsewhere. Just as he shrank from using monetary policy to fight bubbles because it was hard, so he understood that getting financial regulation right was virtually impossible.[9] Volcker had failed at it, presiding over the banks' disastrous lending to Latin America and over the creation of the first too-big-to-fail precedent in the Continental Illinois bailout; now the derivatives mess showed that Greenspan too might fail at it. To a politically astute Fed chairman, the smart course was to avoid entanglement in regulation in the first place—to leave it to lesser colleagues at the Fed, to maintain that markets would manage their own risks, to define financial instability as something other than his problem. The upshot was that Greenspan shrank from deploying both of the tools he might have wielded against financial excess. He would not use monetary policy to target bubbles. He would not use regulatory policy to clamp down on crazy risk taking.

Seven years earlier, at his confirmation hearing in the Senate, Greenspan had previewed one part of his response to the Bankers Trust imbroglio. "History tells us that we become overenthusiastic about certain types of financial arrangements, certain types of ideas, and we overdo it," he reflected. But then he expressed faith that such errors would be self-correcting: their senses sharpened by salutary losses, financiers would mend their ways and regulatory reform would be superfluous.[10] By way of an example, Greenspan cited Mexico's default in 1982. Before, Wall Street bankers had lent heedlessly to Mexico; after, they had learned their lesson. "International lending will be significantly more prudent in the years ahead," Greenspan told the senators. "I don't think any new policies have to be implemented."

It was a hope more than a forecast—a hope born of the fact that Greenspan had no appetite for regulatory remedies. But what if the hope turned out to be empty? If financiers committed the same errors, over and over, perhaps it might be time to recognize that the faith in self-correcting prudence was deluded?[11]

Toward the end of 1994, Greenspan booked a room at the Stanhope, the elegant Fifth Avenue hotel across from Central Park that had become his home away from home in Manhattan. He wanted to get away with Andrea after Christmas—they would dine together at Le Périgord, scene of their first date exactly one decade earlier. So much had happened in their relationship since then: Andrea had grown closer to him than anyone had ever been, with the exception of his mother. They had their minor differences, to be sure. She had been lobbying to acquire a chocolate Labrador; he vetoed four-legged intrusions. She liked elegant Merchant Ivory movies; he liked adrenaline-soaked car chases. She had a taste for delicate cooking; he was content with mashed potatoes. But Alan and Andrea clicked in the important ways: in their love of music, politics, A-list parties, and spectator sports; in their clear determination, above all, that work always came first—and that each would willingly make space for the other's devotion to it. In this helter-skelter rush of living, moments of tranquility were to be savored. It would be a pleasure to wander the city where they had first met, away from the fishbowl of the capital.

Before escaping to New York, Greenspan celebrated Christmas Eve with Lane Kirkland, president of the AFL-CIO. Kirkland had been Greenspan's friend since their joint service on the Reagan-era Social Security commission, and the fact that the labor leader and the libertarian remained close reflected the bipartisan spirit of old Washington. The next morning Greenspan consorted with yet more liberals, accompanying Andrea to the usual festival of Christmas presents at the home of Al Hunt and Judy Woodruff. Only a few weeks earlier, the hugely influential conservative talk radio host, Rush Limbaugh, had warned Republicans against fraternizing with the liberal media: "You will *never ever* be their friends. They don't *want* to be your friends. Some female reporter will come up to you and start batting her eyes and ask you to go to lunch. . . . Don't fall for this."[12] Watching Andrea's goddaughter tear open her Christmas loot that morning, Alan was evidently indifferent to Limbaugh's fatwa. He was romantically entangled with a tough liberal reporter who batted her eyes with the best of them.

Greenspan played tennis on Christmas afternoon, but worldly concerns were about to encroach on the spirit of the holidays. Hard on the heels of Orange County's failure, Mexico was on the brink of a default;

contrary to Greenspan's confirmation testimony, financiers had evidently forgotten the lesson about lending recklessly to Mexico. Spooked by a political assassination and an insurgency in Mexico's south, they were now rushing to yank their money out—it was 1982 all over again, except that this time it was scarier. Then, Volcker had rescued Mexico with a mere $3.5 billion; this time, Mexico had debts of fully $28 billion that would come due over the next year. Moreover, the nature of the creditors had changed. In 1982, Mexico's loans had come from banks; Volcker could get their bosses in a room and direct them not to pull their money out. But this time, the creditors were bondholders. They were too numerous and dispersed to be herded.

Fresh from his Christmas tennis game, Greenspan met with Jaime Serra, the Mexican finance minister, and Lawrence Summers, the former Harvard professor who led the international side of the Treasury. Serra explained that the situation was desperate.

The United States had to provide the money to allow Mexico to repay its creditors. But for Greenspan and the Treasury, there were risks in saying yes. The weakening of market discipline that results from any bailout would be replicated on an international scale. Just as Continental Illinois had been revealed to be too big to fail, so Mexico would now appear too big to fail, or too geopolitically important. The resulting "moral hazard"—the precedent suggesting that Wall Street could spray money at emerging markets and expect taxpayers to make good their losses—would be more toxic by far than anything that had happened during the third-world debt crises of the previous decade. Volcker had punished American bankers who lent foolishly: their repayments had been postponed and they had been forced to swallow losses. But Greenspan and the Treasury would be providing taxpayer dollars to Mexico, and Mexico would be shoveling those same dollars straight into the pockets of reckless foreign bondholders. Greenspan's assertion in his confirmation testimony—that financiers would learn from their errors—would be turned upon its head. Far from repeat errors being unlikely in finance, each error would make the next one *more* likely because the incentive to avoid error would have been diluted.

Despite the strong case against a rescue, Greenspan was determined to help Mexico.[13] His softening line toward bailouts, evident in his response to the Continental Illinois rescue in 1984 and to Black Monday in 1987, was now confirmed for a third time. He had no interest in allowing financial disruptions on his watch; he was ready to do whatever it took to defuse them. A default by a major emerging economy such as Mexico, seen until recently as a poster child for promarket reform, could create contagion anywhere, discrediting the market model and playing into the hands of anti-globalization radicals. In a paradox that the young Greenspan would have mocked without mercy, support for free-market principles would have to be shored up by means of government intervention in the market.

Bob Rubin, the White House economic adviser who was about to take over as Treasury secretary, initiated a series of bull sessions on what to do about Mexico. Greenspan was instantly drawn in by the style of these debates: they were intelligent, creative, and collegial—as stimulating as Ayn Rand's Collective but immensely more practical. Larry Summers, particularly, was a source of brilliant plans: at one point he advocated government guarantees for private loans to Mexico, with the government avoiding a taxpayer subsidy for Wall Street by selling its guarantees for an appropriate premium. Bob Rubin, for his part, brought his own form of wisdom to the mix: with his background as a Wall Street trader, he had a sober sense that there was no such thing as a sure bet in finance—all decisions were uncertain. When the bull sessions tilted toward providing assistance to Mexico, Rubin would bring up all the reasons why it would be better to hold back. When the mood of the collective shifted the other way, Rubin turned contrarian in the opposite direction.[14] Either way, he retained his understated calm. He seemed nerveless, almost detached—rather like the Fed chairman.[15]

Greenspan stuck around for the deliberations until the morning of December 27. Then he took his leave and headed to New York with Andrea. The Stanhope beckoned.

No sooner had the couple checked in at the hotel than the phone began ringing. Bob Rubin was not so easy to escape. Mexico's currency was continuing its dive and Rubin wanted Greenspan's input.

"So much for romance," Andrea sighed. She went out into the city on her own, leaving Alan in the hotel room.

After two days holed up at the Stanhope, Greenspan returned to Washington and convened an FOMC conference call on December 30. The Rubin team was heading toward a Mexico bailout, and it wanted the Fed's backing. If Greenspan was going to acquiesce, he needed to get his committee behind him.

There were, not surprisingly, some frosty reactions. The FOMC members were being asked to assent to a rescue whose details they had no part in negotiating. But Greenspan sold the Mexico operation forcefully. The crisis presented a textbook case for last-resort lending, he explained— Mexico was temporarily illiquid, not irredeemably insolvent. If the Fed could help the country survive the equivalent of an irrational bank run, the crisis would soon pass. Besides, the Fed's assistance would be conditional. The Mexicans would have to commit to reforms before they borrowed the Fed's money.[16]

His committee more or less appeased, Greenspan returned to the bull sessions with Rubin. The Fed was willing to help Mexico, he reported, but the Mexicans should also help themselves: to persuade investors to keep cash in their country, they should be instructed to raise interest rates.[17] But over the next week or so, Greenspan contributed another perspective, too—one that drew inspiration from General Colin Powell, the victor of the Gulf War. In the buildup to that conflict, Powell had insisted that the United States should deploy force at such an overwhelming scale that victory would be all but certain. The basic rule, Greenspan now argued to the Clinton team, was to figure out how much money it would take to stabilize Mexico—and then to provide more of it. In bailout strategy as in religion, there was nothing quite like the zeal of the converted.[18]

On January 10, 1995, Rubin met with Greenspan and Summers to finalize a rescue plan.[19] The Greenspan-Powell doctrine was duly embraced: Mexico was too big to fail, and the rescue would be too big to argue with. When Rubin presented the proposal to the president later that day, he found Clinton surprisingly willing to sign on.[20] "After all this chicken-shit ethical stuff," the president said, referring to the various scandal investigations that lapped at his administration's door, "I'm doing this because I think it's the right thing to do, even if we lose the election."[21]

The politics of the bailout were indeed perilous. Newt Gingrich, the new Republican House Speaker, was ready to support the administration, despite the usual conservative resistance to foreign assistance. But Gingrich warned the Clintonites that rank-and-file Republicans would paint the bailout as a global version of welfare. With a class of fire-breathing House freshmen who took their cues from Rush Limbaugh, the chances of Republican support for a taxpayer rescue were almost zero.

Gingrich suggested that there was only one way to get the bailout through Congress. The administration would have to convince Limbaugh himself of its merits. Moreover, there was only one way to achieve that. Greenspan would have to call him.

"I don't know Rush Limbaugh," Greenspan objected.

"He'll listen to you," Gingrich predicted.[22]

Sitting in his studio at WABC, high above Penn Station in New York City, Limbaugh duly got a call from the Fed chairman. It was as though William McChesney Martin were telephoning Ayn Rand: the central bank chief was lobbying the high priest of the do-nothing caucus. Limbaugh listened to Greenspan respectfully, the scorn and bombast of his radio persona undetectable. It was not clear whether Limbaugh was going to change his mind, but Greenspan was pleasantly surprised to have been treated politely.

The next day, January 12, the White House staff dimmed the lights in the press briefing room. Two figures stepped up to the podium, their figures silhouetted against the murky light behind them.[23] The press corps had been told that no photographs would be allowed; the sources would brief journalists on the details of the Mexico program, but they were to remain anonymous. Somehow, however, the careful arrangements failed. The face of the new Treasury secretary, Bob Rubin, was caught on television. Next to him was Greenspan.

Twenty-four hours later, Greenspan served as pitchman for the Mexico operation a third time, appearing before a large gathering of senators and representatives to urge quick passage of the bailout legislation. "Officials at the notoriously reticent Federal Reserve say they have seldom seen anything like it," reported the *New York Times;* the chairman had morphed from monetary technocrat to the administration's rescue salesman, reviving the old qualms about his willingness to compromise the Fed's hard-won political independence. But although there was a rich irony in Greenspan's behavior—he was siding against his own history and his own party—the Fed chairman was doing only what Fed chairmen always do. Greenspan was echoing Arthur Burns's concern for financial stability following the bankruptcies of Penn Central and New York. He was following in the tradition of Paul Volcker, who managed the fallout from Mexico's earlier debt crisis and rescued Continental Illinois. He was anticipating Ben Bernanke's reaction to the 2008 crisis. The Fed had been created after the 1907 crisis because the nation needed a lender of last resort. With Greenspan in charge, it had one.

Despite Greenspan's efforts, there was no way to get the rescue plan through Congress. Rush Limbaugh refused to moderate his denunciations of a big-government bailout, and Congress showed no inclination whatever to pass the needed legislation promptly. Instead, lawmakers promised to festoon the bailout bill with irrelevant add-ons: Mexico should clamp down on emigration; Fidel Castro was a bad guy. While the politicians dawdled, the Mexican peso continued its collapse. Investors staged sympathy panics as far afield as Thailand.

On January 30, Gingrich informed the Clinton team that it would have to wait at least a fortnight for congressional action. Meanwhile, the Mexicans warned the Treasury privately that the moment of default was approaching.[24] Rubin and Summers hurried over to the chief of staff's office at the White House to discuss what was to be done. At eleven p.m., Clinton returned from a fund-raiser and strolled into the meeting, still dressed in his tuxedo. He gazed longingly at the Domino's Pizza boxes strewn across the office.

Seizing the opportunity, Rubin told Clinton it was time for a different remedy. The president could do without the bailout money he was seeking from Congress; instead, thanks to an assist from Greenspan and the Fed, he could tap an alternative source of financing. Ted Truman, the head of the Fed's international division, had come up with a way of using the Fed's muscle to augment an obscure instrument, the Exchange Stabilization Fund (ESF), which had been created to dampen swings in the dollar. The Fed could buy the ESF's holding of German marks and Japanese yen, supplying the fund with more U.S. dollars with which to help Mexico; the ESF would buy back the foreign currency from the Fed when the world economy calmed down again. With Greenspan's backing, the idea could be pushed through the FOMC. The Stabilization Fund would then be large enough to make congressional support unnecessary.

The next day Clinton announced that Mexico would get a $20 billion line of credit from the Exchange Stabilization Fund—it was almost four times more, in inflation-adjusted dollars, than Volcker and the Reagan team had mustered. To bring the total package up to a truly Powell-doctrine magnitude, the International Monetary Fund's commitment to Mexico was increased by $10 billion, and an impressive-sounding but meaningless promise from the Bank for International Settlements was added for good measure. Mexico would be expected to reciprocate with reform: the budget deficit would be cut so as to control the public debt; the central bank would tighten monetary policy and gain greater independence. In response to Clinton's announcement, Mexico's currency and stock market recovered by a tenth. After six weeks of hair-raising chaos, the run on Mexico was finally slowing.

Greenspan had been central to the Mexico rescue, and the result was yet another step in his emergence as a maestro.[25] Since the start of the Clinton administration, Rubin and his colleagues had urged the president not to speak out against the Fed, knowing that such criticism would backfire. But Mexico marked the moment when the deference toward Greenspan ceased to come through gritted teeth—when the Clintonites embraced him as a trusted ally.[26] The Fed chairman had the respect of the media and of the newly powerful Republicans in Congress, and he was prepared to use his influence to advance Clinton's projects.[27] Even the White House political advisers now recognized the advantages of having him on their side. In a capital riven with partisan splits, a bipartisan sage could be invaluable.

Whether Greenspan's intervention had been good for global finance was of course a different question. Traditionalists were appalled by the expansion of moral hazard: the Fed chairman was guilty of "providing long-term financing to another country that has mismanaged its financial affairs," St. Louis Fed president Thomas Melzer complained at the FOMC meeting at the start of February. A minority among the Fed's staff experts gave this argument an extra twist, asserting that Greenspan could have fought harder for a Volcker-style solution that imposed losses on private creditors, thereby limiting moral hazard.[28] The most telling criticism, advanced only in retrospect, was that Greenspan and the Treasury could have taken advantage of the fact that Mexico's bonds had been issued under Mexican law. In theory, Mexico could have changed the bond contracts by passing a new law, ending the exodus of capital by defaulting on its obligations: it could have hit the investors who deserved to be hit and spared U.S. taxpayers. But this nuclear option was anathema to a technocratic Mexican government eager to attract foreign investment by forswearing abrupt legal changes. Perhaps understandably, Greenspan and the Treasury opted for the surest way to bring the crisis to an end, even at the risk of more crises later.

In the aftermath of Mexico, Greenspan was left to contemplate the emerging bubble in his own status. He was asked with ever greater frequency to testify on Capitol Hill—and on an ever broader range of topics. "The Federal Reserve has now become the honest broker," Greenspan mused to his FOMC colleagues the day after the bailout, noting that he had just been invited to speak "not on Mexico but more or less on the world at large." Whatever the topic of the moment, Greenspan was regarded as the man who knew, and Congress expected him to hold forth on it.

"It is like asking me to umpire the new game of Zipswitch," Greenspan protested to his committee, drawing deferential laughter. "I would say, what? I don't know what the rules are. I don't know who the players are. I don't know what is going on, but am I to be the umpire? And they say, sure, why not?"

"Even though you have not been asked, it has been reported that you have agreed!" Lawrence Lindsey shot back, a bit mischievously. It was an obvious tease. Congress might be responsible for the demand-side factors behind the rise of the maestro, but Greenspan was responsible for the supply side.

There was more laughter at this, but then Greenspan turned serious. A new risk was menacing the Fed—the mirror image of the one the central bank was used to. Rather than being attacked for its failure to contain inflation, or for its callous determination to eliminate inflation at the expense of jobs, the Fed was *not* being attacked; rather, it was being elevated to the point that too much was expected of it. "People are trying to get us to do things that I suspect cannot possibly be done effectively, efficiently, or otherwise," Greenspan fretted. "That is a problem that we are going to have to confront."

Greenspan did not say how this risk would show itself, but the answer was hiding in plain sight—in the debates of recent weeks on derivatives and bailouts. Unseen, unmeasured dangers were building up within finance; the trouble with Greenspan's guru status was that it encouraged people to assume that the dangers would be managed. Nobody was more conscious of this vulnerability than the guru himself. "The markets truly believe that we know what is going on in the economy to a degree that no one else really does," Greenspan marveled to his colleagues in March 1995. "The real danger is that things may get too good. When things get too good, human beings behave awfully." Underscoring the perils in the maestro bubble, the chairman sounded a warning about "the degree of credibility that the Federal Reserve has accumulated in the last year or so. . . . I worry about that, and I worry about that basically because we could be our own worst enemies."

In the years after the 2008 meltdown, the world showed a fresh interest in observations of this kind: success had bred confidence; confidence had blurred into complacency; complacency had caused human beings to behave awfully. By common agreement, the unsung prophet of such cycles had been Hyman Minsky, an American economist who warned that calm periods in markets naturally stimulate an appetite for extra risk, so that finance is never truly stable. But Greenspan understood the Minsky message before Minsky was in vogue—indeed, he understood it at a time when most of the economics profession erroneously believed that macroeconomic stability bred financial stability.[29] In this sense, tragically, Greenspan also was the man who knew. He was the maestro who presided over global finance. He was the skeptic who understood that maestro worship can fuel bubbles.

I n August 1995, Andrea was in Vietnam, on assignment for her network. Alan managed to reach her there with a message. At the age of ninety-two, his mother had died, ending his routine of visits to her apartment on West Sixty-eighth Street. Rose had withered away gradually rather than succumbing with a jolt; but her death, however foreseeable and merciful, was nonetheless a bleak milestone. Andrea cut short her trip to return home as soon as possible and attend the graveside ceremony in New York. For some time afterward, Alan would reflexively reach for the phone in the morning, as if to dial Rose's number.

Years earlier, in the mid-1980s, ex-President Gerald Ford had attended a board meeting in New York at which Greenspan was mentioned. "Oh Alan, yeah, he's the guy we always said would never get married before his mother dies," Ford blurted out, to the embarrassment of everybody present. After Rose's shadow faded to nothing, this prophecy came true. For most of Greenspan's adulthood, his mother's undivided devotion had been all that he needed to keep driving ahead. But now his routines with

Andrea were filling the gap: the mornings that he spent soaking in a hot tub while she was out running, the evenings that they spent watching TV and listening to music. Like his mother years earlier, Andrea cooked Alan the simple food he preferred. "I've forgotten how to cook the good stuff," she laughed. "He's not a fancy eater."

Twenty-two

IRRATIONAL
EXUBERANCE

In the spring of 1995, Susan M. Phillips prepared for an unusual meeting. A personable white-haired economist who had previously served as the nation's chief derivatives regulator, Phillips was now the Fed governor in charge of administrative affairs—affairs that included the shabby state of the Fed's boardroom. After two decades of laissez-faire indifference, the chamber's walls were faded and its chair coverings tattered; visitors with electronic slides had to be told that there was no means of displaying them. Even more annoying, the sound system was so atrocious that it was difficult to hear, and the lights seemed to beam directly into the governors' eyes, as though the space were conspiring to frustrate not just listeners but lip-readers. A year or so earlier, a plan to renovate the boardroom had been precipitately shelved; Congress had been looking for excuses to attack the Fed, and a lavish redecoration seemed impolitic. But after some creative brainstorming, Phillips had come up with an ingenious plan. The boardroom would not be renovated. It would be refurbished.

Phillips hired an interior designer to fix things without changing them. Together, they identified the supplier who had produced the carpet that was now threadbare, and they commissioned a fresh replica. They tracked down the weaver who had made the gold silk covering the walls and ordered new rolls of material. The chairs were to be covered with a pattern almost indistinguishable from the old one, and the chandelier was to be cleaned rather than supplanted. No doubt this quest for continuity rendered the whole facelift more expensive, not less; but if the boardroom looked brighter yet fundamentally unchanged, the expenditure might not attract unwanted chatter. All that Phillips needed now was a green light from Greenspan.

And so Phillips found herself waiting in the boardroom with the designer. They laid out swatches of material for the chairman's perusal; in the case of the new coverings for the chairs, they readied various subtly different options for him to take a view on. The designer, in particular, was imbued with the historic significance of the occasion, and prepared a thoughtful gift: a miniature version of the new boardroom rug for Greenspan to keep as a memento. After all, the Fed was about to spend $1 million on a single room.[1] It was not every year that the world's economic control center got a makeover.

Presently, the door from the chairman's office opened. Greenspan entered and addressed Phillips.

"It doesn't look as though you are doing too much damage," he offered. Then he turned and left. The interchange had lasted less than thirty seconds.[2]

Figuring she had received all the feedback she was going to get, Phillips pressed ahead with the refurbishment. When the FOMC convened on August 22, Greenspan duly acknowledged its completion. "This is the first meeting in our rejuvenated Board Room," he announced; and then, alluding to the large display that dominated the east wall, he assured his colleagues, "The map of the Federal Reserve Districts has been enhanced but not redrawn, so your Districts are what they were; you need not worry about that.

"However, as in the old James Bond movies, there are a lot of buttons here that you can't see. If I push one in an appropriate manner, you fall through the floor with your chair, and there is a pool down there with sharks and all sorts of other creatures.

"That is not meant to influence your vote," he added.

The committee members laughed, possibly a bit nervously. The joke was a little close to the bone. The truth was that Greenspan's dominance of the FOMC really did call to mind that of James Bond's nemesis, the cat-stroking Ernst Stavro Blofeld of the nefarious Special Executive for Counter-Intelligence Terrorism Revenge and Extortion.[3]

"I support your proposal," one regional Fed president exclaimed.

"Whatever it is!" another added.

"Will this be part of the transcript to be released five years from now?" somebody asked.

"It's recorded," a colleague responded grimly.

"I don't think there is anything else that has to be discussed with respect to the Board Room. What you see is what you get," Greenspan concluded. "We will soon find out if it is a major improvement or just more expense."

At the end of the meeting, Greenspan recommended that interest rates stay put and met with absolutely no resistance. The committee's instant submission exceeded even the customary deference that Greenspan usually enjoyed. The obedience was due to the sharks circling below, an FOMC member suggested.

Of course, it was political economy, not sharks, that explained Greenspan's growing dominance. By August 1995, Greenspan was presiding over the eighteenth consecutive quarter of growth. Unemployment was down at 5.7 percent, significantly below the previous decade's average of 6.3 percent, and there was no sign of the overheating that brought most booms to an end: core inflation was running at under 3 percent, almost the lowest it had been since the Johnson era.[4] On top of this remarkable performance, Greenspan's prestige had benefited from the successful Mexico bailout, which had endeared him to the Clinton team; and from the continual fights over the budget between the president and Congress, which played to his long-standing strength as an arbiter of fiscal questions. The more acrimonious the battles between Newt Gingrich's conservatives and the Clintonites, the more Greenspan stood out as a rare leader who commanded universal respect. "I seek Fed advice on almost every serious issue before us," confessed Jim Leach, the Iowa Republican who presided over the House Banking Committee.[5]

In a city filled with tough reporters and scalp-hunting investigators, Greenspan somehow managed to avoid putting a foot wrong: he played Washington so well, he actually enjoyed it. One time, when he was chatting with the head of the Federal Deposit Insurance Corporation before testifying about a rogue trader at a Japanese bank, Greenspan said something that made his fellow regulator laugh. "Be careful!" he quickly warned her in a low voice: news photographers were lurking everywhere, and no regulator should allow herself to be pictured chortling merrily when the news of the day was a bank scandal.[6] Testifying before Congress with increasing frequency, Greenspan would deflect irksome questions with a flick of his disarming wit: "If I seem unduly clear to you, you must have misunderstood what I said," he teased a congressman; "I know you believe you understand what you think I said, but I am not sure you realize that what you heard is not what I meant," he told another.[7] The thrill of dancing through the minefields entertained Greenspan so thoroughly that he took evasive action even when there was no requirement to do so. Arthur Levitt, the chairman of the Securities and Exchange Commission, ran into Greenspan one day as he was holding court at a Kennedy Center reception. "Alan, how are you?" Levitt asked. The Fed chairman turned conspiratorially and held a finger to his lips. "I am not allowed to say," he answered.[8]

Toward the end of 1995, the Clinton administration pondered its choice for the next Fed chairman. It quickly concluded that the best successor to Greenspan would be none other than Greenspan. The president's economic advisers drew up a list of alternative options—William McDonough, the New York Fed chief, as well as Gerald Corrigan, his predecessor—but they were merely going through the motions. In the view of Rubin and his newly elevated deputy Treasury secretary, Lawrence

Summers, Greenspan was doing the Fed job just about as well as it could be done. The fact that he was a Republican was all to the good. It would smooth his path to confirmation by a Republican Senate.

After Greenspan's help with Mexico, Clinton was happy to accept his economists' recommendation, but he wanted to couple Greenspan's reappointment with that of a loyal Democrat to the vice chairmanship—the number two slot vacated by the defeated Alan Blinder. The president's top choice for the vice chairmanship was Felix Rohatyn, a headstrong investment banker and a loquacious monetary dove; Rohatyn's conviction that the economy could grow faster without triggering inflation chimed with Clinton's own view that globalization and de-unionization had suppressed price pressures. The way the president saw things, a robust debate on the economy's potential would be healthy for the Fed. If it spilled out into the open, that would be no bad thing in a democracy.

That was not Greenspan's view, however. Even though he knew Rohatyn from the New York social circuit and was ostensibly his friend, the truth was that another outspoken vice chairman was just about the last thing he wanted. The fact that Rohatyn was dovish on inflation only made things worse. By weakening the Fed's perceived commitment to price stability, Rohatyn might perversely force Greenspan to run a tighter policy to compensate for lost credibility.

With Bob Rubin at the Treasury privately sympathizing with his reservations, Greenspan resolved to block Rohatyn's path. Never mind that Rohatyn had Clinton's backing. Greenspan would defy both of them.

It quickly became evident who had the stronger hand in this battle. The key figures in the Senate had got into the habit of formulating economic opinions by first asking Greenspan where he stood; he was the man who knew, and they would not stray far without consulting him. Clinton, in contrast, was just a political rival; most Senate lions felt they owed him nothing. One after another, influential lawmakers indicated to the administration that Rohatyn could never be confirmed: his grasp of economics was shaky and his monetary views were suspect.[9] Seeing that his way forward was obstructed, Rohatyn bitterly withdrew. The backing of the president had turned out to matter less than the shadowy resistance of the Fed chairman.

In January 1996, Greenspan flew to Paris to attend a meeting of the Group of Seven (G7) advanced economies. During a break in the proceedings, Bob Rubin led him off toward the edge of the room, a view of the Champs-Elysées spread out below them.[10] "When you get back," Rubin said, "the president's going to want to talk to you." It was obvious from Rubin's body language what he was trying to say.[11] Clinton was about to become the third successive president to nominate Greenspan.

A little while later, Greenspan ran into Gerald Corrigan, one of his notional competitors for the chairmanship. Corrigan announced happily that he had lost weight. Never to be outdone, Greenspan grasped his own suit jacket, pulling it outward to show off the ample slack around the waist. He had shed twenty pounds recently.[12]

In the first half of 1996, the Goldilocks economy continued to amaze observers.[13] Growth came in at 7.2 percent in the second quarter of the year—a startling performance so long into a recovery. Core inflation telegraphed no signs of overheating at all. To the contrary, in June it stood at a mere 2.7 percent—the United States was experiencing the polar opposite of stagflation. Now nearing the height of his authority, Greenspan was to interpret this improbable mix of data in a way that would make him a legend, accomplishing yet another step in his progress toward maestro status. And yet with the unfair benefit of hindsight, it is possible to see his decisions in an alternative light. His judgments in 1996, often regarded as his finest achievement, can also be viewed as a harbinger of trouble.

The context for these fateful judgments came into focus in July, when the FOMC tiptoed stealthily across a sort of monetary Rubicon. Seven years earlier, in February 1989, the committee had dismissed a suggestion from Lee Hoskins, the president of the Cleveland Fed, that it should set an explicit target for inflation.[14] In January 1995, the FOMC had considered an inflation target once again, but the Clinton appointee, Janet

Yellen, had successfully championed the case against adoption.[15] Now, in the changed intellectual climate of the summer of 1996, the FOMC reopened the question; and this time the Fed resolved to follow the example set by New Zealand, Canada, and several others. Following a formal debate, the inflation targeters emerged with three quarters of a victory.

It was a strange kind of a victory.[16] It did not come about because the FOMC could prove there were large benefits from suppressing inflation; indeed, Yellen lectured the committee on the lack of such evidence, and nobody contradicted her.[17] Nor was it the case that the committee knew how to define inflation: there were multiple indices that attempted to measure price changes, and more than one way of calculating each of them. Nor, finally, was it the case that the Fed understood what rate of inflation would be most desirable: 2 percent, zero percent, or some other more or less arbitrary number. Rather, the truth was that by 1996—nine years into Greenspan's tenure, and fourteen years after Volcker had ended the 1979–82 monetarist experiment—the FOMC was tired of inhabiting a doctrinal no-man's-land. It was eager to focus its discussions by clarifying its long-term objective, even if the case for that objective had yet to be established.[18]

The prospect of clarity was especially alluring because its supposed drawbacks were receding. During the FOMC debate eighteen months earlier, Yellen had resisted an inflation target because of the presumed sacrifice of jobs. Now, with falling inflation accompanied by falling unemployment, that sacrifice seemed to have evaporated. Eighteen months earlier, similarly, Yellen had argued that an inflation target might squander the Fed's credibility because the Fed might announce a target and then miss it. Now, with inflation falling almost magically, the risk of missing seemed modest.[19] Years later it would often be asserted that the Fed's conversion to inflation targeting had brought inflation down. But causality flowed equally in the opposite direction. Falling inflation brought the FOMC to the point where it was ready to embrace inflation targeting.

Greenspan might have reflected on the irony in this development. In the 1960s, rising inflation had destroyed the gold standard and ushered in the era of discretionary monetary policy; as he had later argued to Reagan, it was wishful to think that a return to gold would restore price stability because inflation determined which monetary regime was feasible, not the other way around.[20] Now, in the 1990s, falling inflation was opening up the possibility of an inflation target, which would reduce monetary discretion—even though, if inflation was falling anyway, the switch in monetary regime might have limited significance.

But for now Greenspan's mind was not focused on this history. After listening to Yellen revisit the merits of inflation targeting, the chairman asked for her bottom line on the Fed's objectives.

"To the extent that there is no trade-off," Yellen replied, covering her back carefully, "then price stability, literally zero inflation, is good and we should go for it."

This seemed like a dodge. Maybe, if Yellen was still around when the United States next experienced a harsh recession, she would decide that there was actually a trade-off—in which case she might go back to worrying about unemployment rather than just targeting inflation.

"Is long-term price stability an appropriate goal of the Federal Reserve System?" Greenspan pressed her.

"Mr. Chairman, will you define 'price stability' for me?" Yellen parried.

"Price stability is that state in which expected changes in the general price level do not effectively alter business or household decisions."

"Could you please put a number on that?" Yellen demanded. Now Greenspan himself was being called out for dodging. The committee laughed appreciatively.

"I would say the number is zero, if inflation is properly measured."

"Improperly measured, I believe that heading toward 2 percent inflation would be a good idea," Yellen countered. She was alluding to the fact that inflation indices tended to overstate the true extent of price pressures, although the overstatement was generally reckoned to be less than 2 percent—meaning that her target was still somewhat arbitrary. Still, with that contention, Yellen nudged the Fed over its Rubicon. Having adamantly opposed inflation targeting eighteen months earlier, she had now morphed into a cautious proponent—even going so far as to endorse a specific rate of inflation.

Yellen's 2 percent objective stuck. Other committee members seized upon it approvingly, and it quickly emerged as the consensus.[21] "Since we have now all agreed on 2 percent, my question is, what 2 percent?" Greenspan soon asked, and the discussion moved on to a debate about rival inflation benchmarks. There had been no collective epiphany—no moment of lucidity when the committee had decided on its new objective because of the force of the arguments marshaled on its behalf. But in a curious, crablike fashion, the FOMC had arrived at a monetary regime change. From July 1996 on, the Fed's leaders understood that they were aiming to get inflation down to 2 percent, though they were not entirely sure what they would do when they arrived there.[22]

Greenspan seemed torn about this new development. Part of him hankered for a more ambitious objective: not 2 percent but zero. If the Fed's explicit policy was to devalue the currency by 2 percent per year, was it not perpetrating a fraud upon the saving public? For a few fleeting moments, the gold standard libertarian bubbled to the surface. "We just have to make our dollar bills smaller and smaller to reflect the loss of purchasing power," he sniffed sarcastically, sounding like a character from *Atlas Shrugged*. "The total amount of paper would be the same," he added. Then he harkened back to his failed efforts to prove a connection between inflation and productivity. "My own view, which is probably going to be determined to be correct eventually—in the year 2252—is that as the inflation rate goes down, [it] will enforce cost-cutting improvements and technological changes," he said, managing to fuse humorous humility with stiff-necked obstinacy in one brief intervention.

Even as he yearned for zero inflation, Greenspan was pulled in another direction. More than other members of the committee, he was comfortable with the doctrinal chaos of his early tenure; and he cherished the freedom to improvise as he went along, unfettered by any formal objective. This led him to insist that whatever the Fed's new policy might be, it was vital that it should be kept secret—so long as it was under wraps, the commitment would be reversible. Although he had himself granted an interview to the *Financial Times* a week earlier, infringing the Fed's informal communications blackout during the days around FOMC meetings, Greenspan now waxed lyrical about the evils of leaks.[23] "The discussion we had yesterday was exceptionally interesting and important. I will tell you that if the 2 percent inflation figure gets out of this room, it is going to create more problems for us than I think any of you might anticipate."

The previous summer, Greenspan had marked the opening of the Fed's new boardroom by casting himself as a James Bond villain. Now he had unwittingly recalled another classic movie. In Stanley Kubrick's cold-war parody, *Dr. Strangelove,* a Germanic wheelchair-bound defense scientist propels himself alarmingly toward the camera and lays out the logic of nuclear deterrence: "Ze whole point of ze Doomsday Machine is lost if you keep it a secret!" Of course, the same doomsday logic holds for inflation targets: just as world-destroying weapons deter enemies only if their existence is well publicized, so an inflation target will work better if the public knows about it. By embracing an inflation target, a central bank aims to convince workers that their cost of living will not jump; therefore, they can go easy on their pay demands. Likewise, by embracing an inflation target, a central bank aims to convince bosses that input costs will be stable; therefore, they need not raise prices. Inflation targets, like nuclear arsenals, work by altering expectations and therefore behavior. In his preference for improvisation, in his wariness of a promise that might constrain his freedom, Greenspan had done the equivalent of building a doomsday weapon—in secret.[24]

The Fed's embrace of an unannounced inflation target set the stage for Greenspan's next pivotal moment, which came later that same summer. Starting in August 1996, Greenspan and his colleagues latched on to a statistical mystery: workers were being paid more, but somehow rising wage bills were not stoking inflation. This would not have been a mystery if productivity had been rising: workers who produce extra can naturally be paid extra without forcing up the cost of widgets. But the curious thing was that no such productivity acceleration was showing up in the data. Mike Prell, the Fed's head of Research and Statistics, concluded that it was only a matter of time before rising wages triggered inflation.

Not everyone accepted Prell's verdict. A few FOMC members felt that productivity might be accelerating, even if official data did not capture it. Buoyed by sizzling growth and a hot stock market, business executives were brimming with anecdotes about efficiency gains—gains that resulted from information technology; from innovations such as just-in-time inventory management; and from the multiple opportunities presented by deregulation, de-unionization, trade liberalization, and globalization. "Mike, I agree with your characterization of the productivity data," Gary Stern, the president of the Minneapolis Fed, exclaimed during the August FOMC meeting. "But I think the business community would take sharp exception to it. Everywhere I go, they talk about the tremendous productivity improvements that they are achieving."[25]

Greenspan was on both sides of this debate. He believed in listening to managers who were on the front lines of the economy, and he had faith that technology could deliver accelerating progress.[26] But he also suspected that the stock market was getting ahead of itself—some of the bullish business sentiment might be exaggerated. The S&P 500 index was up 45 percent since the beginning of 1995. "You've got stocks selling at absolutely unbelievable multiples of earnings and revenues," a Wall Street seer had protested recently. "You've got companies going public that don't even have any earnings."[27] Americans seemed to be entering one of those phases when they believed too much in their own brilliance and forgot that bad things could happen.

Hoping to resolve the mismatch between statistics and anecdotes, Greenspan took advantage of a break in the August FOMC meeting to seek out Larry Slifman, an associate director in Prell's research division.

"Look at these numbers," Greenspan said, pointing to a data set he had obtained from one of Slifman's colleagues. The series added a new dimension to the productivity mystery: corporate profits were growing. In an environment of rising wages and stable prices, profits usually suffered.

"Does this make sense to you?" Greenspan demanded.

Slifman thought there might be a mistake in the way profits had been calculated. But Greenspan suggested an alternative view. The statistics on profits might be exactly right; the error was far more likely to be found in the productivity data. In Greenspan's view, profits were relatively simple to measure. Productivity could be trickier, particularly in service businesses.[28]

Greenspan directed Slifman to take a hard look at the productivity numbers. Then he escaped to Jackson Hole for the Fed's summer symposium; and from there he flew on with Andrea to their annual tennis vacation in Carmel, California. Returning to Washington in the second week of September, he summoned Slifman again, along with Carol Corrado, a colleague from the research division.

Neither Slifman nor Corrado had come up with an explanation for the contradiction between rising profits on the one hand and the apparently flat rate of productivity growth on the other. But Greenspan insisted that they try harder: there was too much at stake to simply note the mystery without resolving it. If productivity was truly flat, Mike Prell was right that inflation was looming—and the Fed ought to raise interest rates. But if productivity was accelerating, it followed that there was no pressing need to head off inflation. Until this confusion was resolved, the Fed would be navigating blindfolded. Greenspan instructed the researchers to break down the productivity data by business sector. There was a chance that an anomaly would reveal itself this way, supporting Greenspan's hunch that productivity was rising faster than the aggregate numbers indicated.

While the staff worked on their assignment, Greenspan aired his hunch at one of his breakfasts at the Treasury. Larry Summers, usually an ally, expressed doubts about his hypothesis. Rather like Greenspan, Summers would later be unfairly caricatured as an avid believer in the efficiency of markets; but he refused to buy the bullish mood that was emanating from the stock market.[29] To the contrary, Summers was doing his best to push back against the sunny view of the economy's potential that was popular among business chiefs, challenging even the president in the process—Clinton was "too yippity on productivity," Summers declared, cheekily. Now addressing Greenspan, Summers pointed out that even if a measurement error was causing the level of productivity to be understated, it did not necessarily follow that the rate of change was picking up. "Alan, maybe there's a constant error and it should've been plus 1 percent for the past 40 years! How do you know it's accelerated?"[30]

Summers's skepticism was shared by several members of the Federal Open Market Committee. By the middle of September, eight of the twelve regional Fed presidents had joined Mike Prell's camp and were petitioning for higher interest rates. What's more, the position of these Fed presidents was reported by Reuters, much to Greenspan's fury.[31] A follow-on article in *BusinessWeek* described the leaks as a revolt against the chairman—an attempt to force him into tightening. Greenspan hit back by asking the Fed's inspector general to find out who the leaker was, and the Federal Bureau of Investigation was called in to help. Finding that both the inspector general and the FBI were demanding to see him, Laurence Meyer, a newly appointed governor at the Fed, decided to visit a lawyer.[32]

Summers's caution about the economy's potential, together with the hawkish signals from the regional Fed presidents, served to convince Greenspan only that he needed a resolution to the productivity mystery. On September 19 the Fed staff researchers duly assembled detailed statistics for productivity across 155 separate categories of firm, going back to 1960. It was a prodigious trove of data, even by the standards of the Fed; and poring over the numbers, Greenspan found what he was looking for. He could see that productivity in manufacturing had been rising robustly, consistent with the anecdotal evidence from company bosses, and with the fact that profits had been strong despite rising wages and flat prices. But weak productivity in the service sector seemed to be depressing the economy-wide numbers: according to the detailed data, productivity in services had actually fallen. Here, surely, was the error that explained the mystery. It was one thing for productivity to be flat—that seemed questionable but possible. It was another thing for the data to indicate that productivity in services was actually declining: that seemed implausible. Given the competitive pressure on law firms, business consultancies, and other service outfits, they had every incentive to extract new efficiencies from their teams. Given their enormous investments in information technology, they could scarcely be getting *less* out of their workers.

When the FOMC convened again the following week, the pressure from the regional Fed presidents to raise interest rates was common knowledge on every bond desk on Wall Street, and the markets were fully expecting a rate hike. Sure enough, as the committee began its deliberations, the hawks went on the offensive. Boston Fed president Cathy Minehan reeled off the names of hometown economists from Harvard and MIT who unanimously believed that interest rates should be higher.[33] Janet Yellen, normally a dove, declared that the economy was "operating in an inflationary danger zone." But Greenspan stood against the tide. Flourishing the results of his statistical sleuthing like a magician unfurling a silk scarf, he laid out the solution to the productivity conundrum. The "bias in service prices," he announced, "is obviously the source of this problem"—productivity was growing faster than the official data suggested, so inflation posed less of a threat than the committee might imagine. Duly impressed, the monetary hawks backed off. Interest rates remained unchanged, and Wall Street scrambled to adjust bond prices.

Years later, Greenspan's productivity call was remembered as a high point of his Fed tenure. Drawing on his unrivaled feel for economic data, he saved the economy from a premature interest rate hike that even doves like Yellen had supported. Greenspan's belief in the productivity acceleration "was intuited," Larry Summers would marvel. "It must have come from some combination of good luck and a very deep acquaintance with a lot of data. And a very great feel for a lot of data. And I think the Fed staff didn't see it. I don't think most other people who could have been Fed chairman would have seen it. And I think we probably got lower unemployment for several years than we would have gotten if he had not had that perception."[34]

As well as standing up for workers, Greenspan had scored a brilliant victory on behalf of the empirical New York school. In the half century since he had studied economics under Arthur Burns at Columbia, the economics profession had come to be dominated by the rising tide of quantitative modeling; the work of collecting basic measurements of the economy had come to seem mundane by comparison. But sometimes the most important insights came not from computation, no matter how dazzling. They came from picking apart data.[35]

The FOMC debate of September 1996 was not just about productivity, however. It also featured an argument that is less often remembered. Echoing the position he had taken during the bond-market boom in 1993, Lawrence Lindsey gave warning that Greenspan's recommendation not to raise rates might stoke a financial bubble. In the five weeks since the previous FOMC meeting, the S&P 500 index had jumped by a further tenth. Real estate prices around New York were taking off; luxury German carmakers had recorded the best summer on record. "The long-term costs of a bubble to the economy and society are potentially great," Lindsey reminded his colleagues. "As in the United States in the late 1920s and Japan in the late 1980s, the case for a central bank ultimately to burst that bubble becomes overwhelming," he continued. "I think it is far better that we do so while the bubble still resembles surface froth and before the bubble carries the economy to stratospheric heights. Whenever we do it, it is going to be painful, however."

Lindsey was hinting at a dilemma that came to be well recognized by monetary experts. On the one hand, the productivity surge that Greenspan had identified created a basis for keeping interest rates low: firms were passing some of their efficiency gains through to consumers, reducing inflation. On the other hand, that very same productivity surge was creating a boom, and loose money from the central bank might turn the boom into a bubble. Higher productivity fueled higher profits, hence the jump in stock prices; feeling confident about the future, and observing that borrowers' balance sheets were strengthening as their real estate and other assets gained in value, financiers were rushing to lend, threatening to inflate asset prices further. Meanwhile, forces elsewhere in the economy added to the go-go atmosphere. As higher productivity allowed for higher wages, workers, feeling richer, borrowed and spent more; as high productivity and high growth increased returns for businesses, companies stimulated the economy by purchasing machine tools, computers, warehouses, and so forth. If the central bank surveyed this flaming undergrowth and then hosed it with monetary kerosene, it would be asking for trouble. Lindsey was surely right: the risk of financial overshoot would be considerable.

Over the years to come, economists learned to frame Lindsey's concern by focusing on the distinction between a "demand shock" and a "supply shock."[36] Central banks were used to dealing with the first sort of challenge, which was in any case relatively straightforward. If demand jumped because, for example, the government ran a larger budget deficit, then inflation, growth, and stock market sentiment would all head in the same direction: upward. This would allow the central bank to kill three birds with one stone: by raising interest rates, it would simultaneously reduce inflation, bring growth down to its sustainable level, and let the air out of an incipient stock bubble. By contrast, a supply shock—a sudden change in the economy's capacity to produce things—confronted the central bank with an altogether trickier problem, because inflation and the economy would head off in opposite directions. As Lindsey was suggesting, a surge in productivity would push inflation down, creating a predicate for lower interest rates. But that same surge in productivity would also push growth, corporate profits, and the stock market upward, creating a predicate for higher interest rates.[37]

There was not much doubt about how Greenspan would respond to Lindsey's intervention. He had brushed him off in 1993, and even though the bond bubble had subsequently burst, the performance of the real economy had vindicated the Fed's policy. Now, having more or less come to terms with the unannounced 2 percent inflation objective, Greenspan was almost bound to prioritize stable inflation over stable asset prices. He freely conceded that Lindsey's diagnosis was correct. "I recognize that there is a stock market bubble problem at this point," he allowed; "I agree with Governor Lindsey that this is a problem that we should keep an eye on." But he still planned to ignore Lindsey, despite the fact that he might be right. Even if the central bank's mission was to deliver stable growth, and even if bubbles could destabilize growth just as surely as inflation, the Fed had decided to target inflation, mainly because the disinflationary forces in the world were making this the easy option. Following Lindsey's advice, in contrast, would be hard. "We have very great difficulty in monetary policy when we confront stock market bubbles," Greenspan declared to his colleagues. "To the extent that we are successful in keeping product price inflation down, history tells us that price-earnings ratios [and hence stock prices] under those conditions go through the roof. What is really needed to keep stock market bubbles from occurring is a lot of product price inflation. . . . There is a clear tradeoff. If monetary policy succeeds in one, it fails in the other."

In the last years of his tenure, and into retirement, Greenspan attempted to rewrite this phase of his history. He would argue that bubbles were impossible to spot. But in 1996, he was quite willing to call one. He would argue, likewise, that bubbles were impossible to deflate. But in 1996 he suggested in passing to his colleagues that increasing "margin requirements"—that is, making it harder to borrow money to buy stocks—might take the air out of the market. Despite what he asserted later, the real reason Greenspan shrank from acting against the 1990s stock bubble was not that it was impossible to identify, and not that it was impossible to pop. It was simply that, for an inflation-targeting central bank, worrying about bubbles was a secondary priority.[38]

Greenspan's diagnosis of the productivity acceleration represented a clear triumph. But his policy response to that acceleration was a mixed blessing. By using the space created by productivity-driven disinflation, Greenspan presided over a glorious period of growth, high-tech investment, and job creation that boosted living standards among low-skilled workers; in the era of globalization, the late 1990s stand out as one of the few periods in which inequality retreated. But by allowing this bonanza, Greenspan also signaled an unwillingness to confront bubbles, with consequences that ultimately proved more serious than he imagined.

O n October 30, 1996, Alan arranged a surprise dinner for Andrea. They had been together—at first loosely, then tightly—for a dozen years, and Alan gathered a few friends at Galileo, an upscale Italian restaurant in Washington. The evening marked Andrea's fiftieth birthday—she was just over twenty years younger than her consort—and Alan presented her with a ring: a diamond. When he interrupted the dinner to toast her, he spoke so warmly and emotionally that his friends thought he might have something bigger on his mind. The TV host Jim Lehrer agreed with the World Bank president's wife, Elaine Wolfensohn, that Alan had come within a whisker of proposing marriage.

The couple was certainly getting to the point where marriage would seem natural. A couple of times recently, Alan had failed to drink sufficient fluids, fainted, and been whisked off to the hospital; when Andrea had rushed to be with him, Alan had reacted first with surprise, then later with warm gratitude. A few days after the birthday dinner at Galileo, Alan had a chance to repay the debt. Determined to strike a blow against encroaching age, Andrea entered the New York marathon. It was a splendid day in Manhattan, with the temperature rising through the forties and a westerly wind blowing at the runners' backs; and Andrea realized her ambition to complete the race, finishing in 5 hours, 19 minutes, and 37 seconds, and earning 24,783rd place, with 3,291 runners straggling in behind her.[39] Partway through the contest, Andrea strained a hamstring, and she stopped to call Alan from a pay phone; when she arrived at the next mile marker, her man was waiting for her with a leg brace and a tube of anti-inflammatory cream, not to mention bananas. A small item in the *Philadelphia Inquirer* reported coyly that the famous television correspondent had summoned help from "a friend."[40] But the fact that the Fed chairman had stayed out of the newspapers did not diminish the force of his gesture. For possibly the first time in his life, Alan was caring physically for someone other than his mother.

Two days later, on November 5, Bill Clinton was reelected. It was a triumph over personal scandal, and over the humiliation of the 1994 midterms—against all odds, Clinton had become the third Democrat in the twentieth century to secure two terms in the White House. Surveys of voters leaving the polls left no doubt as to the reason: the strong economy had carried Clinton to victory, just as the lingering credit crunch of 1991–92 had destroyed the reelection prospects of his predecessor.[41] For the Republican Greenspan, the irony that he had made possible a Democratic victory paled next to the irony that this victory came as a relief. Greenspan's relations with the Clinton team could scarcely have been better; in contrast, the opposing Republican ticket had featured his old supply-side nemesis Jack Kemp as the vice presidential candidate. Yet while prosperity had delivered an electoral outcome that suited Greenspan perfectly, it brought challenges, too. The news of Clinton's victory caused the stock market to take off on a fresh sprint.[42] Lawrence Lindsey's warnings were becoming harder to brush off with confidence.

At the FOMC meeting in mid-November, it was not just Lindsey who was fretting. "We are risking a major asset price bubble," Cathy Minehan of the Boston Fed declared to her colleagues.

A few days later, Mike Prell invited a who's who of stock market experts to the Fed's headquarters in Washington. His invitation laid out the questions that the Fed was wrestling with. "Are there signs of speculative excess?" his memo asked. Did the crush of new company flotations on the stock exchange signal "over-exuberance?"[43] Evidently, the clandestine adoption of an inflation target was not preventing the Fed from pondering bubbles, even if it was unlikely to use interest rates to deal with them.

Lindsey sensed the tide was moving his way. He told David Wessel, a *Wall Street Journal* economics reporter, that the Fed was increasingly worried about a stock market bubble.

Wessel recognized a good story, but he wanted to check it with Greenspan. He drafted a column that led with the sentence "If you were Alan Greenspan, wouldn't you be worried about the soaring stock market?" Then he sent a copy of his draft to Greenspan's press chief, Joe Coyne, and awaited the reaction.

Coyne duly called him back. "I showed your column to the chairman," he informed Wessel. "He said it was very interesting."[44]

Wessel had the confirmation he needed. On November 25 his column appeared on the front page of the *Journal*. "Worried Fed Watches Stock Market's Climb," announced the title.

The following week, on December 3, Mike Prell's invited experts trooped into the Fed's boardroom, where Greenspan and his fellow governors awaited them. The chairman opened the proceedings by calling on Abby Joseph Cohen, the chief stock market strategist at Goldman Sachs. Cohen was a reassuringly unflashy figure, a small, plainspoken ex–Fed economist who favored conservative gray suits. But her message was bracingly vivid: there was no need to worry about speculative excess, because the market had plenty of room to rise further. Corporate profits were growing, helping to justify the market's rise; the economy was stronger than the official data showed; and an environment of low interest rates rendered equities attractive to investors.[45] In Cohen's estimation, the S&P 500 might be undervalued by as much as a quarter.[46]

Greenspan listened to Cohen, not giving anything away.[47] The fact that Goldman's top strategist was so strikingly bullish proved how hard it was to diagnose a bubble. But there was another lesson, too. Investors valued equities highly partly because interest rates were low. If there was a bubble, in other words, the Fed might be encouraging it.[48]

The next speaker was David Shulman of Salomon Brothers. Shulman had attended a similar meeting of outside experts in 1991—the one that had brought home to Greenspan the full extent of the real estate market's troubles. As he eyed Greenspan this time, Shulman felt that a change had come over him. The Fed chairman was no longer grappling with a financial system riddled with rotten property lending and bankrupt S&Ls, and he was no longer at loggerheads with the White House. He was comfortable in his job, and he was evidently enjoying himself.

Unlike Cohen, Shulman was bearish. He presented a table showing that the S&P 500 index was trading at almost nineteen times earnings, a level that signaled danger—in 1968, 1972, and 1987, the market had crashed after peaking at this sort of level.[49] The signs of bubble psychology were ubiquitous: scarcely a month went by without the appearance of a breathless new stock market publication; and a whole new class of day traders was getting in on the game, using Internet platforms to buy Internet stocks that they discussed in Internet chat rooms.

Greenspan turned next to Morgan Stanley's Byron Wien. He was evidently going alphabetically.

"Wien!" said the chairman.

Wien was sixty-three years old. He had a bald head and a lined face. He thought to himself, "I haven't been called by my last name since I was in the army."

"You are optimistic, aren't you?"

"Yes," Wien answered. Like Abby Cohen, he was using a model that compared the valuation of the stock market to interest rates on bonds. Thanks to the low rates engineered by the Fed, the bull market would continue.

Wien saw that Greenspan was listening attentively. He had a feeling that the chairman was nodding in agreement.

After the three Wall Streeters were done, the microphone was passed to the two academics in the group: John Campbell of Harvard and Robert Shiller of Yale. The professors presented a series of charts comparing stock prices to dividends. According to this means of valuing equities, the market was wildly overvalued. If the Fed raised interest rates, the market would crater.

After a morning of meetings, the experts filed into the Fed dining room. They sat down to lunch, and Cohen remarked that the food had improved since her visits to the employee cafeteria in the 1970s.[50] Alluding to the question that had been debated that morning, Robert Shiller asked Greenspan when a Fed chairman had last used his bully pulpit to sound a warning about the stock market's level. A Fed staff economist gave the answer—1965—suggesting a precise knowledge of precedent that would later seem revealing.[51]

When the lunch was over, Byron Wien called his colleagues at Morgan Stanley to report on the discussion. The way he saw things, the key takeaway was that Greenspan had agreed with his bullish view on equities. He could sense it from the way Greenspan had been watching him; the man's body language said everything. The stock market had just been given a green light, Wien confided to his firm. The Fed would not stand in the way of a continued rally.

A couple of days later, Wien flew off to see a Morgan Stanley client in Houston. Emerging from the airport late on December 5, he checked into a hotel and went to sleep.

That evening, Greenspan delivered the dinner address at the annual black-tie gala of the American Enterprise Institute. A cavernous ballroom at the Washington Hilton was filled to the gills, and Greenspan launched into a speech freighted with history and philosophy. "Money—serving as a store of value and medium of exchange—is the lubricant that enables a society to organize itself," he pontificated. "The ability to store the fruits of one's labor for future consumption is necessary for the accumulation of capital." Because money was essential, central banks with the power to manipulate it were bound to attract scrutiny, the chairman continued. He invoked Alexander Hamilton, the object of pervasive suspicion after he created America's first quasi-central bank; he recalled William Jennings Bryan, the mesmerizing populist who had decried the gold-based monetary order on behalf of indebted farmers. Across the vast width of the ballroom, a sea of earnest figures toyed with their desserts and struggled to keep up with Greenspan's meaning.

Three quarters of the way into his soliloquy, Greenspan abandoned circuitous statements in favor of rhetorical questions. He ruminated aloud about what stable money really meant. Inflation had been easy to measure when the bulk of the economy had consisted of manufacturing: a ton of cold rolled steel was roughly the same in 1950 as in 1960; if the price went up, inflation was the reason. But in a high-tech and service-based economy, the old verities were gone. "What is the price of a unit of software or a legal opinion?" Greenspan mused; the software of 1986 had been altogether different from the software of 1996, so comparing prices was meaningless. "Where do we draw the line on what prices matter?" Greenspan continued. "Certainly prices of goods and services now being produced—our basic measure of inflation matter. But what about futures prices or more importantly prices of claims on future goods and services, like equities, real estate, or other earning assets?" Then, with most of his audience safely reduced to a stupor, Greenspan wondered: "How do we know when irrational exuberance has unduly escalated asset values?" He plodded to a close and retreated from the podium.

Regaining his seat near Andrea, Greenspan asked if anything about his speech had struck her. As a lifelong reporter, Mitchell seldom hesitated in picking out a lede. On this occasion, however, she came up blank: nothing in Alan's torturous remarks had struck her as newsworthy. But the Fed reporters present had been primed by reading Wessel's column in the *Journal,* and they pounced in unison upon one line in the speech—the one about irrational exuberance. In fact, even before Greenspan had begun speaking, the Reuters news agency had sent out an alert based on the advance text: "Fed must be wary when irrational exuberance affects stocks, assets—Greenspan."[52]

The chairman had judged the news reporters perfectly. He had given them just enough fodder to feed their need for a story, while not risking his reputation by issuing an explicitly alarmist warning. Sure enough, as headlines about the irrational exuberance comment reached financial trading desks, markets reacted just as Greenspan knew they would. The Fed seemed to be promising action against bubbles; and futures on stock prices, which remain open for trading overnight, began to fall sharply. Markets in Australia and New Zealand started to fall next; Japan followed, then Europe. John Makin, a hedge-fund economist who attended the speech, had left the Hilton ballroom feeling that there was nothing to report. When he got back to his hotel, he was peppered with phone calls. The traders who were watching his fund's positions overnight had seen the news and panicked.[53]

At around six the next morning, Byron Wien was awakened in his Houston hotel room. The phone was ringing. It was Morgan Stanley's chief bond trader.

"You asshole," screamed the trader. "You told us you had convinced Greenspan that the market wasn't overvalued."

A little while later, Wien's phone rang again. This time it was Morgan's head equity trader on the line. He was not brimming with charity, either.[54]

When the New York Stock Exchange opened, it followed foreign markets downward. Robert Shiller was driving his child to school in New Haven when he heard the news about Greenspan's remarks. "I wonder if I had anything to do with that," he said to himself.[55]

But then, just as quickly, the market recovered. Once traders got hold of the text of Greenspan's comments, the gap between his speech and the alarming headlines became obvious. To be sure, Greenspan had deliberately sounded a warning; he was gratified that the market had heard him.[56] But a reading of his speech showed clearly that his warning had been hedged to the maximum extent; it was hardly a bold sign that he meant to clobber the market by raising interest rates. "The Fed has no intention of tightening policy simply to push the equity market down," said Bruce Steinberg, a Merrill Lynch economist. "It will only tighten when it believes the inflation climate requires it." The diffidence of Greenspan's warning paradoxically assured investors that they had nothing to fear. "Instead of raising rates, he is going to make speeches," one Wall Streeter remarked dismissively.[57]

By the end of the day, the S&P 500 index had recovered almost all its losses. If this was the worst the central bank was going to do, there would be no stopping the bull market.[58]

Greenspan almost reveled in his lack of influence. The passive part of him—the lingering sideman—seemed happy to gesture at the stock market's exuberance without being taken seriously. By speaking out, he had preserved his intellectual integrity, satisfying his residual loyalty to the fierce warnings about bubbles he had issued as a young man. But by failing to make an impact, he was absolving himself of responsibility to do more: the stock market was not his problem, because there was little he could do about it. Of course, this claim to impotence was doubtful—if he had at least implied a willingness to stomp on equities by tightening policy, the market reaction would surely have been different.[59] When the Fed eventually did tighten by a modest quarter of a percentage point the following March, the S&P 500 duly fell 5 percent in just over a week. But after that, the Fed backed off, and the market headed up again.[60]

If this refusal to confront bubbles would ultimately prove to be a mistake, it was a mistake that was bigger than just Greenspan. The global inflation-targeting consensus made it almost inevitable that central banks would downplay the significance of bubbles; relative to that consensus, the Fed chairman was admirably alert to the fragility of markets. The tragedy of Greenspan's tenure is that he did not pursue his fear of finance far enough: he decided that targeting inflation was seductively easy, whereas targeting asset prices was hard; he did not like to confront the climate of opinion, which was willing to grant that central banks had a duty to fight inflation, but not that they should vaporize citizens' savings by forcing down asset prices.[61] It was a tragedy that grew out of the mix of qualities that had defined Greenspan throughout his public life—intellectual honesty on the one hand, a reluctance to act forcefully on the other. At his confirmation hearing nine years earlier, Senator Proxmire had summed up Greenspan's tenor during the Ford years: he had been a "a get along, go along, comfortable and increasingly popular chairman" of the Council of Economic Advisers; when he had gone up against rivals like Kissinger, he had hidden behind passive-aggressive delay tactics rather than confronting him directly. In the Reagan years, similarly, Greenspan had battled the supply-side fantasists on deficits and gold; but he had always acted stealthily, often at one remove, through proxies. Now, as Fed chairman, Greenspan had risked unpopularity by pushing down inflation during George H. W. Bush's tenure, and he had defied Clinton, Gingrich, and Blinder with his hike of 75 basis points in November 1994. But when it came to heady equity markets, his analytical lucidity about the dangers of bubbles was trumped by his reluctance to act boldly.

Lawrence Lindsey, Greenspan's leading critic on the FOMC, attended his last meeting as a Fed governor on December 17. He predicted that the market would charge even higher in 1997, storing up trouble for the future. He obviously believed that the Fed should do something about it.

"I will make another speech," Greenspan deadpanned.

"Don't wait a whole year," Lindsey shot back, forlornly.

The rest of the committee was laughing. By mocking his own helplessness, Greenspan had reduced the whole issue of stabilizing finance into something of a fatalistic in-joke.

However much Lawrence Lindsey might brood about bubbles, Greenspan was increasingly preoccupied with other matters. On Christmas Day, 1996, after the habitual carnival of presents with Judy Woodruff and Al Hunt, he drove back with Andrea to their secluded home on a winding, wooded road in Washington. It was a curiously warm Christmas, with the temperature approaching 60 degrees, as though nature had suspended winter. Alan turned to Andrea and asked whether she would like a big wedding or a small one.

That was as close to a formal proposal as he was going to manage. It was "as ambiguous as some of his testimony before government committees," Andrea recalled; if she wanted a clear expression of his love, she would have to make do with Alan's toast at her birthday dinner, two months earlier. Like Alan's irrational exuberance lecture, that birthday speech had evidently concealed a vital message wrapped in code—it had been encrypted to preserve some scope for course correction and retreat; encrypted to safeguard the thing that Alan feared to lose the most, his freedom of action. Greenspan's Randian convictions, once the fount of his public-policy positions, had by now mostly dried up. But the personal part of his individualism survived. Marriage involved a formal renunciation of autonomy. It had taken until the age of seventy—it had taken Rose's death—for Alan to get there a second time.

A few days later, on the twelfth anniversary of their first date in New York, Alan and Andrea had some friends over to dinner. When they announced to their guests that they were finally engaged, Kay Graham, the *Washington Post* proprietor, let out a shriek, and Jim Lehrer, the news anchor, jumped up to phone his wife, who was at home nursing an illness. "No one had imagined that we'd ever become respectable," Andrea would write, betraying a surprisingly traditional sentiment for a trailblazing career woman.[62]

A little while later, Alan confided to a friend that he should have proposed marriage a long time earlier. When the friend relayed the words to Andrea, she looked overcome.

"He said that?" she asked softly.[63]

Twenty-three

"THE BEST ECONOMY I'VE EVER SEEN"

T he bride wore a short cream Oscar de la Renta dress with a pill-box hat. She carried a bouquet of roses: cream, champagne, and pink.[1] Her father was beaming; Ruth Bader Ginsburg, the Supreme Court associate justice, was officiating; the bride's seven-year-old goddaughter, serving as flower girl, bubbled on the borderline between terror and excitement.[2] Meanwhile, the bride's betrothed was almost provocatively himself. Eschewing a tuxedo, he wore a navy blue pinstriped business suit, hoisted from his closet with no particular fanfare; and he smiled impishly at the friends assembled in the garden of the picturesque inn, nestled in Virginia's horse country an hour outside Washington. Just as the ceremony was finishing—just as Justice Ginsburg was pronouncing them married—rain began to spit on the assembled company, lending the faux English setting a genuine touch. As the guests got wet, the groom leaned down and planted a long kiss on his wife. He came up for air and planted another one.

"He's an animal, he's just an animal," whispered Al Hunt, the father of the nervous flower girl.

"Sensual exuberance," agreed General Colin Powell, the victor of the Gulf War and a much-hyped presidential prospect.

Right up until their wedding day, April 6, 1997, Alan and Andrea had hoped to keep the ceremony private. Andrea had gone so far as to appeal personally to the *New York Times* to publish the marriage announcement without giving away the location. But nothing stays private when your guests are so public—here was Henry Kissinger, complete with his security guard; here were Senators Daniel Patrick Moynihan and John Warner; here was Katharine Graham, the *Washington Post* proprietor and grande dame of Washington society. Inevitably, gossip writers were on hand to capture the occasion, not least Roxanne Roberts, the *Post*'s very own society portraitist.

Did those kisses mark the emergence of a new, romantic Alan Greenspan, Roberts demanded.

Greenspan laughed mischievously, raising his eyebrows. "You'll never know," he answered.[3]

The couple posed for the press photographers, who pleaded repeatedly for another of those kisses.

"Later," Andrea said slyly.

The guests moved from the damp garden to the dining room. The food served by the Inn at Little Washington was justifiably famous, and the wedding-goers were made to run the gauntlet of a seven-course meal: bell-pepper soup, asparagus with pickled quail eggs, charcoal-grilled salmon, parsley-crusted rack of baby lamb—all building inexorably toward the four-tiered wedding cake with mocha and crushed toffee. "It was a four-star meal and a four-star kiss," declared the TV newsman Tim Russert. When the feasting was over, the guests boarded buses back to Washington, where the celebrations continued the next evening with a party at the home of James Wolfensohn, the World Bank president.

By marrying Andrea, Alan would say with a chuckle, he had pulled off a historic feat. No other suitor had ever contrived to marry two unrelated Jewish Mitchells.[4] But Greenspan had also pulled off something more: after four decades, he had ended a singular chapter in his life, ceding some of his autonomy. He was evidently not opposed to marriage—he had now done it twice. But he had nonetheless remained a bachelor between the ages of twenty-seven and seventy-one, choosing serial semiattachments that would not obstruct his drive to prove he could be more than a mere sideman. During forty-four years of bachelordom, as he had once said, he had dated news anchors, senators, and beauty queens; but now, remarkably, he was committed to one person. "I intend to make her happy and I will succeed," he announced proudly to his wedding guests. From any other bridegroom, it might have sounded trite. But coming from the strangely honest figure in the blue business suit, it was an earnest confession of the distance he had traveled.[5]

Alan and Andrea felt too busy for a honeymoon. They spent their wedding night at home, and two days later they were doing one of the things they liked best: attending a state dinner at the White House. Andrea wore another Oscar de la Renta creation, this one a black lace gown; conveniently, the designer was a friend, and never mind the fact that Alan had first come to know him when he was dating Barbara. Sitting at the president's table at the state dinner, Andrea found herself with Dan Aykroyd, famous for his starring roles in *The Blues Brothers* and *Saturday Night Live;* and Marylouise Oates, who had befriended the Clintons during the anti-Vietnam protests of the 1960s. At one point in the evening, Aykroyd and Oates burst into song, belting out an old Beatles number as though Bobby Kennedy had not yet been shot and Richard Nixon were still the enemy. Andrea could not help feeling that the solemn portrait of Abraham Lincoln hanging in the State Dining Room clashed oddly with the sixties ballad; for Alan, naturally, the dissonance was even more awkward.[6] The Clintonites' roots were in the counterculture he had battled as a Nixon aide. Now they had taken over, and he was sitting among them, and his own economic stewardship had given them four more years in the White House.

As well as channeling the Beatles, Marylouise Oates had some advice. She and her husband, the political consultant Bob Shrum, insisted that honeymoons could not be skipped so casually. Alan and Andrea had to go somewhere. Shrum recommended Venice.

Alan studied his diary. He could fit Venice in that June, right after a planned trip to a monetary conference in Switzerland. And so Andrea accompanied him there, suffering through a tedious luncheon speech by the German chancellor, Helmut Kohl, and trying to avoid reporters who now saw her as a route to the Fed chairman. By the time the couple left Switzerland, Andrea was complaining of "the least romantic honeymoon in history," but the stay at the Cipriani in Venice put things right. Alan and Andrea ate at open-air cafés, went shopping, and toured churches and the old Jewish ghetto. Eventually Alan asked, "What is the value-added produced in this city?"

"You're asking the wrong question," his wife laughed.

"But this entire city is a museum. Just think of what goes into keeping it up."

Andrea stopped walking and looked at him. "You should be looking at how beautiful it is," she chided gently.[7]

Greenspan's happy life was mirrored by the happy goings-on in the economy. By the summer of 1997, things looked even better than they had the previous fall, when the chairman had first diagnosed a surge in productivity. The jobless rate was slipping below 5 percent; meanwhile, inflation was inching down to around Janet Yellen's 2 percent target. Greenspan was now so confident of his productivity thesis that he began to broadcast it in public. In July he testified before Congress about a potential "once- or twice-in-a-century phenomenon that will carry productivity trends nationally and globally to a new higher track." The S&P 500 index promptly jumped more than 2 percent by the end of that day. Greenspan might still worry about the danger of a stock bubble, but his techno-optimism was inflating it.

Looking back on this period, the *Wall Street Journal* writer David Wessel noticed how Greenspan's shifting stance was picked up by newspaper cartoonists. For years, they had portrayed him as a dour killjoy: "Just when the recovery starts to sprout, stomp on it!" yelled out a Greenspan-like gardener, maniacally tramping on minuscule seedlings.

As recently as the occasion of his wedding, a cartoonist had drawn a pajama-clad Fed chairman calling, "Honey, would you mind checking under the bed for signs of inflation?" But now that Greenspan's cheery productivity thesis was buoying the market, the punch lines underwent a change. One two-panel cartoon began with an upward-pointing chart labeled "U.S. economy"; this was titled "Remarkable." A second panel showed Greenspan pronouncing himself optimistic. This one was titled "Truly Remarkable."[8]

By the start of August 1997, the S&P 500 had risen fully 27 percent since that evening the previous December when Greenspan had questioned its level. Journalists could not resist quoting the "irrational exuberance" phrase, which appeared on average twice per day in news outlets across the nation.[9] But the more the cliché was repeated, the more the market seemed to soar. If Greenspan's attempt to slow the rally had been reduced to an ironic meme, surely there was nothing that could stop it.

"What do we do with monetary policy when there is no inflation but asset prices are booming?" Boston Fed president Cathy Minehan asked at the August 1997 FOMC meeting.

Greenspan reminded her that he had posed precisely that question in his irrational exuberance speech. Eight months later, he was no closer to answering his own question. The Fed's policy tool kit contained only one proven tool: the power to change the short-term interest rate.

"We have one instrument and conflicting goals," Greenspan pleaded. "What do we do?" Then he added, "What should the Japanese have done?" In the late 1980s, Japan had experienced flat consumer prices combined with a ruinous bubble in equities and real estate.

"Hindsight tells us to prick the bubble sooner, but how does foresight tell us we have a bubble?" Minehan wondered.

"I do not know what to do," Greenspan responded. Faced with the problem of one instrument and two goals, the Fed had tried to conjure up a second instrument: it would use interest rates to guide inflation while using public rhetoric to guide assets. But in Greenspan's mind, at least, that strategy had proved useless. The stock market had simply shrugged off his irrational exuberance speech.

"It had some success," countered one FOMC member.

"Temporarily," Greenspan retorted.

A mid the surfeit of exuberant news, there was one cloud on the horizon. The strong U.S. economy and the related strength of the dollar were causing ructions elsewhere. The first casualty was Thailand, which had pegged its currency to a basket consisting mainly of dollars. As the Thai baht followed the greenback up, Thailand lost competitiveness and its trade deficit swelled alarmingly. To pay for the excess of imports over exports, Thailand resorted to borrowing from foreigners. But this strategy could be sustained for only so long, and pretty soon speculators woke up to the fact that it was a matter of time before the currency peg shattered. The speculators sold baht aggressively, and their prophecy fulfilled itself. On July 1, 1997, the peg duly broke and the currency began a headlong fall, causing the economy to shrink by one sixth and transferring more than $1 billion of Thai savings from the central bank to the speculators.[10]

Once Thailand fell, the panic spread to its neighbors. In August, Indonesia was forced to let its currency fall by 11 percent, and Malaysia came under attack from the markets. But in contrast to Mexico's crisis, two and a half years before, the disruptions in East Asia caused barely a flicker on Greenspan's radar screen. Mexico had been a neighbor, a partner, a member of the North American Free Trade Agreement; East Asia was half a world away. Moreover, the Mexico rescue had triggered recriminations from Congress, and neither the Clinton Treasury nor the Greenspan Fed wanted to deploy U.S. taxpayers' dollars in Asia.[11] In September, Greenspan traveled to Hong Kong for the annual meeting of the World Bank and International Monetary Fund, and furious arguments about the crisis raged—Prime Minister Mahathir Mohamad of Malaysia called for a ban on "unnecessary, unproductive and immoral" currency trading. Greenspan sat through several meetings with Asian financial officials, but he did his best to keep his head down, possibly encouraged by the fact that Andrea was with him.[12] Their friend James Wolfensohn kept telling people that they were newly married, and Elaine Wolfensohn took Andrea to shop for pearls. "You spent what?" Alan demanded, when Andrea returned with her booty.[13]

Over the next weeks, the rumblings from Asia grew louder. The crisis spread to Hong Kong; and on October 27, after a few particularly bad days, Wall Street staged a sympathy fit, suffering its steepest one-day drop since 1987. But the way Greenspan saw things, there was still no reason to worry. If Asians needed rescue packages, the International Monetary Fund would arrange them; if Wall Street swooned, there might even be a silver lining. A stock market correction would ameliorate the Fed's problem of having two objectives and one instrument—given that Greenspan had failed to talk the market down, Asia was welcome to spook it. Testifying before Congress two days after Wall Street's drop, Greenspan cautiously welcomed the sell-off, noting that the real economy was unlikely to suffer. East Asia represented too small a share of U.S. trade to derail America's growth bonanza.

If there was one potential exception to Greenspan's relaxed view, it was South Korea. The country's economy was far bigger than the others—more than twice the size of Indonesia's, more than three times bigger than Thailand's—and its international borrowing was on a sufficient scale to damage American banks if it defaulted.[14] But a South Korean meltdown did not seem likely. Admittedly, Korea's lenders had taken losses on their exposure to bankrupt companies in Thailand, and the Korean won was sliding. But the central bank had stockpiled foreign-currency reserves worth $24 billion. If Korea's finance companies ran short of dollars because of losses in Southeast Asia, the central bank could lend them the foreign currency they needed. There would be no need for a U.S. bailout.

On November 20, Ted Truman, the chief of the Fed's international division, flew into South Korea. He suspected that something might be wrong: the finance minister had recently been fired for suggesting that Korea needed an emergency loan from the IMF. But when Truman visited Lee Kyung Shik, the central bank governor, the full extent of the trouble was laid bare. Nearly all of Korea's foreign-currency reserves were gone. They had already been used to prop up the country's banks, which needed dollars to replace loans from global lenders that were running from Korea.

As Truman realized the hopelessness of Korea's position, he wondered why the country's new finance minister had agreed to take on the portfolio.

"Because he had not seen the books yet," Lee responded.[15]

A few days later, on November 25, Lee visited Greenspan for breakfast at the Fed headquarters in Washington. Having been warned by Truman that Korea's true reserves were far below the publicly announced amount, Greenspan probed his visitor for confirmation. This time, however, the central bank chief put on a brave face. Everything was fine. Korea could handle the situation.

Greenspan concluded that Lee was either uninformed or unforthcoming. If Lee wanted Greenspan's help, he had not played his cards skillfully.[16]

Early the next morning, Charles Siegman, the senior Fed economist with responsibility for Korea, was visited by a Korean central-bank official who was part of the delegation accompanying the governor.[17] Now Korea's message changed again. The official informed Siegman that Korea might default in a matter of days; it needed Fed assistance urgently, and the visitor proposed that this should take the form of a central-bank swap line. The Fed would provide the Koreans with dollars; Korea's central bank would provide the Fed with an equivalent amount of its own currency.

Seeking to get a clearer reading on the true state of Korea's reserves, Siegman asked how a default could be so imminent. Surely the central bank could use its foreign-currency reserves to deal with the crisis?

The official responded that the reserves were already gone. Evidently, the governor had not been straight during his breakfast with the Fed chairman.

When Siegman relayed the message to Greenspan, the chairman ruled out the idea of a Fed swap line. It was not just that he was irritated by the governor's dissembling; the larger point was that if Korea was on the ropes, the Treasury and the International Monetary Fund should take the lead in assisting the country. At various times during the Fed's history, its leaders had conceived of their responsibilities in international terms. But Greenspan was inclined to take a less expansive view. If foreign developments affected the United States, then the Fed would respond: as a neighbor, Mexico had qualified. But in general Greenspan would prefer to avoid foreign entanglements, and never mind the fact that he reigned in an era of globalization.

Whatever he thought about Korea, Greenspan certainly wanted to do right by his allies in the Clinton administration. After hearing from Siegman, he placed a call to Larry Summers to update him about Korea's plight. Then he hurried over to the Treasury to brief Rubin.

The Treasury secretary gathered his international team around him and went into his characteristic listening mode. He asked questions, took notes on a yellow legal pad, and insisted on clear thinking. But there was no obvious way forward. On the one hand, if Korea was left to default to its foreign creditors, the damage would be considerable; financial panic might spread, engulfing other emerging economies. On the other hand, rescuing Korea would not be straightforward. The country's debts were huge, and international confidence in its economic management would be shredded once its reserves were understood to be fictitious. Nor did it help that South Korea was on the eve of an election. A rescue package would have to be predicated on reforms by the Korean government. With politics in flux, it would be hard to extract a meaningful commitment.[18]

The next day was Thanksgiving. Rubin embarked upon another round of brainstorming and conference calls, now drawing Clinton's foreign policy advisers into his orbit. Because of the holiday, the scattered members of the Clinton brain trust had to be reached at home: at one point, Secretary of State Madeleine Albright held her phone in one hand while basting her turkey with the other. The more Rubin listened to the advisers, the more he could see that they supported the idea of a bailout: Korea was too strategically important to abandon. American troops were stationed on Korean soil, and a deepening of the crisis might embolden communist North Korea to attack. U.S. military security could be affected.

As the discussions progressed, Greenspan accepted the case for a rescue. If his friends in the administration wanted to act, he was not going to oppose them. But when he spoke publicly about the crisis, his pronouncements were not exactly calculated to build confidence in a bailout. In a speech in New York on December 2, Greenspan lamented the rotten state of banks in the emerging world: government meddling had resulted in mountains of bad loans to political cronies. In many countries, the entire banking system was "at severe risk of collapse," he worried, apparently untroubled by the effect that he might have on already jumpy investors. In the Q&A session that followed, Greenspan added that no amount of rescue money could end a run on a nation that failed to embrace reform. The implication was that speculators should not be overly impressed by the mere announcement of a bailout.

On December 3, South Korea received precisely the sort of bailout that Greenspan had warned against. Acting in close consultation with Rubin and the Treasury, the International Monetary Fund announced that Korea would get $55 billion in official loans, an amount intended to calm the banks that were yanking cash out of the country. But within a few days of this announcement, Greenspan's bleak warnings proved correct. Starting on December 8, Korea's currency resumed its free fall.

When the FOMC convened on December 16, Greenspan sounded oddly detached from Asia's turmoil. "It will be fascinating to watch what happens," he mused to his colleagues. "Our financial institutions have not lent that much to borrowers in that part of the world. Even if they lost 90 percent of those loans, it would not be a big deal," he added, rather too sweepingly.[19] Besides, the do-nothing libertarian within Greenspan doubted that a further attempt at a bailout would be healthy anyway.

"If there is a big flood of IMF money into Asia, I think we will find that they are going to continue doing whatever they did before," he predicted, reprising an argument he had used during the New York crisis in 1975. "They are going to behave the way they think they ought to, which is what got them into trouble."

The next day South Koreans elected a new president. The markets fell again—the victor, Kim Dae-Jung, had threatened to renegotiate the conditions attached to IMF assistance. Rubin visited Congress to brief lawmakers on the gravity of Korea's position, bringing Greenspan along to reinforce his arguments. Whatever the Fed chairman's skeptical musings to his FOMC colleagues, he remained a loyal member of the Treasury team.[20]

That evening Rubin gathered his advisers at the Jefferson Hotel, the elegant establishment a few blocks north of the White House where he lived during his time as Treasury secretary.

"Some problems have no solutions," he remarked grimly.[21] If the United States mounted a second rescue attempt that failed to impress the markets, it would damage confidence in U.S. leadership.

Casting around for a solution, Rubin's advisers dusted off an approach not seen since the Volcker era. For Mexico and for the first Korea rescue, the Clintonites had relied upon emergency assistance plus policy reform in the crisis-hit country. Now, for its second stab at fixing Korea, it would add a third ingredient: it would twist the arms of private creditors so that they stopped yanking their money out. Unlike in the case of Mexico, Korea's foreign debts consisted mainly of bank loans, not bonds held by thousands of dispersed investors. The government could get the bankers in a room and tell them to keep lending. Instead of being bailed out, private creditors would be bailed in.

There was one obstacle, however. Greenspan was of two minds about the arm-twisting strategy. He could see that bailing in the banks was better than disbursing U.S. taxpayers' money to South Korea, and better than allowing a major economy and military ally to default chaotically. But he felt leery of browbeating the banks to keep lending to Korea, just as he had felt uneasy about Gerald Corrigan's pressure on banks to keep lending to brokers after the crash of 1987. After all, the central message of his New York speech had been that governments should stay out of private credit decisions.

Greenspan indicated to Rubin that he was not going to call the bankers. If Rubin wanted to squeeze them, he would have to do the calling.[22]

Rubin accepted the role of chief enforcer. Over the next days, he called the heads of a few banks, even threatening to shame one lender in public if it failed to cooperate. But he was not going to act entirely alone. Whatever the chairman's misgivings, the Fed would have to help corral the bankers—even if Greenspan wasn't going to get involved personally.

A week later, on Christmas Eve, Bill McDonough of the New York Fed summoned the heads of the nation's six major banks to his boardroom.[23]

"I have been authorized by the international institutions and the United States government to tell you the game is over," McDonough announced to the bank chiefs. Taxpayers were not going to pour cash into Korea only to see it used to repay imprudent creditors. "If you continue to have your bank lines paid down, the flow of international money into Korea will end immediately," McDonough growled. "I didn't bring you here on Christmas Eve to say Merry Christmas."[24]

The banks asked for time to confer among themselves, and McDonough retreated to his office. It was an echo of that moment, ninety years earlier, when J. Pierpont Morgan had locked Wall Street's leaders into his library, demanding that they come up with the money to stem the 1907 panic. Fittingly, it was J.P. Morgan's chief executive who sought McDonough out a little while later to convey the bankers' joint decision.

"We've decided that we want to make an announcement," the Morgan man said. The banks were ready to roll over their loans to Korea as they came due, rather than demanding their money back. But he added that such an announcement would take time. The banks' communications people had gone home for the holidays.

"Bill, it's Christmas Eve," he pleaded.

"My public information officer is here, on duty. He'd be happy to put out an announcement," McDonough countered. Then, perhaps remembering the sensibilities of the Fed chairman, he added a rider: "Not on Fed stationery."

A statement was duly drafted in the name of the assembled banks. "It is our firm belief that a market-oriented private sector financing initiative offers the best solution," it announced, in language that might have been deliberately chosen to assuage Greenspan's free-market scruples.[25] But the truth was that this "private" initiative was the result of government muscle. Besides, the simultaneous provision of official loans to Korea meant that taxpayers were still helping to protect the bankers from their follies.

Greenspan did not voice qualms about McDonough's manhandling of the banks—he remained a team player. To the contrary, when the head of a major bank called him to complain about official bullying, Greenspan retorted that creditors had a strong interest in averting a Korean meltdown.[26] But other free-marketers in Washington showed no hesitation in denouncing the rescue. "If we were to put purple dye on the taxpayers' money that we are today sending these countries," grumbled the libertarian congressman Ron Paul, "Wall Street fat cats would be walking around with purple pockets tomorrow."[27] Paradoxically, the more free-marketers attacked the rescue, the more Greenspan came to be identified as a supporter of the deal. To shield himself from right-wing congressional critics, Rubin took to calling attention to Greenspan's backing—if a libertarian Republican had helped to formulate the Korea plan, surely it could not be described as welfare for bankers.[28] In this manner, strangely, Greenspan emerged as a key architect of a policy about which he had initially expressed ambivalence. There would be lasting implications for his reputation.

By the spring of 1998, South Korea was on the mend. Whether Greenspan liked it or not, the Fed was emerging as the central banker to everybody.

W ith South Korea safely stabilized, Wall Street kept humming. By the last week of March 1998, the S&P 500 index was up 50 percent since the beginning of 1997, and up fully 140 percent since Greenspan's celebrated soft landing. The hot stock market made capital cheap and abundant, fueling a frenzy of mergers. Bank stocks were up threefold in as many years, powered by a wave of takeovers.[29]

On March 26, 1998, Greenspan came face to face with Wall Street's wild euphoria. At eleven o'clock that morning, Sanford Weill, the stocky, sixty-five-year-old Brooklyn native who had built the Travelers insurance group out of practically nothing, arrived in the Fed chairman's office accompanied by John Reed of Citicorp, the second-largest bank in the country. The two financial chieftains had gone out of their way to escape notice, traveling from New York by separate jets and separate cars, slipping through the back entrance of the Fed's Eccles Building. But once installed with Greenspan, Weill and Reed revealed their hands. They were plotting the creation of the largest financial firm on the planet.

The proposed merger between Travelers and Citicorp was doubly audacious. Not only would it be the biggest corporate marriage ever, it would also test the borders of legality. Since 1987, the Fed had expanded the first breach of Glass-Steagall into a cavernous loophole: there was no longer an effective bar to combining securities underwriting and bank lending in a single holding company. But a Travelers-Citi tie-up would still exceed what was allowed because it fused underwriting and lending with insurance. The way the laws were written, the two Wall Street bosses could press ahead with their union. But unless Congress passed a reform to permit their merger retrospectively, they would eventually have to unpick it.

Weill had the advantage of a long-standing relationship with Greenspan. He had hired him as a consultant in 1977, and Greenspan had provided his take on the economy at weekly Monday sessions, impressing Weill particularly with his feel for commodity prices. One summer in the late 1970s, Weill's son had worked at Greenspan's firm, and the two men shared a close relationship with Gerald Ford, who had served on the boards of several Weill companies. Now, sitting in the Fed chairman's office, Weill laid out his plan to his old friend. He wanted to be sure that he had the chairman's blessing.

Greenspan responded guardedly to Weill's presentation. Precisely because of their past friendship, he had to be cautious. Whenever he met Weill to discuss a regulatory issue, he was careful to have the Fed general counsel sit in on the meeting.

"Well, we'll consider it," Greenspan said. "You can expect it to be a rigorous examination." But he evidently was not saying no. Weill and Reed felt encouraged.[30]

Greenspan's poker face concealed conflicting reactions. On the one hand, a Travelers-Citi merger would represent the culmination of the trend toward financial silo busting that Greenspan had championed since his service on Nixon's financial-reform commission almost three decades earlier. On the other hand, Weill was taking a risk, and his chutzpah was unnerving. Despite his confident presumption, Congress might not pass the law he needed to ratify his combination of banking with insurance; after all, it had tried and failed to remove barriers to "universal banking" on ten occasions over the past decade.[31] Meanwhile, the merger would encourage yet more exuberance in markets. When Weill's deal went public, bank stocks would soar and Wall Street would no doubt break all records.

Five days after Weill's visit, the FOMC convened for its next meeting. Even though the Travelers-Citi deal was still not public, the committee members could see that the economy might be approaching that phase when a boom descends into self-parody. Unemployment was down at 4.6 percent, its lowest rate in twenty-five years, and workers with particularly sought-after skills were dashing from one employer to the next in search of ever fatter pay packets. The president of the Dallas Fed reported on a billboard that had appeared across the freeway from the Texas Instruments headquarters. WHY DID THE ENGINEER CROSS THE ROAD? the billboard asked. TO GET A BETTER JOB.

Alone among the committee members, Greenspan knew that Travelers-

Citi was in the works, but he did not breathe a word of it. Instead, he conceded to his colleagues that "the economy's performance is absolutely unusual." The stock market, in particular, was possessed by "an utterly unrealistic expectation" of corporate earnings; meanwhile, risky companies were borrowing at interest rates scarcely higher than the rate on risk-free government bonds, and bank officers were behaving as though risk had somehow vanished. "There is too little uncertainty in this system," Greenspan observed. "Human nature has not changed and when it reasserts itself, things are going to look a lot different."

If that sounded like a cogent argument for raising interest rates, Greenspan assured his colleagues that it wasn't. That time was approaching, to be sure: "Unless this system starts to self-correct fairly shortly," Greenspan stipulated, "we will have no choice but to move." But for the time being, he continued, inflation remained quiescent and there was no harm in waiting. "I do not think it is appropriate to move at this stage," he said. "Were we to do so, I believe we would create too large a shock to the system." Forgetting his earlier lectures about the importance of getting ahead of the curve, and unmoved by his insider knowledge of the Travelers-Citi merger, Greenspan had become a procrastinator.

"Our actions in early 1994, properly viewed, prevented the recession of 1996," Jerry Jordan of the Cleveland Fed reminded him. "What we are faced with today is how to prevent the next credit crunch and recession of the year 2000."[32]

It was a prescient observation.

The following Monday, April 6, Weill and Reed waltzed into a ballroom at the Waldorf Astoria in Midtown Manhattan. Weill's tie matched the blue of the Citicorp logo; Reed's was red, the color of Travelers. The two cross-dressers sat in front of a large sign emblazoned with the name CITI-GROUP. The crisp capital letters *tilted forward*, as if pointing to the future.

A frenzy of flashbulbs and boisterous news crews greeted the grinning pair.

"Some business we're in, huh?" a rising Travelers star named Jamie Dimon whispered to his neighbor. "It's like Michael Jackson, Michael Jordan."[33]

Weill launched into his case for the merger. Universal banks, offering every conceivable financial service, were already accepted in Japan and Europe; it was time for the United States to produce a champion that could aspire to compete globally. It was simply not right that Chase, the biggest U.S. lender, ranked only seventeenth in the world; or that Citicorp, second in the United States, trailed in at number twenty-seven in the international league tables. Moreover, Weill continued, the Fed itself had blessed the silo busting embodied in his plan, recently praising a deregulatory reform bill that had unfortunately stalled—again—in Congress. "Maybe what we're doing will cause that legislation to change," Weill mused.[34] By the end of that day, ecstatic investors had lifted the Travelers and Citi stock prices by 20 and 25 percent.[35] For the first time ever, the Dow Jones Industrial Average closed above 9000.

It was not just investors who reacted swiftly. Within hours of the Weill-Reed press conference, armies of lobbyists descended upon the Senate and House banking committees, and staff experts set to work resuscitating the abandoned reform bill; by the end of the day, it had found its way back onto the House calendar for fresh consideration.[36] The usually sober *New York Times* splashed the front page of its business section with a giant illustration depicting Weill and Reed as twin King Kongs, perched on the iconic slanted roof of the Citicorp Center; and the *Times* editorial board assured readers that there was nothing to fear from this marriage of two monsters.[37] "The fact is that Citigroup threatens no one because it would not dominate banking, securities, insurance, or any other financial market," the *Times* wrote confidently. "A collapse in the company's securities and insurance operations could drag down its commercial bank. But that will happen only if Federal regulators fall sound asleep."[38]

The following week, on April 13, Wall Street woke up to the fact that something broader might be stirring. Two midwestern lenders, Banc One and First Chicago, unveiled plans for a merger that would forge the nation's fifth-largest bank.[39] That same day, the Waldorf Astoria played host to another surprise corporate wedding, as executives from North Carolina–based NationsBank and California-based BankAmerica announced an even bigger deal; the newly formed Bank of America would have nearly five thousand branches sprinkled like Starbucks stores from one coast to the other.[40] Although neither of these deals eclipsed Travelers-Citi, they confirmed that Weill's audacious announcement was not a mere fluke. Whereas in the 1970s, each financial subindustry had feared competition from the rest, stymieing the silo-busting deregulation that Greenspan had favored, now America's insurers and bankers were focused on a different threat: foreign competition. In consequence, the logic of conglomeration had been broadly accepted. A new era of megalenders was dawning.

Five days later, with the Dow up another 1.5 percentage points since Weill's press conference, the cover of the *Economist* showed a gloomy lower Manhattan skyline, menaced by an enormous bubble floating fatefully toward the sharpened tip of the torch on the Statue of Liberty. "Evidence of speculative excesses is widespread," the *Economist* asserted; the real economic gains associated with lower inflation, shrinking federal deficits, and better technology were not enough to justify the stratospheric level of the stock market. "The Federal Reserve needs to tighten the monetary screws," it proclaimed. "It would have been better if the Fed had raised interest rates sooner to prevent a bubble in the first place."[41]

On May 5, Greenspan paid a formal visit to the White House for the first time in more than a year. The president wanted to know: Had Greenspan seen the *Economist* article?

Greenspan had seen it. But he also understood that Clinton would appreciate an upbeat rejoinder; the staff had organized the meeting because the president needed an antidote to the Monica Lewinsky scandal. So Greenspan accentuated the positive, emphasizing to Clinton that the changes in the real economy were truly impressive. Thanks to computerized logistics, companies knew how many parts to order for their factories and how many widgets to ship to each outlet; the old production bottlenecks were gone, and with them a main driver of inflation. As a result, the unemployment rate was down at an incredible 4.3 percent, and yet prices were still stable.

"This is the best economy I've ever seen in fifty years of studying it every day," Greenspan assured the president.[42]

Twenty-four

"UNCLE ALAN WILL
TAKE CARE OF US"

A s American prosperity advanced, the cable business-news network CNBC gained traction with a fetching gimmick.[1] On mornings when the FOMC was due to meet, a camera crew would lie
in wait outside the Fed building. When the powerful figure of the Fed
chairman hove into view—pin-striped, proceeding purposefully, curled-
top briefcase in one hand—a telephoto close-up would interrogate his
face. If Greenspan looked tense, the network would couple the footage
with the suspenseful theme tune from *Mission Impossible,* the old CBS TV
series recently remade as a shoot-'em-up movie. If Greenspan looked carefree, the producers might roll out Jean Knight's jaunty soul hit, "Mr. Big
Stuff."[2] Then the camera lens would home in on that briefcase, swinging
lightly in the Fed chairman's hand. If the case looked fat, it signified a
heavy reading load—evidently, Greenspan was working himself up to a
fateful decision about interest rates. If the case looked slim, then Greenspan was presumably relaxed. The Fed could be expected to leave rates
unchanged, and Americans could breathe easily.

CNBC's "briefcase indicator" conveyed no real monetary intelligence,
as everybody understood—Greenspan joked that the size of his bag
depended on whether he had packed a sandwich. But the indicator spoke

volumes about the Fed chairman's cult status, and the pleasure he took in it. That portentous stroll to the office—the central-banking equivalent of a double-holstered Gary Cooper advancing manfully across a dusty square—was a matter of deliberate choice: if Greenspan had wanted to avoid the cameras, his driver could have whisked him into the Fed's underground garage rather than dropping him off a few blocks from the Eccles Building. But by the summer of 1998, Greenspan enjoyed Greenspan gags as much as the next guy—indeed, he reveled in them. Andrea had started a collection of Greenspan-alia: there were Alan Greenspan postcards, Alan Greenspan cartoons, Alan Greenspan T-shirts, and even a doll fashioned after the Fed chairman.[3] Three years earlier, Greenspan had worried to his FOMC colleagues about the bubble in his own status: he had become the "Zipswitch chairman." But now he had given up fighting this overvaluation, just as he had given up resisting the stock market's exuberance.

"How many central bankers does it take to screw in a lightbulb?" went a joke of the time.

"One," the answer went: "Greenspan holds the bulb and the world revolves around him."[4]

The sideman's emergence as Mr. Big Stuff reflected a change in the culture. CNBC was one of several cable news channels that sprang up in the 1990s, hungry for daytime fodder to feed their audiences of day traders. The oracular Fed chairman was a ratings godsend; his least significant remarks were carried live and unexpurgated. Whenever he popped up in public, his lined face and large spectacles were beamed to screens around the world: "Greenspan Speaks," the TV caption would announce, as though no further proof of newsworthiness were necessary.[5] Given that billions of dollars of wealth were created or destroyed on the basis of the chairman's pronouncements, nobody thought this particularly odd—which said something about monetary policy. In the wake of his irrational exuberance speech, Greenspan had concluded that his rhetoric was powerless to bring the stock market down. Now that investors hung upon his every word, his modesty appeared exaggerated.[6]

The emerging cult of Alan Greenspan also reflected exceptional prosperity. The United States was reclaiming a preeminence not seen since the aftermath of World War II. From Europe to Asia, America's postwar rivals had been thoroughly humbled. The Soviet Union had disintegrated. Japan was experiencing its first lost decade. China was as yet too poor to pose a threat. West Germany was resting, python style, having swallowed up its eastern neighbor. And the keys to American ascendancy lay precisely in those forces with which Greenspan was identified: in the new computing and communications wizardry, whose impact on productivity the Fed chairman had been early to divine; in the superiority of the market-based system that he had championed since his youth; in the quantitative and pragmatic approach to the world, which he exemplified so perfectly. Two decades earlier, Henry Kissinger had become the improbable celebrity of an era shaped by geopolitical forces, from the Soviet challenge to Vietnam. Now America's fate hinged on economic and technological currents that Greenspan interpreted—and embodied.

Of course, this brave new economy was not without its worries. As well as crises in East Asia and the perplexing emergence of the megabanks, the nation was facing a bewildering proliferation of derivatives. In the three and a half years since the shocking losses at Orange County, Procter & Gamble, and Gibson Greeting Cards, swaps of all varieties had roughly tripled in volume: if they had proved their potential to cause trouble back in 1994, they were now even scarier.[7] At his breakfasts with his friends at Treasury, Greenspan would occasionally ponder this problem, siding with Lawrence Summers and against Bob Rubin. The way Rubin saw things, zippy financial instruments could easily go wrong—after all, plenty of supposed professionals had only a flimsy grasp of risk, and plenty of unscrupulous salesmen were ready to take advantage of them. Summers countered by accusing Rubin of being against anything modern. If the trio had been discussing tennis, Rubin would have insisted on the virtues of wooden rackets.[8]

In the spring of 1998, around the time Weill and Reed were plotting the Travelers-Citi merger, this friendly banter among allies gave way to something serious. The change was forced from outside their tight circle by Brooksley Born, an accomplished club buster who was the first woman to become president of the *Stanford Law Review*. A black-and-white photo of the *Law Review*'s 1964 editorial board shows an elegant feminine figure sitting incongruously amid five men; and Born went on to graduate at the top of her class, a triumph that led naturally to a clerkship with a federal judge on the prestigious Court of Appeals for the District of Columbia. Now, three decades later, Born was chairwoman of the Commodity Futures Trading Commission, the body that regulated traditional derivatives that were traded on U.S. exchanges. In March 1998, Born boldly suggested that she ought to be regulating untraditional derivatives also.

When it came to debates about derivatives, Born knew as much as Greenspan, Summers, or Rubin; after her time on the D.C. Circuit Court, she had risen to the helm of the derivatives practice at Arnold & Porter, a top international law firm. Moreover, the thrust of her regulatory instincts came to be widely accepted after the 2008 crisis, providing a belated vindication.[9] In essence, her chief worry was that the fastest-growing parts of the derivatives market lacked the stabilizing institutions of traditional, exchange-traded equities or futures, with the result that the whole market could descend into chaos if a large trading firm declared bankruptcy. One such stabilizing institution was the central clearinghouse, which stood between buyer and seller and guaranteed payments on trades; unnervingly, non-exchange-based derivatives were traded "over the counter," with banks entering into swap contracts directly with each other—there was no third-party guarantee that obligations would be honored. Another stabilizing institution was the requirement that traders put down money, or "margin," to cover their potential debts; in over-the-counter markets, there were no standard margin requirements, so the potential losses from nonpayment were larger. In the absence of these safeguards, proliferating over-the-counter swap contracts were connecting corporations, banks, and hedge funds in long chains of IOUs. The links in these chains could snap at any moment.

Given the merits of her position, and given that Bob Rubin was predisposed to take her side, Born started out with a reasonable chance of

winning the argument. But in order to prevail, she would have to outmaneuver the laissez-faire faction in Washington. She would have to get past
Alan Greenspan.

Born phoned Susan Phillips, the Fed governor who had overseen the
makeover of the Fed's boardroom. Phillips was also the head of the Fed
committee dealing with derivatives and a former chairwoman of the Commodity Futures Trading Commission. She was a fellow woman and a fellow derivatives expert. Born presumed she was an ally.

"She called me up one day and said, 'Alan does not agree with me and
does not understand,'" Phillips recalled later.

"Would you go down and straighten him out?" Born demanded.

Phillips was stunned. Who did this woman think she was? Born had
badly underestimated Phillips's sense of loyalty to the Fed chairman.

"Brooksley, I can't do that," Phillips retorted. "He understands this
stuff and he has a view. Alan thinks about things. He doesn't just get
straightened out."

Sometime later, Born called Phillips again. Having failed to "straighten
out" Greenspan, she now proposed to circumvent him. Her plan was to
issue a "concept release," inviting public comment on the regulation of
derivatives. This would be a prelude to regulating over-the-counter swaps,
just as the CFTC already regulated exchange-traded futures.

Born told Phillips that her concept release was already written. If Phillips wanted to look at it before it went public, she should come over to the
CFTC with one Fed staff person only and sit in a room and read it.

"Can't you just send me a copy?" Phillips objected.

Born refused—she was not going to let her discussion paper out of the
CFTC building. Years later, when Born's attempt to regulate derivatives
became the stuff of legend, she was frequently portrayed as the victim of
sexism. According to this narrative, her reform plans were squashed
because she was not part of the boys' club. But in the spring of 1998, Born
was managing to alienate just about everyone, including women such as
Phillips.[10]

"Okay, I'll come over," Phillips said. She recruited Pat Parkinson, the
top staff expert on derivatives at the Fed, and they went over to the CFTC

office a couple of days later. There they spent two hours in confinement, reading Born's proposals. Born herself was not around to say hello, much less take account of their reactions.

Phillips and Parkinson were alarmed by what they read. Even though the concept release took no positions, merely asking for comment, its long list of questions promised to stir up a hornet's nest of trouble. The CFTC regulated futures, and futures were required to be traded on exchanges; some lawyers believed that if the CFTC asserted the right to regulate swaps, then a court might regard swaps as futures, in which case all swaps would have to be traded on an exchange—otherwise, they might be illegal and unenforceable. Trillions of dollars of outstanding over-the-counter contracts could be consigned to a legal limbo.

The news of Born's unpublished concept release soon filtered back to Greenspan. No doubt he celebrated silently. Born was making a spectacular blunder: the prospect of putting the entire stock of over-the-counter swaps into legal jeopardy would convert Bob Rubin from a potential Born ally into a committed opponent. Born might be accomplished, intelligent, and right. But she was possessed of a litigator's aggression. She evidently had no idea how to finesse the complex interagency politics of U.S financial regulation.[11]

Greenspan mentioned the Born problem to Arthur Levitt, the chairman of the Securities and Exchange Commission, while the two men were playing golf at the Chevy Chase Club. The CFTC chairwoman had gone rogue. She was a danger to everybody.[12]

Levitt readily agreed. Born had done nothing to win him over in advance; he did not know her more than superficially, and he found her intimidating. Besides, if any agency was going to expand its regulatory authority, Levitt thought it ought to be his SEC, not its junior cousin.[13]

On the afternoon of April 21, 1998, Born was summoned to a meeting at the Treasury. Greenspan met with Pat Parkinson that morning to make sure he was on top of all the details; then he went over to the Treasury a bit early to huddle with Rubin and Arthur Levitt so that they could agree on a common position.[14] By the time Born arrived in the Treasury secretary's ornate conference room, the high command of the nation's regulatory army had assembled. There was Gene Ludwig, the comptroller of the currency; Ellen Seidman, director of the Office of Thrift Supervision; Bill McDonough, the president of the New York Fed; and, of course, Lawrence Summers.[15]

Born took a seat toward the end of the table. Rubin was seated in the middle of one side. Greenspan was seated in the middle of the other.

Speaking in front of the assembled witnesses, eliminating all ambiguity as to where the administration stood, Rubin asked Born to hold off on her concept release. There were complex issues to be worked out. Half-baked regulatory proposals could call into question the legality of the over-the-counter market, potentially triggering panic.[16]

Greenspan weighed in, now happily aligned with the Treasury secretary. The group needed to avoid the error of supposing that just because an absence of regulation entailed risk, the imposition of regulation would reduce it. History was littered with examples of regulation that misfired: the 1960s caps on interest rates had merely caused dollar savings to flee to Europe, spawning the so-called Eurodollar market; similarly, a precipitate lunge against over-the-counter derivatives might drive the whole business to London. In the back of his mind, Greenspan recalled that during the crash of 1987, the clearinghouses in Chicago had been on the brink of failing; if regulators now chased derivatives risk out of over-the-counter products and onto exchanges, they might concentrate and so compound the problem.[17] Besides, the policy of not regulating derivatives might have some benefits, Greenspan maintained. In the absence of regulation, traders understood clearly that they must monitor their own risks. They seemed to be managing just fine—Orange County and Procter & Gamble had been an aberration.

Several more voices piled on, urging Born to reconsider. Finally, when she was sufficiently subdued, Rubin offered her a way forward. If Born would put off the publication of her concept release and spend some time working with Treasury lawyers, they might find a way of addressing her legitimate concerns without jeopardizing the entire stock of outstanding swaps contracts.

To many in the room, Born appeared to accept Rubin's olive branch.

But compromise was not her natural style, and she viewed the scare stories about the potential invalidation of outstanding swaps as a smoke screen for industry apologists. No matter what the alarmists asserted, the concept release stated explicitly that it was not the CFTC's intention to raise doubts about the validity of existing swaps. If the Treasury's lawyers still worried, so what? They were wrong, and the right course was to ignore them.

In May, after a few unproductive efforts to contact Treasury's lawyers, Born did just that: she ignored them. She pressed ahead with her concept release, publishing it in defiance of just about every other senior figure in the government. Just as she had predicted, no legal turmoil ensued; the arguments advanced by Rubin and Greenspan had evidently been exaggerated. But without waiting to discover this, the Treasury immediately joined with the Fed and the SEC to release a joint statement rubbishing Born's proposal, ensuring that the concept release never gained traction in Congress. The upshot was that an opportunity for progress was missed. The cause of derivatives regulation, which would in any case have faced an uphill battle because of the power of Wall Street's lobbyists, was set back by more than a decade.[18]

A little while later, on June 17, 1998, Greenspan offered an ironic coda to this fight over the new financial instruments. "When we observe a phenomenon emerging which could threaten the stability of the system, if we don't get ourselves emotionally exercised on it, we shouldn't be in office," he testified to the Senate. But Greenspan was not talking about destabilizing derivatives, a threat to the stability of the system that apparently left him cold. Rather, he was expounding on the advent of the new megabanks, and explaining why they were not actually threatening. With the benefit of hindsight, the Fed's refusal to be emotionally exercised by the disruptive proliferation of unregulated swaps was a failure of the Greenspan era.

If there was one institution that embodied Greenspan's optimism about the new finance, it was Long-Term Capital Management. Founded four years earlier by quantitative wizards from Salomon Brothers, Long-Term's partners included the financial economists Myron Scholes and Robert Merton, who had received the Nobel Prize for their "new method to determine the value of derivatives." David Mullins, the former Fed vice chairman who had lectured Mike Prell about the efficiency of markets, was another principal at LTCM; and for its first two and a half years, the firm performed spectacularly. Its approach was to use the new science of risk management to identify hazards that others feared too much—and then to be paid handsomely for absorbing them. For example, if banks were leery of bonds issued a year ago because they might be hard to sell in a panic, LTCM would buy these illiquid bonds at a discount, calculating that the odds of a panic were sufficiently small to make this a profitable strategy. Equally, if pension funds fretted too much about the peril of a stock market collapse, LTCM would sell them financial derivatives that acted as volatility insurance. In this way, the new financial instruments facilitated the transfer of risks away from those who misjudged them and toward those who understood them minutely. It was just as Greenspan envisaged.

Around the time that Greenspan was fending off Brooksley Born's derivatives proposal, Long-Term Capital Management ran into trouble. Its risk calculations were based on historical patterns, which showed what any given trade could lose in normal circumstances. Combining all potential losses across their portfolio, the partners determined, with confident precision, exactly how much they could lose on any given time horizon. But if markets neglected to behave as they had done historically, this reckoning would be thrown off; and in August 1998, the markets stopped cooperating. Russia, once the darling of Western investors, stunned the world by defaulting. The country's debts to foreigners, far larger than those of East Asia, were suddenly impossible to collect; an aptly named hedge fund, High-Risk Opportunities, blew up; there were rumors that Lehman Brothers might go under. In this febrile environment, LTCM's confidently precise bets went disastrously awry. By the end of August, the partners had lost $1.9 billion—44 percent of the fund's capital and more than three times the maximum that the partners had thought possible.[19]

In principle, this bonfire of Long-Term's vanities was of no concern to Greenspan. The fund's investors had chosen to take risks; if they lost, that was their problem. Indeed, letting LTCM suffer was essential to Greenspan's laissez-faire vision of finance—he could scarcely argue that derivatives traders could be trusted to manage their own risks while simultaneously responding to their pain and so dulling their incentives to be prudent. But not for the first time, Greenspan lacked the fortitude to live up to his vision. Paul Volcker might have acquired Churchillian status by offering the nation blood, toil, tears, and sweat. But Greenspan's cult status had come to depend on continual growth, exuberant finance, and miraculously low unemployment.[20] His identity had fused with the national expectation of prosperity without limit. He was imprisoned by his reputation.

On September 4, 1998, the maestro appeared on a stage at Berkeley's business school to deliver a long-planned speech on technology and the new economy. Given America's extraordinary performance, he might have stuck to his script. The markets were jittery, with the S&P 500 index down by around a tenth since Russia's default; but this did not amount to a crisis—during the Asian crisis the previous autumn, Greenspan had welcomed the sharp sell-off on Wall Street as a salutary correction. This time, however, he took the opposite approach. Working from an amended version of his prepared remarks, he warned his Berkeley audience that the United States could not expect to be an "oasis of prosperity" amid global turmoil; and he hinted that the Fed might be ready to offset this turmoil with looser-than-expected policy. Greenspan might conceive of the Fed's mission in American terms. But the reality of globalization made it impossible to ignore the world around him.

Naturally, Greenspan's hints of a rate cut had their desired effect. Cable television and financial newspapers seized on the Fed chairman's words, and the markets rallied sharply.

Fresh from that victory, Greenspan had dinner in San Francisco with Bob Rubin and Japan's finance minister, Kiichi Miyazawa. Following the success of the Korea rescue, Rubin was intent on responding vigorously to

Russia; he wanted Greenspan's help in badgering Japan to stimulate domestic growth as part of a broader plan to prop up the world economy. Rubin hoped that Europe and Canada would play their part as well; the more buy signals that governments could send to investors, the better the chances of arresting a meltdown in the markets. Greenspan duly joined Rubin in an international lobbying effort, calling his counterparts in capitals around the world, urging them to do something to boost spending. The Group of Seven leading economies duly issued a joint statement on September 14, pledging to support the world economy.[21]

Five days later, on Saturday, September 19, Bill McDonough of the New York Fed took a call from Long-Term Capital.[22] The fund's troubles had gone from bad to existential. Thanks to its use of over-the-counter derivatives, LTCM's leverage was huge; the loss of $2 billion in equity required it to liquidate an astronomical $500 billion of market bets supported by that capital.[23] But unwinding complex derivative positions was easier said than done. Because swaps were not traded on exchanges, they had no clearly established price; in moments of market stress, they could be impossible to exit. The more markets panicked, the more the panic fed itself; there was no central clearing system to guarantee payments on trades, so nobody wanted to strike deals with derivatives shops that could blow up at any moment. Brooksley Born's instincts were proving right. Over-the-counter derivatives lacked the stabilizing institutions that markets needed.

McDonough listened to Long-Term Capital's report and then phoned Greenspan. He proposed sending a Fed official to the LTCM office in Greenwich, Connecticut, to determine how bad the mess was. Whatever Greenspan's laissez-faire scruples, his stimulus efforts with Bob Rubin were not going to be enough. If LTCM unleashed a $500 billion fire sale, other banks and hedge funds with similar positions would go up in flames. Such was the nature of the new finance.

Greenspan gave his approval for McDonough's plan. It was too risky to do otherwise.[24] That evening, he and Andrea accompanied Vice President Al Gore, the Canadian ambassador, and their families to a performance of Cirque du Soleil, celebrated for the wizardry of its acrobatics.

Surrealistic figures bounced off one another's heads and shoulders as if propelled by springs. A gold-dusted man and woman balanced on each other in impossible poses, seemingly defying gravity.[25]

The next day was Sunday. Peter Fisher, McDonough's deputy at the New York Fed, hitched a ride in an assistant's Jeep to the LTCM headquarters in Greenwich. There were no acrobats present, and no gold dust to be found; there were only empty rooms and unmanned computer terminals. Working with a colleague from the Treasury, Fisher soon determined that the mess was worse than he had dreamed. Not only was Long-Term's leverage enormous, but its positions were concentrated in particular niches; Fisher reckoned that Long-Term's holding of futures on British government bonds might represent as much as half of the open interest in that market. If Long-Term was forced to dump these bets in a rush, some markets might freeze up; they would not merely fall—they would cease functioning. Moreover, in past financial collapses, regulators had been able to avert a fire sale by seizing control of the assets held by the bust bank. But the plumbing of the over-the-counter swaps market made the standard approach impractical this time. Every asset in LTCM's possession had been pledged as collateral to a lender or trading partner. In the event of a default, the counterparties would seize everything and probably sell immediately.

Fisher reported what he had found to Greenspan the next morning. The markets were in turmoil, and some commentators were speculating that the release of Clinton's videotaped deposition in the Monica Lewinsky sex scandal, scheduled for later that morning, was rattling investors— a theory that Fisher found grimly amusing. Leveraged derivatives, not sex, were the real source of the panic.

Greenspan listened carefully to Fisher. Then he made it clear that he did not want more calls like this one. In future, LTCM updates should be reported to Don Kohn, Greenspan's most trusted staff adviser. This would be in keeping with standard procedure. Besides, just as in 1987, and just as with Korea, Greenspan wanted to keep his distance from the New York Fed's actions.

After hanging up the phone, Greenspan arranged for an FOMC conference call. Even if he preferred to avoid direct entanglement with LTCM, he had no qualms about stepping up his monetary response to the fallout. The world economy was in a precarious state. Following Russia's default, Brazil was on the ropes. A few days earlier, President Clinton had delivered a speech at the Council on Foreign Relations, worrying that global financial turmoil could halt the tide of freedom and prosperity.[26]

Once the FOMC members had assembled on the line, Greenspan proposed that he should take up a standing invitation from the Senate to testify that Wednesday. He would use the occasion to double down on his Berkeley hints about cutting interest rates. Although U.S. output was still growing, there was a risk that market turmoil would derail its advance. The Fed should signal its willingness to act now, to buy insurance for the economy.

Not all Greenspan's colleagues were convinced that a rate cut was necessary. Despite the post-Russia correction, the S&P 500 was up 38 percent since the time of the chairman's irrational exuberance outburst; and in the fortnight since Greenspan's reassuring Berkeley speech, the market had stabilized. Meanwhile, the real economy was not just growing; it was strong—the data would later show that growth in the third quarter of 1998 came in at 5.3 percent. Even if the Russia shock was more serious than East Asia, the economy had enough momentum to absorb it.

"There may be a little Main Street/Wall Street dichotomy here," Al Broaddus of the Richmond Fed said drily.

Greenspan was not to be put off. Unlike his FOMC colleagues, he had heard Peter Fisher's message. Wall Street was far more vulnerable than was signaled by stocks; the real danger lay in a potential freeze-up in derivatives. As usual, the committee deferred to the chairman. Greenspan would signal a rate cut when he appeared before the Senate.

The next morning, Tuesday, September 22, Greenspan took a call from Gerald Corrigan, the former New York Fed president who was now a senior Goldman Sachs executive.

"Alan," Corrigan said, "I want to pass along some information. I neither expect nor want any reaction or comment from you."

Greenspan indicated he was listening.

The liquidity in the marketplace had just evaporated, Corrigan stressed. It had become impossible to sell. It was not quite as bad as the 1987 crash, but it was close to that.

Greenspan thanked Corrigan and the call ended.[27] Peter Fisher's warning was evidently accurate. The freeze-up was beginning.

That evening in New York, Fisher convened the heads of sixteen banks that had lent extensively to Long-Term Capital. By now, the hedge fund needed an emergency infusion of $4 billion to prevent a collapse and a fire sale. Replaying the drama of previous crises, Fisher encouraged the assembled creditors to recapitalize LTCM; if they let it go down, a fire sale would ensue and everyone would suffer. The bankers understood the message, but there was no obvious formula for apportioning the costs. At the height of the Korea crisis, the New York Fed had asked the banks not to pull their money out, but this time it was telling them to put new money in. The haggling over which bank should kick in how much spilled over into Wednesday morning.

As the negotiations deadlocked in New York, Greenspan had other business to attend to. The Travelers-Citi question had not gone away, and on Wednesday morning the Fed's board met in Washington to authorize the combination. Some of the Fed governors questioned whether supervisors would prove capable of controlling the risks in the merged behemoth, given its fantastical complexity. But a majority of the governors favored marching on. Even though the Fed was grappling, right at that very moment, with a vast failure of risk management among the banks that had lent recklessly to LTCM, the board pronounced itself confident that Sandy Weill's audacious union would produce a bank that behaved prudently. "Citigroup is expected to have in place a risk-management structure sufficient to monitor and manage the risks of a diverse organization," the board's ruling declared.[28] Armed with this approval from the Fed, the merger was allowed to go forward.

Greenspan emerged from the board meeting at lunchtime. There was still no resolution in New York, and he headed over to Congress, where he was due to testify in the Senate. No matter what LTCM's creditors decided, the chairman was determined to deliver a message to the world. The Fed was not going to sit on its hands while the markets descended into panic.

"The most recent, more virulent phase of the crisis has infected our markets," he told the senators.

Virulent. Infected. The force of his language could not possibly be missed by those ever-vigilant Fed journalists.

"We're *fraying* at the edges," Greenspan went on, in case anyone had dozed through the first hints.

Sure enough, the markets jumped in response to Greenspan's remarks. By the end of that afternoon's trading, the Dow Jones Industrial Average was up by more than 2 percent. "These are about as blunt statements as you ever get from the chairman," a Wall Streeter observed appreciatively.[29]

An hour after the stock market closed, the standoff in New York came to an end. Eleven of LTCM's creditor banks agreed to increase their contributions to the recapitalization, allowing a foot-dragging minority to put up less, which in turn made possible an agreement. Shortly after seven o'clock that evening, a press release conveyed the news to relieved traders around the world.[30] Thanks to the combined efforts of the Washington and New York Feds, the worst of the crisis was over.

There was still a crisis of ideas, however. In ratifying the Travelers-Citi merger, the Fed had blessed a new species of megabank, proclaiming itself competent to oversee such behemoths. But the Long-Term Capital shock had shown that supervisors were unable to prevent banks from financing LTCM thoughtlessly. In shooting down Brooksley Born's derivatives proposal, the Fed had contended that over-the-counter traders could police their own risks. But LTCM had underlined the danger in these chains of paper promises.

At the FOMC meeting at the end of September, Greenspan's much telegraphed monetary loosening came into effect with a cut of 25 basis points. But the loose nature of the Fed's intellectual moorings was the more urgent subject of discussion.

Greenspan demanded to know how the Long-Term Capital debacle could have come about. Why had banks lent so heedlessly to LTCM? Why hadn't the Fed's bank examiners stopped them?

"We still have to look into that," conceded Rich Spillenkothen, the Fed's chief of supervision.

"I know that we check to see whether bank policies are being implemented," Greenspan persisted. "But how did we do that with respect to, say, Morgan and LTCM?"

Spillenkothen responded that the Fed probably hadn't done anything with respect to Morgan and LTCM. His team of bank examiners did not have the resources to parse every loan. "We do a spot check," he offered.

"Where we are most vulnerable is with regard to the adequacy of our examinations," Greenspan concluded. "If we had to meet the standards that people think exist, we would have five times as many examiners," he went on. "We would examine them to death, and they would not have any breathing room." The bottom line was that government supervision could never save Wall Street from blowing itself up; the inevitability of crises just had to be accepted. And yet, on the other hand, the LTCM episode showed how frightening such crises could be. It was not just a single hedge fund that had failed. Just about every major creditor on Wall Street had thrown money at Long-Term Capital, even though its strategy was built on hubris.

"It is one thing for one bank to have failed to appreciate what was happening," Greenspan lamented. "But this list of institutions is just mind-boggling."

Of course, there might have been a middle way—between laissez-faire fatalism and hyperactive regulation. If supervision was doomed to failure, and if banks' risk management could fail to a "mind-boggling" extent, then at least the Fed could limit the size, complexity, and leverage of lenders, containing the scope of the problem. Finance would never be fail-safe, as Greenspan correctly understood. But it could perhaps be rendered safer to fail: over-the-counter derivatives could be centrally cleared so that panic in one fund would not spread panic to the rest;

simpler banks, easier to manage during good times and easier to dismember if they went bust, could be favored over complex ones. Yet Greenspan showed no inclination to explore this middle way.

Two days later, on October 1, Greenspan testified before Congress. Now speaking in public, he did his best to accentuate the advantages of modern finance—because he had no plan to rein it in, he had no choice but to extol it. Hedge funds such as LTCM were mostly positive for the economy, he maintained: they contributed to a "sophisticated pricing system which is one of the reasons why the use of capital in this country is so efficient." Playing on the politicians' patriotism, Greenspan continued, "It is why productivity is the highest in the world, why our standards of living, without question, are the highest in the world. . . . The average American is far better off than at any time in our history."

"How many more failures do you think we'd have to have, Mr. Chairman, before you might think that some regulation in this area might be appropriate?" somebody asked.[31]

"This is a risky business and I would expect a lot of failures to occur," Greenspan responded, not very encouragingly.[32]

Later that day, Brooksley Born appeared before the same House committee. She sat in Greenspan's seat, though she could not aspire to fill it. Most of the press corps had melted away. A small woman from an obscure regulatory agency looked up at the assembled lawmakers.

"You're welcome to claim some vindication if you want," the committee chairman told her.

Up until this point in early October, Greenspan's handling of the LTCM debacle invited a double verdict. On the negative side of the ledger, he had failed to seize the opportunity to revise his views—either on complex megabanks or on over-the-counter derivatives. Having rightly opposed the financial silos of the 1970s, the distortive interest-rate caps of Regulation Q, and the arguably outdated constraints of Glass-Steagall, he did not prove agile enough to pivot when the new leveraged finance demanded it. But on the positive side of the ledger, Greenspan had handled the immediate crisis well, expanding moral hazard as little as possible. He had talked up the markets and delivered a small interest-rate cut, but that was easily reversible. He had allowed the New York Fed to orchestrate LTCM's rescue, but at least the Fed had not contributed taxpayer money to the effort—this was not a replay of Continental Illinois, when U.S. government funds were committed. After watching LTCM's partners lose their personal wealth in the meltdown, other hedge-fund managers generally avoided crazy leverage over the next decade; after seeing the fund's creditors being forced to pick up the pieces, banks grew more careful in how they financed hedge-fund trading. Come 2008, freestanding hedge funds (as distinct from those whose discipline was compromised by deep-pocketed banking parents) emerged as one of the more stable parts of the financial system.

But over the next weeks, this dual verdict on Greenspan had to be revised—in a negative direction. For one thing, the chairman rebuffed a second attempt to regulate derivatives, this one advanced by officials from within Rubin's Treasury. Unlike Brooksley Born's proposal, the Treasury initiative did not threaten to outlaw the entire stock of outstanding swaps; it endorsed the sensible notion of moving over-the-counter contracts to centralized clearing, and it suggested that the unregulated derivatives subsidiaries of the investment banks might be subjected to SEC examinations. But Greenspan poured scorn on both proposals. So long as he opposed them, Congress would oppose them, too. The Treasury retreated.[33]

Meanwhile, Greenspan's monetary response to LTCM went from measured to excessive. On October 15, with the FOMC not due to meet for another month, Greenspan convened his colleagues by conference call and cut interest rates by an additional 25 basis points. It was a dramatic gesture—the Fed had not changed rates between meetings in more than four years—and it was almost certainly unwarranted. On the eve of Greenspan's action, the S&P 500 index was down barely 5 percent since Russia's default—hardly cause for worry. The economy, moreover, was accelerating; having racked up growth of 5.3 percent in the third quarter, output was on its way to growing by 6.7 percent in the fourth one. And although the credit markets remained stressed, LTCM had been recapitalized by its bankers, neutralizing the immediate danger of a fire sale.[34] Given that the risks were minimal, Greenspan was demonstrating an extreme risk aversion.

Several FOMC members doubted there was any need for a rate cut. "Action today could be viewed, by some anyway, as an effort to help bail out the hedge funds," William Poole of the St. Louis Fed said pointedly.

Greenspan ignored Poole, and went ahead anyway.

When the rate cut was announced at 3:15 p.m., the stock market and the bond market raced each other upward. By the end of the day, the S&P 500 was up fully 4 percent, and the next day it rose further. "My traders were high-fiving each other and whooping like after a touchdown," one fund manager recalled. "I watched the screens"—color coded to distinguish falling stocks from rising ones—"as they turned from red to green."[35] Up and down Wall Street, Greenspan's surprise intervention cemented his status: he was not just a guru; he was a guardian angel. "This is a way of telling everyone, the lifeguard is back on duty; you can go back in the pool," Goldman Sachs's chief economist commented after the intermeeting rate cut.[36] "We used to call him Uncle Alan," the Wall Street veteran David Shulman recalled of this period. "We would say, 'Uncle Alan will take care of us.'"[37]

And the uncle was not done yet. The following month, at the FOMC's regular November meeting, Greenspan cut rates a third time. Addressing his committee, he did not try to argue that the easing was necessary because markets were fragile. After all, both the stock market and the bond market had maintained their upward momentum since the intermeeting rate cut.[38] Nor did the chairman pretend that a rate cut was needed to boost growth: "The economy is in fact doing reasonably well," he acknowledged. But he nonetheless insisted on easing by a further quarter point. "A little insurance at this stage is probably wise," he asserted. Far from opposing financial rescues, Greenspan now wanted to roll them out preemptively.

"I am concerned that we are pouring gasoline rather than water onto this economy," William Poole of the St. Louis Fed objected.

"A bubble economy scenario may be building," agreed Tom Hoenig of Kansas City.

The chairman was not listening.

G reenspan's preemptive rescue boosted his stature even further. Wall Street celebrated, and markets soared: by the end of 1998, the S&P 500 index was up 28 percent since its low point at the end of August. Far from exhibiting concern about such heady valuations, Greenspan had become their central source. "There is a sense now that if this is a bubble and it bursts, the Fed will lower interest rates and everything will be fine," the Harvard economist Gregory Mankiw assured the *New York Times* in January.[39] "America's domestic policy is now being run by Alan Greenspan and the Federal Reserve Board," declared Clinton's former labor secretary, Robert Reich.[40] The nation seemed delighted with this distribution of responsibility.

On February 15, 1999, Greenspan's worldly, sagelike face appeared on the cover of *Time* magazine. The chairman loomed proudly in the foreground while smaller images of Bob Rubin and Larry Summers hovered on his flanks; beneath, bold yellow letters identified the trio as "The Committee to Save the World"—the title was more evocative of comic-book heroes than of financial technocrats. A year or so earlier, the "briefcase indicator" film sequences had cast Greenspan as Mr. Big Stuff, but that had been a knowing joke; now *Time* was deadly serious. Greenspan and his Treasury comrades were "economist heroes," the magazine proclaimed; they were the "Three Marketeers," stars who had "outgrown ideology," and without their valiant efforts, the U.S. economy would have crumpled under the impact of the Asian and Russian crises. The fact that Greenspan had occasionally doubted the case for assistance to the Asians did not factor into *Time*'s thinking, nor did the possibility that Greenspan might have cut interest rates too much after Russia's default in the summer. Greenspan, Rubin, and Summers shared "a mania for analysis that has bred a rigorous, unique intellectual honesty," *Time* insisted. "What holds them together is a passion for thinking and an inextinguishable curiosity."

The irony in this encomium cannot have been entirely lost on the Zip-switch chairman. Four decades earlier, in his magisterial article for the American Statistical Association, Greenspan had ripped apart the excessive faith in financial statesmen that fueled the bubble of the 1920s. Thanks to the creation of the Fed, investors had believed that risk had been banished—the business cycle was dead; there was no longer any danger in piling into the stock market. That confidence in central bankers had set the 1920s stock market up for a fall. "The sharp upward gyrations in stock prices—and other capital values—made the subsequent stock market reversal inevitable," Greenspan had concluded.

Twenty-five

ALAN.COM

On March 29, 1999, the Dow Jones Industrial Average closed above 10,000 for the first time in its history. Thanks to the spillovers from the technology revolution, even a stock index dominated by old-economy blue chips had doubled in four years, while the tech-heavy Nasdaq index had tripled. Companies such as eBay and Amazon were reinventing the economy from the ground up. Whereas during the cold war, technology had seemed to threaten a nuclear apocalypse, now it promised a utopia. "Computing is not about computers anymore. It is about living," declared one prominent seer. "We will socialize in digital neighborhoods in which physical space will be irrelevant."[1] "We are seeing a revitalization of society," another guru chimed in; "a new more democratic world is becoming possible."[2] Bestriding the globe as the sole superpower, the United States was creating the electronic building blocks of a thrilling new order—naturally, with itself at the center. "You've got to be a bull," crowed Richard Grasso, the shiny-headed New York Stock Exchange chairman, as he tossed caps emblazoned with "Dow 10,000" to cheering traders on the floor. "Our country has never been stronger."[3]

The day after the Dow passed its milestone, an obscure start-up named Priceline.com made its stock market debut. Priceline had begun operations just one year before, and for anyone who paused to contemplate its headlong rise, it stood as a warning. The company consisted of virtually no assets, an untested brand name, and fewer than two hundred employees; in its first eight months in business, its signature achievement had been to sell $35 million worth of discounted air tickets—for which it had paid $36.5 million. On top of this $1.5 million operating loss, Priceline had burned upwards of $100 million on Web development, marketing, and free stock options for suppliers; by one reckoning, the company had incinerated $114 million of investors' money.[4] But Priceline's ebullient founders were unencumbered by self-doubt. They experimented boldly, selling car rentals, hotel rooms, and mortgages on their Web site; they rented a ball-room in a grand Manhattan club and pitched a vision of a cyberretailing empire to captivated investors. Amid the euphoria on Wall Street, every go-go fund manager wanted a piece of the action. By the end of its first day of trading, on March 30, 1999, Priceline's value had quadrupled to $10 billion—more than United Airlines, Continental Airlines, and Northwest Airlines put together.

While Priceline's stock price was exploding, Greenspan was seated in the Fed's conference room, chairing an FOMC meeting. As usual, a vocal minority on his committee was worried by Wall Street's advances.

"The stock market remains exuberant, to say the least," Boston Fed president Cathy Minehan observed. "The cost of capital is too low." The fact that inflation was quiescent provided only false comfort. "The exuberance of the economy may well come back to haunt us, even if inflation does not take off in the near term," she cautioned. If Greenspan had cut rates back in the autumn for fear that markets might crater, a symmetrical policy surely required him to undo those cuts now.

"Now that the markets are mostly back to normal, I believe it is time to unwind those cuts," agreed William Poole, the St. Louis Fed president.

Greenspan refused to budge, ruling out higher interest rates. His determination to stay loose posed something of a mystery. He had explicitly justified his post-LTCM rate cuts on the ground that the economy needed insurance; as Minehan and Poole said, this rationale was no longer credible. He had once upbraided his vice chairman for what amounted to a "Manley Johnson put"; yet now traders were celebrating a "Greenspan put" that took the risk out of investing. Greenspan was no doubt conscious that 45 percent of American households held equities, three times the proportion of twenty years before; if he raised interest rates with the clear purpose of bringing stocks down, he would no longer be a national hero. But Greenspan had proved himself capable of toughness, especially when resisting pressure from President George H. W. Bush. Why was he so steely in 1990, and yet so soft in 1999? Was it age, marriage, a desire to protect a reputation that had soared to such extraordinary heights? Or was there some other reason for his reluctance to tighten?

The best reason—at least, the one most persuasive to the economics profession—was that inflation was quiescent. The underlying "core" rate of consumer price inflation was running at 2.1 percent, right around the informal 2 percent target.[5] To be sure, this rationale for loose money was still somewhat surprising given that Greenspan had been careful not to commit himself publicly to inflation targeting. Three years earlier, during the Fed's debate on the merits of a target, he had insisted that the 2 percent goal should be kept secret: he had been determined to retain policy discretion. Yet now he was refusing to exercise that discretion—so why had he demanded it? Three years earlier, moreover, Greenspan had raised the possibility of an inflation target of zero. If that was his view, why not raise interest rates and push inflation below 2 percent, meanwhile addressing the evident froth in the equity market? At a minimum, higher interest rates might have let a little air out of the bubble, preventing it from expanding further—not a transformative achievement, perhaps, but certainly one worth having. Or depending on the unpredictable reaction of investors, higher interest rates might have had a more powerful effect, jolting the stock market back to its senses much as the Fed's rate hike in February 1994 had jolted the bond market.

In refusing to tighten rates in early 1999, Greenspan was revealing himself to be far more committed to inflation targeting than he had previously admitted. His undeclared policy was now perfectly simple: he would allow the economy to grow as fast as it could, consistent with the preservation of Paul Volcker's legacy. But the new Greenspan doctrine was based on flimsy foundations. The Fed and the economics profession had yet to prove that an unchanging rate of inflation should trump other central-bank objectives. The attempts to show a link between low inflation and high productivity growth had failed. Where was the evidence that price stability mattered more than financial stability?

At the end of August 1999, Greenspan flew to Jackson Hole for the Fed's summer gathering. The action on Wall Street had grown crazier; both the Dow and the Nasdaq had gained another tenth since Priceline's flotation. Greenspan had done the minimum to respond. He had held interest rates down through April and May, then raised them by a cautious 25 basis points at the end of June, following up with another 25 points on the eve of the Jackson Hole meeting. Interest rates were still 25 basis points below their pre-LTCM level.

Addressing the central-banking priesthood in Jackson Hole, Greenspan refused to defend his passivity in the face of the stock market's exuberance. To the contrary, his opening speech at the symposium emphasized the economy's vulnerability to market crashes. As more companies sought public listings, and as the value of those companies increased, stock market wealth was growing relative to national income, Greenspan observed. If this enormous stock of paper wealth were to evaporate, the consequences would be awful. Prudent central bankers should therefore prepare for the worst. "History tells us that sharp reversals in confidence happen abruptly, most often with little advance notice," Greenspan reminded his colleagues. He understood the frailty in finance, even if he was not doing much about it.

If Greenspan would not defend his policies, others were more forthcoming. After the chairman left the podium, the distinguished company at Jackson Hole heard from two academic economists: Ben Bernanke, the Princeton professor who had written shrewdly on the 1987 debacle and the early 1990s credit crunch; and Mark Gertler, a coauthor of Bernanke's from New York University. In hindsight, the professors' presentation came to be seen as a pivotal moment: it marked Bernanke's emergence into the public spotlight, leading ultimately to his selection as Greenspan's successor; it marked the most impressive effort yet to establish the case for targeting inflation rather than responding to asset bubbles. Yet although the presentation set Bernanke on the path to future prominence, and although it had a profound impact on the Fed's hardening commitment to inflation targeting, its conclusions were strangely unpersuasive.

Echoing the Fed chairman's speech earlier that day, Bernanke and Gertler began by acknowledging the challenge posed by asset prices. The advanced economies had experienced an increase in financial instability, they conceded; such instability menaced jobs and incomes. But the professors nonetheless argued that central bankers should take account of the stock market only insofar as it affected inflation. In and of itself, the bursting of a bubble need not be too painful if monetary policy came to the rescue, the authors said—this was what the Fed had done after 1987. It was hard to distinguish a dangerous bubble from a healthy rise in the market, the professors continued; and besides, central banks need not target bubbles because there was a more practical option. "By focusing on the inflationary or deflationary pressures generated by asset price movements, a central bank effectively responds to the toxic side effects of asset booms," they asserted.[6] Resorting to italics to drive their point home, the professors insisted, "*A key advantage of the inflation-targeting framework is that it induces policy-makers to automatically adjust interest rates in a stabilizing direction in the face of asset-price instability.*"

This, of course, was oddly optimistic. It was true that cleaning up after the crash of 1987 had proved relatively easy, although the Fed's loose policy had allowed the New England property bubble to inflate—and that bubble had proved toxic. Likewise, it was true that diagnosing bubbles could be hard—but sometimes hard challenges might be too important to duck, and Greenspan had diagnosed plenty of bubbles during

FOMC meetings. As to the claim that inflation targeting would dampen bubbles automatically, Bernanke and Gertler were glossing over the distinction between a demand shock and a supply shock—a distinction that had been recognized by several members of the FOMC, and that Bernanke himself would ponder in a speech five years later.[7] In the face of a productivity revolution that created an increase in supply, the Fed might confront downward pressure on inflation combined with upward pressure on assets—the choice between price stability and financial stability could not be avoided. Indeed, the late-1990s bubble resulted precisely from the fact that Greenspan had followed the inflation-targeters' advice. The core measure of inflation had averaged 2.2 percent in the past twenty-four months—from an inflation-targeting perspective, Greenspan's policy had been immaculate. But because he had targeted inflation, Greenspan had been content to keep interest rates, and thus borrowing costs, low, which encouraged investors to bid up financial assets. It was just as Larry Lindsey, Cathy Minehan, and the other FOMC skeptics had feared. It was the opposite of what Bernanke and Gertler asserted.[8]

The professors made another claim that helped to solidify the inflation-targeting consensus. "Macroeconomic stability, particularly the absence of inflation or deflation, is itself calming to financial markets," they suggested. Financial assets would be easier to value in a stable setting, the idea went: spared the need to worry about swings in inflation or interest rates, fund managers could focus on assessing the business prospects of firms, and their decisions would steer asset prices toward their efficient, nonbubbly level. But this proposition was excessively optimistic, too. It neglected the point for which the economist Hyman Minsky later became famous: if you remove inflation and interest-rate risk, investors are liable to compensate with extra risk of other kinds, leaving markets no more stable. Since the time when he had dubbed himself the Zipswitch chairman, Greenspan had understood this point. "When things get too good, human beings behave awfully," he had stated then. "To the extent that we are successful in keeping product price inflation down, history tells us that price-earnings ratios [and hence stock prices] under those conditions

go through the roof," he had observed, a year later. A stable macroeconomic environment was no guarantee of stable capital markets. Again,
Bernanke and Gertler were mistaken.

The doubts about the professors' inflation-targeting prescription would
be aired in scholarly papers over the next decade. One school argued that
central banks should pay more attention to leverage and bubbles.[9] Another
pointed out that inflation responded to changes in the real economy only
with a lag, so that central banks would do better to respond to nominal
GDP—a combination of inflation and the growth rate. Either way, pure
inflation targeting attracted thoughtful attacks, and at Jackson Hole in
1999, several flaws in the Bernanke-Gertler stance were pointed out
immediately. Alan Blinder, who had left the Fed vice chairmanship to
return to Princeton, echoed Greenspan's past objections to the contention
that low inflation would stabilize finance. "Stock market investors get
irrationally exuberant when inflation gets low," Blinder pointed out. "You
have a central bank that is doing exactly what it should do, that delivers
low inflation and smooth output performance. The central bank may
therefore, unwittingly—and not because it is doing the wrong thing—
contribute to a financial bubble. Indeed, that is the way a lot of people
characterize the United States today," he declared pointedly.

Blinder was by no means the only critic. Rudiger Dornbusch, a prominent MIT economist who was serving as the official respondent to Bernanke and Gertler, accused the authors of basing their findings on
"channels and effects that are not altogether apparent." Moreover, Dornbusch continued, both the Bernanke-Gertler prescription and the Fed's
historical practice involved a troubling bias: when asset markets rose, the
central bank was supposed to ignore them; but when they fell, the
clean-up-afterward doctrine required it to react forcefully. Mike Mussa,
the formidable chief economist of the International Monetary Fund,
weighed in on this point, too. If the Fed was going to respond to asset
busts, Mussa argued, then it should respond to asset bubbles as well.[10]
Otherwise, traders would expect to ride bull markets without resistance
from the Fed, and then expect a safety net when the market reversed
direction. Confronted with such lopsided incentives, rational investors

would take as much risk as possible. It was a formula for ever greater lever-age and instability.

After the discussion was over, Greenspan walked past Bernanke and Gertler, who were now seated a safe distance from the microphones. As quietly as he could, he said, "You know, I agree with you."[11]

Despite the chairman's long preoccupation with bubbles, and despite the flaws in the Bernanke-Gertler view, Greenspan was giving the infla-tion targeters the benefit of the doubt. If he was not going to jack up inter-est rates to fight a speculative mania, he needed a theory that would justify his actions.

G reenspan flew from Jackson Hole to his annual tennis retreat on the West Coast—he was a creature of habit. Landing with Andrea at San Jose airport, he boarded a car for Carmel Valley, and the couple wound their way through a secluded countryside of gentle mountains, gnarled oak forests, and crystal streams. As the resort grew nearer, the road relaxed into quiet curves, passing cowboy bars and boutiques, sad-dlery shops and spas, and acres of vineyards planted with pinot. It was the perfect counterpoint to the East Coast. A five-car backup on Carmel Val-ley Road amounted to a traffic jam, a local magazine boasted.[12]

Alan was almost six months past his seventy-third birthday. His tennis was still solid: most Saturdays and Sundays, he would be on court at the Chevy Chase Club by nine a.m.—there would be one coach for Andrea and another one for him, and when they were done with their respective drills, they would sometimes get together for a game of doubles. But the question of aging was nonetheless a real one. Andrea worried about the toll the Fed was taking. After a dozen years in office, perhaps Alan deserved a break—a chance to sleep past 5:30 a.m.; to travel, maybe even to the beach; to enjoy an entire opera without having to leave early to pre-pare for congressional testimony.[13] His third term as chairman would be up the following summer; and although he could theoretically serve a fourth term and even part of a fifth term—he would be forced into retire-ment only when his simultaneous appointment as a Fed governor expired in January 2006—Andrea sometimes wondered whether three terms might be enough. Already Alan had served for almost twice as long as Bob Rubin, his ally at the Treasury. Rubin had recently called it quits, stepping down from public office to return to Manhattan.

Alan regretted Rubin's leaving. To help mark the moment, he had made an appearance in a spoof movie directed by the White House economics staff; the film told the story of the Treasury secretary's kidnapping by the nefarious Japanese, and Alan accepted a walk-on role in which he starred as none other than the Fed chairman. "Alan Greenspan and Woody Allen have one thing in common," a Clinton adviser said with a chuckle, "they both know how to play only one character."[14] But the Woody Allen comparison was not just a joke; it was precisely the issue confronting Andrea in Carmel. In the gaps between the tennis games and snoozes, she and Alan contemplated the question: After so many years of playing Washington, could Alan reinvent himself?

Alan felt he was still equal to the responsibilities of office. As far as he could tell, his mind remained as sharp as ever; he would know when he was fading when he had trouble with calculus, and there was no sign of that. As to the prospect of retirement, Alan and Andrea had tried, at least a little bit, to take time off and travel; there had been that honeymoon in Venice—at least Alan hadn't hated it.[15] But the truth was that by the end of their stay in Italy, the economist inside him had elbowed aside the romantic, clamoring to estimate the city's value-added. There was no point in fantasizing that he was going to change. He was deeply contented with the established patterns of his life. He had no desire to shuffle them.

If the president offered Alan a fourth term at the Fed, he would not hesitate to accept it.

A bit more than a month later, on October 11, Greenspan appeared in Phoenix at the Arizona Biltmore, an iconic castle made from patterned blocks under Frank Lloyd Wright's direction. Almost half a century earlier, Ronald and Nancy Reagan had celebrated their honeymoon at this resort, but Greenspan had come on a less joyous mission. Standing in the

Biltmore's capacious ballroom, looking out on seven hundred or so members of the American Bankers Association, Greenspan laid out the Fed's approach to financial supervision. What followed was the regulatory counterpart to the Bernanke-Gertler paper on the Fed's monetary stance. Greenspan honestly acknowledged the risks in too-big-to-fail banks. Then he proceeded to explain why the Fed should not address them.

"The megabanks being formed by growth and consolidation are increasingly complex entities that create the potential for unusually large systemic risks," Greenspan began.

Megabanks; complex entities; large systemic risks. The chairman seemed to have embraced the language of the bankers' critics.

"No central bank can fulfill its ultimate responsibilities without endeavoring to ensure that the oversight of such entities is consistent with those potential risks," Greenspan continued.

At this point, opponents of the Travelers-Citi merger might have rubbed their hands expectantly.

"At the same time, policymakers must be sensitive to the tradeoffs," Greenspan pivoted. "Heavier supervision and regulation designed to reduce systemic risk would likely lead to the virtual abdication of risk evaluation by creditors," he cautioned. "The resultant reduction in market discipline would, in turn, increase the risks in the banking system, quite the opposite of what is intended." Faced with a choice between extra regulatory discipline on the one hand and continued market discipline on the other, Greenspan had no difficulty in taking sides. "Supervisors have little choice but to try to rely more—not less—on market discipline," he announced to the audience.

Greenspan's conclusion invited questions—to put it mildly. Surely market discipline had a history of failing, stretching back to Continental Illinois, and before that to Penn Central? Surely such failures were even likelier now, given the complexity of the megabanks? With his usual tragic honesty, Greenspan acknowledged these dangers, just as he acknowledged the risks in stock market crashes. For one thing, market discipline could function only if creditors had sound information about banks' portfolios, but banks were not in the habit of transparency. "The best way to encourage more disclosures is not yet clear," Greenspan admitted. For another thing, market discipline required banks to borrow from someone other than federally insured depositors, because only uninsured creditors facing the possibility of losses could be expected to monitor banks' risks. Unfortunately, only the largest banks met this condition, and even they relied on insured deposits for much of their funding. Market discipline—imperfect at the best of times—would have limited power under these conditions.[16]

Undeterred by the admitted flaws in his argument, the chairman pressed onward to his conclusion. The Fed favored supervision that was "the least intrusive, most market based," he declared to his audience at the Biltmore. With that, he exited through a doorway at the back of the stage, not pausing to take questions.[17]

One month later, after cantankerous negotiations between the Treasury, Congress, and the Fed, President Clinton signed a law that realized Greenspan's regulatory philosophy. Thanks to Sandy Weill's ferocious lobbying, Congress had finally coughed up a financial reform bill: by legalizing the silo-busting combination of insurance, lending, and the underwriting of securities, the measure completed the ratification of the Travelers-Citi merger. Cynics quipped that the Financial Services Modernization Act of 1999 would be better named the "Citicorp Authorization Act."[18] But what was more astonishing was the nature of the debate leading up to the reform. Rather than questioning whether the nation could afford too-big-to-fail banks, the Treasury had focused on a turf question: whether securities operations of banks should be structured as subsidiaries, implying that they would be overseen by the Treasury, or as affiliates, in which case the Fed would supervise them. Congress, for its part, had staged a battle royal over banks' obligations to low-income communities— a worthy issue, perhaps, but not one that came close to the too-big-to-fail question. Greenspan's dubious bet on market discipline was left unaddressed. The elephant in the room was too enormous to confront directly.

One year after the sidelining of Brooksley Born, the banking reform of

1999 represented another missed opportunity to grapple with the fragilities in finance. At a minimum, the consolidation of the banking sector should have been coupled with a corresponding consolidation of regulators, whose overlapping mandates allowed firms to shop around for the laxest overseer. But no such consolidation was attempted. Instead, the authorities stumbled on, trusting that rival banking regulators would collaborate successfully with the Securities and Exchange Commission, the Commodity Futures Trading Commission, and state-level insurance regulators. By retaining this army of Inspector Clouseaus, the government was setting itself up for a regulatory fall. "History is liberally dotted with crises caused by liberalizing finance without improving supervision," the *Economist* observed presciently.[19]

When the dust eventually settled on the Citicorp Authorization Act, Sandy Weill mounted a four-foot-wide slab of wood on the wall of his office. "The Shatterer of Glass-Steagall," it proclaimed proudly; and the caption ran alongside a portrait of the shatterer himself, in all his insolent glory.[20] Meanwhile, Weill picked up another trophy, too: Citigroup announced a prize hiring—Bob Rubin. The erstwhile Treasury secretary had had no shortage of offers, and Weill's winning bid cemented his status as the top dog on Wall Street.[21] Yet Rubin's arrival at Citigroup also hinted at a darker tale. In the months since the merger, the effort of integrating two sprawling empires with contrary cultures had poisoned Weill's relationship with his cochief, John Reed; the only thing the two could still agree on was that they needed outside mediation.[22] Even-tempered and judicious, Rubin would act as conciliator and coach—a "buffer that could allow them each to do their jobs without running afoul of each other," as one chronicler put it.[23]

One year earlier, when approving Weill's merger in the heat of the LTCM crisis, Greenspan and his fellow governors had expressed faith in the quality of Citi's management. Now Citi's top team felt it needed help from Rubin. The Fed evidently had a weak grasp of what it took to make a megabank function, which meant that its supervisors would be hard-pressed to distinguish sound lenders from shaky ones. The central bank was in over its head. The financial system was about to grow more vulnerable than anyone dreamed possible.

Even as he grappled with bubbles and banks, Greenspan faced another challenge. The computer chips that powered the new economy were flawed: because of a programming shortcut that had been popular in the days when silicon memory was scarce, the chips might confuse the year 2000 with the year 1900 when the millennium rolled over at midnight on January 1. Computers running on processors not protected from this "Y2K bug" could suffer debilitating glitches. And because trillions of dollars existed as 1s and 0s in banks' hard drives, a software failure threatened to ignite panic throughout the economy.

By the summer of 1999, the ripples from the Y2K problem were already apparent. Market interest rates rose that summer as businesses scrambled to lock in funding ahead of possible disruptions to credit markets; the corporate bond market was "acting like all Four Horsemen of the Apocalypse are playing polo on Wall Street," one commentator said, in a fit of galloping hyperbole.[24] Spying a textbook case in which the lender of last resort ought to step in, Greenspan readied his response to the apocalypse.[25]

Greenspan rolled out his Y2K plan in late October. It was both imaginative and vigorous. The Fed would pre-position emergency stocks of shrink-wrapped currency at ninety locations across the nation; crisis-management teams would be prepared in every Federal Reserve district. Meanwhile, armed with a newly created Y2K fund, the Fed offered to sell banks a promise of liquidity: they could buy options on short-term loans around the century date change. Greenspan hoped that merely dangling these options would calm Y2K fears; perhaps no one would actually purchase them.[26] But the banks snapped up the options the way ordinary citizens were expressing their millennial anxieties by stockpiling canned goods—at the first auction on October 20, banks submitted bids to buy five times more options than the central bank was offering. The Fed duly responded by auctioning more options over the next days. By the time of the next FOMC meeting, on November 16, it had sold more than $300 billion of them.[27]

The sale achieved its purpose: market interest rates subsided. But it also allowed equities to set off on a fresh tear: the Nasdaq jumped by fully one fifth during the first month of the auctions. Anticipating that consumers would now spend cash they previously had planned to hoard, analysts pushed up growth forecasts—and growth duly hit an annualized rate of 7.1 percent in the fourth quarter.[28] Fund managers who had fretted about Y2K-panicked customers withdrawing their money now reported the opposite problem, with the result that yet more cash was searching for a home in Wall Street's bubbly markets.[29] Even though Greenspan raised interest rates by 25 basis points at the November FOMC meeting, lifting the federal funds rate to 5.5 percent and finally undoing his post-LTCM cuts, this was effectively a nonhike hike. Tightening money with one hand, Greenspan was permitting exuberance with the other.[30]

As Christmas approached, the nation reveled in astonishing prosperity. A jeweler in Chicago sold a $100,000 man's pinkie ring adorned with a massive diamond that slid along the top on its very own rail system. A boutique reported hot demand for a $12,000 beaded cardigan.[31] The average new home in Scottsdale, Arizona, was fully 50 percent larger than ten years before. In Tucson, an establishment called PetsHotel Plus provided upscale canine guests with telephones, allowing absent masters to call in and coo at their dogs on the speakerphone.[32]

Greenspan's reputation continued to soar with the stock market. Vice President Al Gore, by now focusing on his bid for the White House, called himself Greenspan's "biggest fan" and rated the chairman's performance as "outstanding A-plus-plus."[33] Republican front-runner and Texas governor George W. Bush put aside his family's lingering resentment toward Greenspan and credited him for his "great job of managing the monetary side of our economy."[34] Not to be outdone, Republican senator John McCain wished the chairman could stay at his post into the afterlife. "I would do like we did in the movie *Weekend at Bernie's*," McCain joked during a Republican presidential primary debate. "I'd prop him up and put a pair of dark glasses on him and keep him as long as we could."[35]

By the time of the next FOMC meeting, on December 21, Wall Street was expecting another round of tightening. With tech stocks rocketing upward and the economy at boiling point, surely it was time for rates to rise above their pre-LTCM benchmark. Unemployment had fallen to an unsustainably low 4.1 percent, and the trade deficit was widening alarmingly. Unless demand was reined in, the economy would run out of workers to produce additional output, or run out of foreign loans to pay for its imports. But with the Y2K date changeover just days away, Greenspan lacked the will to move. "We want to communicate as effectively as we can that we have no intention of doing anything through the year-end and maybe for a short period thereafter," he argued.

"One always hates to see a marathon runner trip up at the end, and we certainly don't want to be the person from the stands who runs out and trips that runner up," another governor observed supportively.[36]

Performing her familiar function, Cathy Minehan of the Boston Fed attempted to push back. "It is hard to find any Y2K panic or even deep worries out there, and believe me we've tried to find it," she objected. But as usual, she was ignored, and because she was among the regional Reserve Bank presidents who lacked a vote at this meeting, ignoring her was particularly easy. The committee voted unanimously to leave the fed funds rate unchanged. The Dow, the S&P 500, and the Nasdaq responded in unison, hitting record highs on the last trading day before Christmas.

As the markets rocketed skyward, Greenspan received his own gift from the White House. The chief of staff, John Podesta, called him on the president's behalf to offer a fourth term in office. The Clinton team had briefly contemplated the possibility of an alternative chairman, but nobody could imagine how anyone could surpass the incumbent. Someone sounded out Bob Rubin to check whether he might be interested in the job. Rubin responded that Greenspan was perfect for it.

"I bet he'll stay there until they carry him out," Clinton remarked to his advisers.[37]

On the last day of 1999, the three major stock market indices raced each other up, setting a new set of records. That evening similar euphoria suffused the White House, where the first couple staged the American Creators' Millennium Dinner, a tribute to the innovation and ideas that powered American supremacy. Not everybody present was technically an innovator, it had to be confessed; Elizabeth Taylor, Robert De Niro, and Sophia Loren were no doubt great in their own way, though the last of these was not actually American. "I cannot help but think how different America is, how different history is, and how much better because those of you in this room and those you represent were able to imagine, to invent, to aspire," President Clinton oozed to the assembled throng. The Hollywood composer John Williams gave the singer Jessye Norman a bear hug. Mary Wilson, a former Supreme, sang the old-time hits that baby boomers loved as the White House rang in the new century.[38]

Alan and Andrea caught the first part of the evening; it was, as Alan said later, Clinton's "Camelot moment."[39] But well before midnight the first couple of finance slipped out of the White House, boarding a car that carried them through Washington's dark streets to the Fed's Y2K command center. There, in the William McChesney Martin Building, a hundred or so people sat in a large room, watching the celebrations on their TV screens as the millennium advanced westward from Asia and through Europe. Countless hours of preparation were about to be tested. If the Y2K bug so much as reared its head, the Fed was ready to swat it.

Greenspan looked around the room. He was dressed up in black tie, a grand, slightly dried-out figure with thin wisps of hair, peering through large spectacles. The staffers wore red T-shirts prepared especially for the occasion. They were young enough, or old enough, to be the chairman's children.

Earlier in his Fed tenure, Greenspan might have stayed up to take charge, but he no longer felt a need to linger. He had inspected the troops, and now he headed home with Andrea. By the time midnight arrived in Washington, he was tucked snugly in bed; and when he awoke the next morning, he found that the millennium had rolled over without drama. Nothing much happened over the next few days. Some cash registers at a Godiva chocolate shop in New York malfunctioned temporarily.[40]

On Tuesday, January 4, President Clinton played host to another Camelot moment. The White House announced Greenspan's fourth appointment to the Fed, and it was less of an announcement than a coronation. An eternal philosopher-king was to be enthroned, and his aura would rub off on those fortunate enough to be around him. Indeed, Greenspan's term in office was not due to expire for a further six months, but the Clinton team was eager to get the news out now, at a time when it might give the president an extra bounce as he prepared for his final State of the Union address before a joint session of Congress. The man without effective term limits was thus being recruited to elevate the man running up against his cap, and the press commentary served only to underline the power of seniority. Greenspan had become, as the *New York Times* put it, "an institution in his own right."[41] Nobody would have said the same about Bill Clinton.

Soon after ten o'clock on an unseasonably warm January morning, Greenspan headed over to the White House.[42] He had a brief private meeting with Clinton, who extended the official invitation to serve another term, which he accepted graciously. Then he prepared to follow the president into the Oval Office, which had been turned into an improvised press briefing room.

A gaggle of reporters lay in wait. Cameramen stood ready to capture the event, which would naturally be broadcast live. Indeed, CNN had been teasing it all morning.

"He had a very tough act to follow in Paul Volcker," CNN anchor Bill Tucker announced, striving valiantly to fill the airtime before the press conference began. "There were a lot of people who didn't feel like Alan Greenspan would be able to live up to Volcker's term at the Fed. But he has done so, and surpassed."[43]

Presently, Clinton and Greenspan strode into the Oval Office, trailed by Larry Summers and a few White House advisers.[44] As the reporters' chatter died down and the live TV feed switched on, Clinton stood alone at a podium that had been set up in front of the *Resolute* desk. Greenspan lingered shyly in the background.[45] His suit was black; his shoes were black; his expression seemed a little black as well. The only relief came from the faintly red-and-white variegations on his otherwise black necktie.[46]

"You're supposed to stand over here today," Clinton said, beckoning the sideman. He wanted Alan Greenspan close. That was the whole point of the occasion.

"This is the only time I'm interfering with the independence of the Fed!" he added.

Greenspan walked over to the president and stood at his left. The president began speaking.

"Chairman Greenspan's leadership has always been crucial. . . . With his help, we were able . . . to enact historic financial reform legislation, repealing Glass-Steagall and modernizing our financial systems for the twenty-first century. He was also, I think it's worth noting, one of the very first in his profession to recognize the power and impact of new technologies on the new economy, how they changed all the rules and all the possibilities.

"In fact, his devotion to new technologies has been so significant, I've been thinking of taking 'Alan.com' public. Then we could pay the debt off even before 2015." At this, Clinton grinned triumphantly.

The president stopped, turned, and shook the nominee's hand. The cameras captured the moment, and Clinton yielded the podium.

Greenspan stepped forward and a broad smile flashed across his face. The leader of the world's sole superpower was beside him. A rapt press corps was before him. A global television audience was watching.

"Is the market irrational?" the veteran White House reporter Helen Thomas demanded as soon as it was time for questions.

There was scattered laughter in the room.

"Helen, I've—"

"Do you still stick by your previous statements on the stock market?"

"You surely don't want me to answer that?"

"Yes I do."

"You do? Well, I—I don't think I will." There was more laughter in the Oval Office. "Helen, you've been asking me questions now for decades—"

"Since you reformed the Social Security system."

"—and I usually answer them, so my record's not bad."

Another reporter had a turn. Why had Greenspan decided to stay in the job? "After a decade there, one might expect that you might want to retire or move on," the reporter observed. Perhaps Greenspan ought to quit while he was gloriously ahead, he seemed to be suggesting.

"There's a certain really quite unimaginable intellectual interest," Greenspan began, warming to the subject. "You have to put broad theoretical and fairly complex conceptual issues to a test in the marketplace.

"Unlike a straight academic career, you end up fully recognizing that hypotheses matter, that actions matter, and the ideas that you come up with matter.

"And that is a challenge which, I must say to you, is—as I said to the president before, it's like eating peanuts. You keep doing it, keep doing it.

"You never get tired, because the future is always, ultimately, unknowable."

Greenspan appeared at his Senate confirmation hearing on January 26, while the rest of the capital was digging out from a foot of snow dumped on the city by an unexpectedly powerful nor'easter.

Senator Phil Gramm, the savvy Republican chairman of the Senate Committee on Finance, captured the spirit of the occasion.

"If you were forced to narrow down the credit for the golden age that we find ourselves living in," Gramm said in his slow Texas drawl, "I think your name would have to be at the top of the list."

Speaking for the Democrats, Senator Charles Schumer of New York described Greenspan as a "national treasure."

"Why have three successive administrations appointed Alan Greenspan to be chairman of the board of governors of the Federal Reserve System?" Gramm asked during the final debate.

"Because he is the best central banker we have ever had," Gramm said, answering his own question.[47]

Then, just a little over a month later, the Nasdaq stock index peaked, and by the middle of May it had lost fully one third of its value. Priceline.com was among the big losers, and initial public offerings came to a standstill. As Americans dusted themselves off after that sickening slide, the question was whether Alan.com would collapse with the overvalued new economy.

Twenty-six

"A VERY SURREAL
ENVIRONMENT"

On a rainy morning in December 2000, Greenspan set off for breakfast with America's next president. It had been a strange few weeks in politics: after a disputed election count in Florida, dueling demands for recounts, and arcane arguments about card-punch voting contraptions, the Supreme Court had put an end to the uncertainty, handing the presidency to George W. Bush. Now Dubya, as people called him, had moved his court to Washington. His first appointment on his first day in the capital was with the Fed chairman.

The president-elect's father, the first President Bush, blamed Greenspan for his electoral defeat at the hands of Bill Clinton. But the younger Bush was not in a position to indulge the family grudge. The Fed chairman was now the undisputed architect of American prosperity; and even though growth had slowed since the stock market's dive in the spring, the Goldilocks glow still radiated powerfully. Greenspan presided over an economy that had expanded in fifty-one out of fifty-three quarters during his tenure; unemployment in December 2000 stood at an astonishingly low 3.9 percent. A bestselling biography of Greenspan, published on the eve of the election, had formally anointed him the maestro. Whoever succeeded Bill Clinton would hold office in the Greenspan era, the biography asserted.[1] To most of the book's readers, that seemed about right.

Greenspan's driver deposited him at the Madison Hotel, a stuffy Washington establishment across the road from the *Washington Post*. There, seated with the president-elect, the Fed chairman acknowledged the likelihood of short-term economic trouble. The tech-heavy Nasdaq had by now lost half its value since its peak in March, and even blue-chip stocks were sliding. But Greenspan reserved his emphasis for a sunnier message: America's future was bright.

Bush seemed to like the sound of that; but in any case, he had no choice. "I want you to know," he said toward the end of the breakfast, "that I have full confidence in the Federal Reserve and we will not be second-guessing your decisions."[2] The lesson of the past decade had not been lost on him. No president had anything to gain from bashing a Fed chairman, especially not one who seemed to reign over the economy as if by divine right.

The elect and the elected finished their breakfast and walked out of the hotel. Camera crews and reporters had staked out the exit, and Bush wrapped an arm around Greenspan as they approached the throng. In contrast with his father, he was unencumbered by New England diffidence. He was as tactile and Texan as the elder Bush had been patrician and proper.

"I talked with a good man right here," the Texan told the press, with Greenspan still close by him. "We had a very strong discussion about my confidence in his abilities."[3]

It was not just the incoming president who was telegraphing positive signals. The new vice president was Dick Cheney, a Greenspan friend since the Ford administration. As defense secretary in the elder Bush's presidency, Cheney had shared intelligence about the Gulf War; as a corporate chieftain he had attended Alan and Andrea's Fourth of July parties at the Fed headquarters; the previous summer, he had met Greenspan to discuss the search criteria for Candidate Bush's running mate. Admittedly, Cheney could be inscrutable: during that running-mate conversation, for

example, Greenspan could not tell whether his old friend's selection criteria amounted to a perfect self-description by design or by coincidence—
Cheney appeared to be organizing a nationwide search for none other
than himself. But Greenspan did not hold that against him. If Cheney was
scheming to make himself vice president, Greenspan was happy to support the plot.[4]

On December 18, the same day he breakfasted with Greenspan, Bush
offered the job of Treasury secretary to Paul O'Neill, another Greenspan
friend from the Ford administration. As in the case of Cheney, the bond
had grown deeper with time. As a director of the aluminum giant Alcoa in
the 1980s, Greenspan had helped to install O'Neill as chairman and chief
executive; later, as O'Neill had gone from strength to strength at Alcoa, he
and Greenspan had remained close, bonding over a shared fascination
with economic data as well as the shared experience of exalted professional status. It helped, perhaps, that the Fed chairman had spent his for-
mative years as a consultant to industrialists. Greenspan's connection to
O'Neill had a particular significance because it doubled as a connection to
his youthful self.

When O'Neill got Bush's call offering him the Treasury job, he responded by hedging evasively. He was a somewhat obsessive figure, upright
and uptight. He was not sure he was ready to return to government. He
would accept a cabinet position only if he could make a difference.

"He's got two pages of pros and cons," Cheney reported to Greenspan
after O'Neill had failed to jump at the president's offer. "Can you talk
to him?"

O'Neill had by now left Washington for Manhattan, where he
checked into the Hyatt hotel next to Grand Central station. He had just
hung up his suit jacket and turned on the TV news when the telephone
rang.[5]

O'Neill recognized a familiar voice. "Alan?" he said.

"So, I hear you had an interesting day."

"News travels fast."

"Paul, I'll be blunt," Greenspan told him, winding up for the pitch that Arthur Burns had used to lure him to the Council of Economic Advisers. "We really need you down here.

"There is a real chance to make some lasting changes," Greenspan continued. "We could be a team at the key moment, to do the things we've always talked about." Greenspan mentioned Social Security reform as an example, knowing that O'Neill favored replacing government pensions with private retirement accounts. Of course, Greenspan owed his own job partly to the fact that he had avoided consideration of privatization when presiding over Reagan's Social Security commission. But the thought of a political suicide mission would appeal to O'Neill. He was principled to the point of self-righteousness.

"We have an extraordinary opportunity," Greenspan reiterated. "Paul, your presence will be an enormous asset in the creation of sensible policy."[6]

O'Neill hung up the phone and thought over what Greenspan had said. Since their joint service in the Ford administration, he had made more money than Greenspan, but he nonetheless admired the chairman for living a life "guided by inquiry," as he put it. Besides, O'Neill had already decided to step down from the helm of Alcoa, and he needed a new challenge. It was not in his character to relax: as Ford's deputy budget director, he had worked every day except Christmas, as he had once informed an interviewer, stipulating that his definition of a workday involved a twelve-hour minimum.[7] He had no more interest in wandering around Venice than Greenspan did.

O'Neill phoned his wife to tell her he would accept Bush's offer. He met with no resistance, but he knew she was crying.

Greenspan, for his part, was delighted. The new Bush administration would not be like the old Bush administration: instead of the hostile Nick Brady, Greenspan would have a friend at Treasury.

On the morning of January 5, 2001, Paul O'Neill went over to the Federal Reserve building for breakfast with Greenspan. He showed up punctually at 8:30 a.m. The Fed chairman was nowhere to be seen.[8]

An apologetic sagelike figure appeared after some moments.

"Jesus, Alan, I read all the papers already and, you know, there's really not a whole lot to do around here. . . ."

Greenspan took the tease in stride and muttered something about traffic.

A waiter appeared, and both men ordered healthy meals involving slices of grapefruit. O'Neill's silver hair was always cropped and parted perfectly. Greenspan could look pleasantly disheveled.

How was the economy? O'Neill asked.

What was going on with metal prices? Greenspan wondered.

The two friends discussed the data like "mariners discussing tides and winds," as the writer Ron Suskind put it. Then they got down to the policy issue that was consuming Washington.

The issue was tax, and a sizable cut appeared inevitable. Candidate Bush had promised a reduction worth $1.6 trillion over a decade; now, as president, he was determined to deliver. And whereas his father had been forced to renege on his "no new taxes" pledge, the younger Bush was in a stronger position. Thanks to the deficit-reduction packages enacted under Bush senior and Clinton—and thanks, just as powerfully, to a tax windfall from the Greenspan boom—the federal government was running budget surpluses for the first time since Neil Armstrong walked on the moon. The Congressional Budget Office had recently projected that the federal government would take in nearly $4.6 trillion more than it would spend over the next decade.[9] Bush's proposed tax cut seemed eminently affordable.

The budget office's projection, however, was just that: a projection. Anybody who recalled the disastrous budget forecasts of the early Reagan years would treat it with caution. Indeed, just in the fortnight since Greenspan had met Bush at the Madison, the economy had slowed appreciably, driving the Fed to announce a hefty rate cut of 50 basis points on January 3. A weaker economy meant weaker tax revenues. Just as the windfall from the Greenspan boom had fueled the unexpected budget surplus, so a prolonged slowdown might cause the surplus to evaporate.

"It's certainly not money in the bank," Greenspan remarked of the projected surplus. After years of resisting deficits, he did not want the federal government to go back into the red.

O'Neill nodded.

What if the surplus turned out to be smaller than expected? Greenspan wondered. Already Congress was intending to use half the projected savings to shore up the federal pension and health programs for retirees. What if the other half of the surplus failed to materialize?

"Triggers," O'Neill answered. The tax cut should be made conditional upon the surplus really being there. If the budget went back into the red, triggers would automatically suspend the tax cut so as to contain the deficit.

It was an elegant idea—too elegant, perhaps, to survive the rough-and-tumble of the legislative process. For starters, the president would have to be convinced.

"Think you could find a way to mention triggers in one of your upcoming pronouncements?" O'Neill asked slyly.

"Why me?" Greenspan protested.

"Because I thought of it," O'Neill answered. "That means you have to sell it."

A week or so later, on Sunday, January 14, 2001, O'Neill and Greenspan visited the future vice president at his gated-community town house in McLean, Virginia, just outside Washington. With six days to go until Bush's inauguration, it was time to fix priorities so that they could hit the ground running.

Cheney was set to play a larger role in the new administration than most vice presidents. Having served as Ford's chief of staff, he knew precisely how to wield power that formally resided elsewhere, and no detail escaped him. When managing the Ford White House, Cheney had laid down the law on which salt shakers to use on which occasions; discovering that nine people in the West Wing had consumed $101 worth of coffee in a single summer month, he had launched a weeks-long inquisition followed by a stern clampdown.[10] For the incoming vice president, command and control were ends in themselves, not just the means to policies he believed in.

Cheney was clear that the president's tax cut had to be the first priority. Bush had campaigned on the issue; it was a political imperative. Besides, the softening economy created a new urgency. Early in his campaign, Bush had advocated the tax cut mostly on the ground that the nation was booming—if the proceeds of the surplus were not returned to the people, Congress would lavish the money on big-government programs.[11] Now Cheney thought the tax cut could be sold on the opposite theory. The economy was slowing. A tax cut would revive it.[12]

Cheney's new stance was bad news for the Greenspan-O'Neill triggers plan. According to the vice president's logic, if the economy slowed even more sharply and the budget deficit returned with a vengeance, that would be all the more reason to press ahead with tax cuts.

O'Neill tried to suggest that tax cuts were not the only way to fight a slowdown. "The best, first stimulus, truth be told, may be monetary policy," he objected.

Greenspan agreed, hinting as strongly as he could that the Fed stood ready to cut interest rates.

Cheney listened, not giving anything away. He was low-key, nonconfrontational, and noncommittal. He was more Greenspan than Greenspan.

Presently, the discussion moved on. Neither the Fed chairman nor the Treasury secretary had summoned up the nerve to mention triggers.

Ten days later, on January 24, 2001, Greenspan visited Kent Conrad, the senior Democrat on the Senate budget committee. At the start of the Clinton presidency, Conrad had successfully baited Greenspan into endorsing a specific target for deficit reduction. Now he had an advance copy of Greenspan's testimony, due to be delivered before the budget committee the next day. The Fed chairman was about to endorse Bush's proposed tax cuts.[13]

Conrad was not happy. "If you endorse these tax cuts, Alan, you're going to unleash the deficit dogs," he protested. The Fed chairman had championed budget responsibility in the Clinton years. Now what had happened?

"There are a lot of caveats attached to my statement," Greenspan answered. His testimony would constitute a conditional endorsement of the tax cuts, not a blank check for the White House. True to his breakfast promise to O'Neill, Greenspan was advocating triggers.

Conrad persisted. Nobody would notice the triggers proposal. The newspapers would be looking for a clear headline: "Fed Chairman Supports Tax Cuts." What's more, Conrad continued, those cuts would deprive the government of revenues it needed in the long run. If you extended the budget projection out beyond ten years, the deficit was destined to grow bigger than ever, fueled by soaring health costs for retirees.

Greenspan tried to mollify the senator. To be sure, an excessive tax reduction might be risky. But a cautious one could be risky in its own way, too—what if the huge budget surpluses did actually materialize? If the Congressional Budget Office projection was right, the government would soon pay off the entire national debt; it would then have no choice but to invest its accumulating cash pile in the financial markets. All of a sudden, the Feds would be buying up chunks of the equity market, effectively nationalizing the commanding heights of the economy.

Greenspan was resorting to a curious argument. To a libertarian, naturally, the prospect of government accumulation of stakes in private companies was anathema. But to a pragmatist—a label the mature Greenspan generally wore comfortably—this was a fuss about nothing. The government could create an investment fund to hold financial assets passively, without meddling in the companies whose shares it owned.[14] Besides, the problem of zero national debt was not exactly imminent.

"You have a lot of debt to pay down before you get there," Conrad observed.

It might happen as soon as 2008, Greenspan parried.

"Let's worry about that, Mr. Chairman, when we get close to that point. We have plenty of time, if that develops."

After Greenspan left, Conrad put a call in to Bob Rubin. As the architect of the 1990s deficit reduction, the former Treasury secretary would surely be alarmed at the prospect of Greenspan's testimony. Perhaps he could persuade his old friend to recalibrate his message?

Rubin agreed to try. He had recently lunched with Greenspan at the Fed, and he remained on good terms with him.

When Rubin reached Greenspan by phone, he urged him to anticipate perceptions. If the Fed chairman delivered his draft testimony unchanged, the headlines would proclaim that he was endorsing the tax cut. The nuance about triggers would be lost on the public.

"I can't be in charge of people's perceptions," Greenspan replied. "I don't function that way. I can't function that way."

Again, it was a curious argument. Contrary to Greenspan's assertion, he absolutely did function by manipulating perceptions. Perceptions lay at the heart of everything the Fed did—that was how it influenced market interest rates. More to the point, perceptions lay at the heart of what Greenspan himself did. The media watched everything from his body language to the bulge in his briefcase, and he understood this perfectly.

On the morning of Greenspan's testimony, January 25, 2001, *USA Today* published a triumphant scoop. "Greenspan to Back Tax Cuts," the newspaper's front page proclaimed, even before Greenspan had said anything. By the time the Fed chairman appeared in Congress, the reporters were intent mainly on confirming the established story line, and several slipped out of the hearing room once they had heard what they needed. Kent Conrad watched them as they left. So much for those triggers, he thought bitterly.

As the Bush administration settled into the White House, Greenspan was a frequent visitor—more frequent, by far, than during the Clinton administration. But his conversations with the president's economic team were not always easy. The head of Bush's National Economic Council was none other than Lawrence Lindsey, the former Fed governor who had repeatedly warned Greenspan about asset bubbles. Now installed in the White House, Lindsey demanded payback. Having allowed the bubble to inflate, the Fed chairman could hardly oppose a tax cut that protected the economy from the fallout.

Lindsey could be difficult to argue with. He was smart, stubborn, and possessed of an annoyingly good memory. Visiting Greenspan as the tech bubble inflated in 1998 and 1999, he had pressed the Fed chairman to say how policy makers would cope when the bubble eventually imploded.

"There's no guarantee that even if you get a 1929, you'll end up with a 1932," Greenspan had replied. In other words, a crash would not harm the economy if the government responded with a determined stimulus.[15]

Now that the crash had duly arrived, Lindsey reminded Greenspan of that comment. How could the Fed chairman oppose a stimulus that he had privately endorsed earlier? Besides, Lindsey continued, Greenspan needed to respect democracy. Bush had won a mandate to deliver the tax cuts; Greenspan had no business obstructing him. The administration was committed to respecting the monetary independence of the Fed. Greenspan should reciprocate by respecting the president's primacy on the budget.

As well as hearing from Lindsey, Greenspan kept up his visits to Dick Cheney. The Fed chairman regarded the vice president as his back channel to Bush: if the president was set on a tax cut, perhaps Greenspan, working through Cheney, could aspire to rein him in a bit. But the vice president's objective was precisely the reverse: not to augment the maestro's influence but to contain it. If Greenspan felt as though he had a private channel to the top, he was less likely to denounce the tax plan in public; so Cheney invited the chairman over to his office, nodded along, and said enough to humor him. Despite the real bond between the two men, Cheney was resorting to the same pretend-to-listen tactic that Greenspan had deployed on Dick Darman during the administration of Bush senior—but now Greenspan was on the receiving end.[16]

In February 2001, Greenspan testified in the Senate once again, this time before the banking committee.[17] Its chairman was the wily Republican Phil Gramm, who had teased Greenspan for appearing next to the first lady at Bill Clinton's deficit-cutting State of the Union address. Now, with the opposite party in the White House and the opposite momentum on taxes, Gramm could see what Greenspan was up to: a U-turn, pure and simple.

"I got the idea in listening to some of my colleagues that at least they perceive that you had been misquoted in your testimony," the senator began, referring to the fact that Democrats were still claiming Greenspan as their ally in opposing the tax cuts. The Fed chairman's mention of deficit triggers showed that he did not really support Bush's cuts, or so the Democrats suggested.

"But I have noted in the past, when you thought people got it wrong, you issued a clarification," Gramm continued. "I saw no clarification as a result of that testimony.

"In your opinion, were your views misconstrued?" Gramm demanded.

The question left Greenspan nowhere to hide. Contrary to what he had pleaded to Rubin, he *could* be in charge of people's perceptions—Gramm was asking him to say how Congress should construe his tax testimony. If Greenspan wanted to force politicians to reckon with his triggers proposal, this was his moment. If not, he would have to come clean. The game of cozying up simultaneously to both sides was not going to be sustainable.

Greenspan refused Gramm's invitation to reiterate his support for deficit triggers. "Mr. Chairman, I do think that because of the complexity of the issue which I addressed in the Senate Budget Committee—complex of necessity, because things are changing in ways that we had not been required to evaluate previously—that a number of the reports that I saw were quite selective of the general position that I took," he waffled masterfully. "But I don't find that unusual. I find that sort of more general rather than otherwise. I don't know what to do about it."

With that, Greenspan passed up the opportunity to press his triggers proposal, effectively endorsing the administration's position. The triggers idea had been just the latest instance of his tendency to speak the truth, but quietly. As an adviser in the Ford White House, he had waffled on the 1975 tax cut, allowing the president to construe his lack of an objection as an endorsement. As Fed chairman during the tech bubble, he had muffled his musings about irrational exuberance in a cloak of history and philosophy. Given his stature, Greenspan might at least have tried to sway the tax debate. But he was not about to clash with the president's national economic adviser. He was not going to fight his good friend the vice president.[18] He was not going to risk the Fed's monetary independence by challenging the White House on fiscal policy.

"We did what we could on conditionality," O'Neill reflected to his friend in May, after a last-ditch trigger amendment had been defeated in the Senate.

"Without the triggers, that tax cut is irresponsible fiscal policy," Greenspan observed.[19]

Arguably, in not insisting on the same point publicly, Greenspan himself had acted irresponsibly.

As he agitated from the sidelines of the tax debate, Greenspan confronted a challenge that fell directly within his own bailiwick. In March 2001 the economy entered a recession, the first since the previous Bush presidency.[20] Not at all surprisingly, the Fed chairman reaped some of the blame. A survey of money managers in March found a sharp decline in his standing.[21]

The blame for the recession could be laid at Greenspan's door in two senses. The previous spring, he had committed a rare tactical error, misjudging the outlook for growth and inflation. In February and March 2000, he had delivered a pair of quarter-point rate hikes, responding to evidence that inflation was rising; then, in May, he had followed up with a double dose of tightening, hiking by a further 50 basis points. The logic was straightforward: the most recent data on core inflation suggested that it was still heading up.[22] But the last hike in Greenspan's sequence turned out to be too much. The chairman had overestimated the underlying growth in productivity and underestimated the drag on the economy from the recent collapse of the Nasdaq. Ten months later, with the May 2000 tightening having taken its effect, the recession started.

In a larger sense, however, Greenspan's error was not tactical but strategic. Because he had allowed the stock market to run wild in 1999, a period of exuberant growth would now be followed by a hangover. Just as Greenspan had argued in his 1959 paper, booming asset prices had driven companies to splurge on machinery and equipment; likewise, the collapse of the Nasdaq in 2000 portended a retrenchment. Sure enough, business investment collapsed by 25 percent in the first quarter of 2001, precisely as the young Greenspan would have predicted.[23] The question this posed was whether the Fed should have been thinking on a longer horizon. At the end of the 1990s, it had aimed for the maximum amount of noninflationary growth possible over the next year or so. Now it turned out that maximizing growth over a period of a year might mean undershooting growth over a period of, say, three years. Perhaps the Fed should stabilize the economy over a longer horizon—which would mean paying more attention to asset prices?

Whether this critique was right would ultimately depend on the depth of the recession. The Fed had bet its reputation on the proposition that it could clean up after a bubble; if it succeeded in that task, perhaps the downturn would be mild enough for the earlier boom to have been worth it. Recognizing the stakes involved, Greenspan loosened policy aggressively from the start of 2001: he cut by 50 basis points in early January, then eased again in late January, March, April, and May, bringing the federal funds rate down by a cumulative 2.5 percentage points. It was a dramatic intervention, more forceful by far than anything Greenspan had undertaken in response to the recession during the first Bush administration.[24] But the ferocity of the Fed's action carried a warning. Perhaps, in the face of some future financial implosion, the Fed might run out of space to ease? Perhaps rate cuts this rapid and this deep might risk unpleasant side effects?

"Banks in our region are beginning to lend more aggressively on real estate," Tom Hoenig, the president of the Kansas City Fed, observed at the FOMC meeting in March 2001. Low interest rates "might cause some— for lack of a better word—overbuilding," he ventured.

While Greenspan struggled with tax politics and recession, he sensed another challenge from the White House. A vacancy had opened up on the Fed's board, and Lawrence Lindsey was backing the appointment of an obscure community banker named Terry Jorde.

Jorde was more or less the antithesis of Greenspan. A petite blonde with a toothy smile, she ran a small community bank headquartered in the minuscule North Dakota frontier town of Cando—the name, pronounced *CAN-do,* had been chosen by Captain Prosper Parker in 1884, in a flourish of pioneer punning. Unfamiliar with Manhattan's high-rises and high finance, Jorde could boast an intimate knowledge of farming; indeed, she was married to a durum wheat planter. As a community banker, she had met Larry Lindsey in the 1990s, when he had been leading the Fed's outreach to community groups; the two had stayed in touch, and Lindsey had invited Jorde to participate in an economic forum with President-elect Bush shortly before he took office. If Lindsey succeeded in getting her appointed to the Fed's board, she might feel more loyalty to her political patron than to the Fed chairman.[25]

Jorde also boasted a prominent ally in the Republican-led Congress. Richard Armey, the House majority leader, was a family friend and fellow Cando native. Reports that Jorde might be elevated to the Fed "are just tickling me plum," Armey announced in early May 2001. "She's a bright young woman who I'm sure studied finance and economics," he ventured by way of an endorsement. "I've spoken to the President about her twice," he added.[26]

A little while later, the bright young woman trooped into the Fed building as part of a delegation of community bankers. Despite their modest role in American finance, the community banks packed political punch: with networks all over the country and the power to sway votes at the grassroots, they were respected in Washington. Ken Guenther, the community bankers' top lobbyist, occasionally played tennis or golf with the chairman. When Guenther and his posse visited the Fed, Greenspan knew he had better see them.

Guenther had planned his team's agenda carefully. Toward the end of the meeting, the visitors would raise the matter of Terry Jorde's impending nomination as a Fed governor. They wanted Greenspan to understand that Jorde had their full support. She was not just a nobody from a mom-and-pop outfit. She represented thousands of community banks from states across the country.

When the time came, Guenther and his entourage duly spoke up.

With Jorde looking on, Greenspan replied, "The Board knows everything it will ever want to know about durum wheat."[27]

That was "the execution of Terry Jorde in front of her peers," Guenther would say later. Despite his best efforts to mount a lobbying blitz to get around Greenspan, there was nothing he could do to revive Jorde's prospects. In July 2001, the White House abandoned her nomination.

Greenspan might cave in to the White House on issues like tax. But when it came to appointments to his board, he remained a force to be reckoned with.

On September 8, 2001, Greenspan left for a central bankers' gathering in Basel. Three days later, he boarded an Airbus A330-200 for the long flight home to Washington.[28] About halfway into the journey, he rose for a stroll. There were still several hours before the plane would land. A busy schedule awaited him, starting with a meeting with the prime minister of Australia.

"Mr. Chairman, the captain needs to see you up front," a voice said.

It was Bob Agnew, chief of the security detail.

"Two planes have flown into the World Trade Center," Agnew continued quietly. There was a beat. "I'm not joking."

Once Greenspan entered the cockpit, the captain briefed him on the limited information he had received. Hijacked planes. Two into the World Trade Center. One into the Pentagon. One missing. The pilot had been ordered to return to Zurich, but he did not intend to panic passengers by sharing the news of the hijacks.

A dash for the seat phones nevertheless ensued when the captain announced the change of flight plan over the cabin intercom. Greenspan, by now back in his seat, also tried to place a call. It was no use. All the lines were busy.

Isolated in his flying tin can, Greenspan stared out of his cabin window. His thoughts were normally a place of refuge, but now they could not shelter him.

He wanted to call Andrea. Fortunately, she was not in New York, and she had not been planning to visit the Pentagon on that particular Tuesday. Even so, Alan worried. What if she had gone to the Pentagon on some last-minute visit?

Greenspan's thoughts turned to the Fed. Was everybody safe? What about their families? This was the first attack on U.S. soil in more than fifty years. How far would the economy be damaged?[29]

It was clearly not good news that two of the four planes had hit the financial district of lower Manhattan. Paralysis among the banks and brokerages in and around the World Trade Center might in turn paralyze their Main Street clients, setting off a chain reaction of insolvencies. But the ultimate nightmare would involve Fedwire, the electronic network that financial institutions used to transfer funds. The Fed could fight a liquidity panic by pumping money into the system so long as Fedwire functioned; but if Fedwire was crippled, a crisis would be inevitable.[30] In principle, the system was fortified with multiple redundancies, supposedly allowing it to maintain operations even after a nuclear attack. Now those defenses would be tested.

Unbeknownst to Greenspan, part of the Fedwire system had indeed been clobbered. The data centers that serviced one of the two main Fedwire clearinghouses were damaged, creating a logjam in the payments network. Moreover, even if most of the Fedwire infrastructure had survived, the staff experts who operated it faced a horrifying challenge. Debris from the World Trade Center towers rained down on the New York Fed's headquarters at 33 Liberty Street; and One Liberty Plaza, a black steel skyscraper adjacent to the World Trade Center complex and just two blocks west of 33 Liberty Street, seemed to have sustained structural damage—if it toppled, chunks of it might land on neighboring buildings and the area would be choked in clouds of asbestos. Already the electricity in the Fed building had stopped working and the telephones were down. Several of the Fed's trading partners at Wall Street's big bond desks were battling equally chaotic circumstances.

Fearing that the Liberty Street tower was in danger of collapse, a Fed janitor commandeered the public address system and blurted out an evacuation announcement.[31] Even if the order had been authorized, it would have been unprecedented. Someone was always inside the New York Fed to monitor the markets. The building never shut down—there was not even a key to lock it.[32]

Ignoring the janitor's evacuation order, the New York staff hunkered down, coordinating lending operations by cell phone. They could hardly abandon their stations without also abandoning the country to chaos. In the face of a psychological shock of this size, people would hoard cash; and if people who had hoped to borrow were suddenly cut off, chains of IOUs would strain and crack, destroying confidence throughout the economy.

About a hundred Fed officials slept in their offices that night, and armed guards stationed themselves at the building's entrances. More than $70 billion of gold bullion lay stored in the Fed's underground vaults. In the dead dark of an electricity-free night, there would be a risk of looters.[33]

Greenspan's plane landed safely back in Switzerland. He refused to watch video replays of the destruction at the World Trade Center and Pentagon. For a man who had spent much of his life in the shadow of the Twin Towers, the attacks were painful enough just to hear about. The wounded financial district had been the cradle of Townsend-Greenspan; it was where a square-shouldered, forty-one-year-old economist had first met Richard Nixon. Countless Greenspan acquaintances showed up to work there every day. The thought of how many might be injured or dead sickened him.

At just before 3:00 p.m. on the East Coast, Alan finally managed to get through to Andrea on her cell phone. He was relieved to hear her voice, but Andrea was just seconds away from going on television with a live special report.

"Just tell me quickly what's happening there," Alan asked her.

Andrea held the cell phone to one ear. A producer in New York was speaking urgently into her other ear, warning her to be ready.

"Listen up," Andrea said. With that, she dropped the cell phone in her lap. The cameras blinked on, and she launched into her report: United Flight 93 had crashed in Pennsylvania.[34]

Assured that Andrea was safe, Alan's next call was to Roger Ferguson Jr., the Fed vice chairman who was leading the emergency response in Washington. Ferguson was a calm presence, and he was doing everything right: he had lost no time in assuring the Fed's member banks that the discount window would remain open, and so far he had delivered on his promise.[35] Indeed, thanks to the heroic efforts of the Fed's staff, the discount window was on its way to pumping more than $37 billion worth of reassurance into the country's banks by the end of that first day: it was nearly two hundred times more than the Fed normally lent—Black Monday looked trifling by comparison.[36] Meanwhile, faced with disruptions to the nation's check-clearing system, the Fed announced that it would shoulder the "risk of ride": banks receiving checks would get their money from the Fed immediately, even before the paying banks had made good on their obligations.[37] The Fed also stemmed the panic among foreign financial institutions. It lent to the central banks of Britain, the Eurozone, and Canada, allowing them to support domestic lenders that found themselves abruptly short of dollars.[38]

Greenspan listened as Ferguson ticked off the steps he was taking. "You are in charge," he told his deputy. "You go forward and make the decisions."[39]

Thus far the Fed had averted disaster. But there were still many unknowns. The trading floors of several exchanges had suffered structural damage. In the bond market alone, data representing $170 billion worth of trades were missing.[40]

You'll never believe this," the pilot said, offering Greenspan a headset. It was Wednesday, the morning after the attacks, and the Fed chairman was standing in the cockpit of an air force fueling tanker. With American airspace shut down to commercial flights, Greenspan had taken the only possible ride home.[41] It was not exactly comfortable.

Taking the headset from the pilot, Greenspan listened in.

There was nothing. Just static.

"Normally the North Atlantic is full of radio chatter," the pilot said. "This silence is eerie."[42]

As the tanker entered U.S. airspace, it was met and escorted by two F-16 fighters. The captain got permission to fly over the site of what had been the Twin Towers, now a smoking ruin of mud and twisted metal.[43]

When Greenspan got back to the Fed, he found an atmosphere of embattled paranoia. The security staff refused to allow him to work out of his office. Fearing an attack by a sniper, they moved him to a room with no window over Constitution Avenue.

Roger Ferguson was running the crisis-response work partly out of his own office, and partly out of the boardroom and the nearby Special Library. Far from seeking to impose himself on Ferguson's efforts, Greenspan continued to let him run the practical side of the emergency response. He retreated to his temporary office and plotted the Fed's next monetary move, monitoring the markets to the extent that they were functioning.

Like the victim of a trauma who curls up into a fetal crouch, Greenspan was gravitating instinctively to his comfort zone. He had never taken much interest in financial plumbing; he was and remained an economic forecaster. Separated from the chairman's formal quarters, studying the data on his own, he was the same introverted consultant he had always been. He took refuge in his office just as he had once hidden away in his walk-in closet at Townsend-Greenspan.

"We seek, virtually hour by hour, positions of comfort," Greenspan reflected later. "There are people who I know very well who get anxiety attacks if they are by themselves. I was just the opposite."[44]

On Thursday, September 13, Greenspan convened his FOMC colleagues by conference call. The stock exchanges were still not functioning, despite a personal appeal from President Bush that they should open as soon as possible. Telephone workers hoped to restore 90 percent of the exchanges' phone lines over the weekend, but that might not be enough: no one expected trading on the first day back from the attacks to be anything but torrential. Meanwhile, falling debris had destroyed two electrical substations on which the exchanges depended. To get the power back up, utility workers planned to run giant extension cords through the streets of lower Manhattan. "It will look a bit like a Third World solution," New York Fed president Bill McDonough said grimly.

McDonough was even more concerned about One Liberty Plaza. Engineers had pronounced the skyscraper structurally sound in three different surveys, but occupants of the nearby buildings were still terrified. Loud bangs and booms from the rubble-clearing effort at Ground Zero sent people racing out into the streets.

"Somebody is going to have to figure out once and for all whether the building is really likely to fall or not," McDonough pleaded. "Nobody is quite sure whether people are just traumatized and overreacting or whether something is really wrong.

"So we're living in a very surreal environment," he concluded.

Greenspan listened to McDonough's report in silence. The New York Fed chief was evidently distraught—understandably, because he was operating in the shadow of a possibly unstable tower, and with a phone system that was still only half working. Greenspan, for his part, seemed almost to be shutting down; he was not one for emotional entanglement, with situations or with people. When McDonough finished talking, the chairman responded numbly, from a place of pure reason.

"This event came at a most inopportune time if one really wants to look at it purely from an economic forecaster's point of view," he observed. The economy had already been weak before the terrorist attacks. Now the shock to confidence might send it into free fall.

On Friday, Alan and Andrea joined the country's political elite in Washington's National Cathedral. President Bush led his fellow Americans in a National Day of Prayer and Remembrance, and the service glowed on television screens in homes and offices around the nation. Ushers passed out red, white, and blue ribbons to be pinned on mourners' lapels; Andrea put one on, then quickly took it off again before going on air after the ceremony was done—she was struggling with her dual roles as insider-spouse and outsider-reporter.[45] In bagel shops in lower Manhattan, exhausted recovery workers stared at the proceedings on the TV screens, finished their coffees, and returned to the rain-soaked muck.[46]

Slowly but surely, the recovery work was paying off. Tests at the NYSE and Nasdaq over the weekend established that electricity and phone lines were working well enough to allow the exchanges to reopen on Monday. In preparation for that moment, President Bush declared on Sunday, "The markets open tomorrow, people go back to work, and we'll show the world." On NBC, Andrea's network, Vice President Cheney asked the American people to "stick their thumb in the eye of the terrorists and say that they've got great confidence in the country, great confidence in our economy, and not let what's happened here in any way throw off their normal level of economic activity." The renowned investor Warren Buffett appeared on CBS's *60 Minutes* and announced that he would not be selling anything when the market opened: "There's something I might buy," he added. Buoyed by this tide of patriotism, a New York Fed official went to a store in Midtown and bought $1,500 worth of bunting and American flags. By Monday, 33 Liberty Street was decked out as though for Victory Day, and rousing music blasted from loudspeakers at the building's parapet.[47]

At 7:30 a.m. on Monday, Greenspan convened another FOMC conference call. This was the moment for which he had been preparing in the solitude of his office: he had decided to cut interest rates by another 50 basis points. The idea was to do enough to reassure markets, but not so much as to telegraph panic. By timing the announcement just before the markets' reopening, Greenspan was aiming for the maximum possible psychological impact. The committee quickly rallied behind him.[48]

When the markets reopened at 9:30 a.m., the sell-off was as mild as the Fed could possibly have wished for. Stocks closed the day around 7 percent lower; but the trading was orderly and the infrastructure functioned, accommodating the highest volume of orders on any day, ever. What could have been several days of Black Monday–style panic turned out to be a measured market correction—painful, certainly, but bereft of self-feeding terror.

The value of an active central bank had seldom been clearer.

The attacks of 2001 brought an end to the euphoric mood that had persisted through the 1990s. What the Nasdaq collapse had initiated, the destruction of the World Trade Center completed. It turned out that dot-com companies were not actually building a utopia with America at its apex; it turned out that the symbols of U.S. preeminence could become propaganda props for terrorists. Americans were left to reckon with the fact that their sense of post-cold-war invulnerability had been punctured. They would henceforth set aside more of their resources for airport security, border security, policemen, and air marshals. They would endure longer waits outside sporting events and concerts. They would lose some of their openness to immigrants, and hence a measure of their economic vitality.

For Greenspan, too, life became more complicated. His low-key security team was replaced by an officious Secret Service detail, with rules about who sat where in the back of the car and about not getting out until the door was opened for you. The post office stopped delivering mail to the Greenspan-Mitchell home—letters and packages had to be cleared first by security. Wandering off to a movie unaccompanied was now out of the question. Alan and Andrea's secluded residence was rigged up with surveillance cameras. And rather than just dropping Alan off in the evening, his guards now camped there permanently.

For Andrea especially, these changes took some getting used to. Their relatively modest house was not designed to accommodate a permanent visit from a large team of well-built strangers. There was no basement or rec room for the Secret Servicemen to shed boots and watch TV, so they were forced to linger awkwardly in the small hall outside the kitchen. Later, when it became clear that this was not sustainable, the agents retreated to an RV trailer installed in the driveway—it was not a welcome addition to one of the prettiest residential streets in Washington. Andrea asked a landscape designer to come up with a system of flowered trellises to disguise the eyesore. But the security men were having none of that. The line of sight through the windows of the RV was not to be cluttered with hanging roses or begonias.

Andrea went to lunch with the CIA chief, George Tenet. He was a voluble source on all matters terrorism related.

"Do we have to live this way?" she asked him.

"Yes, you do," came the reply. "And just don't ask me."

After that, Andrea made her peace with the security presence. If the terrorists were out to hit the symbols of America's economic prowess, her husband was certainly among them. But she never said anything to Alan about the CIA chief's ominous hint. There were some things he did not want to know. Threats were a waste of his energy.

A year later, on the anniversary of the attacks, Andrea watched a documentary about them. Alan refused to sit and watch with her.

"I worked by those Twin Towers," he said. "I'm not going to ever look at this."[49]

Twenty-seven

LOWFLATION

G rowing up as an economist, Greenspan had lived through many of the debates that preoccupied him as Fed chairman. Thanks to Bill Townsend's focus on finance, he had pondered the interactions between monetary policy and asset prices. Thanks to Arthur Burns's empiricism, he had developed a lifelong skepticism of models, a trait that set him apart from economists who trained a generation later. Thanks to John Gurley and Edward Shaw, he had formed a firm conviction that financial innovation was positive for the economy, even though markets were only approximately efficient. Now, in the wake of the attacks of September 2001, another debate from Greenspan's youth floated up from the deep past. The controversy unleashed by Alvin Hansen, the distinguished Keynesian at Harvard who predicted "secular stagnation," came back with a vengeance.

As an undergraduate at New York University, Greenspan had been unimpressed by Hansen's forecast. He had sided instead with the far less illustrious George Terborgh, rejecting the contention that America had run out of scope to innovate, or that companies' anemic appetite for investment would saddle the economy with excess savings and inadequate demand— and hence with stagnation and deflation. Greenspan had been vindicated in this youthful judgment: the postwar consumer boom brought a surge of investment, consumer credit, and double-digit inflation—exactly the opposite of stagnation. The memory of that vindication no doubt reinforced Greenspan's later optimism about America's potential, particularly when he was talking up the New Economy in the late 1990s. As a young autodidact, Greenspan had raised himself on stories about the heroic railway pioneers of the nineteenth century; he had marveled at the early prototype of a television set at the World's Fair in 1939; he had embraced Ayn Rand's worship of inventors. He was almost programmed to believe in progress.

Yet in the aftermath of the 2001 terrorist attacks, the debate between Hansen and Terborgh took on a different complexion. The U.S. economy, already listing, now suffered a debilitating loss of confidence. Business investment collapsed. Before, it had been held back by the overhang of excess investment during the tech boom; now the overhang was compounded by the unfamiliarity of a new world, one in which goods no longer rolled across borders without paranoid inspection. The Fed, which had battled inflation continually since the Hansen-Terborgh debate, now confronted the opposite challenge. Spending was so weak—the animal spirits of investors so muted—that the Fed's preferred measure of core inflation fell to 1.2 percent in the month of the attacks; and in November the University of Michigan reported that inflation expectations had plunged to 0.4 percent. It was an extraordinary descent. In thirty-five years of tracking inflation expectations, the Michigan survey had never recorded a reading below 1 percent, ever.[1]

The collapse of inflation was rendered particularly disconcerting by Japan's recent experience. Like the United States in the late 1990s, Japan in the late 1980s had succumbed to a wild stock market and investment bubble; more than a decade on, Japan had yet to recover. Households were intent on rebuilding their savings, and businesses refused to invest; there was not enough spending to absorb the supply of goods pumped out by the factories created during the boom years. As a result, Japanese prices had drifted downward for eight years. The Bank of Japan had cut interest rates to zero; but in yet another echo of the debates of Greenspan's youth, monetary policy seemed impotent. Hansen had been wrong to predict secular stagnation in the United States after the war. But his writings had anticipated Japan circa 2000.

At its meeting in November 2001, the FOMC grappled with the risk of a Japan-style deflation. Already it had cut the federal funds rate from 6.5 percent to 2.5 percent that year, but its medicine was having no discernible effect: investment remained weak and inflation was still falling. With rates now at their lowest since the 1960s, the central bank might soon be out of ammunition.

Don Kohn, the normally unflappable chief of the monetary affairs division, seemed worried. In the face of economic weakness, the Fed had sometimes found it necessary to drive real borrowing costs into negative territory.[2] But if inflation itself turned negative, there would be no scope to push the inflation-adjusted interest rate below zero—for example, if inflation was minus 0.5 percent, the Fed could not set nominal interest rates at minus 1 percent, because savers would respond by hoarding cash rather than paying banks to accept deposits from them. Because of this "zero lower bound" on interest rates, negative inflation blunted the Fed's power. If prices started heading down, the central bank would run out of ammunition faster than it expected.

Summarizing the research literature, Kohn told the FOMC that in the face of the deflation threat, it might want to act preemptively. The committee should cut interest rates before the impact of its cuts was undermined; if it waited, seeking to "keep its powder dry," deflation might render the powder useless. An economy facing a Japan-type risk must avoid being "pinned to the lower bound," Kohn urged. The language conjured up the image of a boxer pinned against the ropes, with deflation pummeling him.

Greenspan might once have ridiculed Kohn's argument.[3] In one of his Randian lectures, he had observed that persistent deflation under the nineteenth-century gold standard had "in no way inhibited the expansion of economic activity." Between 1865 and 1900, U.S. prices had fallen by an average of 1.7 percent per year, a far steeper decline than anything experienced in Japan; and yet, as Greenspan said, "The latter half of the 19th century was perhaps the period of the greatest advancement in standards of living that has ever existed."[4] The lesson seemed to be that deflation that resulted from cost-cutting new technologies might be entirely harmless.

By this stage in his life, however, Greenspan's Randian convictions had faded; at the FOMC meeting in November 2001, Greenspan backed Kohn's side of the argument. For one thing, the downward pressure on prices was not simply the result of tech-driven economies; rather, the nation was suffering a sudden weakness in demand, as Americans licked their wounds after the tech crash and as confidence suffered after 9/11.[5] For another, the structure of the U.S. economy had changed profoundly since the late nineteenth century. Companies and individuals had accumulated vast debts, which would be harder to pay off if deflation increased their real value. Likewise, incomes had grown "stickier" than they had been in the past. In the nineteenth century, price falls had been followed by falls in wages, keeping the system in equilibrium; but now the existence of unemployment benefits could be expected to embolden workers to fight cuts in wages, with the result that deflation would cause wages to increase in real terms, perhaps leading to a rise in unemployment. Meanwhile, government benefit payments were even stickier. Pensions, disability pay, or other support payments would not be cut if prices fell; the upshot would be a larger government deficit. Pre–World War I deflation might have been benign, as the young Greenspan had argued, but it was harder to imagine the same phenomenon in the early twenty-first century.

Building on Kohn's comments, Greenspan proposed that the Fed cut interest rates by another 50 basis points, to the extraordinarily low rate of 2 percent. It was the FOMC's duty to "put in enough shot to knock down the opponent before the opponent eventually does us in," he said gravely. Confronted with the prospect of a duel to the death, the committee supported him unanimously. At the following meeting, Greenspan cut the rate again, to 1.75 percent. He was not going to sit on his hands and follow Japan into stagnation.

Greenspan's battle against deflation, running from November 2001 until June 2004, would later be debated furiously. In his determination to insure the economy against a Japanese-style slump, he pushed down borrowing costs about as far as they could go; and his actions fueled the climb in house prices that built steadily in 2002 and 2003, reaching its wildest and frothiest extremes in the two years that followed.[6] John Taylor, the Stanford professor who had worked for Greenspan on Ford's Council of Economic Advisers and as a part-timer at his consulting firm, lambasted the Fed repeatedly for cutting rates too much, focusing particularly on the phase starting in 2003. In the view of Taylor and his allies, Greenspan's monetary policy in this period was more reckless than anything during the tech boom. In the late 1990s, after all, the chairman had diagnosed productivity correctly, and although the Nasdaq bubble eventually burst, it caused a mild recession rather than a meltdown. In the 2000s, by contrast, Greenspan held down interest rates without the justification of the New Economy. And in the place of the shallow recession of 2001, the nation reaped the Great Financial Crisis.[7]

This comparison can be reversed, however.[8] Greenspan's productivity call of 1996 was brilliantly correct, but it does not necessarily follow that monetary policy itself was correct; there is a reasonable case for saying that Greenspan should have kept interest rates higher in 1997–98 in order to dampen asset markets.[9] There is an extremely strong case, moreover, for criticizing Greenspan's looseness from late 1998, when he cut more than was necessary following Long-Term Capital Management's collapse and then failed to undo the cuts until November 1999, by which time the stock market had lost all touch with reality. In contrast, the rate cuts starting in November 2001 had a better rationale, as we have seen: the fear of Japan-style deflation.

Moreover, the standard comparison of consequences—a relatively harmless tech bust in 2000, a full-blown financial meltdown in 2007–8— should also be qualified. The tech bust proved relatively harmless because the Fed loosened aggressively to avoid stagnation; if this aggressive loosening was partly to blame for the property bubble, it follows that the tech bubble planted the seeds for the 2008 crisis. Indeed, by creating a risk of deflation, the tech bust put the Fed in a position where it almost needed frothy real estate to keep the economy going, especially after the terrorist attacks compounded the risk of stagnation. Writing in his *New York Times* column in August 2002, the Princeton economist Paul Krugman declared, "Alan Greenspan needs to create a housing bubble to replace the Nasdaq bubble."[10]

On January 17, 2002, Greenspan visited his friend Paul O'Neill for one of their weekly Fed-Treasury breakfasts. O'Neill was pondering the administration's response to the collapse of the energy company Enron, a microcosm of the economy's difficulties. Enron had invested feverishly during the bubble years, splurging on everything from wastewater treatment plants to fiber-optic cable. Its behavior proved that, as Greenspan had written in 1959, crazy market valuations for corporate assets would induce executives to create more such assets, crazily. Then the boom had turned to bust and Enron had tried to cover up its losses with a series of accounting tricks, hiding them in off-balance-sheet vehicles named after the velociraptors of *Jurassic Park:* there was Raptor I, Raptor II, and so on. Shareholders and employees had been bamboozled into thinking that everything was fine. Now Enron was bankrupt.

Greenspan agreed with O'Neill that the Enron fiasco showed it was time to reform audit standards. In the wake of Enron's failure, a parade of public corporations had confessed to doctoring their accounts: evidently, the exuberance of the tech bubble had been sustained partly by fraud, and Enron was by no means a freakish bad apple. According to a Fed staff calculation, large public companies had overstated their profits by an *average* of 2.5 percentage points per year between 1995 and 2000.[11]

O'Neill thought the solution lay with chief executives. Derivatives and other modern financial tools made it easy to doctor company accounts, and there was no way to uninvent them. But if CEOs were held to a higher standard of legal responsibility for their companies' disclosures, they would have every incentive to ensure their accuracy.

Greenspan was not convinced at first: O'Neill's plan sounded too simple. But then he gave ground. "It may be the thoughtful solution," he allowed. "Nothing else has worked."

"So, I guess we're a team again," O'Neill said. "Let's see how we do this time."[12]

The following month, on February 12, 2002, Greenspan e-mailed O'Neill his thoughts on accounting reform, confessing that he had "gone further than originally intended." The more Greenspan had thought about the Enron scandal, the more indignant he had become. In a market-based system, investors were supposed to allocate savings to the companies that would use them best; there was no way they could get this right without reliable corporate disclosures. Likewise, advanced economies took it for granted that central banks should smooth inflation and growth; there was no way that Greenspan could deliver on that hope if corporate data were rotten. "Quarterly earnings results have become increasingly subject to anticipation, spin, and rumor," Greenspan complained. It would take regulation to fix this.

O'Neill read the memo with delight. It showed the Fed chairman's pragmatic side: he was no laissez-faire ideologue. If only the public got a chance to meet this Greenspan, he reflected.[13]

On February 22, O'Neill convened the administration's top financial brass in one of the Treasury's large conference rooms.[14] He lost no time in laying out his main idea. The legal standard for triggering litigation against a CEO ought to be lowered—from recklessness to negligence.

Harvey Pitt, the SEC chairman, was skeptical. "Shifting the standard to negligence is a huge problem," he objected. "We'll be overwhelmed with litigation."

More voices intervened, and the discussion descended into legal detail. Some agreed with Pitt that the negligence standard was undesirable; others pointed out that chief executives could already be sued under existing law if their accounts were misleading. Everybody had questions. It was hard to keep the big picture in focus.

Presently, Greenspan weighed in. He slapped his hand on the table and spoke in an insistent voice. "There's been too much gaming of the system until it is broke. Capitalism is not working!"[15]

The room fell silent. Greenspan, usually so measured, was speaking with surprising vehemence. Perhaps his maestro status had gone to his head. Perhaps this whole question of the reliability of corporate data had touched a special nerve. Or perhaps it was just that the Bush economics team was frustratingly incoherent: the Treasury, the National Economic Council, and the Council of Economic Advisers were frequently at loggerheads. For whatever combination of reasons, the sideman was uncharacteristically forceful.

"There has been a corrupting of the system of capitalism," Greenspan announced. "There's a hole in the present system."

"It's not the job of government to protect shareholders from the risk of bad management," the SEC chief retorted. He was in the odd position of lecturing Greenspan on the perils of regulation.

"This is a moral and ethical issue," Greenspan replied. The Randian was welling up within: capitalism was not merely efficient; it was morally superior—if only it could be made to function properly. "The President needs to speak to the nation about the moral issues—something he does so well."[16]

Sun streamed through the windows of the Treasury's large conference room, bathing the whole scene in a cinematic glow. Later, some participants would recall this moment vividly. They were witnessing the grand drama that made it worth serving in Washington.[17]

Greenspan's intervention refocused the meeting. His political instincts were right: whatever the legal merits of the SEC chief's position, the administration could hardly respond to the Enron scandal by doing nothing. Plenty of battles lay ahead, and Greenspan and O'Neill lost several of them. But in July 2002, President Bush signed a comprehensive corporate governance reform, the most far-reaching legislative overhaul of business rules enacted since the 1930s.

Even as it created momentum for accounting reform, Enron's collapse rekindled the debate over derivatives. The company had virtually invented online energy trading, and it had pleaded unsuccessfully for a government bailout on the ground that, like Long-Term Capital Management, it was too interconnected to be allowed to go under. In the face of this new setback, Greenspan mostly stuck to his old line: "New financial products, including derivatives, have enabled risk to be dispersed," he assured the Senate in March 2002. "Shocks to the overall economic system are accordingly less likely to create cascading credit failure."[18] But Greenspan also seized on public suspicion of the new instruments to push a fresh agenda. In April he took a stealthy shot at Fannie Mae and Freddie Mac, the two government-chartered mortgage giants whose distortive effects on the economy he had documented in the 1970s.

Greenspan was firing at formidable targets. Since 1990, the first year in which Fannie and Freddie both operated as profit-seeking public companies, the growth of the two housing finance giants had been almost as astounding as the growth of derivatives. By 2001, their combined balance sheets had swelled nearly ninefold: they now held $1.2 trillion of mortgages and mortgage-backed securities. Meanwhile, they also guaranteed payments on another $1.5 trillion of mortgage securities held by other investors. All told, Fannie and Freddie shouldered the risk associated with almost half of all outstanding residential mortgage debt—a market share that had nearly doubled in the span of just over a decade.

Greenspan usually saw the bright side of financial innovation and agglomeration, but the near doubling of Fannie and Freddie's market share was an exception. The explosion of over-the-counter derivatives reflected free choices by investors, leading Greenspan to give it the benefit of the doubt; in contrast, the rise of Fannie and Freddie reflected a sinister subsidy. Because the mortgage giants had originally been chartered by the government, and because they maintained formidable lobbying machines, investors assumed that they would never go bankrupt: they were not merely too big to fail; they were too politically connected. Perceiving no risk in lending to Fannie and Freddie, their creditors extracted no risk premium; the resulting reduction in borrowing costs amounted to a subsidy worth more than $10 billion per year, according to the Congressional Budget Office.[19] No wonder Fannie and Freddie were ranked number one and number two, respectively, on *Fortune*'s list of the most profitable companies per employee.

On April 22, 2002, Greenspan used a speech in New York to tweak the mortgage giants. His message was deliberately muffled: if he had been leery of speaking out forcefully about the stock market's irrational exuberance in 1996, taking on Fannie and Freddie was even more daunting. But noting that the stability of derivatives markets depended on traders' monitoring one another's financial soundness, he raised a ticklish question. If Fannie and Freddie were assumed to enjoy a government backstop, why would their trading counterparties bother with due diligence? "We need to be careful not to allow subsidies to unduly disturb an efficient financial structure," Greenspan reflected.[20] The existence of large players that were insured from risk could undermine risk-management standards throughout the derivatives market.

Just as with the irrational exuberance speech, journalists zeroed in on Greenspan's veiled message with uncanny accuracy. Headlines such as "Fears for Fannie and Freddie" and "Greenspan Faults Mortgage Agencies" quickly appeared. Reflecting on this media storm, the *New York Times* credited the Fed chairman's comments with creating an opportunity for reform. "By making derivatives and disclosure, rather than the subsidy itself, the center of debate," the paper observed, "the critics have for the first time in two years put some real pressure on Fannie and Freddie."[21] Congress and the Treasury quickly piled on, and within three months the mortgage giants were forced into a concession. Both Fannie and Freddie volunteered to register with the Securities and Exchange Commission and to disclose more about the quality of the mortgages backing their securities. Registration was supposed to underline the fact that, legally speaking, the housing lenders' debt was not backed by the government.

It was not exactly a clampdown, but it was perhaps a small beginning. And for the second time in two months, Greenspan had discreetly pushed the cause of tighter regulation.

Greenspan was still a frequent visitor to the Bush White House. Once every fortnight or so, a car would ferry him from the Fed garage to the southwest gate—sometimes he would meet a senior economic official;

sometimes he would see Dick Cheney or the president. On one of these visits, Greenspan was walking through the Roosevelt Room with Bush beside him.

"Mr. President, there is an opening at the Fed," Greenspan said, leaning in toward him. "If you would be willing, Don Kohn would be a fantastic nominee."

"Oh yeah?" said Bush. "Tell me about it."

Greenspan seized the opening. When it came to lobbying the administration on tax cuts or accounting reform, he had met with mixed success. But when it came to personnel issues, the barriers were lower. "He's one of the finest economists I've ever known," Greenspan said simply.

A young White House adviser heard the interchange and marveled. This was not the way appointments to the Fed board were meant to be decided. When a governorship became open, the White House personnel office was expected to survey the field of compelling candidates and draw up a short list. Even if the president and his senior entourage ended up choosing someone whom they knew, they were supposed to send their person over to the central bank. The Fed chairman was not supposed to do the choosing.[22]

But on this occasion, Greenspan's intervention worked. The word in the president's ear all but settled the question of the Fed vacancy. Don Kohn was interviewed by the White House personnel office and then by Bush himself. But he was prepped before each meeting by none other than Greenspan, and his elevation from top staff member to governor followed smoothly.

For years, successive administrations had aimed to surround the Fed chairman with presidential loyalists: even the formidable Volcker had had to face a board that was willing to outvote him. Greenspan, more than any of his predecessors, had maneuvered deftly to protect his freedom, blocking unwanted nominees, as in the cases of Felix Rohatyn and Terry Jorde. But now he had taken a step further, all but nominating his own man.[23]

By the summer of 2002, the economy was looking stronger. Having expanded by 3.8 percent in the first quarter, it managed 2.2 percent in the second—the recession was clearly over. But the recovery was lopsided: even the lowest federal funds rate in forty years was failing to revive business investment, which would languish below its prebubble level for another several quarters, demonstrating that cleaning up after the tech bust was by no means easy.[24] In the absence of business investment, the recovery was being fueled by real estate.[25] With the Fed's loose policy pushing down on mortgage interest rates, home prices took off; scarcely imagining what might come later, the *New York Times* lamented that prices were "so far out of line with incomes" that even a run-down California ranch house could sport a million-dollar sticker.[26] Among savvy New Yorkers, housing replaced tech start-ups as the hot investment. "People are buying real estate instead of going into the stock market," a Manhattan-based designer proclaimed after trading in his portfolio for a condo on Miami's South Beach.[27]

Eager to keep the recovery going, the Bush administration did everything it could to promote the housing boom. In June 2002 the president announced a "Blueprint for the American Dream," a plan to help poor families to buy property. Stretching logic fearlessly, Bush drew a connection between the security of home ownership and security against terror: "Part of being a secure America is to encourage homeownership, so somebody can say, 'This is my home, welcome to my home.'"[28] The next day the president warmed to his theme. "Let me first talk about how to make sure America's secure from a group of killers," he proclaimed. "You know what they hate? They hate the idea that somebody can go buy a home."[29] To lend substance to his rhetoric, Bush called upon Congress to boost home ownership with tax credits and grants. The housing market was rising at its fastest rate in over fifteen years, but Bush wanted it to rise faster.

Congress was normally happy to encourage more spending on housing. Inducements from the building lobby and the rhetoric of the American Dream had captured both political parties. But not wanting to take chances, the administration reached for a faster way to realize its housing ambitions: it enlisted Fannie and Freddie. The giants had the means to funnel money into low-cost housing, and they had the incentive, too. "Subprime" loans to risky borrowers generated higher revenues than ordinary mortgages; meanwhile, Fannie and Freddie could cite them in their lobbying campaigns as proof they were socially inclusive. By volunteering as the agents of the president's initiative, moreover, Fannie and Freddie could effectively undo the regulatory concession they had offered under pressure from Greenspan. If they served as presidential foot soldiers, their de facto government backstop would surely be beyond doubt. "To get those high homeownership goals, you cannot rein in Fannie and Freddie," a financial analyst commented.[30]

Within a week of Bush's home-security speeches, the housing giants were in action. Fannie Mae announced one hundred new partnerships with church groups to increase home ownership among racial minorities. Freddie Mac unveiled a twenty-five-point program aimed at minorities and immigrants.[31] Soon executives from the mortgage giants showed up at a White House conference brimming with good news. Fannie had accelerated and even automated the underwriting of subprime loans. As a result of its Expanded Approval program, thousands of previously uncreditworthy families had gotten mortgages. Freddie had reached out to customers with "nontraditional" financial profiles, such as immigrants with no bank accounts or credit cards in the country.[32]

Despite his efforts to contain Fannie and Freddie, Greenspan accepted the administration's housing drive quietly. He had ignored the first Bush administration's pleas to support growth in 1991 and 1992; he did not want to relive those battles. Besides, neither he nor his Fed colleagues were impressed by the newspaper chatter about a housing bubble.[33] The real estate takeoff might simply reflect demography: baby boomers were hitting their financial prime and splurging on housing; immigration was bringing new home buyers to the country. And the possibility of a housing bubble had to be weighed against other risks. Given the continuing dearth of corporate investment, a bit of real estate euphoria seemed like a necessary tonic. In the absence of a housing boost, there might be Japan-style deflation.

"Being concerned about stimulating the housing market should not slow us down here," Vice Chairman Roger Ferguson reflected to his FOMC colleagues at the end of September 2002, summing up the majority view on the committee. "To put the philosophical question on the table: If the choice is between unbalanced growth that gets the economy back to trend or a perfectly balanced economy that's growing infinitely below trend for a long period of time, I know what my loss function looks like." A recovery that relied to an unnatural extent on housing was better than Alvin Hansen's secular stagnation.

"I'm not as convinced as others seem to be that creating an environment where people extract still more equity from their houses is all good," countered Jack Guynn of the Atlanta Fed. But nobody was listening.

When the FOMC convened again in November 2002, Greenspan remained preoccupied with the risk of stagnation: he still wanted to cut interest rates. This time it was not just Guynn who seemed uncomfortable. On the one hand, an even lower federal funds rate might cause home prices to accelerate into some crazy never-never land; on the other hand, a lower funds rate was not going to stimulate corporate investment, the missing element in the recovery. The dearth of investment reflected the glut of unused factories and fiber-optic cables created during the bubble—the problem was not that businesses could not afford to invest; it was that they did not want to. If a rate cut stimulated the economy, it would not be by inducing productive investment; it would be by inducing consumers to borrow and spend more. But household debt was already approaching a milestone: it was nudging 100 percent of disposable income, up from 72 percent when Greenspan had assumed office. By treating the hangover from the last bust, the Fed might store up trouble for the future.[34]

Pushing back against the naysayers, Greenspan returned to the specter of deflation. If the Fed did not act, it faced the danger of the zero lower bound, at which monetary policy would be neutered. "I don't think we could adjust all that easily if we were to fail to move and the economy began to deteriorate and we were looking into a deep deflationary hole," he said darkly.

With that, resistance melted. The chairman wrapped up the meeting by calling for a cut of fully 50 basis points, and everyone supported him.

"Not surprisingly, I do think that you're right," William McDonough of the New York Fed declared enthusiastically.

"I support a cut of 50 basis points. I'm delighted to support 50," announced Governor Edward Gramlich.

"I agree enthusiastically," said Bob McTeer of Dallas.

Dropping to 1.25 percent, the federal funds rate now sat at its lowest since the Kennedy era.

If Greenspan was determined to avoid stagnation, the Bush administration was even more eager. Starting in the summer of 2002, Vice President Dick Cheney had begun plotting to stimulate the economy with a second tax cut, and never mind the fact that the vast budget surpluses projected in 2001 had already evaporated. When O'Neill and Greenspan registered their concern about the return of budget deficits, Cheney simply pressed on. He would ignore "the munchkins at Treasury," as one confidant explained, and he cynically invoked the old supply-side myth that tax cuts would pay for themselves.[35]

Attempting to block Cheney, O'Neill took his objections directly to the president: he let it be known that if Bush wanted to go forward, then Bush would have to fire him.[36] But by now the Treasury secretary had played out his hand; his indignant self-righteousness had exhausted colleagues' patience. Unlike his friend Greenspan, O'Neill lacked the personality to survive Washington for long. In the first week of December 2002, Cheney called O'Neill with the president's response to his tax stand. Bush was indeed firing him.

With O'Neill out of the picture, Greenspan became the sole advocate of budgetary responsibility. He avoided threats and ultimatums and stuck scrupulously to facts, presenting Cheney with a Fed study on the effects of deficits. As he had explained to Clinton one decade earlier, higher government borrowing would drive long-term interest rates up, hurting the economy. A second round of tax cuts might stimulate spending, but only in the short run. Within a couple of years, the nation would be poorer for them.[37]

Greenspan hoped that Cheney would pass his warning to the president. Instead, Cheney passed the study to an adviser with instructions to poke holes in it. The Fed was "completely wrong" about its own data, the adviser faithfully concluded.[38]

"Reagan proved deficits don't matter," Cheney reportedly insisted at a White House staff meeting. "We won the midterms. This is our due."[39]

In January 2003, the administration went public with the details of its second tax cut. It was stunning in its scale: despite the fact that the budget was in the red, Bush proposed to wave good-bye to $700 billion worth of revenues over the next decade. Greenspan's advice had been ignored. The spirit of Jack Kemp was finally outmaneuvering him.

In February, Greenspan testified to Congress. He did not mince words.

"I am not one of those who is convinced that stimulus is desirable policy at this point," he declared.

"Fiscal stimulus is premature," he added for good measure.

Senator Jim Bunning, a supply-side supporter of the Bush tax cuts, looked for a way to hit back at him. He took aim at what he presumed must be Greenspan's weak spot. "You have been in this position for a long time," he growled. "Some would say too long."[40]

A few days later, a Bloomberg headline asked, "Greenspan's Days Numbered?"[41]

Greenspan's supply-side critics may have hoped that the chairman was a spent force, but others saw him differently. A month after the tax testimony, on Monday, March 24, the president himself summoned Greenspan to his office. Bush needed the Fed chairman's assistance at a time of national peril. American troops had invaded Iraq, supported by a rather short roster of allies.[42]

After the fight over the tax cuts, Greenspan was happy to be helpful. He had no trouble supporting the invasion, believing Iraq to be hiding weapons of mass destruction—this in a region that was critical to the world's oil supplies.[43] As the president requested, Greenspan stepped up his visits to the White House, often attending the 8:30 a.m. meetings convened by Stephen Friedman, who had replaced Lawrence Lindsey as chairman of the National Economic Council. The administration's top economic figures crowded around a table in Friedman's office on the second floor of the West Wing, poring over what they called the dashboard—data on everything from oil prices to airline bookings, which were updated and e-mailed several times each day to key government officials. Greenspan was in his element: he had analyzed the impact of war on the economy since Douglas MacArthur's landing at Inchon, and he dominated the bull sessions with his minute grasp of the energy market. By the middle of April, the peril seemed to be passing. Coalition forces secured Baghdad, and an American M88 armored recovery vehicle tore down the symbol of the dictator's cult of personality, a supersized bronze statue. The U.S. economy seemed to have survived. There had been no serious spike in oil prices, no major hit to global trade, and no panic on Wall Street.

On April 22, Greenspan made a trip to Baltimore and checked into the Johns Hopkins University Hospital, where he was to undergo surgery for an enlarged prostate. Even with the Iraq invasion dominating the nation's attention, the Greenspan watchers on cable television seized upon this urological news hook. The chairman would not need general anesthesia, a CNN financial reporter confided, "so perhaps the big question may be whether or not he'll reveal anything about interest rate policy to the surgeon."[44] By unplanned coincidence, other financial reporters were due to interview President Bush that same morning. Somebody asked about the Fed chairman's status. "I think Alan Greenspan should get another term," the president replied, almost casually.[45]

The answer caught everyone off guard. The S&P 500 staged an instant 2 percent rally, and no doubt Senator Bunning cursed silently. Given Greenspan's age and his opposition to the tax cuts, commentators had assumed that he might go when his fourth term expired the following summer. By then, Greenspan would have completed nearly seventeen years as the world's most powerful economist; and in any case, his reign had to end by early 2006, for although there were no limits to the number of times he could be appointed as chairman, his simultaneous appointment as a governor of the Fed was term limited. But, apparently, he was not leaving quite yet. "The president and I have not discussed this, but I greatly appreciate his confidence," Greenspan announced after returning home from his surgery. He sounded as surprised as anyone.[46]

However abrupt and premature it seemed, Bush's declaration of support was understandable. Greenspan's length of service made him difficult to replace; the longer he stayed, the more reassuring his presence. With the fighting in Iraq continuing, Bush wanted to keep economic headaches to a minimum, and the rally on Wall Street proved that continuity would boost confidence. In the judgment of the president's advisers, moreover, Greenspan showed no sign whatever of losing his edge. One senior White House figure noted that in addition to his tennis passion, Greenspan seemed particularly happy in his marriage, a factor that would ward off aging. "Did he seem old?" another one recalled. "No! I thought I was with Babe Ruth in 1927." Yet by postponing the eventual transition, the administration was courting trouble down the road. The reflexive faith in Greenspan built up his stature at the expense of the institution he led. Monetary policy was all maestro and no machine. A commentator in the *New York Times* complained that the Fed might be subsumed under a "cult of personality."[47]

By the summer of 2003, the modern iteration of the Hansen-Terborgh debate had yielded a split verdict. Aided by the short-run stimulus from the second Bush tax cut, which became law in May, growth was running at above 2 percent. The fear of secular stagnation appeared exaggerated. On the other hand, there was still no revival in business investment, and inflation remained disconcertingly below target. Having ticked up to 1.8 percent the previous autumn, the inflation rate had slipped back down to 1.5 percent in April and May 2003: the economy was apparently producing less than it could—there must be idle workers and machines, because otherwise supply bottlenecks would be pushing prices upward.[48] Still determined to root out deflation, Greenspan cut rates yet again in June, from 1.25 percent to 1 percent.

And then he went further. With the federal funds rate now perilously close to the zero lower bound, he embraced the manipulation of expectations he had resisted since the 1970s. Given that there was a limit to how much he could cut short-term interest rates, he shifted to pulling down longer-term interest rates by guiding the markets about his future policy. And what was most surprising was the driver of this intellectual switch. For the first time in Greenspan's tenure, the prime mover of monetary policy was not actually Greenspan himself. Instead, it was Ben Bernanke, the quiet Princeton professor who had made the case for inflation targeting in Jackson Hole four years earlier.

The Bush administration had appointed Bernanke to the Fed's board the previous summer. His elevation had come alongside that of Don Kohn, Greenspan's close ally; this was a case of wining some and losing some, for Greenspan had not been thrilled at Bernanke's arrival—the last eminent Princeton economist to serve on the FOMC had been the disputatious Alan Blinder. But whereas Blinder had immediately been touted as a likely contender for the Fed chairmanship, Bernanke generated no such talk, and the mild modesty of his manner betrayed no hint of ambition.[49] Precisely because he seemed so unassuming, Greenspan allowed him space to stretch. A few months into his tenure, Bernanke made a widely noted speech about strategies to get around the zero lower bound. Now, in the summer of 2003, Bernanke weighed in again, extending his thinking on the response to lowflation.

True to the arguments he had made at Jackson Hole, Bernanke believed that the Fed should publicly commit to an inflation target. If the commitment was explicit, investors would understand that low inflation would cause monetary policy to stay loose for an extended period; as a result, they would bid down longer interest rates, creating the economic stimulus the Fed wanted. But Bernanke was a wilier politician than his ivory-tower manner suggested. Knowing that Greenspan was determined to preserve monetary discretion, Bernanke devised a more modest proposal: the Fed should announce what it regarded as an acceptable *range* for inflation.[50] By communicating that range clearly to the public, the Fed could multiply the power of its interest-rate tool "many times over," Bernanke insisted at the FOMC meeting in June 2003. Monetary policy, he would later say, is 98 percent talk and 2 percent action.

"Ambiguity has its uses but mostly in non-cooperative games like poker," Bernanke explained to his FOMC colleagues. "Monetary policy is a cooperative game. The whole point is to get financial markets on our side and for them to do some of our work for us."

Greenspan thanked Bernanke for his remarks and then largely ignored them.[51] He was not yet ready to compromise his precious discretion by telling the markets what he planned for the future. But over the next weeks, the economy conspired to bring him around. The strange combination of recovery and lowflation grew more pronounced: in the third quarter of 2003, growth accelerated to 6.9 percent, yet inflation slipped downward. This paradoxical mixture left the bond market guessing about the Fed's response. Perhaps the Fed would focus on the growth part of the picture, raising interest rates to cool things down. This would follow the pattern of 1994, when the Fed had raised interest rates in response to strong growth, before inflation had materialized. Or perhaps the Fed would focus on the fall in inflation, in which case it would pursue the opposite policy: it would cut interest rates. In the absence of clear communication, investors were fumbling in the dark. Wrongly plumping for the first theory—that the Fed would focus on strong growth and so raise the interest rate—they drove long-term rates up by a full percentage point by the end of July. It was the opposite of what Greenspan had wanted.

"I have some concerns about our communication," Bernanke reiterated at the next FOMC meeting, in August. So long as the Fed refused to speak clearly, perverse misunderstandings were inevitable.

"We've seen in the last two meetings that our words have been far more powerful than our policy decision in terms of changing markets," Bernanke added later in the discussion. "Our communications are a very, very powerful tool.

"Now, the reaction of the Committee has been that it's so powerful that perhaps we want to stay away from it completely," he added, drawing laughter from around the table.

"But if we give no information about our future intentions, then somehow or another the market has to make an assumption or come to some conclusion about what our policy is going to be. The presumption, therefore, is that we are so bad at giving information that we better leave it to the market to draw information from nothing. I don't want to be that pessimistic."

Bernanke's logic was irrefutable: he had exposed the Dr. Strangelove quality of Greenspan's unannounced inflation target. Whether the Fed should focus exclusively on inflation was doubtful, given the disruptive power of financial bubbles. But if the Fed decided to target inflation, it would be better off saying so.

Early in Greenspan's tenure, Don Kohn had headed off an early call for inflation targeting, declaring, "It's what we do more than what we say—read our actions rather than our lips."[52] Now, however, Kohn acknowledged Bernanke's point. "We need to work on how we talk about our assessments and judgments," he conceded.

Some wrangling ensued about how to put Bernanke's insight into practice, and the committee converged on the idea of extending the FOMC's postmeeting statement. The staff was ready with a draft that said low interest rates were likely to be maintained "for a considerable period."

Not everyone was happy. The statement had already stipulated that the FOMC viewed "undesirably low" inflation as the main risk for the foreseeable future. Why take the additional step of spelling out that low inflation called for low interest rates?

"I would appeal to the Committee to retain the sentence because in my view it makes a very big difference," Bernanke insisted. Once upon a time, an earlier generation of central bankers had swayed gentleman financiers with the flicker of eyebrows. Now that clubby bankers had been displaced by impersonal markets, arched eyebrows were giving way to arch sentences.

Rather unusually, Greenspan put the matter to a vote. Seven of eighteen FOMC members wanted to drop the extra sentence. A narrow majority sided with Bernanke in favoring it.

With that, a shortened version of the additional sentence made its way into the postmeeting statement. The FOMC had gone from guiding the markets about its view of the economy to telling them explicitly what it expected to do with interest rates. This experiment with "forward guidance" fell short of the proposal for a publicly announced inflation target, and it was timid compared with the experiments conducted by the Fed when the problem of the zero lower bound returned with a vengeance after 2008. But it was a new departure nonetheless. In its long march from secrecy to transparency, the Fed had crossed another watershed.

At the FOMC's next meeting, in September 2003, Greenspan grumbled that he regretted the experiment.[53] But the promise to keep interest rates low for a "considerable period" stuck, and by the end of the year, the chairman had embraced it. Contemplating an inflation rate that had at last stabilized and growth that continued to be strong, he acknowledged that Bernanke had been right. "Our effort to communicate that message succeeded," he declared in December.

And yet, not for the first time, success created its own dangers. Rock-bottom interest rates, coupled with the assurance that they would remain low "for a considerable period," achieved exactly what they were supposed to achieve: more borrowing. In the last quarter of 2003, the number of outstanding subprime mortgages doubled, according to an industry survey.[54] The nation's home-ownership rate climbed to 68.5 percent, its highest level ever.[55]

Twenty-eight

THE FOUR WINDS

In the last months of World War I, the British government convened a commission on the future of monetary policy. Weighing the opinions of twenty-three experts, it found unanimous support for a return to the prewar gold standard.[1] Gold was seen as a pillar of a free society, a bulwark against government abuse; there was no other tried and tested basis on which to rebuild international finance. And yet despite this expert unanimity, the decision to return to the gold standard proved disastrous, both in Britain and abroad: until it was abandoned, it deprived the monetary authorities of the tools to fight the Depression. At the end of his life, Montagu Norman, the revered governor of the Bank of England and chief personifier of the gold pledge, offered a poignant confession. "With all the thought and work and good intentions, which we provided, we achieved absolutely nothing . . . we collected money from a lot of poor devils and gave it over to the four winds."[2]

Three quarters of a century later, an idea that could be thought of as the opposite of the gold standard was similarly tarnished. It consisted of a broad faith in financial innovation: the conviction that a few spectacular mishaps notwithstanding, the paraphernalia of tradable risks and income streams was a force for progress. Whereas the gold standard had promised sober discipline—it would prevent governments and private lenders from creating money and credit promiscuously—modern finance promised exhilarating license. By isolating risks and dispersing them, it would allow companies and families to borrow more, and safely: the primitive strait-jacket of gold would be displaced by the permissive elegance of risk-measurement models. But just as the progold consensus of 1918 led to disaster, so the modern tolerance for financial innovation turned out to be too trusting. Alan Greenspan, the revered chairman of the Fed and chief personifier of the new instruments, would see his reputation suffer—although he would never quite match Norman in declaring his life's work to have been futile.

When ideas succeed in one period and then fail in the next one, it is because the conditions required for their success have been eroded. The gold standard underpinned a period of advance in the late nineteenth century; then, after World War I brought about a lopsided distribution of gold among the main economies, it became a catastrophe waiting to happen. Similarly, the faith in modern finance served the advanced economies well for some four decades, spanning the first breaches of Regulation Q in the early 1960s to the profusion of securitization and derivatives in the early 2000s. But then, by an alchemy that almost no contemporary appreciated, finance tipped into a dark zone. Experiments that had once been merely bold became outrightly brazen. Risks that had never been large enough to threaten the entire system took on an unimaginable scale.

The tipping point came somewhere around 2004, when the fans of the Texas Rangers baseball team were introduced to a new name—not Alfonso Soriano or Joaquín Arias, the players traded by the New York Yankees earlier that year; and not Gerald Laird, the team's new starting catcher. Rather, the new name belonged to the ballpark—Ameriquest Field in Arlington—after the Rangers signed a $75 million sponsorship deal with the nation's largest subprime mortgage lender.[3] Around the same time, Ameriquest's chief rival, an upstart named Countrywide, splurged on underwriting golf tournaments; and the mortgage division of the big West Coast lender Wells Fargo almost courted an image of imprudence by sponsoring extreme sailing.[4] Angelo Mozilo, the boss of Countrywide, would stand up in front of investors in this period and rattle off a startling list of mortgages. "We have ARMs, one-year ARMs, three-year, five-year, seven- and 10-year," he would say dizzily, referring to the adjustable-rate mortgages that Countrywide peddled. "We have interest-only loans, pay-option loans, zero-down programs, low-, no-doc programs, fast-and-easy programs, and subprime loans."[5] He sounded for all the world like a carnival barker.

The new mortgage mania was a grotesque caricature of the healthy innovation that had come before. In the past, borrowers with slightly dubious credit had turned to subprime lenders who overlooked their weaknesses in return for higher interest payments; this was financial flexibility of the reasonable sort. Now borrowers with truly awful credit could borrow without even documenting their earnings, which was not reasonable at all.[6] In the past, similarly, borrowers with temporarily low incomes—for example, a couple in which one partner was taking time out to complete college—could get a mortgage with a low initial rate that would go up after a year or two. Now adjustable-rate mortgages were abused to give borrowers an early repayment holiday in exchange for punitive rates later, with no obvious reason to expect the borrowers' incomes to rise commensurately. The old practice of requiring home buyers to make a down payment out of their own savings was thrown to the four winds also, so that now a decline in house prices would leave them with no equity in their homes. "Ten years ago, if I offered to buy your house with a 100 percent loan, you would have called it 'creative financing' and thought I was crooked," observed a real estate agent in Anaheim. "Today, everybody wants a 100 percent loan."[7]

By the middle of 2004, the mortgage industry was on track to pump out almost double the volume of subprime loans it had made one year earlier.[8] Even more alarmingly, fully one third of subprime mortgages were being extended without meaningful assessments of borrowers' financial status, and borrowers were seduced with all manner of payment holidays that increased their indebtedness later.[9] Far from registering anxiety about this mania, the mortgage firms presented it as progress. Thanks to computerized mortgage underwriting, default risks could be calibrated without formal documentation of income, or so the lenders asserted; loans with minimal credit checks were gloriously liberating, not menacingly dangerous. But the reality was less comforting, for this blizzard of new-fangled mortgages was intimately connected with another financial trans-formation. Increasingly, the firm that originated a mortgage was not the firm that held it for the long term; instead, banks and other lenders were selling the mortgages to firms that bundled them together and sliced them into securities that were then resold to distant investors. Not only did this allow lenders like Ameriquest and Countrywide to maximize the number of mortgages they could churn out on relatively little capital, but it also minimized the amount of risk they took on in the process. If borrowers defaulted, it was not Ameriquest's or Countrywide's problem. No wonder Angelo Mozilo stood ready to lend to just about anyone.

This packaging and securitizing of mortgages was another example of a practice that had worked well for a long period and then tipped into a crazy zone. Like the earlier, more reasonable incarnations of subprime lending, the early mortgage-backed securities had mostly been healthy for the financial system—the claim that they allowed default risks to be dispersed widely was in fact true. But then this trend reached its extreme limits. Rather than merely turning mortgages into mortgage securities, financiers began to issue securities backed by other securities, creating strange instruments known as "collateralized debt obligations, squared." A complex tiering was superimposed on these confections, with "senior" tranches of CDOs and CDOs-squared having the first claim on repay-ments and "junior" tranches accepting greater default risks in exchange for higher interest payments. The more byzantine the construction, the harder it became for investors to understand what they were purchasing. "We had meetings where I would say, 'Are you sure you're comfortable with that?'" one mortgage executive recalled later. "And they would bring in the quants!"[10]

Taken by themselves, none of these experiments would have been too dangerous. But the cocktail of "no-doc" lending, zero-down payments, and opaquely complex mortgage derivatives mixed perilously with other factors. The government was pushing Fannie and Freddie to lend more to low-income borrowers, and the GSEs responded by loading up on sub-prime mortgages, stoking the mania with a big increase in demand. Meanwhile, the loose monetary policy Greenspan had adopted out of fear of a Japan-style slump was bearing down on interest rates, and investors grew desperate for the income promised by mortgages, no matter how opaque the tiering or how scant the documentation. So strong was the appetite that three out of every four new conventional, "prime" home loans were securitized in 2004, up from one out of two just four years earlier. The securitization rate for higher-yielding subprime loans took off like a rocket, soaring from 40 percent to 73 percent over the same four years. It would peak at nearly 93 percent on the eve of the financial crisis.

Because of investors' insatiable demand for mortgage securities, mortgage originators had no incentive to lend carefully; all that mattered was to lend copiously. Loan officers at Ameriquest were made to put in "power hours," nonstop cold-calling sessions to potential borrowers; those who racked up big numbers won trips to Hawaii and the Super Bowl, while those who failed to win new customers were thrown overboard. "I was told I was going to be fired at least 200 times," an Ameriquest employee recalled later; the boss would constantly be asking him, "Why can't you do more?" A movie called *Boiler Room,* which captured the culture of fast-talking stock swindlers, became required watching at some Ameriquest branches. The film imbued employees with "the energy, the impact, the driving, the hustling"—the full menu of qualities, in other words, that would spur a frightened sales team to inflate the mother of all bubbles.[11]

By this stage in his life, none of these developments should have surprised Greenspan. He had watched financiers overreach repeatedly since the collapse of Penn Central in 1970; he had seen Charles S. Sanford, the hapless boss of Bankers Trust, fail to understand the complex swaps that his sorcerers supplied to Procter & Gamble and Gibson Greeting

Cards. If the Bankers Trust traders had talked about the "ROF factor," or rip-off factor, back in 1994, it ought to have been obvious that the byzantine CDOs-squared were intended to bamboozle clients—"to lure people into that calm and then just totally fuck 'em," as a Bankers Trust trader had put it. But Greenspan had long since arrived at a position about finance that mirrored his position on bubbles. He understood that financiers could be foolish, and sometimes even fraudulent, but he doubted that the Fed had the manpower or the political mandate to restrain them. "Where we are most vulnerable is with regard to the adequacy of our examinations," Greenspan had observed after the Fed's failure to restrain the banks that had lent heedlessly to Long-Term Capital Management. "If we had to meet the standards that people think exist, we would have five times as many examiners."

Having arrived at this conclusion, Greenspan had embraced a pair of assumptions that he knew to be precarious. First, however reckless financiers might sometimes be, their risk managers would generally restrain them, perhaps prodded by regulators who might help at the margin. Second, when risk management did fail, the Fed would clean up afterward—disciplining miscreants like Bankers Trust, bailing out banks like Continental Illinois, cutting interest rates aggressively in the face of shocks such as the failure of Long-Term Capital Management. Like the pre-1914 gold standard, these assumptions had held up over a long period.[12] There had been crises, certainly. But cleaning up afterward had more or less succeeded.

Because of this mind-set, Greenspan refused to act preemptively to curb the feverish mortgage market in 2004. "American consumers might benefit if lenders provided greater mortgage product alternatives," he told an audience in February, apparently unperturbed by the eye-popping buffet of mortgages that was already on offer.[13] "Risk modeling has improved in accuracy and will continue to do so," he announced cheerfully in April, as though the quants at Ameriquest and Countrywide could be relied upon to manage risks safely.[14] With the unfair benefit of hindsight, this sunny complacency was a clear error, because a regulatory clampdown on wild mortgages and securitization could in principle have addressed the 2008 crisis at the source, mitigating the damage far more directly than tighter monetary policy could have. But if we are to draw the right lessons from this episode, it is important to be clear that Greenspan did not commit this error absentmindedly, and he was not alone. Just as the gold standard commanded near-universal confidence in Britain in 1918, so Greenspan's complacency on housing was shared by nearly everyone.

This point bears emphasizing because, in the years after the crisis, a contrary narrative emerged. According to this imagined history, Greenspan was warned about the coming real estate meltdown and took it upon himself to do nothing. For instance, the Greenlining Institute, an organization seeking to protect minorities from predatory lending, sent Greenspan a pile of mortgage documents showing how opaque the new loans could be. "Even if you had a doctorate in math, you wouldn't understand these instruments and their implications," Greenspan reportedly acknowledged during a follow-up meeting.[15] In another example, a delegate from the National Community Reinvestment Coalition pointed Fed officials toward examples of predatory lending. "Their response was that the market would correct any problems," the delegate recalled after the crisis; "Greenspan in particular believed that the market would not produce, and investment banks would not buy, loans that did not make sense."[16] But quite apart from the question of whether a handful of suggestive conversations constitutes a real warning, the key problem in the anti-Greenspan narrative lies in what the consumer advocates were saying. They were not predicting a threat to the financial system; rather, they were advancing a narrower claim that the Fed should protect vulnerable groups from imprudent borrowing.[17] Most prominent mortgage critics, in other words, failed to connect the dots between sharp sales practices and the risk of a financial crisis.[18] And this was only natural. Subprime lending and mortgage securitization had been around for years without triggering a catastrophe.

This failure to connect the dots between abusive lending and systemic risk is illustrated by the story of Edward Gramlich. Tall, affable, and possessed of a kindly humor, Gramlich was the Fed governor in charge of the consumer and community affairs committee, the perfect platform from which to sound the warning about predatory home lending. As early as the summer of 2000, Gramlich duly held hearings around the country, soliciting complaints from residents and activists about abusive mort-gages.[19] Sure enough, he found horror stories aplenty. Borrowers had been bamboozled with surprise fees, altered documents, unnecessary refinanc-ings, and disclosure forms more convoluted than a Pynchon novel.

"I wish you guys could do something," fumed one home owner from Brockton, Massachusetts. "We pray to a higher God up above, a spiritual God. These people that are doing these loans, they're praying to a higher money called the color green."[20]

Gramlich was sympathetic. If there was clear evidence of abusive lend-ing, he wanted the details.

At one of the hearings, the chief legal counsel of Countrywide ex-plained why his firm regularly lent to people who could not prove their earnings.

"If you can't document the income, how do you know the income, and how do you know they can pay the loan back?" Gramlich demanded.

"I would say that there are certain reality checks, let's just say," the Countrywide man waffled. If a waiter claimed to earn $300,000, the appli-cation would be denied, he went on. "So it is a more difficult—it's a more difficult task."

The answer sounded shifty. But after sitting through hours of hearings in four cities, Gramlich was still uncertain of how much abuse was really going on. He had to weigh complaints of predatory lending against com-plaints of the opposite variety: activists frequently lamented that banks refused to lend to low-income borrowers, even at a premium interest rate. A blanket clampdown on subprime mortgages would deprive some legiti-mate borrowers of a shot at home ownership; if the Fed acted heavy-handedly, the poor might suffer. And even if Countrywide's legal counsel was annoyingly evasive, presumably the risk managers at his company had quantified their exposure? Not knowing what to make of all this, Gram-lich asked his staff to design a "pilot program" of spot checks on six to eight mortgage lenders in the hope of gathering more evidence.

What happened next would later be the subject of controversy. At some point in the late summer of 2000, Gramlich suggested the pilot program privately to Greenspan, and Greenspan expressed doubts; in the years after the crisis, this was held up as the moment when the laissez-faire chairman condemned the nation to the subprime meltdown. "He was opposed to it, so I didn't really pursue it," Gramlich told the *Wall Street Journal* in 2007; "Did Greenspan Add to Subprime Woes?" ran the title of the *Journal*'s article.[21] Up to a point, the implied criticism was justified: if Gramlich's pilot program had been pursued, the Fed might have curbed lending abuses, slowing the gusher of uncollectable loans that fueled the financial crisis. Perhaps, to push the point a little further, the pilot program might have led the Fed to a broader understanding of the mortgage mania, which in turn might have alerted it to the perils in extreme securitization: on this theory, predatory lending was the smoke that might have led Greenspan to the fire.[22] But the awkward truth is that Gramlich left Greenspan plenty of room to doubt his pilot program. The spot checks would be "limited in scope," as a Fed staff memo noted, but they would also be "resource intensive"—hardly a seductive combination. It was by no means certain that the checks would turn up evidence of abuses sufficient to warrant a clampdown; yet they were likely to "raise expectations," as the staff memo put it, exposing the Fed to "more intense public and political criticism if it decides not to go forward."[23] In sum, Gramlich was proposing an expensive fishing expedition that might cause political trouble and have limited effect. It is understandable—if not, in hindsight, commendable—that Greenspan balked.

Gramlich himself seems to have believed that Greenspan was being reasonable. Once the chairman had registered his resistance, Gramlich dropped his proposed pilot program quietly—hardly a sign that he had overwhelming faith in it. "When Ned was on to something, he was tenacious," a fellow governor recalled later, citing Gramlich's insistent advocacy on other issues. In this instance, however, Gramlich chose not to press his case.[24]

That was neither man's last word on predatory lending, however. Over the next weeks, Gramlich's staff considered other ways of reining in the kinds of abuses reported at that summer's hearings. This time, rather than proposing a pilot program of inspections, they crafted a series of consumer-protection rules for the most abusive lending practices.

Writing these rules involved delicate judgments. There was a fine line between measures that prevented consumer rip-offs and measures that smothered consumer choice. If the Fed banned all no-doc loans on the ground that they were too risky, for example, shopkeepers and other small-business owners might have trouble buying a home: because they were self-employed, they lacked standard wage documents.[25] If the Fed banned adjustable-rate mortgages, it might likewise penalize workers who could genuinely expect to earn more in the future. To get around this sort of problem, the Fed staff decided against banning a specific set of mortgage practices. Instead, it required lenders to make a good-faith judgment about a loan's impact on the borrower.

In December 2001, the staff presented the proposed rules to the Fed's board. The directives aimed among other things to stop lenders packing mortgages full of exorbitant insurance fees. They also prohibited refinancings that were not "in the borrower's interest."

Greenspan was uncomfortable with that last provision. "In the borrower's interest" sounded vague. He preferred bright lines to mushy exhortations.

"Who makes that calculation?" Greenspan demanded.

The staff replied that the creditor would make it.

"How does he make that?" Greenspan pressed.

It's the "totality of the circumstances," the staffer answered.

"In other words, it's their judgment, but they are responsible to defend it if challenged?"

"That's correct."[26]

Evidently, if the rules were approved, lenders would have to retain lawyers to advise them on the meaning of "borrower's interest," not to mention "totality of circumstances." The cost of compliance would push mortgage costs up, perhaps hurting the very borrowers whom the Fed sought to protect. The advantages of regulation had to be weighed against the costs. It was hard to be sure what the right balance was.

To make matters worse, approval of the rules did not guarantee their enforcement. The Fed had the authority to inspect bank-holding companies and, at least in theory, their subsidiaries, but myriad lenders fell outside its net; the Fed would have to depend on an alphabet soup of other regulatory agencies to help enforce its mortgage policies. Some of these agencies were underfunded and short on expert staff; the Federal Trade Commission, which had authority over nonbank mortgage originators, did not conduct any on-site inspections.[27] Uneven supervision would surely drive unscrupulous lenders into the arms of the agencies least equipped to restrain them.

Presently, Edward Gramlich spoke up. Contrary to the later myth that grew up around him, he downplayed the gains to be had from writing stricter mortgage rules. Instead, he pinned his hopes elsewhere, telling the board that "the very best defense is education and financial literacy."[28]

Despite these reasonable misgivings about the proposed rules, the board voted unanimously to approve them. Again contrary to later myth, the Greenspan Fed did at least attempt to curtail mortgage abuses. Years later, with the benefit of hindsight, it became obvious that the Fed should have gone further: in 2008, the Fed issued tougher rules, requiring among other things that borrowers' tax and insurance payments be factored into the calculation of the size of mortgage they could afford. But in the early 2000s, almost nobody wanted to go that far—not the regulators on the Fed staff, not Edward Gramlich, and certainly not Congress. Moreover, the results of Greenspan's regulatory effort seemed partially to validate the misgivings. Subprime lenders skirted the new regulations by tweaking their methods; for example, when they were forbidden to extract extra fees by refinancing a home more than once in a year, they simply waited 366 days before flipping a customer from one mortgage to the next one. Within a few years, the Fed's 2001 rule making had been almost entirely evaded: originally, the Fed's staff had estimated that the rules would affect 38 percent of subprime loans; by the end of 2005, they affected about 1 percent.[29] Perhaps discouraged by this experience, nobody at the Fed pushed for additional mortgage restrictions until the end of Greenspan's tenure.

In August 2007, a fortnight before dying of cancer, Gramlich wrote a farewell letter to Greenspan.

"I thought you were a magnificent central banker and a great leader,"

Gramlich wrote graciously, before adding, "I suppose we all go out with one item of unfinished business."

Referring to the recent *Wall Street Journal* article, which recounted how Greenspan had blocked his pilot program, Gramlich went on, "For me it is that I truly wish the press would stop kicking you around on this subprime supervision issue. What happened was a small incident, and as I think you know, if I had felt that strongly at the time, I would have made a bigger stink.

"But that aside, I will always treasure our days together."[30]

The Fed's attempted clampdown on mortgage abuses in 2001 underlined Greenspan's pragmatism. Despite his reputation as a laissez-faire ideologue, he was prepared to countenance regulation when the case seemed reasonable, even though he generally believed that private risk managers would perform better than government overseers. The same pragmatism was evident following the Enron scandal, when Greenspan advocated tougher regulation of corporate accounting and spoke out against Fannie Mae and Freddie Mac, the two GSEs that owned or guaranteed nearly half of all mortgages. Moreover, in 2004, Greenspan went back on the offensive against the mortgage giants.

Greenspan's position on the GSEs had not always been a profile in courage. Ever since his diagnosis of the 1970s housing boom, he had understood how they could warp finance; but whereas he had fought doggedly to protect the Fed's monetary independence and its supervisory turf, he had deliberately sidestepped the challenge of reining in Fannie and Freddie. In the early 1990s, for example, a staff economist in the Senate conceived a plan to curb the GSEs by empowering the Fed to regulate them; as soon as Greenspan got wind of this idea, he placed a call to the startled economist and bluntly declared that the Fed would not accept this mission.[31] Later in the 1990s, Greenspan learned that Richard Baker, the Louisiana congressman who chaired the House Subcommittee on Capital Markets, was plotting legislation to contain the GSEs; Greenspan invited Baker over to breakfast, congratulated him on doing the right thing, but stressed that he could support his efforts only privately.[32] In the last year of the Clinton administration, both Baker and the Treasury revived the notion that the Fed could oversee Fannie and Freddie. Again, Greenspan declined. He was happy to advise behind the scenes. He was not going to risk a head-on fight with the GSEs' lobbyists.

Greenspan's veiled attack on the mortgage giants in 2002 had signaled a new willingness to stick his neck out. Egged on by politicians from both parties who loved to preach the merits of home ownership while pocketing campaign contributions from Fannie and Freddie, the housing giants had grown to such a size that they could not be ignored any longer. Whereas individual mortgage originators such as Ameriquest and Countrywide appeared too small to pose a risk to the financial system as a whole, the GSEs were clearly large enough to do so. Worse, the logic of the GSEs' subsidies created a perverse incentive to grow even bigger. The more they expanded, the nastier the mayhem if they went bust—and therefore the stronger the presumption of a government backstop, which in turn enabled them to borrow even more cheaply. The subsidy from the implicit backstop empowered them to grab market share, which in turn empowered them to grab more subsidies.

In February 2004, Greenspan testified before the Senate. Pointing to the fact that the GSEs' expanding portfolios were backed by extraordinarily thin buffers of capital, he gave warning of "a systemic risk sometime in the future."[33] To avert such a crisis, Greenspan continued, the government would have to step in. The GSEs needed a serious regulator, and that regulator should cap the size of their portfolios.

Senator Richard Shelby, the chairman of the banking committee, followed Greenspan's observation to its natural conclusion. If the GSEs were too big to fail, weren't megabanks also a problem?

"What about large banking institutions like Citigroup or Bank of America?" Shelby asked. "Do they receive a similar funding advantage?"

"I think they receive some," Greenspan answered, frankly acknowledging the risk posed by behemoths that had grown up on his watch.

"Have you ever quantified that, has anybody at the Federal Reserve?" Shelby wondered. He was inviting Greenspan to explain why the GSEs should be singled out for special attention. Was the Fed chairman merely acting on his libertarian bias—on a prejudice that government-chartered lenders were intrinsically more troubling than private ones?

Greenspan insisted otherwise. Yes, he told the senator, the megabanks could borrow slightly more cheaply because they might be too big to fail, but these subsidies had indeed been quantified—and they were far smaller than for the mortgage giants. Besides, banks maintained thicker capital cushions and were subjected to more supervision. Greenspan was targeting Fannie and Freddie on the basis of facts, not ideology.

"But there is a perception by some people that some of the largest banks are too big to fail," Shelby pressed again.

Greenspan stood his ground. "If you look at the prices of their securities in the marketplace," he said, referring to the banks, "it's fairly evident that there is very considerable question as to whether in the event of failure that they will in fact be bailed out. That is far less the case on the part of the securities of Fannie and Freddie."

Greenspan was right. Market data, not Friedrich Hayek or Ayn Rand, informed his regulatory focus. And the market's response to his testimony underlined his point. By the end of the day, the GSEs' stock prices had fallen by around 3 percent. Evidently, their valuations were based on the presumption that Washington would underwrite their expansion. Some tough words from the Fed chief were enough to raise doubts about that.

Even before Greenspan finished speaking, however, the mortgage giants counterattacked. Showing remarkably little deference to Greenspan's stature, Fannie Mae rushed out a statement, brazenly accusing him of misunderstanding the mortgage business.

"The testimony does not appreciate the role of our mortgage portfolio," Fannie's statement complained. Limits "on Fannie Mae's mortgage portfolio business would force the housing finance system to rely more on large banks, which are not required—or structured—to . . . lower mortgage costs."

There was barely any truth in Fannie's complaint: the GSE portfolios did almost nothing to make mortgages cheaper for home buyers. Indeed, Fed researchers had recently measured the reduction and found it to be vanishingly small. The GSEs' borrowing subsidies enriched their shareholders and executives, not their borrowers.[34]

Fannie's denunciation of Greenspan was soon followed by Freddie's. It was regrettable that the chairman had diverted attention from important matters "to a more theoretical discussion," Freddie said gravely; restricting the GSEs' portfolio size would "increase the cost of mortgages for America's homebuyers."[35] There was that same lie, again. The giants were clearly not going to give up on it.

Five weeks later, the Senate returned to the question of restrictions on GSEs. The day before the hearing, an ad appeared on television.

The screen showed a worried-looking Hispanic couple.

Man: "Uh-oh."

Woman: "What?"

Man: "It looks like Congress is talking about new regulations for Fannie Mae."

Woman: "Will that keep us from getting that lower mortgage rate?"

Man: "Some economists say rates may go up."

Woman: "But that could mean we won't be able to afford the new house."

Man: "I know."

This time the big lie demonstrated an even bigger truth. Government subsidies to the mortgage giants might not reduce the cost of housing loans; but they did generate a political war chest, enabling Fannie to run TV commercials. Subsidies paid for ads aimed at perpetuating subsidies.

"Here is an organization that was created by the Congress . . . spending money questioning the Congress's right to take a serious look at oversight . . ." sputtered Senator Chuck Hagel. "I find it astounding. Astounding!"[36]

As shameless as Fannie and Freddie might be, there was no doubting their effectiveness. The TV commercial sent out an unmistakable message: members of Congress who voted to cap the GSEs' portfolio size would have to run for reelection against a barrage of mendacious ads in their home districts. Not at all surprisingly, the majority of lawmakers took fright; and by the late spring of 2004, the mortgage giants had emerged victorious. Never mind what the White House and the Fed chairman might urge. There would be no new regulation.

Greenspan's failure on the GSEs compounded his inaction on the mounting excesses in the private mortgage market. He had attempted to curb Fannie and Freddie, testifying insistently to Senator Shelby on why they posed unusual risks, but his efforts had proved inadequate. He had averted his eyes from private mortgage originators like Countrywide, although, in his defense, neither consumer advocates nor his own staff flagged them as a systemic menace. The fact that Greenspan's actions were ineffectual and yet somewhat understandable stands as a warning to his successors. After the 2008 meltdown, central bankers resolved to use regulatory policy, not monetary policy, to head off the next crisis. But regulatory tools are hard to wield. They involve confronting brutal lobbies: witness Fannie's TV ad. They involve interpreting vague reports of market abuses: witness Edward Gramlich's diffident advocacy of a pilot supervisory program. And they involve writing rules that are flexible enough not to be oppressive, yet tough enough to change behavior. This is a tricky balance to strike: witness the failure of the Fed's attempt in 2001 to clamp down on subprime abuses. Moreover, these challenges in implementing regulation extended beyond mortgage origination to other bits of the food chain—notably to the Wall Street banks that packaged, securitized, or invested in home loans.

In November 2003, Greenspan acquired a new lieutenant at the New York Fed: a hard-charging forty-two-year-old named Timothy Geithner. Fit, foulmouthed, boyishly cherubic in his looks, Geithner was a protégé of Bob Rubin, whose ability to catapult favorites into lofty jobs was legendary. Now, having spent the 1990s at the Treasury handling emerging-market crises, Geithner brought his experience with collapse to the task of regulating Wall Street. Knowing that regulators could not anticipate where the next shock would come from, Geithner aimed to boost the financial system's overall resilience. He notched up some considerable victories—in particular, the plumbing of the derivatives market, which had consisted of a frightening mess of unconfirmed paper trades, was modernized, silencing one dog that would otherwise have barked during the 2008 crisis. But Geithner also wanted to increase Wall Street's capital buffers so that the big houses could weather unanticipated shocks. On this goal, he soon ran up against the limits of regulation.

The idea of requiring banks to hold more capital had enthralled regulators, including Greenspan, since the 1980s. Paul Volcker had conspired successfully with the Bank of England to force the Basel Accord on banks, laying down the minimum amount of capital relative to loan portfolios. But as Greenspan had noted after the Continental Illinois disaster, there was no certain way to determine how much capital was right—much depended on the types of risks that banks shouldered. Now, as Geithner tried to build more robust buffers into the financial system, this lack of objective criteria became a problem. He could form his own judgment about the right amount of capital, and attempt to force it on the banks that came under his jurisdiction. But then borrowing and lending would migrate to institutions that lay outside the Fed's purview: to investment houses such as Bear Stearns; to Fannie and Freddie; to myriad "shadow banks"—money-market funds, auto-loan providers, and so on. Because it was hard to demonstrate conclusively how much capital these players required, nobody was going to stop them from carrying on as they were: the difficulty in specifying bright-line rules combined with the fragmentation of the regulatory system to frustrate Geithner's quest for resiliency. "Our capital buffers were too thin, but they were already thick enough to drive trillions of dollars of assets—more than were in the entire commercial banking system—outside our direct supervision," Geithner recalled ruefully.[37]

Determined not to give up, Geithner attempted to gain traction over investment banks and shadow banks via what he called the indirect channel. He prodded the banks he did supervise to demand larger buffers at the less regulated players they dealt with. If the New York Fed lacked the direct authority to get shadow banks to build up more resiliency, perhaps it could get at them by generating peer pressure.

To ensure he had support for this approach, Geithner checked in with the Fed chairman.

"That's what you're supposed to do," Greenspan assured him.[38]

And yet, despite Greenspan's blessing, Geithner's push for extra capital ended in failure. It was one thing to demand better plumbing in the derivatives market—the banks recognized that this was in their own interest. It was quite another to demand thicker capital buffers in a financial environment in which traders lusted for more risk. And so, in the end, the Fed's efforts did little to promote resiliency. "The Wild West with better plumbing was still the Wild West," Geithner conceded.[39]

If the Fed's regulatory defeats stand as a warning to Greenspan's successors, its monetary debates challenge the postcrisis consensus on interest rates and asset bubbles. After 2008, central bankers and economists generally concluded that monetary policy had been almost irrelevant to the mortgage bubble. In a speech in January 2010, for example, Ben Bernanke, who by then had succeeded Greenspan as Fed chairman, declared that "only a small portion of the increase in house prices earlier this decade can be attributed to the stance of U.S. monetary policy"; and in a paper published by the Brookings Institution the following spring, Greenspan presented his own version of this argument.[40] And yet at the time the bubble was inflating, this claim of monetary impotence would have been regarded as strange. Greenspan and his FOMC colleagues took it for granted in 2004 that monetary policy was affecting asset prices, including house prices.

This recognition was evident during the FOMC discussion at the end of January 2004, for example. By now the federal funds rate had been down at 1 percent for seven months, and the Fed had pledged to stay loose for a "considerable period" after four successive meetings. Over the same seven-month period, the S&P 500 index had gained almost a fifth. Investors had bid down the interest rates on mortgage securities until they were barely higher than safe government bonds. As a result, mortgage lending was booming. House prices had leaped by a tenth over the period.

"These markets have the potential over time to feed into the types of speculative excesses that were so damaging . . . in the late '90s," Cathy Minehan of the Boston Fed worried to her FOMC colleagues.

"Financial conditions are now very accommodative," agreed Timothy Geithner. "These factors make the fundamentals look better than they probably are. They make us more vulnerable to the buildup of distortions in financial markets that can only be unwound with some drama."

"Bankers are willing to take on more risk than I have heard them admit to in recent years," added Governor Mark Olson, who was himself a former banker.

Vice Chairman Roger Ferguson pushed the argument further, linking the financial exuberance with the Fed's forward guidance about future interest rates. "Perhaps we are anchoring the yield curve more than we'd like," he suggested. "The fixed-income markets in particular are not in fact doing the appropriate job of pricing risks." He was suggesting that the Fed's forward guidance had made life too predictable, lulling speculators into complacency. "We need in some sense to remove the anchor that we have placed on those markets," he concluded.

Greenspan also sounded worried. "It sounds as though we're back in the late '90s or perhaps early 2000," he said, recalling the extremes of the tech bubble. "When we get down to the rate levels at which everybody is reaching for yield, at some point the process stops and untoward things happen."

After the crisis, those who downplayed the relevance of monetary policy would argue that the low federal funds rate affected only short-term borrowing rates; therefore, because mortgages were mostly long-term, the Fed could not be held responsible for the housing bubble. This was in itself a dubious claim: in 2003 and 2004, about one third of home-loan applications were for mortgages with teaser rates linked to the fed funds rate.[41] But as Greenspan's "reaching for yield" comment recognized, the larger point was that a low and predictably stable federal funds rate set off a general scramble on Wall Street. Banks and investment houses felt safe in borrowing cheap overnight money because the Fed had assured them that the cost of such borrowing would not rise suddenly. They used this short-term borrowing to buy higher-yielding longer-term debt—including, not least, securitized mortgages. In this way, credit funds known as "SIVs" and "conduits" bridged the supposed divide between the federal funds rate and longer-term market interest rates. The general scramble for yield explained why, as Roger Ferguson observed, risky bonds were not being priced appropriately.[42]

"The potential snapback effects are large," Greenspan went on. "We are always better off if equity premiums are moderate to slightly high or yields are moderate to slightly high because the vulnerability to substantial changes in market psychology is then obviously less." Exuberant markets posed a risk, in other words. "In my view we are vulnerable at this stage to fairly dramatic changes in psychology," Greenspan said ominously.

Summing up this threat of a "snapback," Greenspan was certain where it came from. "We are undoubtedly pumping very considerable liquidity into the financial system," he declared. If a bubble was growing, in other words, monetary policy was at least partially responsible.

The FOMC discussion of January 2004 confirms the weakness in the postcrisis consensus about excess leverage and asset bubbles. It is true that a regulatory clampdown on wild mortgages could have mitigated the crisis more directly than higher interest rates could have, but as we have seen, the regulatory response failed and will likely fail in future. On the other hand, Greenspan's discussion of "reaching for yield" shows that the Fed did at least contemplate ideas that made a monetary response conceivable. The FOMC identified the risk of a market reversal, and it understood that its own policy of low rates and forward guidance was contributing to the frothy markets that would make a reversal painful.

Moreover, if it had chosen to tighten monetary policy, there would have been none of the rule-writing dilemmas or agency turf battles that made regulation difficult: raising interest rates would have been straightforward. And yet by the end of the January meeting, the Fed had decided not to counter the potential speculative snapback by increasing the fed funds rate.

The case against using monetary policy to restrain home prices was advanced by Don Kohn, the FOMC member who was closest to Greenspan. Agreeing with others around the table, Kohn accepted that low interest rates were pumping up markets. In his view, this was hardly a surprise: the Fed's monetary lever always worked by revving up interest-rate-sensitive sectors of the economy such as housing.[43] But Kohn had doubts about the next step in the analysis. Just because house prices were revved up, it did not necessarily follow that there was a bubble.

"It's about second-guessing asset-price levels," Kohn cautioned. "It's something we didn't do in the stock market run-up in the '90s, and I was pretty comfortable with how we handled that. So I'd be a little cautious about using monetary policy to try to damp asset-price movements."

"I certainly agree with that," Greenspan responded.

Greenspan and his chief lieutenant were not willing to act against potential bubbles unless they had conclusive proof of their existence, which was another way of saying that they would never act against them.[44] Having weathered the implosion of previous bubbles, in 1987, 1994, and 2000, they had reason to believe that history was on their side. If house prices did turn out to constitute a bubble, they could always clean up afterward. The danger of a snapback had to be weighed against more certain and immediate goals: to allow as much growth and employment as possible, consistent with a stable consumer-price index.[45]

For the next few months, the Fed continued to guide investors about its future policy, oblivious to Roger Ferguson's warning that this might "anchor" the yield curve and lull investors into complacency. In March

2004 the FOMC repeated its promise to be patient about raising interest rates; in May it declared it would tighten "at a pace that is likely to be measured." It was only in June, after fully twelve months with a 1 percent federal funds rate, that the FOMC ventured a quarter-point hike. By this point, house prices had risen by 20 percent in a year.[46] It was the same amount that they had gained during the entire decade of the 1990s.

The June 2004 rate hike marked the start of a long tightening cycle. But it was nothing like the tightening cycle of ten years earlier. In 1994, the Fed had kept the market guessing, sometimes hiking by 25 basis points, sometimes by 50 basis points, and once even by 75 basis points.[47] But in 2004, having promised to tighten at a "measured" pace, the Fed made good on its undertaking. After each FOMC meeting, it tightened by 25 basis points—not more, not less. Far from surprising leveraged speculators and triggering a new version of "Hurricane Greenspan," the Fed proceeded with as little disruption as possible.

The calm in the markets was so complete as to be eerie. Assured of the Fed's "measured" intentions, banks and investment houses remained content to borrow copiously at short-term rates, which were still low by historic standards. They used this cheap funding to bid down long-term rates, with the result that long rates did not follow the fed funds rate upward. In fact, Wall Street was so elated that the tightening would be "measured" that it borrowed short and lent long even more eagerly than before—rather than rising, long rates actually subsided. With mortgages now cheaper than ever, house prices continued to head upward.

At the August 2004 FOMC meeting, Greenspan wondered aloud whether markets might be complacent. But he stuck to his promised path of "measured" hikes, and raised interest rates by the expected 25 basis points. By September, longer-term interest rates had subsided again. The lack of market drama was a marvel in some ways—"a central banker's dream," as Jeffrey Lacker of the Richmond Fed called it.

In October, with mortgage interest rates still heading down, Greenspan appeared before a convention of community bankers in Washington. With mounting speculation in the media about a property bubble, here was an opportunity to remind home buyers of a home truth: "There is no perpetual motion machine which generates an ever-rising path for prices of homes," Greenspan had written in his doctoral thesis, in 1977. But instead, Greenspan cast himself as a cheerleader for the housing boom, just as he had once been a cheerleader for the New Economy. Were home buyers borrowing incautiously? Greenspan thought not: the vast majority of families who took out mortgages were fully capable of repaying on schedule. Did home prices reflect a speculative euphoria? Again, Greenspan said no: people generally bought homes not in order to flip them for a quick profit but because they needed to live somewhere. Besides, Greenspan continued, the so-called national housing market was really a collection of distinct cities and regions. "Local economies may experience significant speculative price imbalances," Greenspan stipulated. But "a national severe price distortion seems most unlikely in the United States, given its size and diversity."[48]

Ever since his irrational exuberance speech in December 1996, Greenspan had doubted that jawboning asset prices could achieve much. But if public rhetoric, like regulatory policy, was not going to succeed, perhaps this reinforced the case for leaning against bubbles using interest rates?

Toward the end of 2004, the Fed's research brain trust set out to steer the boss in a different direction.[49] For the previous couple of years, the staff economists had brushed aside loose commentary about a housing bubble, arguing that the run-up might be justified by the fundamentals of demography, and further that house prices would abate naturally if they were in fact overvalued. But now the economists were worried. Home prices seemed to be deviating from their normal relationships, either to incomes or to rents; rather than borrowing some crazy multiple of wages to buy a home, a sensible family should prefer to rent one more cheaply. The only rationale for buying was that prices, already elevated, would head even higher. But as Greenspan had recognized in the 1970s, price rises supported by nothing more than the expectation of further price rises tend not to be sustainable.

Greenspan listened to the staff economists. Even though they were evidently prodding him to worry more, they seemed to be offering more questions than answers. They were not certain, for example, how to establish basic facts: different measures of home prices showed different rates of appreciation. Comparing uncertain home prices to uncertain rental prices introduced a further level of complexity, especially because houses in the rental market were generally lower quality than owner-occupied houses, creating an apples-to-oranges problem. The one clear conclusion from the economists' research was that concluding anything was difficult.[50] By late 2004, moreover, economists who thought that property was overvalued were on the defensive. Similar predictions had been offered for the previous couple of years. The pessimists had been discredited.

At a different point in his career, Greenspan might have responded to his staff's presentation more forcefully. If there were ambiguities in the data, surely these could have been resolved with some determined prodding from the chairman—after all, this was what Greenspan had demanded when confronted with anomalies in productivity measures eight years earlier. But this time Greenspan seemed detached, even incurious. His usual appetite for data had apparently deserted him, and at least one staff member guessed that having recently declared publicly that house prices did not constitute a bubble, the chairman was not interested in revising his position. But there was another factor, also. Since his early years as a young data sleuth, Greenspan had loved mechanical relationships: if military procurement went up, aircraft makers' demand for metal would *necessarily* go up; if profits rose while prices and wages remained flat, then productivity *must* be increasing. But house prices, like all asset prices, eluded such clear-cut results. After a lifetime of observing markets, Greenspan was at one with Kohn. He did not believe that markets were always efficient, but he was reluctant to second-guess them.

By the start of 2005, the Fed's successive quarter-point hikes had created something of a mystery. The fed funds rate had climbed by a cumulative 125 basis points, but ten-year rates had continued to slide— they were now considerably below where they had been at the start of the tightening. The consequences for real estate were hardly a surprise. On the Gulf Coast of Florida, investors snapped up condominiums that were as yet unbuilt; contrary to Greenspan's reassuring pronouncements, apartments were being bought, flipped, and sometimes flipped again before anybody so much as lived in them. Property developers dazzled prospective buyers with extravagant parties. At the launch of one ambitious Miami development named Aqua, hostesses in fringed hot pants coaxed home buyers to salsa, and chefs whipped up model crepes in Aqua's model kitchen. The Mortgage Bankers Association reported that risky adjustable-rate and interest-only loans accounted for nearly two thirds of all mortgage originations in the second half of 2004. An industry insider called the shift to the new products a sure sign of "the end of the housing cycle."[51]

At the FOMC meeting on February 1, 2005, Greenspan appeared to show concern at the euphoria. Reacting to another iteration of the long-running discussion about the case for a publicly announced inflation target, he objected that the Fed's job might have to be defined more broadly. "Are we dealing solely with the prices of goods and services, or do asset prices enter into the evaluation?" he demanded. "Is macroeconomic stability, and specifically financial stability, a factor that must be taken into account?" Rather than using the Fed's interest-rate lever solely to target inflation, Greenspan was saying, there might be a case for using it to restrain leverage and bubbles. Again, the postcrisis insistence that monetary policy was irrelevant to asset prices was not always evident before the crisis.

"I have a suspicion that future FOMCs will eventually come to decide . . . that asset prices are a relevant consideration," Greenspan continued.[52] The Fed should "try to mold a level of financial stability that cannot be achieved without advertence to asset prices." Hinting at the gathering mortgage storm, Greenspan went on, "Unless human nature has changed beyond my expectations, I believe it's extraordinarily unlikely that we will be as fortunate as we've been in recent years." Perhaps the Fed staff's warning about house prices had unsettled him after all.

Now that Greenspan was the one sounding a warning about bubbles, it was the turn of others in the room to seem detached, even incurious.

After all, the chairman was not offering a clear bottom line: like the Fed's housing experts, he was raising questions rather than providing answers. It was all very well to pronounce vaguely about how asset prices might matter. He was not saying *how* the Fed should respond to them.

One after another, the FOMC members spoke up, pointedly ignoring Greenspan's musings.

Presently, one said, "Mr. Chairman, you raised the question of asset prices, and I notice that nobody has commented on that, so let me.

"Asset prices are a fundamentally different breed of cat," the governor insisted flatly.[53]

Greenspan said nothing. He could not really object; even if some part of him liked to relive the bubble preoccupations of his younger days, he basically agreed that asset prices should be left to find their own level. After a few more apocalyptic hints during the next day's discussion, the chairman retreated to safe ground. The chief risk confronting central bankers, he now said, was an acceleration of inflation.

It was a strange mixture, this combination of prescient foreboding and conventional wisdom, of musings that recalled a youthful preoccupation with finance and conclusions that fitted perfectly within the inflation-targeting straitjacket. Nearing his seventy-ninth birthday, Greenspan had lived many lives. Sometimes he seemed to want to be both icon and iconoclast.

Two weeks later, on February 16, 2005, Greenspan attached a name to the unusual behavior of long-term interest rates. "The broadly unanticipated behavior of world bond markets remains a *conundrum*," he testified to Congress. Normally, he lectured, a 150 basis point rise in the fed funds rate would drive long rates up; after all, the ten-year interest rate could be thought of as the average of the short rates over the period. So if long rates remained weirdly low, why might this be? Inflation expectations had certainly not fallen dramatically enough to provide an explanation. Nor were investors expecting a weak economy. Greenspan even doubted the leading theory among his colleagues.[54] During an FOMC meeting two months earlier, Ben Bernanke had pointed to a "savings glut." Long-term loans were cheap because capital was in plentiful supply, Bernanke had observed. Savings were flooding into the United States from China and other countries.

The savings-glut theory was more plausible than Greenspan acknowledged, and later he would come around to it. China, like other emerging economies, was buying up long-term bonds issued by the U.S. government and other Western powers, helping to explain why long-term rates were low—including rates on long-term mortgages. In keeping with this theory, the housing bubble of the mid-2000s was not confined to the United States, encouraging Bernanke and his allies to argue that global savings patterns were the culprit. Yet although there was some truth to this analysis, it was not the whole story. Later research confirmed that Chinese savings patterns did indeed influence U.S. long-term interest rates, but also that this effect could be swamped by changes in Fed policy.[55] Moreover, to the extent that the U.S. housing bubble had analogs in Europe, a glut of foreign savings was not mainly to blame. In some smaller European economies, notably Spain, the housing bubble was the result of the new common currency, the euro, which had brought about a collapse in borrowing costs. Elsewhere the bubble reflected the policies of central banks that shared the Fed's inflation-targeting mind-set: Britain was a good example. But the chief omission in the savings-glut theory was the Western financial system itself. In the United States especially, but also in Europe, the cause of the housing bubble was not simply a general surfeit of savings. It was that banks and various species of investment fund were scooping up those savings and pumping them into real estate. If financiers had chosen differently, there would not have been a bubble.

In the years after the crisis, Greenspan suggested that there was nothing the Fed could have done to change financiers' choices. If long rates remained low despite rising short rates, it followed that the Fed was powerless. This claim of central-bank impotence was part of a tradition: in 1975 Arthur Burns had lamented that the Fed could not be expected to bring inflation down because "all of us recognize that the influence the Federal Reserve has on long-term rates is negligible."[56] But as Greenspan should have recalled from his own observations of the 1970s, this claim of impotence was false. In the 1970s, long rates had stopped rising in tandem with short rates because Fannie and Freddie were creating a new source of long-term loans; the answer, as Volcker ultimately showed, was to hike short rates more aggressively. In the 2000s, similarly, long rates had stopped rising with short rates. The answer, again, was to hike short rates more—and to stop coddling investors with advance warning of the Fed's decisions.[57]

Greenspan might also have reflected on another episode from his career: the 1993 bond market bubble. Then, in keeping with the tradition of claiming monetary impotence, Greenspan had ascribed the collapse of long-term interest rates to factors other than the Fed: inflation expectations were falling. The following year, when the Fed hiked the short-term interest rate, the bond bubble popped: the Fed turned out to be the opposite of impotent. Moreover, Mike Prell and the research department had explained why Greenspan had been wrong: low long-term rates in 1993 were the product of an extended spell with a rock-bottom federal funds rate. Prell's point was that monetary policy determined investors' expectations about interest rates in the future, and that those expectations fed through into long-term interest rates: "The persistence of low short rates will gradually lower investors' perceptions of what is normal and sustainable," Prell had concluded. If that had been true in the era before the Fed guided expectations deliberately, it was presumably all the more true now that the Fed was promising to raise rates only gradually.

A month after the conundrum speech, at the FOMC's meeting in late March 2005, Timothy Geithner put his finger on the trouble with the Fed's forward guidance, noting "a remarkable reduction in uncertainty about monetary policy expectations." Because there were no surprises left in monetary policy, investors sated their risk appetites by leveraging their portfolios and buying higher-yielding bonds. The result was "this broad pattern now evident of lower risk premia across financial markets."

"Part of this is due to fundamentals," Geithner stipulated, alluding to the possibility that a flood of savings from China might indeed be suppressing long-term interest rates. "But part seems due to our monetary policy signal," he added pointedly. So long as Wall Street remained confident that Fed tightening would be "measured," it had absolutely no reason to stop borrowing short and lending long.[58] The Fed's soothing pronouncements were stoking a dangerous appetite for risk—an appetite that was not going to be suppressed by the New York Fed's regulatory efforts.

If Geithner worried about the incentives created by forward guidance, other thoughtful figures on Wall Street were even more nervous. Through 2004 and 2005, Tom Maheras, the head of trading operations at Citigroup, conducted a running conversation with his top Fed-watching economists, Lewis Alexander and Kim Schoenholtz. The way Maheras saw things, the Fed was too predictable and too soft. In 1998, it had cushioned the shock of LTCM's failure by overreacting with rate cuts, encouraging Wall Street to believe that it was safe to take on leverage: if markets blew up, the Fed would put things right and protect traders from losses. Now the Fed was compounding its post-LTCM error by telegraphing its moves in advance, Maheras thought. Greenspan ought to hit speculators with a surprise rate hike of 50 or 75 basis points, as he had in 1994. Otherwise, Wall Street would leverage itself indefinitely.[59]

Alexander and Schoenholtz listened to their boss, but they rejected his prescription. By now every serious Fed watcher had absorbed Ben Bernanke's case for clear central bank communication. The Fed had signaled it would tighten at a "measured" pace, and Greenspan had to stick to the plan; in a modern, financialized economy, a central bank did not so much set interest rates as seek to guide them, so its credibility was everything. Besides, inflation was just about on target, at a touch over 2 percent. There was no case to be made for hiking the fed funds rate more aggressively.

A curious pattern was emerging. Monetary experts wanted to preserve their interest-rate tool to stabilize inflation and, secondarily, employment. They therefore hoped that financial stability would take care of itself, that some combination of market self-discipline and regulatory discipline would contain excesses—and that if they did not, the Fed could clean up afterward. But the creators of those excesses lacked faith in this approach: they wanted to be smacked around by a sterner monetary authority. In the view of Tom Maheras and other senior Wall Streeters, the faith in market self-discipline was a dangerous delusion: bank shareholders did not care about long-term risk; they wanted immediate profits. Likewise, the faith in regulatory discipline was a delusion, too: regulators struggled to define clear rules; balkanized agencies could not coordinate their efforts. And the shattering of these delusions could be scary to behold, potentially swamping the Fed's ability to clean up afterward. Perhaps not surprisingly, traders in the markets sensed these risks more viscerally than monetary experts.

Although he had laid out the problem with forward guidance, Timothy Geithner stopped short of demanding a tougher monetary policy. He had been at the Fed for just over a year, and like everybody there, he deferred to Greenspan's record of success over almost two decades. Besides, as Geithner himself conceded, there were risks in being tough: even if the Fed's forward guidance lulled traders into taking too much risk, it seemed perverse to address the problem of a potential future shock by shocking markets preemptively.[60] As a result, nobody around Greenspan really challenged his thinking; and at successive FOMC meetings through the rest of the year, Greenspan persisted serenely with his "measured" strategy. Far from viewing the conundrum of low long rates as a problem to be fixed, he marveled at the smoothness with which monetary policy was operating. "The market now pretty much anticipates how we're going to respond to various events," he rejoiced in May 2005. "The markets will do our work for us until we come and sit at this table and formalize it." In these circumstances, the Fed's goal was to "continue to convey to the marketplace where our priorities are." Forward guidance would ensure "as little reaction to our post-meeting statement as possible."[61]

In the space of eighteen months, Greenspan had fretted that Wall Street was "reaching for yield," anticipating that "untoward things" might happen. He had objected to an explicit inflation target, musing that a future FOMC might come to regard asset prices as "a relevant consideration." He had listened to colleagues' concerns about the risks in forward guidance, and had come close to embracing their anxiety by diagnosing a "conundrum." And yet despite the chairman's depth of understanding, Fed policy remained unchanged. Greenspan was the man who knew. He was not the man who acted.

Comfortable in his pattern of measured quarter-point rate hikes, Greenspan was savoring his last months as Fed chairman. He had recently visited Scotland to deliver a lecture in Adam Smith's birthplace, Kirkcaldy; his friend, the brainy British finance minister, Gordon Brown, had shown him around the seaside town and presented him with an early edition of Smith's *The Wealth of Nations*. In Washington, Greenspan kept up a full social schedule, courting the press and lunching with cabinet officials; he still played tennis and golf regularly at the Chevy Chase Club. In May 2005, the press speculated briefly that Greenspan's Fed tenure might be extended beyond its scheduled expiration, on January 31, 2006; if he could hang on into May, he would become the longest-serving Fed chairman, overtaking William McChesney Martin.[62] But the speculation did not last. Although Greenspan's latest appointment as chairman would not expire until 2008, his term as a Fed governor was due to end; the rules allowed a governor to complete his predecessor's appointment, and then to be appointed to a single fourteen-year term—beyond that, extensions were impossible. One of the most extraordinary careers in Washington was thus drawing to a close. Soon, the Greenspan era would be over.

On Saturday, August 20, 2005, Greenspan flew to Jackson Hole, leaving a few days earlier than usual. Rather than playing tennis in Carmel afterward, he had opted for a break ahead of the symposium. This year's proceedings were to be titled "The Greenspan Era: Lessons for the Future." He wanted to be ready.

Greenspan had every reason to expect a rapturous send-off. In the eighteen years since Reagan had appointed him, the U.S. economy had experienced only two recessions: in 1990–91 and in 2001. Taking these two episodes together, the United States had been in recession for just 7 percent of Greenspan's tenure, whereas Burns had presided over a recession for 26 percent of his time, and Volcker had done so for 23 percent. Greenspan's record on price stability had been better still. Since the soft landing in the spring of 1994, core inflation had never risen above 2.3 percent; it had been lower and less volatile than at any time since the 1960s. Economists had dubbed this miracle the Great Moderation. A few journalists and dissidents might fret about forward guidance and bubbles. But when it came to the central bank's main mission of stabilizing growth and inflation, Milton Friedman's verdict was correct. Greenspan had "set the standard."

On Friday, August 26, the monetary priesthood gathered expectantly in the Jackson Lake Lodge, with its picture windows looking out over the mountains. After introductory remarks from Greenspan, in which he modestly invoked the "inevitable and ongoing uncertainty" that central bankers faced, the stage was taken by none other than Alan Blinder. As Fed vice chairman in the mid-1990s, Blinder had frequently quarreled with Greenspan, accusing him of substituting his own mysterious intuition for model-driven forecasts. But now, assessing the cumulative evidence from Greenspan's long chairmanship, Blinder had revised his view. Together with Ricardo Reis, a Princeton colleague, he showered Greenspan with extraordinary praise, piling superlative upon superlative.

Greenspan had a "legitimate claim to being the greatest central banker who ever lived," the paper delivered Blinder and Reis contended.

"There is no doubt that Greenspan has been an amazingly successful chairman of the Federal Reserve System," they added.

"Financial markets now view Chairman Greenspan's infallibility more or less as the Chinese once viewed Chairman Mao's."

He had demonstrated "subtlety, a deft touch, and good judgment."

He had handled the Fed "with great aplomb, and with immense benefits to the U.S. economy."

If there was any criticism of Greenspan, it was that he had been *too* commanding and brilliant. "Alan Greenspan has become what amounts to the nation's unofficial economic wise man—on just about any subject," the professors chided. He had boosted his stature to the point that he overshadowed his own institution.

But then Blinder and Reis conceded, "If the nation wants a wise man, it could do a lot worse than Alan Greenspan."

The praise started again.

"The coming replacement of Alan Greenspan by a mere mortal in January 2006 will not . . . be like changing dentists."

Greenspan was "a living legend."

He was the "*maximum maximorum.*"

"His job performance has, in the current vernacular, been awesome."

At the end of the symposium, Greenspan rose to address the priesthood one last time. "Difficult challenges lie ahead," he said, "some undoubtedly of our own making."[63]

Twenty-nine

"I FOUND A FLAW"

O n January 31, 2006, Alan Greenspan awoke to his last day as the world's most powerful economist. On the radio that morning, National Public Radio broadcast the perky strains of "Irrational Exuberance," a Pennsylvania man's orchestral ode to the departing Fed chairman.[1] On television, a twenty-five-year-old art student named Erin Crowe installed herself in the CNBC studio and began painting live, on air, a portrait of the hangdog sage in all his lugubrious glory. Crowe's televised artistry turned out to be a publicity stunt for her "Good-bye Greenspan" show at the Broome Street Gallery in New York, where thirty likenesses of the great man were up for sale at $6,000 per canvas. She was cashing in on Greenspan fever because the next Fed chairman, Ben Bernanke, would be harder to monetize. "His beard is covering his face, and I don't think he has the same facial expressions," the artist said, regretfully.[2]

Greenspan's final weeks in office had been a blur of adulation. In November, he found himself sandwiched between the singer Aretha Franklin and the actor Andy Griffith on a White House stage, waiting to receive the Presidential Medal of Freedom.[3] In December, the G7 club of leading finance ministers convened a special meeting to bid him good-bye: his favorite public official, Britain's Gordon Brown, presented him

with an armful of well-chosen gifts, among them a letter from George
Washington to the Bank of England, inquiring about the interest on his
deposits.[4] Greenspan was granted the Freedom of the City of London, an
honor that conferred an ancient privilege to drive sheep across London
Bridge; and a few days later, after donning a violet gown and accepting
an honorary doctorate from his undergraduate alma mater in New York,
the sage was feted once again at the White House. The dinner guests
included both Republicans and Democrats, from Dick Cheney to Bob
Rubin. In his long career in Washington, Greenspan had made remarkably few enemies.

On that last morning in January 2006, a light rain dampened the capital. Greenspan put on a black pinstriped suit and a confident red tie, and
set off to chair his final FOMC meeting. When he arrived in the Fed's
conference room, his colleagues stood up and broke into applause. Greenspan motioned with his hands for everyone to be seated.

"It's fitting for Chairman Greenspan to leave office with the economy
in such solid shape," said Janet Yellen, who was now the president of the
San Francisco Fed. "The situation you're handing off to your successor is
a lot like a tennis racquet with a gigantic sweet spot."

Another regional Fed president wheeled out some lines from Shakespeare, and compared Greenspan to Henry V.[5]

Roger Ferguson, the vice chairman, professed Greenspan to be "the
monetary policy Yoda."

"Yoda, of course, is a complimentary word in my household," Ferguson stipulated, lest the comparison to a gnarled nine-hundred-year-old
alien be taken badly.

"I'd like the record to show that I think you're pretty terrific, too,"
Timothy Geithner chimed in. "And thinking in terms of probabilities, I
think the risk that we decide in the future that you're even better than we
think is higher than the alternative."

Geithner's colleagues chuckled merrily.

When his turn arrived, Greenspan said little. He had not prepared a
final speech; throughout his efficient and productive life, he had never
wasted time on sentimentality. Rather, he was eager to finish the meeting

punctually so that nobody would be late for the next item of the day, a farewell luncheon.

"I think it's fairly clear that there's consensus around the table that we'll move 25 basis points today," he ventured.

His colleagues fell in line: it was the fourteenth consecutive meeting at which the Fed had delivered on its promise of a "measured" tightening. Then the committee broke for lunch, and Andrea arrived to accompany Alan out into the cavernous marble atrium of the Eccles Building.

A crowd of 1,500 awaited them, from the top economists on the Fed's staff to the lowliest janitors and cleaners; and despite Greenspan's reputation as an imperial chairman, the feeling in these last moments of his reign was touchingly affectionate. The staff presented him with a chair from the Fed's boardroom; an old baseball glove signed by each president of the Federal Reserve's twelve district banks; and the Federal Reserve flag that had flown during his last FOMC meeting.[6] But the highlight of the party was a giant cookie, propped up on an easel; it was cut in the shape of Greenspan's silhouette, and lines of colored frosting traced his shirt, tie, and thick-rimmed glasses.[7] Alan posed with Andrea for photographs in front of his chocolate-chip likeness, and silver fountains flowed with bubbly champagne.[8] The metaphor for the economy was clearly not intended.

Greenspan was not about to fade into the sunset. He had prepared for a life without chauffeurs by occasionally taking the wheel in Andrea's car, and he soon got used to the eerie solitude of riding an elevator alone, with no minder beside him. When his security detail decamped from Andrea's garden, he felt temporarily exposed: "Okay, is somebody going to shoot me?" he wondered to himself, before realizing with a jolt that he was no longer worth targeting.[9] But these adaptations were incidental to his main focus, which was to hold fast to the habits that defined him. He would still wake early in the mornings, eager for fresh facts about the world. He would still maintain his network of social and professional contacts, accompanying Andrea to A-list parties and lunching with politicos, economists, and journalists. He would still play tennis at the Chevy Chase Club, even if that meant occasional trouble with his back and bouts with a physiotherapist.

One week after leaving the Fed, Greenspan showed up in the executive dining room at Lehman Brothers, the storied Wall Street investment bank, and delivered remarks on the economy to a handful of Lehman's hedge-fund clients. He collected a fee of $250,000 for his opinions, more than an entire year's salary as Fed chairman. Next, Greenspan embarked on the writing of a memoir, his arm strengthened by a publishing contract worth more than $8 million, not to mention by the services of an accomplished ghostwriter. To round out his portfolio, Greenspan set up a new consulting firm, installing himself with three young assistants in a suite a few blocks north of the White House; there was an imposing pair of screens upon his desk, and photographs of Andrea, Gerald Ford, and Margaret Thatcher. The new firm of Greenspan Associates launched with just one client—Britain's Gordon Brown—and the relationship was pro bono. But soon paying customers signed on, notably the West Coast fund-management giant, Pimco. Greenspan would show up at Pimco's quarterly conferences and weigh in on the outlook—he still seemed to be stewing data in his head and letting out just a little of the steam for his public to sniff, as a client had recalled of his performances in the seventies. But now for every issue that economists encountered, Greenspan could cite a precedent—he had experienced every circumstance before, and he was in no doubt what he thought of it. Having attained the age of eighty, he was coming at the present through the past. The younger economists tired of him.

Inevitably, the deference that Greenspan had taken for granted began to ebb slightly. After the outsized Lehman paycheck, there was a clucking chorus of complaint. Greenspan had delivered his talk with the inside knowledge of his last FOMC meeting still fresh in his mind, and before the minutes of the proceedings had been released to the public; his comments had moved markets, and presumably Lehman's plutocratic clients had profited.[10] Meanwhile, the institution that Greenspan had dominated was starting to move on. Beginning with his very first FOMC meeting, Ben Bernanke set about changing the tone of the debates, and the implied criticism of Greenspan was obvious. Under Bernanke's leadership, committee members would be permitted to interrupt their colleagues with two-handed interventions; the goal was to encourage a meaningful exchange, not a series of canned speeches. And whereas Greenspan had quashed dissent from colleagues by firmly laying out his preferences at the start of the policy discussion, Bernanke reserved judgment until the end. This gave other committee members a chance to state their recommendations openly, without feeling obliged to mold them to the chairman's view. It was a more collegial approach, and the deliberations were the richer for it.

But the real challenge to Greenspan's reputation lay elsewhere: not with unseemly Wall Street lecture fees or FOMC procedures, but rather with the economy. In his last months in office, Greenspan had come to recognize that the housing market might indeed be in the grip of a bubble, though he had done little about it. Now, in the first months of his retirement, the question was what the deflating of that bubble might mean. If home prices leveled off or even fell, new home construction would grind to a halt, silencing one engine of the economy. At the same time, consumers would lose the ability to borrow against the rising value of their homes; because this "home-equity extraction" accounted for a large chunk of consumption growth, another engine would shut down abruptly. In the final portion of his tenure, Greenspan had cemented his status as folk hero by turning ordinary homeowners into mortar millionaires. But this bonanza was reversible.

By the spring of 2006, the slow march of quarter-point rate hikes was finally biting. Borrowers who had accepted risky mortgages now faced much higher repayments when their fixed teaser rates expired, rendering their loans impossible to service. Moreover, the old escape from this dilemma might soon be cut off. Before, financially strapped homeowners had simply borrowed more against the rising value of their houses, using the cash to pay off auto loans or credit-card debt, so freeing income for their mortgage payments. But this stratagem depended on house prices continuing to rise. The moment they fell, homeowners would lose the ability to borrow more. Unrepayable mortgages would be revealed as just that: unrepayable.

In May 2006, the Fed nudged the federal funds rate to 5 percent, up from 1 percent two years earlier. That same month, the Case-Shiller index of house prices registered its first monthly decline in more than a decade. The moment of truth was approaching.

O ne year later, in the summer of 2007, Greenspan prepared for the September launch of his autobiography. In June his publisher achieved both publicity and secrecy by wheeling him out at a booksellers' convention, taking care to ensure that recording devices were banned from the auditorium.[11] A few weeks later, Greenspan sat for an interview on CBS's *60 Minutes,* while *Newsweek* bought the rights to publish excerpts from the memoir, to be titled *The Age of Turbulence.* Industry gossips speculated that the book would break all records for the genre.[12] And after all, why not? Greenspan's public appearances still generated reverential attention. House prices were down by 5 percent over the past year, but he was still the maestro.[13]

The first reactions to the book were not about housing. The newspapers seized on Greenspan's criticisms of the Bush administration: he was damning about the two budget-busting tax cuts; and in a passing but much-quoted comment, he declared that the Iraq War had been "largely about oil." The Bush administration and its allies fanned the story by responding with contempt: if Greenspan had entertained these misgivings, he should have made them clear earlier, when his opinion actually mattered. A newspaper cartoon showed a gesticulating former Fed chairman announcing, "The war is about oil!" while a minuscule Bush retorted, "Hippie!"[14] At a glitzy publication party attended by Bob Rubin and Henry Kissinger, Bill Clinton gave a toast.[15] Bush administration heavyweights were conspicuous by their absence.

But the fun of pitting Greenspan against Bush could not obscure the flashing signs from the economy. Now that house prices were falling and interest rates were higher, the option of refinancing was gone and almost one in six subprime mortgages was delinquent.[16] In turn, dozens of subprime lenders had filed for bankruptcy; and, in July 2007, two hedge funds operated by the investment bank Bear Stearns had collapsed under the weight of subprime investments. At the Fed, the new chairman and his allies hoped that this shock would prove fleeting.[17] But just as Greenspan was out flacking his book, the questions were accumulating.

Greenspan seemed unsure how best to answer them. In a speech in London on October 1, 2007, he stated that he had long regarded the housing market as "an accident waiting to happen." However, as he explained in his memoir, he had been content to let it rip in 2004 and 2005 because "I believed then, as now, that the benefits of broadened home ownership are worth the risk." In fact, Greenspan elaborated, the bubble had been good: "Because of the housing boom and the accompanying explosion in new mortgage products, the typical American household ended up with a more valuable home and better access to the wealth it represented."[18] At other times, however, Greenspan sounded more defensive. Far from painting the real estate boom as a desirable gamble, he claimed instead to have resisted it. But in this telling, his efforts had been thwarted by the "conundrum" of low long-term interest rates. The Fed had done what it could by steadily raising the short-term rate, but the bond market had refused to budge. The central bank had been impotent—and therefore innocent.

"We tried to raise the rate in 2004 and we failed," Greenspan told the TV host Tim Russert in a *Meet the Press* interview on September 23, one week after publication of his memoir. "We tried again in 2005 and we failed. And so it's very clear to me that central banks, ourselves, the Federal Reserve, included, had very little control over the extent of that boom."[19]

The worse the news on housing grew, the more Greenspan backed off his suggestion that the boom had been a boon, doubling down on his alternative claim of central-bank impotence. On December 12, 2007, he reiterated in the *Wall Street Journal* that the conundrum had rendered the Fed powerless, adding that loose policy had been justified by the fear of deflation.[20] The next day he appeared on NPR and was asked whether the Fed could have prevented, or eased, the real estate bubble. "There's only one thing we could have done—cutting off short-term credit," Greenspan replied. "But that would have broken the back of the economy." Short of a murderously high fed funds rate, in other words, "the evidence is very clear that there was nothing that any central bank could have done, or tried to do."[21]

Of course, Greenspan's pleading was mostly unpersuasive. The threat of Japanese-style deflation had been a worry until the spring of 2004; but after that, core inflation had actually risen slightly above 2 percent, allowing Greenspan scope to tighten more rapidly. Contrary to Greenspan's claims on NPR, moreover, there was no reason to suppose that monetary policy had to be either impotent or lethal: the Fed could have steered a middle course simply by abandoning forward guidance and "measured" gradualism.[22] Anna Schwartz, the coauthor, with Milton Friedman, of the magisterial *Monetary History,* skewered Greenspan on this point. "There never would have been a sub-prime mortgage crisis if the Fed had been alert," she charged. "Monetary policy was too accommodative. Rates of 1 percent were bound to encourage all kinds of risky behavior." The contention that the mortgage bubble reflected a global savings glut did not impress Schwartz in the least. "The Fed failed to confront something that was evident. It can't be blamed on global events," she concluded.[23]

Even though Greenspan's monetary policy was vulnerable to attack, the majority of his critics focused instead on his regulatory policy. Aside from a few mavericks such as Schwartz and Stanford's John Taylor, not many people wanted to denounce Greenspan for setting interest rates too low—after all, he had delivered broadly on-target inflation and strong growth, the opposite of stagflation. But there had always been an anti–Wall Street, regulation-minded caucus; and now that finance was fraying, critics rounded on Greenspan for believing in a laissez-fairey tale. In December a columnist in *Slate* magazine accused Greenspan of "a combination of incompetence and ideology. . . . When Fed governor Edward Gramlich urged Greenspan to crack down on predatory mortgage lending, Greenspan shrugged."[24] Writing in his *New York Times* column a few days later, Paul Krugman dredged up Greenspan's extreme anti-antitrust writings from the early 1960s, brandishing them triumphantly as though they were a smoking gun. Confidently assuming that the Fed chairman's convictions had remained unchanged over the space of four decades, Krugman lamented, "It's no wonder, then, that he brushed off warnings about deceptive lending practices, including those of Edward M. Gramlich."[25]

If the myth of Gramlich's prescience cast a shadow over Greenspan, a strange amnesia about the Fed's attempt at mortgage regulation served to compound his troubles. On December 18, 2007, the Fed proposed new restrictions on abusive mortgages, and they were greeted as though the 2001 rules had never been promulgated. "Reading these proposals today is almost painful," harrumphed a liberal economist in Washington. "These are all just simple, common-sense regulation. Why couldn't Greenspan have done this seven years ago?"[26]

More than a decade after he had worried about becoming the Zip-switch chairman, Greenspan was confronting the risks in his preeminence. He made an irresistible target, this magus who embodied American omniscience and power; anyone who hungered for a scapegoat was certain to come after him. Americans love to celebrate success stories, from Horatio Alger to tech pioneers, but they have a taste for retribution, too. If the bubble in Greenspan's reputation was about to pop, it would do so loudly—and not necessarily fairly.

On March 16, 2008, Greenspan attempted a defense of his approach to regulation. Writing in the *Financial Times,* he confessed that market discipline had failed to contain mortgage excesses. But he pleaded nonetheless that readers recognize "financial self-regulation as the fundamental balance mechanism for global finance." After all, Greenspan continued, government regulation often fared no better than imperfect market discipline. Some of the worst mortgage problems were concentrated at banks "whose regulatory oversight has been elaborate for years."[27]

Greenspan's timing could not have been less fortunate. The day his op-ed appeared, the *Financial Times* led its front page with the collapse of the investment bank Bear Stearns—a textbook illustration of how market discipline could fail spectacularly. Bear had collapsed, moreover, because oversight had been lax: like the other big investment banks, it had contrived to escape supervision by any of the main safety-minded regulators—the Fed, the Office of Thrift Supervision, and the Comptroller of the Currency. Instead, Bear came under the Securities and Exchange Commission, which allowed it to operate with almost no equity buffers; whereas a bank like Citigroup had more than sixty government supervisors stationed permanently on its premises, Bear got away with annual supervisory visits.[28] The fragmentation of the regulatory system had encouraged risk taking to migrate to banks where oversight was weakest. The "financial self-regulation" that Greenspan touted had not been enough to compensate.

Greenspan's unlucky timing left him looking isolated. Deutsche Bank had recently signed on as a Greenspan consulting client, but the day after the *FT* op-ed appeared, Deutsche's boss staked out the opposite position: "I no longer believe in the market's self-healing power," he declared flatly.[29] Martin Wolf, the *FT*'s chief economics commentator, had recently published an upbeat book titled *Why Globalization Works*. But now he sounded dark. "The dream of global free-market capitalism died," Wolf declared after the failure of Bear Stearns. "Deregulation has reached its limits."[30]

Amid mounting doubts about markets, Greenspan tried again to defend his perspective. "Would a material tightening of regulation improve financial performance?" he demanded in another *FT* article, three weeks later. "I doubt it," he continued firmly. "The problem is not the lack of regulation but unrealistic expectations about what regulators are able to prevent," he carried on, trying to shift the argument back to the familiar ground on which he had traditionally won it. Laissez-faire policies ought to be judged not against some imagined utopia of watertight rules, Greenspan was saying; rather, critics should reckon with the dispiriting reality of frayed red tape, the product of dysfunctional rulemaking in Washington. Invoking the recent collapse and nationalization of the British lender Northern Rock, Greenspan pressed his point. The failure of regulation was not just an American story; it was an international one. Regulation was *always* doomed because it was impossible to implement successfully. "How can we otherwise explain how the UK's Financial Services Authority, whose effectiveness is held in such high regard, fumbled Northern Rock?" Greenspan asked. Or how to explain why "in the US, our best examiners have repeatedly failed over the years. These are not aberrations."[31]

It was a reasonable riposte, but nobody was listening. Greenspan, a *New York Post* columnist scolded, was "the real culprit in this whole mess"; the *Wall Street Journal* published a short guide to Greenspan haters.[32] A vituperative blogger named W. C. Varones was tracking "mortgage-related suicides" under the header "Greenspan's body count."[33] A slim book with the self-explanatory title *Greenspan's Bubbles: The Age of Ignorance at the Federal Reserve* had entered its fourth printing. Another anti-Greenspan hit job would be published soon. *Deception and Abuse at the Fed,* proclaimed its title.[34]

"Do you worry that, as time goes by, the critical interpretations of your record—that monetary policy was too easy, and regulatory policy too hands-off—will become the conventional wisdom?" the *Wall Street Journal* inquired in early April 2008.

"Yes," Greenspan replied bluntly.

Then he continued.

"If that's the conclusion people are going to come to, then the evaluation of this period will produce the wrong answers and the wrong policies.

"It's important that mistakes of policy and policymakers be critically examined. But it's equally important that the diagnoses be accurate."[35]

After the failure of Bear Stearns, the next leg down in the financial crisis was less embarrassing to Greenspan. As losses in the housing market continued to mount, Fannie and Freddie hit the rocks; they owned or guaranteed almost half of all mortgages, so they were bound to take big losses. Not surprisingly, their stock prices collapsed. In June 2008 alone, Fannie was down 28 percent and Freddie was down 34 percent.

Greenspan had never been in doubt that the collapse of the GSEs was possible. He had stressed their extraordinarily thin capital buffers in testimony to Congress: with a capital-asset ratio of less than 2 percent, Fannie and Freddie were more leveraged even than Bear Stearns and the other big investment banks.[36] Likewise, he had given warning that the government would have to mount a rescue in the event of a collapse, and now he would be vindicated. At the beginning of July, seeing the *Titanic* heading toward the iceberg, Treasury Secretary Hank Paulson resolved to ask Congress for the authority to seize control of the two housing lenders.

On July 10, 2008, as he was preparing his request, Paulson consulted Greenspan. The two had not spoken in a while—a testament, perhaps, to the distance between the administration and Greenspan since the publication of his memoir. After some confusion about tracking down Greenspan's phone number, Paulson and half a dozen staff members huddled over the Polycom on the Treasury secretary's desk. A faint voice came at them through the speaker.

Greenspan endorsed Paulson's plan to prepare the ground for a rescue. Thirty-three years had passed since he had told Ford to deny aid to New York; he had long since given up opposing bailouts. But as well as blessing Paulson's preparations, Greenspan could not resist a madcap, Randian tease: now that he had returned to private life, there was nothing to prevent him from following the logic of his ideas to their most radical conclusions. At bottom, Greenspan told the Treasury team, the spreading mortgage crisis reflected excess housing supply. Therefore the government should buy up vacant homes and burn them.

After the call, Paulson told his staff: "That's not a bad idea. But we're not going to buy up all the housing supply and destroy it."[37]

Fannie and Freddie went from bad to terrible over the next weeks, and on September 7 Paulson exercised his power to take them into "conservatorship"—effectively, to nationalize them. Over the next three years, the Treasury would kick in a total of $188 billion to prevent the GSEs from defaulting to their bondholders, an infusion of money that was twenty-eight times larger than the sum required to rescue the entire financial system in 1907, even after adjusting for inflation.[38] But the size of the bailout did not capture its full cost. As part of the nationalization, private shareholders were wiped out; and because those shareholders included banks, the contagion was instant. Ten lenders collapsed into the arms of the government's deposit-insurance fund, and some three dozen others faced doubts about their soundness. The events surrounding the GSE takeover amounted to "a massive, underreported, underappreciated jolt to the system," the market-savvy Fed governor Kevin Warsh later recalled vividly.[39]

With the unfair benefit of hindsight, Greenspan might have done more to avert this catastrophe. On at least two occasions, he had refused to allow the Fed to take on the mission of regulating the GSEs, preferring to prioritize the Fed's monetary independence. But the GSE failure was not a shock to Greenspan's worldview. To the contrary, he had expected it.

The next shock was more challenging. The day after the government takeover of the GSEs, Lehman Brothers entered its own death spiral.

Unlike Fannie and Freddie, Lehman Brothers fell into the Bear Stearns category: it was a poster child for the financial practices that Greenspan had defended.[40] It was party to almost a million bilateral derivatives contracts, those over-the-counter deals that Brooksley Born had wanted to move into centralized clearinghouses. It was also an enthusiastic responder to the incentives created by the Fed: it had borrowed billions in short-term funds, loading up on cheap money while interest rates were low and using it to buy higher-yielding mortgages. In Greenspan's more hopeful moments, he had trusted that Lehman would take such risks only if it had sufficient capital to absorb losses. In the absence of adequate capital buffers, after all, other savvy institutions should have refused to trade with it: Why enter into a swap contract with a firm that might fail and renege on it? In the absence of adequate capital buffers, likewise, creditors might be expected not to lend: Why hand money to a firm that might go bankrupt? But this system of counterparty discipline failed. The Fed chairman had expected far too much of it.

If Greenspan was dismayed by Lehman's recklessness, he did at least know how to respond to its impending failure. On September 14 he appeared on a Sunday-morning talk show and called for a public rescue.

"There are certain types of institutions which are so fundamental," he pleaded. "On very rare occasions, and this is one of them, it's desirable to prevent them from liquidating in a sharply disruptive manner."[41]

Greenspan's words would soon appear prophetic. Having rescued Fannie and Freddie, Hank Paulson was tired of being Mr. Bailout; and when a plan to have a British bank absorb Lehman was blocked at the last moment by the authorities in London, the Treasury secretary ignored Greenspan's advice, allowing Lehman to declare bankruptcy early on Monday morning. The news immediately put the financial system into a tailspin. The spectacle of a legendary investment bank reneging on its debts spread panic up and down Wall Street. It no longer felt safe to lend to anyone.

The first casualty of the Lehman fallout was Merrill Lynch, America's best-known stockbroker, which was also staggering under the weight of disastrous subprime investments. A few hours after Lehman was denied government help, Merrill sold itself hastily to Bank of America in order to avoid bankruptcy. The next day, Tuesday, September 16, the panic spread to the giant insurer American International Group (AIG), where a financial-engineering unit had accumulated enough derivatives exposure to bring the company to its knees—again, counterparty surveillance had done nothing to prevent it from gambling recklessly. If AIG defaulted on its swap contracts, the knock-on effects would bring several other Wall Street houses down. This time the Fed mounted an emergency rescue, pumping in a loan of $85 billion and seizing ownership of four fifths of the company.

While the Fed averted a default by AIG, it was too slow to prevent another disaster that unfolded that same Tuesday. The Reserve Primary Fund, the oldest money-market fund in the country, held Lehman paper that was now in default: as a result, a dollar deposited in the Primary Fund was now worth only ninety-seven cents. This was the first time in history that a money-market fund had "broken the buck"—puncturing the myth that money-market accounts were as safe as federally insured bank deposits. Investors who had parked around $3 trillion in money-market funds woke up to the horrifying prospect that their cash might go up in smoke; they rushed to yank their money out, forcing the funds to liquidate their portfolios of Treasury bills and other short-term paper. After years in which the Fed's reassuring policies had made short-term credit plentiful and cheap, the run on money-market funds cut off the supply almost completely.

Since the 1990s, commentators had mocked the Fed's hair-trigger readiness to protect Wall Street from shocks. Now they were about to experience life outside the shelter of the "Greenspan put," and they were not going to like it. Companies that had relied on the money market to meet obligations to workers or suppliers were suddenly unable to do so: confidence collapsed, and spending fell off a precipice. Leveraged financial institutions were in even more trouble: with short-term loans no longer available, they were forced to liquidate portfolios just when everybody else was selling. In this environment, only banks with access to an alternative source of short-term funding—loans from the Fed's discount window—were likely to survive. In the absence of the "Greenspan put," the vast shadow-banking sector that had grown up on Greenspan's watch was in danger of imploding.

A quarter of a century earlier, the Fed and the Reagan administration had responded to history's first electronic bank run, on Continental Illinois, by extending its safety net to the bank's uninsured creditors. On Friday, September 19, 2008, a terrified Bush administration responded to history's first shadow-bank run in the same way: it extended its safety net to cash parked in money-market funds, even though these had been explicitly excluded from federal deposit insurance. Over the weekend, the new government backstop was expanded even more. With Bear Stearns, Lehman Brothers, and Merrill Lynch already extinct, the Fed acted to save the two survivors among the big five investment banks: Goldman Sachs and Morgan Stanley. To protect them from the run on short-term lending, the Fed reclassified Goldman and Morgan as bank-holding companies, entitling them to emergency loans from its discount window. Meanwhile, the Securities and Exchange Commission banned short selling of the two firms' stock. The metaphorical Greenspan put had been replaced by a direct ban on speculative attacks on Wall Street.

The post-Lehman chaos vindicated Greenspan's earlier readiness to respond forcefully to market shocks; later even Hank Paulson would refer to Lehman's collapse as "an economic 9/11." But the chaos also made Greenspan's bet on market discipline look disastrous. It was not that a few firms had failed; the entire money-market industry had required a bailout. It was not that Greenspan's faith had been unwarranted in a few exceptional cases: both the housing-finance giants and all five major investment banks had either failed or been rescued. Ever since the 1980s, when he had endorsed the rescue of Continental Illinois, Greenspan had known that his worldview was contradictory: whereas in the 1960s and 1970s he had preached market discipline while opposing bailouts that might weaken it, from 1984 onward that consistency was gone—he had continued to trust market discipline even as he embraced the bailouts that would undermine it. For a quarter of a century, Greenspan had straddled this incongruity without paying a steep price. But now a lifetime of judgments was being made to look complacent.

Had he known what was to come, what might Greenspan have done differently? Understanding that market discipline was fallible, but fearing correctly that regulation might also fail, Greenspan could have pushed harder for that regulatory third way: mechanisms to ensure that when the inevitable failures did occur, the damage could be minimized. Thicker capital cushions were an obvious example—Timothy Geithner had tried and failed to get this done, but he might have achieved more given stronger support from the Fed chairman. Pushing over-the-counter derivatives into central clearinghouses was another example: had Greenspan thrown his weight behind a sounder version of Brooksley Born's proposal, it might have been harder for AIG to accumulate a swaps portfolio so large that it menaced the entire economy.[42] Discouraging too-big-to-fail lenders was yet a third example of a path not taken: during the crisis, large banks, investment banks, and shadow banks were exposed as having been more reckless than supposedly risky hedge funds, because the latter were small enough to fail, and so had fewer corrupting incentives.[43] Forcing more regulation onto the shadow-banking sector could have been the final item on a resiliency agenda. During the Greenspan era, investment banks, money-market funds, and Fannie and Freddie had all grown prodigiously without being subjected to real supervision. None of these creatures were the direct responsibility of the Fed. But Greenspan's extraordinary stature conferred a duty to at least try to curtail them.

After the failure of Bear Stearns, Greenspan had tried to defend his philosophy of finance. Now, after Lehman, he was closer to venturing an apology.

On October 23, 2008, Greenspan appeared before a House committee. His face was etched with lines and his white shirt collar was rumpled. It was the first time he had submitted to an open-ended grilling on Capitol Hill about his role in the mortgage meltdown.

"I would like to provide my views on the sources of the crisis," Greenspan began. "I would also like to discuss how my thinking has evolved and what I have learned this past year."

At the root of the crisis, Greenspan explained, lay a failure of Wall Street's risk models. In assessing mortgage securities, investors had placed their faith in "a vast risk management and pricing system . . . combining the best insights of mathematicians and finance experts." But as Greenspan had known since his days a young consultant, no mathematical model was worth anything if the data that went into it were flawed, and Wall Street had made the fatal mistake of basing expectations of the future on a few scant years of good performance. Having thus convinced themselves of the safety of mortgage securities, investors had rushed in to buy; and lenders had responded by creating mortgages of all kinds, with no regard to quality. Here, in a nutshell, lay the cause of the troubles. The "whole intellectual edifice . . . collapsed . . . because the data inputted into the risk management models generally covered only the past two decades, a period of euphoria."

The chairman of the committee, Henry Waxman, listened to Greenspan's confession. With a bald head and a precisely clipped mustache, he had the air of a joyless functionary, not a glad-handing politician.

Waxman was not satisfied with Greenspan's story. The former Fed chairman was apologizing for Wall Street's mistakes, not for his own.

"You were, perhaps, the leading proponent of deregulation of our financial markets," Waxman said accusingly. "You have been a staunch advocate for letting markets regulate themselves.

"Let me give you a few of your past statements," the congressman continued menacingly.

"In 1994, you testified at a congressional hearing on regulation of financial derivatives. You said, 'There's nothing involved in Federal regulation which makes it superior to market regulation.'

"In 1997, you said, 'There appears to be no need for government regulation of off-exchange derivative transactions.'

"In 2002, when the collapse of Enron led to renewed congressional efforts to regulate derivatives, you wrote the Senate, 'We do not believe a public policy case exists to justify this government intervention.'

"Earlier this year, you wrote in the *Financial Times,* 'Bank loan officers, in my experience, know far more about the risks and workings of their counterparties than do bank regulators.'"

Waxman looked up from his script and fixed his gaze on Greenspan. "My question for you is simple," he announced.

"Were you wrong?"

Greenspan could have hit back directly. He was not simply an ideologue who believed in deregulation as a matter of faith. He was a pragmatist who had surveyed the evidence and concluded that private risk managers, however fallible, might be better than regulators. One conspicuous failure—albeit a huge one—did not necessarily prove that his judgment had been wrong. Private risk management had worked for many years. Perhaps it would work again in the future.

But instead of confronting Waxman, Greenspan tried to evade him.

"Let's separate this problem into its component parts," he parried professorially. He was willing to concede that credit derivatives—the sort that AIG had sold to customers seeking to protect themselves against a counterparty's default—had "serious problems." But derivatives on currencies and interest rates were fine; and at the time of the debate with Brooksley Born, those were the ones that had existed. Greenspan had green-lighted virtuous swaps, in other words. On evil swaps, not guilty.

Waxman realized that Greenspan could hide in the details of derivatives for a long time, running out the clock on him. So he interrupted.

"You said in your statement that you delivered, the whole intellectual edifice of modern risk management collapsed. You also said, 'Those of us who have looked to the self-interest of lending institutions to protect shareholders' equity, myself especially, are in a state of shock, disbelief.'

"Now that sounds to me like you are saying that those who trusted the market to regulate itself, yourself included, made a serious mistake?"

Greenspan tried to dive back into the long grass of the swaps market. But Waxman was not having it.

"Where did you make a mistake?" he insisted.

"I made a mistake in presuming that the self-interest of organizations, specifically banks and others, were such that they were best capable of protecting their own shareholders and their equity in the firms," Greenspan offered.

Now Waxman was closing in. But Greenspan was already running on to safer ground, explaining why for forty years he had doubted the efficacy of regulation.

"It's been my experience, having worked both as a regulator for eighteen years and . . . in the private sector, especially ten years at a major international bank, that the loan officers of those institutions knew far more about the risks involved and the people to whom they lent money than I saw even our best regulators at the Fed capable of doing," Greenspan pleaded.

"So the problem here is something which looked to be a very solid edifice . . . did break down. And I think that, as I said, shocked me."

"Do you have any personal responsibility for the financial crisis?" Waxman asked. He was not interested in the subtleties.

Greenspan set off on a new tack, seeking to put the record straight about his dealings with Edward Gramlich. He still spoke in the same mesmerizing way: he was dense, circuitous, and difficult to follow; yet somehow his listeners were encouraged to believe that the difficulty was their fault. Five, ten, or fifteen years earlier, the magic of his manner might have worked—Waxman himself had fallen under Greenspan's spell occasionally. But now the maestro effect was gone. Waxman was not going to defer to him.

"Dr. Greenspan, I am going to interrupt you," the congressman broke in. "You had an ideology. You had a belief." Then he quoted Greenspan's own admission on this score. "I do have an ideology," Greenspan had once said. "My judgment is that free, competitive markets are by far the unrivaled way to organize economies. We have tried regulation, none meaningfully worked."

"That was your quote," Waxman declared fiercely. "You had the authority to prevent irresponsible lending practices that led to the subprime mortgage crisis. You were advised to do so by many others. And now our whole economy is paying the price. Do you feel that your ideology pushed you to make decisions that you wish you had not made?"

Waxman's windup had combined an exaggeration of the Fed's power to enforce lending standards at nonbanks; an exaggeration of the force with which Edward Gramlich had spoken; and an exaggeration of the link between reckless mortgage lending and the collapse of leveraged finance. But his question was a masterstroke. The hunter had pushed his quarry out of the long grass: rather than going after him on regulatory detail, he was gunning for nothing less than his entire ideology.

Now Greenspan made a fatal error. Rather than unpicking Waxman's exaggerations, he urged him to refine his thoughts on the nature of ideology.

Ideology, Greenspan explained earnestly, was "a conceptual framework . . . [governing] . . . the way people deal with reality.

"Everyone has one," Greenspan continued. "You have to. To exist, you need an ideology.

"The question is, whether it is accurate or not. What I am saying to you is, yes, I found a flaw, I don't know how significant or permanent it is, but I have been very distressed by that fact."

It was an unremarkable observation. Of course, all ideologies had flaws; the fact that Greenspan had acknowledged his went only to show his pragmatism. By the same token, the opposite ideology had flaws. How often had regulation failed? Would proregulation ideologues match Greenspan's honesty in acknowledging the fissures in their framework? In Greenspan's understanding, the statement that his ideology was flawed was almost a statement of the obvious.

Having offered his token philosophic concession, Greenspan wanted to return to the matter of Edward Gramlich. He seemed oblivious to the fact that Waxman had wounded him.

"But if I may, may I just finish an answer to the question—" Greenspan began.

"You found a flaw?" Waxman interrupted.

"A flaw, a flaw in the model that I perceived is the critical functioning structure that defines how the world works, so to speak," Greenspan confirmed. He was impatient to move on to his next argument.

"In other words, you found that your view of the world, your ideology, was not right, it was not working?" Waxman asked. He was intent on wounding his target as many times as possible.

"Precisely," Greenspan acknowledged. "That's precisely the reason I was shocked, because I had been going for forty years or more with very considerable evidence that it was working exceptionally well."[44]

After Greenspan's duel with Waxman, commentators pounced on his apparent recantation of his ideology. The maestro had confessed to "a flaw in the model"; an "edifice" had collapsed; it was the end of an era. The confession was received as proof, moreover, that the revered Fed chairman had been monstrously naïve; by his own admission, he had been "shocked" that financiers had failed to manage risks successfully. "The system of unregulated incentives, compensation systems, and business practices Greenspan oversaw—or at least tolerated without comment— was riddled with obvious conflicts of interest," the New Yorker's Steve Coll pointed out; how could Greenspan be surprised by the collapse of this rotten ant hill?[45] "Did Greenspan really believe that the people in power, presented with a chance to make a killing, would put the interests of their institutions and stockholders ahead of their own?" the *Los Angeles Times* asked incredulously.[46] In 2010, *The Flaw* became the title of a celebrated documentary. Quoted and requoted without proportion or context, Greenspan's confession threatened to define his legacy.

Of course, the "flaw" was more subtle than Greenspan had apparently admitted. Greenspan had always known that private risk management could fail; his only new discovery in 2008 concerned the scale of the consequences. Moreover, not only had Greenspan *not* believed in the rationality of economic agents; he had doubted it far more insistently than the majority of economists. Summing up the state of the profession after the crisis, Paul Krugman described how both rational-expectations conservatives and Keynesian liberals had been wrong: the first school had believed so fervently in rationality as to deny the possibility of a serious recession; the second had recognized the possibility in theory, but had nonetheless constructed mathematical models based on rational agents, making a slump hard to envisage.[47] Yet Greenspan was innocent of both kinds of mistake. Ever since his debates with Milton Friedman in the 1970s, he had doubted the power of rational expectations; and throughout his tenure at the Fed, he had poked holes in the staff's Keynesian models, frequently warning that the economy could screech to a far more brutal stop than conventional forecasts indicated. It was precisely because he feared the irrationality of finance that Greenspan had created his eponymous put. If the world had sought out a Fed chairman who was equipped to avoid the errors identified by Krugman, it would have awarded the job to none other than Greenspan.

Six months before the "flaw" confession, Greenspan had told the *Wall Street Journal* that sticking him with facile blame would cause the wrong lessons to be drawn from the financial crisis. Now this was proving right: by fixating on the maestro's supposed flaw, the world was achieving catharsis, not enlightenment. If Greenspan really had assumed that markets were perfectly rational, the fragility of finance would have been easy to fix: his removal from public office would have made the world safer.

But the truth was less convenient. Greenspan had understood the limits of market rationality better than most. It followed that future Fed leaders might be ambushed by the same forces.

Because of the distraction of the supposed "flaw" confession, Greenspan's more significant admissions went largely unnoticed. In October 2009, addressing the Council on Foreign Relations in New York, Greenspan embraced the resiliency agenda on which he had been culpably passive. Lenders should be better capitalized, he now said; derivatives should be pushed into central clearinghouses; and megabanks like Citigroup were a mistake—"If they're too big to fail, they're too big," he observed forcefully.[48] The following spring, in a paper for the Brookings Institution, Greenspan criticized the "jerry-built regulatory structure that has evolved over the decades in the United States"; and he went so far as to estimate how much capital banks should be required to hold: an amount equivalent to 14 percent of assets.[49] Given his long-held position that the right amount of capital defied definition, and that megabanks should be welcomed, these were striking departures. They were far more relevant to the future of finance than that philosophic quip to Waxman.

By this time, however, Greenspan's audience was dwindling. Cable news channels no longer hung upon his words, and his public interventions began to veer between the predictable and the eccentric. In April 2010, he was called to testify before the Financial Crisis Inquiry Commission, but rather than expand on his lucid confession about resiliency, he curled up into a defensive crouch, emphasizing an account of the meltdown designed mainly to protect his reputation: monetary policy had been blunted by the global savings glut; there was little that regulators could have done; there would be more crises in the future.[50] As the public debate pivoted to the monetary experiments of the Bernanke Fed, Greenspan contributed warnings of excess money creation, complete with misguided predictions of impending inflation. In 2013, Greenspan published a sequel to his memoir, billed as an attempt to make sense of the crash. But its main contention—that investors could be systematically irrational—was neither new to economics nor even to Greenspan. At eighty-seven years old, Greenspan was forgetting his own history.

The public that had revered him in his prime now turned upon him cruelly. Only a few years earlier, the painting that Erin Crowe had created live on television had fetched $150,400 in an online charity auction. Now the businessman who bought it refused to display it publicly. A financial consultant in Manhattan proposed to turn two Greenspan portraits into dartboards: "All I see when I look at these paintings are two market crashes, a bear market, and the current economic crisis," he said viciously. Another of Erin Crowe's clients complained, "Man, everyone thought he was hot, but he turned out to be a dog." After tracking down multiple collectors across the nation, an intrepid newspaper reporter found only one with a charitable view of the ex-maestro.

"Alan Greenspan at one time was a hero to most of us, and now he is being called a villain," said a man in Jupiter, Florida.

"Who knows what history will say about Alan Greenspan?"[51]

Conclusion

THE BLIND
ROLLER SKATER

In the spring of 1916, ten years before Greenspan was born, the *New York Times* published an obituary of one of his early heroes: "J. J. Hill Dead," the headline proclaimed, "Fortune Put at $75,000,000." James J. Hill had been built like "a buffalo," his teeth "seemingly fit to crunch iron," and although he had amassed interests in shipping, farming, and banking, his greatest monument by far was his audacious rail network, a six-thousand-mile web that stretched from the Minnesota boundary to the Pacific. Hill had willed this system into existence by sheer obstinacy of spirit, laying tracks through virgin wilderness bereft of produce or people, then building up the farms and settlements that would make his lines profitable. Herds of hogs and cattle populated the plains, and towns sprang up where none had been, hurrying into life before the weeds had grown over the railroad embankments. Moreover, whereas lesser railroad magnates had relied on government subsidies and land grants, Hill had pursued his vision without federal assistance. "The greatest constructive genius of the Northwest is gone," Minnesota's governor lamented after Hill's passing.[1]

Such were the grand industrialists who stirred a bookish autodidact from Washington Heights to seek out his own form of greatness. Until he passed the age of forty, Greenspan duly pursued his ambition in a way that Hill might well have recognized, rising from modest origins as the captain of an independent firm, driving himself forward by dint of a strong will and a keen mind, identifying naturally with Ayn Rand's swashbuckling enterpriser heroes. But then, when he signed on with the Nixon campaign in 1967, Greenspan's life turned down a different path: he forsook the individualistic endeavor of an enterpriser for the collective work of politics; he left a realm in which success could be measured neatly in dollars, embarking on a murkier quest for influence and reputation. Greenspan's new habitat—Washington, D.C., as it existed from the late 1960s—could scarcely have been more different from James J. Hill's unplowed frontier. Nothing could be accomplished in the nation's capital without cynical tactics and inglorious compromise. Having chosen government as his calling, Greenspan could never hope to match the tycoons who had inspired him.

For any chronicler of any outsized life, the great-man theory of history stands as a temptation. The lure is especially enticing during periods that empower heroes, periods featuring military conquest or dramatic change; or periods featuring especially egregious inequality, which concentrates power among a handful of leaders. Philosophers of history, reaching for circumstances in which great men made a clear difference, frequently invoke antiquity: "If there had been no Themistocles there would have been no victory of Salamis," mused John Stuart Mill, "and had there not, where would have been all our civilization?"[2] But if antiquity provided the ideal playground for greatness, James J. Hill's era came a close second. The technological frontier and the physical frontier were receding at once; the combination of rail power and the momentum of westward expansion gave Hill his opportunity. Perhaps not surprisingly, many nineteenth-century intellectuals shared the young Greenspan's romantic fascination with outsized individuals. "[A]ll things that we see standing accomplished in the world are properly the outer material result . . . of the thoughts that dwelled in the great men sent into the world," proclaimed the British historian Thomas Carlyle in the classic statement of Victorian hero worship.[3]

For the biographer of Alan Greenspan, however, the great-man theory of history is a trap. Far from inhabiting a playground for Randian supermen, Greenspan came of age in a very different time: a time of cookie-cutter suburbs, mass-produced consumer goods, an absence of heroic wars, and relatively low inequality. Rather than living in the heyday of individualism, Greenspan confronted imposing collectives: big corporations, big unions, and increasingly big government. With his imagination fired by the tycoons of the nineteenth century, Greenspan resisted as stoutly as he could, pronouncing Ayn Rand's atavistic hero worship in *Atlas Shrugged* to be "radiantly exact," and rejecting the homogenizing bonds of family life even as baby making boomed around him. But limited mortals cannot escape their times, and Greenspan's entry into the public arena sealed his fate. By the late twentieth century, nobody, not even the U.S. president, could evade the checks and balances of political life: rival government departments that fought selfishly for turf; lobbies that captured portions of Congress; an intellectual climate that threw open some paths and rendered others all but impenetrable. The paradox of Alan Greenspan is that by embodying the American economy in a period of prosperity, he came to seem all-knowing and all-powerful. But a fair evaluation must place him in his true context—a context that made it extraordinarily hard for individuals to stamp their mark on progress.

A ll this being said, how should we judge Greenspan? As an observer, analyst, and forecaster, he was formidable. Thanks to his early training in the old-fashioned empiricism of the New York school, he focused more on data than on fallible econometric models, avoiding the mathematical hubris of the next generation of economists. Thanks to his early education in finance, courtesy of his mentor Bill Townsend, he understood the interactions between markets and the real economy better than most of his contemporaries. Aside from the times during his thirties when he fell under Ayn Rand's eccentric spell, he managed to be right about most things: right about the interaction between asset values and growth, which he laid out in 1959; right about the inflationary bias in an overregulated economy, starting in the 1960s; right about the interplay between monetary policy and housing finance in the late 1970s; right about the irresponsibility of Reaganite supply-siders in the 1980s; right about the productivity acceleration in the mid-1990s; and right about the threat of lowflation in the 2000s. In this long string of successes, the productivity call was by far the most noted. "I don't think most other people who could have been Fed Chairman would have seen it," Lawrence Summers said, summing up the consensus in the economics profession; the "call on the productivity acceleration was truly a great one," the Fed governor Laurence Meyer agreed—"He got it right before the rest of us did."[4] But the truth is that Greenspan's less remembered pre-Fed judgments were equally prescient. Unlike Milton Friedman, he anticipated the failure of Nixon's price controls in the early 1970s; unlike almost everybody, he argued that the public's revulsion at inflation later in the decade would create a predicate for its conquest. Academic economists, unaware of Greenspan's record as a forecaster and observing his empiricism and his impatience with models, occasionally expressed doubts about his grasp. But those who worked closely with him almost always took a different view. "Alan is one of the smartest people I've ever known in my life," declared the eminent Princeton economist Burton Malkiel, after serving with Greenspan in the Ford White House.[5]

Setting aside his early Randian lapses, Greenspan was ultimately guilty of one serious analytical error—admittedly, a consequential one. Although he understood the frailty in finance, he underestimated the cost in doing little about it. His nonchalance in the face of proliferating derivatives and leveraged shadow banking recalled the classic silent movie *Modern Times,* in which Charlie Chaplin puts on roller skates and a blindfold and pirouettes about the floor of a department store, oblivious to the fact that he is inches from a steep drop over an open balcony.[6] How this costly misjudgment should be weighed against a lifetime of wise insight is itself a matter of judgment, as we shall see presently. But in fairness to Greenspan, the collective nature of this error should at least be recognized. As late as the spring of 2007, Greenspan's successor, Ben Bernanke, assured the public that the impact of falling house prices on the broader economy was "likely to be contained," and the International Monetary Fund declared that global economic risks were declining. Greenspan may have resembled Chaplin's blind roller skater, but so did virtually all forecasters.

As a doer rather than an observer, however, Greenspan's record was not so distinguished. His participation in the Nixon campaign was often immature or craven, especially when he attacked Bobby Kennedy for supposedly stoking racial violence after Martin Luther King's assassination. Later, during Nixon's presidency, he allowed himself to be co-opted into a plot to neuter an economist whom he revered and an institution that he would embody. As chairman of Ford's Council of Economic Advisers, he began by reassuring Senator William Proxmire that he would not force his libertarianism on the president if he was in "a minority of one." But then he delivered on this promise almost too much, failing to resist an increase in the federal budget deficit even when his weekly GNP estimates indicated that no stimulus was necessary, and even when other presidential counselors were urging budgetary responsibility. The clearest instance in which Greenspan urged Ford to stand on principle turned out to be misjudged. He offered impractical antibailout purism when New York flirted with bankruptcy.

After Ford's presidency, Greenspan's performance as a doer remained checkered. He resisted the supply-side radicals who gathered around the new Republican standard-bearer, Ronald Reagan, but he was not always a profile in courage. When the moment of truth came at the Palmer House Hilton in Chicago, Greenspan signed off on the dangerously rosy forecasts that disguised the recklessness of Candidate Reagan's budget plan; then he went out and convinced the press that the plan was responsible. After Reagan's election, Greenspan ducked the challenge of using the Social Security commission to reform government pensions, even though, from the perspective of a libertarian, his appointment represented a golden opportunity to offer more than tweaks and patches. Finally, as Fed chairman, Greenspan was not quite the all-powerful leader that most Americans supposed. The recovery from the 1987 crash owed less to him than to a cast of lesser-known players: Gerald Corrigan, the domineering boss of the New York Fed; Leo Melamed, the scrappy chief of the Chicago Mercantile Exchange; Stanley Shopkorn of Salomon Brothers and Bob Mnuchin of Goldman Sachs, who bought the market at a crucial time, perhaps averting catastrophe. Likewise, the remarkable moderation of inflation in the 1990s reflected, at least partly, the downward pressure on prices from deregulation and globalization. As Greenspan himself was the first to acknowledge, these were not of the Fed's making.

Greenspan's specialty as a political actor lay in a sort of manipulative genius. As a business consultant who served fee-paying executives, he had learned to combine data-infused counsel with a dash of flattery and guile: he taught clients to depend on his advice, but he knew better than to alienate them by contradicting them directly. Thanks to his apprenticeship in the Nixon campaign, Greenspan learned to maneuver politically as well—he watched Patrick Buchanan perform a U-turn on farm subsidies when chased by the "Dakota wolves," then switched from penning strident denunciations of the Great Society to offering calibrated political advice, informed by his keen polling analysis. By 1975, Ayn Rand's unworldly chief economist had mastered Washington so completely that he could stymie no less an infighter than Henry Kissinger on the question of the Iranian oil deal—a fact that did not stop him from teaming up with Kissinger five years later in an attempt to maneuver Ford onto Reagan's presidential ticket. From this period forward, Greenspan went to extraordinary lengths to cultivate the media, instructing his assistants to pull him out of meetings if a big newspaper called, and emerging as a favorite talking head on television. As a result, as Fed chairman, Greenspan enjoyed an almost reverential press. He captured the credit for stabilizing the economy after the 1987 crash; he dominated *Time*'s cover showing "The Committee to Save the World," even though the two smaller figures at his flanks (the Treasury secretary and deputy Treasury secretary, no less) had spearheaded the emerging-market rescues. To an extent that had never been true before for central bankers, Greenspan's pronouncements on all manner of subjects came to be treated as gospel. He was, as he joked nervously, the Zipswitch chairman. He was the maestro.

Despite his extraordinary prestige, Greenspan knew he could survive in Washington only by avoiding fights, or by engaging them passively and deviously. It was an approach that came naturally to a sensitive, shy man. Haunted by the absence of a pale father, intimidated by the presence of a vivid mother, he often lacked the confidence to confront others personally and directly. And so, from early in his public service, Greenspan became a master of passive aggression, pretending to sympathize with Kissinger while stalling him, inviting anti-supply-side economists to difficult meetings in the early Reagan period so that they would make his arguments for him, feigning sympathy with the gold bugs of 1981 while deliberately sabotaging their project. Later, as Fed chairman, Greenspan turned away suggestions that the Fed should regulate the GSEs, preferring to encourage reformers privately behind the scenes rather than joining the front lines of the struggle. Even at the start of the George W. Bush administration, when Greenspan was supposedly at the height of his powers, he caved in to the White House on the first tax cut, despite having been a budget hawk for the previous four decades. On financial regulation, similarly, Greenspan was a follower more than a leader. He took care to vote with the majority on the Federal Reserve Board, deferring to the Fed's general counsel whenever possible. The exceptions to this pattern of passivity came when the Fed's turf was threatened, notably at times when the Treasury proposed to usurp its authority to supervise the banking system. Although he shrank from open conflict when he could, Greenspan adored power and was prepared to fight for it.

Greenspan's passivity as a political actor exacerbated his single error as an analyst—his underestimation of the potential costs from financial fragility. With the explosion of derivatives, megabanks, shadow banks, and leverage, the financial system changed out of all recognition during his tenure; he should have demanded commensurate change in the apparatus of regulation. His failure to do so is commonly ascribed to his libertarian bias: he "deregulated" finance, it is often said, because he was a laissez-faire ideologue. But by the time Greenspan became Fed chairman, his ideology was mostly gone: he was "a get along, go along, comfortable and increasingly popular" figure, as Senator Proxmire observed at his confirmation in 1987; he was a pragmatist capable of actively backing regulation, as he did during the post-Enron debate on corporate auditors. The real reasons for Greenspan's tolerance of the new finance therefore lay elsewhere. First, he made a pragmatic judgment that megabanks, derivatives, and securitization might be stabilizing, seeing in them risk-spreading advantages as well as evident pitfalls—and even if this judgment ultimately proved wrong, the fact that it was shared by most Democratic experts as well as the technocrats on the Fed's staff suggests that it was scarcely ideological. Second, Greenspan made the equally pragmatic judgment that fighting for new regulation would be politically impossible. It would mean forging a united front among multiple regulatory bodies, and it would involve battling powerful lobbies that had the ear of Congress. With his reflexive passivity, Greenspan had no stomach for this fight. "He was not an in-your-face personality; he was an around-the-corner personality," one close acquaintance said. He was first and foremost a political survivor. He wanted to make friends, not alienate them.

Quite how harshly Greenspan should be judged for this timidity comes back to the question of individuals and history. If Greenspan had demanded a bolder response to the challenge of leverage, megabanks, and derivatives, would he have made a real difference? The best guess is that he would not. The moments when Greenspan did stick his neck out are instructive on this point. He opposed the second George W. Bush tax cut, and the White House rolled over him. He pushed belatedly for GSE regulation, this time with the White House on his side, and he was beaten back by lobbyists. He supported the Fed's efforts to clamp down on risky mortgages, and the housing lenders soon found ways around the restrictions. He backed the drive for Wall Street resilience conducted by Timothy Geithner at the New York Fed, but this came to almost nothing. It is worth recalling that the redoubtable Paul Volcker resisted the unraveling of the Glass-Steagall regulations to absolutely no avail—why then should we suppose that Greenspan could have made a greater difference? Likewise, it bears noting that Paul O'Neill, the Treasury secretary in the early 2000s, broke Washington's code of caution and fought hard for his beliefs. He was fired for his trouble.

Greenspan may have been hailed as the maestro, and the width of his briefcase may have been scrutinized by news pundits. But the truth is that there were limits to his power. He was not an Athenian general or a nineteenth-century railroad pioneer. He was maneuvering in cramped political terrain, boxed in by a clamorous multitude of turf fighters and string pullers and influence peddlers. If he often behaved passively, it was partly because he was hemmed in by these constraints. He should not be condemned, for with limited power comes limited responsibility.

There was, however, one area in which Greenspan exercised untrammeled power: the setting of short-term interest rates. From the time of his first FOMC meetings, when he clashed boldly with the Fed's top staff forecaster, Mike Prell, Greenspan set about establishing control over this lever. A series of challengers, from the economics team in the George H. W. Bush administration to FOMC members such as Alan Blinder and Lawrence Lindsey, attempted to tell him which way he should pull—he dispatched them forcefully. Much of the economics profession, including the Fed's in-house brain trust, believed he should give up some of his authority by publicly committing to an inflation target—he rebuffed them repeatedly. Presidents and senators had long been in the habit of sniping at the Fed chairman—in the Greenspan era, they learned to defer to him. Because Greenspan dominated monetary policy so completely for almost two decades, his impact on history is best viewed through a monetary lens. The smoothness of economic growth—the prevalence or absence of humanly costly shocks—is the best test of Greenspan's legacy.

By now there should be no suspense about the verdict on Greenspan's monetary policy. On the one hand, he brilliantly limited fluctuations in inflation—even if deregulation and globalization partly explained inflation's low level, monetary policy also played a part, and Greenspan's steadying presence deserves credit for its low variance. On the other hand, Greenspan utterly failed to limit leverage and bubbles, and this failure magnified financial fragility. Because he conducted monetary policy with a view to ensuring price stability, not financial stability, Greenspan allowed this fragility to grow and grow. Like Chaplin's blind roller skater, he underestimated the abyss that lay beneath him.[7]

How did the man who knew the risks in financial cycles back in 1959 nonetheless commit this error? It is not enough to invoke Greenspan's own explanation here, for the Fed chairman was capable of making arguments that he only half believed if he saw tactical gain in them. Thus, in the aftermath of the tech crash and even more insistently during his retirement years, Greenspan and his sympathizers would repeat a three-part mantra: central banks should not raise interest rates to combat asset bubbles because bubbles are impossible to identify in advance; they should not do so because the debris from bust bubbles can be cleaned up after the fact; and they should not do so because interest rates would have to be raised by such a large amount that they would puncture the economy. Yet none of these assertions is really persuasive. To be sure, bubbles cannot be identified with certainty; but Greenspan had no hesitation in diagnosing bubbly markets at countless FOMC meetings, and the post-Greenspan consensus among central bankers, which holds that incipient bubbles should be deflated with regulatory tools, presumes the possibility of diagnosis. Likewise, it is true that central banks can sometimes clean up after bubbles, but this option is neither reliable nor cost free: the Fed's cleanup operation following the tech bust contributed to the next bubble in housing; and when the housing bubble burst in 2008, no amount of cleanup work could prevent a prolonged downturn. Finally, the assertion that it would require a crippling amount of tightening to let the air out of a bubble is merely that—an assertion. The impact of higher interest rates on asset prices depends on market psychology, whose shifts are too fickle to predict confidently.

Because Greenspan's three-part mantra is not convincing, there are times when it makes sense for central banks to raise interest rates to fight asset bubbles. They should not do this when other considerations point strongly the other way: when unemployment is high or when deflation threatens. But just as it would be wrong to give up on the quest for better regulation, despite the many obstacles that lie in its way, so it is unreasonable to rule out the use of interest rates to fight bubbles at all times and in all circumstances. During Greenspan's Fed tenure, he should have raised rates to fight bubbles on two occasions—in late 1998 and early 1999, and again in 2004–5. In both instances, unemployment was low, deflation was not threatening, and yet markets were evidently too hot. The Fed should have raised rates more aggressively, accepting somewhat lower growth in the short term in exchange for a more stable economy in the medium term.

Why did a man as historically conscious as Greenspan fail to do more to fight bubbles? A clue to the answer can be found in the 1960s, when another school of economists found itself in an analogous position. At that time, the fathers of modern portfolio theory confronted a highly inconvenient truth: contrary to their efficient-market assumptions, price changes in asset markets do not follow the "normal distribution" depicted by a bell curve; rather, very large price moves occur far more frequently than the thin tails of the bell curve anticipate. At first the efficient marketers responded open-mindedly to this objection, acknowledging that its main proponent, the maverick mathematician Benoit Mandelbrot, was right. But then they swept Mandelbrot's protests under the carpet because his message was too difficult to live with. Deprived of their bell-curve assumption, the efficient marketers' mathematical techniques would cease to work. "Mandelbrot, like Prime Minister Churchill before him, promises us not utopia but blood, sweat, toil and tears," Paul Cootner, an efficient marketer, objected. "If he is right, almost all of our statistical tools are obsolete—least squares, spectral analysis, workable maximum-likelihood solutions, all our established sample theory, closed distribution functions. Almost without exception, past econometric work is meaningless."[8]

Greenspan is misleadingly remembered as an efficient-market believer, even though he spent much of his life worrying about bubbles. Paradoxically, he is not usually remembered for what he and the efficient marketers genuinely shared. Like the efficient-markets school, Greenspan grasped a crucial weakness in his outlook: if the central bank's job is to protect workers from economic shocks, then price stability is not enough—financial stability is as essential. Indeed, given Greenspan's failure to establish that driving inflation below, say, 5 percent would bring faster gains in productivity or other obvious boons, he might have concluded that financial stability was *more* essential. But like the efficient marketers, Greenspan turned his eyes from the weakness in his outlook because it was too awkward to live with. If he had tried to make bubbles and leverage a central part of his mission, the Fed's mandate from Congress, requiring it to focus on inflation and employment, would have needed revision. Likewise, the expectations of politicians and the public, which created the enabling environment around the Fed, would have required reshaping. For a man who was averse to picking unnecessary fights, it was all too daunting.

In moments of honesty, Greenspan admitted this. In March 1994, reflecting on the recent bond-market collapse, Greenspan mused to his FOMC colleagues that price stability might coexist dangerously with financial instability, as it had done in the 1920s. The implication was that fixating exclusively on stable inflation might involve missing the main threat to the economy. But then he quickly backed away, acknowledging that the implications of his hypothesis were impossibly unsettling. "All of our concepts about how the monetary system works will have to go into a radical revision, which I can't at this stage even remotely contemplate," he confessed, sounding as desperate as the efficient marketer Paul Cootner. For the rest of his tenure, Greenspan danced around this dark problem. In 1996, when he mused aloud about "irrational exuberance," he was not merely suggesting that the market was too high; he was asking whether monetary policy should do something about it: "Evaluating shifts in balance sheets generally, and in asset prices particularly, must be an integral part of the development of monetary policy," he stated. Likewise, in the twilight of his tenure, in February 2005, Greenspan confronted his colleagues with tantalizing questions. "Are we dealing solely with the prices of goods and services, or do asset prices enter into the evaluation?" he wondered. "Is macroeconomic stability, and specifically financial stability, a factor that must be taken into account?"

In short, Greenspan knew that financial instability mattered. But he focused instead on inflation for a simple and not entirely good reason. Controlling asset prices and leverage was hard; fighting inflation was easier. At a time when deregulation and globalization were bringing down prices anyway, and when Paul Volcker had established the legitimacy of an inflation-fighting Fed, Greenspan chose the path of least resistance. To be fair, even this easier path was no cakewalk: during the first third of his tenure, when the battle against inflation was not yet won, Greenspan bravely fought off public attacks from the George H. W. Bush administration. But as inflation abated and financial excesses started to build up, the chairman should have pivoted to face the new challenge—he should have conducted monetary policy with an eye to stabilizing finance. Failing to execute that pivot was Greenspan's most consequential error, one that he did not have to make. Although he presided over the Fed during the years when inflation targeting came to be accepted internationally, he did not have to follow this fashion. In the world of monetary technocrats, as distinct from the world of regulatory politics and deep-pocketed lobbies, he was powerful enough to kick away constraints—the Fed's monetary policy was whatever he wanted it to be. Inside the Fed's boardroom, Greenspan was as mighty as his hero James J. Hill. With great power comes great responsibility.

As I conclude my writing in early 2016, the conventional verdict on Greenspan seems doubly perplexing. He is commonly condemned for his regulatory errors. And yet, as I have tried to show, he made pragmatic judgments about finance that were widely accepted at the time; he backed regulation more than his critics care to recall; and it is not at all clear that a stronger push would have made a difference. In contrast, Greenspan's monetary policy, entailing a single-minded focus on inflation, is commonly lauded. And yet, as I have argued, focusing on inflation distracted the Fed from the perils of finance. By committing itself more formally to inflation targeting after Greenspan's retirement, the Fed has unfortunately compounded this problem.

If the life of Alan Greenspan teaches us one thing, it is that democracies must be realistic about what they expect from their leaders. Greenspan was honest, decent, and profoundly wise—he was a model of a public servant. But he was not infallible or omniscient or endowed with magical courage, particularly when it came to confronting powerful adversaries. Precisely because modern American democracy is so gridlocked, there is a tendency to wish for superman saviors—a tendency that is evident, incidentally, in the current fashion for "macroprudential" regulation, which involves central bankers identifying pockets of troubling financial risk and then coolly commanding mighty banks to pull back from them. But systems of public administration that presume the existence of omniscient saviors will inevitably fail—and the cycle will then turn, and the supermen will be condemned bitterly. America's political culture adores leaders, but it is merciless when they fall short. In this sense, also, Alan Greenspan teaches a lesson. From hero to antihero, from maestro to villain, his story is a fable of the land that made him.

Acknowledgments

This book could not have been written without the support of the Council on Foreign Relations, where I have worked since 2007. Thanks to the patience of the Council's leadership—in particular, that of Richard N. Haass, the president, and James M. Lindsay, the director of studies—I have been able to devote five years to the chronicling of Alan Greenspan's life, and have benefited from the help of researchers whose combined efforts make this the equivalent of a fourteen-year undertaking. My family points out that each of my four books has taken longer than the previous one, and that this is not obviously a good thing. But it has been a privilege to indulge my most perfectionist instincts: to immerse myself in a project of this scope with no thought other than to write the best book possible. Whenever I encountered archives that might yield fresh material, or interview subjects who might fill in missing pieces, I was in the fortunate position of having the time and resources to go after them.

Among the researchers who joined me, Jon Hill stands out for his sheer stamina. When I hired Jon in 2011, I had read his graceful writing and could see that he was smart: he came to the Council from Columbia University, where he double-majored in economics and political science and edited *The Blue & White,* the undergraduate magazine. But there was no way I could have anticipated his tenacity as an investigator. Jon dug up the census records from 1940 to establish how much Greenspan's mother earned. He wrote the code needed to download and search the otherwise unmanageable tape logs from the Nixon library, then documented Greenspan's involvement in the Nixon administration's plot against the Fed by deciphering the cracked voices of the president and his henchmen. Combining George Washington University's National Security Archive and the State Department's Office of the Historian, he reconstructed Greenspan's epic battle with Henry Kissinger in 1975 over the Iranian oil question. On the crucial matter of how far the Fed tried to tamp down irresponsible mortgage lending in the early 2000s, Jon filed the requests under the Freedom of Information Act that helped me to relate the real story, which is not the story told in most accounts of the period. Jon stuck with the project for more than four years. He was an exceptional collaborator.

I was also fortunate to have the assistance of Matthew C. Klein and Jeremy Cohen, each of whom spent two years at the Council. Matt, who now writes for the *Financial Times* section Alphaville, devoted one year of his time with me to reading the twelve thousand pages of FOMC transcripts spanning 1987 through 2006—I doubt that any other researcher has completed this monetary Iron Man. Jeremy, who has gone on to a doctorate at Princeton, pieced together Greenspan's strange role at the 1980 Republican convention; his fights with supply-siders in the 1970s and early 1980s; and his intellectual evolution on the question of bailouts during Paul Volcker's Fed chairmanship. When it came to statistical questions, I sought help repeatedly from Dinah Walker, who was working at the Council between stints at the New York Fed; Dinah's masterful spreadsheets, displaying decades of data on interest rates, inflation measures, asset prices, and much else, were always an Alt-Tab flip away while I was writing. A succession of wonderful interns—Sahana Kumar, Michael Ng, Sebastian Beckmann, Shannon Prier, Alex Lloyd George, Lauren Waugh, and Asha Banerjee—provided additional feedback and much faithful fact-checking. The Council's library team tolerated endless requests for obscure books, journal articles, and microfilm news clips from predigital archives. Laura Puls spearheaded the effort to pull together the best possible collection of photographs. David De La Fleur, Gabriel Lafuente, Simon Lee, and their colleagues in IT were patient when my computers stalled, which is sadly more than I can claim.

Writing this book at the Council also allowed me to draw on the experience of its members. Toward the end of my writing, I benefited from feedback from three circles of readers: Daniel Yergin, a Council board member and Pulitzer Prize–winning historian, chaired a study group of experts in Washington, D.C.; Michael Levi, the director of the Council's Greenberg Center for Geoeconomic Studies, did the same in New York; and Stacey LaFollette and Kate Dinota of the Council's meetings team convened a group of younger members to provide additional reactions. Liaquat Ahamed, Lewis Alexander, Theresa Barger, Douglas Elmendorf, Stephen Freidheim, Karen Johnson, Jonathan Kirshner, Donald Kohn, Peter Osnos, Michael Prell, Jonathan Rauch, Kim Schoenholtz, Brad Setser, David Wessel, and Robert Zoellick were among those who read parts of the manuscript and provided extensive challenge and counsel; many others, too numerous to mention, provoked me to reexamine my analysis or storytelling. I should also like to thank Adam Posen for arranging a study group for me at the Peterson Institute for International Economics, of which he is president. Several friends at Peterson, including Joseph Gagnon, David Stockton, Ted Truman, and Steve Weisman, read chapters and helped me with extensive comments. Finally, and most cryptically, the Council on Foreign Relations appointed two anonymous reviewers, who wrote trenchantly about the manuscript's strengths and gaps. I have done my best to reflect this collective wisdom in revisions to the final draft. Remaining open to reader comments, even when stamina is failing and the finish line looms temptingly in sight, is an indispensable part of the book-writing process.

For the third time in my career, I have benefited from that publishing dream team: my agent, Andrew Wylie, and my editor at Penguin Press, Scott Moyers. Despite the delays that I inflicted upon them, they were unfailingly supportive. Reading the chapters as I wrote them, Scott would usually react with masterful morale-building e-mails—he is the sort of editor who refuses to meddle when meddling is not needed. But on at least one occasion, Scott bounced a chapter back to me and commanded a rewrite. He is the sort of editor who intervenes decisively when intervention is needed. In the United Kingdom, I was lucky to be taken on a second time by Michael Fishwick of Bloomsbury. Always pretending to know less than he does, Michael prompted me helpfully on matters of clarity and pace, insisting in particular that I lay out the nature of my sources in a preface.

Finally, thanks to my family: Felix, Maya, Milo, and Molly; and my beloved wife, Zanny. They are not everything, as my former colleague David Maraniss once wrote in his acknowledgments; they are the only thing.

Appendix

THE GREENSPAN EFFECT

INFLATION TAMED

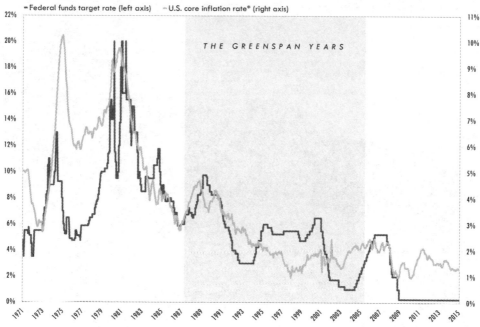

■ Federal funds target rate (left axis)   ~ U.S. core inflation rate* (right axis)

THE GREENSPAN YEARS

Sources: Bloomberg, U.S. Bureau of Economic Analysis   * Year-over-year change in the core personal consumption expenditures price index   Jon Hill / Council on Foreign Relations

THE GREAT MODERATION

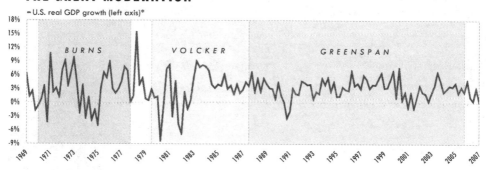

■ U.S. real GDP growth (left axis)*

BURNS   *VOLCKER*   *GREENSPAN*

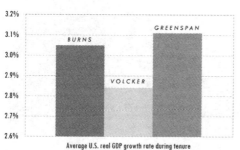

Average U.S. real GDP growth rate during tenure   Volatility of U.S. real GDP growth, standard deviation in percentage points

Source: U.S. Bureau of Economic Analysis   * Annualized quarter-over-quarter growth rate   Jon Hill / Council on Foreign Relations

LEVERAGING AMERICA

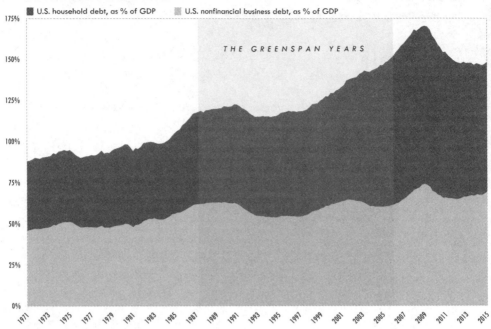

■ U.S. household debt, as % of GDP   ▨ U.S. nonfinancial business debt, as % of GDP

THE GREENSPAN YEARS

Sources: U.S. Bureau of Economic Analysis, Board of Governors of the U.S. Federal Reserve System   Jon Hill / Council on Foreign Relations

THE SHADOW

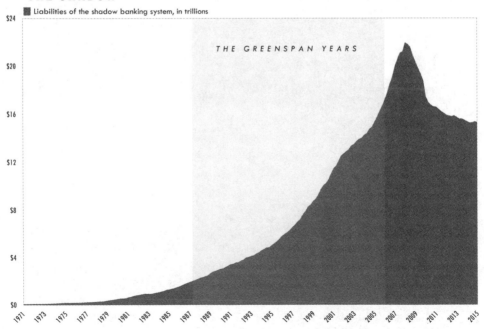

■ Liabilities of the shadow banking system, in trillions

THE GREENSPAN YEARS

Source: Board of Governors of the U.S. Federal Reserve System data, presented according to methodology in Federal Reserve Bank of New York Staff Report No. 458, "Shadow Banking" (2010).   Jon Hill/Council on Foreign Relations

Notes

INTRODUCTION

1. The following dialogue is reconstructed from contemporaneous notes taken by Martin Anderson, a White House adviser. I am grateful to Martin and Annelise Anderson for making these notes available to me.

2. William L. Silber, *Volcker: The Triumph of Persistence* (New York: Bloomsbury Press, 2012), 149.

3. In 1975 Greenspan was asked for an interview by *Penthouse*. He declined. See Justin Martin, *Greenspan: The Man Behind Money* (Cambridge, Mass.: Perseus Publishing, 2001), 127.

4. Alan Greenspan, Economics of a Free Society (lecture series presented at the Nathaniel Branden Institute, Roosevelt Hotel, New York, December 1963–February 1964, sec. VIII–17). Greenspan delivered a set of ten weekly lectures between December 1963 and February 1964. A detailed script of each presentation was drawn up. The author wishes to thank Lowell Wiltbank for providing a complete copy of these scripts, which runs to a little more than three hundred pages. Section numbers reflect the order of the lecture in the series followed by the page number for that lecture.

5. Toward the end of his life, Greenspan often rediscovered his youthful convictions. Thus, in an interview in 2010, Greenspan vigorously denied the usefulness of central-bank activism. "There's an implication out there that if you have a lethargic economy the way to get it going is to kick it. Now if you have a manic depressive and you kick him, he will go into a deeper manic depression. This assumption that is taken as a given, that you have to 'spark' the economy, is an incredible hypothesis. It's just false! There is no evidence that 'sparking' an economy actually turns it on. . . . We've had centuries of business cycles which go up and which go down. There hasn't been a single business cycle which has not recovered on its own." Alan Greenspan, interview by the author, October 29, 2010.

6. While Friedman expected the Fed to succumb to political pressure, others thought the central bank was powerless because rational individuals would adjust their behavior in an offsetting direction. For the rational expectations view, see Finn E. Kydland and Edward C. Prescott, "Rules Rather Than Discretion: The Inconsistency of Optimal Plans," *Journal of Political Economy* 85, no. 3 (June 1977): 473–91; Robert J. Barro and David B. Gordon, "A Positive Theory of Monetary Policy in a Natural Rate Model," *Journal of Political Economy* 91, no. 4 (August 1983): 589–610.

7. Quoted in Silber, *Volcker: The Triumph,* 149.

8. William Greider, *Secrets of the Temple: How the Federal Reserve Runs the Country* (New York: Simon & Schuster, 1989), 714.

9. Friedman's article compared inflation under Greenspan with the postwar rate, using the GDP deflator, a measure that is broader than the more familiar consumer price index. The comparison given here sharpens Friedman's point: Greenspan's record was superior even to Volcker's second term—that is, it was superior to Volcker's *after* his celebrated victory over inflation.

10. Milton Friedman, "'He Has Set a Standard,'" *Wall Street Journal,* January 31, 2006.

11. Greenspan tried to reconcile his two selves by saying that he had run America's fiat currency "as though we were on the gold standard." *House Committee on Financial Services, Monetary Policy and the State of the Economy: Hearing Before the Committee on Financial Services,* 109th Cong., 1st sess., 2005, http://www.gpo.gov/fdsys/pkg/CHRG-109hhrg23738/pdf/CHRG-109hhrg23738.pdf. Greenspan offered versions of this remark at other hearings of the House committee, always at the prompting of Congressman Ron Paul. See also his House Financial Services Committee testimonies of July 18, 2001; February 12, 2003; and July 21, 2004. Greenspan made the same point during interviews with the author on October 29, 2010; November 8, 2010; December 10, 2010; and May 4, 2012. The claim is justified in the sense that the Greenspan Fed contained inflation, but not in the sense that it abstained from manipulating the money supply, especially when the financial system was strained following crises.

12. Writing about the lead-up to the crash of 1929, the young Greenspan had observed that the Fed's narrow focus on consumer price stability was folly—the Fed should have raised rates to head off an asset bubble. "Those who claimed that the famous policy of monetary ease by the Fed in 1927 was the spark to the 1929 speculative boom were, almost certainly, making a proper evaluation. . . . The sharp upward gyrations in stock prices—and other capital values—made the subsequent stock market reversal inevitable." Alan Greenspan, "Papers on Economic Theory and Policy" (PhD dissertation, New York University, 1977), 102.

13. In congressional testimony in 1994, Greenspan observed that derivatives

linked financial institutions in ways that could exacerbate crises: "The very efficiency that is involved here means that if a crisis were to occur, that crisis is transmitted at a far faster pace and with some greater virulence." At times, although not consistently, Greenspan also foresaw the too-big-to-fail problem. To cite one example, in a speech in 1999, he stated that "the megabanks being formed by growth and consolidation are increasingly complex entities that create the potential for unusually large systemic risks." See Alan Greenspan, "The Evolution of Bank Supervision" (speech, American Bankers Association, Phoenix, October 11, 1999). Greenspan also warned of the systemic risk posed by Fannie and Freddie. See chapter twenty-eight.

14. Between 1970 and 1990, the hardware costs needed to support securitization fell from about 4 percent of the value of a $2 billion basket of mortgages to about one tenth of a basis point. Over the same period, the share of mortgages securitized rose from 1.7 percent to 43.2 percent. I am indebted to Lewis Alexander for this comparison.

CHAPTER ONE

1. Stewart H. Holbrook, *The Story of American Railroads* (New York: Crown Publishers, 1947), 1. Greenspan's mentor Ayn Rand cites Holbrook in her "Notes on the History of American Free Enterprise" from *Capitalism: The Unknown Ideal* (New York: Signet, 1967), 108–16. Greenspan himself remembers reading Holbrook, who captured the excitement that Greenspan shared about the railways.

2. Alan Greenspan, interview by the author, October 12, 2010.

3. Greenspan's childhood is briefly described in his autobiography, *The Age of Turbulence*, and at somewhat greater length in *Greenspan: The Man Behind Money*, by Justin Martin. Martin's rich account is based on interviews with Greenspan's childhood friends and cousins. I have relied on both sources, as well as on extensive Greenspan interviews. See Alan Greenspan, *The Age of Turbulence: Adventures in a New World* (New York: Penguin Books, 2008); and Justin Martin, *Greenspan: The Man Behind Money* (Cambridge, Mass.: Perseus Publishing, 2001).

4. Greenspan recalls, "It's not that we ever starved or anything like that but I mean to this day I turn lights off, lord knows that's the last

thing I should be spending my time on but it's still built into my personality. I still eat everything on my plate, that's the way I was brought up." Greenspan, interview by the author, May 4, 2012.

5. Steven M. Lowenstein, *Frankfurt on the Hudson: The German-Jewish Community of Washington Heights, 1933 to 1983, Its Structure and Culture* (Detroit: Wayne State University, 1989).

6. Ernest Stock, "Washington Heights' 'Fourth Reich': The German Émigrés' New Home," *Commentary*, June 1951.

7. Census records in the National Archives show that in 1940 Rose Goldsmith was working forty hours a week and earning a bit over $1,000 a year. *Sixteenth Census of the United States: 1940* (U.S. Census Bureau, April 2, 2012), National Archives, http://1940cen sus.archives.gov/search/?search .result_type=image&search.state= NY&search.county=New+York+ County&search.city=&search .street=163rd+W#filename= m-t0627-02677-00216.tif&name= 31-2139&type=image&state=NY.

8. Greenspan, *Age of Turbulence*, 21.

9. Greenspan, interview by the author, February 6, 2013.

10. Bonnie Angelo, *First Mothers: The Women Who Shaped the Presidents* (New York: William Morrow, 2000).

11. Quoted in Ernest Jones, *The Life and Work of Sigmund Freud* (New York: Basic Books, 1953), 1:5.

12. "She was a very buoyant lady . . . very optimistic . . . nothing bothered her." Greenspan, interview by the author, July 10, 2012.

13. "I was more inclined to sit in the corner." Greenspan, *Age of Turbulence*, 21.

14. The manifest recording the arrival of Haim Grunspann and his family is on record at the Ellis Island Passenger List Database of the Statue of Liberty–Ellis Island Foundation, Inc.

15. "He promised me things and never delivered." Greenspan, interview by the author, July 10, 2012.

16. Martin, *Greenspan: The Man Behind Money*, 2.

17. Greenspan links his early interest in mathematics to his lack of familial ties: "There is something about growing up in a household where there's a mother and a father and siblings all of whom love each other. . . . I never had that. I was never consciously aware that I missed it but I go back now in retrospect with an adult's understanding of how the human species works and realize that it did have an effect on me. . . . Why I was

originally drawn to math I think is the certainty of it. There is an incredible degree of security, intellectual security, in the feeling that I don't need to go and ask other people, 'Is this right?'" Greenspan, interview by the author, October 29, 2010.

18. Justin Martin writes that Greenspan refused to be bar mitzvahed. But Greenspan's recollection is that he went through with the ceremony, although studying for it had been "my least favorite time." Explaining why he went through with it, he says, "I'd have been rebelling against my mother, which I wasn't going to do." Greenspan, interview by the author, July 10, 2012.

19. Martin gives the uncle's name as Jacob, but the true name was Irwin. See New York Public Library 1940 census records and 1940 telephone directory. (*Sixteenth Census of the United States: 1940* [U.S. Census Bureau, April 2, 2012], National Archives, http://1940census.archives.gov/search /?search.census_year=1940&search .enumeration_district=31-577& search.page=1&search.result _type=image&search.state=NY #filename=m-t0627-02636-00987 .tif&name=31-577&type=image& state=NY&index=19&pages=47& bm_all_text=Bookmark).

20. Martin, *Greenspan: The Man Behind Money*, 3.

21. "I've never been a moody kid if I may put it that way. Even in my own world I enjoyed it. I had a good time being by myself." Greenspan, interview by the author, July 10, 2012.

22. Irwin Kantor's memories were relayed by his son, Larry Kantor. Lawrence Kantor, interview by the author, May 15, 2012.

23. Greenspan reflects, "I'm sure coming from a family where my mother basically brought me up and she was working, and I spent an awful lot of time by myself, listening to the radio, playing games with myself . . . if I reach back in time it made me sort of an introverted person. There are people I know very well who get anxiety attacks if they're by themselves. I can't even remotely understand that, but it's a common phenomenon. I was just the opposite." Greenspan, interview by the author, February 6, 2013.

24. Andrea Mitchell, interview by the author, May 14, 2012.

25. "I was acutely aware of the fact that there was something special about what I could do at a young age. It goes back to several years earlier when my mother used to parade me

out in front of my relatives and say add 236 and 447 and I could do it. I can't do it now without a calculator." Greenspan, interview by the author, February 6, 2013.

26. H.R. Regan & Co., display ad 40: "1935 Marches On!" Advertisement, *New York Times,* January 6, 1935, N11.

27. It seems possible that Greenspan's father was a more compelling person than he acknowledges. He did, after all, remarry, unlike his mother. He was intelligent and focused enough to write a book. Perhaps Alan could not relate to him and resented his absence, and therefore judged him too harshly.

28. Greenspan, interview by the author, March 1, 2013.

29. "When I was at a ball game in Yankee Stadium at one point when I was young, I said, this is the most marvelous place in the world to be. It was the center of the universe." Greenspan, interview by the author, July 10, 2012.

30. Greenspan became a Brooklyn Dodgers fan around 1939 because he was taken with Red Barber, the Dodgers commentator, who combined a folksy southern style with an impressive grasp of statistics. Greenspan, interview by the author, March 1, 2013.

31. Walter Isaacson, *Kissinger: A Biography* (New York: Simon & Schuster, 2005), 35.

32. Andrea Mitchell reflects, "We react to music in similar ways, viscerally, emotionally . . . we grew up with music around us. Having a mother who plays the piano, I know in my case, the house was always filled with her playing the piano. And we would go to sleep at night with her playing Chopin and Rachmaninoff, so there's music that I always associate with my mother. And I think with him, it's sort of the same way." Mitchell, interview by the author, May 14, 2012.

33. Greenspan, *Age of Turbulence.*

34. Greenspan, interview by the author, June 18, 2014.

35. Martin, *Greenspan: The Man Behind Money,* 10.

36. The bandleader Leonard Garment later told the *New Yorker's* John Cassidy, "He had exactly the same face, a slightly ironic, self-measuring smile, very interior-oriented." John Cassidy, "The Fountainhead: Alan Greenspan Faces the Biggest Challenge of His Career," *New Yorker,* April 24, 2000.

37. "I was on a train from Birmingham to Atlanta, and I happened to find myself seated next to a young southern woman with whom I conversed for the next couple of

hours. I can truthfully say that I didn't understand half of what she was saying, and I am sure she had the same difficulty with my New York accent. I knew she was speaking English, but it sounded as if she was speaking in a foreign tongue." Alan Greenspan, *The Map and the Territory: Risk, Human Nature, and the Future of Forecasting* (New York: Penguin Press, 2013), 234; Greenspan, interview by the author, July 10, 2012.

38. Ira Gitler, *Swing to Bop: An Oral History of the Transition in Jazz in the 1940s* (New York: Oxford University Press, 1985), 202.

39. Ted Gioia, *The History of Jazz* (Oxford: Oxford University Press, 2011); Geoffrey C. Ward, *Jazz: A History of America's Music* (New York: Knopf, 2000).

40. Gitler, *Swing to Bop,* 202.

41. A 1947 Childs' restaurant menu from the Paramount location was uploaded on the Internet in 2011, when it was auctioned.

42. Charles G. Shaw, *Nightlife: Vanity Fair's Intimate Guide to New York After Dark* (New York: John Day Company, 1931), 66. George Chauncey, *Gay New York: Gender, Urban Culture, and the Making of the Gay Male World, 1890–1940* (New York: Basic Books, 1994), 166. Chauncey quotes a Manhattan resident recalling the Childs' being regularly "taken over" by "hundreds" of gay men after midnight in the late 1920s.

43. Quotation heard on Henry Jerome Orchestra, *The Henry Jerome Orchestra, 1944–45* (Love Records, 1997).

44. Greenspan reflected, "I essentially concluded that having seen what some of the really good people could do, and fundamentally recognizing that it's not an issue of studying and you'll learn, there are certain inherent qualities that you're born with, and if you don't have them, you'll never achieve certain levels. Mozart had it when he was 4. I never had it, period. I was a fairly good amateur musician, and I was an average professional." Someone who measured himself against Mozart would not be content to be "average." Devin Leonard and Peter Coy, "Alan Greenspan on His Fed Legacy and the Economy," *BusinessWeek,* August 9, 2012.

45. Kelly-Ann Franklin, "Norwich Native, Grammy-winning Musician Lived Generously and Humbly, Friends Say," *Bulletin,* April 6, 2011.

46. Reflecting on why he had felt able to stand outside the culture of the band, Greenspan says, "I was getting support from my mother all

the time." Greenspan, interview by the author, July 10, 2012.

47. Looking back, Greenspan acknowledges the influence of his father in his choice of reading as he was getting ready to leave the music business. "Why I pulled this stock market book off the shelf in the public library I don't know. I do think the reason for doing that was largely my father's Wall Street experiences. I wanted to learn more about it. I was not conscious of it at the time but it is conceivable that it was he who directed me, more by example than by anything else." Greenspan, interview by the author, October 12, 2010.

CHAPTER TWO

1. Alexander Feinberg, "All City Lets Go: Hundreds of Thousands Roar Joy After Victory Flash Is Received," *New York Times,* August 15, 1945.

2. James T. Patterson, *Grand Expectations: The United States, 1945-1974* (New York: Oxford University Press, 1996), 3.

3. Ibid, 4.

4. "The American soldier is depression conscious," *Fortune* magazine opined, "worried sick about postwar joblessness." William H. Chafe, *The Unfinished Journey: America Since World War II* (New York: Oxford University Press, 1986), 29; Patterson, *Grand Expectations.*

5. Patterson, *Grand Expectations,* 5.

6. Thanks to the war, the federal budget alone became larger than the entire gross national product had been a decade earlier. Chafe, *Unfinished Journey,* 7.

7. Patterson, *Grand Expectations,* 55.

8. George H. Nash, *The Conservative Intellectual Movement in America Since 1945* (New York: Basic Books, 1976), xiii.

9. A fellow student remembers shirts and ties as normal for serious students at the School of Commerce in the 1940s. Robert Kavesh, interview by the author, March 5, 2013.

10. Lawrence B. Glickman, "Ryan Revives Old National Fixation on 'Free Enterprise,'" *Bloomberg View,* August 17, 2012.

11. Mark Skousen, *The Making of Modern Economics: The Lives and Ideas of the Great Thinkers* (Armonk, NY: M. E. Sharpe Publishers, 2009).

12. Paul A. Samuelson, *Economics: An Introductory Analysis,* 1st ed. (New York: McGraw-Hill, 1948), 152–53.

13. William F. Buckley, *God and Man at Yale: The Superstitions of "Academic Freedom"* (South Bend, Ind.: Gateway Editions, 1977), 42.

Samuelson appeared to enjoy riling conservatives, writing in his textbook that "the capitalistic way of life is on trial."

14. Walter E. Spahr, "The March into the Death Valley of Socialism" (speech, Economic Club of Detroit, March 7, 1949).

15. Robert Kavesh, interview by the author, February 27, 2013. See also John Cassidy, "The Fountainhead: Alan Greenspan Faces the Biggest Challenge of His Career," *New Yorker*, April 24, 2000. Cassidy identifies the book as Dudley Dillard, *The Economics of John Maynard Keynes: The Theory of a Monetary Economy* (New York: Prentice-Hall, 1948).

16. Recalling his time at NYU, Greenspan says, "What I realized is that if the only thing you learn is what you get from sitting in the classroom or even reading the assignments, you are not getting, I was not getting as much as I wanted." Alan Greenspan, interview by the author, October 29, 2010. In another interview Greenspan reflected, "I'm sort of an odd, eclectic sort of person. I did not go through the standard curriculum that everyone else did. I did a *vast* amount of my learning on my own through reading; not sitting in classrooms." Greenspan, interview by the author, November 22, 2010.

17. Kavesh, interview by the author, February 27, 2013. Martin, *Greenspan: The Man Behind Money*, 26.

18. Greenspan later expanded on Hill's significance in lectures given at the behest of Ayn Rand. See Alan Greenspan, Economics of a Free Society (lecture series presented at the Nathaniel Branden Institute, Roosevelt Hotel, New York, December 1963–February 1964, sec. IX).

19. Stewart H. Holbrook, *The Story of American Railroads* (New York: Crown Publishers, 1947), 3. Greenspan's enthusiasm for late-nineteenth-century industrialists extended beyond the railways. "I had an idealized version of the nineteenth century, from the 1880s forward through Teddy Roosevelt. It was a very deep-seated sense of awe." Greenspan, interview by the author, October 12, 2010.

20. "I was unaware of the Depression when I was growing up in it. I just thought the 1930s were normal." Greenspan, interview by the author, March 1, 2013.

21. George W. Terborgh, *The Bogey of Economic Maturity* (Chicago: Machinery and Allied Products Institute, 1945), 2.

22. Patterson, *Grand Expectations*.

23. "7,773 Get Degrees from N.Y.U. Today," *New York Times*, June 9, 1948.

24. Economics barely existed as a separate field in the United States before World War II. When Milton Friedman enrolled at the University of Chicago in 1932, he joined what was then the Department of Political Economy.

25. Greenspan, *Age of Turbulence*, 31.

26. As noted in the previous chapter, endnote 16, Greenspan acknowledges this connection between his personality and his intellectual preferences. "There is an incredible degree of security, in the feeling that I don't need to go and ask other people, 'Is this right?'" Greenspan, interview by the author, October 29, 2010. On another occasion, Greenspan said, "A solved equation is an absolute. There's no judgment involved and that fits very well with my basic introverted view of the world." Greenspan, interview by the author, July 22, 2010.

27. Greenspan recalls, "The biggest surprise of my life was that I ended up with four years of college with two Bs and the rest As. I was never that good a student and it really surprised me. One B was for physical training. The other must have been conduct, or something." Greenspan, interview by the author, October 12, 2010.

28. Greenspan says of his father, "He had great aspirations but he never converted them. . . . And I never fully trusted him. He'd tell me things which he was going to accomplish, like fictional heroes aspiring to great things who never achieve them. . . . There must have been deep disappointment on his part for what he had achieved." Greenspan, interview by the author, October 12, 2010. In another conversation, Greenspan said, "[E]verything he ever did sort of quasi-failed. He was never an inspiration to me." Greenspan, interview by the author, October 29, 2010.

29. Greenspan's future friend Daniel Patrick Moynihan wrote of his relationship with his own estranged father, "I find thru the years this enormous emotional attachment to Father substitutes—of whom the least rejection was cause for untold agonies—the only answer is that I have repressed my feelings toward dad." See Steven R. Weisman, *Daniel Patrick Moynihan: A Portrait in Letters of an American Visionary* (New York: PublicAffairs, 2012), 15.

30. Martin, *Greenspan: The Man Behind Money*, 29.

31. Lanny Ebenstein, *Milton Friedman: A Biography* (New York: St. Martin's Griffin, 2007), 16.

32. Greenspan, interview by the author, December 22, 2010.

33. Greenspan, interview by the author, September 6, 2011.

CHAPTER THREE

1. James T. Patterson, *Grand Expectations: The United States, 1945–1974* (New York: Oxford University Press, 1996), 22.

2. The account of the clash between Truman and the Fed is drawn from Robert L. Hetzel and Ralph F. Leach, "The Treasury-Fed Accord: A New Narrative History," *Economic Quarterly* 87, no. 1 (Winter 2001): 41.

3. Most economists believed it would take a huge shift in interest rates to make any difference to inflationary bottlenecks. See for example Paul Samuelson, *Economics: An Introductory Analysis*, 1st ed. (New York: McGraw-Hill, 1948), 353: "*Investment is likely to be inelastic with respect to the interest rate. The same is even more true about people's decisions on how much of their incomes to spend on consumption.*" [Emphasis in original.] The mistaken belief in the impotence of monetary policy was shared even at the central bank; in 1939 an article in the *Federal Reserve Bulletin* declared, "Experience has shown that prices do not depend primarily on the volume or the cost of money." See Robert L. Hetzel, *The Monetary Policy of the Federal Reserve* (New York: Cambridge University Press, 2008), 35. For more on the assumption that monetary policy was impotent, see Daniel L. Thornton, "The Evolution of Inflation Targeting: How Did We Get Here and Where Do We Need to Go?" (Sixth Norges Bank Monetary Policy Conference, Oslo, 2009). Economists' underestimation of monetary policy was based partly on the perception that low interest rates had failed to stimulate the economy in the 1930s, although this interpretation overlooked the fact that while nominal interest rates had been low, deflation had rendered real interest rates higher. On this point, see also Ben S. Bernanke, "Money, Gold, and the Great Depression" (remarks, H. Parker Willis Lecture, Lexington, Virginia, March 2, 2004), http://www.federalreserve.gov/board Docs/speeches/2004/200403022/default.htm.

4. Samuelson, *Economics: An Introductory Analysis*, 353.

5. Hetzel, *The Monetary Policy*, 35.

6. Hetzel and Leach, "The Treasury-Fed Accord," 52.

7. Ibid.

8. Greenspan, *Age of Turbulence*, 42.

9. Ibid., 44.

10. Bob Kavesh, Greenspan's friend at NYU, has no memory of discussing discrimination against Jews with Greenspan. Robert Kavesh, interview by the author, February 27, 2013. However, Greenspan was conscious that discrimination existed. Referring to the barriers faced by his cousin, Greenspan recalls, "That type of extraordinary discrimination was very evident to me when I was young." Greenspan, interview by the author, January 10, 2013. Given the prevalence of discrimination, Greenspan could hardly fail to be aware of it. In 1935, for example, the dean of the Yale medical school instructed: "Never admit more than five Jews, take only two Italian Catholics, and take no blacks at all." See David M. Oshinsky, *Polio: An American Story* (New York: Oxford University Press, 2005), 98. Discrimination against Jews continued at the school until well into the 1950s. See Jerome Karabel, *The Chosen: The Hidden History of Admission and Exclusion at Harvard, Yale, and Princeton* (New York: Houghton Mifflin Harcourt, 2005), 329. Meanwhile, Chafe notes that the U.S. government showed scandalously little appetite for helping Jews escape from Europe. In one characteristic instance in 1943, Romania offered to allow the evacuation of seventy thousand Jews in return for a bribe of $170,000. Six months later, the offer had not been taken up. William H. Chafe, *The Unfinished Journey: America Since World War II* (New York: Oxford University Press, 1986), 25.

11. Chafe reports that *Fortune* complained of klannishness, not clannishness. Chafe, *Unfinished Journey*, 25.

12. "I would often be at large meetings in which I would be the only Jew in the room." Greenspan, interview by the author, January 10, 2013.

13. "I learned everything about how roller mills were tuned and how cold-rolled sheet was derived from hot-rolled sheet and what the temperatures are and I just loved it! It was the *engineering*." Greenspan, interview by the author, July 22, 2010.

14. Greenspan, interview by the author, November 15, 2010.

15. Greenspan, interview by the author, June 10, 2011.

16. Greenspan recalls that, thanks to the influence of Townsend and Skinner, "there was a lot of monetarism in my thinking. I was learning monetary economics, at least the monetary data, and all the stuff that Friedman would be using later." Greenspan, interview by the author, December 16, 2010.

17. Chafe, *Unfinished Journey*, 144. In 1946, Americans had taken out short-term loans worth $8 billion. By 1958, that number had more than quintupled, to $46 billion. See ibid., 112.

18. When President Truman made a snide reference to "money changers" on Wall Street, Merrill seized the opportunity to rally the burgeoning ranks of property owners to his banner. "Mr. Truman knows as well as anybody that there isn't any Wall Street," a Merrill advertisement thundered. "That's just legend. Wall Street is Montgomery Street in San Francisco. Seventeenth Street in Denver. Marietta Street in Atlanta. Federal Street in Boston. . . . And it's any spot in Independence, Missouri, where thrifty people go to invest their money, to buy and sell securities." See John Steele Gordon, *An Empire of Wealth: The Epic History of American Economic Power* (New York: HarperCollins, 2004), 369.

19. Testifying before Congress in May 1942, Friedman talked extensively about inflation without mentioning "money" or "monetary policy." See Lanny Ebenstein, *Milton Friedman: A Biography* (New York: Palgrave Macmillan, 2007), 86–87. Later, in a 1951 essay titled *Comments on Monetary Policy*, he assigned fiscal policy and monetary policy a roughly equal responsibility for prices. "Monetary and fiscal measures are the only appropriate means of controlling inflation. . . . Monetary and fiscal measures are substitutes within a wide range." See Milton Friedman, *Essays in Positive Economics* (Chicago: University of Chicago Press, 1953), 264.

20. See John G. Gurley and E. S. Shaw, "Financial Aspects of Economic Development," *The American Economic Review* 45, no. 4 (September 1, 1955), 515–38. Greenspan comments, "Gurley Shaw showed me that all financial intermediaries can be thought of as doing the same thing. They improve the economy by reducing risk through diversification. . . . Gurley Shaw allows you to cut through all the complexity and get to the essence of finance." Greenspan, interview by the author, February 10, 2012.

21. The paper is Alan Greenspan, "Stock Prices and Capital Evaluation," *Proceedings of the Business and Economic Statistics Section of the American Statistical Association* 6, no. 1 (1959): 2–26. In his memoir, Greenspan relates that its arguments were in his mind during FOMC discussions of the stock market in December 1995. Greenspan, *Age of Turbulence*, 166.

22. Greenspan, "Stock Prices and Capital Evaluation," 21. In an interview, Greenspan elaborates, "If the market value of GM were greater than the cost of building it new, leaving out the tricky problem of reputation and goodwill and all that, I will build GM. If the cost is *above* the market price, I won't. Since 1959 I have been using that relationship in models that I have used to forecast capital gains and it works very well." Greenspan, interview by the author, December 16, 2010.

23. In 1958, Greenspan had also pointed to the relationship between shifts in market psychology and the real economy. He sounded a warning concerning "periods of rapidly changing business and consumer psychology. In periods of high confidence there is a tendency for existing capital assets to be monetized as consumers and businessmen both attempt to pyramid on thin equities." Alan Greenspan, Paul B. Simpson, and Addison T. Cutler, "Monetary Analysis and the Flow of Funds—Discussion," *The American Economic Review*, Papers and Proceedings of the Seventieth Annual Meeting of the American Economic Association, 48, no. 2 (May 1, 1958): 171–77.

24. Greenspan, interview by the author, November 8, 2010.

25. Lawrence H. Summers to Alan Greenspan, letter (October 28, 1997). Copy on file with the author.

26. The wealth effect is known in the economics literature as "wealth elasticity of demand." A search for that term in JSTOR locates the earliest mention in the early 1960s. However, the connection between wealth and spending is acknowledged in some contemporaneous writings; see for example Friedman, *Essays in Positive Economics*, 270.

27. In fairness to the 1920s Fed, it should be acknowledged that hawks within its ranks argued for tighter money precisely to choke off speculation. Between May 1928 and August 1929, the New York Fed duly raised the discount rate from 3.5 percent to 6 percent, precipitating the crash of October.

28. Later scholarship on the Depression did not vindicate Greenspan. Rather, the stock market crash of 1929 was found to create uncertainty among consumers, inhibiting consumption of durables. See Christina Romer, "The Great Crash and the Onset of the Great Depression," *Quarterly Journal of Economics* 105, no. 3 (1990): 597–624.

29. Liaquat Ahamed memorably profiles believers in the gold standard in *Lords of Finance*. The gold standard has been the creed of industrious, thrifty, orderly people, people with a taste for rules and discipline and unbending efficiency. It is a heavy, unmoving, inflexible anchor, and it is beloved by people who like anchors and solidity, who doubt that such things can come from fickle governments, these being social constructs, and any collective enterprise being fragile and suspect. H. G. Wells praised the gold standard for its "magnificent stupid honesty." As Ahamed writes, it "served to reinforce all those Victorian virtues of economy and prudence in public policy . . . [it was] a gift of providence, a code of behavior transcending time and place." Liaquat Ahamed, *Lords of Finance: The Bankers Who Broke the World* (London: Penguin, 2009), 20.

30. As later chapters will show, for practical purposes Greenspan came to see gold as a distraction. But he continued to describe it as the ideal monetary anchor for a laissez-faire economy.

31. Alfred Winslow Jones, creator of the first "hedged fund," launched his groundbreaking venture in 1949 after writing an essay in *Fortune* about predictive financial charts.

32. "When I was very young, you could make money by looking at commodity prices and saying, all commodity prices are volatile and none can go below zero. To the extent that they are crop-induced, you look for those for which the prices are severely depressed and you get five or ten of them, and you load up positions and you don't know when or how or by what means but you know that some external event is going to cause prices to pop. It might be a crop shortage or some dynamic force from the outside but something. If you had maybe five positions, you didn't need to know which one. Four could fail and you could lose maybe 2 percent of your investment and you could do very well because the fifth would take off. You could do that because markets were incomplete. It was so obvious. You'd think everyone would pick that up. You can't do that anymore."

Greenspan, interview by the author, October 12, 2010.

33. "I was very puzzled at how was it possible that somebody trading across the ring from me, who can barely spell the word *copper,* or more interestingly, doesn't know whether he's trading copper or zinc, does better than I do." Greenspan interview by the author, January 10, 2013.

34. "Markets have got *very* little to do with the particular commodity that's being traded. It's human psychology." Greenspan, interview by the author, October 29, 2010.

35. "We're dealing essentially with human fears, human aspirations, human euphoria and it is independent of the particular speculative instrument. . . . [A] goodly part of my view of financial markets was originally crafted in those periods when I was doing individual commodities." Ibid.

36. A search of JSTOR confirms that Greenspan's usage was unusual.

37. Greenspan returned to this theme in *The Map and the Territory*, published in 2013. "Fear induces a far greater response than euphoria. Accordingly, asset prices and other fear-sensitive financial variables move far more rapidly when falling than they do when rising." Greenspan, *The Map and the Territory: Risk, Human Nature, and the Future of Forecasting*, 280.

38. Alan Greenspan, "Papers on Economic Theory and Policy" (PhD dissertation, New York University, 1977), 95.

CHAPTER FOUR

1. In 1949, coal accounted for two thirds of the world's energy consumption; by 1971, oil accounted for two thirds. See David Halberstam, *The Fifties* (New York: Villard Books, 1993), 117–18.

2. Benjamin Fairless, "The Most Dramatic Years in the Story of Steel," *Life*, October 22, 1956, 164.

3. James T. Patterson, *Grand Expectations: The United States, 1945–1974* (New York: Oxford University Press, 1996), 74. Kindle edition.

4. Greenspan's address is shown on his marriage license: 67-14 Juno Street. The building was built in 1947.

5. Joan Mitchell described her first encounter with Greenspan to three writers. See Michael Lewis, "Beyond Economics, Beyond Politics, Beyond Accountability," *Worth*, May 1995, 61. See also John Cassidy, "The Fountainhead: Alan Greenspan Faces the Biggest Challenge of His Career," *New Yorker*, April 24, 2000. See also Martin, *Greenspan: The Man Behind Money*, 31.

6. The marriage license, available on request from the Marriage Bureau of the Office of the City Clerk in New York, states that the union took place on Sunday, October 12, 1952, at 6:30 p.m.

7. Martin, *Greenspan: The Man Behind Money*, 31.

8. Alan Greenspan, *Age of Turbulence*, 40.

9. Andrea Mitchell remarks, "He's not a visually observant person." Andrea Mitchell, interview by the author, May 14, 2012.

10. Lewis, "Beyond Economics, Beyond Politics, Beyond Accountability," 65.

11. Quoted in William H. Chafe, *The Unfinished Journey: America Since World War II* (New York: Oxford University Press, 1986), 111–12.

12. Quoted in Chafe, *Unfinished Journey,* 141.

13. William H. Chafe, *The Unfinished Journey: America Since World War II* (New York: Oxford University Press, 2003), 136.

14. The most popular item among followers of the Foundation for Economic Education was Bastiat's *The Law,* the text that Ronald Reagan invoked a third of a century later during his inflation conversation with Milton Friedman and Greenspan. See George H. Nash, *The Conservative Intellectual Movement in America Since 1945* (New York: Basic Books, 1976), 615–17. Kindle edition.

15. Sources date Greenspan's first encounters with Rand slightly differently. Greenspan says in his memoir that he was twenty-six, meaning that his first meeting with Rand took place before March 1953; but in a subsequent interview Greenspan said that it might have happened later. Greenspan, interview by the author, April 30, 2013. Meanwhile, Justin Martin reports that Greenspan's conversion to objectivism came in 1954. See Martin, *Greenspan: The Man Behind Money,* 40.

16. Anne Conover Heller, *Ayn Rand and the World She Made,* 1st printing edition (New York: Nan A. Talese, 2009), 238–39. Heller's excellent biography of Rand is a key source in the pages that follow.

17. Greenspan, *Age of Turbulence,* 4; and Heller, *Ayn Rand and the World,* 177.

18. Heller, *Ayn Rand and the World,* 176.

19. Ibid., 257.

20. Oswald Hanfling, *Logical Positivism* (New York: Columbia University Press, 1981), 193.

21. Greenspan, *Age of Turbulence,* 41.

22. "What she did was she demonstrated that the position I was at was *syllogistically* inaccurate and

NOTES

wrong. Once I removed that premise, a whole area of examination opened up. Not for *rational* discussion but for the discovery of systematic relationships. . . . It was an *epistemological* change, not a philosophical change." Greenspan, interview by the author, October 29, 2010.

23. Martin, *Greenspan: The Man Behind Money*, 40–41.
24. This quotation comes from Robert Anderson and John Little, *Ayn Rand: In Her Own Words*, Documentary, 2011.
25. Ayn Rand, *The Romantic Manifesto: A Philosophy of Literature* (New York: Signet Books, 1971), 168.
26. Heller, *Ayn Rand and the World*, 139.
27. Ibid., 275. A photo of the gold bar is reproduced in Jeff Britting, *Ayn Rand* (Woodstock, N.Y.: Overlook Press, 2004), 89.
28. Britting, *Ayn Rand*, 85.
29. Heller, *Ayn Rand and the World*, 275.
30. Ibid., 282–83.
31. Whittaker Chambers, "Big Sister Is Watching You," *National Review*, December 28, 1957.
32. The journalist was Claudia Pierpont. See Heller, *Ayn Rand and the World*, 287.
33. Ibid. Two decades later, the Republican vice presidential candidate was Paul Ryan, who had once cited *Atlas Shrugged* as an influence on his monetary thinking.
34. Greenspan recalls that before he met Rand, he had been intrigued by the use of gold as a marker of status and store of value in all ancient cultures. Greenspan, interview by the author, April 30, 2013. Rand, for her part, had been confirmed in her affection for gold by Ludwig von Mises. See Heller, *Ayn Rand and the World*, 248.
35. Robert Kavesh, interview by the author, February 27, 2013.
36. From 1936 through 1940, Roosevelt's appointees to the Justice Department, culminating with Thurman Arnold's selection to head the Antitrust Division, mounted ambitious attacks on horizontal collusion and single-firm dominance. See William E. Kovacic, "The Modern Evolution of U.S. Competition Policy Enforcement Norms," *Antitrust Law Journal* 71, no. 2 (January 1, 2003), 378.
37. Both Rand's *Notes* and Greenspan's antitrust essay are reprinted in the volume Ayn Rand et al., *Capitalism: The Unknown Ideal* (New York: Signet, 1967).
38. "Where monopoly rests on manmade obstacles to entry into a market, there is every case for removing

them." Friedrich A. Hayek, *The Constitution of Liberty* (Chicago: University of Chicago Press, 1960), 266.
39. Friedman argued that monopolies were often preferable to hamfisted attempts to rein them in, but antitrust legislation was nonetheless a welcome restraint on blatant price fixing and collusion. "The Sherman antitrust laws, with all their problems of detailed administration, have by their very existence fostered competition." Milton Friedman, *Capitalism and Freedom*, 40th Anniversary Edition (Chicago: University of Chicago Press, 2002), 199. See also pp. 28 and 132.
40. Greenspan, interview by the author, May 4, 2012, and April 30, 2013.
41. Alan Greenspan, "'Bad History, Worse Economics Spawned Anti-Trust, Says Critic,'" *Barron's*, February 5, 1962.
42. Even as early as 1932, a classic volume by Adolf A. Berle Jr. and Gardner C. Means (*The Modern Corporation and Private Property*) had documented the dominant position of the large corporation in the modern economy, the growing dispersion of corporate stock, and the separation of ownership from control. Adolf A. Berle Jr. and Gardiner C. Means, *The Modern Corporation and Private Property* (New York: The MacMillan Company, 1932). Lamenting that talented mavericks were giving way to bean counters, Russell Leffington, a partner at J.P. Morgan, warned the Senate Committee on Finance in 1935 that "we are becoming a nation of hired men, hired by great aggregates of capital." Halberstam, *The Fifties*, 122.
43. Indeed, GM would have been even more dominant if a team of its executives had not rescued its primary competitor, the Ford Motor Company, after the war—a rescue that Alfred Sloan himself had blessed, fearing that if Ford went bust, GM would be revealed as a monopoly.
44. Greenspan recalls, "If you were to try to understand how the world works, you'd have to start with a structure. If you try to cram all of the qualifications in before you've got a conceptual structure, you will fail. And the ideal way to learn is to get a simplistic system and then start to take the exceptions. That's the reason why younger students or people in their teens are very idealistic. The world is a very simple place. It's black and white. And in my case, it remained black and white longer than for

the average person." Greenspan, interview by the author, June 27, 2010.
45. Greenspan, interview by the author, December 10, 2010.

CHAPTER FIVE

1. Ronald Steel, *Walter Lippmann and the American Century* (New Brunswick, NJ: Transaction Publishers, 1980), 525.
2. Under the surface, there lurked awkward questions as to how precisely the monetary policy worked: "I haven't the faintest idea of how you control the money supply," the Fed chairman, William McChesney Martin, once confessed. "Yet everyone thinks I have it at my fingertips." But for the new breed of confident economists, such details were beside the point. William Greider, *Secrets of the Temple: How the Federal Reserve Runs the Country* (New York: Simon & Schuster, 1989), 329.
3. Paul Samuelson, *Economics: An Introductory Analysis* (McGraw-Hill, 1961), 318.
4. Samuelson, *Economics*, 375. Samuelson's message reached a large audience: in 1964, his textbook sold 440,000 copies.
5. Arthur F. Burns, "Progress Toward Economic Stability" (Presidential Address, Seventy-second Annual Meeting of the American Economic Association, Washington, D.C., December 28, 1959). Reprinted in Arthur F. Burns, "Progress Toward Economic Stability," in *The Business Cycle in a Changing World* (New York: National Bureau of Economic Research, 1969), 128.
6. See Robert J. Gordon, "The History of the Phillips Curve: Consensus and Bifurcation," July 15, 2009, https://ideas.repec.org/a/bla/econom/v78y2011i309p10-50.html.AU.
7. Quoted in William H. Chafe, *The Unfinished Journey: America Since World War II* (New York: Oxford University Press, 1986), 195.
8. Greenspan, interview by the author, December 10, 2010.
9. Greenspan, interview by the author, October 29, 2010.
10. Nathaniel Branden, *My Years with Ayn Rand* (San Francisco: Jossey-Bass, 1999), 212.
11. "Deposits, Earnings Mount at Trans-World Financial," *Barron's*, July 30, 1962.
12. Greenspan recalls that in 1962, TWF—Trans-World's ticker symbol—was trading at fifty times earnings. Greenspan, interview by the author, January 21, 2011. Stocks for the California S&Ls

were trading at twenty-five times earnings in late 1961. See Mitchell Gordon, "Thrift-Land Revisited: Apparently Nothing Can Halt the Growth of California's Savings and Loans," *Barron's*, March 11, 1963.

13. Hubert Kay, "California's S. & L.'s: The Boom the Bankers Knock," *Fortune*, August 1964, 120.

14. Ibid., 122.

15. "Finance: Black Bart's Red Ink," *Time*, April 19, 1968.

16. "Civilization seemed far more advanced in California rather than back East . . . a more exotic nature to the vegetation . . . it was a different world, and it was all new." Greenspan, interview by the author, January 21, 2011.

17. "Hillcrest Country Club," *Los Angeles Times,* August 6, 1972.

18. A summary of Greenspan's argument is contained in the 1962 version of his antitrust essay, reprinted in *Barron's*, February 5, 1962.

19. "And I'm not sure whether I said anything intelligent for the next several years. I was just so awed at the idea of A, he knew Ayn Rand; but B, he would introduce me; and C, I would have coffee with her." Kathryn Eickhoff, interview by the author, November 29, 2011. Eickhoff granted the author approximately ten hours of interviews.

20. Scott McConnell, *100 Voices: An Oral History of Ayn Rand* (New York: New American Library, 2010), 268.

21. "He loved to dance with women who could dance with him. . . . And you know, Alan always came and would dance not only with whoever he was there with, if he came with somebody, but any of the women who were particularly good dancers." Eickhoff, interview by the author, November 29, 2011.

22. "He's the only person I know of who reads a statistical abstract into the footnotes. Many people use a statistical abstract to go look up the number on something. Alan doesn't; he reads it." Ibid.

23. Ibid.

24. "Things he did not like to do, he never found time to do them." Ibid.

25. "Every time I hired somebody and I really got to like them, become good friends with them, Alan would start dating them, and then they would break up, they would quit, and I would no longer have a friend." Ibid.

26. "Alan has always been serially monogamous. . . . I have never known him not to have a woman that he was dating at any point in time." Ibid.

27. James T. Patterson, *Grand Expectations: The United States,*

1945–1974 (New York: Oxford University Press, 1996), 33. Kindle edition.

28. Martin, *Greenspan: The Man Behind Money*, 62.

29. On average, a woman made just over fifty cents for every dollar a man did. See Patterson, *Grand Expectations*. Greenspan's openness to promoting women may have been connected to the fact that he did not share the postwar enthusiasm for the nuclear family, which lay behind much of the prejudice against working women. "The independent woman is a contradiction in terms," a popular book declared in 1947, advising women to strive for "receptivity and passiveness, a willingness to accept dependence without fear or resentment, with a deep inwardness and readiness for the final goal of sexual life—impregnation." See Ferdinand Lundberg and Marynia F. Farnham, *Modern Woman: The Lost Sex* (New York: Harper & Brothers, 1947). See Patterson, *Grand Expectations*, 36. Even Ayn Rand, though she said women could be as intellectually capable as men, considered "hero worship—the desire to look up to man" the essence of femininity. See Ayn Rand, "About a Woman President," in *The Voice of Reason: Essays in Objectivist Thought,* ed. Leonard Peikoff (New York: New American Library, 1988), 268. The essay was originally published in the December 1968 edition of the *Objectivist Newsletter.*

30. Eickhoff, interview by the author, November 29, 2011.

31. "Alan is a very withdrawn person. . . . He did not form close relationships with people easily . . . so he was fond of his mother and recognized her positive attributes. . . . He would have thought of her as a good person, rather conventional, and had absolutely nothing to say to her." Ibid.

32. Ibid. In a follow-up interview, Eickhoff reiterated her point. Eickhoff, interview by the author by phone, March 13, 2012.

33. Eickhoff, interview by the author, November 29, 2011.

34. Ibid. Greenspan recalls in his memoir, "Ayn Rand became a stabilizing force in my life." See Greenspan, *Age of Turbulence*, 51.

35. These letters, sent under the name of Greenspan's financial firm, Townsend-Greenspan, went out on January 4 and March 29, 1963. My thanks to Kathryn Eickhoff for providing me with copies.

36. In his skepticism of forecasts, Greenspan was not alone. William McChesney Martin, the chairman

of the Federal Reserve Board, forbade the staff from making forecasts until 1966. Between 1936 and 1965, moreover, there were no academic economists serving as Fed governors. See Robert J. Samuelson, *The Great Inflation and Its Aftermath: The Transformation of America's Economy, Politics, and Society* (New York: Random House, 2008), 80. Martin once told a visitor, "We have fifty econometricians working for us at the Fed. They are all located in the basement of the building, and there is a reason why they are there. . . . The danger with these econometricians is that they don't know their own limitations, and they have a far greater sense of confidence in their analyzes than I have found to be warranted." Richard T. McCormack, *A Conversation with Ambassador Richard T. McCormack* (Bloomington, IN: Xlibris, 2013). Kindle edition.

37. Month-on-month headline inflation in November and December 1962 had been zero. If Greenspan's readers preferred to consult year-on-year numbers, they would have noted that both core and headline consumer price inflation stood at an unremarkable 1.3 percent in December 1962.

38. Greenspan notes that Gurley and Shaw led him to appreciate the difficulty in choosing monetary targets. The choice of a particular measure of the money supply—currency and checking accounts (M1), or currency plus a broader range of deposit accounts (M2), or any other variable—seemed arbitrary once Gurley and Shaw had pointed out that there was "a whole continuum of Ms." that could potentially be followed. The gold standard had the advantage of avoiding the choice of monetary aggregate. Greenspan, interview by the author, February 18, 2011.

39. Greenspan's letter did not elaborate on the advent of negotiable time deposits, presumably because he assumed that contemporary readers would know of them. For a readable account of this innovation, see Jeff Madrick, *Age of Greed: The Triumph of Finance and the Decline of America, 1970 to the Present* (New York: Knopf, 2011), 18.

40. Greenspan recalls Friedman's influence, but does not specifically recall particular writings from this period. Greenspan, e-mail to the author, May 5, 2013.

41. Milton Friedman, *A Program for Monetary Stability* (New York: Fordham University Press, 1960), 91. Originally delivered as the

Millar Lectures at Fordham University, 1959.

42. Alan Greenspan, "Liquidity as a Determinant of Industrial Prices and Interest Rates," *Journal of Finance* 19, no. 2 (May 1964): 159. Originally delivered at the annual meeting of the American Finance Association, Boston, December 27–29, 1963.

43. The following account comes mainly from Eickhoff, interview by the author, November 29, 2011.

44. Quotation comes from the full transcript of Greenspan's ten lectures that was provided to the author by a former employee of Townsend-Greenspan, Lowell B. Wiltbank.

45. In an apparent contradiction of Greenspan's account, some of the money panics of the late nineteenth century brought about recessions that were more than transitory. The panic of 1873, for example, led to what was known at the time as the Great Depression. Greenspan's lectures deal with this objection by presenting this episode as a result of the dilution of the gold standard during the Civil War, when the government had printed so-called greenbacks. The depression of the 1870s was caused, in Greenspan's account, by a deflation that took place as investors anticipated the retirement of greenbacks in 1879 and the contraction of credit that came with it.

46. The gold constraint was dismantled in stages between the Fed's opening in 1914 and Nixon's abandonment of the dollar-gold link in 1971. But Greenspan was right that after 1914 the government had the power to create bank reserves at will because it could decree relaxations to the remaining constraints whenever they became inconvenient.

47. Barry Goldwater, *The Conscience of a Conservative* (Bottom of the Hill Publishing, 2010), 11.

48. John Chamberlain, "Campus Radicals," *Wall Street Journal*, November 3, 1960, 16.

49. Jennifer Burns, *Goddess of the Market: Ayn Rand and the American Right* (Oxford, England; New York: Oxford University Press, 2009), 190.

50. Rand had refused to vote in 1952 and 1956, disgusted by both Eisenhower and Stevenson. See Heller, *Ayn Rand and the World She Made*, 247.

51. Ayn Rand, *Atlas Shrugged* (New York: Signet Books, 1992), 965.

52. In an interview that appeared the same month in *Playboy*, Rand insisted that "faith . . . is extremely

detrimental to human life: it is the negation of reason." Ayn Rand, "Ayn Rand: A Candid Conversation with the Founder of 'Objectivism,'" interview by Alvin Toffler, *Playboy*, March 1964.

53. Rand argued that objectivists need approve only of Goldwater's *political* philosophy, not his *total* philosophy; a candidate should be expected to represent merely "an approximation" of one's values, a "lesser of two evils." Ayn Rand, "How to Judge a Political Candidate," *Objectivist Newsletter* 3, no. 3 (March 1964), 10.

54. Rick Perlstein, *Before the Storm: Barry Goldwater and the Unmaking of the American Consensus* (New York: Nation Books, 2009), Kindle location 5614.

55. McConnell, *100 Voices*, 271.

56. The following description of the 1964 Republican National Convention comes from C-SPAN video footage and Perlstein, *Before the Storm,* Kindle locations 8618–42. "Goldwater 1964 Acceptance Speech," *C-SPAN Video Library*, accessed July 22, 2015, http://www.c-span.org/video/?4018-1/goldwater-1964-acceptance-speech.

57. Greenspan, interview by the author, April 14, 2011.

58. Ayn Rand, "'Extremism' or the Art of Smearing," *Objectivist Newsletter* 3, no. 9 (1964).

59. "The War Hawks," *Washington Post*, July 14, 1964.

60. Perlstein, *Before the Storm,* Kindle location 8665.

61. Nixon claimed to have felt "almost physically sick" listening to the nominee's speech at the convention. Gary A. Donaldson, *Liberalism's Last Hurrah: The Presidential Campaign of 1964* (Armonk, NY: M.E. Sharpe, 2003), 180–81.

62. Ayn Rand, "It Is Earlier Than You Think," *Objectivist Newsletter* 3, no. 12 (December 1964).

63. Heller, *Ayn Rand and the World,* 323.

CHAPTER SIX

1. This description is taken from the marvelous reporting by Brad Parks of the *Newark Star-Ledger.* See Brad Parks, "Crossroads Pt. 2: 5 Days That Changed a City," *Star-Ledger,* July 9, 2007.

2. Patrick J. Buchanan to Richard Nixon, memorandum, July 17, 1967, personal files of Patrick J. Buchanan. I am grateful to Pat Buchanan and to the archivists of the Richard Nixon Presidential Library and Museum for providing me with an extensive collection of memos by or relating to

Alan Greenspan from the Nixon campaign of 1967–68.

3. Martin Anderson and Annelise Anderson, interview by the author, April 7, 2011.

4. Martin, *Greenspan: The Man Behind Money,* 64.

5. Anderson's memo was delivered on July 10, 1967.

6. This comment of Greenspan's was recorded by Ray Price, a Nixon adviser, in a memo to Pat Buchanan written on August 17, 1967. The author is grateful to Pat Buchanan for sharing the memo. Raymond K. Price Jr. to Patrick J. Buchanan, memorandum, August 17, 1967, personal files of Patrick J. Buchanan.

7. Patrick J. Buchanan, interview by the author, March 20, 2013; Patrick J. Buchanan, e-mail to the author, June 2, 2013. In his memoir, Greenspan recalls a lunch rather than a dinner (Greenspan, *Age of Turbulence,* 57). However, Buchanan's memory of a dinner includes details of the conversation and ambience; being more specific, it is also more credible. A careful analysis of Nixon's campaign memos also shows that Greenspan's account of events leading to his involvement with Nixon is mistaken in some minor details.

8. Greenspan, interview by the author, May 4, 2012. Leonard Garment has claimed that he brought Greenspan into the campaign, but Greenspan convincingly recalls that Anderson was the key connection.

9. The acquaintance was Fred Ikard of the American Petroleum Institute. Quoted in Joseph Kraft, "Right, for Ford," *New York Times,* April 25, 1976. Although the quote was published later, it referred to the 1960s.

10. Richard T. McCormack, *A Conversation with Ambassador Richard T. McCormack* (Xlibris, 2013), 13. Perhaps the key inflection point came in 1966, when the Fed began to lower interest rates despite troubling inflation, with Martin justifying his stance with the dubious claim that it would make Congress more likely to cut the budget deficit. As well as the bullying from Johnson, Martin was under pressure from the economics profession. He had taken tough action against inflation in the late 1950s, with the result that inflation was headed off but the economy went into recession. Paul Samuelson responded by attacking the "disastrously biased tight-money capers of 1956–1960." See Julio J. Rotemberg, "Penitence After Accusations of Error: 100 Years of

Monetary Policy at the U.S. Federal Reserve," in *The First Hundred Years of the Federal Reserve* (National Bureau of Economic Research Conference, Cambridge, Mass., 2013).

11. Robert J. Samuelson, *The Great Inflation and Its Aftermath: The Transformation of America's Economy, Politics, and Society* (New York: Random House, 2008), 95–96.

12. William H. Chafe, *The Unfinished Journey: America Since World War II* (New York: Oxford University Press, 1986), 317.

13. James T. Patterson, *Grand Expectations: The United States, 1945–1974* (New York: Oxford University Press, 1996), Kindle location 11915.

14. See "Chronology of the War in Vietnam and Its Historical Antecedents from 1940," *New York Times*, January 28, 1973. See also "U.S. Vietnam Casualties Exceed Record Again: Weekly U.S. Casualties Exceed Record Again," *Washington Post*, June 2, 1967.

15. George C. Wilson, "1967 Draft-Call Level May Increase in 1968," *Washington Post*, October 13, 1967.

16. "Man of the Year: The Inheritor," *Time*, January 6, 1967.

17. Martin, *Greenspan: The Man Behind Money*, 61.

18. Greenspan, *Age of Turbulence*, 56.

19. Homer Bigart, "City's Welfare Rolls Soar Despite National Prosperity and Decline in Unemployment," *New York Times*, June 30, 1967.

20. "Changes in Center's Plans Are Sought by Architects," *New York Times*, June 11, 1967.

21. Ada Louise Huxtable, "Project, Planned 10 Years, Has Been Called Unsound: Work Starts on Total Renewal Project," *New York Times*, October 21, 1966.

22. Alan Greenspan to Patrick J. Buchanan, memorandum, July 27, 1967, personal files of Patrick J. Buchanan.

23. Price Jr. to Buchanan, August 17, 1967, ibid.

24. See James Reston, "Nixon on What Makes Him Run Again," *New York Times*, October 25, 1967. See also Carey Goldberg, "The Mudge Rose Firm Enters the Tar Pit of Legal History," *New York Times*, October 1, 1995. See also Richard Nixon, *RN: The Memoirs of Richard Nixon* (New York: Simon & Schuster, 1990), 247–50.

25. Terence Smith, "Nixon on Nixon and Other Issues," *New York Times*, September 4, 1966.

26. "I had the sense that here was a once-important figure who had been pushed off into a little room with a lot of memories," Greenspan recalled. Greenspan, *Age of Turbulence*, 57.

27. Martin, *Greenspan: The Man Behind Money*, 68.

28. "And my impression of him is a stiff and a very proper candidate, in other words, very stiff, used exquisitely accurate syntax in his sentences and paragraphs." Greenspan, interview by the author, July 16, 2010.

29. Gladwin Hill, "Clark Notes Drop in Summer Riots," *New York Times*, October 4, 1968.

30. Ibid.

31. See George Gallup, "Domestic Issues Lead List for 1968," *Washington Post*, December 20, 1967, and "Poll Finds Crime Top Fear at Home," *New York Times*, February 28, 1968.

32. Alan Greenspan to Richard Nixon, "The Urban Riots of the 1960s," memorandum, September 26, 1967, personal files of Patrick J. Buchanan.

33. "They [Kennedy-LBJ] argued that the Negro has undergone severe and unjust discrimination (which is true) and exploitation by the white community (which is false)," ibid. Objectivists routinely insisted that Marx's theory of worker exploitation was unfounded. Whether white liberals had this meaning in mind when they referred to American blacks is not a question Greenspan's memo reckoned with.

34. Richard Nixon, "What Has Happened to America," *Reader's Digest*, October 1967.

35. Ibid.

36. Alan Greenspan to Richard Nixon, "Possible Article on 'What's Wrong with the Great Society,'" memorandum, November 3, 1967, personal files of Patrick J. Buchanan.

37. Buchanan, interview by the author, March 20, 2013. Greenspan remembers the story differently: he believes that Buchanan reported to him that the "Nebraska bears" were after him. However, Buchanan's memory is supported by a line in a memo from Buchanan to Nixon dated March 20, 1968, in which Buchanan reports the Dakota senator's irritation with Greenspan. A copy of this memo was provided to the author by Pat Buchanan. Patrick J. Buchanan to Richard Nixon, memorandum, March 20, 1968, personal files of Patrick J. Buchanan.

38. Buchanan, interview by the author, March 20, 2013.

39. Richard J. Whalen, *Catch the Falling Flag: A Republican's Challenge to His Party* (Boston: Houghton Mifflin Harcourt Publishing Company, 1972), 83.

40. Luce had recently lost her husband, Henry, *Time*'s legendary publisher, to a heart attack; but then she had once quipped that "widowhood is a fringe benefit of marriage."

41. Buchanan, interview by the author, March 20, 2013.

42. Eickhoff, interview by the author, November 29, 2011. See also Theodore H. White, *The Making of the President 1968* (New York: Harper Perennial, 2010), 384.

43. Martin Anderson describes Nixon's communications technology and its rapid response briefings in an oral history interview. See Miller Center, "Interview with Martin Anderson," http://miller center.org/president/reagan/oral history/martin-anderson. Greenspan recalls, "Part of my job was to coordinate responses on any issue that came up: we'd scramble to assemble the necessary research and fax it to Nixon and the campaign team overnight." Greenspan, *Age of Turbulence*, 58.

44. For example, Richard Allen, the campaign's foreign policy director, was paid $3,000 monthly. "Spreadsheet," June 27, 1968, folder 17, box 31, Nixon Presidential Returned Materials Collection, White House Special Files, Richard Nixon Presidential Library and Museum, Yorba Linda, California.

45. The hourly employee was Lowell Wiltbank. "Kathryn lodged a real complaint for a couple of weeks, because I was a part-timer and she was on salary, so I was being paid by the hour and she's just being paid for the job, and I logged ninety-six hours one week." Lowell Wiltbank, interview by the author, March 20, 2012.

46. Robert M. Eisinger, *The Evolution of Presidential Polling* (Cambridge, UK: Cambridge University Press, 2003), 89. The analysis ultimately had little impact because the Kennedy campaign and DNC didn't believe its results were reliable.

47. This description is taken from Evan Thomas, *Robert Kennedy: His Life* (New York: Touchstone, 2002), 366.

48. R. W. Apple Jr., "Kennedy Sees Capital Damage After Going to Church in Slum," *New York Times*, April 8, 1968.

49. Thomas, *Robert Kennedy*, 368.

50. Alan Greenspan to DC, memorandum, April 8, 1968, personal files of Patrick J. Buchanan.

51. "Kennedy Deplores Tolerance of Rise in Level of Violence," *New York Times,* April 6, 1968.

52. "We're Not Afraid . . . We're Gonna Die for Our People," *Washington Post,* April 26, 1968.

53. Ward Just, "Nixon Urges Program to Aid 'Black Capitalism,'" *Washington Post,* April 26, 1968.

54. Kennedy had borrowed this line from George Bernard Shaw.

55. William Safire, *Before the Fall: An Inside View of the Pre-Watergate White House* (New Brunswick, NJ: Transaction Publishers, 2005), 48.

56. Ray Jenkins, "George Wallace Figures to Win Even If He Loses," *New York Times,* April 7, 1968. See also Patterson, *Grand Expectations,* 698.

57. Alan Greenspan to Patrick J. Buchanan, memorandum, July 4, 1968, personal files of Patrick J. Buchanan. The issue in this memo was how Nixon should respond to Wallace's populist denunciations of the federal census.

58. Alan Greenspan to Patrick J. Buchanan, "Getting the Wallace Vote," memorandum, July 7, 1968, personal files of Patrick J. Buchanan.

59. The following description is taken from Whalen, *Catch the Falling Flag,* 181.

60. Buchanan, interview by the author, March 20, 2013. It is also notable that Richard Whalen, who describes this retreat brilliantly and in some detail in his memoir, says nothing about Nixon's outburst even though he played up other bruising moments in the campaign.

61. Greenspan, interview by the author, November 15, 2010.

62. Ibid.

63. Greenspan, *Age of Turbulence,* 59. Greenspan had explained his decision not to work in the Nixon administration in similar terms in a 1974 interview. See Erwin C. Hargrove and Samuel A. Morley, eds., *The President and the Council of Economic Advisers: Interviews with CEA Chairmen* (Boulder, CO: Westview Press, 1984), 414–15.

64. *Goldfinger* (1964), filming locations, IMDb, accessed February 28, 2014, http://www.imdb.com/title/tt0058150/locations?ref_=tt_dt_dt.

65. "The Unlikely No. 2," *Time,* August 16, 1968.

66. Patterson, *Grand Expectations,* Kindle location 11958.

67. Hobart Rowen, "Greenspan Views: Right of McKinley," *Washington Post,* August 18, 1968.

68. Steven F. Hayward, *The Age of Reagan: The Fall of the Old Liberal Order: 1964–1980* (New York: Random House, 2009), 215–21; David S. Broder, "Hangover in Chicago," *Washington Post,* August 30, 1968.

69. James Mann, *Rise of the Vulcans: The History of Bush's War Cabinet* (New York: Penguin Books, 2004), 9.

70. Whalen, *Catch the Falling Flag,* 216.

71. "Townsend-Greenspan Polling Analysis," October 4, 1968, personal files of Patrick J. Buchanan.

72. Alan Greenspan to DC, "Short-Term Campaign Strategy," memorandum, August 30, 1968, personal files of Patrick J. Buchanan.

73. Ibid.

74. Alan Greenspan to Martin Anderson, Patrick J. Buchanan, and James Keogh, memorandum, n.d., Economics [1968–70], box 25, White House Central Files, Staff Member and Office Files: Martin Anderson, Subject Files, Richard Nixon Presidential Library and Museum.

75. Hobart Rowen, "Nixon Firmly Committed to Full-Employment Policy," *Washington Post,* October 18, 1968.

76. Ibid.

77. White, *The Making of the President 1968,* 395.

78. Deirdre Carmody, "Pierre Prepares for New Tenant," *New York Times,* November 29, 1968.

79. Deirdre Carmody, "Politics or Not, the Pierre Is Always the Pierre," *New York Times,* November 29, 1968.

80. James Keogh to H. R. Haldeman, memorandum, November 13, 1968, folder 5, box 41, Nixon Presidential Returned Materials Collection, White House Special Files, Richard Nixon Presidential Library and Museum. H. R. Haldeman's notes from the transition confirm that Greenspan was being considered for a White House staff position. See in particular H. R. Haldeman, "Handwritten Notes," November 16, 1968, folder 9, box 41, Nixon Presidential Returned Materials Collection, White House Special Files, Richard Nixon Presidential Library and Museum.

CHAPTER SEVEN

1. The decision to tighten was taken in December 1968. The discount rate went up from 5.25 percent in November 1968 to 5.5 percent in January 1969. See "U.S. Discount Rates, Federal Reserve Bank of New York 11/19140-07/1969," National Bureau of Economic Research, http://www.nber.org/databases/macrohistory/data/13/m13009.db.

2. The data on debt are from the Federal Reserve's Z.1 Financial Accounts of the United States (commonly known as the Flow of Funds report). "Federal Reserve Statistical Release: Z.1 Financial Accounts of the United States, Historical Data," Board of Governors of the Federal Reserve System, June 11, 2015, http://www.federalreserve.gov/releases/z1/Current/data.htm. The data on GDP come from U.S. Bureau of Economic Analysis, "National Income and Product Accounts, Table 1.1.5 Gross Domestic Product," July 30, 2015. It should be noted that government debt as a share of GDP came down over the period. In denouncing Johnson's budget policies, Greenspan had been attacking the wrong target.

3. Adopted in 1933, Regulation Q interest-rate caps prohibited the payment of interest on demand deposits at banks, and capped rates that could be paid on savings or time deposits. Meanwhile, Congress legislated interest-rate caps for S&Ls in 1966, but administrative caps had been applied before that.

4. *Economic Report of the President* (Washington, D.C.: U.S. Government Printing Office, February 1970), 104. Greenspan's firm, Trans-World, was more prudently managed than most. But at the start of 1970, it, too, experienced a sudden outflow of deposits, proving that even a relatively cautious mortgage firm could not escape the consequences of dysfunctional controls on interest rates. Steven S. Anreder, "Building for the Futures? The Worst May Be Over for California's Savings and Loans," *Barron's,* April 27, 1970, 19.

5. Even without regulated deposit rates, savings and loans were vulnerable to a rise in short-term interest rates: their funding costs would go up straightaway while their revenues from long-term fixed-rate mortgages would adjust slowly. However, deposit rate caps turned the problem of a rising cost of funds into a problem of a loss of funds, exacerbating the vulnerability. The economist James Tobin calculated that as of 1970, the S&Ls had sufficient reserves to tide them through a period of high funding costs, but an outright loss of funds posed a graver threat. See James Tobin, "Deposit Interest Ceilings as a Monetary Control," *Journal of Money, Credit and Banking* 2, no. 1 (February 1970): 4–14.

6. "Worldly Philosopher: Alan Greenspan Analyzes Prospects for Interest

Rates, Steel and Gold," *Barron's,* April 22, 1968.

7. Kathryn Eickhoff, interview by the author, July 14, 2013.

8. Eickhoff, interview by the author, November 29, 2011.

9. The minutes of the commission's meetings are notable for the minimal contributions from commissioners with no economics background. See "AVAF—Minutes of Meeting of Pres. Com. on All-Volunteer Armed Force [1969–70] [1 of 4]," n.d., box 38, Richard Nixon Presidential Library and Museum, through "AVAF—Minutes of Meeting of Pres. Com. on All-Volunteer Armed Force [1969–70] [4 of 4]," n.d., box 39, Richard Nixon Presidential Library and Museum, Yorba Linda, California.

10. Milton Friedman and Rose D. Friedman, *Two Lucky People: Memoirs* (Chicago: University of Chicago Press, 1998), 380.

11. When the abolitionists on the staff tried to insert a feisty appeal to natural rights into the commission's final report, Greenspan joined with the generals in swatting it down, despite the fact that the campaign brief he had worked on with Anderson had included a similar argument.

12. "AVAF—Minutes of Meeting of Pres. Com. on All-Volunteer Armed Force [1969-1970] [2 of 4]," n.d., box 38, White House Central Files, Staff Member and Office Files: Martin Anderson, Richard Nixon Presidential Library and Museum.

13. Alan Greenspan, interview by the author, November 15, 2010.

14. Descriptions of scene taken from photograph of Cabinet Room, reproduced in Bernard Rostker, *I Want You! The Evolution of the All-Volunteer Force* (Santa Monica, CA: RAND Corporation, 2006), 88.

15. Presidential Daily Diary Entry, September 28, 1971, Richard Nixon Presidential Library and Museum.

16. The three-page memo resulting from this meeting is in the Richard Nixon Presidential Library and Museum. Paul W. McCracken, "Handwritten Notes," August 30, 1969, Friedman, Tonsor, Greenspan 8-30-1969, box 17, White House Central Files, Staff Member and Office Files: Paul W. McCracken Meeting Files, Richard Nixon Presidential Library and Museum.

17. This interchange took place on October 23, 1969. See John Ehrlichman, *Witness to Power: The Nixon Years* (New York: Simon & Schuster, 1982), 248–49.

18. Stephen Slivinski, "Last Stop Lending," *Federal Reserve Regional Focus,* Winter 2009, 6–9.

19. Martin Arnold, "City Inquiry Is Set in Skyscraper Fire," *New York Times,* August 7, 1970.

20. Richard Stone, "Fatal Blazes in Modern Office Skyscrapers Stir Charges of Unsafe Building Practices," *Wall Street Journal,* December 8, 1970.

21. Lawrence van Gelder, "Fire on 33rd Floor of New Building Kills Two," *New York Times,* August 6, 1970. See also Robert E. Tomasson, "New Fire Code Points to Change in Office Design," *New York Times,* February 25, 1973.

22. The anchor was Howard K. Smith of ABC News. See A. James Reichley, *Conservatives in an Age of Change: The Nixon and Ford Administrations* (Washington, D.C.: Brookings Institution Press, 1981), 220.

23. Nixon's commitment to the Keynesian consensus had been evident even before the inauguration. At the start of December 1968, he had announced the choice of Paul McCracken to head the White House Council of Economic Advisers. His new chief economist understood that "it was not necessary to accept increased unemployment to end inflation," Nixon assured the press, insisting that McCracken was "a centrist, a man who is pragmatic in his economics"; someone who would "not approach the grave economic problems that face us in a doctrinaire manner." The repudiation of laissez-faire advisers such as Greenspan was obvious, and Nixon's references to economics in his inaugural address merely reiterated his status quo approach to the economy. See "McCracken Named Economic Adviser," *Washington Post,* December 5, 1968. See also Sewell Chan, "Paul W. McCracken, Adviser to Presidents, Dies at 96," *New York Times,* August 3, 2012.

24. William Safire, *Before the Fall: An Inside View of the Pre-Watergate White House* (New Brunswick, NJ: Transaction Publishers, 2005), 491.

25. Robert D. Hershey Jr., "Raymond J. Saulnier, Economic Adviser to Eisenhower, Dies at 100," *New York Times,* May 8, 2009.

26. The dialogue is taken from Cabinet Room, Conversation 56-1, May 6, 1971, White House tapes, Richard Nixon Presidential Library and Museum.

27. A version of this testimony appeared as a *New York Times* op-ed, along with a picture of Greenspan smoking a pipe. See Alan Greenspan, "Opening Pandora's Box," *New York Times,* July 25, 1971.

28. Safire, *Before the Fall,* 496. The date of the meeting comes from Charles W. Colson, Notes, July 23, 1971, Presidential Meetings & Conversations [7/1/71-7/30/71] [3 of 3], box 16, Charles W. Colson Collection, Richard Nixon Presidential Library and Museum. Safire writes that Colson told him Weinberger and Kissinger were present, but when Safire asked Weinberger and Kissinger for confirmation, they said they could not recall any such meeting. The Presidential Daily Diary for July 23, 1971, lists Nixon's shipmates that night as Haldeman, Colson, Ehrlichman and Weinberger—no Kissinger, unless his presence was kept secret. Presidential Daily Diary Entry, July 23, 1971, Richard Nixon Presidential Library and Museum.

29. James T. Patterson, *Grand Expectations: The United States, 1945–1974* (New York: Oxford University Press, 1996), Kindle location 12532.

30. Safire, *Before the Fall,* 496, and Colson, "Notes."

31. Safire, *Before the Fall,* 492.

32. Charles W. Colson, Paper, July 26, 1971, Federal Reserve—Arthur Burns, box 61, White House Special Files, Staff Member and Office Files: Charles W. Colson, Subject Files, Richard Nixon Presidential Library and Museum.

33. In interviews with the author, Greenspan recalled brushing off Colson's request. However, Colson's notes from the conversation and tape recordings from the White House indicate that Greenspan cooperated. Colson's notes, spread over one and a half pages of a yellow legal pad, indicate that he first called Greenspan asking him to intervene and then later got a call back from Greenspan to report on Burns's reaction, which consisted of an expression of dismay, a request to see Nixon, and a statement that he might be willing to be more supportive of the administration's economic policy. Confronted with these notes, Greenspan suggested to the author that Colson may have concocted them to support a false claim that he had secured Greenspan's cooperation—the notion being that Colson needed to make that claim in order to impress his boss, White House chief of staff Haldeman. But Colson presumably took these phone notes for his personal office files, not for presentation to

superiors, so Greenspan's defense seems unpersuasive—in all likelihood, the notes would not have impressed Colson's superiors because they would not have been presented to them. Greenspan's complicity in Nixon's dirty trick seems overwhelmingly likely. Greenspan, interview by the author, November 15, 2010, October 30, 2015, and December 14, 2015. See also Charles W. Colson, Call Notes, n.d., Federal Reserve—Arthur Burns, box 61, Charles W. Colson Collection, Richard Nixon Presidential Library and Museum.

34. Quotes taken from Colson, Call Notes, op.cit.

35. Haldeman dialogue taken from Oval Office, Conversation 550-1, July 28, 1971, White House tapes, Richard Nixon Presidential Library and Museum.

36. White House Telephone Conversation 7-18, July 28, 1971, White House tapes, Richard Nixon Presidential Library and Museum.

37. Safire, *Before the Fall*, 495.

38. Monetary historians have debated the extent to which political pressure may have caused the Fed to loosen policy ahead of the 1972 election. See Julio J. Rotemberg, "Federal Reserve Goals and Tactics for Monetary Policy: A Role for Penitence?," *Journal of Economic Perspectives* 27, no. 4 (Fall 2013): 73–74. The incident described here encourages the verdict that political pressure was decisive. It seems overwhelmingly likely that the Fed would have pursued a tighter monetary policy had it not been for Nixon's smearing of Burns. The Fed had raised the discount rate by 25 basis points eleven days before the smear; rather than follow up with a further hike, it reversed course and began cutting. Moreover, at the time of the smear, the M2 measure of monetary growth was rising at a monthly rate of 0.9 percent, much higher than the 0.5 percent average in the three years before Burns took over the chairmanship. Absent Nixon's bullying, Burns would have wanted to steer monetary growth back down to the earlier average. Instead, he allowed the pace to accelerate: between the smear and the 1972 election, M2 grew at an average monthly rate of 1.0 percent. Burns's incentive to restrain monetary growth was all the stronger given that Nixon was simultaneously running an expansionary budget deficit. The inflation penalty for the postsmear monetary looseness was delayed by the wage-price freeze of August

1971, but it set the stage for the sharp inflationary acceleration of 1973.

39. The details of the Camp David meeting are taken mostly from Don Oberdorfer, "Planning Took Several Weeks," *New York Times,* August 17, 1971.

40. H. R. Haldeman, *The Haldeman Diaries: Inside the Nixon White House* (New York: G.P. Putnam's Sons, 1994), 341.

41. Since 1933, the U.S. pledge to convert dollars into gold had applied to foreign governments only, and in the postwar period the big ones undertook not to test the U.S. government's ability to deliver on its promise. But as foreign governments feared that the U.S. might devalue, their commitment not to demand gold broke down. By the start of 1968, the U.S. gold stock was down to $12 billion. Meanwhile, foreign central banks held more than $15 billion in dollar reserves, and European commercial banks held $25 billion in dollar deposits—accumulations that reflected U.S. spending abroad on war and foreign direct investment (the U.S. current account was not the driver of foreign holdings of dollars because it was in surplus). It was obvious that the United States might not make good on its pledge to convert dollars into gold, and the fears were self-fulfilling.

42. Alan Greenspan, *The Age of Turbulence: Adventures in a New World* (New York: Penguin Books, 2008), 61–62. Greenspan recalls in an interview: "It's funny because whenever people ask me, 'When is it when you had your back problems?' and I say I know exactly when it was, it was in a weekend in mid-July 1971!" Greenspan, interview by the author, November 8, 2010.

43. Greenspan's affection for the gold standard was reserved for the more restrictive nineteenth-century version. By 1971, the dollar-gold link had long since ceased to restrain credit creation. In Senate testimony in 1968, Milton Friedman had rightly argued that whatever one might think in principle about the virtue of monetary restraint, the gold cover did not provide it. See Senate Committee on Banking and Currency, *Hearings on the Gold Cover: Hearing Before the Committee on Banking and Currency, United States Senate*, 1968, 152–66.

44. "When he injured his back and was laid up for so long, his mother was there every day for him and whatever he needed, she got it for him. She did it willingly. And after

that Alan had a different view of her and started calling her every morning. And that went on for the rest of her life. He had been changed. He was not calling just out of a sense of duty. His mother had become important to him. It meant a great deal to him." Eickhoff, interview by the author, by phone, March 13, 2012. "He began to appreciate his mother and what she did for him. And why what she did for him showed her values. And that she did hold values strongly.... For once in his life he needed things, somebody had to do things, and she did." Eickhoff, interview by the author, November 29, 2011.

45. Herbert Stein, *Presidential Economics: The Making of Economic Policy from Roosevelt to Clinton* (Washington, D. C.: American Enterprise Institute for Public Policy Research, 1994), 178.

46. Ibid., 179.

47. This list is taken directly from Dick Cheney's memoir. See Dick Cheney, *In My Time: A Personal and Political Memoir* (New York: Threshold Editions, 2011), 60.

48. Ibid., 61.

49. "Alan was a political and judicious person. He did not want to get out on a limb. In a larger group, he was fairly quiet. He was not a big leader and he should have been." Donald Jacobs, interview by the author, June 27, 2013. Jacobs was the staff director of the commission.

50. The ordinary saver was unable to circumvent regulation, Tobin wrote, because he was hampered "by the significant minimum denominations and lot sizes of market instruments, by brokerage fees, by his own unfamiliarity and ignorance." James Tobin, "Deposit Interest Ceilings as a Monetary Control," 9.

51. The first money-market fund appeared in 1970. By 1980 Americans had invested nearly $100 billion in them.

52. Cabinet Room, Conversation 86-5, December 22, 1971, White House tapes, Richard Nixon Presidential Library and Museum.

53. The regulator was Preston Martin, chairman of the Federal Home Loan Bank Board, which oversaw S&Ls. Richard Erb to Peter Flanigan, "Hunt Commission Report," memorandum, December 21, 1971, President's Commission on Financial Structures and Regulation 1/1/71, box 1, White House Central Files, Subject Files: FG 267, Richard Nixon Presidential Library and Museum.

54. Oval Office, Conversation 640-6, December 22, 1971, White House

tapes, Richard Nixon Presidential Library and Museum.

55. Alan Greenspan, presentation, American Finance Association, New Orleans, December 28, 1971.

56. Alan Greenspan to Milton Friedman, letter, October 2, 1972.

57. Milton Friedman to Alan Greenspan, letter, October 10, 1972.

58. Alan Greenspan, "The Mirage of Wage-Price Controls," *Wall Street Journal,* April 30, 1973. This op-ed column was a précis of an address to the American Statistical Association.

59. Alan Greenspan, "Do-Nothingism," *New York Times,* July 31, 1973.

60. "Business Outlook: Inflation: The Longer View" (New York: Townsend-Greenspan & Company, January 23, 1974), personal files of Kathryn Eickhoff; and "Business Outlook" (New York: Townsend-Greenspan & Company, January 28, 1974), personal files of Kathryn Eickhoff.

61. Patterson notes: "The very high hopes of the previous decades—a key to the drive, the optimism, the idealism, and the rights-consciousness of the era—were becoming harder to achieve." Patterson, *Grand Expectations,* 783.

CHAPTER EIGHT

1. "Economists: Super-Capitalists at the CEA," *Time,* August 5, 1974.

2. See Senate Committee on Banking, Housing, and Urban Affairs, Nominations of Philip A. Loomis Jr. and Alan Greenspan: Hearing Before the Committee on Banking, Housing, and Urban Affairs, United States Senate, 1974.

3. Alan Greenspan, *The Age of Turbulence: Adventures in a New World* (New York: Penguin Books, 2008), 63.

4. Ibid.

5. "Economists: Super-Capitalists at the CEA."

6. Soma Golden, "Why Greenspan Said 'Yes,'" *New York Times,* July 28, 1974. In addition, the *New Republic* described Greenspan as a "fundamentalist mystic." See Richard L. Strout, "Economic Fundamentalist: Chairman Greenspan," *New Republic,* September 14, 1974.

7. The fact that Nixon by now seemed likely to resign made it easier to condemn his record—Nixon resigned in a speech the evening of Greenspan's hearing. However, at the time when news of Greenspan's nomination first surfaced, in early July 1974, Nixon's departure was by no means certain, so the expectation that he would serve a different president

probably did not drive Greenspan's decision to accept the nomination.

8. The financial sacrifice did not bother Greenspan. "I've never had a problem making money so I'm not worried about [that]—I make more than I could possibly use. That wasn't a factor." Alan Greenspan, interview by the author, December 10, 2010.

9. After the hearing, Proxmire told his staff researcher that Greenspan's extreme views might cost the nation dearly in the future. See "An Oral History Interview with Morton Schwartz," *Wisconsin Historical Society,* accessed March 25, 2014, http://content.wisconsinhistory.org/cdm/ref/collection/proxmire/id/2260. Like Proxmire, Biden voted against Greenspan's confirmation. Greenspan recalls, "I got two negative votes in the committee. One I've always considered to be a compliment. It was a freshman senator by the name of Joe Biden. He said: 'I'm going to vote "no" for your confirmation, frankly because I think you hold political views far different from mine and you are much too smart not to have some impact. Therefore, I will vote "no."' To which I said, 'Thank you, Senator.'" Greenspan, interview by the author, November 8, 2010.

10. Carroll Kirkpatrick, "Nixon Resigns," *Washington Post,* August 9, 1974.

11. James T. Patterson, *Restless Giant: The United States from Watergate to Bush v. Gore* (New York: Oxford University Press, 2005), 1.

12. "Policy: Seeking Relief from a Massive Migraine," *Time,* September 9, 1974.

13. Gerald R. Ford, "The President's News Conference," White House, August 28, 1974, http://www.presidency.ucsb.edu/ws/?pid=4671.

14. Kathryn Eickhoff says of Rand's relationship with Greenspan at the time when he took office, "She had that sort of mother's pride in what Alan had done and what his success was. Certainly when he asked her what she thought about his going down to Washington, he took [her answer] very seriously. She was . . . very concerned that he might sacrifice some of his own values by doing so." Kathryn Eickhoff, interview by the author, November 29, 2011.

15. "So I said I will accept with your understanding that I will be taking a thirty-day lease and I will have my suitcase parked at the door." Greenspan, interview by the author, December 10, 2010. In his memoir, Greenspan recalls

telling White House chief of staff Alexander Haig, "If I come in as chairman and the administration starts implementing policies I can't agree with, I'd have to resign. You don't need that." Greenspan, *Age of Turbulence,* 63. Kathryn Eickhoff corroborates Greenspan: "Alan went down to Washington believing he would be back in New York in less than six months because he did not think he could last longer than that without running into someone asking him to do something which would violate his values." Eickhoff, interview by the author, November 29, 2011.

16. The description is taken from Julia Duscha, "Economists at the White House—Telling It Like It Is," *New York Times,* September 8, 1974.

17. The historian Douglas Brinkley notes that Ford embraced the civic-movement approach with touching simplicity. "Once you had 213 million Americans recognizing that inflation was a problem and joining in the effort to do something about it, positive results would have to follow," Ford wrote. "If both the government and the people tightened their belts voluntarily and spent less than they would have before, that would reduce demand, and the inflation rate would start going down." Douglas Brinkley, *Gerald R. Ford,* The American Presidents Series (New York: Times Books, 2007), 77.

18. Greenspan recalls, "I remember vividly. I said to myself, 'Now, do you dare to say this? It's accurate. The question was "Whose incomes fell the most?" Any other answer is wrong!' I'm now in government for the first time and in a matter of weeks . . . I don't think I would have done that again any time thereafter. It was an early lesson in truth-telling." Greenspan, interview by the author, December 22, 2010.

19. Justin Martin, *Greenspan: The Man Behind Money* (Cambridge, Mass.: Perseus Publishing, 2001), 103.

20. Ibid.

21. Michael Lewis, "Beyond Economics, Beyond Politics, Beyond Accountability," *Worth,* May 1995.

22. Martin, *Greenspan: The Man Behind Money,* 103.

23. Greenspan, interview by the author, December 22, 2010.

24. The economist was IBM vice president David Grove. His study assumed moderate monetary growth. See "Inflation: Summing Up the Summit," *Time,* October 7, 1974. Okun, for his part, conceded in 1975 that Greenspan's policies

would cure inflation in the same way that "decapitation can be one answer to a headache." Henry Mitchell, "Atlas Shrugged, Greenspan Accepted," *Washington Post,* January 12, 1975.

25. Alan Greenspan, "Reflections on the Economists Meeting September 5, 1974," draft memorandum, September 5, 1974, Summit Conference on Inflation—September 1974, box 52, Alan Greenspan Files: Subject File, 1974-1976, Gerald R. Ford Library.

26. In a diary entry dated November 18, 1974, John Casserly, a Ford speechwriter, noted, "The Whip Inflation Now campaign was evaluated as a complete bust but the most interesting thing about it from the inside was that Ford men and women called it a bust. This would never have happened under Nixon." John J. Casserly, *The Ford White House: The Diary of a Speechwriter* (Boulder: University Press of Colorado, 1977), 12. "Every time the 'WIN' issue came up we at the Economic Policy Board would hide our heads in embarrassment," said Simon. "I still have a box of old 'WIN' buttons at home which I look at any time I develop partisan delusions." William E. Simon, *A Time for Truth* (New York: Reader's Digest Press, 1978), 105. In his memoir, Greenspan describes Whip Inflation Now as "a low point of economic policymaking." Greenspan, *Age of Turbulence,* 66.

27. James P. Sterba, "New 'Advice' to Curb Inflation: Buy Now, Buy More—Spend!" *New York Times,* November 16, 1974.

28. Ibid.

29. Alan Greenspan to Jerry Jones, "Effort to Ensure Continuation of Citizens' Action Committee (WIN)," February 27, 1975, Alan Greenspan Files: White House Correspondence, box 4, Jerry Jones, Gerald R. Ford Library.

30. A month into his tenure, he had urged that Ford delay the launch of the WIN campaign, but when the president declined to do so, he had lodged no further protest. Dick Cheney, *In My Time: A Personal and Political Memoir* (New York: Threshold Editions, 2011), 76. Equally, on October 15, the day that Ford pressed forward with his WIN initiative by urging his fellow Americans to "clean up your plate before you get up from the table," Greenspan was asked to comment on a draft of the president's speech. Rather than rubbishing the whole thing, Greenspan suggested only marginal edits to the text, most of

which were ignored anyway. Alan Greenspan to Paul Theis, memorandum, October 15, 1974, personal files of Alan Greenspan. This memo is among the files of Ford-era material provided to me by Alan Greenspan. I am grateful to Katie Broom for her assistance.

31. "Rumsfeld wanted me to be chief economic spokesman for the administration. I said I'll never do that. The reason I didn't was you can see what it means, you get up there and whatever the policy is you have to stand up with a straight face and say it's the right thing to do. . . . My view was that the CEA was supposed to be an economic consulting firm with one client, and you just tell 'em what the facts are and what's going on and what the alternatives are. But the political decisions are made elsewhere, and I was very uncomfortable getting involved in that stuff." Greenspan, interview by the author, June 27, 2012.

32. Greenspan, interview by the author, July 16, 2010.

33. Steven F. Hayward, *The Age of Reagan: The Fall of the Old Liberal Order: 1964–1980* (New York: Random House, 2009), 448.

34. Earlier in December, Greenspan had lobbied to have the draft of a presidential speech altered so as to focus more on inflation and less on the potential need for a stimulus. Casserly, *Ford White House,* 17.

35. "If we could keep our hand off the panic button, the economy would correct itself." Greenspan, *Age of Turbulence,* 67.

36. Not wanting to be held responsible for failing to anticipate bad outcomes, Greenspan had told White House colleagues in November, "We think this is going to be a rather deep but short recession, but we could fall off the cliff." Ron Nessen, interview by the author, December 21, 2010. Greenspan's insistent pessimism alienated colleagues; one White House aide called Greenspan "a goddam gloom-and-doom artist." Larry Martz et al., "The Economy: Can They Fix It?," *Newsweek,* February 24, 1975. Even so, Ford felt in December that he had not been warned of the bad economic news. "An economist, someone once remarked to me, is a person who tells you that there is definitely not going to be a hurricane," Ford wrote in his memoir. "Then, shortly thereafter, he volunteers to repair and rebuild your roof." See Gerald R. Ford, *A Time to Heal: The Autobiography of Gerald R. Ford* (New York: Harper & Row, 1979), 202.

37. Stanley J. Sigel, "Round Table of GNP Users," in *The U.S. National Income and Product Accounts,* ed. Murray F. Foss (Chicago: University of Chicago Press, 1983), 318. At Townsend-Greenspan, Greenspan had produced a monthly GNP measure.

38. David Hume Kennerly, White House Photograph, December 27, 1974, White House Photographic Office Photographs, 1974–77: Series A&B, Volume 26, Roll A2598, Frames 9-36, Color, Gerald R. Ford Library.

39. Casserly, *The Ford White House,* 26. Burton Malkiel, interview by the author, June 25, 2012.

40. The colleague was Bill Seidman. See John Cassidy, "Moneyman," in The Talk of the Town, *New Yorker,* February 6, 2006.

41. Again, the colleague was Seidman. See Lewis, "Beyond Economics, Beyond Politics, Beyond Accountability."

42. In his memoir, Ford describes Greenspan as dovish on the tax cut, even though Greenspan had testified against such a cut in the August Senate hearing. See Ford, *A Time to Heal,* 84.

43. Casserly, *Ford White House,* 26.

44. Greenspan, *Age of Turbulence,* 68. A quarter of a century later, at the start of the administration of George W. Bush, Greenspan would offer another qualified approval of a tax cut, and the Bush team would seize on his endorsement while ignoring the nuances in Greenspan's statement. Greenspan claimed to be startled, all over again.

45. The speechwriter was Robert Hartmann. He had conceived the WIN campaign, and since then Rumsfeld, Greenspan, and Cheney had been at pains to prevent him from writing speeches that committed the president to policies of which they did not approve. Numerous memoirs of the Ford White House record the bitterness of this faction fighting. See for example Donald Rumsfeld, *Known and Unknown: A Memoir* (New York: Penguin, 2011), 182.

46. Nessen, interview by the author, December 21, 2010. See also Ron Nessen, *Making the News, Taking the News: From NBC to the Ford White House* (Middletown, CT: Wesleyan University Press, 2011), 150.

47. The colleague was Jim Lynn, Ford's budget director. Greenspan, interview by the author, December 22, 2010.

48. Nessen, interview by the author, December 21, 2010. See also Nessen, *Making the News, Taking the*

News: From NBC to the Ford White House, 151–52.

49. Alan Greenspan to William E. Simon, memorandum, January 15, 1975, personal files of Alan Greenspan.

50. Alan Greenspan to Economic Policy Board, memorandum, January 12, 1975, personal files of Alan Greenspan.

51. Murray Seeger, "Has No Faith in Ford or Congress: AFL-CIO to Plan Own Recession War," *Los Angeles Times,* January 22, 1975. The quotation is also excerpted in a collection of quotes from Meany in Alan Greenspan's personal files.

52. The critic was Walter Fackler of the University of Chicago. See Martz et al., "The Economy: Can They Fix It?," 58.

53. U.S. Congress, *Congressional Record,* 94th Cong., 2nd sess., January 23, 1975.

54. "He did not waste time. He was forty-eight years old. He knew his way around the ladies." Kaye Pullen, interview by the author, October 15, 2012.

55. Ibid.; and Kaye Pullen interview by the author, April 23, 2012.

56. Mitchell, "Atlas Shrugged, Greenspan Accepted."

57. Allen J. Mayer, Jane Whitmore, and Pamela Lynn Abraham, "Greenspan—Atlas Jogs," *Newsweek,* February 24, 1975.

58. Martz et al., "The Economy: Can They Fix It?"

59. "The Economy: How Far Is Down?," *Newsweek,* February 24, 1975.

60. Between January and March 1975, Gallup put Ford's approval rating in the 37–39 percent range, a far cry from the 71 percent at the start of his presidency and lower than any reading taken later. "Presidential Approval," Roper Center, 2015, http://www.ropercenter.uconn.edu/polls/presidential-approval/.

61. Greenspan's weekly GNP gauge was correct. The economy returned to growth in the second quarter of 1975.

62. Greenspan quotes taken from Erwin C. Hargrove and Samuel A. Morley, eds., *The President and the Council of Economic Advisers: Interviews with CEA Chairmen* (Boulder, CO: Westview Press, 1984), 445; and from Sigel, "Round Table of GNP Users," 318.

63. Arthur F. Burns to Gerald R. Ford, memorandum, March 28, 1975; 1975 March 2–1977 Nov. 16, box 1, Arthur Burns papers, 1911–2005, Duke University Libraries.

64. On March 28, 1975, the same day he advised Ford to accept the Democrats' tax cut, Greenspan wrote to Senator Edmund Muskie objecting to the idea of commitment to reduce unemployment to 7 percent by the end of the following year. "Your question assumes there is an amount of stimulus which, if applied, could reduce unemployment by the dimensions that you specify," Greenspan wrote. He had not lost the capacity to denounce the more ambitious versions of fine-tuning. See Alan Greenspan to Edmund S. Muskie, correspondence, March 28, 1975, Davis Subject, Congressional Correspondence (2), Box 151, CEA Staff Economists Files (1982 Accretion), 1974–77, Gerald R. Ford Library.

65. Alan Greenspan to Gerald R. Ford, memorandum, March 28, 1975, Alan Greenspan Files, White House Correspondence, James Cannon, box 3, Gerald R. Ford Library.

66. Describing Greenspan's influence over Ford, Dick Cheney recalls, "Alan combined economic expertise with an appreciation of practical politics. No less important, he had a real knack for capturing large and complicated ideas in a few well-chosen words. The president liked him and put a lot of stock in his judgment." Cheney, *In My Time,* 79.

67. Patterson, *Restless Giant,* 96.

68. To be sure, the big deficits of Ford's tenure were primarily driven by the recession, but the tax cuts also contributed. In fiscal 1975, U.S. GDP was $1,560 billion, so the March 1975 tax cut of $22.8 billion represented about 1.5 percent of GDP. That was much less than the huge stimuli enacted in 1933 and 2009, both of which came to more than 5 percent of GDP, but it was still hard to reconcile with Greenspan's professed commitment to budgetary restraint. For data cited here, see Office of Management and Budget, "The Budget for Fiscal Year 2012," Historical Tables, Table 1.2, n.d., 24.

69. In July 1975, when the first tax rebate had yet to take full effect and the second one was still months off, Greenspan wrote to Ford that the latest economic news "virtually guarantees a significant recovery throughout the rest of this year." He then noted that the only disappointing feature of the economy was that long-term interest rates remained too high, a fact he blamed on high inflation expectations. The remedy, Greenspan told the president, was "continued vigilance on the fiscal side."

But Ford acceded to congressional pressure for further tax relief five months later. Alan Greenspan to Gerald R. Ford, memorandum, July 25, 1975, personal files of Alan Greenspan.

70. Greenspan's *Wall Street Journal* op-ed, titled "The Politics of Inflation," had appeared just one year earlier, on March 14, 1974. "I see inflation as essentially a political, not an economic problem," Greenspan wrote. "The ever-increasing political focus on short-term benefits at the expense of long-term costs has been particularly evident in the budgetary process as candidates for political office have vied with each other to capture votes by proposing new or bigger expenditure programs." Alan Greenspan, "The Politics of Inflation," *Wall Street Journal,* March 14, 1974. Given those words, it is hard to believe that Greenspan expected Congress to go along with spending cuts when he proposed them in 1975. Sure enough, federal outlays in the year to June 1976 came to 21.4 percent of GDP, a touch higher than the previous year and considerably above the 18.7 percent of GDP in fiscal years 1973 and 1974.

71. Asked about this episode, Greenspan said that he "was making a political economy judgment" and that "no matter how convinced you are that something is going to come out a certain way, you've got to hedge against being wrong." He continued, "There is no doubt that the type of judgment I was making was that Ford would be much better off if he signed the bill. Suppose I was wrong and things were worse, he would be better off having signed it. If I were right, signing it would not cause much of a problem." Greenspan, interview by the author, December 22, 2010.

CHAPTER NINE

1. Peter Kihss, "Tory Chief, Here, Deplores Statism," *New York Times,* September 16, 1975.

2. "Margaret Thatcher: A Cut Above the Rest," *Economist,* April 8, 2013, http://www.economist.com/blogs/blighty/2013/04/margaret-thatcher-0.

3. Deirdre Carmody, "First Woman to Head Major British Party Makes Some Political Points as She Winds Up Tour Here," *New York Times,* September 18, 1975.

4. Charles Moore, *Margaret Thatcher: The Authorized Biography, from Grantham to the Falklands* (New York: Alfred A. Knopf, 2013), 317.

5. Ibid., 318.

6. Ibid.
7. Graham was speaking to Lady Hartwell, the wife of the owner of the London *Daily Telegraph*. Ibid., 319.
8. Alan Greenspan, *The Age of Turbulence: Adventures in a New World* (New York: Penguin Books, 2008), 282. In his magisterial biography of Margaret Thatcher, Charles Moore says that Thatcher and Greenspan met at Katharine Graham's house. But Greenspan, for whom the encounter remained vivid, recalls that the dinner took place at the British embassy. Press accounts make no mention of a Graham dinner but confirm that there was a dinner for Mrs. Thatcher at the embassy on September 19. See Jeannette Smyth, "Thatcher Midst the Colonials," *Washington Post*, September 20, 1975.
9. The definition of monetary aggregates including M3 was changed by the Federal Reserve in 1980. See Table 2 in Thomas D. Simpson, "The Redefined Monetary Aggregates," *Federal Reserve Bulletin* 66 (1980), 99.
10. In 1974, the Bundesbank had become the first central bank to publish monetary targets. The Fed followed in 1975, but the targets were not taken seriously until October 1979.
11. Kaye Pullen, interview by the author, October 15, 2012.
12. Later in her U.S. trip, Thatcher would tell an audience, sounding remarkably like Greenspan, "When money can no longer be counted on to act as a store of value, savings and investment are undermined, the basis of contracts is distorted and the professional and middle-class citizen, the backbone of all societies, is disaffected." Moore, *Margaret Thatcher*, 329.
13. Pullen, interview by the author, October 15, 2012.
14. Greenspan had been watching the travails of the British economy for months before Thatcher's visit. In April 1975, he sent the president a clipping from the *Economist* detailing the "crumbling financial and fiscal condition" of the United Kingdom. "Observe that the British economy appears to be at the point where they must accelerate the amount of governmental fiscal stimulus just to stand still," Greenspan told Ford. "This is clearly a very dangerous situation. The frightening parallels, with a lag, between the financial policies of the U.S. and those of the U.K. should give us considerable pause." Alan Greenspan to Gerald R. Ford, April 23, 1975, Memoranda for the President, August 1974–

September 1975, box 1, Records of the U.S. Council of Economic Advisers (1969), 1974–1977, Gerald R. Ford Library.
15. James Q. Wilson, "The Riddle of the Middle Class," *Public Interest*, no. 39 (Spring 1975): 128. A copy complete with a White House circulation list was found in Greenspan's personal files.
16. Louis Harris, speech (National Press Club, Washington, D.C., June 26, 1975). The speech was circulated in the White House. A copy was found in Greenspan's personal files.
17. The dean was Arnold Weber of the business school at Carnegie Mellon University. See James P. Gannon, "Future Fear: Is the Economy Sliding into Five or Ten Years of Stagnation, Unrest?," *Wall Street Journal*, May 15, 1975.
18. Steven F. Hayward, *The Age of Reagan: The Fall of the Old Liberal Order: 1964–1980* (New York: Random House, 2009), 517.
19. Hobart Rowen, "Humphrey-Javits Bill Urges Long-Term Economic Plans," *Washington Post*, May 13, 1975.
20. Alan Greenspan to Gerald R. Ford, memorandum, June 3, 1975, personal files of Alan Greenspan.
21. Alan Greenspan to Gerald R. Ford, memorandum, June 24, 1975, personal files of Alan Greenspan.
22. The Harvard colleague was Stanley Hoffmann. Quoted in Niall Ferguson, *Kissinger 1923–1968: The Idealist* (New York: Penguin Press, 2015), Kindle location 625.
23. Walter Isaacson, *Kissinger: A Biography* (New York: Simon & Schuster, 2005), 319.
24. Edwin L. Dale Jr., "Kissinger's Worldwide Economic Design," *New York Times*, June 8, 1975, sec. 3.
25. In early 1974, at the height of the boom, basic foodstuffs were up by 100 percent in four years, fertilizer by 170 percent, and petroleum by more than 350 percent. These percentage changes refer to the rise in commodity prices relative to manufactured goods between a benchmark period, 1968–70, and the peak of the commodity boom in 1974. See Hollis B. Chenery, "Restructuring the World Economy," *Foreign Affairs* 53, no. 2 (January 1975): 244.
26. Henry Kissinger, speech (Kansas City International Relations Council, May 13, 1975), http://www.ford.utexas.edu/library/docu ment/dosb/hak1975.pdf.
27. Ibid.
28. "Henry and I have been working together for years but we're not personally very close. I know his

wife very well and I know him very well but there's always a little distance that prevented me from making that kind of connection. . . . He's got a different personality from mine. We actually worked together one time in the private sector. And as well as I know Kissinger, there are deep, deep secrets in that man that I'm not sure even he knows about." Alan Greenspan, interview by the author, October 12, 2010.
29. Kissinger had made this appeal for a new Bretton Woods in a speech on April 17, 1975, at the National Press Club. In response, Greenspan argued that if Kissinger regretted its passing, he should press for a return to national budget discipline. See Alan Greenspan to Donald Rumsfeld, "The Financial Crises of New York City," memorandum, September 12, 1975, Alan Greenspan Files: White House Correspondence, box 4, Rumsfeld, Donald, Greenspan, Gerald R. Ford Library.
30. G. Edward Schuh to Alan Greenspan, memorandum, April 22, 1975, personal files of Alan Greenspan.
31. G. Edward Schuh to Alan Greenspan, memorandum, May 23, 1975, personal files of Alan Greenspan.
32. G. Edward Schuh to Alan Greenspan, memorandum, June 4, 1975, personal files of Alan Greenspan.
33. Bernard Gwertzman, "Kissinger's New Role: His Speeches on Economic Policy Irk Officials Who Prefer More Research," *New York Times*, June 4, 1975.
34. The lieutenant was Thomas Enders, his assistant secretary for economic affairs.
35. Henry Kissinger and Thomas Enders, "Memorandum of Telephone Conversation," June 1, 1975, Kissinger Telephone Conversations, http://gateway.pro quest.com/openurl?url_ver= Z39.88-2004&res_dat=xri:dnsa& rft_dat=xri:dnsa:article: CKA13689.
36. Andrew Scott Cooper, *The Oil Kings: How the U.S., Iran, and Saudi Arabia Changed the Balance of Power in the Middle East*, Reprint edition (New York: Simon & Schuster, 2012), 262–63.
37. By the spring of 1975, Iran's oil production was down by a sixth since the previous year, and it was building up an unsold stockpile.
38. Gerald R. Ford, Henry Kissinger, and Brent Scowcroft, "Memorandum of Conversation," June 12, 1975, Gerald R. Ford Library, http://www.fordlibrarymuseum .gov/library/document/0314 /1553120.pdf.

39. Henry Kissinger, Alan Greenspan, et al., "Memorandum of Conversation," June 16, 1975. in Monica L. Belmonte, ed., *Iran; Iraq, 1973–1976*, vol. 27, *Foreign Relations of the United States, 1969–1976* (Washington, D.C.: United States Government Printing Office, 2012), 403–6.

40. The problems with Kissinger's oil plan had been pointed out earlier to him by the economists on his National Security Council staff. On June 6, 1975, Robert Hormats and Robert Oakley had written to him that "for 500,000 barrels of oil per day out of our total consumption of roughly 18,000,000 bpd you are, in short, running a major policy and personal risk by advancing this proposal. The profound changes called for in the way the US does business and conducts its financial relations holds virtually no hope that the plan could succeed and will expose you to the worst sort of criticism." Memorandum from Robert Hormats and Robert Oakley of the National Security Staff to Secretary of State Henry Kissinger, June 6, 1975, in Monica L. Belmonte, *Iran; Iraq, 1973–1976*, 27:401–3.

41. Henry Kissinger and Charles Robinson, "Memorandum of Telephone Conversation," June 16, 1975, Kissinger Telephone Conversations, http://nsarchive.chadwyck.com/cat/displayItemId.do?queryType=cat&ItemID=CKA13749.

42. Henry Kissinger and Alan Greenspan, "Memorandum of Telephone Conversation," June 17, 1975, Kissinger Telephone Conversations, http://nsarchive.chadwyck.com/cat/displayItemId.do?queryType=cat&ItemID=CKA13753.

43. Table 11.1a, "World Crude Oil Production: OPEC Members" (U.S. Energy Information Administration, Monthly Energy Review, September 25, 2013).

44. Greenspan later observed that "the major job of the Council of Economic Advisers is to shoot down crazy schemes that people on the Hill have, or in the Administration. Productive things are not visible." Greenspan, interview by the author, December 10, 2010.

45. Following conversation from Henry Kissinger, Frank Zarb, Alan Greenspan, and Charles Robinson, "Memorandum of Conversation," n.d., Classical External Memcons, May–December 1975, folder 2, box 23, Record Group 59, Department of State Records, National Archives.

46. This meeting with Kissinger took place one day before Greenspan wrote the second of two June memos to Ford emphasizing the case for deregulation, as mentioned earlier in this chapter.

47. The frustrated CEA memos of the spring, cited above, were followed on July 1, 1975, by a memo from CEA economist Bob Stillman. "I always feel perplexed anytime I deal with people from State," Stillman wrote. "Their language is so rhetorical that it is difficult to know whether to accept their statements at face-value and label the perpetrators 'economic ignoramuses' or whether to conclude that the rhetoric is a necessary façade in international politics." Stillman inclined toward the first hypothesis, noting that Kissinger's speeches were suffused with the "hand-in-hand down the primrose path" view of international economics. Robert Stillman to Paul W. MacAvoy, memorandum, July 1, 1975, personal files of Alan Greenspan.

48. Cooper, *Oil Kings,* suggests that the June 30 meeting with the shah and his foreign minister was unsuccessful. But a memo from Kissinger to Ford on August 15, declassified after publication of *Oil Kings,* indicates otherwise. See Document 140, Monica L. Belmonte, *Iran; Iraq, 1973–1976.*

49. Henry Kissinger, Frank Zarb, Alan Greenspan, Charles Robinson, et al., "Memorandum of Conversation," July 14, 1975, Classified External Memcons May–December 1975, folder 3, box 23, Record Group 59, Records of Henry Kissinger, 1973–77, Department of State Records, National Archives.

50. Henry Kissinger and Charles Robinson, "Memorandum of Telephone Conversation," August 7, 1975, Kissinger Telephone Conversations, http://nsarchive.chadwyck.com/cat/displayItemIdImages.do?queryType=cat&&ItemID=CKA13923.

51. Gerald R. Ford, Henry Kissinger, and Brent Scowcroft, "Memorandum of Conversation," August 7, 1975, box 14, National Security Adviser, Memoranda of Conversations 1973–1977, Gerald R. Ford Library, http://www.fordlibrarymuseum.gov/library/document/0314/1553204.pdf.

52. Henry Kissinger, memorandum, August 15, 1975, National Security Adviser, Kissinger-Scowcroft West Wing Office Files, box 16, Iran (5), Secret, Nodis, Cherokee, Gerald R. Ford Library.

53. Charles Robinson to Henry Kissinger, memorandum, August 17, 1975, WikiLeaks, https://www.wikileaks.org/plusd/cables/1975STATE195265_b3.html.

54. Charles Robinson to Henry Kissinger, memorandum, August 30, 1975, WikiLeaks, https://www.wikileaks.org/plusd/cables/1975STATE207021_b.html.

55. Charles Robinson to Henry Kissinger, memorandum, September 8, 1975, in Monica L. Belmonte, *Iran; Iraq, 1973–1976*, 27:430–32.

56. Henry Kissinger, interview by the author, September 5, 2012.

57. Ibid.

58. Whether Greenspan had been right to block the deal was a slightly different question, however. In the long run, he was correct that untrammeled price signals would balance demand with supply more efficiently than government deal making. In the short run, however, the shah worked out his irritation with his U.S. partners by joining other hawkish producers in demanding a price increase, ultimately securing a price hike of 10 percent.

59. Roderick M. Hills, interview by the author, April 24, 2012. Hills was the administration colleague who was bundled into the same car as Greenspan.

60. Alan Greenspan to Donald Rumsfeld, Dick Cheney, and Robert Goldwin, memorandum, September 25, 1975, James Cannon (3), box 2, Records of the U.S. Council of Economic Advisers (1969), 1974–1977, Gerald R. Ford Library. Sara Jane Moore, the shooter in the second incident, did her best to vindicate Greenspan's perspective; at her trial she described her attempt to kill Ford as "a correct expression of my anger."

61. Martin Tolchin, "General Negative Feeling Toward City Shown in Congressional Refusal of Aid," *New York Times,* May 25, 1975. For his part, Representative Thomas P. O'Neill Jr. of Massachusetts, the House majority leader, complained of New York's municipal employees, "Their salaries are too high, their pensions are too high, and they have too much vacation."

62. Greenspan advised on the draft of the May 14 letter from Ford rejecting New York's request. See Alan Greenspan to James Cannon, note, May 1975, Seidman files, box 78, New York City, Gerald R. Ford Library. Carey quotation is from Frank Lynn, "Carey and Mayor Express Anger," *New York Times,* May 15, 1975.

63. Frank Lynn, "Carey and Mayor Express Anger."

64. Greenspan contended that far more than money was at stake.

"America is better off economically than it was fifteen years ago, but are we spiritually better off?" he demanded of his colleagues. "Resurrecting respect for leadership in government can only be done by moving away from short-term expediency." See Alan Greenspan et al., "Memorandum of Conversation," September 25, 1975, James Cannon (3), box 2, Records of the U.S. Council of Economic Advisers (1969), 1974–1977, Gerald R. Ford Library.

65. See also Federal Open Market Committee, "Memorandum of Discussion" (Board of Governors of the Federal Reserve System, November 18, 1975), 67.

66. Seymour P. Lachman and Robert Polner, *The Man Who Saved New York: Hugh Carey and the Great Fiscal Crisis of 1975* (New York: SUNY Press, 2010), 152.

67. "President Sees No Justification for Help to City," *New York Times,* October 8, 1975. See also Hobart Rowen, "Burns Says Haste Is Vital for NY," *Washington Post,* October 9, 1975.

68. "Around City Hall," *New Yorker,* October 27, 1975, 154.

69. These arguments were made in three memos, one of which was finalized six days after Ford's October 29 speech even though its gist was probably deployed in oral form in the debates leading up to it. See Greenspan to Rumsfeld, "The Financial Crises of New York City"; Paul W. MacAvoy to Gerald R. Ford, memorandum, October 27, 1975; personal files of Alan Greenspan; and Burton G. Malkiel to William Seidman, memorandum, November 4, 1975, personal files of Alan Greenspan.

70. *Adequacy of Federal Agency Studies into National Impact of a New York Default,* vol. 1, 2 vols., Hearings Before a Subcommittee of the Committee on Government Operations, House of Representatives, 94th Cong., 1st sess., October 8 and November 7, 1975 (Washington, D.C.: United States Government Printing Office, 1975), http://hdl.handle.net/2027/pur1.32754076878366. The study revealed that 546 banks held "significant" amounts of New York State and City securities, which the House subcommittee's chairman, Benjamin Rosenthal, noted was "approximately 100 more banks than had been previously known to hold such securities." Edwin L. Dale Jr., "Large Banks Hold Big Stakes Here," *New York Times,* November 14, 1975.

71. John Scadding to Alan Greenspan, memorandum, November 10, 1975, personal files of Alan Greenspan. Scadding was forwarding a memo written by David Brazell three days earlier.

72. John J. Casserly, *The Ford White House: The Diary of a Speechwriter* (Boulder: University Press of Colorado, 1977), 206.

73. Robert Trowbridge Hartmann, *Palace Politics: An Inside Account of the Ford Years* (New York: McGraw-Hill, 1980), 358.

74. Gerald R. Ford, "Remarks on the Subject of Financial Assistance to New York City" (National Press Club, October 29, 1975).

75. Ford's speechwriter, Bob Hartmann, later wrote that there were hidden hands behind the speech, "and the hands were the hands of Greenspan." Hartmann, *Palace Politics,* 358.

76. Francis X. Clines, "Beame and Carey Decry Ford Plan," *New York Times,* October 30, 1975.

77. Ibid. "I'd say the President spoke out to the hinterlands and tried to reach a certain audience, and he's very mindful of an apparition called Ronald Reagan who somewhere beclouds his future," Carey suggested.

78. A CBS–*New York Times* poll taken in the wake of the speech found that a small majority of all Americans—55 percent—supported some kind of federal aid for New York, an increase over a Gallup poll taken just days before the speech that pegged public support at 42 percent.

79. "Default Anticipation Notes Bow at Follies," *New York Times,* November 15, 1975.

80. Ibid.

81. The witness was Felix Rohatyn. See Lachman and Polner, *Man Who Saved New York,* 163.

82. Gerald R. Ford, "Statement on Measures Taken to Improve the Financial Situation of New York City" (President's News Conference, White House, November 26, 1975).

83. There is a lesson here for the future of finance: commentators repeatedly assert that the system can be rendered safer if the government conducts fewer bailouts, but the reality is that governments will always provide bailouts. Thus, in the wake of the chaos of 2007–9, free-market commentators asserted that the government could have reduced the damage by allowing the investment bank Bear Stearns to fail. Likewise, the efforts to put the financial system back together again featured strenuous attempts to reduce the odds of future government rescues. But history shows that bailouts will be forever with us; nobody wants to trust the market when the market threatens pandemonium. Conservatives of all people should accept this truth about human nature, not pretend that human nature can be otherwise.

84. Pullen, interview by the author, April 23, 2012.

85. "Television: Not for Women Only," *Time,* February 21, 1972. See also "The Press: Bah-Bar-Ah's Bow?," *Time,* October 18, 1976.

86. Barbara Walters, *Audition: A Memoir* (New York: Vintage Books, 2009), 260.

87. Ibid.

88. Stephen F. Hayes, *Cheney: The Untold Story of America's Most Powerful and Controversial Vice President* (New York: HarperCollins, 2007), 102.

89. Burton Malkiel, interview by the author, June 25, 2012.

90. John B. Shoven, interview by the author, April 7, 2011.

91. Walters, *Audition,* 262.

92. Ibid., 263–64.

93. Ibid., 261.

94. Jeannette Smyth, "Personalities," *Washington Post,* May 11, 1976.

95. Walters, *Audition,* 263.

96. Alan's call on ABC's balance sheet turned out better than another financial tip he gave Barbara later. Flush with her big salary, she wanted to buy a $250,000 Fifth Avenue co-op. "The way New York City is going, it's not a good investment," Alan told her, sagely. Thirty-five years later, the apartment was worth more than $30 million. Ibid., 264.

97. Frank Zarb, interview by the author, May 22, 2012.

98. Greenspan, *The Age of Turbulence,* 81.

99. "I really hoped that that would go someplace, because I thought she was the first one he'd gone out with that could work. Because her job was more important than his job." Kathryn Eickhoff, interview by the author, November 29, 2011. Kaye Pullen also expected that the two might get married. Pullen, interview by the author, April 23, 2012.

100. Greenspan recalls, "She knew all the musicians, Isaac Stern and everybody else. But she was not really emotionally drawn to music the way I was. Very few people are. And Andrea was. And that was a necessary, but not sufficient condition. That was a filter which separated how I looked at women." Greenspan, interview by the author, January 10, 2013.

101. At the 1977 White House Correspondents' Dinner, Greenspan

was overheard saying that he and Barbara Walters are "very good friends. We see each other quite often. But no, there are no announcements." Nancy Collins, "The Gossip Column," *Washington Post,* May 2, 1977.

102. Marian Burros et al., "Inauguration: Establishment Crowd a Day of Citywide Celebrating," *Washington Post,* January 20, 1977.

103. Pullen, interview by the author, October 15, 2012.

104. Alan Greenspan to Frank Zarb, memorandum, December 13, 1975, personal files of Alan Greenspan.

105. Alan Greenspan to Nathan Haywood, memorandum, December 24, 1975, personal files of Alan Greenspan.

106. Alan Greenspan to James M. Cannon, memorandum, April 6, 1976, personal files of Alan Greenspan.

107. Fearing systemic fallout from the untested municipal bankruptcy option, state governments rescued cities such as Chicago, Boston, Camden, Harrisburg, and Detroit; in effect, the new bankruptcy option became a threat used by cities to snag the bailouts it was designed to prevent. See Clayton P. Gillette, "Fiscal Federalism, Political Will, and Strategic Use of Municipal Bankruptcy," *University of Chicago Law Review* 79, no. 1 (Winter 2012): 309.

108. James W. Singer, "The Humphrey-Hawkins Bill—Boondoggle or Economic Blessing?," *National Journal,* June 12, 1976.

109. Margaret Weir, *Politics and Jobs: The Boundaries of Employment Policy in the United States* (Princeton, NJ: Princeton University Press, 1992), 135.

110. Joint Economic Committee, *Thirtieth Anniversary of the Employment Act of 1946: Hearings Before the Joint Economic Committee, United States Congress* (Washington, D.C., 1976).

111. The quotes in this paragraph come from Singer, "The Humphrey-Hawkins Bill," 815.

112. Greenspan told Reichley that he remembered "real pressure" within the administration to ramp up spending at the beginning of '76, but he and Ford resisted. "We could not be sure that increased spending would have a positive effect in the short run, and then we would have to deal with the effects of having unleashed inflationary pressures into the economy.... Actually, the extent to which economists can predict the effects of economic decisions is really quite limited." A. James Reichley, *Conservatives in an Age of Change: The Nixon and Ford Administrations* (Washington, D.C.: Brookings Institution Press, 1981), 401. And the economy was improving, so it seemed additional stimulus would have been wasteful.

113. Alan Greenspan to Gerald R. Ford, "Reasons for Better Than Expected Economic Improvement," memorandum, April 16, 1976, Alan Greenspan Files: White House Correspondence, box 2, Gerald R. Ford Library.

114. In 1976 the federal government changed the close of its fiscal year from the end of June to the end of September, leading Greenspan to expect that the slow growth in the second quarter would be offset during the third.

115. Malkiel, interview by the author, June 25, 2012.

116. Greenspan, interview by the author, June 27, 2012.

117. Greenspan, interview by the author, December 22, 2010.

CHAPTER TEN

1. Alan Greenspan, interview by the author, December 22, 2010.

2. Kathryn Eickhoff, interview by the author, November 29, 2011.

3. Wealth effects are partially recorded in the Federal Reserve's Flow of Funds data set, but the transfer of wealth from housing stock to other parts of the consumer balance sheets is hard to track. Robert Parker, who worked on these issues at the Bureau of Economic Analysis in the 1970s, received multiple calls from Greenspan to debate the data. Robert Parker, interview by the author, June 13, 2011.

4. Greenspan's method is described in the appendix to a Townsend-Greenspan client letter. See Alan Greenspan, "Business Outlook" (New York: Townsend-Greenspan & Company, August 26, 1977).

5. The finding that home-equity extraction boosted purchasing power by almost 5 percent is taken from Greenspan's memo. However, repeating his calculation with today's revised data indicates that the effect was closer to 4 percent. The finding that home-equity extraction boosted total spending by almost 3 percent is based on the author's calculation, and assumes that all proceeds of the home-equity extraction were spent in the same quarter.

6. Greenspan, "Business Outlook."

7. Donald Pitcher, interview by the author, December 19, 2011. Pitcher was a portfolio manager at MFS Boston.

8. Howard Hudson, interview by the author, September 12, 2011.

9. "We had to have post-Greenspan meetings to parse what in fact he had been saying. He would leave us with more than one conclusion, intentionally." Ibid.

10. David Rowe, interview by the author, October 11, 2011.

11. Greenspan, interview by the author, January 31, 2013.

12. Burton Malkiel, the Princeton professor who worked with Greenspan on macroeconomic forecasting at the Council of Economic Advisers, emphasizes that Greenspan worked from Keynesian models, often seeking to add his own empirical insights from his days as an industrial economist. "He's perfectly willing to use Keynesian forecasting models ... he would want to tease the models and shock the models with this, that, and the other thing." If Greenspan's skepticism about policy activism made him look like a Friedmanite anti-Keynesian, his appetite for complex forecasting models made him look like a Keynesian anti-Friedmanite. Burton Malkiel, interview by the author, June 25, 2012.

13. Greenspan built home-equity extraction into his firm's model. "It became a very important independent variable for personal consumption expenditures, especially on large, big-ticket items. And you could see the correlations were really extraordinary." Greenspan, interview by the author, January 17, 2012.

14. Greenspan did believe (correctly) that markets were efficient to a first approximation. But he was more preoccupied with examples of market inefficiency than most economists in the late 1970s. Indeed, his writing about feedback loops and their propensity to inflate bubbles often resembles that of George Soros, the hedge-fund speculator who turned an obsession with far-from-equilibrium feedback loops into an astonishing fortune. (For a discussion of Soros's belief in feedback loops, see Sebastian Mallaby, *More Money Than God: Hedge Funds and the Making of a New Elite* [New York: Penguin, 2010], especially chapter four.) Confusingly, Greenspan's 2013 book recants a faith in market efficiency, leaving a false impression that he had believed in market efficiency for much of his career. Alan Greenspan, *The Map and the Territory: Risk, Human Nature, and the Future of Forecasting* (New York: Penguin Press, 2013). The

same confusing impression is encouraged by Greenspan's "confession" to Congressman Henry Waxman in October 2008 that he had discovered a "flaw" in his worldview. On this, see chapter twenty-nine.

15. Versions of this idea predated Keynes. Money was frequently described as a "veil" that hid the real working of the economy; or to use a different metaphor, it was the grease of trade, not the wheel. See Robert B. Ekelund Jr. and Robert F. Hébert, *A History of Economic Theory and Method*, third international edition (New York: McGraw-Hill, 1990), 517.

16. Justin Martin, *Greenspan: The Man Behind Money* (Cambridge, Mass.: Perseus Publishing, 2001), 139.

17. Leonard Silk, "Greenspan, White House Days Behind, Picks Up as Before Economic Scene: Greenspan Resumes Old Career," *New York Times*, April 28, 1977.

18. Ibid.

19. Rowe, interview by the author, October 11, 2011.

20. Eickhoff, interview by the author, November 29, 2011.

21. "A Difference of Opinion," *Fortune*, February 13, 1978. In this interview, Greenspan opposed a "general tax cut" and emphasized the inflationary consequences of deficits. He devoted much of the interview to arguing in favor of a business tax cut, which would boost growth more and expand the deficit less than other tax cuts. Neither Proposition 13 nor the Kemp-Roth tax cuts followed this logic, but he endorsed them anyway.

22. Romer and Romer examined the effect of tax cuts on future spending decisions. After analyzing tax cuts enacted in 1948, 1964, 1981, and 2001/2003, they found that tax cuts tended to be followed by increases in spending—the opposite of what the starve-the-beast theory predicted. Policy makers addressed increased deficits not by cutting spending but by raising taxes again. Christina Romer and David Romer, "Do Tax Cuts Starve the Beast? The Effect of Tax Changes on Government Spending," *Brookings Papers on Economic Activity*, Spring 2009, 139–214.

23. "Nation: Economists Eye the Impact," *Time*, June 26, 1978.

24. "A Difference of Opinion," *Fortune*.

25. Congressional Budget Office, "Understanding Fiscal Policy," April 1, 1978, 128.

26. Walter Heller, "The Kemp-Roth-Laffer Free Lunch," *Wall Street Journal*, July 12, 1978.

27. Greenspan stipulated that "if we continue to have unrestrained expenditure growth on the one hand and sharp cuts in receipts on the other, we will have horrendous deficits." Then, embracing the Prop 13 faith, he added: "That is clearly true but irrelevant."

28. Alan Greenspan, "Economic Conditions and Outlook" (George S. Eccles Distinguished Lecture Series, Utah State University, October 23, 1978).

29. At the time of Greenspan's speech, house prices were rising by more than 6 percent per year after adjusting for inflation.

30. It should be noted that the Fed's policy was less tight than it seemed because inflation was high: the real short-term funds rate (the rate after subtracting core PCE inflation) was a bit above 2 percent at the time of Greenspan's speech. However, the decoupling of short rates and mortgage rates is clear. Between the start of October 1975 and the start of October 1978, the Fed had pushed the short-term interest rate up from 6.2 percent to 8.9 percent, but the thirty-year conventional mortgage rate rose by only 0.6 percentage points, from 9.22 percent to 9.86 percent. Mortgage data are from the St. Louis Fed's Federal Reserve Economic Data (FRED) database.

31. In the year to September 1978, inflation-adjusted growth had come in at 5.3 percent.

32. The existence of a "conundrum" with respect to mortgage interest rates is omitted in scholarly examinations of this period. See, for example, Julio J. Rotemberg, "Penitence After Accusations of Error: 100 Years of Monetary Policy at the U.S. Federal Reserve," in *The First Hundred Years of the Federal Reserve* (National Bureau of Economic Research Conference, Cambridge, Mass., 2013), and Daniel L. Thornton, "The Evolution of Inflation Targeting: How Did We Get Here and Where Do We Need to Go?" (Sixth Norges Bank Monetary Policy Conference, Oslo, 2009). However, retrospective analysis shows Greenspan was right. Between 1954 and 1969, the correlation between the effective federal funds rate and the seasonally adjusted growth in home mortgages had been strong (showing an R² of 0.4, according to calculations by Dinah Walker of the Council on Foreign Relations). Between 1970 and 1984, the correlation broke down (R² of 0.06). By 1978, in other words, the previously tight relationship between interest rates and the growth in

mortgage lending had indeed been broken.

33. After 2007, Greenspan implied that the "conundrum" had rendered the Fed powerless. But in 1978 he argued that it merely meant that in order to get its way, the Fed would have to act forcefully.

34. Greenspan, interview by the author, January 25, 2011.

35. "The Fed vs. Jimmy's Aides: Seeing Slowdown Instead of Surge, Bill Miller Declines to Tighten Policy," *Time*, April 30, 1979.

36. Edwin McDowell, "He Even Counsels Kennedy," *New York Times*, December 9, 1979. It was a point he would raise again in 1983 on the PBS show *Open Mind*. "Regulating the Economy," *Open Mind* (New York: PBS, August 12, 1983).

37. In January 1979, Carter enjoyed a 57–35 lead over Reagan. He also held a wide lead over Ford, 53 to 39 percent. But by early July 1979, Carter was losing in hypothetical head-to-head contests with Reagan, Ford, and Howard Baker.

38. Quoted in James T. Patterson, *Restless Giant: The United States From Watergate to Bush v. Gore* (New York: Oxford University Press, 2005), Kindle location 2023.

39. For Anderson's discussion of how he persuaded advisers to help Reagan, see Martin Anderson, *Revolution: The Reagan Legacy* (Stanford, CA: Hoover Press, 1990), 168.

40. See Edwin Meese, "Campaign Planning Meeting Notes," n.d., all April and May 1979 Notes, Meese, Ed—Campaign Planning—Meetings, April 1979/May 1979, Box 103, 1980 Campaign Papers, Ronald Reagan Governor's Papers, Ronald Reagan Library.

41. Martin, *Greenspan: The Man Behind Money*, 141.

42. Edwin Meese, "Notes and Agendas from Meeting on Public Policy Issues," September 8, 1979, Meese, Ed—Campaign Planning—Meetings, September 1979, box 103, 1980 Campaign Papers, Ronald Reagan Governor's Papers, Ronald Reagan Library. The following account derives from these sources.

43. Greenspan, interview by the author, April 11, 2011.

CHAPTER ELEVEN

1. In January 1978, Burns had lamented, "We need an anti-inflation policy on the part of the Administration," as though it were not the Fed's responsibility to deliver one. The view that fiscal policy and not monetary policy

caused inflation is reflected in staff briefings as well. For example, in a March 21, 1978, FOMC staff briefing, James Kichline suggested that "in the absence of an effective Administration antiinflation program, the risks appear weighted toward higher rather than lower rates of inflation." Daniel L. Thornton, "The Evolution of Inflation Targeting: How Did We Get Here and Where Do We Need to Go?" (Sixth Norges Bank Monetary Policy Conference, Oslo, 2009), 3.

2. Burns gave this testimony on July 24, 1975. It should be noted that during his Fed tenure Burns was occasionally capable of acknowledging his power. For example, in congressional testimony in July 1974, he said, "From a purely theoretical point of view, it would have been possible for monetary policy to offset the influence that lax fiscal policies and the special factors have exerted on the general level of prices.... But an effort to use harsh policies of monetary restraint to offset the exceptionally powerful inflationary forces of recent years would have caused serious financial disorder and dislocation." However, statements emphasizing monetary policy impotence were more common. See Julio J. Rotemberg, "Penitence After Accusations of Error: 100 Years of Monetary Policy at the U.S. Federal Reserve," in *The First Hundred Years of the Federal Reserve* (National Bureau of Economic Research Conference, Cambridge, Mass., 2013), 13.

3. In his February 2, 1970, *Newsweek* column, even Milton Friedman had expressed satisfaction that his "close friend and former teacher Arthur Burns" would become Fed chair, and urged the Fed to "shift promptly to a less restrictive policy." See Rotemberg, "Penitence After Accusations of Error."

4. The "Great Inflation" of the 1970s is sometimes invoked as proof that inflation can take off with little warning, and therefore that modern central banks should be wary of risking even temporary periods of inflation. But the Great Inflation of the 1970s owed much to the lack of an expert consensus in favor of fighting inflation. The conclusion is that modern central banks have more scope to risk temporary inflation surges than is sometimes recognized.

5. As Burns put it in his Belgrade speech, "We look in vain to technical reforms as a way of eliminating the inflationary bias of industrial countries." Arthur F. Burns, "The Anguish of Central Banking"

(1979 Per Jacobsson Lecture, Belgrade, September 30, 1979).

6. William Greider, *Secrets of the Temple: How the Federal Reserve Runs the Country* (New York: Simon & Schuster, 1989), 46.

7. Volcker's reaction to Burns's speech is described in William L. Silber, *Volcker: The Triumph of Persistence* (New York: Bloomsbury Press, 2012), 168.

8. Ibid., 15.

9. Ibid., 33.

10. González accused Volcker of usury during a House hearing on July 14, 1981; July was the month in which the federal funds rate topped 22 percent.

11. Charles Goodhart, "The Conduct of Monetary Policy," *Economic Journal* 99, no. 396 (June 1, 1989): 301. After leaving office in 1987, Volcker delivered his own retrospective lecture, contrasting his legacy pointedly with that of Burns by titling it "The Triumph of Central Banking?" Paul Volcker, "The Triumph of Central Banking?" (1990 Per Jacobsson Lecture, Washington, D.C., September 23, 1990), http://www.perjacobsson.org/lectures/1990.pdf.

12. Quoted in Silber, *Volcker: The Triumph,* 149.

13. Neil Irwin, *The Alchemists: Three Central Bankers and a World on Fire* (New York: Penguin, 2013), 70.

14. Alan Greenspan, interview by the author, November 8, 2010. Greenspan added, "The most important action that the Federal Reserve ever did was what Volcker did in 1979–80. That was critical to this country to an extent that few people could imagine."

15. The pollster was Daniel Yankelovich. See William Bowen, "The Decade Ahead: Not So Bad If We Do Things Right," *Fortune,* October 8, 1979.

16. Robert L. Hetzel, *The Monetary Policy of the Federal Reserve* (New York: Cambridge University Press, 2008), xiv.

17. Silber, *Volcker: The Triumph,* 172.

18. William Bowen, "The Decade Ahead." To the suggestion that forcing down inflation would cause a recession, Greenspan answered, "Is there an alternative? We don't have either the option of doing nothing or the option of applying a painless cure."

19. "Right Move at the Eleventh Hour: Time Board of Economists Generally Backs Fed's Decision," *Time,* October 22, 1979, 24.

20. "Will the Last Remain First? A Cooler Ronald Reagan Enters the Race," *Time,* November 26, 1979.

21. "'President Reagan,'" *New Republic,* December 1, 1979. For further

doubts about Reagan's seriousness, see "Where Did He Get Those Figures? G.O.P. Front Runner Seems to Pluck Facts from Thin Air," *Time,* April 14, 1980.

22. Notes from a meeting with Milton Friedman, January 21, 1980, folder "Meese, Ed—Campaign Planning—Meetings, January 1980," Box 103, Ronald Reagan Campaign Papers, Ronald Reagan Governor's Papers, 1965–1980, Ronald Reagan Presidential Library.

23. Arthur Laffer, "The Laffer Economic Report," January 11, 1980, Research Policy (Hopkins/Bandow)—[Correspondence], box 453, Ronald Reagan 1980 Campaign Papers, Ronald Reagan Library. Emphasis original.

24. David A. Stockman, *The Triumph of Politics* (New York: Harper & Row, 1986), 50.

25. Ibid., 49–50.

26. Dennis Farney, "Reaching Out: Reagan Seeks to Shed His Doctrinaire Image but Keep His Loyalists," *Wall Street Journal,* November 9, 1979.

27. Nancy Collins and Carla Hall, "Super Mania: Weekend of Parties and a World Premiere for the Special Olympics," *Washington Post,* December 11, 1978.

28. William Bowen, "Better Prospects for Our Ailing Productivity," *Fortune,* December 3, 1979.

29. Alan Greenspan, "The Great Malaise," *Challenge* 23, no. 1 (April 1980): 37–40.

30. Steven F. Hayward, *The Age of Reagan: The Fall of the Old Liberal Order: 1964–1980* (New York: Random House, 2009), 624.

31. Lou Cannon, "Ford Will Reassess His 1980 Prospects," *Washington Post,* September 23, 1979.

32. Elisabeth Bumiller and Joseph McLellan, "Ford at a Grand Old Party," *Washington Post,* March 13, 1980.

33. Martin Schram, "Ford Says He Won't Be a Candidate," *Washington Post,* March 16, 1980.

34. Thomas M. DeFrank, *Write It When I'm Gone: Remarkable Off-the-Record Conversations with Gerald R. Ford* (New York: Berkley Books, 2008), 82.

35. William J. Casey to Ronald Reagan, memorandum, June 4, 1980, Meese, Ed—Campaign Planning—Political Memos, June 1980, box 103, Ronald Reagan 1980 Campaign Papers, 1965–1980, Ronald Reagan Library.

36. In an interview with AP the day of his appointment, Greenspan sounded softer on government spending than he had done in his private conversation with Bill Casey one month earlier. "I'm not

arguing for or recommending that specific programs be curtailed. I don't think that's necessary. It might be necessary in three or four years if we continue doing what we're doing. I'm merely arguing we stand still and keep existing legislation where it is . . . the equivalent is if Congress went home all year long." This was the ultimate in do-nothingism. Associated Press, "Reagan Budget Aide Has Spending-Cut Plan," July 8, 1980.

37. Walters recounted this episode in an on-air discussion with ABC colleagues on Wednesday, July 16, 1980. See "1980 Republican National Convention," *ABC News* (Nashville, Tenn.: WKRN, July 16, 1980), Vanderbilt Television News Archive. The author thanks Vanderbilt University's Television News Archive and the Motion Picture and Television Reading Room of the Library of Congress for assistance in accessing this video and others cited in this chapter.

38. Justin Martin, *Greenspan: The Man Behind Money* (Cambridge, Mass.: Perseus Publishing, 2001), 142.

39. James M. Perry and Albert R. Hunt, "Canceled Ticket: The Reagan Ford Deal Was Built Bit by Bit—and Then Fell Apart," *Wall Street Journal*, July 18, 1980.

40. Henry Kissinger, interview by the author, September 6, 2012.

41. Perry and Hunt, "Canceled Ticket." Hunt later recalled that Greenspan was a wonderful source for this story, providing yet another example of Greenspan's focus on cultivating the media. Albert Hunt, interview by the author, February 4, 2014.

42. Greenspan said later of this meeting and the idea of the "Dream Ticket," "The more I thought about it, the more I thought it was a good idea." Perry and Hunt, "Canceled Ticket."

43. David M. Alpern et al., "How the Ford Deal Collapsed," *Newsweek*, July 28, 1980. See also Martin, *Greenspan: The Man Behind Money*, 143.

44. The following account is drawn from multiple sources, but especially from Richard Allen's vivid account. Although Allen published his memory of events twenty years after the fact, it was based on detailed contemporaneous notes. See Richard Allen, "George Herbert Walker Bush: The Accidental Vice President," *New York Times Magazine*, July 30, 2000.

45. "Campaign '80/Republican Convention," *World News Tonight*, *ABC News* (Nashville, Tenn.: WKRN, July 16, 1980).

46. Perry and Hunt, "Canceled Ticket."

47. Various elaborate claims have been advanced concerning Walters's conduct in securing this interview. According to one account, Walters told Ford, "Mr. President, you've got to do this for old times' sake, for Alan's sake." See "Barbara Walters and Senator Edward Brooke: The Secret Was Already Out," *New York Magazine Daily Intelligencer*, May 2, 2008. See also Tom Shales, "Camera Madness: Network Showdown at Republican Convention," *Washington Post*, July 18, 1980. See also "1980: It's Reagan-Bush, Not Reagan-Ford," *National Journal*, August 26, 2012.

48. Robert Shogan, "Bush Ends His Waiting Game, Attacks Reagan," *Los Angeles Times*, April 14, 1980.

49. Allen, "George Herbert Walker Bush."

50. Ronald Reagan, *An American Life* (New York: Simon & Schuster, 1990), 215.

51. Allen, "George Herbert Walker Bush."

52. Looking back, Greenspan plays down the odds that the Dream Ticket might have worked, emphasizing that Ford was happy with his life in California. "It was the first time he was making any money. He was playing golf, which he loved to do." Greenspan, interviews by the author, July 16, 2010, and January 25, 2011. On the other hand, Kissinger told the *Washington Post* that "if it had been possible for both the principals to go to bed, sleep on it, meet again in the morning, we could have wrapped up this thing in two hours in the morning," adding, "that's how close it was." (Haynes Johnson et al., "The Republicans in Detroit: The Cement Just Wouldn't Set on GOP's Alliance," *Washington Post*, July 17, 1980.) Kissinger also said that Greenspan believed at the time that the deal could work, and that Greenspan "probably was tempted by being secretary of Treasury." Kissinger, interview by the author, September 6, 2012.

53. "Campaign '80/Republican Convention," *World News Tonight*, *ABC News* (Nashville, Tenn.: WKRN, July 17, 1980), Vanderbilt Television News Archive.

54. "1980 Republican National Convention," *ABC News* (ABC, July 17, 1980), ABC News Archive. The author would like to thank ABC News for providing a copy of the Walters-Greenspan interview. Greenspan recalls of this Walters interview, "It was the only time she ever interviewed me. We had a Chinese wall, so to speak." Greenspan, interview by the author, January 25, 2011. In another interview

with Tom Brokaw about an hour later, Greenspan reprised his managerial defense of the Dream Ticket. "There was never any intention or any discussion of changing the constitutional prerogatives of the presidency. And the only alterations that were being involved in an enhanced vice presidency really represented shifting of various managerial functions which would allow the vice president to do the types of things which probably is inappropriately now being done by the chief of staff." See "1980 Republican Convention" (Nashville, Tenn.: NBC, WSMV, July 17, 1980).

55. Greenspan's assumption of a 17 percent recovery rate from tax cuts was broadly vindicated by later research. A 1986 National Bureau of Economic Research report estimated that between just under 17 percent and 25 percent of the cost of the Reagan tax cuts was recouped as a result of "changes in taxpayer behavior." See Lawrence B. Lindsey, "Individual Taxpayer Response to Tax Cuts 1982–1984 with Implications for the Revenue Maximizing Tax Rate," Working Paper (Cambridge, Mass.: National Bureau of Economic Research, December 1986). Similarly, Mankiw and Weinzierl find a 17 percent payback for a tax reduction on labor income. N. Gregory Mankiw and Matthew Weinzierl, "Dynamic Scoring: A Back-of-the-Envelope Guide," Working Paper (Cambridge, Mass.: National Bureau of Economic Research, December 2004).

56. "A Warning to Reagan on Kemp-Roth," *BusinessWeek*, August 11, 1980.

57. Martin Anderson, *Revolution: The Reagan Legacy* (Stanford, CA: Hoover Institution Press, 1990), 129.

58. Ibid., 132. Anderson writes, "Greenspan was one of the few economists in the country who enjoyed almost universal respect among the press."

59. Anderson's numbers assumed real growth in defense expenditures of 5 percent per year, lower than the 7 percent annual increase the campaign had talked about. He also assumed a business tax cut that would be less costly than the version Congress was most likely to enact. See Stockman, *The Triumph of Politics*, 70–71. See also Elizabeth Drew, "A Reporter at Large: 1980: Reagan," *New Yorker*, September 29, 1980, 123. Sixteen months later, on January 17, 1982, Greenspan was called to account for the Chicago forecast on NBC's

NOTES

Meet the Press. He confessed that, relative to that forecast, Reagan's defense expenditures had turned out higher, other spending cuts had turned out lower, and economic growth had been much slower, even though the Chicago growth projection had been in line with the consensus in the fall of 1980. *Meet the Press* (Washington, D.C.: NBC, January 17, 1982).

60. This description is taken from Anderson's vivid account. See Anderson, *Revolution,* 133.

61. Ibid., 134.

62. Drew, "A Reporter at Large; 1980: Reagan," 123. The article also observes, "Greenspan is actually a very conservative man, but, compared with some of the people who had been advising Reagan, he is conventional." Meanwhile, *Time* magazine was suitably impressed as well. In place of smoke and mirrors, Reagan now had an economic platform that was "debatable, but plausible," in the judgment of *Time*'s editors. The fact that Greenspan had close ties to *Time* was surely not irrelevant. See George J. Church, Laurence I. Barrett, and William Baylock, "Conservative Conservatism," *Time,* September 22, 1980. Likewise, the *Washington Post* quoted Greenspan's reassuring verdict: "This is an exercise in reasonable budget making." See Lou Cannon, "Reagan Scales Down Plan for Patching Up Economy," *Washington Post,* September 10, 1980.

CHAPTER TWELVE

1. Lou Cannon, *President Reagan: The Role of a Lifetime* (New York: PublicAffairs, 2000), 95–114.

2. Alan Greenspan, *The Age of Turbulence: Adventures in a New World* (New York: Penguin Books, 2008), 88.

3. Ronald Reagan to Alan Greenspan, letter, September 23, 1980, Political Ops—General—Debate (1/3) (Timmons), box 250, Ronald Reagan Campaign Papers, 1965–80, Ronald Reagan Governor's Papers, Ronald Reagan Library.

4. Murray L. Weidenbaum, interview by the author, June 12, 2013.

5. Robert G. Kaiser, "High Visibility and Higher Stakes," *Washington Post,* February 5, 1981. See also Walter Shapiro, "The Stockman Express," *Washington Post,* February 8, 1981.

6. David A. Stockman, *The Triumph of Politics* (New York: Harper & Row, 1986), 74.

7. Ibid., 75.

8. Gail Fosler, interview by the author, October 3, 2011.

9. Weidenbaum, interview by the author, June 12, 2013.

10. Stockman, *Triumph of Politics,* 95.

11. Ibid., 103.

12. As a share of GDP, the fiscal 1982 and 1983 budgets produced deficits of 4.0 percent and 6.0 percent. This was a worse performance than the deficits of 3.4 percent and 4.2 percent over which Greenspan had presided in the Ford years, and also the worst performance in the post–WWII era. See Office of Management and Budget, "The Budget for Fiscal Year 2012," Historical Tables, Table 2, n.d.

13. CPI inflation was 12.6 percent in November 1980.

14. Coordinating Committee on Economic Policy, "Economic Strategy for the Reagan Administration" (Los Angeles, November 16, 1980). The author thanks George Shultz for providing a copy of this document.

15. This scene is brilliantly described in William L. Silber, *Volcker: The Triumph of Persistence* (New York: Bloomsbury Press, 2012), 194–95.

16. Paul Volcker, interview by the author, December 8, 2010.

17. Silber, *Volcker: The Triumph,* 194–95. See also Stockman, *Triumph of Politics,* 71. Stockman's presentation, "Avoiding a GOP Economic Dunkirk," had emphasized the danger that monetary policy would stifle growth before tax cuts could stimulate it.

18. Volcker, interview by the author, December 8, 2010.

19. The meeting took place on Friday, January 23, 1981. Martin Anderson, *Revolution: The Reagan Legacy* (Stanford, CA: Hoover Institution Press, 1990), 250.

20. Associated Press, "Lass Gets Presidential Hug," *Sarasota* (Florida) *Herald-Tribune,* January 24, 1981.

21. The following scene, including the passage on Volcker's gratitude to Burns, is taken from Silber, *Volcker: The Triumph,* 200–201.

22. Weidenbaum, interview by the author, June 12, 2013. Weidenbaum would become Reagan's first CEA chairman and was present at the meeting.

23. Steven Rattner, "Greenspan's Widened Influence," *New York Times,* March 9, 1981. In 1980, the pitcher Nolan Ryan earned $1 million, according to the Society for American Baseball Research.

24. "Talking Business with Alan Greenspan; Reagan Policy and Congress," *New York Times,* March 24, 1981. A little while

later, Greenspan added that corporations with short-term borrowing were also in trouble: their debt payments were rising through the roof, forcing them to lay off workers. "A sustained recovery may be difficult to achieve until order is restored to the balance sheets of financial institutions and nonfinancial companies," Greenspan told the *Wall Street Journal.* Thanks to his understanding of the linkages between finance and the real economy, Greenspan's forecast proved better than most, at least on this occasion. The *Journal* noted that "administration officials and most private economists believe that interest rates will turn down soon and spark a business recovery in the fourth quarter." As it turned out, growth in the fourth quarter of 1981 was negative 4.5 percent, followed by negative 6.5 percent in the next quarter. Greenspan's projection that the recovery would be delayed until the second quarter of 1982 was closer to the mark: growth in that quarter came in at positive 2.2 percent, although the economy did not start growing strongly until 1983. See Kenneth H. Bacon, "Budget Blight: Economic Slowdown Could Widen Deficit, Some Reaganites Fear," *Wall Street Journal,* August 12, 1981.

25. "Watch on the Rhine," *Wall Street Journal,* May 21, 1981.

26. In the last months of Carter's tenure, supply-side forces in Congress had slipped a gold clause into the law, requiring that the secretary of the Treasury convene a high-level commission on the role of gold in monetary policy. However, it took further pressure the following year to get the administration to appoint the commission.

27. Kiron K. Skinner, Annelise Graebner Anderson, and Martin Anderson, eds., *Reagan: A Life in Letters* (New York: Free Press, 2003), 298–99. Quoted in Silber, *Volcker: The Triumph,* 195.

28. Ronald Reagan to Murray L. Weidenbaum, "Handwritten Note on Gordon Luce Correspondence," 1981, box FG 143033198, Ronald Reagan Library. The author is grateful to Jerry L. Jordan for bringing this evidence to his attention.

29. Murray L. Weidenbaum to Ronald Reagan, memorandum, August 11, 1981, box FG 143033198, Ronald Reagan Library. The author is grateful to Jerry L. Jordan for providing a copy of this document.

30. Ronald Reagan to Gordon Luce, letter, August 14, 1981, Ronald

Reagan Library. Copy obtained from Jerry L. Jordan.

31. Hobart Rowen, "Reagan Might Just Join the New Gold Rush," *Washington Post,* August 20, 1981.

32. On Anderson's unsuccessful effort to have Greenspan appointed to the commission, see Kevin Hopkins to Martin Anderson, memorandum, April 29, 1981, Gold Commission (1), box CFOA84, Martin Anderson Files, Ronald Reagan Library. The memo offers Anderson a list of possible commission members; Anderson scrawls at the bottom: "Rec[ommend] Alan Greenspan."

33. Citing a conversation with Greenspan, Anderson wrote in an internal memo that Reagan should support Greenspan's idea of gold-linked bonds, adding that this would mean extending the gold commission's deadline. See Martin Anderson to Edwin Meese, memorandum, August 31, 1981, Gold Commission (1), box OA9540, Edwin Meese Files, Ronald Reagan Library. Coupled with evidence from other administration sources, who recall that the White House aimed to use the gold commission to defuse the pressure for a return to the gold standard, Anderson's memo strongly suggests that Greenspan's mission was to kill the gold campaign by delaying it. This is consistent with the delay tactics that Greenspan deployed against Kissinger in 1975, and is consistent with the role he played, at the Reagan administration's behest, when he strung out the Social Security commission beyond the 1982 midterm elections.

34. It was "a remarkable turnabout from an ardent supporter of hard money," *Newsweek* noted. Harry Anderson et al., "Reagan's Ailing Economy," *Newsweek,* September 7, 1981.

35. Committee on the Budget, United States Senate, *Second Concurrent Resolution on the Budget—Fiscal Year 1982,* 1981. See also Silber, *Volcker: The Triumph,* 207.

36. Empirical studies support Greenspan's concern about the effect of deficits on interest rates. Eric Engen and R. Glenn Hubbard estimate that a 1-percent-of-GDP increase in the federal deficit raises interest rates by 18 basis points on five-year-ahead rates and 24 basis points on current rates. See Eric M. Engen and R. Glenn Hubbard, "Federal Government Debt and Interest Rates," in *NBER Macroeconomics Annual 2004,* ed. Mark Gertler and

Kenneth Rogoff, vol. 19 (Cambridge, Mass.: MIT Press, 2004), 83–138. William Gale, Peter Orszag, and colleagues find larger effects: an increase of 25 to 35 basis points on five-year-forward interest rates for each percent-of-GDP increase in the future unified deficit and 40 to 70 basis points for each percent-of-GDP increase in the future primary deficit. William G. Gale et al., "Budget Deficits, National Savings, and Interest Rates," *Brookings Papers on Economic Activity,* no. 2 (2004): 101–210. The effect was almost certainly more powerful in the early 1980s than later, when more capital flowed across borders. See Richard J. Sebula and James V. Koch, "Federal Budget Deficits, Interest Rates, and International Capital Flows: A Note," *Quarterly Review of Economics and Finance* 34, no. 1 (Spring 1994): 117–20.

37. Lewis Lehrman, a member of the gold commission, asserted that "the road to the balanced budget is paved with the gold standard." See Lewis Lehrman, "The Case for the Gold Standard," *Wall Street Journal,* July 30, 1981.

38. Jude Wanniski to Alan Greenspan, letter, September 25, 1981, Correspondence: Greenspan, Alan, 1991–1993, box 14, Jude Wanniski, Hoover Institution Archives.

39. "For the first time in fifty years, they seriously considered it," Congressman Ron Paul told a reporter. See Robert Furlow, "Gold Backer Sees Victory in Rejection," Associated Press, March 9, 1982.

40. Kenneth Duberstein, a White House aide at the time, recalls of the gold bandwagon, "Alan blew it up." Kenneth Duberstein, interview by the author, February 20, 2014.

41. Robert M. Ball, *The Greenspan Commission: What Really Happened* (New York: Century Foundation, 2010), 21.

42. The Cato Institute proposed individual Social Security accounts in its newsletter in 1979. The next year it published a book advocating individual accounts titled *Social Security: The Inherent Contradiction.* Peter J. Ferrara, *Social Security: The Inherent Contradiction,* Studies in Public Policy (Cato Institute, 1980). Moreover, back in the summer of 1975, Donald Rumsfeld had written to Greenspan, asking whether the administration should tackle the subject, and Greenspan had responded by commissioning a memo on various options, including private savings

accounts. Donald Rumsfeld to Alan Greenspan, memorandum, August 1, 1975, personal files of Alan Greenspan; and Barry R. Chiswick and June O'Neill to Alan Greenspan, memorandum, August 6, 1975, personal files of Alan Greenspan.

43. On Greenspan's support for Stockman, see John S. DeMott, "The Outlook Brightens," *Time,* June 1, 1981. Greenspan had also argued the point privately to the administration. According to Martin Anderson's notes of an earlier President's Economic Policy Advisory Board meeting, on June 11, 1981—generously provided to the author—Greenspan suggested that the introduction of Social Security reform legislation had caused long-term interest rates to moderate.

44. Martin Feldstein, interview by the author, January 30, 2013. Feldstein chaired the Council of Economic Advisers starting in 1982.

45. William A. Niskanen, who served on Reagan's Council of Economic Advisers between 1981 and 1985, later called the May Social Security package "the major domestic policy mistake of the Reagan administration—an extraordinary political misjudgment." See William A. Niskanen, *Reaganomics: An Insider's Account of the Policies and the People* (New York: Oxford University Press, 1988), 38.

46. James Baker, the White House chief of staff, recalls, "Greenspan never mentioned private Social Security accounts to me. He knew that they would not work. Politically it was hopeless." James Baker, interview by the author, June 12, 2013. Similarly, Greenspan recalls, "Trying to push private accounts was not my job." Greenspan, interview by the author, February 18, 2011. Together with other evidence, these recollections contradict (and almost certainly correct) a suggestion in Robert M. Ball's memoir, *The Greenspan Commission: What Really Happened.* Ball, who was one of the leading Democrats on the commission, recounts that Greenspan had to be talked out of a free-ranging philosophical discussion of federal retirement provision. See Ball, *Greenspan Commission,* 15. Given Greenspan's experience in the Ford administration and his highly developed political skills, it seems implausible that he would have risked splitting the commission at the outset with a divisive debate about fundamental principles.

47. Alan Greenspan, "Briefing for Reporters," December 16, 1981, National Commission on Social Security Reform, box CFOA89, Martin Anderson Files, Ronald Reagan Library.

48. Anne Conover Heller, *Ayn Rand and the World She Made*, 1st printing edition (New York: Nan A. Talese, 2009), 397.

49. Susan Chira, "Followers of Ayn Rand Provide Final Tribute," *New York Times,* March 10, 1982.

50. Scott McConnell, *100 Voices: An Oral History of Ayn Rand* (New York: New American Library, 2010), 326.

51. David Rowe recalls that Rand's death seemed to affect Greenspan. "Around the office, the one time he seemed gloomy was when Ayn Rand died. Alan was hit hard by that. That was the one time when he seemed more subdued, a little testier. You did not see his dry wit for a while." David Rowe, interview by the author, October 11, 2011.

52. Edwin Harper, "Notes: President's Economic Policy Advisory Board," March 18, 1982, Economic Policy Advisory Board, box OA9449, Edwin Meese Files, Ronald Reagan Library.

53. See Rowland Evans and Robert Novak, "The Economics of Pain," *Winchester Star,* March 12, 1982. See also Hobart Rowen, "Does Reagan Seek an Economic Czar?," *Washington Post,* July 18, 1982.

54. In 1983, Greenspan told the *New York Times,* "When I was asked to be the chairman, I wondered whether I had enough time to take the job on. But then I thought about it, and I thought the commission would produce a report that would sit on a shelf, and how much time could that possibly take?" Tamar Lewin, "The Quiet Allure of Alan Greenspan," *New York Times,* June 5, 1983. David Rowe recalls, "The commission did not take more than 5 or 10 percent of Alan's time. Alan is good at delegating things. It was not a big deal for him." Rowe, interview by the author, October 11, 2011.

55. Greenspan "bent over backward to show procedural fairness," Nancy Altman recalls of Greenspan. "He was serious about it and he understood that something had to be done. It was the pragmatic side that was being pulled out. He kept his personal views to himself." Nancy Altman, interview by the author, February 18, 2011. Even Robert M. Ball, whose later account of the commission's success played down Greenspan's role, told the *New York Times,* "He was easy to deal with on procedural matters, and his conduct at meetings was low-key. He talks very quietly, and his manner does defuse people who might disagree." Lewin, "The Quiet Allure of Alan Greenspan."

56. Christopher Connell, "Saturday AM Cycle Bulletin," Associated Press, February 27, 1982.

57. Nancy J. Altman, *The Battle for Social Security: From FDR's Vision to Bush's Gamble* (Hoboken, NJ: John Wiley & Sons, 2005), 240.

58. Ibid., 241.

59. Ball, *Greenspan Commission,* 18.

60. Ibid., 28.; Altman, *Battle for Social Security,* 244.

61. Altman, *Battle for Social Security,* 244–45.

62. Feldstein, interview by the author, January 17, 2013.

63. Ball, *Greenspan Commission,* 34.

64. Ibid., 35.

65. Ball writes, "This point seems to have been lost on everyone who sees the Greenspan Commission as an unqualified success and as a model for the future. The reality was that the commission as such had just about struck out by the end of its originally appointed term in 1982, having reached agreement on nothing more than the size of the problem and the desirability of extending Social Security coverage to newly hired employees." Ibid., 42.

66. Altman, *Battle for Social Security,* 250.

67. Greenspan, interview by the author, February 18, 2011.

68. Ball, *Greenspan Commission,* 55.

CHAPTER THIRTEEN

1. William Greider, *Secrets of the Temple: How the Federal Reserve Runs the Country* (New York: Simon & Schuster, 1989), 483.

2. James M. Boughton, "The Mexican Crisis: No Mountain Too High?," in *Silent Revolution: The International Monetary Fund 1979–1989* (Washington, D.C.: International Monetary Fund, 2001), 281–318.

3. In 1979, regulators did begin to caution banks about Latin American exposure. However, an analysis of the program by the U.S. General Accounting Office in 1982 suggested that these cautions "had little impact in restraining the growth of specially commented exposures." Banks continued to lend freely to Latin America right up to the outbreak of the crisis in August 1982. See Timothy Curry, "The LDC Debt Crisis," in *History of the Eighties—Lessons for the Future,* vol. 1, 2 vols. (Washington, D.C.: FDIC, 1997), 191–210. Further, in December 1981 the Fed, in cooperation with the Office of the Comptroller of the Currency, issued new regulations requiring banks to hold more capital—a 5 percent capital-asset ratio for larger banks and 6 percent for smaller ones. The seventeen largest banks, however, were exempted from the regulation, largely because they were unable to comply with it. In 1981, the seventy largest banks averaged capital-asset ratios of 4.37 percent, with many of the largest well below that. See Greider, *Secrets of the Temple,* 423–33.

4. Adding together the top eight banks' exposure to Latin America, federal officials found that it came to 232.6 percent of their capital. See Federal Deposit Insurance Corporation, Timothy Curry, "The LDC Debt Crisis," *History of the Eighties: Lessons for the Future.* Vol. 1. Federal Deposit Insurance Corporation.

5. These loans were structured as currency swaps. Volcker informed the Reagan administration and key congressional chairmen of his actions, but he took advantage of the rules governing central-bank swaps, which allowed him to avoid public reporting for several months.

6. The Department of Energy would buy $1 billion of oil from Mexico and pay immediately instead of waiting for delivery. The Department of Agriculture would kick in another $1 billion, dressed up as a line of credit for the future purchase of U.S. farm produce. The Fed would provide—which meant, print—$925 million, and it would persuade foreign central banks to come up with a further $925 million between them.

7. Quoted in Robert D. Hershey Jr., "In Remembrance of Real Money," *New York Times,* December 10, 1985.

8. Greenspan had repeatedly predicted a crisis in the savings-and-loan industry. He had picked the wrong example, at least for the moment. But his broader point was right.

9. Before Volcker's arrival, blue-chip corporate borrowers had faced long-term interest rates of around 9.5 percent; by April 1981, rates were up at 14 percent. Bond yields cited here are from Moody's AAA corporate bond index, which reflects yields on bonds with maturities of between twenty and thirty years.

10. Senate Committee on Banking, Housing, and Urban Affairs, *International Debt: Hearings Before the Subcommittee on International Finance and Monetary Policy of the Committee on Banking, Housing, and Urban Affairs,* 98th Cong., 2nd sess. February 17, 1983.

11. William L. Silber, *Volcker: The Triumph of Persistence* (New York: Bloomsbury Press, 2012), 222.

12. See, for example, Robert D. Hershey Jr., "The Fed and Its Credit Dilemma," *New York Times,* October 11, 1982; and Clyde H. Farnsworth, "Monetarists Divided on Fed's Stand," *New York Times,* October 12, 1982.

13. Steven F. Hayward, *The Age of Reagan: The Fall of the Old Liberal Order: 1964–1980* (New York: Random House, 2009), 197. Echoing Baker, Reagan's campaign director, Ed Rollins, noted that "there's only one man who can cost the President reelection all by himself, and that's the chairman of the Federal Reserve. We need to control that guy."

14. Harry Anderson and Rich Thomas, "Voting for Volcker to Stay," *Newsweek,* June 20, 1983.

15. Jeremiah O'Leary, "Volcker Won't Get 2nd Term," *Washington Times,* April 18, 1983.

16. See, for example, Tamar Lewin, "The Quiet Allure of Alan Greenspan," *New York Times,* June 5, 1983.

17. Walter Shapiro et al., "Will Reagan Reappoint Volcker?," *Newsweek,* May 23, 1983.

18. Quotes from Eckstein come from Lewin, "The Quiet Allure of Alan Greenspan."

19. Joseph Vitale, "Profile: Alan Greenspan," *NYU Business,* n.d., 28–33. It is clear from the content that the profile ran in the first months of 1983.

20. Lewin, "The Quiet Allure of Alan Greenspan." The quote from Walters comes from Linton Weeks and John M. Berry, "The Shy Wizard of Money," *Washington Post,* March 24, 1997.

21. This passage is taken from William L. Silber's masterful *Volcker: The Triumph,* 229.

22. Ibid., 232. William Greider says that Volcker and Reagan met in the Oval Office. But press reports shortly after Volcker's renomination report that the meeting took place in the residence, suggesting that Silber's version of events is accurate. See "Paul Volcker—Federal Reserve Board Chairman," United Press International, June 18, 1983.

23. Anderson and Thomas, "Voting for Volcker to Stay."

24. James T. Patterson, *Restless Giant: The United States from Watergate to Bush v. Gore* (New York: Oxford University Press, 2005), 159.

25. This exchange comes from Silber, *Volcker: The Triumph,* 232.

26. Ronald Reagan, *The Reagan Diaries,* ed. Douglas Brinkley (New York: HarperCollins, 2007), 157.

27. Tom Herman, "Volcker Has 76.9% Support to Remain Fed Chief, in Poll of Investment Leaders," *Wall Street Journal,* June 8, 1983, 18.

28. Not only was inflation down, but growth had by now recovered powerfully. In the second quarter of 1983, output grew at an annualized rate of 9.4 percent.

29. George Will, "The Idea of Replacing Volcker," *Washington Post,* May 12, 1983.

30. Reagan, *Reagan Diaries,* 157.

31. Silber, *Volcker: The Triumph,* 233.

32. Milton Friedman to Alan Greenspan, letter, July 13, 1983, folder 149–9. Correspondence: Greenspan, Alan, 1971–2002, box 149, Milton Friedman Papers, Hoover Institution Archives.

33. Greenspan was being interviewed on *Open Mind* by Richard Heffner, a professor of communications and public policy at Rutgers University. "Regulating the Economy," *Open Mind* (New York: PBS, August 12, 1983). Press accounts of the contest for the Fed chairmanship frequently suggested that Greenspan might not want the job; but this only showed Greenspan's skill in disguising his ambition. When the job was offered to him four years later, Greenspan had no hesitation in taking it.

34. Keith H. Hammonds, "What's New on the Lecture Circuit; The Superstars," *New York Times,* September 11, 1983. The article reported that Greenspan gave eighty speeches per year, at fees of between $10,000 and $13,000.

35. Alan Greenspan, interview by the author, January 31, 2013.

36. Ibid. Rory O'Neil, interview by the author, October 11, 2011. Dyan Machan, "One Plus One Plus One Equals Zero," *Forbes,* April 20, 1987.

37. In 1982, Greenspan reflected, "I sit on the boards of a number of major corporations and often wonder how much I contribute, or in fact should contribute, to the forming of general policy for the enterprise.... The vast majority of meetings are dull and that probably is good news for shareholders.... The truth of the matter is that boards of directors do not have a significant function except when something is going disastrously wrong. It's on those rare occasions when the directors earn their fees.... As you thumb through your annual reports of the companies in which you own shares, hope that your directors are being well paid, but that they are never called upon to really exert themselves." "Commentary

by Alan Greenspan," *Nightly Business Report* (Miami: South Florida Public Television, WPBT, February 15, 1982).

38. J.P. Morgan was also known by the name of its bank subsidiary, Morgan Guaranty Trust.

39. "When I became a director of J.P. Morgan and I walked into 23 Wall Street and I sat down in the boardroom and there was this picture hanging over me, it was a real thrill. I had an idealized vision of the nineteenth century." Greenspan, interview by the author, October 12, 2010. In another interview, Greenspan recalled his sensation upon entering the boardroom: "What am I doing here? How the hell did I get here? It was like a kid dreaming of being a major-league baseball player, and he's standing up at the plate, and the catcher behind him is a very famous ballplayer or something like that." Greenspan, interview by the author, March 11, 2011. See also Alan Greenspan, *The Age of Turbulence: Adventures in a New World* (New York: Penguin Books, 2008), 78–79. The impressive Morgan chandelier is noted in Ron Chernow, *The House of Morgan: An American Banking Dynasty and the Rise of Modern Finance* (New York: Grove Press, 2001), 719.

40. Michael Patterson, interview by the author, November 9, 2011.

41. John F. Ruffle, a senior J.P. Morgan executive who presented regularly to the board during Greenspan's tenure, remembers Greenspan as among the three board members who challenged him with penetrating questions. (The others were George Shultz and Frank Cary, the boss of IBM.) John F. Ruffle, interview by the author, September 14, 2011. However, two other Morgan veterans with less specific memories said that Greenspan was as passive as the other directors.

42. One of the girls on the receiving end of this lecture was Gail Collins, who recalled the experience in a column for *Newsday.* (Gail Collins, "Anti-Porn Banker Kept Dirty Books," *Newsday,* December 9, 1991.)

43. Quoted in Robert Scheer, "Of Saviors and Loans," *Playboy,* September 1, 1990.

44. Ever since his service on Nixon's financial commission, Greenspan had opposed regulatory silos, arguing that consumers would gain from freer competition among firms, and that the firms themselves would be safer if they could diversify their risks more widely. About a year before he met

Keating, in July 1983, Greenspan had testified to a House committee that he saw "no danger in allowing a continued unwinding of the regulatory mechanism"—an unwinding that had already unleashed a "veritable explosion of new financial services in recent years." (See Lisa J. McCue, "Greenspan Denounces Moratorium; Says Further Deregulation Will Benefit Consumers, Market," *American Banker,* July 15, 1983.) The following September, Greenspan restated his message in the *Wall Street Journal,* insisting that competition would drive the financial sector to produce worthwhile services that lowered the cost of capital. To those critics who contended that much financial innovation was aimed merely at sidestepping regulation, Greenspan replied that this went only to show that regulation was "outmoded." (Alan Greenspan, "Onward the Revolution in Financial Services," *Wall Street Journal,* September 16, 1983.)

45. Greenspan's November 1984 letter is reprinted in House Committee on Government Operations, *Federal Regulation of Direct Investments by Savings and Loans and Banks; and Conditions of the Federal Deposit Insurance Funds: Hearings Before a Subcommittee of the Committee on Government Operations* (Washington, D.C., 1985). Emphasis in original. A further description of Greenspan's study is reported in David LaGesse, "Thrifts Face Crucial Fight on Investments," *American Banker,* December 7, 1984.

46. LaGesse, "Thrifts Face Crucial Fight on Investments."

47. Nathaniel C. Nash and Philip Shenon, "A Man of Influence," *New York Times,* November 9, 1989. After the downfall of his business empire in April 1989, Keating told reporters: "One question, among many raised in recent weeks, had to do with whether my financial support in any way influenced several political figures to take up my cause. I want to say in the most forceful way I can: I certainly hope so."

48. The letter, dated February 13, 1985, and addressed to Thomas Sharkey, principal supervisory agent for the San Francisco Federal Home Loan Bank Board, is reprinted as "Appendix C" in Martin Mayer, *The Greatest-Ever Bank Robbery: The Collapse of the Savings and Loan Industry* (New York: C. Scribner's Sons, 1990).

49. Greenspan made this comment on March 29, 1985, on Louis Rukeyser's *Wall Street Week. Wall Street Week with Louis Rukeyser* (Owings Mills, Maryland: PBS, MPT, March 29, 1985).

50. Nathaniel C. Nash and Philip Shenon, "A Man of Influence." See also Greg Evans, "The Desert Fox," *Cincinnati Magazine,* August 1989.

51. Lincoln's assets doubled in size over the course of 1984. In contrast, the assets of the savings-and-loan industry as a whole in California, Arizona, and Nevada grew 30 percent that year. The growth of Keating's S&L is described in Nathaniel C. Nash, "Greenspan's Lincoln Savings Regret," *New York Times,* November 20, 1989. Industry statistics are reported in "Asset Growth at Western S&Ls Slowed Sharply," *Los Angeles Times,* July 23, 1985.

52. Greenspan, *Age of Turbulence,* 115.

53. Richard L. Berke, "Savings and Loan Executives Accused of Tapping Phones," *New York Times,* October 27, 1989.

54. Joseph W. Cotchett and Stephen Pizzo, *The Ethics Gap: The Erosion of Ethics in Our Professions, Business, and Government: Greed and the Casino Society* (Carlsbad, CA: Parker & Son Publications, 1991), 144. The source on the rerouting of Greenspan's calls is Michael Bradfield, the Fed's general counsel. Michael Bradfield, interview by the author, February 21, 2014.

55. For more on these projects see Evans, "Desert Fox." The sale of these assets cost taxpayers dearly. In 1988, several months before it took over Lincoln Savings and Loan, the government estimated the thrift's controlling stakes in this hotel, the Phoenician, and another, the Crescent, to be worth $179 million. In October 1991, the stakes in these hotels—now on the government's balance sheet—were sold to the Kuwaiti Investment Office for $111.5 million, a loss of $67.5 million. See "U.S. Sells 2 Hotels in Lincoln S&L Case to Kuwaiti Investors," *Wall Street Journal,* October 24, 1991. In 1993, when the Resolution Trust Corporation—the government entity created to clean up the thrift mess—moved Keating's half-built housing community, Estrella, off its books, the highest bid came in at $28 million, compared to a book value of $295 million. See James S. Granelli, "Keating's 'Dream' Is Devalued," *Los Angeles Times,* June 2, 1993. It should be noted, though, that the RTC hoped to recoup some of its loss by maintaining an equity partnership with the property's new developer. See Terry McDonnell, "RTC Rings Up Big Sale in Arizona," *Chicago Tribune,* May 23, 1993; and Dean Foust, "Now They're Really Down to the Dregs," *BusinessWeek,* March 7, 1993.

56. Citing RTC sources, the *Los Angeles Times* put Lincoln's estimated cost to taxpayers at $3.4 billion in October 1993. An RTC spokeswoman cited in the article described Lincoln as "by far . . . the costliest thrift failure ever." See James S. Granelli, "Forecast Is Now $3.4 Billion to Liquidate Lincoln Savings," *Los Angeles Times,* October 31, 1993.

57. Nash, "Greenspan's Lincoln Savings Regret."

58. Having hit a trough of 2.4 percent in July 1983, consumer price inflation was back up at 4.6 percent the following April.

59. Paul Blustein, "Feldstein to Quit Economic Job at White House," *Wall Street Journal,* May 10, 1984.

60. Chernow, *House of Morgan,* 658. Chernow's reconstruction of the Continental Illinois saga is a fine example of his wonderful writing. See also Jeff Bailey, John Helyar, and Tim Carrington, "Anatomy of a Failure: Continental Illinois: How Bad Judgments and Big Egos Did It In," *Wall Street Journal,* July 30, 1984; and R. C. Longworth and Bill Barnhart, "How Panic Followed the Sun in Debacle at Chicago Bank: The Run on Continental," *Chicago Tribune,* May 27, 1984.

61. Chernow, *House of Morgan,* 658.

62. Ibid., 659.

63. Robert A. Bennett, "$4.5 Billion Credit for Chicago Bank Set by 16 Others," *New York Times,* May 15, 1984.

64. Chernow, *House of Morgan,* 659.

65. Between the run on the Knickerbocker Trust on October 22, 1907, and the calming of the crisis in mid-November, J. Pierpont Morgan and his associates worked to stem the panic. Morgan browbeat fellow bankers into providing $25 million in emergency credit to equity traders on October 24, 1907. He then assembled the bankers in his library and extracted a further $25 million in the early hours of November 3, 1907. In addition, the Treasury had put $25 million at Pierpont's disposal. On October 27, Morgan had put together $30 million in emergency financing for New York City. To provide liquidity to the system, New York's top bankers approved the creation of $100 million in clearinghouse certificates to shore up interbank

lending. Counting all these actions together, and adding in a host of smaller interventions, the most expansive estimate for the total size of the 1907 rescue comes to $300 million—about $3.3 billion in 1984 dollars. Thus the total 1907 rescue was more than a billion dollars smaller than the Morgan syndicate loan for Continental Illinois, and was dwarfed by the total response to Continental Illinois, counting in loans from the Fed's discount window and action by the FDIC. The estimate given here for the size of the 1907 bailout is pieced together from Robert F. Bruner and Sean D. Carr, *The Panic of 1907: Lessons Learned from the Market's Perfect Storm* (Hoboken, NJ: John Wiley & Sons, 2007).

66. The account of the Morgan meeting comes from the vivid reconstructions in Silber, *Volcker: The Triumph*, 245–46; Chernow, *House of Morgan*, 660; and Greider, *Secrets of the Temple*, 628.

67. "Commentary by Alan Greenspan," *Nightly Business Report* (Miami: South Florida Public Television, WPBT, June 4, 1984); and "Commentary by Alan Greenspan," *Nightly Business Report* (Miami: South Florida Public Television, WPBT, June 18, 1984). Greenspan calculated that if the FDIC guaranteed all creditors to all U.S. banks, "the U.S. Treasury would pick up a new contingent liability of $1.1 trillion."

68. Greenspan emphasized this point in the *Times* discussion, and again when he addressed the conservative Heritage Foundation the following spring. Addressing the Heritage Foundation on March 23, 1985, Greenspan said, "At some point I would like to see a system with no federal deposit insurance at all. I do not expect to see that, but I am not the only one opposed to the whole issue of federal deposit insurance." Warming to his theme, he denounced deposit insurance as "the use of the sovereign taxing and money-printing processes of the state," because governments could deliver on their insurance promise only by extracting resources from the long-suffering public via taxes or inflation. In short, Greenspan's Randian lucidity remained acute, even as he gave up expecting any of these principles to determine policy. "Fallout from Continental's Collapse," *New York Times*, August 5, 1984.

69. *The Map and the Territory*, Greenspan's postcrisis apologia, acknowledged that he had paid too little attention to the individual irrationality documented by behavioral economists. But it gave short shrift to the other big weakness in the rational-agent view of the economy: distorted incentives within institutions that lead rational individuals to choices that cut against the interests of both the institution they work for and the broader common good. For more on this, see the closing section of chapter four. Alan Greenspan, *The Map and the Territory: Risk, Human Nature, and the Future of Forecasting* (New York: Penguin Press, 2013), chapter four.

70. Greenspan wrote later, "During my tenure as a director of JPMorgan (just prior to joining the Federal Reserve), I was impressed by the value the bank accorded to its AAA rating. They recognized that in the short run, they could achieve a higher return on equity through increased leverage. But they feared that that could lower the bank's AAA rating, an important factor in their long-term ability to attract low-cost liabilities. Most important, the rating was required to sustain a reputation for prudence, an essential characteristic of their historic franchise that dated back to the time of John Pierpont Morgan himself. Similar considerations led to constrained leverage on the part of many nonfinancial corporations for which I have worked over the years." Ibid., 87.

71. "Fallout from Continental's Collapse."

CHAPTER FOURTEEN

1. "On our very first date, music was a bonding experience for us. We react to music in similar ways, viscerally, emotionally." Andrea Mitchell, interview by the author, May 14, 2012.

2. Alan Greenspan, *The Age of Turbulence: Adventures in a New World* (New York: Penguin Books, 2008), 98.

3. In her autobiography, Mitchell comments that "except for a few women far more glamorous than I, the big anchor jobs have always been reserved for men." Walters was the most prominent exception to the rule Mitchell was describing. Andrea Mitchell, *Talking Back: . . . to Presidents, Dictators and Assorted Scoundrels* (New York: Penguin Books, 2006), Kindle location 2900.

4. Kathryn Eickhoff, interview by the author, November 29, 2011.

5. Mitchell, *Talking Back*, Kindle location 2152.

6. Mitchell, interview by the author, May 14, 2012.

7. "He's unique in that way. He always understood my changing plans or getting up in the middle of the night to do work, because to him, work was always the most important thing. So if I, even to this day say, 'I'm so sorry. I have to do this.' Go to the NATO meeting next week, which is pretty much going to be a useless exercise. And I had agreed to go to New York with him on Sunday night for dinner, and totally forgot that I have to be in Chicago Monday, and he said, 'Well, that's your job. Of course you have to do that.'" Ibid.

8. Mitchell, *Talking Back*, Kindle location 1539.

9. Ibid, Kindle location 2894.

10. Sean Wilentz, *The Age of Reagan: A History, 1974–2008* (New York: HarperCollins, 2008), 180. See also Timothy J. McNulty, "In the End, Regan's Storied Foresight Failed Him," *Chicago Tribune*, February 28, 1987.

11. Sprinkel had worked for Regan at the Treasury. His near elevation to the Fed chairmanship is recalled by his friend and fishing partner, Richard McCormack. Richard T. McCormack, interview by the author, June 21, 2012.

12. Mitchell, *Talking Back*, Kindle location 2292.

13. James Baker recalls, "The feeling on our part was that a president is entitled at some point in his presidency to have his own chairman of the Federal Reserve. And there wasn't anybody else in America that I thought, or that we thought, would be suitable." James Baker, interview by the author, June 12, 2013. Greenspan recalls, "I don't know but I must assume that there was some general view that being a good friend of Jim Baker, Howard Baker, and Ronald Reagan that I would be flexible." Alan Greenspan, interview by the author, November 15, 2013.

14. Ronald Reagan, *The Reagan Diaries*, ed. Douglas Brinkley (New York: HarperCollins, 2007), 484.

15. The Fed "is not supposed to be a one-person show," Governor Martha Seger had growled after the vote, anticipating the criticism of the "imperial chairmanship" that would later be heard under Greenspan. See William L. Silber, *Volcker: The Triumph of Persistence* (New York: Bloomsbury Press, 2012), 255.

16. On Volcker's reaction, ibid. On fears of deflation, see John M. Berry, "Price Declines Spark Fears of Deflation," *Washington Post*, June 22, 1986.

17. "The business has changed," Morgan's chairman, Lewis Preston, said. "Basic lending is never going

to return to the profitability that existed in the Fifties and Sixties." Gary Hector, "Morgan Guaranty's Identity Crisis," *Fortune,* April 28, 1986.

18. J.P. Morgan's paper, "Rethinking Glass-Steagall," appeared in the *Morgan Economic Quarterly* in December 1984.

19. Morgan's research was vindicated by academic authors. See, for example, Eugene Nelson White, "Before the Glass-Steagall Act: An Analysis of the Investment Banking Activities of National Banks," *Explorations in Economic History* 23, no. 1 (January 1986): 33–55.

20. Hector, "Morgan Guaranty's Identity Crisis." In 1986, J.P. Morgan underwrote more Eurobond issues for American companies than any U.S. investment bank. See "Banking on Greenspan," *Economist,* June 13, 1987.

21. Ron Chernow, *The House of Morgan: An American Banking Dynasty and the Rise of Modern Finance* (New York: Grove Press, 2001), 716. Although Greenspan supported the report, its principal author, Ned Kelly, then of Davis Polk, recalls that Greenspan was not involved in the drafting of the text. Edward W. Kelly Jr., interview by the author, September 19, 2011. Expounding on the case for financial deregulation in front of an audience at the conservative Heritage Foundation on March 23, 1985, Greenspan declared, "I have never seen a constructive regulation yet." Alan Greenspan, "Address on Interest Rates and Banking Reform" (Heritage Foundation, Washington, D.C., March 23, 1985).

22. Volcker recalls that the article was delivered to him by Lewis Preston. Paul Volcker, interview by the author, September 13, 2011.

23. Troland Link, interview by the author, September 13, 2011.

24. Kelly Jr., interview by the author, September 19, 2011.

25. The Treasury's plan for banking deregulation had crystallized by early June 1987, when it was described in a long *New York Times* article. But it is safe to assume that the Treasury's ideas had been germinating for a period of at least a couple of months before the *Times* article surfaced. See Nathaniel C. Nash, "Treasury Now Favors Creation of Huge Banks," *New York Times,* June 7, 1987.

26. The study was conducted by First Manhattan Consulting Group. Ibid.

27. The executive was Richard S. Simmons, vice chairman of Chemical New York Corporation, the fourth-largest U.S. bank at the time. Ibid.

28. Some later research suggested that countries were less likely to suffer a financial crisis if they had a more concentrated banking system and fewer restrictions on bank activity. In other words, the case for restricting bank size was not clear ex-post, let alone ex-ante. See Thorsten Beck, Asli Demirgüç-Kunt, and Ross Levine, "Bank Concentration and Crises" (National Bureau of Economic Research working paper no. 9921, August 2003), http://www.nber.org/papers/w9921.

29. Nathaniel C. Nash, "Bank Curb Eased in Volcker Defeat," *New York Times,* May 1, 1987. The point about the limits to the Fed's statutory authority is also reported in Barbara A. Rehm, "Fed Approves Four More Banks' Securities Bids," *American Banker,* May 20, 1987. Volcker also declared that if the banks set up securities units, they should at least give them names that sounded different to their parents, adding that the proposed 5 percent ceiling on securities revenues should be defined in such a way as to minimize the banks' headroom. (Silber, *Volcker: The Triumph,* 260.) Volcker's view on how the underwriting of Treasuries should be treated is reported in John E. Yang, "Fed Vote on Banks' Securities Dealing Blurs Legal Line," *Wall Street Journal,* May 1, 1987.

30. Even his loyal general counsel, Michael Bradfield, thought he was fighting a hopeless battle. Michael Bradfield, interview by the author, February 21, 2014.

31. James Baker recalls, "We saw Alan as an anti-regulation chairman. We understood that when we brought him in." Baker, interview by the author, June 12, 2013.

32. Greenspan's assurances to the Treasury are quoted extensively in Nash, "Treasury Now Favors Creation of Huge Banks." Nash had apparently gained access to a transcript of Greenspan's answers to questions put to him by the Treasury as part of his preparation for the Fed job. In his confirmation testimony, Greenspan claimed that the *Times* report had captured his perspective "only partly."

33. Greenspan was more clearly in favor of bank deregulation than he was in favor of big banks. He asserted that the Treasury's conviction, that deregulation would lead to banking concentration, might be wrong. For instance, on March 23, 1985, he argued during an appearance at the Heritage Foundation that there was "no evidence of economies of scale in banking. On the contrary," he continued, "evidence suggests that the smaller institutions fare better and, therefore, there is no evidence to suggest that the small commercial bank, operating with local knowledge and fairly good relationships with the community, has anything to fear from Citibank or anybody else who wants to move in." Greenspan pointed to Citibank's recent failure to penetrate the upstate New York market as evidence to support his view. Greenspan, "Address on Interest Rates and Banking Reform." History proved Greenspan wrong, however.

34. Paul Volcker recalls, "After he was appointed Greenspan came in and provided a green light without any change in the law. My view was that it was not the role of the central bank to approve something that was against the law." Volcker, interview by the author, September 13, 2011.

35. Rehm, "Fed Approves Four More Banks' Securities Bids."

36. Volcker, interview by the author, December 8, 2010. See also Silber, *Volcker: The Triumph,* 260.

37. Greenspan, *Age of Turbulence,* 99.

38. Ibid.

39. Mitchell, *Talking Back,* Kindle location 2618.

40. David Rowe recalls, "One of my grad school colleagues who was at Townsend-Greenspan said everyone in the office found out about it on television." David Rowe, interview by the author, October 11, 2011.

41. Karin Nye, interview by the author, February 8, 2012.

42. "That picture flashes in my mind every now and then, it was very sad." Vivian Gold, interview by the author, March 14, 2012.

43. Greenspan, interview by the author, November 15, 2010.

44. Steven V. Roberts, "Proxmire Thrives in His Chosen Role as Senate Maverick," *New York Times,* September 19, 1977; see also Richard Severo, "William Proxmire, Maverick Democratic Senator from Wisconsin, Is Dead at 90," *New York Times,* December 16, 2005.

45. Video of the hearing is available from C-SPAN. *Greenspan Nomination* (Washington, D.C., United States, 1987), http://www.c-span.org/video/?150949-1/greenspan-nomination.

46. Kenneth McLean, interview by the author, January 27, 2014. (McLean worked for Proxmire.)

47. The Senate transcript records Proxmire as invoking forecasts "in" 1976, 1977, and 1978. But it is clear from the context that Proxmire was referring to forecasts for those years, not forecasts made in those years.

48. For example, see William Fleckenstein and Frederick Sheehan, *Greenspan's Bubbles: The Age of Ignorance at the Federal Reserve* (New York: McGraw-Hill, 2008), 8.

49. Proxmire was citing a study that did not single out Greenspan's Ford administration forecasts but instead heaped scorn on all three administrations covered in its analysis. See "Are We on the Road to a Balanced Budget?," Staff Study prepared for the Joint Economic Committee of Congress, February 1986, Table 4, 8.

CHAPTER FIFTEEN

1. William Greider, *Secrets of the Temple: How the Federal Reserve Runs the Country* (New York: Simon & Schuster, 1989), 48.

2. Alan Greenspan, interview by the author, July 16, 2010.

3. "By that point I was no George Selkirk, I was a Babe Ruth." Greenspan, interview by the author, July 18, 2014.

4. Numbers for end-1987 staff count were supplied by the Federal Reserve Board press office. Federal Reserve Board press office, February 5, 2014.

5. The frequency of Federal Reserve board meetings varied over the years, but in 1987 one meeting per week was typical.

6. Greider, *Secrets of the Temple*, 66.

7. "The Markets Wonder Whether Alan Can Fill Paul's Shoes," *Economist*, June 6, 1987.

8. Greider, *Secrets of the Temple*, 714.

9. Manley Johnson recalls that the newsletter was written by Pierre Rinfret, a fabulist who later ran for New York's governorship. (Manley Johnson, interview by the author, January 27, 2014.) Although no copy of the newsletter could be found, its essence was recalled by Johnson, and Rinfret's views are evident from a speech delivered in June. For the gist of the speech, see William Gruber, "Greenspan's a Political Hack: Economist," *Chicago Tribune*, June 5, 1987. Rinfret was a flamboyant character who claimed a nonexistent doctorate and filed lawsuits liberally—including, in two cases, against members of his own extended family. His newsletter was known for blunt language and wild opinions. In 1974, Rinfret had been the runner-up for the job of CEA chairman—which may help explain his animosity toward Greenspan.

10. This dialogue from the FOMC meeting is taken from the official transcript, available on the Web site of the Federal Reserve Board. Throughout the rest of this book, all quotations from FOMC meetings will come from the same source, though this will not be noted.

11. There was no change in the target federal funds rate immediately after this meeting. Just over a week later, however, it was raised by a token amount—12.5 basis points. (Note that at the time, the FOMC formally targeted the level of bank reserves, but also expressed this policy as in terms of the federal-funds target that became standard later.)

12. "By the time I got to the Fed, I had already decided that I could lead. . . . I had enough experience to realize that I knew more than most of the people who were in the room." Greenspan, interview by the author, June 18, 2014.

13. Ricki Tigert Helfer, interview by the author, July 14, 2013. Greenspan recalls, "I decided very early on that I was going to let other people lead because they knew more than I did. . . . I did not know as much as the bank lawyers at the Federal Reserve Board about the intent of the Congress. And the reason they knew was they wrote the legislation." (Greenspan, interview by the author, July 16, 2010.) In addition, Greenspan's former colleagues at J.P. Morgan recalled that Greenspan was sensitive to accusations that he would show the bank favoritism. Therefore he distanced himself from regulatory decisions that would benefit it.

14. Michael J. Prell, interview by the author, May 15, 2013. Prell recalls that whereas Greenspan doubted the staff's forecasts sometimes, Volcker often disparaged quantitative analysis. Similarly, Don Kohn, another top Fed staff member at the time, recalls that Greenspan's appetite for forecasting detail came as a surprise. Volcker "was at 5,000 feet and Greenspan was down in the weeds in terms of the data. It's just different tastes, different ways of looking at things. And Greenspan wanted to see the statistical results. I remember one of the first memos reported on a regression, and it just kind of reported the results. And he said no, no, no, I want to see the R-squared, and I want to see this, that, and the other thing that Volcker probably wouldn't have wanted to see." Donald L. Kohn, interview by the author, March 13, 2011.

15. Prell, interview by the author, May 15, 2013.

16. Greenspan believed that the hit to GDP from lower factory orders would depend on the value of the inventory as it left the factory gates, not on the inventory's reported value, which reflected the price at which retailers planned to sell it.

17. Prell, interview by the author, May 15, 2013. Another example of the difference of approach between Greenspan and Prell was in house prices. The Fed's forecasting model incorporated the standard wealth effect: if rising house prices made families richer, some fraction of that extra wealth would show up in extra consumption. But Greenspan wanted to go further. In order to turn higher house prices into consumption, families would have to take out bigger mortgages, so Greenspan wanted information on whether banks were in the mood to lend freely. To Prell's way of thinking, this was another cul-de-sac: at least for most periods, mortgage availability was roughly constant, so whatever wealth effect had been observed in the past would likely hold into the future. But remembering his work on home-equity extraction in the 1970s, Greenspan was constantly on the lookout for swings in financial conditions. If banks grew suddenly keener to make loans, the relationship between housing wealth and consumption could change quite radically.

18. At the late September FOMC meeting, the Greenbook prepared by the staff projected that growth in the second half of 1987 would come in at an annualized 3.3 percent, up from 2.6 percent in the Greenbook prepared for the August FOMC meeting. Board of Governors of the Federal Reserve System, "Greenbook" (Federal Open Market Committee, August 12, 1987), http://www.federalreserve.gov/monetarypolicy/files/fomc19870818gbpt219870812.pdf. Board of Governors of the Federal Reserve System, "Greenbook" (Federal Open Market Committee, September 16, 1987), http://www.federalreserve.gov/monetarypolicy/files/fomc19870922gbpt219870916.pdf.

19. Stanley Fischer, "Recent Developments in Macroeconomics,"

Economic Journal 98, no. 391 (June 1988): 331.

20. N. Gregory Mankiw, "Recent Developments in Macroeconomics: A Very Quick Refresher Course," *Journal of Money, Credit, and Banking* 20, no. 3, part 2 (August 1988): 436.

21. Mitchell recalls that her mother came to Washington to help Greenspan furnish his Watergate apartment. Andrea Mitchell, interview by the author, May 14, 2012. In her memoirs, Mitchell writes that she was the one who helped on the interior design front. Andrea Mitchell, *Talking Back: . . . to Presidents, Dictators, and Assorted Scoundrels* (New York: Penguin Books, 2007), Kindle location 2629.

22. Justin Martin, *Greenspan: The Man Behind Money* (Cambridge, Mass.: Perseus Publishing, 2001), 157. Martin interviewed Wesley Halpert's wife, who was present at the lunch.

23. Mitchell, *Talking Back*, Kindle location 2628.

24. Kenneth Guenther, interview by the author, January 31, 2014. Guenther was the president of the Independent Community Bankers of America and Nash's tennis partner.

25. *This Week* (ABC News, October 4, 1987). The author thanks ABC News for providing a copy of the footage from this interview.

CHAPTER SIXTEEN

1. Kenneth Duberstein, interview by the author, February 20, 2014.

2. Andrea Mitchell, *Talking Back: . . . to Presidents, Dictators, and Assorted Scoundrels* (New York: Penguin Books, 2007), Kindle location 2157.

3. Carla Hall and Donnie Radcliffe, "Hands Across the Americas: A Night of Tributes as Reagan Hosts Duarte," *Washington Post,* October 15, 1987.

4. Greenspan's breakfast with Baker, and many other meetings whose dates are pinpointed in the following chapters, are recorded in the diary kept by Greenspan's secretary at the Fed. I am grateful to Alan Greenspan for access to the full set of diaries. Alan Greenspan's Diary, n.d.

5. In an early sign of the fraught nature of open central-bank communication, observers debated whether Greenspan's comments on Brinkley's show amounted to a tightening signal. See contrasting accounts in Matthew Winkler, "Bonds Slump as Prices Near Lows for 1987," *Wall Street Journal,* October 6, 1987; and Hobart Rowen, "Big Banks Raise Prime

Rate a Half Point," *Washington Post,* October 8, 1987.

6. James A. Baker III, *Work Hard, Study . . . and Keep Out of Politics!* (Evanston, Ill. Northwestern University Press, 2008), 440–441.

7. Justin Martin, *Greenspan: The Man Behind Money* (Cambridge, Mass.: Perseus Publishing, 2001), 172.

8. This meeting is recounted in Leo Melamed and Bob Tamarkin, *Escape to the Futures* (New York: John Wiley & Sons, 1996). Richard T. McCormack, interview by the author, June 21, 2012.

9. Ronald Reagan, *The Reagan Diaries,* ed. Douglas Brinkley (New York: HarperCollins, 2007), 538.

10. Corrigan recalls, "We discussed everything under the sun in terms of the Fed, its responsibilities, what were the hot issues. The topic that we probably spent more time on than any other single topic was financial stability issues." Gerald Corrigan, interview by the author, January 22, 2014.

11. See, for example, "Commentary by Alan Greenspan," *Nightly Business Report* (Miami, South Florida Public Television, WPBT, May 9, 1983).

12. The leveraging of the American economy was discussed in detail at the Federal Reserve's Jackson Hole symposium in 1986. See in particular Henry Kaufman, "Debt: The Threat to Economic and Financial Stability"; and Benjamin Friedman, "Increasing Indebtedness and Financial Stability in the United States." Both appear in *Debt, Financial Stability, and Public Policy* (Jackson Hole, Wyo.: Federal Reserve Bank of Kansas City, 1986). Friedman pointed out that in the depths of the recession of 1980, the rate of business failures had stood at 42 failures per 10,000 concerns. Five years later, the rate had tripled to 123 per 10,-000—despite the fact that the economy had recovered. Leverage had increased fragility in other ways: In the mid-1970s, fourteen American bank-holding companies had enjoyed a triple-A credit rating, but by 1987 only J.P. Morgan was solid enough to qualify. The share of corporate debt rated as risky "junk" had more than doubled in the same period, with the result that any bank or investment house with an inventory of bonds was likely to be shakier.

13. Corrigan also voiced concerns about financial fragility in FOMC discussions. On November 3, 1987, for example, he noted that the ratio of nonfinancial debt to GNP had risen sharply, reaching a level last seen in the 1920s. Presciently, Governor Kelley countered, "If there is

a good side to all of this debt creation, it lies in the fact that it puts tremendous pressure on everybody to be productive and, thus, it should have a long-term downward drag on the inflationary concerns that we all have." In other words, debt was bad for financial stability but good because it kept inflation down. Here was another way in which the objectives of financial stability and price stability could work against each other.

14. Both Kaufman and Friedman made versions of this argument. Friedman argued: "A higher debt ratio raises the cost of business contractions, and hence makes policymakers less likely to accept them," which "imparts an inflationary bias." Benjamin Friedman, "Increasing Indebtedness and Financial Stability in the United States" (Symposium on Debt, Financial Stability, and Public Policy, Jackson Hole, Wyo., August 1986), 48. More dramatically, Kaufman declared that "monetary policy must take the risk and err even further on the side of accommodation. . . . [T]his monetary approach runs the risk of rekindling inflation, but the alternative is also punishing. Deflation is the more immediate threat to our economic and financial stability. . . . [T]he new financial world has rendered obsolete the once simple rules for conducting policy." Henry Kaufman, "Debt: The Threat to Economic and Financial Stability" (Symposium on Debt, Financial Stability, and Public Policy, Jackson Hole, Wyo., August 1986), 23. Kaufman's views would certainly have been known to Greenspan: the two had lunch at the Fed on August 13, 1987. (Alan Greenspan's Diary.)

15. The following scene was recalled by Patrick Lawler, the Fed staff economist responsible for tracking the stock market. Patrick Lawler, interview by the author, February 13, 2014.

16. Lawler recalls that two of the economists in the meeting had researched the effect of margin requirements. "The staff view was that margin requirements were useless." Ibid.

17. Manley Johnson, interview by the author, June 19, 2013. Bob Woodward, *Maestro: Greenspan's Fed and the American Boom* (New York: Simon & Schuster, 2000), 37.

18. Johnson, interview by the author, June 19, 2013.

19. Greenspan recalls having J. P. Morgan's example in mind. Alan Greenspan, interview by the author, March 11, 2011.

20. Ruder later claimed he was misquoted. But that evening's PBS *MacNeil-Lehrer NewsHour* showed a clip of Ruder floating the idea of a temporary market closure. "Selling Frenzy; Returning Fire," Transcript, *MacNeil-Lehrer NewsHour* (PBS, October 19, 1987), Transcript #3146.

21. As Peter Sternlight, the head of the New York Fed's open market operations, noted in the institution's bloodless prose at the FOMC's November 1987 meeting: "There were widespread concerns about the very functioning of the financial system as worries developed that steep losses would disable major market participants."

22. This account follows Alan Murray, "Fed's New Chairman Wins a Lot of Praise on Handling the Crash," *Wall Street Journal*, November 25, 1987. Greenspan's response to "down five oh eight" is also recorded in Alan Greenspan, *The Age of Turbulence: Adventures in a New World* (New York: Penguin Books, 2008), 105, and Woodward, *Maestro*, 36–37, with minor variations. Murray's account is preferred because it was published so soon after the events.

23. Johnson, interview by the author, June 19, 2013. Edwin M. Truman, interview by the author, January 26, 2012.

24. Corrigan, interview by the author, January 22, 2014. Woodward describes Corrigan saying something similar on Tuesday morning, but Corrigan reports a clear recollection that the key conversation occurred on Monday night. Corrigan's memory is corroborated by that of Manley Johnson.

25. Beryl Sprinkel was one participant who opposed interfering in the markets. A. B. Culvahouse, interview by the author, February 6, 2013. Culvahouse was White House counsel.

26. Greenspan, *Age of Turbulence*, 106.

27. This account of Melamed's evening is drawn from Melamed and Tamarkin, *Escape to the Futures*, 358–61.

28. Bob Tamarkin, "Melamed, 'Godfather' at Chicago Merc, to Devote Time to Private Firm, Writing," *Wall Street Journal*, December 3, 1984.

29. Melamed and Tamarkin, *Escape to the Futures*, 359.

30. Johnson, interview by the author, June 19, 2013.

31. Woodward, *Maestro*, 39. Greenspan, *Age of Turbulence*, 106, has the same quote without the middle sentence, "Goddamn it . . ."

32. This account is drawn from Melamed and Tamarkin, *Escape to the Futures*, 361–63. It is also recounted in Donald A. MacKenzie, *An Engine, Not a Camera: How Financial Models Shape Markets* (Cambridge, Mass. MIT Press, 2006), 1–3.

33. Tamarkin, "Melamed, 'Godfather' at Chicago Merc, to Devote Time to Private Firm, Writing."

34. Melamed recounts that Continental promised the money just three minutes before the Merc was due to open. Meanwhile, Mark Carlson reports that the Merc was not alone. Morning settlement for the Options Clearing Corporation, which cleared transactions for the CBOE, was not completed on October 20 until two and a half hours after the usual time. See Melamed and Tamarkin, *Escape to the Futures*, 363. Mark Carlson, "A Brief History of the 1987 Stock Market Crash" (Board of Governors of the Federal Reserve System, November 2006), 13–14, http://www.federalreserve.gov/pubs/feds/2007/200713/200713pap.pdf.

35. Greenspan, *Age of Turbulence*, 106–7.

36. James Baker, interview by the author, June 12, 2013. See also James A. Baker III, *Work Hard, Study . . . and Keep Out of Politics!* (New York: G.P. Putnam's Sons, 2006), 440–41.

37. Woodward, *Maestro*, 39.

38. There is some confusion as to who deserves credit for making the statement concise and direct—success has many fathers. But interviews with six participants lead to the conclusion that Corrigan was far more influential than Greenspan.

39. Greenspan later reflected on the trade-off between financial stability and price stability in a speech to the American Economic Association in December 1988: "[I]t was important that our actions not be perceived as merely flooding the markets with reserves. Haphazard or excessive reserve creation would have fostered a notion that the Federal Reserve was willing to tolerate a rise in inflation, which could itself have impaired market confidence. We were cautious to attack the problem that existed, and not cause one that didn't." See Alan Greenspan, remarks (Joint Meeting of the American Economic Association and American Finance Association, New York, December 29, 1988).

40. Greenspan writes of the statement in Greenspan, *Age of Turbulence*, 108, "It was as short and concise as the Gettysburg Address, I thought, although possibly not as stirring."

41. "I remember that morning, after the statement was issued, Alan was very nervous about me making these calls. . . . [He] probably did not want me to call those banks that morning." Corrigan, interview by the author, January 22, 2014.

42. High-frequency traders were widely blamed for the "Flash Crash" of May 6, 2010, in which the stock market abruptly lost 9 percent of its value and then recovered just as quickly. In hindsight, some commentators have suggested that the destabilizing impact of "portfolio insurance" in 1987 should have taught regulators to fear newfangled trading. But the old-fashioned specialist system was the larger source of the fragility. See Carlson, "A Brief History of the 1987 Stock Market Crash," 15.

43. Corrigan, interview by the author, January 22, 2014.

44. Andrew F. Brimmer, "Central Banking and Systemic Risks in Capital Markets," *Journal of Economic Perspectives* 3, no. 2 (Spring 1989): 3–16. The linkages between clearinghouses, member firms, and their customers are lucidly described in Ben S. Bernanke, "Clearing and Settlement During the Crash," *Review of Financial Studies* 3, no. 1 (1990): 133–51.

45. The "TED spread"—the gap between the three-month London Interbank Borrowing Rate and the three-month Treasury bill rate—hit 3 percent on October 19, 1987. The extraordinary stress that this implied can be gauged from the fact that, the first day after the Lehman Brothers collapse, the TED spread was only 2 percent. Later in the post-Lehman panic, the spread rose, peaking at 4.6 percent on October 10, 2008.

46. Woodward writes that Corrigan discussed with Manley Johnson the option of Fed guarantees for loans to brokers. Interviewed much later, Corrigan denies Woodward's account but says he might have been willing to countenance loans from the discount window. However, the law at the time might have made this difficult: until a reform passed in 1991 as part of the regulatory overhaul known as the Federal Deposit Insurance Corporation Improvement Act—or FDICIA—sec. 13-3 of the Federal Reserve Act, governing the use of the discount window for borrowers other than banks, effectively excluded securities firms. See Woodward, *Maestro*, 43. Corrigan, interview by the author, March 25, 2014.

47. Johnson, interview by the author, June 19, 2013. See also Greenspan, *Age of Turbulence*, 107; and Woodward, *Maestro*, 44.

48. According to the Brady Report, questioned trades in the NYSE were 4.02 percent of the total on October 19 and 4.25 percent of the total on October 20, about double the normal rate. Presidential Task Force on Market Mechanisms, *Report of the Presidential Task Force on Market Mechanisms* (Washington, D.C.: Government Printing Office, 1988), 51. See Bernanke, "Clearing and Settlement During the Crash." See also Floyd Norris, "The Crash of 1987," *Barron's*, October 26, 1987.

49. Norris, "The Crash of 1987."

50. A. B. Culvahouse, interview by the author, February 16, 2013.

51. "A number of people, including [Howard] Baker and [Dan] Crippen, the other [James] Baker and [John] Whitehead, started calling the Street and saying that it is really important for the country that you start buying, and some did." Ibid. and A. B. Culvahouse, interview by the author, March 28, 2014. John Gutfreund, the head of Salomon Brothers, reportedly said that if the president wanted him to buy, he would buy, even though he feared that the crash might have cost his firm $1 billion by late morning on Tuesday.

52. Norris, "The Crash of 1987."

53. The dominant account of the crash credits corporate stock buybacks with helping to spark the rally that began around 12:30 p.m. (See Presidential Task Force on Market Mechanisms, *Report of the Presidential Task Force on Market Mechanisms*, 4, sec. III, 26.) However, rules governing buybacks forbid companies from bidding up their own stock prices. Presuming these rules were observed, buybacks could have helped the market by absorbing selling pressure on the way down; and the announcement of buybacks would have encouraged other investors to act as buyers. However, as soon as the price of a stock registered an "uptick," the buybacks would have been required to stop. Buybacks are therefore not a completely satisfying explanation for a sustained rally.

54. Stanley Shopkorn, interviews by the author, January 14, 2013, and March 21, 2014. Shopkorn remembers speaking frequently with Dan Crippen at the White House, getting a more pointed call from Richard Grasso at the NYSE, and then conferring with Mnuchin.

The last of the three calls is also reported in Floyd Norris, "It Never Happened," *New York Times*, October 24, 2007, Economix blog, http://economix.blogs.nytimes.com/2007/10/24/it-never-happened/ and in Floyd Norris, "The Crash of 1987." The Shopkorn-Mnuchin theory of what rescued the market is different from, but more persuasive than, the standard history of the crash. The corporate buyback theory is unpersuasive for the reason cited in endnote 52. Another theory holds that the recovery began with a buying attack in Chicago, where futures contracts on the closely watched Major Market Index staged a miraculous recovery. But nobody has ever explained who initiated the Chicago rally. The analysis embraced here—that the rally was sparked by the Salomon-Goldman actions in New York—has the merit of featuring two named protagonists. Nevertheless, the official Brady Commission report followed the *Wall Street Journal* in suggesting that Chicago led the rally. See Presidential Task Force on Market Mechanisms, *Report of the Presidential Task Force on Market Mechanisms*, sec. III, 26.

55. "I remember Alan vividly saying we have to flood the market with liquidity. We believed that anyway. Nobody resisted Alan." Baker, interview by the author, June 12, 2013.

56. Greenspan, *Age of Turbulence*, 109.

57. Woodward, *Maestro*, 45–46.

58. Ibid., 46.

59. Murray, "Fed's New Chairman Wins a Lot of Praise on Handling the Crash."

60. Invited to comment on the verdict that he had been less important during the crash than Corrigan had been, Greenspan endorsed it. Greenspan, interview by the author, November 2, 2015.

61. In 1994 to the Senate banking committee, Chairman Greenspan indicated that "[t]elephone calls placed by officials of the Federal Reserve Bank of New York to senior management of the major New York City banks helped to assure a continuing supply of credit to the clearinghouse members, which enabled those members to make the necessary margin payments." Alan Greenspan, *Banking Industry Regulatory Consolidation: Hearings Before the Committee on Banking, Housing, and Urban Affairs*, Senate, Second Session, March 2, 1994. See also

Bernanke, "Clearing and Settlement During the Crash," 148.

62. The verdict that Corrigan must have pushed Citi forcefully is supported by Bernanke's observation that the expected value of the loans to brokers must have been negative—in the climate of extreme uncertainty, borrower default must have seemed likely. See Bernanke, "Clearing and Settlement During the Crash." On the impact of banks' lending to securities firms, see also Brimmer, "Central Banking and Systemic Risks in Capital Markets." See also Carlson, "A Brief History of the 1987 Stock Market Crash."

63. Wayne Angell, interview by the author, June 13, 2013.

64. If the great inflation of the 1970s had proved the pitfalls of excessive government activism, the great crash of 1987 was the first in a series of contrary lessons, demonstrating that markets also had their pitfalls.

65. "The limits to arbitrage" was a phrase coined by the economists Andrei Shleifer and Robert Vishny. For a longer explanation of the triple critique of the efficient markets hypothesis, see Sebastian Mallaby, *More Money Than God: Hedge Funds and the Making of a New Elite* (New York: Penguin, 2010), 104–8.

66. As illustrated repeatedly in this book, the common view of Greenspan as a believer in efficient markets is mistaken. He believed that markets are efficient to a first order of approximation, which they are; he never believed they were perfectly efficient or, for that matter, stable. After retiring from the Fed, Greenspan announced a conversion to behavioral economics, implying that he had previously viewed investors as rational. But he had actually seen markets as prone to overshooting since the 1950s. As will be argued later in this book, it is hard to take his supposed conversion at face value.

67. Senate Committee on Banking, Housing, and Urban Affairs, *Testimony by Alan Greenspan, Chairman, Board of Governors of the Federal Reserve System Before the Committee on Banking, Housing, and Urban Affairs*, 100th Cong., 2nd sess., 1988.

68. All data are from the Fed's Z.1 Financial Accounts. Corporate bonds include bonds issued by financial and nonfinancial companies. "Federal Reserve Statistical Release: Z.1 Financial Accounts of the United States, Historical Data," Board of Governors of the Federal

Reserve System, June 11, 2015, http:// www.federalreserve.gov /releases/z1/Current/data.htm.

69. The growth figure is quarter on quarter, annualized. Unemployment fell from 5.9 percent in September 1987 to 5.7 percent in December 1987. Board of Governors of the Federal Reserve System, Greenbook (Federal Open Market Committee, December 15, 1987), 6, http://www.federalre serve.gov/monetarypolicy/files /fomc19971216gbpt219971211.pdf. Board of Governors of the Federal Reserve System, Greenbook (Federal Open Market Committee, February 9, 1988), 14, http://www .federalreserve.gov/monetarypol icy/files/fomc19880210gbpt 219880203.pdf.

70. Alan Greenspan testimony in Senate Committee on Banking, Housing, and Urban Affairs, *Testimony by Alan Greenspan, Chairman, Board of Governors of the Federal Reserve System Before the Committee on Banking, Housing, and Urban Affairs.* Greenspan gave another version of his argument at a joint meeting of the American Economic Association and the American Finance Association in December 1988. See Greenspan, remarks, December 29, 1988.

71. A few years later, Greenspan would refer to "the 1987 stock market crash, which is the first and perhaps the only major stock market crash in history that actually was beneficial to the economy."

72. It should be noted that Greenspan did not give up worrying about bubbles after 1987. But he worried less than he had done. For an example of his continued concern with financial instability, see "Federal Open Market Committee Meeting Transcript," March 22, 1994, http://www.federalreserve .gov/monetarypolicy/files/FOMC 19940322meeting.pdf.; as well as his famous "irrational exuberance" speech. Alan Greenspan, remarks (Annual Dinner and Francis Boyer Lecture of the American Enterprise Institute, Washington, D.C., December 5, 1996).

73. Bernanke, "Clearing and Settlement During the Crash."

CHAPTER SEVENTEEN

1. David Hoffman, "Bush's Maine Event," *Washington Post,* May 28, 1988.

2. Steve Lohr, "Bush, They Say, Is Indeed a Connecticut Yankee from King Henry's Court," *New York Times,* July 5, 1988.

3. This quotation is taken from a Ford Library transcript of author Yanek Mieczkowski's interview with Paul MacAvoy, who advised Bush in 1980.

4. David Hoffman, "Bush Says Tight Monetary Policy Could Hurt," *Washington Post,* June 1, 1988, first sec.

5. Steven K. Beckner, *Back from the Brink: The Greenspan Years* (New York; Chichester: Wiley, 1999), 91.

6. The range of Greenspan's acquaintances is evident from the diaries kept by his secretary at the Fed.

7. A dozen years earlier, gossip columnists had marveled about this awkward intellectual's appetite for parties he seemed too shy to enjoy; it was as though the sideman's insecurity compelled him to be seen—to bask in the recognition that flowed from his White House position. Now that he had scaled the heights of the Fed chairmanship, Greenspan felt more comfortable in his own skin. But he still wanted to be a visible figure on Washington's A-list.

8. Andrea Mitchell, interview by the author, May 14, 2012; and Alan Greenspan, interview by the author, June 26, 2014.

9. Greenspan, interview by the author, June 18, 2014.

10. Ibid.

11. Mitchell, interview by the author, March 14, 2012.

12. Greenspan, interview by the author, July 18, 2014.

13. "I could not believe for weeks after the 1987 crash that there would not be more consequences. So I was not anxious to tighten up." (Greenspan, interview by the author, April 4, 2014.) It should be noted that Greenspan had to manage doves such as Wayne Angell, who believed that even this gradual tightening of monetary conditions would upset the markets and be counterproductive. At one point during the June 1988 FOMC meeting, Greenspan offered to resolve the dispute with Angell on the tennis court, prompting Corrigan to remark, "I feel sorry for that ball!"

14. New England's home values had leaped by a fifth in 1985 and another fifth in 1986, roughly three times faster than the national housing market; they had carried on surging through 1987; and through the first half of 1988, when Greenspan was fretting to his FOMC colleagues about the stock market's stability, they continued to head upward.

15. David Hoffman, "Bush Says Tight Monetary Policy Could Hurt," *Washington Post,* June 1, 1988.

16. Indeed, Morris suggested that, with the economy already operating at full capacity, anything higher than growth of 2 percent was likely to stoke inflation. Woodward notes that by the middle of July 1988, nine of the twelve district Fed presidents would have submitted requests to the Federal Open Market Committee for tighter policy. See Bob Woodward, *Maestro: Greenspan's Fed and the American Boom* (New York: Simon & Schuster, 2000), 51. In addition, the S&P 500 was up by about a tenth in the first half of 1988, making fears of renewed market instability seem far-fetched. The growth figure for Q2 1988 is quarter on quarter, annualized.

17. Sarah Bartlett, "Many Economists Criticize the Fed," *New York Times,* August 3, 1988. In the ten days before the appearance of the article, Greenspan had had lunch with the *Wall Street Journal,* granted two separate interviews to the *Washington Post* as well as one to the *San Francisco Chronicle,* and met with a writer from the *New York Times Magazine.* But he was evidently unable to reach every potentially hostile reporter.

18. Michael Kernan, "The Marines' Sunset Ballet," *Washington Post,* August 8, 1986.

19. Robert D. Hershey Jr., "Job Surge Spurs Inflation Worry," *New York Times,* August 6, 1988.

20. Woodward, *Maestro,* 52.

21. Alan Greenspan, *The Age of Turbulence: Adventures in a New World* (New York: Penguin Books, 2008), 111.

22. Ibid., 112.

23. Woodward, *Maestro,* Kindle location 953.

24. Woodward also reports that Baker complained to Johnson, calling him a traitor, and told Fed governor Kelley that the Fed had kicked the Bush campaign in the teeth.

25. Reuters, "Baker Backs Fed's Move to Suddenly Raise Rates," *Toronto Star,* August 15, 1988. On the day of the increase, White House spokesman Marlin Fitzwater also said there was a "sound reason" for the rate hike and the Fed was "doing a good job" of keeping inflation under control.

26. Annualized quarter-on-quarter growth was 5.4 percent in the second quarter, 2.3 percent in the third quarter, and 5.4 percent in the fourth quarter.

27. Paul Blustein, "Brady Sees No Indication Interest Rates Will Rise; Concerns About Dollar's Slide Also Dismissed," *Washington Post,* November 19, 1988.

28. Manley Johnson, interview by the author, July 15, 2013.

29. Lloyd Grove, "The Kemp Constituency: Reagan, Bush & the Supply-Siders," *Washington Post,* December 2, 1988.

30. Michael J. Prell, "Federal Open Market Committee Meeting Notes: Economic Outlook" (Federal Open Market Committee, December 13, 1988), 20, http://www.federalreserve.gov/monetarypolicy/files/FOMC19881214material.pdf.

31. U.S. nonfinancial, nongovernmental debt had grown more than 75 percent from the end of 1983 to the end of 1988. Board of Governors of the Federal Reserve System, "Households and Nonprofit Organizations; Credit Market Instruments; Liability, Level," *FRED, Federal Reserve Bank of St. Louis,* October 1, 1949, https://research.stlouisfed.org/fred2/series/HSTCMDODNS/. Board of Governors of the Federal Reserve System, "Nonfinancial Corporate Business; Credit Market Instruments; Liability," *FRED, Federal Reserve Bank of St. Louis,* October 1, 1949, https://research.stlouisfed.org/fred2/series/NCBTCMDODNS/.

32. Following the December 1988 FOMC meeting, the target federal funds rate was raised on December 15 and again on January 5, for a total move of 64 basis points.

33. Greenspan's testimony shows him consciously embracing a policy of erring on the side of monetary tightness, despite political pressure not to do so and despite fears of colleagues such as Governor LaWare about financial fragility. "The pursuit of such a strategy on the part of the Federal Reserve embodies an acute awareness of the great cost to our economy and society should a more intense inflationary process become entrenched," Greenspan said. "In the long-run costs of a return to higher inflation, and the risks of this occurring under current circumstances, are sufficiently great that Federal Reserve policy at this juncture might well be advised to err more on the side of restrictiveness than of stimulus." House Committee on Banking, Finance, and Urban Affairs, *Domestic Economic Issues, Financial Providers, and Safety and Soundness of the U.S. Financial System: Hearings Before the Committee on Banking, Finance, and Urban Affairs* (U.S. House of Representatives, 1989), http://babel.hathitrust.org/cgi/pt?id=mdp.39015019122913;view=1up;seq=1.

34. Robert D. Hershey Jr., "Bush Cautious on Anti-Inflation Steps," *New York Times,* January 26, 1989.

35. Barbara Rudolph, "The Savings and Loan Crisis: Finally, the Bill Has Come Due," *Time,* February 20, 1989.

36. Greenspan's presence on the stage was captured on video. See *Savings and Loan Proposal,* News Conference (White House, Washington D.C., United States, 1989), http://c-spanvideo.org/program/LoanPr.

37. The governor was Martha Seger.

38. The quantification of the S&L hit was offered by Richard Syron, president of the Boston Fed. Further demonstrating the FOMC's preoccupation with financial stability, Governor Mike Kelley observed, "There are some very major problems in the United States, and indeed in the world, that could be severely exacerbated if we are too aggressive, too fast: S&Ls, LDCs, the budget deficit. . . ."

39. Even as the Fed's leaders were meeting, the White House was admitting that its $90 billion estimate for the cost of the S&L bailout might be too low, not least because it excluded $36 billion in interest costs. If the Fed allowed a recession, the White House might have to explain to voters why its blockbuster bailout turned out to be even more expensive than promised. In 1996, the government's General Accounting Office put the final cost to taxpayers at well over $100 billion.

40. David Hale, a Chicago-based economist, commented on the way that monetarism had made Volcker's task easier than Greenspan's. "Greenspan first will have to fight a guerrilla war, then trench warfare and finally full-scale, hand-to-hand combat." By contrast, "Volcker just dropped the atomic bomb." See Tom Redburn, "Fed's Greenspan Is Likely to Play Key Policy Role," *Los Angeles Times,* December 11, 1988.

41. Colin James, "Govt Formalizes Inflation Target," *Australian Financial Review,* March 5, 1990.

42. Kohn had considered the pros and cons of inflation targeting in the presentation that he had prepared for this meeting. See Donald L. Kohn, "Federal Open Market Committee Meeting Notes: Long-Run Policy Alternatives Briefing" (Federal Open Market Committee, February 7, 1989), http://www.federalreserve.gov/monetarypolicy/files/FOMC19890208material.pdf.

43. Correspondence held in Alan Greenspan's personal files.

44. Mitchell, interview by the author, July 28, 2014.

45. Barbara Carton, "Bankrupt: After a Decade of Miracles, New England Revisits the Perils of Going Bust," *Boston Globe,* May 14, 1989. See also Doug Bailey, "The Trouble at Eliot Savings," *Boston Globe,* June 20, 1989. Eliot had expanded its portfolio of loans by 500 percent between 1985 and 1988.

46. Michael Boskin to George H. W. Bush, "April Employment and Unemployment," memorandum, May 4, 1989, 5/5/89 1:15 pm Budget Team Meeting, Oval Office, [OA/ID 08061], Michael Boskin Files—Meeting Files, Council of Economic Advisers, Bush Presidential Records: Staff and Office Files, George Bush Presidential Library.

47. The commentator was John Makin, a hedge-fund adviser and scholar at the American Enterprise Institute. See Jonathan Rauch, "Greenspan's Fed," *National Journal* 21 (April 8, 1989).

48. The commentator was *New York Times* columnist William Safire. Art Pine, "Treasury Chief's Fortunes Slip, but Bush Is Loyal," *Los Angeles Times,* March 18, 1990.

49. Marjorie Williams, "The Long and the Short of Richard G. Darman," *Washington Post,* July 29, 1990.

50. Darman's *Meet the Press* appearance took place on August 13, 1989. Woodward, *Maestro,* 62. Greenspan's official Fed diary confirms he was there from Friday to Sunday. Alan Greenspan's Diary, n.d. Joey Ford, Transcript, *Meet the Press* (NBC, August 13, 1989).

51. Woodward, *Maestro,* 62.

52. Richard Darman, *Who's in Control? Polar Politics and the Sensible Center* (New York: Simon & Schuster, 1996), 228.

53. Ibid.

54. The son of an immigrant Irish blacksmith, Syron had studied economics at Boston College and run the Boston Home Loan Bank; he knew as much about New England's real estate finance as anyone.

55. Data from the Bureau of Economic Analysis show New England's personal income growing by less than 1 percent, quarter on quarter, in Q2, Q3, and Q4 1989. By comparison, the rate in the previous four quarters had averaged over 2 percent. U.S. Bureau of Economic Analysis, "SQ1 Quarterly Personal Income: 1988–1989 New England," March 10, 2015, 1, http://www.bea.gov/iTable/iTableHtml.cfm?reqid=70&step=30&isuri=1&

7022=36&7023=0&7024=non-industry&7033=-1&7025=0&7026=91000&7027=1989,1988&7001=336&7028=10&7031=0&7040=-1&7083=percentchange&7029=36&7090=70.

56. The impression created by Syron's accent is noted in John M. Berry, "For the Fed's Man in Boston, Battling Inflation Is Job No. 1," *Washington Post,* March 24, 1989.

57. Johnson, interview by the author, June 19, 2013.

58. Bob Woodward, *Maestro,* Kindle locations 1185–1204.

59. Associated Press, "Visitors Line Up for View of Trading Spasms on Floor," *Los Angeles Times,* October 16, 1989.

60. On Monday, October 16, 1989, the federal funds target rate was unchanged but the "effective" rate—that is, the average rate at which short-term borrowing actually occurred—fell to its lowest level that year, reflecting an injection of Fed liquidity.

61. Greenspan's meeting with Berry and Graham appears as described in his official Fed diary. Two weeks after the lunch, on November 2, 1989, Greenspan went to Greenfield's for dinner. Then on November 6 Greenspan joined Greenfield for lunch at her habitual restaurant in the Madison Hotel, across from the *Post* building.

62. Six years of inflation below 5 percent had pushed the issue off the public's radar—whereas voters overwhelmingly selected inflation as the nation's most important problem in polls during the 1980 elections, inflation failed to make the top five in the 1988 cycle. By then, the national deficit had emerged as the primary economic concern. Even when Gallup conducted a survey the following year asking specifically about personal financial anxieties, only 2 percent of American households named inflation as their top worry. See Roper Center Public Opinion Archives, "1988 US Presidential Election," http://www.ropercenter.uconn.edu/elections/presidential/presidential_election_1988.html; Robin Toner, "Optimistic Mood Greets 41st President," *New York Times,* January 20, 1989; and Marc Rice, "Survey: Top Money Worry Among Americans Is Paying the Mortgage with AM-Housing," Associated Press, May 16, 1989.

63. At the FOMC meeting of March 23, 1993, Greenspan laid out a doctrine of asymmetrical response to recoveries and downturns: the Fed should act quickly to prevent a recovery from overheating, but it should act slowly in counteracting a recession. The purpose was to complete Volcker's efforts to squeeze inflation out of the system. This bias toward toughness was the mirror opposite of the bias associated with Greenspan later. "I think that's in the nature of a central bank because if we are too easy coming down, we set into motion a secular upward bias [in inflation]. There should be asymmetry in that respect; we should be ahead of the curve on the up side and behind the curve on the down side."

64. Jack Nelson, "Interest Rates Peril Fed Chief's Job," *Los Angeles Times,* March 9, 1990.

65. Alan Murray and Jackie Calmes, "The Great Debate: How the Democrats, with Rare Cunning, Won the Budget War," *Wall Street Journal,* November 5, 1990.

66. The conservative was United Conservatives of America chairman Richard Viguerie. See Dan Balz and John E. Yang, "Bush Abandons Campaign Pledge, Calls for New Taxes," *Washington Post,* June 27, 1990.

CHAPTER EIGHTEEN

1. Kevin M. Woods, "Um Al-Ma'arik (The Mother of All Battles): Operational and Strategic Insights from an Iraqi Perspective," *Institute for Defense Analyses* 1 (May 2008), www.dtic.mil/cgi-bin/GetTRDoc?AD=ada484530.

2. "By then, Alan and I were living together, quietly. I didn't want to be away from him for such a long time, but as always, my domestic instincts were fighting my hunger for adventure." Andrea Mitchell, *Talking Back: . . . to Presidents, Dictators, and Assorted Scoundrels* (New York: Penguin Group, 2006), Kindle locations 3234–35.

3. Molly Moore, "Cheney Says Emirates to Host U.S. Forces; Secretary Visits Air Crews in Abu Dhabi," *Washington Post,* August 21, 1990.

4. Alan Greenspan, interview by the author, June 2, 2014.

5. Greenspan had had dinner with Richard and Lynne Cheney on August 7, 1990, for example.

6. Oil-price data are from "EIA Short-Term Energy Outlook, Real and Nominal Price Dataset Series: Crude Oil-M Tab" (U.S. Energy Information Administration, February 2014).

7. DGS10 data series from FRED. Board of Governors of the Federal Reserve System, "10-Year Treasury Constant Maturity Rate," FRED, Federal Reserve Bank of St. Louis, January 2, 1962, https://research.stlouisfed.org/fred2/series/DGS10/.

8. In July the underlying "core" rate hit 5 percent, its fastest pace in nearly six years; and the headline consumer price index seemed set to surge, thanks to the spike in oil prices.

9. The Fed governor was David Mullins.

10. Greenspan recalled later, "When Saddam went into Kuwait, I was very strongly of the view that the only reason he's in Kuwait is as a staging area to go into Saudi Arabia. And ultimately to control the Straits of Hormuz." Greenspan, interview by the author, May 4, 2012.

11. The skeptic was Edward Boehne, the president of the Philadelphia Fed.

12. Richard Darman, *Who's in Control? Polar Politics and the Sensible Center* (New York: Simon & Schuster, 1996), 276.

13. Darman had agreed with the main thrust of a CEA report prepared for Bush in August that both cited Fed tightness as "a key factor in creating the slowdown during the last one and a half years" and suggested the Fed could stave off recession by easing soon. Ibid., 275.

14. A well-connected journalist who was close to Darman recalls, "Darman thought he owned Greenspan."

15. Two weeks before Greenspan's phone call, Darman had taken delivery of a memo from an economist at the Office of Management and Budget, underlining the vulnerability of the banks. See Ahmad Al-Samarrie to Richard Darman, "Banks: The Next Deposit Insurance Crisis?," memorandum, August 10, 1990, Darman (OMB) (1990), OA/ID 29187, John Sununu Files, Bush Presidential Records: Staff and Office Files, George Bush Presidential Library.

16. Janet L. Fix, "FDIC Had Set Aside Funds to Cover the Bank of New England's Failure," *Philadelphia Inquirer,* January 9, 1991, http://articles.philly.com/1991-01-09/business/25820869_1_bank-failures-fdic-fund-alan-whitney.

17. On September 11, 1990, a GAO study reported that the FDIC held a meager 70 cents in reserves to cover every $100 in insured deposits—its lowest ratio ever.

18. Kenneth Duberstein, interview by the author, May 2, 2014.

19. Andrea Mitchell, *Talking Back,* Kindle locations 3194–3203.

20. Greenspan's diary shows a meeting with Scowcroft on September 28, the day of the dinner with Cheney. Alan Greenspan's Diary, n.d.
21. Ken Duberstein recalls that developments in the Gulf were discussed at the dinner. Interview by the author, February 20, 2014.
22. The agreement was to reduce the budget deficit by $500 billion over five years. See John E. Yang, "Bush, Hill Leaders Approve Budget Package," *Washington Post,* October 1, 1990.
23. The FOMC member was Richmond Fed president Robert Black.
24. The FOMC member was Governor David Mullins.
25. The FOMC member was St. Louis Fed president Thomas Melzer.
26. The FOMC member was Cleveland Fed president Lee Hoskins.
27. The FOMC member was New York Fed president Gerald Corrigan.
28. Alan Murray, "The New Fed: Democracy Comes to the Central Bank, Curbing Chief's Power," *Wall Street Journal,* April 15, 1991. By the time Greenspan left office, he was seen as an imperial chairman, and his successor was greeted as a democratizer. The lesson is that Fed chairmen tend to become imperial with time. This may be a good argument for term limits.
29. House Committee on Government Operations, *Deposit Insurance Issues and Depositor Discipline: Hearing Before the Commerce, Consumer, and Monetary Affairs Subcommittee of the Committee on Government Operations,* 101st Cong., 2nd sess., 1990, http://hdl.handle.net /2027/pst.000017881975.
30. "1990–1991 might be the only recession since the 1950s in which tight money was *not* a significant factor in the slowdown of lending." See Ben Bernanke, "Credit in the Macroeconomy," *Federal Reserve Bank of New York Quarterly Review* 18, no. 1 (Spring 1993): 64.
31. The term "balance sheet recession" was used in a retrospective colloquium on the 1990–91 downturn, organized by the New York Federal Reserve in February 1992. However, the term was unfamiliar enough that it was bracketed with inverted commas. See "The Role of the Credit Slowdown in the Recent Recession," *Federal Reserve Bank of New York Quarterly Review* 18, no. 1 (Spring 1993): 2.
32. David Wessel, "Pushing Policy: Fed's Vice Chairman, Seeking Lower Rates, Furthers a Bush Goal," *Wall Street Journal,* October 6, 1992.
33. "Darman once said to me, 'Larry, I dreamed about you last night. I saw you running down the halls tossing grenades into every office as you went by,'" Lindsey recalled later. "Darman figured out I was a monetary dove, and he knew I was a pretty effective troublemaker. He figured he could send me to cause trouble to Alan instead of causing trouble to him." Lawrence Lindsey, interview by the author, August 26, 2011.
34. Alan Greenspan, *The Age of Turbulence: Adventures in a New World* (New York: Penguin Books, 2008), 121.
35. Senate Committee on Banking, Housing, and Urban Affairs, *Deposit Insurance Revision and Financial Services Industry Restructuring: Hearing Before the Committee on Banking, Housing, and Urban Affairs,* 101st Cong., 2nd sess., (Federal News Service, 1990).
36. C-SPAN video archive from January 23, 1991. *Progress of the Resolution Trust Corporation* (U.S. Senate Banking, Housing, and Urban Affairs Committee, 1991), http://www.c-span.org/video/?15872-1/progress-resolution-trust-corporation.
37. Steven Mufson, "Sweeping Bank-Reform Plan Unveiled: Treasury Package Would Bring Down Interstate, Ownership Barriers," *Washington Post,* February 6, 1991.
38. The Treasury's plan for a single bank regulator emerged in January 1991. See, for example, Stephen Labaton, "Plan to Pare Financial Supervision," *New York Times,* January 7, 1991.
39. William Safire, "Bush's Cabinet: Who's Up, Who's Down," *New York Times,* March 25, 1990. Another *New York Times* article quoted a noted Brookings Institution economist: "You're just not very conscious of his presence. . . . It's hard to characterize the absence of a presence." David E. Rosenbaum, "The Treasury's 'Mr. Diffident': Nicholas Brady Wields Power in Washington Because He Is the President's Best Friend," *New York Times,* November 19, 1989.
40. David Wessel, "Is Brady's Treasury Up to Doing Its Job? Many People Doubt It," *Wall Street Journal,* January 31, 1991.
41. Quotes and scene come from C-SPAN video: *Progress of the Resolution Trust Corporation.*
42. James Risen, "Administration Plans to Weaken Fed's Power," *Los Angeles Times,* January 8, 1991. Kenneth H. Bacon, "White House Alters Plan on Banking Laws," *Wall Street Journal,* February 5, 1991.
43. Kenneth H. Bacon, "White House Alters Plan on Banking Laws," *Wall Street Journal,* February 5, 1991.
44. Under the Treasury's February proposal, the Fed would gain power over local banks previously supervised by the FDIC.
45. R. W. Apple Jr., "Allied Forces Storm Iraq and Kuwait After Hussein Ignores U.S. Deadline; Bush Sees a Swift, Decisive Victory," *New York Times,* February 24, 1991.
46. Rick Atkinson, "U.S. Victory Is Absolute," *Washington Post,* March 1, 1991.
47. Andrew Rosenthal, "Bush Halts Offensive Combat," *New York Times,* February 28, 1991. See also George E. Jordan, "Gulf Heroes Will Get Our 'Biggest' Parade," *Newsday,* March 4, 1991.
48. "Music Briefs," *BPI Entertainment Newswire,* February 27, 1991.
49. Greenspan's message in private meetings is recalled by Virgil Mattingly, the Fed's general counsel at the time, who was in awe of Greenspan's skill as a behind-the-scenes lobbyist for the Fed's regulatory interests. Virgil Mattingly, interview by the author, February 18, 2014.
50. David E. Rosenbaum, "Fed to Fight Part of Plan on Banks," *New York Times,* March 5, 1991. Of course, the Treasury was also responsible for the financial system insofar as taxpayers might be called upon to rescue it.
51. The lobbyist was Kenneth Guenther. See "In the Bank; Paradise Lost; Conversation; Strikeout," Transcript, *MacNeil-Lehrer NewsHour* (PBS, July 31, 1990), Transcript #3827.
52. Barbara A. Rehm, "Lawmakers Attack Fed Lending," *American Banker,* May 13, 1991, 2. Mattingly, interview by the author, February 18, 2014.
53. Barbara A. Rehm, "Lawmakers Attack Fed Lending." To the Fed's embarrassment, González's committee staff found 90 percent of the 377 banks that had extended use of the discount window in the preceding six years had ultimately failed, and a House investigation into the Bank of New England collapse later revealed that the FDIC's cleanup costs could have been cut nearly in half had the Fed not propped up the bank for months with discount window loans while billions of dollars in uninsured deposits fled. Representative Tom Ridge (the future DHS secretary), who was one of González's allies on the committee, likened the situation to a sinking ship wherein "the stowaways were getting off with their luggage."
54. Jerry Knight, "Panal Drops Provisions to Limit Fed," *Washington Post,* June 21, 1991.

55. Brady made this pronouncement in a March 24 interview with ABC's David Brinkley on *This Week*. The headline consumer price index had risen by 5.3 percent in the year to February, and would come in at 4.9 percent in the year to March. David Brinkley, *This Week with David Brinkley* (ABC News, March 24, 1991).

56. Hollis McLoughlin, interview by the author, January 17, 2014.

57. On May 15, the *Wall Street Journal* had speculated that the administration's dawdling on Greenspan's reappointment had caused a slide in stock prices. See "Asides: A Nervous Market," *Wall Street Journal,* May 15, 1991.

58. Alan Murray, "Fed Chief Is Expected to Be Reappointed," *Wall Street Journal,* May 17, 1991.

59. McLoughlin, interview by the author, January 17, 2014.

60. At the time, Lawrence Lindsey's confirmation to the Fed Reserve Board was still pending in Congress five months after its submission, underlining the risk in attempting to install an alternative to Greenspan.

61. "We delayed reappointment because we kept waiting for the easing shoe to fall." John Sununu, interview by the author, January 10, 2014. Hollis McLoughlin, Brady's aide, recalls that Bush's chief of staff John Sununu was influential on the timing of the Greenspan announcement. McLoughlin, interview by the author, January 17, 2014.

62. Michael Duffy and Dan Goodgame, *Marching in Place: The Status Quo Presidency of George Bush* (New York: Simon & Schuster, 1992), 249.

63. Bob Woodward, *The Agenda: Inside the Clinton White House* (New York: Simon & Schuster, 2005), 50.

64. Nicholas F. Brady, "A Way of Going" (Unpublished Manuscript, 2008), 241–42.

65. Ibid.

66. Bob Woodward, *Maestro: Greenspan's Fed and the American Boom* (New York: Simon & Schuster Inc., 2000), Kindle location 1654. Darman later seethed privately to colleagues at Brady's incompetence in failing to extract a firm commitment from Greenspan to go for growth.

67. At the May 1991 FOMC meeting, Greenspan and Corrigan had concurred that balance-sheet adjustments might temper the recovery, but that a classic inventory-restocking bounce-back was nonetheless likely. For these reasons, the Fed had decided

against a cut in the federal funds rate from the existing target of 5.75 percent. The fact that the FOMC later resumed cutting, bringing the target rate down to 4 percent by December 1991 and 3 percent by September 1992, constituted a retrospective admission that the policy of mid-1991 had been excessively tight. For an exposition of the lessons learned from this error, see Ben Bernanke, "Credit in the Macroeconomy," 50–70.

68. See Ben Bernanke, "Credit in the Macroeconomy." Bernanke's paper applied new research on asymmetric information to the field of monetary policy, pointing out that borrowers paid a premium to lenders that reflected lenders' imperfect information. This premium increased when falling asset prices, higher interest rates, or a recession heightened doubts about creditworthiness. Although Greenspan would not have couched his arguments in terms of information asymmetries, he would certainly have recognized that stressed economic conditions could disrupt the credit channel.

69. This meeting was recalled by two participants, David Shulman and Ken Rosen. Both had been involved in real estate research at Salomon Brothers, and Shulman continued to direct the firm's real estate research unit. David Shulman, interview by the author, August 5, 2011, and Kenneth Rosen, interview by the author, May 6, 2014.

70. Alarmingly, the scale of this problem dwarfed even the Latin American debt mess: U.S. banks had lent far greater sums to domestic real estate projects than they had ever lent to developing nations. In 1990, government data showed that banks' exposure to commercial real estate amounted to 19 percent of all loans, or five times their exposure to third-world debt as of 1987. See Stephen Kleege, "Fate of Banking in the 1990s Hinges on Real Estate Loans," *American Banker,* October 15, 1990, 1.

71. Ibid. Darman was widely recognized to be a champion Washington leaker. See for example Marjorie Williams, "The Long and the Short of Richard G. Darman," *Washington Post,* July 29, 1990.

72. Bob Woodward, *The Agenda,* 53.

73. Greenspan recalls that when he realized he was being frozen out, his main feeling was "hallelujah." Greenspan, interview by the author, April 1, 2011. Brady affirms that he viewed Greenspan as socially insecure. Nicholas F. Brady, interview by the author, September 19, 2011.

74. Steven Greenhouse, "Bush Calls on Fed for Another Drop in Interest," *New York Times,* June 24, 1992.

75. Lawrence Lindsey was the only FOMC member to even mention Bush's remarks, and then only to declare himself appalled by them. "We'd clearly establish credibility if we stood tall," Lindsey told the FOMC meeting. "Perhaps we could even raise rates and, who knows, really show our independence."

76. In the Fed staff forecast prepared for the June 30 meeting, the projection for growth in 1992 had been revised down from 2.6 percent to 2.4 percent. Lawrence Lindsey summed up the divided sentiment in the Fed boardroom. Although he wondered aloud about tightening policy in order to rebuff the president, he also advocated looser policy because the economy needed it.

77. "George Bush: A President's Story," *One on One with David Frost* (A&E, June 1998).

CHAPTER NINETEEN

1. Marion Burros, "Bill Clinton and Food: Jack Sprat He's Not," *New York Times,* December 23, 1992.

2. Joe Klein, "Clinton: The Survivor," *Newsweek,* July 20, 1992.

3. Bob Woodward, *The Agenda: Inside the Clinton White House* (New York: Simon & Schuster Inc., 2005), 64.

4. Alan Greenspan, *The Age of Turbulence: Adventures in a New World,* (New York: Penguin Books, 2008), 143.

5. Bob Woodward, *Maestro: Greenspan's Fed and the American Boom* (New York: Simon & Schuster, 2000).

6. Clinton's advisers had already warned him that the Bush team had achieved nothing by pressuring the Fed. Alan Blinder, interview by the author, January 23, 2012.

7. Greenspan, *Age of Turbulence,* 143.

8. Greenspan's argument to Clinton is summarized in Woodward, *Maestro;* Bob Woodward, *The Agenda,* 67–68; and Greenspan, *Age of Turbulence,* 144. These sources are corroborated by contemporaneous primary sources that capture Greenspan's thinking about long-term interest rates at this time. Both in testimony to Congress and in FOMC meetings, Greenspan made it clear that he believed deficit reduction led to diminishing inflation expectations and hence to lower long-term bond rates.

9. A former Fed economist recalls that Greenspan asked the staff to

do statistical work that might support his inflations-expectation hypothesis.

10. These quotes are reported in Bob Woodward, *The Agenda,* 60, and Greenspan, *Age of Turbulence,* 144. Ted Truman, the head of the international division of the Fed, also recalls Greenspan returning from Arkansas favorably impressed. Ted Truman, interview by the author, January 26, 2012. Greenspan reiterated his favorable view of Clinton in an FOMC conference call on December 14, 1992.

11. Albert Hunt, interview by the author, February 4, 2014.

12. Robert Rubin, interview by the author, March 5, 2015.

13. The argument for expansionary austerity assumed that deficit reduction would bring down interest rates fast enough to offset the economic drag from budget austerity; and further, that lower interest rates would pull down the dollar. Part of the projected boost to the economy came from a stimulus to exports.

14. Blinder, interview by the author, January 23, 2012.

15. Bob Woodward, *The Agenda,* 92.

16. The visit from Bentsen and Rubin is recorded in the Fed chairman's official diary. Alan Greenspan's Diary, n.d.

17. Woodward, *Maestro,* 98. According to Greenspan's official diary, he met Hillary Clinton at the White House on March 1, 1993, presumably to discuss health reform. Alan Greenspan's Diary.

18. Tyson recalls that Greenspan advised her to clasp her hands under her chin. This pose had the dual function of projecting earnestness and controlling hand gestures. Laura Tyson, interview by the author, July 2, 2014.

19. Greenspan's movements back and forth to New York are recorded in the diary kept for him by his Fed secretary. Alan Greenspan's Diary.

20. Greenspan recalls, "Lloyd Bentsen listened to me on fiscal restraint, and we talked Bill Clinton into it." Alan Greenspan, interview by the author, June 18, 2014. See also Woodward, *Maestro,* 99.

21. On the length of the meeting see Stephen A. Davies and Dean J. Patterson, "President Meets with Greenspan, Requests Backing to Aid Economy," *Bond Buyer,* January 29, 1993. On Clinton's reaction, see Woodward, *Maestro,* 99.

22. Robert Solow is quoted in Linton Weeks and John M. Berry, "The Shy Wizard of Money: Fed's Enigmatic Greenspan Moves Easily in His Own World," *Washington Post,* March 24, 1997.

23. Greenspan also predicted that if bond rates fell back toward 5 percent, the result would be "a far greater stimulus effect . . . than any of these numbers we are talking about." Senate Committee on the Budget, *Statement by Alan Greenspan Before the Committee on the Budget,* 103rd Cong., 1st sess., 1993. Greenspan's testimony gave his audience room to believe that the economy might speed up under the impact of deficit cuts. Hence the Clinton administration memo of February 5, 1993, citing him in favor of the idea that interest rate declines would more than offset the drag from a tighter budget.

24. In the first half of 1967, the ten-year government bond rate had moved between about 4.5 percent and 4.9 percent. The thirty-year bond had not existed until 1977; but between then and the time of Greenspan's testimony, the average spread between thirty-year and ten-year rates was 6 basis points. Therefore the ten-year rate in 1967 implied a thirty-year rate under 5 percent.

25. As it turned out, inflation expectations five to ten years ahead (as measured by the University of Michigan surveys) subsided gradually over the 1990s; they did not fall suddenly in response to the budget deal of 1993, contrary to what Greenspan appeared to be predicting. Moreover, over the first five years of Clinton's presidency, long-run inflation expectations fell by only half a percentage point, implying a reduction in the long-bond rate substantially smaller than the reduction Greenspan dangled before the Senate.

26. Steven Greenhouse, "Fed's Chief Also Likes Clinton Plan on Deficit," *New York Times,* January 29, 1993.

27. Wil S. Hylton, "Alan Greenspan Takes a Bath," *GQ,* April 2005, 7, http://www.gq.com/news-politics/newsmakers/200503/alan-greenspan-budget-federal-reserve?currentPage=1.

28. Bob Woodward, *The Agenda,* 113.

29. Nicholas F. Brady, "A Way of Going" (Unpublished Manuscript, 2008), 242–43.

30. Senate Committee on Banking, Housing, and Urban Affairs, *Federal Reserve's First Monetary Report for 1993: Hearing Before the Committee on Banking, Housing, and Urban Affairs,* 103rd Cong., 1st sess., 1993.

31. This sequence was reported in "1994 Economic Report of the President," February 1994, 84, https://fraser.stlouisfed.org/title/?id=45#!8093.

32. In a speech delivered to the Economic Club of New York on April 19, 1993, Greenspan reiterated the view that inflation expectations were oddly elevated and therefore presented an opportunity for policy makers to bring them down. Alan Greenspan, remarks (Economic Club of New York, New York, April 19, 1993), https://fraser.stlouisfed.org/docs/historical/greenspan/Greenspan_19930419.pdf.

33. The best measure of whether deficit reduction was reducing long-run inflation expectations comes from the University of Michigan's survey of five-ten-year-ahead inflation expectations. Expectations stood at 3.4 percent in February 1993 and 3.5 percent in October 1993. One-year-ahead expectations rose from 2.9 percent to 3.3 percent over this period. "University of Michigan Inflation Expectation," FRED, Federal Reserve Bank of St. Louis, January 1, 1978, https://research.stlouisfed.org/fred2/series/MICH/.

34. Lindsey's position anticipated later debates about using monetary policy to "lean against the wind." "There's probably not a lot of real effect [on asset prices] from 25 basis points on the fed funds rate," he said at the March 1993 FOMC meeting. "I do think, though, that it is a signal to those markets that perhaps we think they are overextended. And I would rather raise the fed funds rate 25 points now to put a little cold water on them than to be in a situation in a few months where we might have to raise it significantly more." Lindsey's explicit advocacy of using monetary policy to combat asset bubbles represents the path not taken by central banks over the next decade.

35. In his 1959 paper, Greenspan had argued that rather than allowing the money supply to expand to "meet the legitimate demands of business," as it did with disastrous consequences in the run-up to the 1929 crash, the Fed should have reacted to the danger posed by "speculative flights from reality." See chapter three.

36. The tension between Greenspan's policy and his former belief in gold was noted at the time by the supply-side gold bug Jude Wanniski, who wrote to Greenspan pointing out that gold prices signaled continued inflation fears, implying that the bond rally might be a bubble. "You've persuaded

the bond market that you're going to maintain a sound money policy, but you haven't persuaded the gold market. Either gold is going to come down or bond yields are going to go up, depending on how you handle yourself in the very near term," Wanniski wrote, suggesting that the Fed should raise interest rates. Jude Wanniski to Alan Greenspan, letter, July 30, 1993, Correspondence: Greenspan, Alan, 1991–1993, box 14, Jude Wanniski, Hoover Institution Archives.

37. The position to which Greenspan began to gravitate in 1993 was cautiously questioned after the financial crisis. In a speech delivered on July 2, 2014, Fed chairman Janet Yellen conceded that higher short-term interest rates can mitigate bubbles, noting that "the level of interest rates does influence house prices, leverage, and maturity transformation." Moreover, unlike the later Greenspan Fed, the Yellen Fed accepted that its responsibilities included fighting asset bubbles. Still, Yellen's preferred tool for doing so was regulatory policy rather than higher interest rates. See Janet Yellen, Inaugural Michel Camdessus Central Banking Lecture, International Monetary Fund Headquarters, Washington, D.C., July 2, 2014, http://www.imf.org/external/np/seminars/eng/2014/camdessus/.

38. The alarming buildup of personal debt was a running theme in Lindsey's commentary throughout this period; at the February 1994 FOMC meeting, he disaggregated elderly and rich Americans from the rest, pointing out that "the non-rich, non-old live paycheck to paycheck, quite literally." To a remarkable degree, Lindsey was pointing to the dynamic that contributed to the fragility of the economy years hence. Low inflation, reflecting cheap imports, allowed monetary policy to stay loose; in turn, low interest rates encouraged excessive personal borrowing.

39. Lindsey was advocating an approach adopted by Nordic central banks two decades later. Norway's central bank increased the policy interest rate in mid-2010 when it faced escalating household debt, undeterred by the fact that inflation was below target; the goal was "guarding against the risk of future imbalances." Sweden's Riksbank held its policy rate "slightly higher than we would have done otherwise" because of financial stability concerns. Both examples are noted by Yellen,

Inaugural Michel Camdessus Central Banking Lecture. Sweden's tightening later proved to be an error, but generalizing from this example may constitute a further error. Sweden embarked on its tightening in 2010, at a time when the economy was weak: the Riksbank's forecast for inflation was below the target and the forecast for unemployment was far above the long-run sustainable rate. As will be suggested in later chapters, Greenspan faced opportunities to tighten policy in pursuit of financial stability when the U.S. economy was stronger than Sweden's in 2010.

40. Bob Woodward, *The Agenda,* 329.

41. The decision to announce the FOMC decision in a public statement contrasted with the practice Greenspan had earlier defended. In October 1989, Greenspan had told a House committee that immediate announcement of FOMC decisions "would be ill-advised and could impede timely and appropriate adjustments to policy." As recently as October 1993, Greenspan had told FOMC colleagues in a conference call that public announcements could roil markets, and that fear of this might inhibit the Fed from moving rates appropriately. Of course, this position was muddled. It was precisely by provoking moves in market interest rates that Fed decisions influenced the economy. Alan S. Blinder and Ricardo Reis, "Understanding the Greenspan Standard," Working Paper (CEPS, September 2005), 35–36.

42. From 1994 to the end of his tenure, Greenspan moved the target rate between meetings on only four occasions, and in all cases he obtained consent from the committee. For analysis of intermeeting moves, see Ellen E. Meade, "The FOMC: Preferences, Voting, and Consensus," *Federal Reserve Bank of St. Louis Review* 87, no. 2, Part 1 (April 2005): 101, http://research.stlouisfed.org/publications/review/05/03/part1/Meade.pdf. One instance of an intermeeting move for which Greenspan secured FOMC approval was to come soon: in April 1994.

43. The target federal funds rate had last been raised in February 1989, from 9.3 percent to 9.75 percent.

44. Greenspan, *Age of Turbulence,* 155.

45. The allegation that Angell footfaulted comes, admittedly, from Greenspan. Greenspan, interview by the author, June 18, 2014. The allegation that Greenspan was deeply keen on winning comes from conversations with several people who played with him.

46. A fuller account of hedge funds' expansion and their interactions with Fed tightening in early 1994 is provided in Sebastian Mallaby, *More Money Than God: Hedge Funds and the Making of a New Elite* (New York: Penguin Group, 2010), Kindle location 3133ff.

47. In the April 1991 Treasury auction, Steinhardt and a hedge-fund manager named Bruce Kovner bid for just over half the Treasury bonds on offer, but then immediately lent them out and bought them back again, ending up with exposure equivalent to more than 100 percent of the auction. Steinhardt and Kovner applied similarly aggressive tactics to the May 1991 auction.

48. The mortgage-trading hedge fund was Askin Capital Management.

49. The thirty-year rate, admittedly, had preserved more of its gain, not least because hedge funds preferred to trade the more plentiful ten-year paper.

50. *Late Edition* (CNN, April 3, 1994).

51. At the May 1994 FOMC meeting, Greenspan reiterated that "the issue of uncertainty as being helpful or unhelpful is really not clear-cut. We experienced periods of relative certainty in the latter part of 1993. . . . That clearly was a very unhappy state of affairs; the mere fact that uncertainty did not exist was not a good; it clearly was a bad."

CHAPTER TWENTY

1. Carrie Mason-Draffen, "One of Clinton's Fed Choices Is Former Syosset High Hoopster," *Newsday,* April 23, 1994.

2. Alan S. Blinder, *Hard Heads, Softer Hearts: Tough-Minded Economics for a Just Society* (Cambridge Mass.: Perseus Books, 1987), ix.

3. John Cassidy, "Fleeing the Fed," *New Yorker,* February 19, 1996.

4. Clay Chandler, "Blinder Tops Candidate List for Fed Post; Princeton Economist Could Be Bank's Next Vice Chairman," *Washington Post,* February 18, 1994.

5. Blinder, *Hard Heads, Softer Hearts,* 33. Blinder also wrote that "inflation's most devout enemies exhibit verbal hysteria." See ibid., 51.

6. Blinder, *Hard Heads, Softer Hearts,* 51.

7. Ibid., 33–34.

8. Bob Woodward, *Maestro: Greenspan's Fed and the American Boom* (New York: Simon & Schuster, 2000), Kindle locations 2608–14.

9. Ibid., Kindle locations 2601–04.

10. Greenspan had described this hypothesis in a speech on April 19, 1993, to the Economic Club of New York. Alan Greenspan, remarks (Economic Club of New

York, New York, April 19, 1993), https://fraser.stlouisfed.org/docs/historical/greenspan/Greenspan_19930419.pdf.

11. Glenn Rudebusch, interview by the author, July 14, 2014.

12. Senate Committee on Banking, Housing, and Urban Affairs, *Testimony by Alan Greenspan, Chairman, Board of Governors of the Federal Reserve System, Before the Committee on Banking, Housing, and Urban Affairs*, 103rd Cong., 2nd sess., 1994, http://fraser.stlouisfed.org/docs/historical/greenspan/Greenspan_19940527.pdf.

13. Addressing his FOMC colleagues in July 1996, Greenspan confessed, "I must admit that several years ago I raised this hypothesis with our staff colleagues and had them take a look at what happens to productivity as the inflation rate moves toward zero. Lo and behold, they got a reasonably good correlation that unfortunately disappeared to a large extent when the data were revised."

14. Keith Bradsher, "New Fuel for the Fed's Rate Fire," *New York Times,* June 9, 1994.

15. The best effort to explain the costs of inflation came from Donald Kohn: "Higher levels of inflation tend to be more variable; you get a lot more uncertainty; people have to interact with the tax system and other things that aren't indexed to inflation rates." But Kohn made his point tentatively, and at the very end of the discussion. Nobody picked up on it.

16. Paul R. Krugman, *The Age of Diminished Expectations: U.S. Economic Policy in the 1990s* (Cambridge, Mass.: MIT Press, 1997). See also Laurence M. Ball, "The Case for Four Percent Inflation," *Central Bank Review* 13 (May 2013): 17–31. Ball's paper summarizes attempts to demonstrate macroeconomic costs from inflation, noting that growth is generally thought to suffer from inflation once the inflation rate rises above only a certain threshold; efforts to quantify that threshold produce estimates ranging from 8 percent to 40 percent. Ball, a professor at Johns Hopkins University, concludes, "Policymakers have developed an aversion to inflation that is out of proportion to its true costs." Ball's verdict as of 2013 was shared contemporaneously by some FOMC members. In an extensive debate on inflation targeting at the FOMC meeting of January/February 1995, several members stressed that the benefits of low inflation had not been empirically established. Likewise,

at the January 1996 FOMC meeting, Governor Janet Yellen cited the work of Truman Bewley of Yale, which suggested that excessively low inflation might be harmful because of downward rigidity in nominal wages; and Mike Prell observed that it was "very hard to get definitive, empirical measures of the costs and benefits of varying inflation between 3 percent and, say, 1 percent as measured by the CPI." The dominant arguments as to why inflation mattered were that firms respond to inflation by adjusting nominal prices at different times, creating inefficient variability in relative prices; and that inflation interacted inefficiently with the tax system. At low levels of inflation, neither cost appeared significant.

17. Warning of the unmeasured cost of inflation, Greenspan said, "The temptation to assume that our forecast point estimates or reduced-form model simulations somehow adequately capture these risks is probably an illusion."

18. Blinder, *Hard Heads, Softer Hearts,* 51. In a similar vein, Blinder had dared to ask whether the popular aversion to inflation was justified: "After all, public opinion also lines up solidly behind the existence of flying saucers, angels, and extrasensory perception." Ibid., 45.

19. Blinder, *Hard Heads, Softer Hearts,* 46.

20. Blinder's past attendance at Jackson Hole symposia distinguished him from Greenspan, who had not been invited before acceding to the Fed chairmanship. Adam Posen, president of the Peterson Institute for International Economics and a former member of the Bank of England's monetary policy committee, recalls that academic economists at Jackson Hole regarded Greenspan as a lightweight into the mid-1990s.

21. "The employment rate of five to ten years from now has nothing to do with today's macroeconomic policy," Blinder said. The long-run role for central banks was to control inflation. Alan S. Blinder, "Overview: Proceedings: Reducing Unemployment: Current Issues and Policy Options" (symposium sponsored by the Federal Reserve Bank of Kansas City, Jackson Hole, Wyo., August 1994).

22. Keith Bradsher, "Fed Official Disapproves of Rate Policy," *New York Times,* August 28, 1994. Bradsher's story seems unfair in light of the fact that in congressional testimony four months later, Greenspan repeated Blinder's view of the Phillips curve. "Over the long run

I don't see any trade off between inflation on the one hand and sustainable economic growth and . . . employment. . . . It is true, however, that in the short run there are trade offs." Joint Economic Committee, *Testimony by Alan Greenspan, Chairman, Board of Governors of the Federal Reserve System, Before the Joint Economic Committee,* 103rd Cong., 2nd sess., 1994. Likewise, on the first day of the FOMC meeting that ran from January 31 to February 1, 1995, Greenspan echoed Blinder, stating, "There still is a short-term Phillips Curve." To be fair, part of the stormy reaction to Blinder's comments came from European central bankers, whom Blinder had accused (correctly) of excessive tightness. But with the notable exception of the *Wall Street Journal,* press accounts built this real disagreement between Blinder and the Europeans into a fake clash between Blinder's Jackson Hole speech and the Fed's monetary orthodoxy. For the *Journal's* commendably fair take, see David Wessel, "Blinder Denies There's a Rift with Fed Chief," *Wall Street Journal,* September 9, 1994.

23. "A Grizzly Subject," *Economist,* September 3, 1994. "Division of Labor Day," *Financial Times,* September 3, 1994. Robert J. Samuelson, "Economic Amnesia," *Washington Post,* September 7, 1994.

24. Alan Greenspan, interview by the author, November 2, 2015.

25. Andrea Mitchell, interview by the author, July 28, 2014.

26. Maureen Dowd, "On Washington, High Up in the Box," *New York Times,* December 12, 1993.

27. Evan Thomas is quoted in Dowd, ibid.

28. Christopher Meyer, interview by the author, May 23, 2013.

29. Greenspan's idea of the proper model for a House Speaker was also influenced by Gerald Ford, who had conducted himself in that job with unflashy decency.

30. John M. Berry, "After a GOP Revolution That Is Likely to Make Greenspan's Job Tougher," *Washington Post,* January 1, 1995.

31. In the first and second quarter of 1995, annualized growth was 1.4 percent. Thereafter the economy accelerated. Greenspan's mentor Arthur Burns had declared in 1969 that "we need to make necessary shifts of economic policy more promptly, so that they may be gradual rather than abrupt." (See Julio Rotemberg, "Federal Reserve Goals and Tactics for Monetary Policy: A Role for

Penitence?," *Journal of Economic Perspectives* 27, no. 4 [Fall 2013]: 73.) Unlike Greenspan, Burns had failed to live by this prescription.

32. From 1994 until the end of Greenspan's tenure, core PCE inflation never exceeded 2.4 percent.

33. As frequently happened with Greenspan, a genuine achievement somehow came to be regarded as an almost superhuman feat. The soft landing of 1995 was frequently referred to as unprecedented in the postwar era, even though the Fed had slowed the economy while avoiding a recession in 1967 and 1986. For an example of the belief that 1995 was unprecedented, see Edmund L. Andrews, "Economy Often Defies Soft Landing," *New York Times,* August 11, 1996. Andrews writes, "The Fed has achieved only one true soft landing—in 1994–95." However, between late 1961 and late 1966, the Fed steered the effective federal funds rate up from 1.2 percent to 5.8 percent, creating a desired slowdown without a recession. Equally, the Fed guided the effective federal funds rate up from 8.5 percent to 11.6 percent between February 1983 and August 1984. Again, growth slowed, but recession was avoided.

34. Putting the same point differently, Blinder said, "He was much, much savvier than the average uncle." Alan Blinder, interview by the author, January 23, 2012.

35. As Greenspan later put it in his memoir, "The soft landing of 1995 was one of the Fed's proudest accomplishments during my tenure." Alan Greenspan, *The Age of Turbulence: Adventures in a New World* (New York: Penguin Books, 2008), 156.

36. Laurence Meyer, a highly respected economic modeler who served as a Fed governor starting in the summer of 1996, later wrote in his memoir, "I ended my term not sure I had ever influenced the outcome of an FOMC meeting. This was one of the frustrating aspects of serving on the Greenspan FOMC." Laurence H. Meyer, *A Term at the Fed: An Insider's View* (New York: HarperBusiness, 2006), 52.

37. Additionally, President Jerry Jordan of the Cleveland Fed argued in the August 16, 1994, FOMC meeting that, over the previous year, the Fed had been more fortunate than skillful. Growth and jobs had outperformed the Fed's expectations, and monetary policy had in retrospect been looser than the staff would have recommended if its growth and jobs

forecasts had been accurate. Yet this policy looseness had not been punished by inflation. The modern state of low inflation had been achieved partly by luck.

CHAPTER TWENTY-ONE

1. "Market Surveys Data, 1987–2010" (International Swaps and Derivatives Association, Inc., June 30, 2010).

2. Carol J. Loomis, "Untangling the Derivatives Mess," *Fortune,* March 20, 1995, http://fortune.com/2012/11/21/untangling-the-derivatives-mess/.

3. Kelley Holland, Linda Himelstein, and Zachary Schiller, "The Bankers Trust Tapes," *Business-Week,* October 16, 1995, http://www.businessweek.com/1995/42/b34461.htm.

4. Richard Spillenkothen, interview by the author, June 5, 2013. Spillenkothen was the head of supervision at the Federal Reserve Board. Susan M. Phillips, a Fed governor from 1991 to 1998, confirms the point that Greenspan did not overtly push deregulation or lax enforcement on regulatory issues, contrary to the widespread assumption that he pursued a Randian agenda. "We used to say, he has never seen a regulation that he liked," she said, adding that he voted with the majority on the board and did not want to use up chips to push regulatory things. He wanted to keep his chips for monetary arguments that he really cared about. Susan Phillips, interview by the author, June 7, 2013.

5. Carol J. Loomis, "Untangling the Derivatives Mess."

6. The quote comes from PaineWebber Inc. analyst Lawrence Cohn. See "Bankers Trust to Revamp Derivatives," *Los Angeles Times,* December 6, 1994, sec. Business, http://articles.latimes.com/1994-12-06/business/fi-5557_1_bankers-trust.

7. Carol J. Loomis, "Untangling the Derivatives Mess." See also Robert A. Rosenblatt, "Orange County in Bankruptcy," *Los Angeles Times,* December 8, 1994.

8. In a similar hearing in the House in 1994, Charles Bowsher, the head of the government's General Accounting Office, testified of derivatives that "the sudden failure or abrupt withdrawal from trading of any of these large U.S. dealers could cause liquidity problems in the markets and could also pose risks to others, including federally insured banks and the financial system as a whole." In contrast, Greenspan testified at

the same hearing that "risks in financial markets, including derivatives markets, are being regulated by private parties.... There is nothing involved in federal regulation per se which makes it superior to market regulation." Later that year, the House considered derivatives regulation but failed to pass it. See Peter S. Goodman, "The Reckoning: Taking Hard New Look at a Greenspan Legacy," *New York Times,* October 8, 2008, sec. A.

9. Greenspan's lucid take on the challenges of successful financial regulation is evident, for example, in a speech delivered on November 16, 1995. Even though he devoted part of his speech to the shortcomings of value-at-risk models used by Wall Street, dwelling at length on these models' underestimation of the probability of extreme market moves, his bottom line was that flawed private risk management was superior to even more flawed regulation. "The effective acceleration of financial events also complicates the task of central banks.... Capital adequacy can be an elusive concept for portfolios that are turning over rapidly. Measurement of capital may be muddled by ... over-the-counter derivative contracts and structured notes.... With instruments trading that represent highly leveraged exposures, a large chunk of capital can disappear, and then reappear, all within the trading day. Supervisors may have to resort to basing their analyses chiefly on assessments of managerial capabilities rather than on the portfolio held at a given instant." After 2008, it became taboo to assert that regulators would have to put their faith in the risk assessments made by private managers. But Greenspan was correct in pointing out the immense challenges involved in the alternative of second-guessing them. After Greenspan's speech, he received a note from Bob Rubin: "I thought your remarks on risk management, and price behavior, were easy to understand and congruent with my experience as a trader. I have saved it for future discussions on regulation. Bob." Evidently, even if post-2008 commentators are quick to condemn Greenspan for his attitude toward financial regulation, and even though Rubin was more sympathetic to the case for regulating derivatives than Greenspan (see chapter twenty-three), his analysis was taken seriously. Alan Greenspan, remarks (Research Conference on

Risk Measurement and Systemic Risk, Washington, D.C., November 16, 1995), https://fraser.stlou isfed.org/docs/historical/greenspan/Greenspan_19951116.pdf. Robert Rubin to Alan Greenspan, note, (n.d.), personal files of Alan Greenspan.

10. Greenspan repeatedly expressed this hope that financiers would learn from errors. In a speech on June 20, 1995, he assured his audience at the Economic Club of New York that "risk-management systems were exposed to a very real life stress test in 1994, when sharp increases in interest rates created large losses in fixed income markets. As a consequence, firms' models and judgments should be sounder today than those that prevailed in early 1994." Alan Greenspan, remarks (Economic Club of New York, New York, N.Y., June 20, 1995), https://fraser.stlouisfed.org/docs/historical/greenspan/Greenspan_19950620.pdf.

11. In Age of Turbulence, published in 2007, Greenspan stuck to the view that financiers would learn from their errors. "It seems superfluous to constrain trading in some of the newer derivatives and other innovative financial contracts of the past decade. The worst have failed; investors no longer fund them and are not likely to in the future." In a footnote, Greenspan noted the danger of "a chain reaction of defaults." But the caveat was consistently buried beneath the sanguine headline. See Alan Greenspan, The Age of Turbulence: Adventures in a New World (New York: Penguin Books, 2008), Kindle Location 9109.

12. Katharine Q. Seelye, "Republicans Get a Pep Talk from Rush Limbaugh," New York Times, December 12, 1994, Late edition. Limbaugh had nearly twenty million listeners. Fully 44 percent of Americans identified him and his fellow conservative talk-radio hosts as their main source of political information. See Richard Corliss, "Look Who's Talking," Time, January 23, 1995, http://content.time.com/time/subscriber/article/0,33009,982262,00.html.

13. Lawrence Summers recalls that Greenspan was in favor of helping Mexico even at the very beginning of their deliberations—before it became clear which way the Clinton administration would come out. Lawrence Summers, interview by the author, March 7, 2012.

14. Bob Woodward, Maestro: Greenspan's Fed and the American Boom (New York: Simon & Schuster, 2000), 139–140.

15. Edwin M. Truman, interview by the author, January 26, 2012.

16. The conditionality is not reflected in the transcript of the call but was part of the committee's understanding. Edwin M. Truman, e-mail to the author, August 2, 2015.

17. Jeffrey Shafer, who was assistant secretary for international affairs at the Treasury, recalls that Greenspan changed his thinking from a bailout solution to a bailout-plus-policy solution. Jeffrey Shafer, interview by the author, July 16, 2014.

18. Rubin's memoir records that "Larry [Summers] and I shared Alan's view that we should put up a significant amount of money, significantly more than we thought would be needed. In this, we were employing a corollary to Colin Powell's doctrine of military intervention." Robert Rubin and Jacob Weisberg, In an Uncertain World: Tough Choices from Wall Street to Washington (New York: Random House, 2003), 12. Looking back on the crisis, Rubin felt his relationship with Greenspan was cemented by the deliberations of this period. "Despite his opposition to government intervention in markets, Alan weighed the moral hazard against the risk of having Mexico go into default. He was a pragmatist." Ibid., 9.

19. Robert Rubin and Jacob Weisberg, In an Uncertain World, 3.

20. Some sources have this as January 11, but Rubin's own memoir has January 10, the day he was sworn in as Treasury secretary. Rubin's memory is corroborated by Ted Truman of the Fed, a key player in the Mexico policy. Ted Truman, e-mail to the author, August 1, 2015.

21. Woodward, Maestro, 141.

22. Greenspan, Age of Turbulence, 159. See also Lucy Howard and Carla Koehl, "Courting Rush," Newsweek, February 13, 1995; and see Robert Novak, "Fed Boss Can't Budge Rush on Mexico," Chicago Sun-Times, January 29, 1995.

23. Keith Bradsher, "Lately, a Much More Visible Fed Chief," New York Times, January 17, 1995.

24. Robert Rubin and Jacob Weisberg, In an Uncertain World, 22.

25. Woodward reports that Greenspan expressed misgivings about circumventing Congress with the rescue from the Exchange Stabilization Fund. However, Truman recalls specifically and vividly that Greenspan's willingness to take the heat from FOMC conservatives made the ESF plan workable. "Greenspan deserves all the credit,"

according to Truman. See Woodward, Maestro, 143. Truman, e-mail to the author, August 1, 2015.

26. Gene Sperling, a White House economics official, recalls, "When Mexico happened, Clinton saw the point of being on good terms with Greenspan. He helped when we had our backs to the wall." Gene Sperling, interview by the author, May 20, 2014.

27. Greenspan's support for the administration's Mexico rescue cost him some support among conservatives. On February 16, 1995, the supply-sider Jude Wanniski wrote to warn him that "despite what Rubin thinks are the commitments of Dole and Gingrich, the Republicans are building a base from which to lob grenades at Treasury and Clinton when Mexico falls apart." Jude Wanniski to Alan Greenspan, letter, February 16, 1995, Correspondence: Greenspan, Alan 1995–1997, box 14, Jude Wanniski, Hoover Institution Archives. On February 27, Wanniski wrote again: "Please tell me you do not really think the Rubin-Summers plan for Mexico will do good. There has to be a gun at your head on this fiasco.... Some of our mutual friends are saying you should be horsewhipped for endorsing the Rubin plan. There is more than a suggestion that you are willing to endorse all kinds of silliness in order to win renomination next year...." Jude Wanniski to Alan Greenspan, letter, February 27, 1995, Correspondence: Greenspan, Alan 1995–1997, box 14, Jude Wanniski, Hoover Institution Archives.

28. One half-developed idea was that the Fed could induce bondholders to accept losses by putting pressure on the banks that held the bonds in custody, but it is not clear that this was ever legal or practical.

29. In a National Bureau of Economic Research paper published in 2011, Frederic S. Mishkin wrote, "Before the recent financial crisis, the common view, both in academia and in central banks was that achieving price and output stability would promote financial stability. This was supported by research (Bernanke, Gertler, and Gilchrist, 1999; and Bernanke and Gertler, 2001) which indicated that monetary policy which optimally stabilizes inflation and output is likely to stabilize asset prices, making asset-price bubbles less likely. Indeed, central banks' success in stabilizing inflation and the decreased volatility of business cycle fluctuations, which became known as the Great Moderation, made policymakers

complacent about the risks from financial disruptions." It is striking that this hypothesized complacency inside central banks is an inadequate description of Greenspan. See Frederic S. Mishkin, "Monetary Policy Strategy: Lessons from the Crisis," Working Paper (Cambridge, Mass.: National Bureau of Economic Research, February 2011). Ben S. Bernanke, Mark Gertler, and Mark Gilchrist, "The Financial Accelerator in a Quantitative Business Cycle Framework," in *Handbook of Macroeconomics*, vol. 1, 1999, 1341–93. Ben S. Bernanke and Mark Gertler, "Should Central Banks Respond to Movements in Asset Prices?," *American Economic Review* 91, no. 2 (2001): 253–57.

CHAPTER TWENTY-TWO

1. Jaret Seiberg, "$1M Fed Boardroom Makeover Gets Warm Reception," *American Banker,* September 5, 1995.
2. Susan Phillips, interview by the author, June 7, 2013.
3. Alan Blinder's failure to influence monetary decisions was the best but by no means the only example of Greenspan's dominance of the FOMC. Laurence Meyer, a respected forecaster who joined the FOMC in 1996, made equally little impact and found himself being discouraged from staking out independent ground. Meyer's memoir relates, "At one of our FOMC meetings, the Chairman said he thought too much 'chatter' was going on between FOMC meetings. By that he means that the press was attributing too many opinions on the outlook or monetary policy to specific FOMC members or to unnamed sources.... The Chairman preferred Committee members to talk as little as possible about the outlook and monetary policy." Laurence H. Meyer, *A Term at the Fed: An Insider's View* (New York: HarperBusiness, 2006), 130–31.
4. In the year to August 1995, core CPI inflation was 2.9 percent. It had been as low or fractionally lower in 1994. But other than that, core CPI inflation had last been lower in July 1966.
5. Keith Bradsher, "The Art and Science of Alan Greenspan: How to Stay Popular in a Divided Washington, and Keep Inflation in Check," *New York Times,* January 4, 1996.
6. The regulator was Ricki Helfer, chairman of the Federal Deposit Insurance Corporation. Ricki Tigert Helfer, interview by the author, July 4, 2013.

7. "Coming in from the Cold," *Economist,* September 25, 1999.
8. Arthur Levitt, interview by the author, November 19, 2012.
9. Given the opportunity to comment on this passage, Greenspan did not do so directly but said that it was broadly right. (Alan Greenspan, interview by the author, November 2, 2015.) In other interviews, Greenspan was open about the fact that he disliked the prospect of Rohatyn's appointment, and the opportunities for him to express this view privately to senators would have been numerous. To pick one suggestive example from his calendar: on December 16, 1995, Greenspan played tennis with Senators John Warner and Larry Pressler, and lobbyist Lloyd Hand. Likewise, Bob Woodward's politically astute account strongly implies that Greenspan obstructed Rohatyn. See Bob Woodward, *Maestro: Greenspan's Fed and the American Boom* (New York: Simon & Schuster, 2000), 161–62. Meanwhile, a Senate staff member observed to the *Washington Post* that at a minimum, Greenspan might have been able to secure Rohatyn's confirmation if he had announced that he wanted it. See Clay Chandler, "Rohatyn Withdraws Name for No. 2 Spot at the Fed," *Washington Post,* February 13, 1996.
10. Greenspan, interview by the author, June 10, 2011.
11. "There was a certain benevolence about him which suggested to me that his body language was communicating more than what his words were saying," Greenspan later recalled. Ibid.
12. Linton Weeks and John M. Berry, "The Shy Wizard of Money," *Washington Post,* March 24, 1997.
13. Sworn in for his third term as chairman in June 1996, Greenspan took care to thank "the American economy." "It has behaved well these last four years," he acknowledged, modestly. "I do not deny that policy has had something to do with it, but history tells us it truly has a mind of its own. It—the economy, that is—can be most cantankerous, wholly oblivious to the ministrations of monetary policy." But even as he warned that the economy had "not been fine-tuned into perpetual tranquility," ever rosier news burnished his reputation further. See John M. Berry, "Greenspan Hails Economy at Swearing-in Ceremony," *Washington Post,* June 26, 1996.
14. See chapter seventeen.
15. Yellen's stance was ironic given that as vice chairwoman and then

chairwoman many years later, she would help to lead the Fed in its full conversion to inflation targeting.
16. The fact that inflation targeting was adopted on the basis of shaky evidence is perhaps unsurprising—monetarism had been adopted in 1979 on an equally uncertain foundation. In 1978 Volcker himself had written an article in the *Journal of Monetary Economics* arguing that the demand for money was sufficiently unstable that fixing the supply of it would lead to excessive swings in interest rates. See Julio Rotemberg, "Federal Reserve Goals and Tactics for Monetary Policy: A Role for Penitence?," *Journal of Economic Perspectives* 27, no. 4 (Fall 2013): 78.
17. Yellen took issue with research by Martin Feldstein of Harvard, which suggested that the interaction between inflation and the tax system distorted savings behavior and imposed significant costs on the economy. Yellen objected that Feldstein's paper brushed over the reality that retirement savings were mostly not subject to tax, and suggested that Feldstein's calculation of a large economic cost was therefore unpersuasive. "Feldstein's number could be off by an order of magnitude," she said, forcefully.
18. As Greenspan said to the FOMC, "The next item on our agenda—the issue of long-term inflation goals—is something that we have been discussing on and off for a long while, and I think we will continue to do so. It is important that we move forward on this issue and more specifically that we agree on what the goals mean before we can find some consensus within the Committee regarding their implementation."
19. In January 1995, Yellen declared, "[W]hen I look at countries that have adopted and carried through inflation targeting programs, I consider the results discouraging.... I do not think inflation targets would raise credibility for the simple reason that they would not be credible."
20. For Greenspan's arguments to Reagan and his progold allies, see chapters ten and twelve.
21. The example set by foreign inflation targeters did not point unambiguously to a 2 percent target, further underlining the sense that it was adopted somewhat arbitrarily. Of three early adopters analyzed in a 1994 Fed paper, Canada had adopted a 2 percent target in 1991; Britain in 1992 had adopted an immediate 1–4 percent target

coupled with a longer-term objective of 2 percent; and New Zealand, following three years of experimentation with other targets, settled in 1993 on a range of 0–2 percent. See John Ammer and Richard T. Freeman, "Inflation Targeting in the 1990s: The Experiences of New Zealand, Canada, and the United Kingdom," International Finance Discussion Papers (Board of Governors of the Federal Reserve System, June 1994).

22. Scholarly attempts to date the start of the Fed's inflation targeting find that monetary policy was consistent with the existence of an inflation target from 1993. (This literature is summarized in David Beckworth, "Inflation Targeting: A Monetary Policy Regime Whose Time Has Come and Gone" [Mercatus Center, George Washington University, July 10, 2014]. See in particular endnote 22.) However, the transcript of July 1996 makes it clear that this was not a target that the FOMC had consciously embraced before 1996; and indeed the discussion of July 1996 resulted in an agreement to move toward 2 percent inflation, with no clarity as to whether the Fed would then decide to stick at 2 percent or push even lower. Consistent with the reading of the transcript presented here, Marvin Goodfriend, a Richmond Fed economist who attended the 1996 meeting and later published a description of the debate, emphasizes his own sense of disappointment that the discussion resulted in a loose understanding of the Fed's inflation goal rather than a formal commitment to a target. See Marvin Goodfriend, chapter in a 2011 book that resulted from an Atlanta Fed Conference, Marvin Goodfriend, "Policy Debates at the Federal Open Market Committee: 1993–2002," in *The Origins, History, and Future of the Federal Reserve: A Return to Jekyll Island*, ed. Michael D. Bordo and William Roberds (New York: Cambridge University Press, 2013). The looseness of the 1996 understanding is captured in the transcripts by Cathy Minehan, president of the Boston Fed: "I am in complete agreement with the two things on which I think they agreed. That is, we should at a minimum hold the line on inflation where it is and go somewhat further if we can do so." The fuzzy nature of the inflation target, even after 1996, is also evident from Greenspan's willingness to call it into question during later meetings. In February 1997, for example, he suggested that

asset prices should be part of the target. "Product prices alone should not be the sole criterion if we are going to maintain a stable, viable financial system whose fundamental goal, let us remember, is the attainment of maximum sustainable economic growth."

23. Greenspan had met Martin Wolf and Michael Prowse of the *Financial Times* on June 25, 1996.

24. At the FOMC meeting beginning February 4, 1997, Greenspan reiterated his view that a public commitment to an inflation target would be unhelpful. "There is no evidence in my experience that words have had the slightest effect. It has not helped the Bundesbank, and if it has not helped the Bundesbank, how is it going to help anybody? The Bundesbank has succeeded because it has taken effective actions. It is what we do, not what we say, that is going to matter." However, in the same meeting Greenspan also insisted that it was essential to signal rate increases before implementing them. Clearly, Greenspan's real objection was not to communicating; it was to any reduction in his room for discretion.

25. Even more than Gary Stern, Mike Kelley was a constant optimist about businesses' ability to drive productivity increases.

26. In his ninth NBI lecture, delivered in 1964, Greenspan had declared that "standards of living tend to grow at an accelerating rate." The more ideas people generated, the more they were in a position to generate further ideas.

27. The Wall Street seer was Barton Biggs, speaking to John Cassidy of the *New Yorker*. See John Cassidy, "Striking It Rich: The Rise and Fall of Popular Capitalism," *New Yorker*, January 14, 2002.

28. Woodward, *Maestro*, 171. See also Alan Greenspan, *The Age of Turbulence: Adventures in a New World* (New York: Penguin Books, 2008), 172. Slifman notes that Greenspan's view that profits were relatively easy to measure was not shared by staff experts. Larry Slifman, e-mail to the author, October 7, 2015.

29. In his academic writing, Summers had pointed to the limits of market efficiency. See, for example, Andrei Shleifer and Lawrence H. Summers, "The Noise Trader Approach to Finance," *Journal of Economic Perspectives* 4, no. 2 (Spring 1990).

30. Woodward, *Maestro*, 171.

31. Isabelle Clary, "Rate Hike Request Reported: Eight of 12 District Banks Are Said to Have Appealed

to the Fed to Raise the Discount Rate," *Philadelphia Inquirer*, September 18, 1996.

32. The result of this investigation is unclear, though Meyer speculates that the chairman discovered the leaker and "dealt with this person directly and quietly." On the leaks and the ensuing tension, see David Johnston, "F.B.I. to Aid Fed in Inquiry of Sensitive Rate Leak Data," *New York Times*, September 22, 1996. See also Laurence H. Meyer, *A Term at the Fed: An Insider's View*.

33. Minehan mentioned, among others, Rudiger Dornbusch and Paul Samuelson of MIT and Ben Friedman and Martin Feldstein of Harvard.

34. Lawrence Summers, interview by the author, March 7, 2012. Similarly, in their retrospective on the Greenspan years delivered at Jackson Hole in 2005, Alan Blinder and Ricardo Reis singled out Greenspan's forbearance in not raising interest rates for particular praise. Alan S. Blinder and Ricardo Reis, "Understanding the Greenspan Standard," Working Paper (CEPS, September 2005), 26 and 60. Laurence H. Meyer, a productivity skeptic on the FOMC, wrote that Greenspan's "call on the productivity acceleration was truly a great one. . . . He got it right before the rest of us did." See Laurence H. Meyer, *A Term at the Fed: An Insider's View*, 125 and 134.

35. Greenspan reflected in his memoir, "This was a classic example of why you can't just decide monetary policy based on an econometric model." See Greenspan, *Age of Turbulence*, 174.

36. For an exposition of the difference between demand shocks and supply shocks, see Ben Bernanke, "The Great Moderation" (remarks, Meetings of the Eastern Economic Association, Washington, D.C., February 20, 2004); and Daniel L. Thornton, "The Evolution of Inflation Targeting: How Did We Get to Inflation Targeting and Where Do We Need to Go Now?," Paper prepared for the 6th Norges Bank Monetary Policy Conference (Federal Reserve Bank of St. Louis, June 11, 2009). Economists had recognized this distinction before in the context of a negative supply shock such as the oil price jumps in the 1970s. But the experience of a productivity-based positive supply shock was novel.

37. In addition to the demand shock/supply shock distinction, some observers have argued that a productivity acceleration combined with an inflation target is likely to

cause the central bank to cut rates just when the equilibrium or "natural" interest rate is rising. As productivity gains raise the expected return on capital, firms will invest more. Unless savings rise commensurately, this extra demand for capital means that interest rates should, all else equal, go up. However, since productivity gains also create deflationary pressure, and since that deflationary pressure is easier to see than the rise in the natural interest rate, an inflation-targeting central bank will tend to cut interest rates. Monetary authorities, therefore, will tend to push interest rates below the stable, market-clearing level. The result will be too much leverage and soaring asset prices: in short, a bubble. This argument was made by Richmond Fed president Al Broaddus during the May 1997 FOMC meeting. For a more recent version, see David Beckworth, "Inflation Targeting."

38. The debate over the costs and merits of inflation targeting continues until the time of writing, but there is evidence that central banks should target the stability of growth and asset prices rather than the stability of inflation when confronted by a supply shock. See for example Gertjan W. Vlieghe, "Imperfect Credit Markets: Implications for Monetary Policy," Working Paper (Bank of England, March 2010). A different line of research has emphasized that, rather than focusing exclusively on inflation, central banks should lean against bubbles by tightening in response to above-trend credit growth, particularly above-trend mortgage credit growth. See Òscar Jordà, Moritz Schularick, and Alan M. Taylor, "The Great Mortgaging: Housing Finance, Crises, and Business Cycles," Working Paper, NBER Working Paper Series (National Bureau of Economic Research, September 2014).

39. John Carmody, "Brinkley's Parting Shots at Clinton," *Washington Post,* November 10, 1996.

40. W. Speers, "Sports of All Sorts," *Philadelphia Inquirer,* November 7, 1996. For color on the race, see Jere Longman, "New York City Marathon: It's Viva Italia! (and Viva Romania! as Well)," *New York Times,* November 4, 1996.

41. Exit polls found that more than 6 in 10 said the economy was in good shape, and Mr. Clinton got most of their votes. R. W. Apple Jr., "The 1996 Election: The Presidency—News Analysis: The Economy Helps Again," *New York Times,* November 6, 1996.

42. In the week of the election, the S&P 500 index rose by almost 4 percent.

43. I am grateful to David Shulman for providing me with a copy of Prell's memo of November 18, 1996, as well as his own presentation at the December 3 meeting.

44. David Wessel to Sebastian Mallaby, June 15, 2015.

45. Abby Cohen, interview by the author, September 12, 2011; John Cassidy, *Dot.con: The Greatest Story Ever Sold* (New York: HarperCollins, 2003), 120–22.

46. I am grateful to Abby Joseph Cohen for providing me with copies of her Goldman Sachs reports on the equity markets from late November and early December 1996.

47. Cohen, interview by the author, September 12, 2011. During the February 1997 FOMC meeting, Greenspan would mock Cohen's model. "I grant Abby Cohen her little relationship, and I wish her well. I hope she spends her bonus, which I gather is very substantial this year, prudently."

48. Ibid. Cohen's estimate of the market's value was based on multiple inputs, one of which was interest rates. If tighter Fed policy had raised both short- and longer-term interest rates, her model would have shown a lower estimate for the stock market's fair value. If the Fed had coupled higher rates with explicit communications indicating that it was targeting equities, Cohen believes that the market might have come down substantially.

49. Shulman also suggested that political cycles signaled danger up ahead. The bull markets of 1968 and 1972 had coincided with elections, and had been followed by falls of 18 percent and 23 percent in 1969 and 1973; perhaps the election year rally of 1996 would be followed by a similar reversal?

50. Abby Cohen, interview by the author, September 12, 2011.

51. John Cassidy, "All Together Now: New Theories on Why We Can't Stay Out of the Stock Market," *New Yorker,* March 27, 2000.

52. Quoted in John Cassidy, "Striking It Rich: The Rise and Fall of Popular Capitalism."

53. John Makin, interview by the author, October 30, 2014. Makin held a position at AEI and was also on the staff of the hedge fund Caxton Associates.

54. "It took me a long time to live that down." Byron Wien, interview by the author, September 9, 2011.

55. John Cassidy, "Striking It Rich: The Rise and Fall of Popular Capitalism."

56. Don Kohn confirms that the "irrational exuberance" phrase was intended to attract notice. "The paragraph on irrational exuberance was debated a lot internally. He wrote it himself, although I wrote some of the rest of that speech." Donald L. Kohn, interview by the author, March 13, 2011.

57. The commentator was Christopher Quick of Quick & Reilly Group. See Floyd Norris, "Greenspan Asks a Question and Global Markets Wobble," *New York Times,* December 7, 1996.

58. Greenspan himself shared the conclusion that the irrational exuberance speech had demonstrated the limits to his own influence. "What was very obvious is that there was no such thing as a verbal intervention in the market. So the question essentially is this, you're sitting with a problem that successful product price inflation engenders asset price inflation. How do you solve that problem? And there is no simple solution to that." Greenspan, interview by the author, September 6, 2011.

59. The message from the visiting Wall Street strategists on December 3 had been precisely that stock prices were supported by low interest rates; if rates went up, equities would adjust downward.

60. In retirement, Greenspan implied that the Fed had made a serious effort to curb the stock market. "I had raised the specter of 'irrational exuberance' over a decade before, only to watch the dot-com boom, after a one-day stumble, continue to inflate for 4 more years, unrestrained by a cumulative increase of 350 basis points in the federal funds rate from 1994 to 2000." (Alan Greenspan, "The Crisis," Brookings Papers on Economic Activity [Washington, D.C.: Brookings Institution, Spring 2010], 208.) But the truth was that in the twenty-one months following the irrational exuberance speech, the Fed raised its rate only once, by 25 basis points; and after that it began cutting. Most of the tightening that Greenspan invoked had come more than two years *before* his speech, in 1994—and had disproved his thesis by triggering a sharp bond-market correction. Barring that one hike in March 1997, the rest of the tightening had come in late 1999 and early 2000—and had again disproved his thesis by triggering the Nasdaq correction.

61. Laurence Meyer, who became a Fed governor in 1996, is among those who stress the courage that

would have been involved in a firm determination to deflate bubbles. "The Fed might find itself in the 'wealth destruction' business. It would be as if the Chairman were telling the American people: 'Sure I just took a trillion dollars out of your portfolios, but believe me, you will come to appreciate the wisdom of my action.'" Laurence H. Meyer, *A Term at the Fed: An Insider's View,* 144.

62. Andrea Mitchell, *Talking Back: . . . to Presidents, Dictators, and Assorted Scoundrels* (New York: Penguin Group, 2006), 444.

63. The friend was Ricki Helfer. Helfer, interview by the author, June 24, 2013.

CHAPTER TWENTY-THREE

1. Roxanne Roberts, "The Groom's Lips Were Sealed: Greenspan Weds Mitchell with a Kiss to Remember," *Washington Post,* April 7, 1997.

2. Andrea Mitchell, *Talking Back: . . . to Presidents, Dictators, and Assorted Scoundrels* (New York: Penguin Group, 2006), 240.

3. Roxanne Roberts, "The Groom's Lips Were Sealed."

4. Alan Greenspan, interview by the author, January 10, 2013.

5. "He had learned something which meant there was an opening up on his part with Andrea that I don't think he had ever visualized." Kathryn Eickhoff, interview by the author, November 29, 2011.

6. Andrea Mitchell, *Talking Back,* 241.

7. Alan Greenspan, *The Age of Turbulence: Adventures in a New World* (New York: Penguin Books, 2008), 181.

8. David Wessel, "Just Call It Irrational Exuberance: Cartoonists Warm to Fed's Chief," *Wall Street Journal,* December 31, 1998.

9. Result based on a Nexis search of American newspapers and wires between January 1 and August 1, 1997, excluding duplicate articles.

10. Sebastian Mallaby, *More Money Than God: Hedge Funds and the Making of a New Elite* (New York: Penguin Group, 2010), Kindle location 3698.

11. The lack of worry about Thailand was such that the FOMC meeting on July 1–2, 1997, held just as the baht was collapsing, barely touched on the subject. The August and September 1997 FOMC meetings also skipped over the Asia crisis quickly. The Fed was more concerned with the dollar/yen exchange rate than with the collapse of Southeast Asia's economies.

12. Greenspan's only contribution to the crisis debates in Hong Kong

was to support the Treasury in thwarting the Japanese, who wanted to set up a new regional rival to the IMF, to be known as the Asian Monetary Fund. Greenspan signed a letter supporting the Treasury's pro-IMF position.

13. Andrea Mitchell, interview by the author, July 28, 2014.

14. As of September 30, 1997, U.S. banks' exposure to South Korea came to $23 billion, considerably more than Thailand or Indonesia, which came to $10 billion and $9 billion, respectively. For the big "money center" banks, Korea exposure probably amounted to about a quarter of Tier I capital, implying that they could have absorbed the hit of a default but that it would have been painful. See David E. Palmer, "U.S. Bank Exposure to Emerging-Market Countries During Recent Financial Crises," *Federal Reserve Bulletin,* February 2000, http://www.federalreserve.gov/pubs/bulletin/2000/0200lead.pdf. The estimate for exposure relative to Tier I capital is derived from Tables 2, 8, and 9.

15. Ted Truman, e-mail to the author, August 26, 2015.

16. Charles Siegman, e-mail to the author, August 28, 2015.

17. This meeting is reported in Greenspan, *Age of Turbulence,* 189, which reports that the conversation took place over Thanksgiving weekend. However, other sources, including Greenspan's official diary, Siegman's recollection, and Blustein's *The Chastening,* make it seem overwhelmingly likely that the interchange took place the day before Thanksgiving. Paul Blustein, *The Chastening: Inside the Crisis That Rocked the Global Financial System and Humbled the IMF* (New York: PublicAffairs, 2001).

18. Robert Rubin and Jacob Weisberg, *In an Uncertain World: Tough Choices from Wall Street to Washington* (New York: Random House, 2003), 228. See also Blustein, *The Chastening,* 136–37.

19. As noted above (endnote 14), U.S. money center banks had exposure to South Korea equivalent to about a quarter of Tier I capital. However, exposure of U.S. money center banks to "troubled Asia" (Thailand, Indonesia, South Korea, Malaysia, and the Philippines) came to slightly more than 60 percent of Tier I capital. (This ratio is estimated using data from Tables 2, 8, and 9 in David E. Palmer, "U.S. Bank Exposure to Emerging-Market Countries During Recent Financial Crises.") Moreover, default in Asia threatened knock-on effects for emerging

economies elsewhere, which might in turn feed back into additional losses for the U.S. banking system. Total international exposure to South Korea alone as of mid-1997 was $114 billion, almost double total international exposure of $63 billion to Mexico three years earlier, according to BIS figures. This would suggest that South Korea in particular and East Asia in general posed a larger threat of contagion than Mexico had done.

20. Looking back, Greenspan said, "Whatever Rubin decided to do, I was on board." Alan Greenspan, interview by the author, December 22, 2010.

21. Bob Woodward, *Maestro: Greenspan's Fed and the American Boom* (New York: Simon & Schuster, 2000), 190–91.

22. Truman recalls, "Greenspan said I am not getting involved in this. 'You, Rubin, must call the bank CEOs and bail them in.'" Edwin M. Truman, interview by the author, June 20, 2013.

23. The banks were Bank of America, Bankers Trust, Bank of New York, Chase Manhattan, Citibank, and J.P. Morgan.

24. William J. McDonough, interview by the author, January 14, 2013.

25. Jill Dutt and John M. Berry, "In Rescue, Banks See Least Pain: Action Called 'Calming Force,'" *Washington Post,* December 25, 1997.

26. Truman, e-mail to the author, August 1, 2015.

27. David Wessel and Stephen E. Frank, "Korean Loan Deal Looks Favorable for Seoul: International Banks Face Possibility for Big Losses on Items Outside Pact," *Wall Street Journal,* January 30, 1998.

28. Ibid.

29. Gordon Matthews, "Market Value Growth of Top 100 in Orbit for 3rd Consecutive Year," *American Banker,* January 12, 1998.

30. Sanford Weill, interview by the author, May 20, 2015.

31. On a strict definition, Weill's desired legislative change did not usher in "universal banking." Fed officials drew a distinction between "universal banking," involving nonbank activities located in bank subsidiaries, and "financial conglomeration," involving affiliations between banks and nonbanks in a single holding company.

32. Jordan went on to say, "I thought that your remarks, Mr. Chairman, developed a persuasive case for acting now. . . . A ¼ percentage point increase in the federal funds rate now would deliver a very important message." He was the lone dissenter

against Greenspan's decision to hold interest rates steady.

33. Peter Pae, "Bank, Insurance Giants Set Merger: Citicorp, Travelers in $82 Billion Deal," *Washington Post,* April 7, 1998.

34. "Travelers-Citicorp Deal Faces Regulatory Hurdles," BestWire, April 6, 1998.

35. Timothy L. O'Brien and Joseph B. Treaster, "Shaping a Colossus: The Overview; in Largest Deal Ever, Citicorp Plans Merger with Travelers Group," *New York Times,* April 7, 1998.

36. Jill Dutt and John M. Berry, "Citicorp-Travelers Deal to Test Regulatory View; Laws Ban Bank-Insurance Mixture," *Washington Post,* April 7, 1998. See also Leslie Wayne, "Deal Jump-Starts a Stalled Banking Bill," *New York Times,* April 8, 1998.

37. Randy Jones, illustration, *New York Times,* April 7, 1998, D1.

38. "A Monster Merger," *New York Times,* April 8, 1998.

39. Peter Pae, "Deal Would Create Nationwide Bank; BankAmerica, NationsBank to Merge," *Washington Post,* April 14, 1998.

40. Sharon Walsh, "What's the Deal? NationsBank Merger Continues Trend of Power Sharing at Top," *Washington Post,* April 14, 1998. See also Jerry Knight, "Banks Now Shift Focus to Global Markets; Creation of Nationwide Firms Through Deals Sets Stage for Worldwide Strategies," *Washington Post,* April 14, 1998.

41. "America Bubbles Over," *Economist,* April 18, 1998.

42. Woodward, *Maestro,* 195. Greenspan repeated this line almost verbatim in testimony before the Joint Economic Committee of Congress on June 10, 1998.

CHAPTER TWENTY-FOUR

1. The CNBC "Briefcase Indicator" was launched at the end of 1997 and gained notice over the course of the following year.

2. Justin Martin, *Greenspan: The Man Behind Money* (Cambridge, Mass.: Perseus Books, 2001), 223.

3. Alan Greenspan, *The Age of Turbulence: Adventures in a New World* (New York: Penguin Books, 2008), Kindle location 3558.

4. Justin Martin, *Greenspan: The Man Behind Money,* 221.

5. Ibid., 223.

6. On at least one occasion, Greenspan asked an aide to track Wall Street's reactions as he testified before Congress. If he said something inadvertently that caused investors to take fright, he wanted a heads-up; that way, he could drive the markets up

again before his testimony was over. Ibid., 222.

7. According to the ISDA market surveys, the notional value of outstanding currency and interest-rate swaps rose from $11.3 trillion in H2 1994 to $37 trillion in H1 1998. "Market Surveys Data, 1987–2010" (International Swaps and Derivatives Association, Inc., June 30, 2010).

8. Robert Rubin and Jacob Weisberg, *In an Uncertain World: Tough Choices from Wall Street to Washington* (New York: Random House, 2003), 287–88.

9. It is sometimes pointed out that Born's concerns related mainly to interest-rate swaps, not to the credit-default swaps that proved dangerous when the insurer AIG failed in 2008. But if Born's instincts on central clearing and margin requirements had been adopted for interest-rate swaps, the same principles would presumably have been applied to credit-default swaps as that market developed in the next decade. Further, it is true that Born did not present a fully fleshed-out proposal; rather, the CFTC issued a "concept release," consisting of a laundry list of discussion points, and Timothy Geithner, then at the Treasury, recalls her ideas as "mostly impenetrable." But the implication of the release was that the over-the-counter market would benefit from safer foundations. When the OTC derivatives market was regulated after 2008, the CFTC based its actions on Born's earlier position. See Timothy F. Geithner, *Stress Test: Reflections on Financial Crises* (New York: Crown Publishers, 2014), 87.

10. Phillips recalls of Born, "Her lack of success was not because she was a woman, but it was the way she went about things. She alienated people, including me." Susan Phillips, interview by the author, June 7, 2013. In addition, at least one senior woman at the CFTC shared Phillips's view that Born was abrasive.

11. Patrick Parkinson, interview by the author, June 18, 2013. Parkinson, e-mail to the author, October 7, 2015.

12. Arthur Levitt, interview by the author, November 19, 2012. Greenspan's official diary confirms that he played golf with Levitt on April 5, 1998. Alan Greenspan's Diary, n.d.

13. A senior Fed official recalls that Levitt was strongly motivated by the SEC's turf concerns.

14. Alan Greenspan's Diary; Arthur Levitt, interview by the author, November 19, 2012.

15. Bethany McLean and Joe Nocera, *All the Devils Are Here: The Hidden History of the Financial Crisis* (New York: Penguin Group, 2010), 104.

16. Michael Hirsh, *Capital Offense: How Washington's Wise Men Turned America's Future over to Wall Street* (Hoboken, NJ: Wiley, 2010), 13.

17. Looking back, Greenspan raised the possibility that concentrating risk in derivatives clearinghouses might backfire, an argument that was credibly revived by some experts after the 2008 crisis. (See, for example, Credit Default Swaps, Clearing Houses, and Exchanges, Squam Lake Working Group on Financial Regulation, July 2009.) However, while clearinghouses are not without risk, they are on balance less threatening to systemic stability than opaque webs of over-the-counter transactions, a point that Greenspan does not contest with any vigor. Alan Greenspan, interview by the author, November 2, 2015.

18. Reflecting on the fact that Born had the advantage of a Treasury secretary who shared her skepticism about derivatives, Pat Parkinson recalls, "She snatched defeat from the jaws of victory." Parkinson, interview by the author, June 5, 2013. However, in addition to the certainty of congressional resistance, it should be noted that swaps were not regulated in other countries at the time, either. Even if Born had played her cards better, the obstacles to reform were considerable.

19. Sebastian Mallaby, *More Money Than God: Hedge Funds and the Making of a New Elite* (New York: Penguin Group, 2010), 233–34.

20. It should be recalled that early in his tenure, Greenspan had shown his grit by driving down inflation from a high of 6 percent and standing up to the Bush administration. But Greenspan's first phase in office was different from the second.

21. Bob Rubin's memoir recalls this communiqué as crucial and emphasizes Greenspan's role in persuading foreign leaders to support it. See Robert Rubin and Jacob Weisberg, *In an Uncertain World,* 283. See also Greenspan, *Age of Turbulence,* 193.

22. The date is given in *When Genius Failed,* by Roger Lowenstein. Woodward's *Maestro* gives the day before, but this would imply an implausibly long lag between the call and the Fed official's visit to LTCM's office. Roger Lowenstein, *When Genius Failed: The Rise and*

Fall of Long-Term Capital Management (New York: Random House, 2000), 183. Bob Woodward, *Maestro: Greenspan's Fed and the American Boom* (New York: Simon & Schuster, 2000), 200.

23. LTCM had leverage of twenty-five to one, but counting in the additional leverage embedded in its derivatives, the ratio was ten times higher. See Mallaby, *More Money Than God,* 388.

24. "When he called to say he'd decided to intervene, I wasn't happy with the idea, but I couldn't disagree." See Greenspan, *Age of Turbulence,* 194.

25. Greenspan's attendance is recorded in his official diary. The performance is described in Pamela Sommers, "A Surreally Big Show," *Washington Post,* September 23, 1998.

26. Bill Clinton, speech before the Council on Foreign Relations, September 14, 1998.

27. Woodward, *Maestro,* 203.

28. "Federal Reserve Press Release: Order Approving Formation of a Bank Holding Company and Notice to Engage in Nonbanking Activities," September 23, 1998, 17, http://www.federalreserve .gov/boarddocs/press/bhc/1998 /19980923/19980923.pdf.

29. The guru was Robert V. DiClemente, cohead of U.S. economic research for Salomon Smith Barney in New York. See Peter G. Gosselin, "Greenspan Hints at Cut; Market Leaps; Fed Chief Says World Woes May Halt U.S. Boom," *Boston Globe,* September 24, 1998.

30. Lowenstein, *When Genius Failed,* 207–8.

31. The question was posed by Representative Maurice Hinchey, a Democrat from upstate New York. See transcript of hearing on LTCM. House Committee on Banking and Financial Services, *Systemic Risks to the Global Economy and Banking System from Hedge Fund Operations: Hearing Before the Committee on Banking and Financial Services,* 105th Cong., 2nd sess., 1998.

32. Ibid.

33. Two administration officials recall pushing for consideration of derivatives reform that would not have involved more power for the CFTC. Greenspan was an implacable opponent. Greenspan's continued opposition to derivatives regulation is evident from "Over the Counter Derivatives Markets and the Commodity Exchange Act," a report of the President's Working Group on Financial Markets, published in November 1999. Endnote 40 of this report states Greenspan's objections to the majority view among his fellow regulators, which favored limited derivatives regulation. President's Working Group on Financial Markets, "Over-the-Counter Derivatives Markets and the Commodity Exchange Act" (President's Working Group on Financial Markets, November 9, 1999), http://www .treasury.gov/resource-center/fin -mkts/Documents/otcact.pdf.

34. Spreads between private borrowing rates and government bond yields had grown, but this was more because of falling government bond rates than because of rising private borrowing rates. "We have these widening spreads, but the question is what kind of impact they are having on the real economy," Tom Hoenig of Kansas City correctly noted.

35. The fund manager was James O'Shaughnessy. See Kenneth Klee and Rich Thomas, "The Party Rolls On," *Newsweek,* December 28, 1998.

36. The economist was William Dudley. See John M. Berry, "Greenspan Orders Interest Rate Cut," *Washington Post,* October 16, 1998.

37. David Shulman, interview by the author, August 5, 2011.

38. Indeed, conceding that the market was buoyant, Greenspan told the FOMC, "Concerns about an asset bubble are not without validity."

39. Louis Uchitelle, "Economists Reject Notion of Stock Market 'Bubble,'" *New York Times,* January 6, 1999.

40. Robert B. Reich, "Trial Ties Up Senate? Don't Worry, Congress Is Irrelevant," *USA Today,* January 7, 1999.

CHAPTER TWENTY-FIVE

1. The seer was Nicholas Negroponte, head of the MIT Media Lab. See John Cassidy, *Dot.con: The Greatest Story Ever Sold* (New York: HarperCollins, 2003), 27.

2. The guru was Michael Hauben. Ibid., 40.

3. Peter Grant and Bill Egbert, "Dow's Batting 10,000: Market's Record Close Signals a New Bull Run," *Daily News,* March 30, 1999.

4. Cassidy, *Dot.con,* 3.

5. On February 17, 2000, Greenspan's Humphrey-Hawkins testimony contained a note saying that the Fed was switching from using consumer price inflation in its report to Congress to the alternative Personal Consumption Expenditure index. But as of 1999, core CPI remained the official measure. "Monetary Policy Report to Congress," Humphrey-Hawkins Report (Federal Reserve Board, February 17, 2000), http://www .federalreserve.gov/boarddocs /hh/2000/february/ReportSec tion1.htm.

6. It should be noted that the Bernanke-Gertler prescription was difficult to implement. The "inflationary or deflationary pressures generated by asset price movements" were hard to anticipate. Indeed, Greenspan had stressed this challenge in his Jackson Hole speech. The Fed had a sketchy grasp of the "wealth effect" that asset prices exerted on economic growth, he explained; more research was needed on how different types of asset price movements affected the behaviors of businesses and investors. He cited three "open questions of particular importance": whether investors responded differently to realized than unrealized gains; how home-equity extraction influenced consumer demand; and what effect speculation-driven movements in stock prices had on business investment spending. Greenspan, "New Challenges for Monetary Policy." Moreover, sharp asset price movements could strongly affect the behavior of the credit channel—as became evident during the 2008 crisis, when wealth effects were dwarfed by the freeze in financial markets.

7. As noted in chapter twenty-two, Bernanke considered the distinction between demand shocks and supply shocks in 2004. See Ben S. Bernanke, "The Great Moderation" (Remarks, Eastern Economic Association, Washington, D.C., February 20, 2004), http:// www.federalreserve.gov/board docs/speeches/2004/20040220 /default.htm.

8. As discussed in chapter twenty-two, a productivity revolution may well lead to higher demand for capital and lower savings, implying a higher natural rate of interest. A central bank that targets inflation will tend to cut interest rates as the productivity shock holds down prices. In some scenarios, therefore, the policy rate will be cut just when the natural rate rises, fueling a bubble. To state the risk in a more general way, inflation is not a reliable signal of when a central bank should tighten, which is why many observers propose the alternative policy of nominal GDP targeting—meaning the targeting of a combination of the growth and the inflation rate.

9. In the years immediately following the Bernanke-Gertler presentation at Jackson Hole, a substantial literature questioned its conclusions. For example, Cecchetti et al. (2000) argue in favor of using interest rates to "lean against the wind" when there is evidence of an asset bubble. (See Stephen G. Cecchetti et al., "Asset Prices and Central Bank Policy," The Geneva Report on the World Economy No. 2 [International Center for Monetary Banking Studies, May 30, 2000].) Anticipating the objection that bubbles are hard to identify, the authors point out that it is also difficult to judge the output gap, which many central banks attempt to infer as part of a standard inflation-targeting policy. Similarly, Bordo and Jeanne (2002) argue that central banks should be open to using interest rates to prick bubbles: "The linkages between asset prices, financial stability, and monetary policy are complex.... The complexity of these linkages does not imply, however, that they can be safely ignored." (See Michael D. Bordo and Olivier Jeanne, "Monetary Policy and Asset Prices: Does 'Benign Neglect' Make Sense?," IMF Working Paper, [December 2002], http://www.imf.org/external/pubs/ft/wp/2002/wp02225.pdf.) Most forthrightly, White (2006) declares that "history also teaches that the stability of consumer prices might not be sufficient to ensure macroeconomic stability. Past experience is replete with examples of major economic and financial crises that were not preceded by inflationary pressures." (See William R. White, "Is Price Stability Enough?," BIS Working Paper [Bank of International Settlements, April 2006], http://www.bis.org/publ/work205.pdf.) After the 2008 crisis, a new wave of research added financial "frictions" (such as the possibility of market freezes and cascading bankruptcies) to Keynesian models; this additional sophistication led to research findings that supported the view that central banks should adopt financial stability as a target. (For a summary of this literature, see Tamim Bayoumi et al., "Monetary Policy in the New Normal," IMF Discussion Note [International Monetary Fund, April 2014], https://www.imf.org/external/pubs/ft/sdn/2014/sdn1403.pdf.) Adopting a more historical approach, Oscar Jorda, Moritz Schularick, and Alan Taylor examine data from seventeen countries extending back to 1870: they find that bubbles, especially those associated with high leverage, merit prophylactic central-bank action. (See in particular, "Leveraged Bubbles," September 2015.) Even skeptics of the view that interest rates should be used to resist bubbles became willing to concede that financial stability required active regulatory attention—and that if this attention failed, there would be no choice but to address bubbles with monetary policy. This position was embraced by most senior central bankers. See, for example, speeches by Ben Bernanke and Janet Yellen: Bernanke, "The Effects of the Great Recession on Central Bank Doctrine and Practice"; and Janet Yellen, "Monetary Policy and Financial Stability" (2014 Michel Camdessus Central Banking Lecture, International Monetary Fund, Washington, D.C., July 2, 2014), http://www.federalreserve.gov/newsevents/speech/yellen20140702a.htm.

10. Greenspan seemed to take Mussa's comment as an implicit criticism and devoted his one intervention—and, coincidentally, the last audience question of the session—to challenging Mussa's premise. "I just wanted to make a very simple point that should be obvious but that I suspect is not," Greenspan began a bit testily, "that there is a form of asymmetry in response to asset rises and asset declines, but not if the rate of change is similar." Asset prices tend to rise gradually and fall sharply, he was saying, so the Fed's response to falls was naturally more dramatic. "New Challenges for Monetary Policy, General Discussion: Monetary Policy and Asset Price Volatility" (symposium sponsored by the Federal Reserve Bank of Kansas City, Jackson Hole, Wyo., August 26, 1999), http://www.kc.frb.org/publicat/sympos/1999/S99disc2.pdf.

11. Mark Gertler, interview by the author, January 7, 2015. See also John Cassidy, "Anatomy of a Meltdown: Ben Bernanke and the Financial Crisis," New Yorker, December 1, 2008, http://www.newyorker.com/magazine/2008/12/01/anatomy-of-a-meltdown.

12. Josh Sens, "Childhood Dreams, Adult Ambitions: Hyatt Heir John Pritzker's Vision of Turning Carmel Valley Ranch into an Always-Open, Everyone-Welcome Version of Summer Camp," Monterey County Weekly, December 16, 2010, http://www.montereycountyweekly.com/news/cover/hyatt-heir-john-pritzker-s-vision-of-turning-carmel-valley/article_ebfe3453-8c14-5fd2-bac9-4cf7499e21e7.html.

13. Bob Woodward, Maestro: Greenspan's Fed and the American Boom (New York: Simon & Schuster, 2000), 219.

14. David E. Sanger, "Rubin Is Kidnapped, but, Hey, Who Cares?," New York Times, July 3, 1999, http://www.nytimes.com/1999/07/03/business/rubin-is-kidnapped-but-hey-who-cares.html.

15. Woodward, Maestro, 219.

16. Greenspan's preoccupation with improved bank disclosures led in April 2000 to the formation of the Working Group on Public Disclosure. However, Greenspan's public statements on banking risks became if anything more complacent. In July 2000, Greenspan testified to the House that "there are no institutions in this country which we perceive as too big to fail"; and further that "the general growth in large institutions has occurred in the context of an underlying structure of markets in which many of the larger risks are dramatically—I should say, fully—hedged." House Committee on Banking and Financial Services, Statement of Alan Greenspan, Chairman, Board of Governors of the Federal Reserve System, Before the Committee on Banking and Financial Services, 106th Cong., 2nd sess., 2000. After 2008, Greenspan admitted his error. Citing his own warnings about megabanks in 1999, he confessed, "Regrettably, we did little to address the problem." Alan Greenspan, "The Crisis," Brookings Papers on Economic Activity (Washington, D.C.: Brookings Institution, Spring 2010), 231.

17. Catherine Reagor, "Greenspan Addresses Bankers' Group in Phoenix," Arizona Republic, October 12, 1999, 1E.

18. Monica Langley, Tearing Down the Walls: How Sandy Weill Fought His Way to the Top of the Financial World . . . and Then Nearly Lost It All (New York: Simon & Schuster, 2003), 341.

19. "Killing Glass-Steagall," Economist, October 30, 1999, http://www.economist.com/node/253588.

20. Katrina Brooker, "Citi's Creator, Alone with His Regrets," New York Times, January 3, 2010.

21. Monica Langley, Tearing Down the Walls, 344.

22. Ibid.

23. Ibid., 341. See also "Three's Company," *Economist*, October 30, 1999. Many observers also suggested that Rubin's move to Citi raised questions about the cozy nexus between government and finance. However, Treasury Secretary Rubin had been a principal obstacle to passage of the banking reform that ratified Citi's structure.

24. John Waggoner, "Fear Sting of Y2K? Try Corporate Bond Funds," *USA Today*, July 30, 1999.

25. At the FOMC meeting in August, Greenspan argued that the staff had underestimated the effects of Y2K.

26. "If we're completely successful in the message we give, we may never have a single one of these options exercised. That would be victory," Vice Chairman McDonough said at the August 24 FOMC meeting. "Not exercised and not even purchased," Greenspan replied.

27. The Fed continued auctioning off Y2K financing options each week until December 1, when the dwindling number of participants signaled that demand had been satisfied. By the time the auctions ended, participating banks had bought options on $489 billion in backup funding. See Evangeline Sophia Drossos and Spence Hilton, "The Federal Reserve's Contingency Financing Plan for the Century Date Change," *Current Issues in Economic and Finance* 6, no. 15 (December 2000), https://www.newyorkfed.org/medialibrary/media/research/current_issues/ci6-15.pdf.

28. Jonathan Fuerbringer, "Year 2000 Insurance Is Hot on Wall St., but Not a Sign of Fear," *New York Times*, November 13, 1999.

29. Ibid.

30. The Fed's Y2K options were designed to avoid a backdoor loosening. The interest rate for borrowing from this facility was set at 150 bps over the fed funds rate, so as to provide insurance against a funding drought without lowering borrowing costs. However, the effect of the policy was nonetheless to ease credit conditions in November, when the spread between rates on December and January monthly LIBOR futures contracts roughly halved. (See chart 1 in Evangeline Sophia Drossos and Spence Hilton, "The Federal Reserve's Contingency Financing Plan for the Century Date Change.") To counteract that easing while leaving the Y2K insurance in place, the Fed could have tightened the funds rate more aggressively.

31. Eddie Baeb, "For Rich Shoppers, the Price Is Right," *Crain's Chicago Business*, December 6, 1999, http://www.chicagobusiness.com/article/19991204/ISSUE01/100013196/for-rich-shoppers-the-price-is-right.

32. Sebastian Mallaby, ". . . East and West," *Washington Post*, April 2, 2000, Op-Ed, B7.

33. Ron Hutcheson, "A Campaign Issue? Candidates' Opinions About the Fed Chairman Vary Widely," *Philadelphia Inquirer*, December 25, 1999, D edition, sec. Business, LexisNexis. John M. Berry, "Rising Campaign Rhetoric over a Reappointment," *Washington Post*, December 21, 1999, Final edition, sec. E, LexisNexis.

34. Hutcheson, "A Campaign Issue? Candidates' Opinions About the Fed Chairman Vary Widely."

35. Fox News, "Republican Presidential Candidates Debate," C-SPAN Video Library, December 2, 1999, http://c-spanvideo.org/clip/4469789.

36. The governor was Roger Ferguson.

37. Woodward, *Maestro*, 220.

38. Roxanne Roberts, "The Clintons Host a Historic Fete," *Washington Post*, January 1, 2000.

39. Alan Greenspan, *The Age of Turbulence: Adventures in a New World* (New York: Penguin Books, 2008), Kindle locations 3665–70.

40. Ibid., Kindle locations 3670–3684.

41. Richard W. Stevenson, "Greenspan Named to Fourth Term as Fed Chairman," *New York Times*, January 5, 2000.

42. The high reached 70 degrees that day, well above the 40-degree temperatures that are typical for Washington at that time of year. "Climate Data Online: Station Data Inventory" (National Oceanic and Atmospheric Administration, n.d.), http://www.ncdc.noaa.gov/cdo-web/datasets/GHCND/stations/GHCND:USC00186350/detail.

43. *CNN in the Money*, January 4, 2000.

44. The description of this scene is based on C-SPAN's video archive. See *Federal Reserve Chairman Re-Nomination* (White House, Washington, D.C., United States, 2000), http://www.c-span.org/video/?154511-1/federal-reserve-chairman-renomination.

45. Ibid.

46. Description based on Reuters photo. MMR/JP—RTR319, Photograph, January 4, 2000, Reuters Pictures.

47. Richard W. Stevenson, "Senate Ratifies Nomination of Greenspan to 4th Term," *New York Times*, February 4, 2000.

CHAPTER TWENTY-SIX

1. Bob Woodward, *Maestro: Greenspan's Fed and the American Boom* (New York: Simon & Schuster, 2000), Kindle locations 3711–37.

2. Alan Greenspan, *The Age of Turbulence: Adventures in a New World* (New York: Penguin Books, 2008), 207.

3. Ron Suskind, *The Price of Loyalty: George W. Bush, the White House, and the Education of Paul O'Neill* (New York: Simon & Schuster Inc., 2004), 7.

4. Barton Gellman, *Angler: The Cheney Vice Presidency* (New York: Penguin Group, 2008), 15.

5. The following passage and others in this chapter involving Paul O'Neill are based closely on Ron Suskind, *Price of Loyalty*. Suskind's account is based mainly on extensive interviews with Paul O'Neill conducted soon after he left office. Critics have accused the book of excessive sympathy with O'Neill's perspective, and its author, a Pulitzer Prize winner and former *Wall Street Journal* reporter, of too much reliance on unnamed sources and occasional sloppiness with facts. (For examples of criticisms of Suskind and O'Neill, see Lawrence Lindsey, "The Value of Loyalty," *Wall Street Journal*, January 14, 2004; and Jacob Weisberg, "Don't Believe Ron Suskind: His Book About Obama Is as Spurious as the Ones He Wrote about Bush," *Slate*, September 22, 2011.) However, O'Neill, a named source, proofread Suskind's manuscript before publication and affirmed its accuracy after publication; Greenspan, for his part, confined his public objection to a single quote in the manuscript. (See David Wessel, "A Tale of Two Treasury Secretaries: Robert Rubin and Paul O'Neill," *Wall Street Journal*, January 15, 2004.) Further, while critics have accused O'Neill of seeking revenge against enemies in the Bush administration, O'Neill had no such motive to distort his account of conversations with Greenspan, who remained an ally and a friend. In sum, although aspects of the Suskind-O'Neill version of history are contested, the reconstructions of meetings involving Greenspan rely on a firsthand witness interviewed soon after the events with no evident ax to grind; they are hard to improve upon. The passage that follows here is drawn from Ron Suskind, *Price of Loyalty*, 28ff.

6. Suskind, *Price of Loyalty*, 30. See also Greenspan, *Age of Turbulence*, Kindle locations 3765–69.

7. Michael Lewis, "O'Neill's List," *New York Times Magazine,* January 13, 2002.
8. The account of the meeting that follows is drawn from Ron Suskind, *Price of Loyalty,* 36ff.
9. "The Long-Term Budget Outlook," Study (Congress of the United States, 2000), http://www.cbo.gov/sites/default/files/long-term%20budget%20outlook.pdf.
10. On the coffee war, see Dick Cheney, "Memoranda for Jim Connor," August 30, 1975, James E. Connor Collection, box 18, Gerald R. Ford Library; and Dick Cheney, "Memoranda for Jim Connor," October 20, 1975, James E. Connor Collection, box 18, Gerald R. Ford Library. On salt shakers, see James Mann, *Rise of the Vulcans: The History of Bush's War Cabinet* (New York: Penguin Group, 2004), 60.
11. In laying out his tax plan on December 1, 1999, Bush provided several rationales, including the possibility that the tax cut might act as insurance against the recession. This last rationale was the one to which Cheney now returned. However, it had not dominated the Bush team's public statements in the interim.
12. Suskind, *Price of Loyalty,* 45.
13. The following interchange is based on ibid., 61.
14. In later congressional testimony, Greenspan argued that the government would buy stock only in politically favored firms, distorting stock prices and hence capital allocation. However, this argument underestimated the response from private investors, who could be expected to shift funds into stocks that were temporarily undervalued as a result of the government's portfolio decisions. See Sebastian Mallaby, "Greenspan on Going Private," *Washington Post,* February 5, 2001.
15. Lawrence Lindsey, interview by the author, March 25, 2015. Greenspan's response is also quoted in Lawrence B. Lindsey, *Economic Puppetmasters: Lessons from the Halls of Power* (Washington, D.C.: AEI Press, 1999), 53. As an adviser to Candidate Bush, Lindsey had ensured that the bubble-insurance rationale for the tax cut had been included in the president's speeches. In laying out his tax cut in Iowa on December 1, 1999, Bush said that his plan would "provide insurance against economic recession."
16. Barton Gellman, *Angler,* 70–71.
17. Senate Committee on Banking, Housing, and Urban Affairs, *Federal Reserve's First Monetary Policy Report for 2001: Hearing Before the Committee on Banking, Housing, and Urban Affairs,* 107th Cong., 1st sess., 2001.
18. Greenspan later claimed to have been surprised by the way his testimony was construed. "I'd misjudged the emotions of the moment," he wrote in his autobiography. Greenspan, *Age of Turbulence,* Kindle locations 4006–9. But he had understood from the beginning how his testimony would be perceived—he was too savvy for it to be otherwise.
19. Suskind, *Price of Loyalty,* 162.
20. According to revised data from the Bureau of Economic Analysis, the economy contracted in Q1 2001 but expanded in Q2; there were not two consecutive quarters of decline, so by some definitions this was not a true recession. However, the chief arbiter of recessions is the National Bureau of Economic Research. Using monthly data, and not using the two-consecutive-quarters test, the NBER determined that a recession began in March 2001 and lasted for eight months. See "The Business-Cycle Peak of March 2001" (National Bureau of Economic Research: Business Cycle Dating Committee, November 26, 2001), http://www.nber.org/cycles/november2001/.
21. The survey was conducted by the Wall Street advisory firm Medley Global Advisers. Previous surveys by the firm had put Greenspan's strong approvals in the 60 percent to 80 percent range. Now they languished below 40 percent. See Glenn Kessler, "Playing to a Larger Audience; Bush Team Starts Sending Its Message to Wall St. and the World," *Washington Post,* March 29, 2001.
22. Core PCE inflation had accelerated from 1.5 percent in January to 1.7 percent in February to 1.9 percent in March. It fell back to 1.7 percent in April, but this was not known at the time of the FOMC's May meeting. (These PCE measures were subsequently revised, though the trend was not much affected.) The FOMC did have an April reading for the less important CPI inflation measure at the time of its May meeting, and this hinted that inflation pressures were ebbing. But this single reassuring data point had to be weighed against several others that pointed toward higher inflation, and the Fed staff supported Greenspan's mistaken decision, a reminder that an inflation-targeting regime is not always easy to operate.
23. "Net Domestic Investment: Private: Domestic Business," FRED, Federal Reserve Bank of St. Louis, http://research.stlouisfed.org/fred2/graph/fredgraph.png?g=RIf.
24. As the economy had softened in the first Bush presidency, in the first part of 1991, Greenspan had taken three months to bring interest rates down by a full percentage point. In January 2001, he cut by that much in a single month. Likewise, in 1991 the second 1 percentage point reduction in interest rates had taken six months. In 2001 it took less than four. The faster loosening in the later episode was made possible by the fact that inflation expectations were so subdued.
25. This was the perception of Kenneth Guenther, and was probably also Greenspan's perception. A White House source with knowledge of these matters finds Guenther's view plausible. Lindsey, for his part, denies any such expectation. Greenspan denies memory of the incident. Kenneth Guenther, interview by the author, January 31, 2014. Lawrence Lindsey, interview by the author, March 25, 2015. Alan Greenspan, interview by the author, November 2, 2015.
26. Nicole Duran, "In Brief: Amrey Says He Lobbied for Friend Jorde," *American Banker* 166, no. 84 (May 2, 2001).
27. Kenneth Guenther, interview by the author, January 31, 2014.
28. Aircraft make and model were determined from airline operating data reported on the Department of Transportation's Form 41 and made available via Bureau of Transportation Statistics at the TranStats Air Carrier Statistics (Form 41 Traffic)—All Carriers' database, http://www.transtats.bts.gov/Tables.asp?DB_ID=111&DB_Name=Air%20Carrier%20Statistics%20%28Form%2041%20Traffic%29-%20All%20Carriers&DB_Short_Name=Air%20Carriers.
29. Greenspan, *Age of Turbulence,* Kindle locations 80–87.
30. From *Age of Turbulence:* "We'd always thought that if you wanted to cripple the U.S. economy, you'd take out the payment systems. Banks would be forced to fall back on inefficient physical transfers of money. Businesses would resort to barter and IOUs; the level of economic activity across the country could drop like a rock." Ibid., 91–93.
31. Emily Walker, "Memorandum for the Record of Meeting with William J. McDonough" (National Commission on Terrorist Attacks upon the United States, January

21, 2004), https://catalog.archives .gov/OpaAPI/media/2610306 /content/arcmedia/9-11/MFR /t-0148-911MFR-00711.pdf.

32. Ibid.

33. Jeff Ingber, *Resurrecting the Street: Overcoming the Greatest Operational Crisis in History* (Jeff Ingber, 2012), Kindle locations 387–88.

34. Andrea Mitchell, *Talking Back: . . . to Presidents, Dictators, and Assorted Scoundrels* (New York: Penguin Group, 2006), 341.

35. Greenspan, *Age of Turbulence,* Kindle locations 120–23.

36. The discount window supplied $200 million in loans on an average day. Bruce Champ, "Open and Operating: Providing Liquidity to Avoid a Crisis" (Federal Reserve Bank of Cleveland, February 15, 2003), https://www.clevelandfed .org/en/newsroom-and-events /publications/economic-commen tary/economic-commentary -archives/2003-economic-com mentaries/ec-20030215-open-and -operating-providing-liquidity -to-avoid-a-crisis.aspx.

37. Jeffrey M. Lacker, "Payment System Disruptions and the Federal Reserve Following September 11, 2001," Working Paper, Working Paper Series (Richmond: Federal Reserve Bank of Richmond, December 23, 2003), 40, http:// www.richmondfed.org/publica tions/research/working_papers /2003/pdf/wp03-16.pdf.

38. Roger W. Ferguson Jr., "September 11, the Federal Reserve, and the Financial System" (Remarks, Vanderbilt University, Nashville, Tenn., February 5, 2003), http:// www.federalreserve.gov/board docs/speeches/2003/20030205/. See also Dina Temple-Raston, "The Week the Fed Saved the World: An Inside Glimpse at the Greenspan-McDonough-Ferguson Team's Backroom Maneuvering," *International Economy,* November 1, 2001.

39. Roger W. Ferguson Jr., interview by the author, March 3, 2015. Greenspan endorsed this account of Ferguson playing the lead role. Greenspan, interview by the author, November 2, 2015.

40. Michael J. Fleming and Kenneth D. Garbade, "When the Back Office Moved to the Front Burner: Settlement Fails in the Treasury Market After 9/11," *Federal Reserve Bank of New York Economic Policy Review,* November 2002, 12, https://www.newyorkfed.org /medialibrary/media/research/ epr/02v08n2/0211flempdf.pdf. See also Donald Donahue and Larry Thompson, "Proposed NSCC Rule Change," September 14, 2006, 7,

http://www.sec.gov.edgekey.net /comments/sr.-nscc-2006-04 /nscc200604-10.pdf.

41. Suskind, *Price of Loyalty,* 183: They were aboard another military cargo plane full of U.S. officials and military brass headed back to the United States from Europe "like a city bus at rush hour." The flight took ten hours and was spare on creature comforts—just a boxed lunch and earplugs.

42. Greenspan, *Age of Turbulence,* Kindle locations 127–28.

43. Ibid., Kindle locations 128–32.

44. Alan Greenspan, interview by the author, February 6, 2013.

45. Andrea Mitchell, *Talking Back,* 345.

46. Dan Barry, "After the Attacks: The Vigils; Surrounded by Grief, People Around the World Pause and Turn to Prayer," *New York Times,* September 15, 2001.

47. "We have the building wrapped in bunting, we have a big flag flying, and we're playing patriotic music from the parapet," Bill McDonough said during the September 17 FOMC conference call. See also Jeff Ingber, *Resurrecting the Street: Overcoming the Greatest Operational Crisis in History,* Kindle locations 2920–35.

48. The Fed's loans to the banking system had already shot up from $13 billion on the eve of the attacks to fully $120 billion. Jeffrey M. Lacker, "Payment System Disruptions and the Federal Reserve Following September 11, 2001," 29.

49. Andrea Mitchell, interviews by the author, March 14, 2012, and July 28, 2014.

CHAPTER TWENTY-SEVEN

1. The University of Michigan began to carry out monthly surveys of inflation expectations in 1978 but had conducted annual surveys since 1966. Until the terrorist attacks, only one reading had come in lower than 2 percent.

2. Core CPI exceeded the federal funds rate in October 1992, and again in five out of the next seven months.

3. The Fed had held a conference on policy in a low-interest-rate environment in Woodstock, Vermont, in October 1999. Research presented there shaped senior staff's thinking, and to a lesser extent Greenspan's.

4. Data on late-nineteenth-century deflation come from Susan B. Carter et al., *Historical Statistics of the United States: Millennium Edition* (Cambridge, UK: Cambridge University Press, 2006).

5. Some economists came to see the early 2000s as a period of good

disinflation: prices were coming down, according to this view, because of the flood of new supply from China, which joined the World Trade Organization in December 2001. While there is some merit to this view, the China surge mostly postdates the FOMC's November 2001 debate, and is inadequate for two further reasons. First, the surge in supply from China resulted in a huge increase in China's trade surplus, which was mirrored in an increase in the U.S. trade deficit. This shift in the balance of payments represented a subtraction from U.S. demand, meaning that the China shock combined elements of good (supply boosting) and bad (demand reducing) disinflation. Second, whatever the nature of the China shock, the overhang from the tech bubble and 9/11 clearly contributed to disinflation, and these two factors were unambiguously in the bad-disinflation category. Ex-post, it is correct to argue that the Fed overreacted to the fear of deflation, and so planted the seeds for the property bubble. Ex-ante, the deflation worry was reasonable, at least until the end of 2003. For a critique of excess fear of deflation, see Claudio Borio et al., "The Costs of Deflations: A Historical Perspective," *BIS Quarterly Review,* March 2015.

6. The extent to which monetary policy after November 2001 fueled the real estate bubble is debated, as will be explained in chapter twenty-eight.

7. For an example of an observer who draws a distinction between the "harmless" tech bubble and the harmful mortgage bubble, see Frederic S. Mishkin, "Monetary Policy Strategy: Lessons from the Crisis," Working Paper (Cambridge, Mass.: National Bureau of Economic Research, February 2011).

8. The critique of Greenspan's monetary policy advanced here is different from that advanced by John Taylor. Whereas Taylor assumes that the Fed seeks to optimize a combination of targeted inflation and full usage of the economy's capacity, the critique here is that the Fed must take account of financial stability, because instability will cause the Fed to deliver poor inflation and capacity utilization over the longer run. The Taylor critique is effectively rebutted by Ben S. Bernanke, "Monetary Policy and the Housing Bubble" (Annual Meeting of the American Economic Association, Atlanta, Georgia, January 3, 2010). The financial stability critique is less

successfully addressed in Bernanke's speech.

9. It is often asserted that plausibly higher interest rates would have made no difference to asset prices. See, for example, Alan S. Blinder and Ricardo Reis, "Understanding the Greenspan Standard," Working Paper (CEPS, September 2005), 71. This assertion cannot be proved because the connection between interest rates and asset prices depends on market psychology, which is fickle and unpredictable. However, as explained in chapter twenty-two, a close study of 1996–97 suggests that the claim of monetary impotence is probably wrong. Market strategists such as Byron Wien and Abby Cohen justified their bullish view of stocks using a dividend discount model. Given a higher discount rate, their view of the market would have been less bullish.

10. Paul R. Krugman, "Dubya Double Dip?," New York Times, August 2, 2002. Krugman was citing Paul McCulley of the investment management firm Pimco. Embracing a similar analysis at the June 2005 FOMC meeting, Janet Yellen acknowledged the link between the tech hangover and the housing boom: "To offset the drags, we've needed to give the economy a strong dose of stimulus, which inevitably boosted the housing sector—and that just to get reasonable economic growth." Equally, staff economist Glenn Rudebusch commented at the same meeting: "The dot-com bubble spurred overinvestment in fiber optic cable and decimated the provision of venture capital for new technology startups for years." He drew the lesson: "It is possible to conceive of a situation in which reducing the bubble in advance is a preferred policy strategy."

11. Alan Greenspan, remarks (Stern School of Business, New York University, New York, March 26, 2002), http://www.federalreserve.gov/boarddocs/speeches/2002/200203262/default.htm.

12. Ron Suskind, The Price of Loyalty: George W. Bush, the White House, and the Education of Paul O'Neill, First paperback edition (New York: Simon & Schuster, 2004), 211.

13. Ibid., 223.

14. Following passage draws on ibid., 224–30.

15. Ibid., 226–27. This passage is also based on the author's background interviews with participants at the meeting.

16. Ibid., 228.

17. Richard Clarida, interview by the author, April 30, 2015.

18. Greenspan was testifying to the Senate on March 7, 2002. His interchange with Senator Jon Corzine offers a good summary of his view of financial innovation. Senate Committee on Banking, Housing, and Urban Affairs, Federal Reserve's First Monetary Policy Report for 2002: Hearing Before the Committee on Banking, Housing, and Urban Affairs, 107th Cong., 2nd sess., 2002, http://hdl.handle.net/2027/pst.000049649147.

19. "Federal Subsidies and the Housing GSEs" (Washington, D.C.: Congressional Budget Office, May 2001), http://www.cbo.gov/sites/default/files/gses.pdf.

20. Alan Greenspan, remarks (Institute of International Finance, New York, April 22, 2002), http://www.federalreserve.gov/boarddocs/Speeches/2002/20020422/default.htm.

21. Alex Berenson, "Market Place: Fannie Mae and Freddy Mac Pressed Again, This Time on Disclosure and Derivatives," New York Times, April 25, 2002.

22. Kevin Warsh, interview by the author, October 21, 2011.

23. In a further sign of the administration's deference to Greenspan on the question of Fed appointments, Greenspan's official diary notes that on March 27, 2002, Glenn Hubbard, the Council of Economic Advisers chairman, visited Greenspan "to discuss Fed. appts." (from Alan Greenspan's Diary, n.d.).

24. Starting in the second quarter of 1996, net private domestic investment had exceeded an annualized rate of $300 billion every quarter until the stock market crash in 2000. Then, from the fourth quarter of 2001 until the first quarter of 2004, it languished below the $300 billion mark. This "investment recession" therefore lasted for ten quarters in total. Although this period was often described as one of "savings glut," the deflationary pressure of the time also reflected weak investment. For data on investment, see "Net Domestic Investment: Private: Domestic Business."

25. In May through August 2002, the S&P/Case-Shiller ten-city house price index sustained four consecutive months of 1.4 percent month-on-month growth, the fastest spurt since the index began in 1987. S&P Dow Jones Indices, "S&P/Case-Shiller 10-City Composite Home Price Index," FRED, Federal Reserve Bank of St. Louis, https://research.stlouisfed.org/fred2/series/SPCS10RSA.

26. Matt Richtel, "Bay Area Real Estate Prices Too Hot for Some to Touch," New York Times, May 29, 2002, http://www.nytimes.com/2002/05/29/business/bay-area-real-estate-prices-too-hot-for-some-to-touch.html.

27. Gregg Fields, "Sales, Prices Rise in South Florida," Miami Herald, June 30, 2002.

28. George W. Bush, "Remarks by the President on Homeownership" (Atlanta, Georgia, June 17, 2002), http://www.prnewswire.com/news-releases/remarks-by-the-president-on-homeownership-77912977.html.

29. George W. Bush, "Remarks by President George W. Bush Re: Homeownership" (Department of Housing and Urban Development, Washington, D.C., June 18, 2002).

30. The analyst was Paul Miller of Friedman, Billings, Ramsey Group Inc. in Arlington, Va. See Tommy Fernandez, "Bush's Minority-Loan Plan Gives GSEs Political Cover," American Banker, June 21, 2002.

31. Kenneth Harney, "Making Dreams Become Reality," Washington Post, June 22, 2002, http://www.washingtonpost.com/archive/realestate/2002/06/22/making-dreams-become-reality/0a5e17ec-4002-4e08-99f8-e5585f6b8cd2/.

32. Brian Collins, "President Bush Calls on Industry to Help Boost Minority Homeownership," National Mortgage News, October 28, 2002.

33. Although the S&P/Case-Shiller housing index was rising at its fastest pace in fifteen years, it would rise even faster during the first half of 2004 and the first quarter of 2005. See S&P Dow Jones Indices, "S&P/Case-Shiller 10-City Composite Home Price Index."

34. The risk of rising consumer debt was raised by Thomas Hoenig.

35. The Treasury munchkins were so dubbed by Grover Norquist, a Cheney ally. See Barton Gellman, Angler: The Cheney Vice Presidency (New York: Penguin, 2008), 264.

36. Suskind, Price of Loyalty, 284.

37. Gellman, Angler, 267–268. The Fed study concluded that long-term interest rates rose 25 basis points in response to a 1 percentage point increase in the projected deficit-to-GDP ratio, and 4 basis points in response to a 1 percentage point increase in the projected debt-to-GDP ratio. Thomas Laubach, "New Evidence on the Interest Rate Effects of Budget Deficits and Debt" (Board of Governors of the Federal Reserve System, May 2003), http://www.federalreserve.gov/pubs/feds/2003/200312/200312pap.pdf.

38. Gellman, *Angler,* 268.
39. Suskind, *Price of Loyalty,* 291.
40. Edmund L. Andrews, "Greenspan Throws Cold Water on Bush Arguments for Tax Cut," *New York Times,* February 12, 2003, http://www.nytimes.com/2003/02/12/business/12FED.html.
41. John Cranford, "Greenspan's Days Numbered?," *Seattle Times,* February 22, 2003.
42. The allies comprised Britain, Australia, and Poland, with the latter contributing a grand total of 194 personnel to the first phase of the operation.
43. In January 2003, Greenspan told the FOMC, "The Iraqis have relatively high-tech chemical and biological warfare capability, and they are likely to spring it on us, perhaps even in advance of our attack."
44. "AOLTW to Sell Stake in Comedy Central," *CNN Live at Daybreak* (CNN, April 22, 2003), http://www.cnn.com/TRANSCRIPTS/0304/22/lad.05.html.
45. John M. Berry, "Bush Signals Another Term for Greenspan," *Washington Post,* April 23, 2003, http://www.washingtonpost.com/archive/business/2003/04/23/bush-signals-another-term-for-greenspan/52f0c11a-db01-4607-8a33-76224a69f4fe/.
46. Edmund L. Andrews, "Greenspan Agrees to Another Term Leading the Fed," *New York Times,* April 24, 2003, http://www.nytimes.com/2003/04/24/business/24FED.html.
47. Daniel Akst, "On the Contrary; Cult of the Personality Lives at the Fed," *New York Times,* May 4, 2003, http://www.nytimes.com/2003/05/04/business/on-the-contrary-cult-of-the-personality-lives-at-the-fed.html.
48. Airing his concern about low inflation during the FOMC's August 2003 meeting, Ben Bernanke observed, "Though I can see that output gaps are extremely hard to measure, the most reasonable guess is that the current gap remains substantial." Looking back on this period in 2010, Bernanke noted that unemployment had remained high in the first half of 2003, and that this may have been another consequence of the tech bubble. Because they had stocked up on capital goods, companies hired relatively few workers. See Bernanke, "Monetary Policy and the Housing Bubble."
49. An FOMC member recalls, "Bernanke did not seem to have any agenda when he joined. He was low key. He was comfortable doing great research without attempting to become the next chair."
50. Bernanke suggested "a working definition of price stability expressed as a range of measured core inflation," adding that "in issuing such guidance, the FOMC would not need to make any explicit commitment." He later acknowledged that he was deliberately couching his proposal in a way that might make it acceptable to Greenspan. Ben Bernanke, interview by the author, September 14, 2015.
51. Greenspan was open to a discussion of how he might communicate the Fed's stance in forthcoming congressional testimony. But he was not ready to change the post-meeting statement.
52. Kohn said this at the February 1989 FOMC meeting. See chapter seventeen.
53. At the FOMC meeting on September 16, 2003, Greenspan said, "In retrospect, I think it was a mistake to include a sentence in our press statement in August indicating that an accommodative policy can be maintained for a considerable period."
54. According to the Mortgage Bankers Association, the number of outstanding subprime mortgages serviced in the fourth quarter of 2003 was double the number serviced in the previous quarter. "U.S. Number of Subprime Loans Serviced," Mortgage Bankers Association via Bloomberg LP, retrieved March 12, 2015.
55. "Homeownership Rate for the United States," *FRED, Federal Reserve Bank of St.. Louis,* https://research.stlouisfed.org/fred2/graph/?g=YYQ.

CHAPTER TWENTY-EIGHT

1. Liaquat Ahamed, *Lords of Finance: The Bankers Who Broke the World* (London: Penguin, 2009), 160.
2. Ibid., 483.
3. Steve Quinn and Katie Fairbank, "What's in It for Texas? Naming-Rights Deal with Ameriquest Will Mean Some Changes," *Dallas Morning News,* May 8, 2004.
4. Ibid.
5. Jody Shenn, "ARMed—Not 'Stuck,'" *American Banker,* June 21, 2004.
6. The share of "low doc" and "no doc" loan originations in the securitized subprime market rose from 20 percent in 2000, to 30 percent in 2004, to 40 percent in 2006. See 12 C.F.R. 226 Revised as of October 1, 2009, 44540–44541, Federal Register, http://www.gpo.gov/fdsys/pkg/FR.-2008-07-30/pdf/E8-16500.pdf.
7. Edmund L. Andrews, "The Ever More Graspable, and Risky, American Dream," *New York Times,* June 24, 2004, http://www.nytimes.com/2004/06/24/business/the-ever-more-graspable-and-risky-american-dream.html.
8. Miguel Segoviano et al., "Securitization: Lessons Learned and the Road Ahead," Working Paper (International Monetary Fund, November 2013), http://www.imf.org/external/pubs/ft/wp/2013/wp13255.pdf, 11.
9. William Shear, "Characteristics and Performance of Nonprime Mortgages" (Washington, D.C.: Government Accountability Office, July 28, 2009), http://www.gao.gov/new.items/d09848r.pdf. See also Andrews, "The Ever More Graspable, and Risky, American Dream." On the proliferation of repayment holidays, see Ben S. Bernanke, "Monetary Policy and the Housing Bubble" (Annual Meeting of the American Economic Association, Atlanta, Georgia, January 3, 2010), Slide 8, 34.
10. Bethany McLean and Joe Nocera, *All the Devils Are Here: The Hidden History of the Financial Crisis* (New York: Portfolio/Penguin, 2010), Kindle locations 2828–32.
11. Mike Hudson and E. Scott Reckard, "Workers Say Lender Ran 'Boiler Rooms,'" *Los Angeles Times,* February 4, 2005, http://articles.latimes.com/2005/feb/04/business/fi-ameriquest4.
12. Greenspan's faith in financial innovation had held up over a longer period than the "classical gold standard," which is commonly dated from 1880 to 1914. (For an example of dating, see Michael D. Bordo, "The Classical Gold Standard: Some Lessons for Today," *Federal Reserve Bank of St. Louis Review,* May 1981.)
13. Alan Greenspan, remarks (Credit Union National Association 2004 Governmental Affairs Conference, Washington, D.C., February 23, 2004), http://www.federalreserve.gov/boarddocs/Speeches/2004/20040223/default.htm. In this speech, Greenspan also suggested that consumers might benefit from variable-rate mortgages. After the crisis, this led him to be painted as a cheerleader for risky borrowing. However, Greenspan's aim was to show that fixed-rate mortgages, as facilitated by the GSEs, were less than indispensable.
14. Senate Committee on Banking, Housing, and Urban Affairs, *The State of the Banking Industry: Testimony of Alan Greenspan Before the Committee on Banking, Housing, and Urban Affairs* (Washington, D.C.: Federal Reserve Board, 2004), http://www.federal reserve.

gov/boarddocs/testimony /2004/20040420/.

15. This interchange was recalled by Robert Gnaizda, the general counsel of the Greenlining Institute. McLean and Nocera, *All the Devils*, Kindle locations 1775–1777.

16. The delegate was John Taylor. Ibid.

17. Whether the advocates were right to emphasize the risks posed to consumers depended on the timing: in the 1990s, subprime lending may have done more good than harm because it allowed marginal borrowers a shot at home ownership in a rising market; by the early 2000s, mortgages had grown wilder and the case for a clampdown was stronger. But whatever the right judgment on consumer protection, the key thing is that these conversations were about just that: consumer protection.

18. One exception to the emphasis on consumer protection was Joshua Rosner, a mortgage analyst who warned about deteriorating underwriting standards and a potential market reversal as early as 2001. However, Rosner's paper did not make the connection between a housing reversal and systemic risk. Senior Fed staff members who recalled hearing from community activists with concerns about housing had no recollection of Rosner. Joshua Rosner, interview by the author, October 14, 2014.

19. The meetings were in Charlotte, Boston, Chicago, and San Francisco.

20. Federal Reserve Board, *Public Hearing on Home Equity Lending* (Boston: Federal Reserve Board, 2000), http://www.federalreserve.gov/events/publichearings /20000804/20000804.htm.

21. Greg Ip, "Did Greenspan Add to Subprime Woes?," *Wall Street Journal,* June 9, 2007, http://www.wsj.com/articles/SB1181 34411823129555.

22. I am indebted to Lewis Alexander of Nomura Securities for this metaphor.

23. Dolores Smith and Glenn Loney to Edward Gramlich, "Compliance Inspections of Nonbank Subsidiaries of Bank Holding Companies," memorandum, August 31, 2000, Financial Crisis Inquiry Commission, http://fcic-static.law.stanford .edu/cdn_media/fcic-docs /2000-08-31_Federal_Reserve _Board_Memo_from_Dolores _Smith_and_Glenn_Loney_re _Compliance_Inspection.pdf.

24. Gramlich's fellow governor recalled, "He never raised a deep concern about housing and subprime with me. I have asked other

governors about this, and nobody can really recall that as a fixed idea in Ned's head." In addition, interviews with Fed staff confirm this interpretation. Greenspan's version of this episode—in House testimony on October 23, 2008, he noted that Gramlich could have pursued the matter further but had chosen to drop it—therefore appears accurate. House Committee on Oversight and Government Reform, *The Financial Crisis and the Role of Federal Regulators: Hearing Before the Committee on Oversight and Government Reform,* 2008, http://www.gpo.gov /fdsys/pkg/CHRG-110hhrg 55764/html/CHRG-110hhrg 55764.htm.

25. When it moved to tighten income documentation rules more decisively in late 2007, the Fed was scolded for burdening borrowers who lack traditional, neatly documented sources of income. "Not every consumer applying for a loan fits into the tight little box of Ward and June Cleaver," lectured one commenter on the Fed's draft proposal. See Brian T. McLaughlin, "Comments on Regulation Z—Truth in Lending" (Federal Reserve Board, December 18, 2007), http://www.federalreserve .gov/SECRS/2007/December /20071227/R-1305/R-1305_36_1 .pdf. After the Fed adopted these rules in 2008, consumer advocates continued to point out that some borrowers were adversely affected. Given these reactions, it is clear that resistance would have been much fiercer in the early 2000s, when subprime delinquencies were actually declining.

26. Board of Governors of the Federal Reserve System, *Regulation Z (Truth in Lending)—Amendments to Implement the Home Ownership and Equity Protection Act (HOEPA) to Address Abusive Lending Practices in Home Equity Lending,* Audio Cassette (Washington, D.C.: 12/12/01, 1 of 1 [Open], 2013), Federal Reserve Board Freedom of Information Office.

27. Of the nearly $600 billion in subprime lending in 2006, about half was originated by lenders that were not beholden to any banking regulator. "Although these lenders were subject to certain federal consumer protection and fair lending laws, they were generally not subject to the same routine monitoring and oversight by federal agencies that their bank counterparts were." "Financial Regulation: A Framework for Crafting and Assessing Proposals to Modernize

the Outdated U.S. Financial Regulatory System" (Government Accountability Office, January 2009), 24, http://www.gao.gov /new.items/d09216.pdf.

28. Board of Governors of the Federal Reserve System, *Regulation Z (Truth in Lending)—Amendments to Implement the Home Ownership and Equity Protection Act (HOEPA) to Address Abusive Lending Practices in Home Equity Lending.*

29. Financial Crisis Inquiry Commission, "The Financial Crisis Inquiry Report: The Final Report of the National Commission on the Causes of the Financial and Economic Crisis in the United States" (Financial Crisis Inquiry Commission, January 2011), http:// fcic-static.law.stanford.edu/cdn _media/fcic-reports/fcic_final _report_full.pdf.

30. Edward Gramlich to Alan Greenspan, letter, August 25, 2007. Greenspan was criticized for releasing this letter to journalists, one of whom provided a copy to the author. See Sewell Chan, "Greenspan Criticized for Characterization of Colleague," *New York Times,* April 9, 2010, http://www .nytimes.com/2010/04/10/busi ness/10gramlich.html.

31. The Senate staff member was an ex–Fed economist named Patrick Lawler. Patrick Lawler, interview by the author, February 13, 2014.

32. Richard Baker, interview by the author, April 21, 2015.

33. Capital-asset ratios at Fannie and Freddie were less than half those at large banks. Wayne Passmore, "The GSE Implicit Subsidy and the Value of Government Ambiguity," Working Paper (Washington, D.C.: Federal Reserve Board, May 2005), http://www.federalreserve .gov/pubs/feds/2005/200505 /200505pap.pdf, 36, Exhibit 7.

34. Ibid. Passmore's study found that GSE lending reduced borrowing costs for some homeowners, but only by around 7 basis points.

35. Barbara Rehm, "How One Day of Testimony Transforms the Debate," *American Banker* 169, no. 37 (February 25, 2004).

36. Bethany McLean, "The Fall of Fannie Mae," *Fortune,* January 24, 2005, http://archive.fortune.com /magazines/fortune/fortune _archive/2005/01/24/8234040 /index.htm.

37. Timothy F. Geithner, *Stress Test: Reflections on Financial Crises* (New York: Crown Publishers, 2014), 96.

38. Ibid., 99.

39. Ibid., 103.

40. Alan Greenspan, "The Crisis," Brookings Papers on Economic Activity (Washington, D.C.: Brookings Institution, Spring 2010); and Ben S. Bernanke, "Monetary Policy and the Housing Bubble" (Annual Meeting of the American Economic Association, Atlanta, Georgia, January 3, 2010). For reasons to suspect that a low federal funds rate materially encouraged dangerous lending and a reach for yield, see numerous citations provided in Frederic S. Mishkin, "Monetary Policy Strategy: Lessons from the Crisis," Working Paper (Cambridge, Mass.: National Bureau of Economic Research, February 2011).

41. Bernanke, "Monetary Policy and the Housing Bubble." Criticizing Bernanke's argument, which later also became Greenspan's argument, Jeremy Stein of Harvard noted that low policy rates may have mattered a great deal for income-constrained borrowers. Adjustable-rate mortgages were used more in expensive cities, a trend that became more pronounced as home prices took off, starting in 2004. See Figure 1 in Jeremy Stein, "Discussant's Comments on: 'The Crisis' by Alan Greenspan," Brookings Papers on Economic Activity (Brookings Institution Press, April 2010).

42. The role of a low federal funds rate in expanding investment-bank balance sheets, and the impact of that expansion on interest-rate-sensitive sectors such as real estate, is explored in Tobias Adrian and Hyun Song Shin, "Financial Intermediaries, Financial Stability, and Monetary Policy," Working Paper (Federal Reserve Bank of New York, September 2008), http://www.econstor.eu/bitstream/10419/60839/1/587563303.pdf. The authors find that greater certainty regarding the future path of short rates also expands longer-term lending by market-based intermediaries, underlining the role of the Fed's forward guidance in boosting real-estate lending. The authors explicitly criticize conventional central-bank thinking for excluding investment banks from the understanding of the relationship between short-term interest rates and sectors such as housing.

43. Kohn was most explicit about this view at the next FOMC meeting, in March 2004. Noting that the Fed's critics feared "that policy accommodation—and the expectation that it will persist—is distorting asset prices," he declared: "Most of this distortion is deliberate and a desirable effect of the stance of policy."

44. Invited to comment on this book's characterization of his view of bubbles, Greenspan emphatically endorsed the significance of his preference for the certainty of mechanical relationships. Fair value for assets could be statistically estimated but not proved, and Greenspan never liked to rely on uncertain models. Alan Greenspan, interview by the author, November 2, 2015.

45. At the March 2004 meeting, Kohn argued: "[A] high burden of proof would seem to be on policies that would slow the expansion, leaving more slack and less inflation in the economy in the intermediate run to avoid hypothetical instabilities later."

46. This gain is based on the Case-Shiller ten-city composite index. S&P Dow Jones Indices, "S&P/Case-Shiller 10-City Composite Home Price Index," FRED, Federal Reserve Bank of St. Louis, https://research.stlouisfed.org/fred2/series/SPCS10RSA.

47. The Fed's unpredictability in Greenspan's early years was not confined to 1994. Prior to June 1989, the Greenspan Fed moved interest rates twenty-seven times in less than two years. Only six of these moves were quarter-point ones. Alan S. Blinder and Ricardo Reis, "Understanding the Greenspan Standard," Working Paper (CEPS, September 2005), 30.

48. Remarks by Chairman Alan Greenspan, "The Mortgage Market and Consumer Debt," (speech, America's Community Bankers Annual Convention, Washington, D.C., October 19, 2004).

49. The following episode is based on an interview with David Stockton, Prell's successor as head of the Fed's research division. David Stockton, interview by the author, June 17, 2013.

50. For a retrospective analysis on economists' difficulty in reaching firm conclusions on house prices, see Kristopher S. Gerardi, Christopher L. Foote, and Paul S. Willen, "Reasonable People Did Disagree: Optimism and Pessimism About the U.S. Housing Market Before the Crash," Public Policy Discussion paper (Boston, Massachusetts: Federal Reserve Bank of Boston, September 2010), http://www.bostonfed.org/economic/ppdp/2010/ppdp1005.pdf.

51. The mortgage strategist was from UBS, a Swiss bank. See "Portrait of a Market on Steroids," Washington Post, May 22, 2005, http://www.washingtonpost.com/wp-dyn/content/article/2005/05/21/AR2005052100118.html.

52. In May and June 2004, the Bank of England had taken a step in this direction, raising interest rates twice in quick succession, partly in response to an overheating housing market.

53. The FOMC member was Edward Gramlich.

54. In his February 2005 testimony, Greenspan declared, "It is difficult to attribute the long-term interest rate declines of the last nine months to glacially increasing globalization." Likewise, in testimony before the Senate on July 25, 2005, Greenspan again downplayed the influence of the savings glut on U.S. bond rates, saying that foreign purchases of U.S. bonds had probably depressed the ten-year rate by less than 50 basis points. The argument that foreign purchases rendered the Fed impotent was one that he emphasized only after retiring.

55. Later research suggested that foreign purchases of U.S. bonds lowered U.S. ten-year rates by about 80 basis points in the year to May 2005. See "International Capital Flows and U.S. Interest Rates," by Francis E. Warnock and Veronica Cacdac Warnock, Journal of International Money and Finance 28 (2009): 903–19. However, this downward pressure could have been counteracted by a different monetary policy; after all, U.S. long-term interest rates rose in the two years following Greenspan's conundrum speech even though net capital inflows grew and gross portfolio inflows remained strong. The limits to the linkage between foreign capital inflows and long-term interest rates are explored in Claudio Borio and Piti Disyatat, "Global Imbalances and the Financial Crisis: Link or No Link," BIS Working Paper No. 346, May 2011.

56. See chapter eleven.

57. In his House testimony, Greenspan himself acknowledged that the federal funds rate was "fairly low."

58. Some economists argue that slowly rising short rates cannot be blamed for encouraging financiers to borrow short and lend long; after all, rising short rates reduced the profit from each dollar allocated to this "carry" trade. However, greater certainty about the path of short rates could magnify the risk-adjusted profit in the carry trade, encouraging banks to increase the size of their bets in order to sustain their earnings. The importance of Fed policy in driving savings into mortgages is underlined by the large yen carry trade in the period before 2007.

Feeling confident that a predictable Fed policy meant a predictable path for the dollar, investment banks borrowed yen and extended loans in dollars, with many of those loans financing the purchase of mortgage securities. See Masazumi Hattori and Hyun Song Shin, "Yen Carry Trade and the Sub-Prime Crisis," IMF Staff Papers (2009) 56, 384–409.

59. Thomas G. Maheras, interview by the author, June 5, 2015. Lewis Alexander, interview by the author, April 28, 2015. Alexander was Citi's chief economist.

60. Geithner, Stress Test: Reflections on Financial Crises, 109.

61. Commenting after reading the manuscript, Greenspan noted with almost passive detachment that his conversion to forward guidance, and to the avoidance of shocks to the markets, was part of a larger shift to central-bank transparency. "I was caught in the middle of a transition. What I did was part of a larger change." Greenspan, interview by the author, November 2, 2015.

62. Nell Henderson, "Administration Considers Delaying Fed Chief's Exit," Washington Post, May 18, 2005, http://www.washington post.com/wp-dyn/content/article /2005/05/17/AR2005051701586 .html.

63. Alan S. Blinder and Ricardo Reis, "Understanding the Greenspan Standard," (speech, Kansas City Fed Economic Policy Symposium, August 2005).

CHAPTER TWENTY-NINE

1. "'Irrational Exuberance': Music Inspired by Greenspan," NPR Music, January 31, 2006, http:// www.npr.org/templates/story /story.php?storyId=5180083.

2. Amy Argetsinger and Roxanne Roberts, "The Reliable Source," Washington Post, February 1, 2006, http://www.washingtonpost.com /archive/lifestyle/2006/02/01/the -reliable-source/1f94edb5-afc3 -4b68-a6f9-95d64cf9532c/.

3. "Presidential Medal of Freedom," C-SPAN Video Library, November 9, 2005, http://www.c-span.org /video/?189856-1/presidential -medal-freedom. Greenspan was one of fourteen Presidential Medal of Freedom recipients that year.

4. Ashley Seager, "Christmas Goodies for Greenspan," The Guardian, December 4, 2005, http://www .theguardian.com/business/2005 /dec/05/useconomy.

5. The comparison of Greenspan to Henry V came from Richard Fisher of the Dallas Fed.

6. Edmund L. Andrews, "Exit Greenspan Amid Questions on Economy," New York Times, February 1, 2006, http://www.nytimes .com/2006/02/01/busi ness/01fed .html?pagewanted=all.

7. "Greenspan Cookie," Flickr, January 31, 2006, https://www.flickr .com/photos/sarah835/310675063 /in/photolist-tshSD-BH9Ei -tsmAA-tsmAB-tshSP-tshSM -tshSJ-tshSB-tshSH/.

8. "The Atrium at the Fed. Greenspan's Retirement Party," Flickr, January 31, 2006, https://www .flickr.com/photos/sarah835 /310675065/in/photolist -tshSD-BH9Ei-tsmAA-tsmAB -tshSP-tshSM-tshSJ-tshSB-tshSH/.

9. Alan Greenspan, interview by the author, July 16, 2010.

10. Richard Beales, Jennifer Hughes, and Andrew Balls, "Life After Fed Proves Tricky for Greenspan," Financial Times, February 9, 2006, http://www.ft.com/intl/cms/s/0 /4fffd952-99aa-11da-a8c3 -0000779e2340.html#axzz3h DZT9Txn; Barbara Hagenbaugh, "Greenspan Steps Up to Microphone Immediately," USA Today, February 14, 2006; Louis Uchitelle, "After the Fed, Exuberance," New York Times, March 10, 2006, http://www.nytimes.com/2006 /03/10/politics/10greenspan .html?pagewanted=all.

11. Amy Argetsinger and Roxanne Roberts, "The Reliable Source," Washington Post, May 31, 2007.

12. Paul Bedard, "Washington Whispers," US News and World Report, May 21, 2007.

13. As late as April 2007, the International Monetary Fund reported that "global economic risks [have] declined since . . . September 2006. . . . The overall U.S. economy is holding up well . . . [and] the signs elsewhere are very encouraging." "World Economic Outlook: Spillovers and Cycles in the Global Economy" (International Monetary Fund, April 11, 2007).

14. Pat Bagley, "Greenspan Speaks," Cartoon, September 19, 2007, Salt Lake Tribune, http://www.politi calcartoons.com/cartoon/095ce19a -2e00-465f-b9f5-31b3484d6aa2 .html.

15. Tribune Media Services, "Celebrity News," Baltimore Sun, October 15, 2007, http://articles.baltimore sun.com/2007-10 15/features /0710150171_1_barbara-walters -rosie-barbra-streisand.

16. "Subprime Mortgage Crisis," University of North Carolina–Chapel Hill, 2012, http://www.stat.unc .edu/faculty/cji/fys/2012/ Subprime%20mortgage%20crisis. pdf.

17. This was the view of Governor Rick Mishkin, for example.

18. Alan Greenspan, The Age of Turbulence: Adventures in a New World (New York: Penguin Books, 2008), Kindle locations 4161–68 and 4187–88.

19. Meet the Press Transcript for September 23, 2007 (NBC, September 23, 2007), http://www.nbcnews .com/id/20941413/ns/meet_the _press/t/meet-press-transcript -sept/#.VbFZGbNVhBf.

20. Alan Greenspan, "The Roots of the Mortgage Crisis," Wall Street Journal, December 12, 2007, http://www.wsj.com/articles /SB119741050259621811.

21. "Greenspan: Recession Odds 'Clearly Rising,'" NPR.org, December 14, 2007, http://www.npr.org /templates/story/story.php?sto ryId=17210282.

22. After the crisis, some commentators drew the lesson that forward guidance could be useful to combat falling inflation but that it should be withdrawn once inflation rose back to target. Thus Angel Ubide, a leading hedge-fund economist, observed, "As slack is being absorbed in a recovery, the best way for monetary policy to preserve financial stability is to avoid generating one way bets and time inconsistent policies. Thus guidance should be softened as the economy approaches the steady state." See Angel Ubide, "Unconventional Monetary Policies—Recent Experiences, Impact, and Lessons," in Monetary Policy After the Great Recession, ed. Javier Vallés (Madrid: Funcas, 2014), 183.

23. Ambrose Evans-Pritchard, "Anna Schwartz Blames Fed for Subprime Crisis," Telegraph, January 13, 2008, http://www.telegraph .co.uk/finance/comment/ambro seevans_pritchard/2782488 /Anna-Schwartz-blames-Fed-for -sub-prime-crisis.html.

24. Daniel Gross, "Heckuva Job, Bernanke!," Slate, December 13, 2007, http://www.slate.com/articles /business/moneybox/2007/12 /heckuva_job_bernanke.html.

25. Paul R. Krugman, "Blindly into the Bubble," New York Times, December 21, 2007.

26. The liberal economist was Dean Baker, codirector of the Center for Economic Policy Research. See Edmund L. Andrews, "In Reversal, Fed Approves Plan to Curb Risky Lending," New York Times, December 19, 2007, http://www .nytimes.com/2007/12/19/busi ness/19subprime.html?_r=1.

27. Alan Greenspan, "We Will Never Have a Perfect Model of Risk," Financial Times, March 17, 2008,

http://www.ft.com/intl/cms/s/0/edbdbcf6-f360-11dc-b6bc-0000779fd2ac.html#axzz3ZBRaIhqN.

28. Financial Crisis Inquiry Commission, "The Financial Crisis Inquiry Report: The Final Report of the National Commission on the Causes of the Financial and Economic Crisis in the United States" (Financial Crisis Inquiry Commission, January 2011), 150–53, http://fcic-static.law.stanford.edu/cdn_media/fcic-reports/fcic_final_report_full.pdf.

29. "Global Credit Crunch: Deutsche Bank Head Calls for Government Help," *Der Spiegel*, March 18, 2008, http://www.spiegel.de/international/business/global-credit-crunch-deutsche-bank-head-calls-for-government-help-a-542140.html.

30. Martin Wolf, "The Rescue of Bear Stearns Marks Liberalization's Limit," *Financial Times*, March 26, 2008, http://www.ft.com/intl/cms/s/0/8ced5202-fa94-11dc-aa46-000077b07658.html#axzz3ZBRaIhqN.

31. Alan Greenspan, "The Fed Is Blameless on the Property Bubble," *Financial Times*, April 7, 2008, http://www.ft.com/intl/cms/s/0/81c05200-03f2-11dd-b28b-000077b07658.html#axzz3ZBRaIhqN.

32. John Crudele, "Paulson's Plan Is More an April Fool's Joke," *New York Post*, April 1, 2008, http://nypost.com/2008/04/01/paulsons-plan-is-more-an-april-fools-joke/.

33. W .C. Varones, *Greenspan's Body Count*, n.d., http://greenspansbodycount.blogspot.com/.

34. "'The Impact Was Larger Than I Expected': Greenspan's Chats with the Journal," *Wall Street Journal*, April 8, 2008.

35. Ibid.

36. In December 2007, Fannie reported capital equivalent to 1.45 percent of assets plus guarantees. The ratio at Freddie was 1.7 percent. Financial Crisis Inquiry Commission, "The Financial Crisis Inquiry Report: The Final Report of the National Commission on the Causes of the Financial and Economic Crisis in the United States," 312.

37. Andrew Ross Sorkin, *Too Big to Fail: The Inside Story of How Wall Street and Washington Fought to Save the Financial System—and Themselves* (New York: Viking Press, 2009), 190.

38. As reported in chapter thirteen, the total rescue in 1907 came to $300 million, or $6.8 billion in 2008 dollars.

39. Financial Crisis Inquiry Commission, "The Financial Crisis Inquiry Report: The Final Report of the National Commission on the Causes of the Financial and Economic Crisis in the United States," 320–21.

40. In a new epilogue to the paperback edition of his memoir, published a week before Lehman's collapse, Greenspan had written, "It seems superfluous to constrain trading in some of the newer derivatives and other innovative financial contracts of the past decade." Alan Greenspan, *The Age of Turbulence: Adventures in a New World* (New York: Penguin Books, 2008).

41. "Economic Downfall," *This Week with George Stephanopoulos* (ABC News, September 14, 2008).

42. "Had AIG been building derivatives exposures on-exchange rather than in the OTC markets, its reckless speculation would have been brought to a halt much earlier owing to minute-by-minute exposure-tracking in the clearinghouse and unambiguous mark-to-market and margining rules." See Benn Steil, "Derivatives Clearinghouses: Opportunities and Challenges": *Prepared Statement by Dr. Benn Steil Before the Committee on Banking, Housing, and Urban Affairs; Subcommittee on Securities, Insurance, and Investment*, May 25, 2011.

43. On superior risk management at hedge funds, the contrast between the disasters of the investment banks and the unaided survival of the hedge fund Citadel is instructive. See Sebastian Mallaby, "The Code Breakers," chapter thirteen in *More Money Than God: Hedge Funds and the Making of a New Elite* (New York: Penguin Group, 2010).

44. House Committee on Oversight and Government Reform, *The Financial Crisis and the Role of Federal Regulators: Hearing Before the Committee on Oversight and Government Reform*, 2008, http://www.gpo.gov/fdsys/pkg/CHRG-110hrg55764/html/CHRG-110hrg55764.htm.

45. Steve Coll, "The Whole Intellectual Edifice," *New Yorker*, October 23, 2008, http://www.newyorker.com/news/steve-coll/the-whole-intellectual-edifice.

46. Tim Rutten, "What the Oracle Didn't See," *Los Angeles Times*, October 25, 2008, http://articles.latimes.com/2008/oct/25/opinion/oe-rutten25.

47. Paul R. Krugman, "How Did Economists Get It So Wrong?," *New York Times Magazine*, September 2, 2009, http://www.nytimes.com/2009/09/06/magazine/06Economic-t.html?page wanted=all&_r=0.

48. Alan Greenspan, "The Global Financial Crisis—Causes and Consequences" (C. Peter McCoulough Series on International Economics, New York, October 15, 2009). The case against megabanks was belatedly supported by research from the International Monetary Fund. "[L]arge banks, on average, create more individual and systemic risk than smaller banks. The risks of large banks are especially high when they have insufficient capital, unstable funding, engage more in market-based activities, or are organizationally complex. This, taken together with the evidence from the literature that the size of banks is at least in part driven by too-big-to-fail subsidies and empire-building incentives, suggests that today's large banks might be too large from a social welfare perspective." See Luc Laeven, Lev Ratnovski, and Hui Tong, "Bank Size and Systemic Risk," IMF Staff Discussion Note (International Monetary Fund, May 2014); www.imf.org/external/pubs/ft/sdn/2014/sdn1404.pdf.

49. Alan Greenspan, "The Crisis," Brookings Papers on Economic Activity (Washington, D.C.: Brookings Institution, Spring 2010), 221–222.

50. Under questioning by Brooksley Born, Greenspan did reiterate his view that capital buffers should be thickened. "We were undercapitalizing the banking system probably for 40 or 50 years, and that has to be adjusted." *The Financial Crisis Inquiry Commission Hearing* (Washington, D.C., 2010).

51. Lucette Lagnado, "After the Bubble, Beauty Is but Fleeting for Greenspan Portraits," *Wall Street Journal*, February 19, 2010, http://www.wsj.com/articles/SB20000142405274870361590457505363238618059 80598.

CONCLUSION

1. "J. J. Hill Dead in St. Paul Home at the Age of 77," *New York Times*, May 30, 1916.

2. Mill also suggested that, without Caesar, "the venue . . . of European civilization might . . . have been changed." John Stuart Mill, "Elucidations of the Science of History," in *Virtual History: Alternatives and Counterfactuals*, Niall Ferguson, ed. (New York: Basic Books, 1999), 32–33.

3. Thomas Carlyle, "Heroes, Hero-Worship, and the Heroic in

History," Echo Library (Teddington: 2007), 1. Lecture originally delivered on May 5, 1840.

4. Lawrence Summers, interview by the author, March 7, 2012. Laurence H. Meyer, *A Term at the Fed: An Insider's View* (New York: HarperBusiness, 2006), 125 and 134.

5. Burton Malkiel, interview by the author, June 25, 2012.

6. For this metaphor I am indebted to my friend the writer Jonathan Rauch.

7. The fact that inflation targeting leads central banks to ignore bubbles and debt buildups is acknowledged even by its advocates. Thus UK chancellor George Osborne declared in his Mansion House speech of 2010 that "the very design of the policy framework [that is, inflation targeting] meant that responding to the explosion in balance sheets, asset prices and macro imbalances was impossible. The Bank of England was mandated to focus on consumer price inflation to the exclusion of other things." George Osborne, speech (Mansion House, London, June 16, 2010), https://www.gov.uk/government/speeches/speech-by-the-chancellor-of-the-exchequer-rt-hon-george-osborne-mp-at-mansion-house.

8. Donald Mackenzie, *An Engine, Not a Camera: How Financial Models Shape Markets* (Cambridge, Mass.: MIT Press, 2006), 114.

Image Credits

Insert pages 1; 2; 5; 6, top; and 20, top: Courtesy of the collection of Alan Greenspan.

Insert page 3: Courtesy of the New York City Municipal Archives.

Insert page 4, top: Courtesy of Henry Jerome Music, Inc.

Insert page 4, bottom: Courtesy of the New York University Archives Yearbook Collection.

Insert page 6, bottom: Courtesy of Photofest/Lebrecht Music & Arts.

Insert pages 7; 10, top; 15, top and bottom: Courtesy of the collection of Kathryn Eickhoff.

Insert page 8: Courtesy of Bettmann/Corbis Images.

Insert page 9, top and bottom: Richard Nixon Presidential Library.

Insert pages 10, bottom; 12; 13, top and bottom; 14, top and bottom: Gerald R. Ford Presidential Library.

Insert page 11: Photograph by David Hume Kennerly, Gerald R. Ford Presidential Library.

Insert page 16, top: Photograph by Michael Evans, courtesy of the Ronald Reagan Presidential Foundation and Library.

Insert page 16, bottom: Photograph by David Hume Kennerly/Getty Images.

Insert page 17, top and bottom: Courtesy of the Ronald Reagan Presidential Foundation and Library.

Insert page 18: William J. Clinton Presidential Library and Museum.

Insert page 19, top: © The Associated Press.

Insert page 19, bottom: Courtesy of the U.S. Department of the Treasury.

Insert page 20, bottom: © The Associated Press/Doug Mills.

Insert page 21: From the pages of *Time* © 1999 Time Inc. All rights reserved. Reprinted from *Time* with permission of Time Inc. Reproduction in any manner in any language in whole or in part without written permission is prohibited.

Insert pages 22, top; and 23, top: Photograph by David Bohrer, the White House.

Insert page 22, bottom: © The Associated Press/Gerald Herbert.

Insert pages 23, middle; and 24: Photograph by Shealah Craighead, George W. Bush Presidential Library and Museum.

Insert page 23, bottom: Cuban News Agency (ACN).

Index

and interest rates, 495, 551
  rise in, 546, 561
  and Sept. 11, 2001, 587
bonds, 148, 214, 219, 312, 362, 466, 472, 536, 539
  decline in, 342, 393
  dollar-dominated, 149, 151, 268
  federal, 40, 42, 92, 264, 300, 441–42, 524, 633, 641
  gold, 267–69
  high-yielding, 129, 385
  inflation-proof, 269
  and interest rates, 219, 257, 502
  junk, 385–88, 394
  and NYC bailout, 196, 198–200
  rates of, 420–21, 426–27, 430–34, 440, 443, 495, 634
  trading in, 420, 423, 441–42
  See also hedge funds
Born, Brooksley, 531–36, 538, 542, 544–45, 559, 660,
  663, 666
borrowing, 196, 218, 524, 616, 633, 643, 660
  and 1990–91 recession, 413–14
  of banks, 559, 634, 636
  by conglomerates, 135–36
  cost of, 41, 77, 264, 311, 379, 393, 420, 423, 427, 435,
    437, 441, 444, 450, 554, 597, 601, 634
  and credit checks, 617–19, 622
  decline in, 400, 432–33
  and the Fed, 328
  of foreign countries, 282–85, 287, 514
  government, 171, 233, 264, 421, 432–33, 441–42
  imprudent, 621–25
  increase in, 47–48, 53, 129, 208–10, 496–97, 606, 614
  by low-income people, 619, 622
  lowest rates of, 416
  risky, 604–5
  and stock market crash, 347–48, 356, 363
Boskin, Michael, 383, 411–12
Boston Federal Reserve, 372, 385, 395, 431, 495, 500,
  550, 563, 633
Bosworth, Barry P., 451
Bradfield, Michael, 348, 353–54, 360
Brady, Nicholas, 375, 377, 384, 400–406, 408, 410–12,
  415, 429, 572
Branden, Barbara, 65, 69
Branden, Nathaniel, 65–66, 69, 79, 82, 85–86,
  89–90, 112
Brash, Donald, 455–57
Brazil, 234, 540
Bretton Woods conference, 145, 183–84, 191
Brinkley, David, 337–39, 342
British Embassy, 179, 410
Broaddus, Al, 540
Brookings Institute, 203, 214, 221, 451,
  632, 670
Brown Brothers Harriman, 34–35, 210
Brown, Edmund, 96
Brown, Gordon, 645, 648–49, 651
Brown, Jerry, 203, 224
Bryan, William Jennings, 111–12, 503
Buchanan, Pat, 102–3, 107–8, 110–12, 117–22, 677
Buckley, William F. Jr., 29, 64, 376–77

budget
  balancing it, 240, 252, 257, 260, 263–65
  bureau, 184
  conservatism, 216, 224, 240
  cuts, 126, 257
  discipline, 134–35, 171, 231, 319, 420, 427–28, 576
  policy, 108, 229, 259, 263
  politics, 429
  stimulus, 167–68, 172, 174–76
  surpluses, 129, 573–76, 607
budget deficits, 32, 110, 181, 212, 218, 229, 394, 596
  under George W. Bush, 575–76, 607–8
  under George H. W. Bush, 389–90, 397–400, 573
  under Clinton, 419–21, 423–30, 433, 443, 573, 575
  and the Fed, 264, 607
  under Ford, 175–76
  Greenspan on, 106, 215–16, 264–65, 278, 419–21,
    428–30, 506
  increase in, 176, 252, 260, 389–90, 420, 676
  and inflation, 264, 421, 428, 431
  and interest rates, 264, 269–70, 270
  under Reagan, 239, 256, 260, 263, 338, 359, 430
  reduction in, 240, 264–65, 275, 359, 398–400,
    419–21, 423–30, 433, 436, 443, 526, 573, 575–77
  support for, 30, 77
  and tax cuts, 251–52
Buffett, Warren, 388, 590
building industry, 149, 164, 210, 218, 233, 372, 383,
  388, 414, 582, 604
bull market, 56, 500–505, 549, 555
Bungay, Jack, 64
Bunning, Jim, 608–9
Burlington Industries, 45
Burns, Arthur, 46, 50, 77, 180, 214, 245, 476
  advises presidents, 125, 134–35, 163, 175–77, 230
  on bailouts, 140–44, 196–200, 300–301
  Belgrade speech of, 228–32, 234, 262, 289, 381, 390
  bullied by Nixon advisers, 4, 140–44, 146, 150, 230,
    415–16
  on central banks, 228–34, 261–63, 289, 381,
    390, 641
  death of, 318–19
  as Fed chairman, 4–5, 134–35, 138, 140–44, 167,
    230, 310, 319–20, 330, 381, 400
  and Greenspan, 37, 156, 572
  on inflation, 40–42, 47–48, 87
  named ambassador, 265
  recessions under, 645–46
  teaches at Columbia, 36–42, 87, 125, 496
Burns, Helen, 214, 318
Bush, George H. W., 385, 396–97, 460, 506, 551, 579,
  605, 680
  and bank reform battle, 403–11
  campaign of, 310, 365–67, 371–74, 389–90
  criticizes Greenspan, 5, 378–79, 389, 437, 569, 684
  deficit-reduction plan, 398–400, 573
  description of, 365–66, 418, 570
  on the economy, 366–67, 371, 378–79, 381, 389–90,
    410–12
  and the Fed, 375, 381, 383–84, 401, 424, 439–40

A Note on the Author

SEBASTIAN MALLABY is the Paul A. Volcker Senior Fellow for International Economics at the Council on Foreign Relations and a contributing columnist at the *Washington Post*. He has been a columnist for the *Financial Times* and spent thirteen years as a staff writer for the *Economist*, serving as Washington bureau chief and writing the Lexington column on American affairs. His three previous books include *More Money Than God: Hedge Funds and the Making of a New Elite*, which was a *New York Times* bestseller. He divides his time between Washington DC, New York and London, where he lives with his wife Zanny Minton Beddoes, the editor of the *Economist*.